NUTRITION

NUTRITION

BASIC CONCEPTS AND APPLICATIONS

William L. Scheider

Assistant Professor
State University of New York College at Buffalo

McGRAW-HILL BOOK COMPANY

New York St. Louis San Francisco Auckland Bogotá Hamburg
Johannesburg London Madrid Mexico Montreal New Delhi
Panama Paris São Paulo Singapore Sydney Tokyo Toronto

NUTRITION

BASIC CONCEPTS AND APPLICATIONS

2 3 4 5 6 7 8 9 0 DODO 8 9 8 7 6 5 4 3

ISBN 0-07-055230-4

This book was set in Century Schoolbook by Progressive Typographers.
The editors were Eric M. Munson, Rhona Robbin, Jeannine Ciliotta, and James S. Amar;
the designer was Nicholas Krenitsky;
the production supervisor was Dominick Petrellese.
The photo editors were Christine L. Reynolds and Jeannine Ciliotta.
The cover and part-opening photographs were taken by DeMarco/Tamaccio;
the drawings were done by Fine Line Illustrations, Inc.
R. R. Donnelley & Sons Company was printer and binder.

Library of Congress Cataloging in Publication Data

Scheider, William L.
Nutrition, basic concepts and applications.

Bibliography: p.
Includes index.
1. Nutrition. 2. Nutrition disorders. I. Title.
QP141.S3425 613.2 81-23695
ISBN 0-07-055230-4 AACR2

With love to
Jay Schrock, Ann Fulton, and Jon Beard

CONTENTS

PART 2 ENERGY AND THE BODY: AN OVERVIEW

Chapter 5 Energy Balance and Weight Control 125

PREFACE

One of the most important tasks of a college education in today's complex world is to train students to make intelligent decisions about issues that affect them and their society. One area of particular concern is nutrition, and an introductory course provides an ideal opportunity to instill and emphasize sound nutritional principles. It can help students select a nutritious diet at a time when they are assuming greater responsibility for their food choices, as well as guide those who want to lose weight, engage in athletic competition, or experiment with vegetarianism. An introductory nutrition course also provides students with information useful when raising families or caring for their parents. In addition, it may influence their thinking on social and political issues, such as hunger in America or malnutrition in developing nations, and inspire some to become involved in solving these problems.

This text, designed for introductory courses, provides nutrition information students can apply to their lives. It can also serve as a good foundation for further studies in nutrition and related fields. Previous coursework in biology and chemistry is not required, although the first chapter includes an optional section for those who wish to examine or review some basic concepts useful in the study of nutrition. The major intent of the first chapter is to present an overview of nutrition that introduces concepts used throughout the book, such as the Recommended Dietary Allowances, the Basic Four Food Group Plan, the U.S. Dietary Goals, and the Dietary Guidelines for Americans.

Parts One, Two, and Three of the book describe the nutrients, including functions, requirements, sources, and the results of deficiency and excess. The vitamins and minerals chapters are organized by topic (functions, requirements, sources, and so on), rather than vitamin by vitamin and mineral by mineral. This approach shows the similarities and relationships among nutrients. For example, the role of the B vitamins as coenzymes is emphasized in the functions section, while the interplay of biological, economic, and cultural factors that has led to beriberi, pellagra, scurvy, and rickets is discussed in the deficiency section. A summary table has been included within these chapters to organize the material in the traditional manner. Part Four, which contains the life cycle chapters, begins with the principles and practice of choosing an adequate adult diet. The rest of the section shows how and why nutrient needs vary during other stages of the life cycle, and the means by which these different requirements can best be met. The book concludes by looking at some of the challenges facing nutritionists in the next decade and placing nutrition in a national and global, as well as personal, context.

Topics of current interest, controversies, and myths are highlighted in the Issue and Focus sections of each chapter. Some, such as lactose intolerance and pica, are designed to provide up-to-date information on specific areas of nutritional interest. When the topic is a genuine controversy, such as the role of cholesterol in causing heart disease, both sides are presented and students are encouraged to draw their own conclusions. Myths relating to the topic are given in a "Fact or Fantasy?" list in each chapter. The myths are evaluated by showing the faulty logic involved and presenting experimental data that refute them. Important statements about a variety of topics are emphasized by setting them off as callouts.

To reinforce the material and encourage application, a Study Guide has been incorporated into the book at the end of each chapter. The summary is a concise, point-by-point outline of important concepts in the chapter. A vocabulary list, study questions, and a self-test provide a comprehensive examination of the material. Students can reinforce their understanding of important terms by defining the vocabulary in their own words and comparing their definitions with those in the glossary. The study questions emphasize concepts of a general nature. The self-test deals with specific points not covered by the vocabulary or study questions; the correct answers are given at the end of the book. Suggested activities are intended to encourage application of information presented in the chapter. For those who wish to pursue topics in more detail, a complete reference list is provided at the end of the book. Some of the more readable and informative references are described in a "For Further Reading" section in the Study Guide.

The text is supplemented with many illustrations and tables. In addition, a "Ready Reference" section is included at the end of the book. It contains the Recommended Dietary Allowances, American Dietetic Association Exchange Lists, several tables of food composition, and other useful data. The book should serve as a valuable reference source long after the course has ended.

An instructor's manual and separate test bank have been prepared for use with this text. The instructor's manual briefly outlines the objectives for each chapter and how the chapter can be used to meet those objectives. Included are a list of concerns my students have expressed about nutrition, as well as suggestions for stimulating discussion in the classroom. Sources of supplementary materials are provided at the end of the manual. Questions in the test bank are drawn from examinations I have given to my own students.

A book of this nature is the collective effort of many people. I would like to thank Elizabeth Raleigh and Karen Fleischer for some timely encouragement in getting the project started, and my editors, Rhona Robbin and Jeannine Ciliotta, for their invaluable advice, editorial efforts, and support throughout its development. I am also grateful to Sharon Antonelli, Carol Bishop, Jan Christian, Lois Farone, Amy Ireson, Naomi A. Peel, Valerie Reid, and Judith Roepke for their comments and criticisms and would particularly like to thank Dr. Jean Bowering, Syracuse University, and Dr. John M. Hill, Brigham Young University, for reviewing the entire manuscript. I am also indebted to Donna Brooks for typing the manuscript. Finally, I would like to thank my family and friends for their support during this lengthy project.

William L. Scheider

THE SCIENCE OF NUTRITION

Interest in nutrition has grown tremendously during the last decade, and, as our knowledge has increased, we have become more and more conscious of the connection between diet and health. We ask more and more questions about what we should eat. Can our foods provide all the nutrients we need? Are food additives dangerous? Will vitamin and mineral supplements give us more energy and prevent disease? How can we lose weight safely and effectively? Is a vegetarian diet better than a conventional one? In 1968 a Citizen's Board of Inquiry into Hunger and Malnutrition in the United States published *Hunger U.S.A.,* which documented an alarming prevalence of nutritional deprivation in this country. In the early 1970s, the Senate Select Committee on Nutrition and Human Needs began to hear testimony linking food-consumption patterns in the United States and other affluent nations with the relatively high incidence of obesity, heart disease, diabetes mellitus, and certain types of cancer in those countries. As a result, in 1977 the committee issued a set of dietary recommendations called the U.S. Dietary Goals. The Dietary Goals were subsequently used by the United States Department of Agriculture (USDA) and the Department of Health and Human Services (HHS) as the basis for their Dietary Guidelines for Americans (1). These Dietary Guidelines are a significant step toward a national nutrition policy.

In the industrialized countries, our problem seems to be one of food choices. People in the developing world, however, are concerned with just getting enough to eat. Much has been said and written about the "protein gap" and the "energy gap," as well as the need to increase food supplies and distribute them better. Drought, crop failures, the increased cost of energy, and political factors resulted in a famine in many parts of the world during the mid-1970s. Although the crisis eases periodically, the problems have not been solved, so we need good nutrition information to protect our health and to be well-informed voters, taxpayers, and members of the world community. First, however, we need to know what nutrition is. We need to know how new information is generated and tested, and we need some reliable sources of this information.

What Is Nutrition?

Nutrition is the science that studies the means by which we obtain, assimilate, and utilize food. It is a discipline with many facets; it draws on many other sciences, including chemistry, biochemistry, physiology, medicine, sociology, economics, geography, agriculture, politics, and food science. Determining the role of a nutrient, such as protein in the body, requires the expertise of biochemists and physiologists. To establish programs to meet the nutritional needs of a developing nation, however, a nutritionist might work with agricultural scientists, economists, and politicians. Treating obesity sometimes requires the help of a psychologist. Nutrition tells us why each nutrient is necessary in the diet, how much of each is required, which foods provide them, the factors that influence food availability and food choices, and the results of deficiency and excess.

WHY WE NEED NUTRIENTS

Nutrients are substances required in the diet for growth, maintenance, and reproduction. Protein, carbohydrate, and fat, for example, provide energy. Proteins perform a variety of other functions, including catalyzing chemical reactions, transporting substances in the blood, muscle contraction, and maintaining fluid and acid-base balances. Vitamins and minerals help other substances do their jobs. Water is also a nutrient; it provides the medium in which all the other nutrients function. Water bathes each cell, transports substances to and from the cells and into and out of the body, regulates body temperature, and participates in chemical reactions.

The relationships between the nutrients and other body substances are very complex. Deficiency of a single nutrient can impair several processes simultaneously, and prolonged deficiency can lead to death. Nutrients also interact with each other in a variety of ways. For example, copper and vitamin C promote the proper functioning of iron, while zinc interferes with copper absorption and utilization. An important part of our study of nutrition will be to look at these relationships, as well as the basic functions of each nutrient.

INFLUENCES ON FOOD CHOICES

Of the thousands of foods known to people throughout the world, each individual selects particular ones to eat. Another important part of nutri-

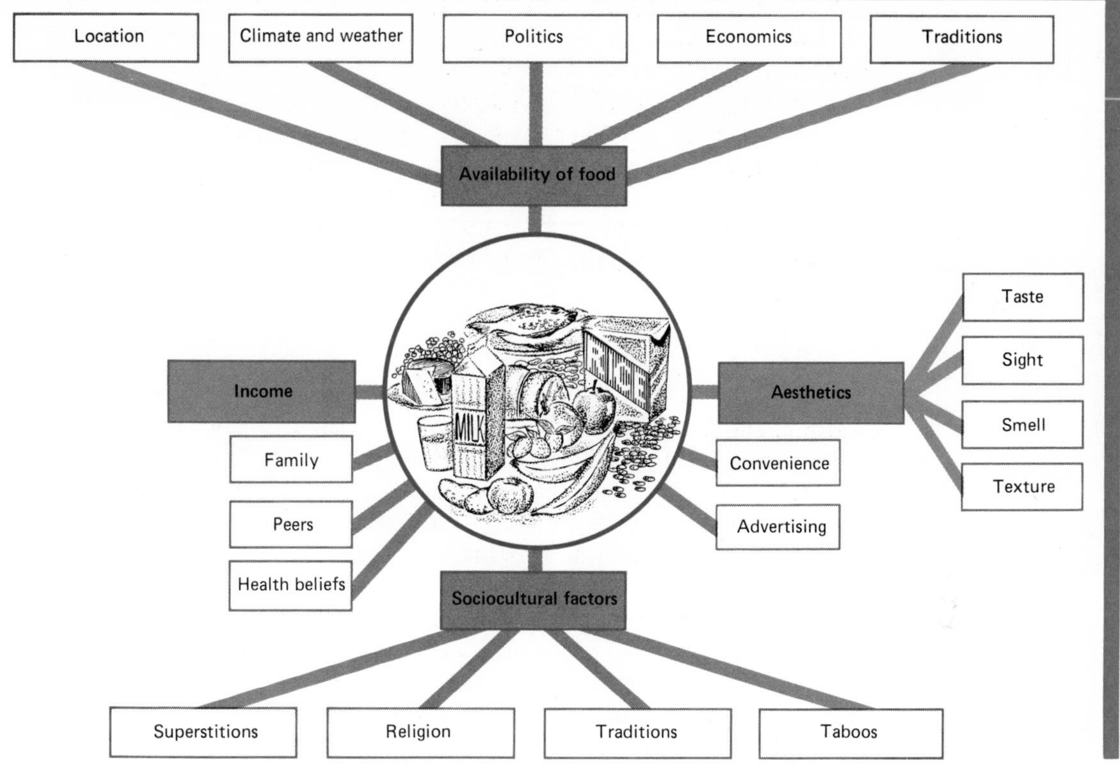

FIGURE 1-1
Factors Influencing Food Choices. The choices we make from the thousands of different foods suitable for human consumption depend on a variety of factors.

tion is the study of the factors that influence these choices (Figure 1-1). A major factor is the availability of different types of food, which in turn is influenced by geographic location, climate and weather, economic policies, political decisions, and cultural traditions. For instance, the climate and geography of southeast Asia are conducive to growing rice rather than other grains, and a cultural pattern has evolved around rice as a staple. In much of the United States, wheat is the major staple. Another factor influencing food choices is income. In the developing nations, meat, dairy products, and eggs are often too expensive to purchase in significant amounts, and many people must do without them. In the United States, rising meat prices have led consumers to buy the less-expensive cuts or to resort to alternatives, such as legumes and grain-based dishes.

Family, peers, health beliefs, convenience, advertising, and sociocultural factors, such as religion, superstition, and taboos, also help determine food choices. Parents shape food preferences by continually exposing their children to particular types of foods at a time when they are forming their likes and dislikes. Forcing a child to eat or using food as a reward or punishment may result in a fondness for or an aversion to certain foods. Peers influence food choices by introducing new foods; many people, especially children, tend to imitate peers they particularly like or respect (see Chapter 12).

The effect of health beliefs on food choices is of great concern to nutri-

FIGURE 1-2
Food Consumption Patterns in Different Cultures. **A** Children eat a lunch of fish, rice, and beverage in Orissa State in India. **B** A South Korean girl enjoys an elaborate formal holiday meal of fish, rice, vegetables, and meat. (Courtesy of the United Nations)

tionists. Some people insist on buying "organic," or "natural," foods; others may fast for extended periods in pursuit of health "benefits." In today's fast-moving world, convenience is another important factor. Fast-food restaurants, for instance, enjoy a thriving business, and frozen foods are eaten at some time by almost every American. Nutritionists also have become concerned about the role of advertising in determining food choices. A convincing pitch made by a celebrity is often a powerful inducement to buy a particular product. In addition, advertising may lead the consumer to believe that some health, athletic, cosmetic, or social benefits can be obtained by eating certain foods. Cultural factors, such as religion, superstition, and taboos, are deeply ingrained influences on what people eat. For example, the Jains in India and the Seventh Day Adventists in the United States practice varying degrees of vegetarianism. Pork is forbidden to Orthodox Jews and beef to Hindus. In parts of Kenya, it is believed that feeding a child eggs causes convulsions, while in other cultures, feeding meat to children is thought to make them greedy.

Probably the most immediate influence on the choice of food is its appeal: how it looks, smells, and feels in our mouths—and tastes. Preferences for certain characteristics are shaped by many of the factors already described. In addition, they may be affected by pleasant or unpleasant associations with particular odors, appearances, and flavors. For example, the first time John ate steamed clams, he enjoyed them. A few hours later he became ill from a digestive-tract infection unrelated to the clams. However, John associated the illness with the clams and has not been able to tolerate the sight or smell of them ever since. That aesthetic qualities exert a powerful influence on food choices is the basis for many current food-processing methods. Manufacturers use a variety of additives and procedures to make the color, flavor, texture, and other characteristics of their foods more desirable.

Throughout this book, we will see how these factors can play a role in promoting obesity, causing malnutrition, and affecting the nutritional status of particular population groups.

HOW MUCH WE NEED: THE RECOMMENDED DIETARY ALLOWANCES

In order to ensure an adequate intake of nutrients, we need to know how much our bodies require. Measuring each individual's nutrient requirements is virtually impossible, so the Food and Nutrition Board (FNB) of the National Academy of Sciences has developed a set of general standards for use in planning to meet the nutrient needs of the American population. These **Recommended Dietary Allowances (RDAs)** are "the levels of intake of essential nutrients considered to be adequate to meet the known nutritional needs of practically all healthy persons" (2).

The RDAs are based on data from several types of studies. **Balance studies** estimate the amount of a nutrient needed to replace that expended by or lost from the body each day. For example, an adult male loses about 1 milligram of iron from his body per day, and since he absorbs only 10 percent of the iron he eats, he must consume 10 milligrams of iron from food to maintain balance. In another type of study, volunteers are deprived of a nutrient and monitored for deficiency symptoms, impairment of specific body functions, and changes in the concentration of the nutrient or its breakdown products in the blood, tissues, and urine. The amount of the nutrient needed to correct the deficiency and return blood and tissue levels to normal can then be measured. Experiments of this type helped clarify human needs for vitamin C.

Surveys of the nutrient intake of whole populations also can help establish requirements: if the population shows no signs of deficiency, impairment of body function, or low blood and tissue concentrations of the nutrient, the requirement must be somewhat less than the amount consumed by the population. For example, the average vitamin E intake in the United States was found to be between 10 and 15 international units per day (IU/day), and no signs of deficiency were observed in the population. So the Recommended Dietary Allowance for vitamin E was lowered from 30 to 12 to 15 IU/day in 1974.

The average human requirement for a nutrient can be estimated on the basis of experimental data. However, if we use this as the standard for the population, many of the people would probably fail to meet their needs with the recommended level of intake. We need a safety factor that takes into account the differences from person to person. In the case of nutrients for which we have sufficient data, the Food and Nutrition Board assumed that the differences in requirements among individuals

The RDAs are not the nutritional requirements of any particular individual; nearly anyone consuming the recommended amounts will meet or exceed his or her needs.

follows a certain pattern. Using statistical methods, it sets the RDA at 2 standard deviations above the average requirement for the population (Figure 1-3). This level is sufficient to meet the needs of 97.5 percent of the people. In addition, because not all nutrients are absorbed completely from the digestive tract, the FNB increased the RDAs for these nutrients. For many nutrients, such as vitamin K, pantothenic acid, biotin, and several trace minerals, data are insufficient to establish RDAs. So the FNB has issued a set of estimated safe and adequate intakes for these substances (Ready Reference 3). A level of intake within the given range is thought to be adequate to meet the needs of most people.

The RDAs are not the nutritional requirements of any particular individual. Instead they are set high enough that nearly anyone consuming the recommended amounts will meet or exceed his or her own particular needs. The slight excesses of nutrients that many people are likely to consume by meeting the RDAs are not considered harmful. The situation is different for energy; even slight excesses over a long period of time will lead to weight gain and perhaps obesity. So the RDA for energy has been set at the requirement of an average individual engaged in light activity. It has no safety factor built into it, and it must be ad-

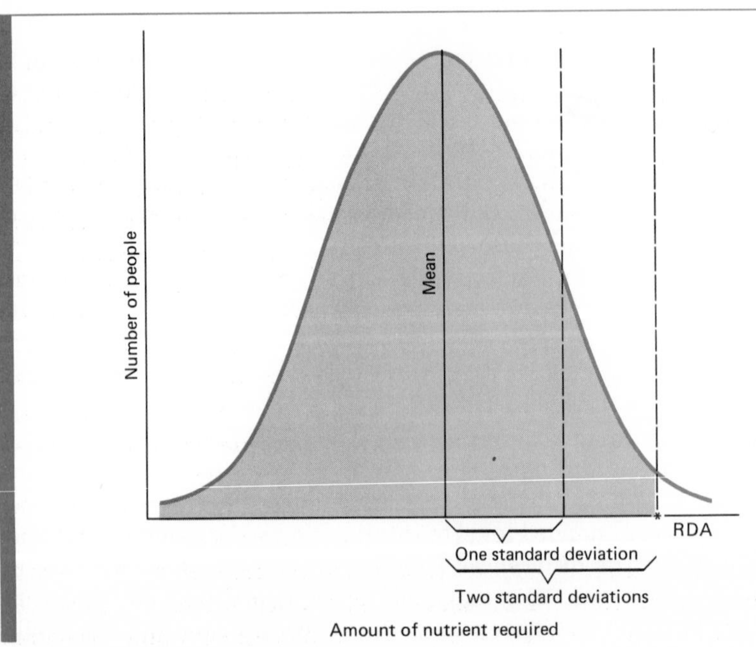

FIGURE 1-3
How the RDAs Are Estimated. The RDAs for protein, vitamins, and minerals are set at two standard deviations above the average requirement for the population. Consuming the RDA level will meet the needs of most healthy people (shaded area).

justed to suit the needs of the individual (see Chapter 5).

The RDAs have many practical uses. A person can use them as a guide against which to judge nutrient intake: the closer the level of intake approaches the RDA, the greater the probability that the individual's needs are being met. The RDAs are most useful in planning diets for large groups of people, such as in hospitals and schools. They also can serve as guidelines for allocating food aid, including food stamps and school lunch programs. Another important application is in evaluating the nutritional status of a population. If the amounts of nutrients consumed fall below the RDAs, some individuals in that population probably are at risk. Food manufacturers may use the RDAs to decide whether or not to fortify their foods and how much of each nutrient to add. The RDAs are also the basis for the **United States Recommended Daily Allowances (USRDAs)**, established by the Food and Drug Administration (FDA) for the labeling of foods. For most nutrients, the USRDA is the highest recommended level of intake for any age group (except pregnant and lactating women) proposed in the 1968 RDAs (see Table 10-4). The nutrient content is expressed on the label as a percent of the USRDA. For example, the USRDA for vitamin C is 60 mg/day, and if the food contains 6 mg/serving, the label states that one serving provides 10 percent of the USRDA for vitamin C (see Chapter 10).

The Food and Agriculture Organization (FAO) and the World Health Organization (WHO) of the United Nations, as well as governments throughout the world, have established their own standards of nutrient intake. The recommendations of FAO/WHO and the Canadian Department of National Welfare are given in Ready Reference 3.

OBTAINING NUTRIENTS FROM FOOD: SOURCES OF INFORMATION

A major problem for many people is choosing a diet that provides sufficient qualities of each nutrient to meet their needs. How do we know which foods contain generous amounts of each nutrient? Chemical analyses of nutrient content have been performed on thousands of foods, and the results have been compiled into food-composition tables such as that in Ready Reference 1, USDA Home and Garden Handbook No. 72, *Nutritive Value of Foods*. More extensive tables are found in Agriculture Handbook No. 456, *Nutritive Value of American Foods in Common Units* (3), Agriculture Handbook No. 8, *Composition of Foods—Raw, Processed, and Prepared* (currently being revised) (4), and Pennington and Church, *Food Values of Portions Commonly Used* (5). Values for nutrients not covered in these tables, such as copper, biotin, and vitamin E, can be found in other publications, such as the *Journal of the American Dietetic Association* and the *American Journal of Clinical Nutrition*.

However, food-composition tables have several disadvantages. For many foods, there is little information on the content of certain nutrients, especially trace minerals such as copper, chromium, selenium, manganese, molybdenum, and zinc. In addition, the listed values are generally averages of analyses made on samples from many geographic locations.

The nutrient content of a food varies widely depending on growing conditions and losses during harvesting, commercial processing, packaging, storage, and home preparation. A particular item purchased at the local supermarket may contain more or less of the nutrient than is listed in the table. Sometimes the value in the table is based on only one or a few analyses, and it may not accurately reflect the content normally found in the food. Food-composition tables also do not give information on the availability of a nutrient. For example, only 2 to 5 percent of the iron in spinach is actually absorbed and used by the body, so the high value for the iron content of spinach is misleading.

Food-composition tables can indicate which foods are relatively good sources of a nutrient, but food plans are far easier to use on a daily basis in the home. The Basic Four Food Group Plan was first published by the United States Department of Agriculture (USDA) in 1957 (6). It divides food into four categories: the meat group, which includes meat, fish, poultry, eggs, nuts, and beans; the milk group, which includes all dairy products; the vegetable-fruit group; and the bread-cereal group, which includes all grain products. At least two servings from the meat group, two from the milk group, four from the vegetable-fruit group (including one good source of vitamin C every day and one good source of vitamin A every other day), and four servings from the bread-cereal group are recommended for adults each day. In a recent publication, a fifth category, the fats, sweets, and alcohol group, has been added (7). These foods supply mainly energy, and no specific number of servings is recommended.

The Basic Four Food Group Plan provides a foundation for an adequate diet, but it must be used intelligently. It is easy to defeat the system by choosing poorer-quality foods from each group, by not making serving sizes large enough, and by preparing the food in a way that results in significant losses of nutrients. Another problem is that the Basic Four Food Group Plan was developed around the need for energy and only eight other nutrients: protein, calcium, iron, vitamin A, vitamin C, thiamine, riboflavin, and niacin. It was hoped that if appropriate foods were chosen, sufficient amounts of the other nutrients would be obtained. However, some nutrients, such as folacin, vitamin B_6, vitamin E, magnesium, zinc, and iron, could be lacking in a diet based on the four food groups, and additional servings of appropriate foods may be needed to provide them (8). In Chapters 5, 7, and 8, we will identify the food groups that make important contributions of each nutrient and the specific items from each group that are particularly good sources. In Chapters 9 and 10, we will return to the Basic Four Food Group Plan and show how it can be used in planning a nutritious diet.

Some experts believe that following the Dietary Goals will have little effect on the nation's health; others contend that the potential benefits are great.

TABLE **1-1**

Nutrition guidelines and goals

A. Dietary Guidelines for Americans

1. Eat a variety of foods.
2. Maintain ideal weight.
3. Avoid too much fat, saturated fat, and cholesterol.
4. Eat foods with adequate starch and fiber.
5. Avoid too much sugar.
6. Avoid too much sodium.
7. If you drink alcohol, do so in moderation.

B. Dietary Goals for the United States

1. To avoid obesity, consume only as much energy (calories) as is expended; if overweight, decrease energy intake and increase energy expenditure.
2. Increase the consumption of complex carbohydrates and "naturally occurring" sugars from about 28 percent of energy intake to about 48 percent of energy intake.
3. Reduce the consumption of refined and processed sugars by about 45 percent to account for about 10 percent of total energy intake.
4. Reduce fat intake to 30 percent of the total calories.
5. Reduce saturated fat consumption to account for about 10 percent of total energy intake and balance that with polyunsaturated and monounsaturated fats, which should account for about 10 percent of energy intake each.
6. Reduce cholesterol consumption to about 300 mg/day.
7. Limit the intake of sodium by reducing the intake of salt to about 5 g/day.

Sources: U.S. Department of Agriculture, Department of Health and Human Services, *Nutrition and Your Health, Dietary Guidelines for Americans,* Superintendent of Documents, Washington, DC, 1980.

U.S. Senate Select Committee on Nutrition and Human Needs, *Dietary Goals for the United States,* 2d ed., Superintendent of Documents, Washington, DC, 1977.

Because considerable evidence has accumulated showing that current intake patterns of energy, fat, cholesterol, sugar, salt, and fiber in the affluent nations may contribute to the relatively high incidence of certain diseases, the United States Department of Agriculture and the Department of Health and Human Services have issued a set of recommendations for modifying the diet called the Dietary Guidelines for Americans (Table 1-1*A*)(1). These were developed from more specific recommendations, the U.S. Dietary Goals, which were issued by the Senate Select Committee on Nutrition and Human Needs in 1977 (Table 1-1*B*)(9). The Dietary Guidelines for Americans can be used with the Basic Four Food Group Plan by selecting foods from each group that conform to the guidelines. The Dietary Goals and the Guidelines for Americans also have generated a great deal of controversy. Some experts, such as A. E. Harper of the University of Wisconsin, point out that the true causes of obesity, heart disease, diabetes, high blood pressure, and cancer are unknown and that the evidence implicating diet is not conclusive. Such experts believe that the recommendations will have no real effect on the health of the nation as a whole and that they should be used only by

TABLE **1-2**

Examples of clinical signs of nutrient deficiency

BODY PART	CLINICAL SIGN	DEFICIENT NUTRIENTS
Eyes	Dryness of the cornea and conjunctiva; foamy spot on the cornea	Vitamin A
Hair	Loss of luster, easy pluckability	Protein
Mouth	Cracked lips	Riboflavin, niacin
	Cracks in corners of mouth	Riboflavin, vitamin B_6, iron
	Bleeding gums	Vitamin C
Tongue	Magenta color	Riboflavin
	Smooth, red, raw	Niacin
Skin	Rough, dry skin with plugged hair follicles	Vitamin A, essential fatty acid
	Oily inflammation of the skin	Riboflavin, vitamin B_6
	Sunburnlike inflammation when exposed to sunlight	Niacin
	Tiny bruises under the skin	Vitamin C
Thyroid gland	Swelling	Iodine
Skeleton	Bowed legs, protruding chest, curved spine in children	Vitamin D
	Joint pains (adults), bone pains (infants)	Vitamin C
Nervous system	Impaired functioning	Thiamine, niacin, vitamin B_{12}, and others
Extremities	Edema (swelling)	Protein, thiamine (wet beriberi)

individuals known to be at risk from one of the diseases they are designed to combat (10,11). However, D. M. Hegsted of Harvard University and other authorities contend that there is little, if any, risk associated with changing the diet to conform to the Senate's recommendations, and the potential benefits are great. So why not make these changes (12)? At many points throughout this book, we will look at the controversies surrounding the role of diet in causing disease, attempt to determine whether altering the diet has any effect, and show how to select a diet that conforms to the Dietary Goals and Guidelines.

EVALUATING NUTRITIONAL STATUS

How do nutritionists determine whether an individual or a population is meeting nutritional needs or is at risk of a deficiency of some kind? Four techniques are generally used to assess nutritional status: clinical examination, anthropometric measurements, biochemical analysis, and estimates of dietary intake (13).

Clinical evaluation involves a physical examination; in deficiency states, the eyes, hair, mouth, tongue, skin, thyroid gland, skeleton, nervous system, and limbs may show abnormalities (Table 1-2). This method is the least sensitive, because some signs can be produced by deficiency of more than one nutrient or in some cases may result from factors other than a nutrient deficiency. Physical changes also may not appear until the deficiency is rather severe. Nevertheless, the signs are useful in confirming the results of the other three methods.

Anthropometric measurements include those made of height, weight, the diameter or circumference of body parts, such as the head, wrist, forearm, chest, waist, and thigh, and the thickness of a pinched skin fold on the triceps, upper back, abdomen, and thigh. They may be used to determine the degree of fatness (see Chapter 5) or to assess growth in infants and children. For example, a child's height and weight can be plotted on growth charts (see Figure 12-1) to show whether the child is gaining weight in relation to height too quickly or too slowly compared with other children of the same age (see Chapter 12). One problem in using anthropometric measurements, however, is establishing the standards that are considered "normal."

Biochemical analysis of the blood and urine is useful in detecting depletion of the body's reserve of nutrients before physical symptoms have appeared. In addition to the nutrients themselves, the analyses can check for products of the breakdown of nutrients or for substances the nutrients work with or act on in the body. Abnormal results do not always indicate a dietary deficiency; they could be because of poor absorption of the nutrient, an increased rate of destruction in the body, or a more rapid rate of excretion. In addition, not all deficiencies are detectable by this method. A person may be consuming inadequate amounts of a nutrient, but blood concentrations will not be reduced because body stores compensate for the reduced intake. For example, when dietary calcium is deficient, the mineral is mobilized from the bones to maintain blood levels.

Dietary intake of nutrients also can provide clues about nutritional status. For a population, intakes can be indirectly estimated by measuring the disappearance of food into commercial channels, although there is no way of knowing whether the food was actually consumed. More direct methods can be used for individuals by whom food was consumed. Food-intake diaries can be kept, or a person may be asked to recall what he or she has eaten during the past 24 hours. Nutrient intake can then be calculated by consulting a food-composition table and comparing the results with the RDAs. These methods rely on the honesty of the subjects in reporting all foods eaten, as well as on their judgment in estimating portion sizes.

All these methods have been used in surveys of the nutritional status of the American population. The two most recent are the Ten-State Nutrition Survey (14) and the First Health and Nutrition Examination Survey (HANES) (15). The Ten-State Survey was carried out by the Department of Health, Education and Welfare at the request of Congress after hearings in 1967 disclosed the probability that serious hunger and malnutrition existed in the United States. Five states (New York, Michigan, Massachusetts, Washington, and California) classified as high-income relative to the poverty index and five states (West Virginia, Kentucky, South Carolina, Texas, and Louisiana) classed as low-income were surveyed. More than 40,000 individuals underwent tests that included a medical history, physical examination, anthropometric measurements, x-ray examination of the wrist, dental examination, and sampling of blood to determine iron status. Blood from selected subgroups representing high-risk populations, such as infants and children (up to 36 months of age), adolescents (10 to 16 years of age), pregnant and lactating women, and the elderly (60 years of age or older) was further analyzed for protein, vitamin A, thiamine, riboflavin, and iodine. In addition, dietary data based on 24-hour recalls were collected from high-risk population groups. The results, published in 1972, are summarized in Figure 14-7. However, because the populations sampled in the survey were weighted heavily in favor of low-income groups, the results are not considered representative of the American population as a whole.

The HANES program was undertaken to provide continuing surveillance of the nutritional status of the American people. The first survey, conducted from 1971 to 1972, looked at a representative sample of the noninstitutionalized civilian population of the United States between the ages of 1 and 74 years. Preliminary results of clinical, anthropometric, biochemical, and dietary evaluations of over 10,000 people were published in 1974. The results of the HANES survey and the Ten-State Survey will be presented at appropriate points throughout this book.

Severe nutritional deficiencies are now relatively rare in the United States and other industrialized nations, although some groups have been found to be at risk. For the people of the developing world, deficiencies are still a serious problem. The greater problem in the industrialized nations, and in the United States in particular, is overnutrition. We will discuss the various nutritional deficiencies and excesses in Chapters 3 through 8 and explore their causes and consequences, as well as the means by which they can be avoided.

Evaluating Nutrition Information

Most people become interested in their eating habits when they hear they will feel more energetic, avoid disease, improve their appearance, and obtain other benefits simply through the proper use of nutrients. Nutritionists are concerned because these claims are often exaggerated or false. Why do people turn to fads? Perhaps one major reason is that all of us like the idea of simple solutions to difficult problems. An obese person, for example, may try a fad diet because he or she has not been able to lose weight by conventional means. Those with incurable conditions ranging from psoriasis to terminal cancer may turn to quacks out of desperation. In addition, proponents of certain foods often present a problem as nutritional in origin when in fact it usually has other roots. For instance, someone who has a demanding job, family responsibilities, and an active social life may feel tired much of the time and begin to take vitamin supplements in order to feel more energetic. Although deficiency of iron and many of the vitamins leads to fatigue, it is more likely that the problem in this case arises from the demands of the person's lifestyle. In some

FOCUS 1-1
SOME DIET-RELATED FALLACIES COVERED IN THIS BOOK

FALLACY	CHAPTER REFERENCE
"Natural" sugars (honey and brown sugars) are more nutritious than refined white sugar.	Chapter 2
White sugar (sucrose) is a poison.	Chapter 2
If you are always feeling tired and irritable, you probably are hypoglycemic.	Chapter 2
Lecithin is a dietary essential and will help prevent or treat atherosclerosis.	Chapter 3
Carbohydrates, not kilocalories, make you fat.	Chapter 5
Fasting, liquid-protein diets, drugs, and spot-reducing devices are safe and effective ways of losing weight.	Chapter 5
It is necessary to have a bowel movement every day.	Chapter 6
Vitamin and mineral supplements are needed by most people.	Chapter 7
Choline, inositol, *para*-aminobenzoic acid (PABA), bioflavonoids, pangamic acid (vitamin B_{15}), and amygdalin (vitamin B_{17}, laetrile) are dietary essentials.	Chapter 7
Massive doses of appropriate vitamins will prevent or cure many diseases, such as the common cold, heart disease, cancer, schizophrenia, and acne.	Chapter 7
Natural vitamins are superior to synthetic ones.	Chapter 7
If you are always feeling tired, you probably have "iron-poor blood."	Chapter 8
The U.S. food supply is so refined and overprocessed it is difficult to choose an adequate diet from foods available in the supermarket.	Chapters 9 and 10
"Organic" and "natural" foods are superior to those produced by conventional manufacturing methods.	Chapter 9
All food additives are poisons and should be avoided.	Chapter 9
Diet can prevent or cure cancer.	Chapter 9
Meat is necessary for good health.	Chapter 10
Protein, vitamin, and mineral supplements will enhance athletic performance.	Chapter 12

cases, the claims do have an experimental basis, but the results do not always apply to the ordinary, everyday life situations of most people, mainly because many of the experiments are done on animals.

A nutritious diet is an important part of feeling good and maintaining health, but there is a limit to the value of nutrition in most situations. In general, a nutrient can only prevent or cure diseases resulting from a deficiency of that nutrient. For example, a variety of nutrients, including protein, vitamin A, vitamin C, and many of the B vitamins, are required to maintain healthy skin. Deficiency of any one produces skin disorders that are cured when the nutrient is returned to the diet. However, consuming more than the recommended amounts of these substances has no effect on, say, acne, the common skin problem of teenagers.

How can we evaluate nutritional claims and separate fact from fallacy? We must rely on the results of well-controlled experiments, which are the basis for the scientific method, rather than on hearsay or the casual observations we make in our lives. The proper design of a controlled experiment can reduce the influence of chance, environmental factors, and psychological bias in evaluating new information. Scientists attempt to reduce the influence of chance by employing large numbers of subjects. To isolate the effects of different environmental factors, researchers divide the subjects into groups, which they attempt to treat in exactly the same manner except for the factor being tested. The aim is to control all variables except one, so that any differences between groups can be attributed to the one difference in the way the groups were treated. For example, T. W. Anderson and his colleagues at the University of Toronto used 818 people in their first experiment testing the effect of vitamin C on the common cold and divided the subjects into two groups, one of which received additional vitamin C and one of which did not. Many characteristics of the two groups matched well, so the effects of factors other than the vitamin C were minimized. Thus any effect on the incidence or severity of colds could probably be attributed to the administration of vitamin C.

Psychological bias in an experiment can be reduced by conducting a **blind experiment**, in which the subjects do not know whether they are receiving the experimental treatment or not. To accomplish this, researchers use a **placebo**, a substance that is identical in all respects to the treatment, but which is inactive. The placebo thus fools the subject into believing he or she is receiving the treatment. The influence of psychological bias can be reduced further by conducting a **double-blind experiment**, in which neither the researchers nor the subjects know who received the treatment until the end of the experiment. Subjects are assigned to groups at random, and only when a code is broken at the end of the experiment can the researchers determine which subjects belong to each group. Anderson's experiments were double-blind, and they showed that vitamin C has no influence on the incidence of colds and only a minor effect on their severity (see Chapter 7).

Choosing foods that will meet our requirements and avoiding costly or potentially harmful fads is the basis for sound nutrition. Equally important is understanding that the foods we eat become parts of complex chemical processes as soon as they enter our mouths. Some basic concepts needed to understand the roles of nutrients in the body are presented in the Optional Overview of Chemistry and Biology at the end of this chapter.

FOCUS 1-2 SOME SOURCES OF GOOD NUTRITION INFORMATION Most people do not have the time or the expertise to locate and interpret research reports about nutrition; they must rely on the interpretations of others. Government agencies, the American Dietetic Association, and other organizations publish a large variety of materials to educate the public as well as nutritionists. Many are available at public and college libraries or can be obtained from the following sources:

1. A complete description of the RDAs:

   Food and Nutrition Board: *Recommended Dietary Allowances,* 9th ed., 1980. ISBN 0-309-02941-1. For sale by:

   Office of Publications
   National Academy of Sciences
   2101 Constitution Avenue, N.W.
   Washington, DC 20418

2. Food-composition tables:

   Adams, C. F.: *Nutritive Value of American Foods in Common Units,* Agriculture Handbook No. 456, 1975. Stock No. 001-000-03184-8. For sale by:

   Superintendent of Documents
   U.S. Government Printing Office
   Washington, D.C. 20402

   Pennington, J. A. T., and Church, H. N.: *Bowes and Church's Food Values of Portions Commonly Used,* Lippincott, Philadelphia, 1980.

   For sale in some bookstores and from the publisher.

3. Basic Four Food Plan:

   Davis, C. A., Fulton, L. H., Light, L., Oldland, T. A., Page, L., Raper, N. R., and Vettel, R. S.: *Food: The Hassle-Free Guide to a Better Diet,* Home and Garden Bulletin No. 228, 1979. Stock No. 001-000-03881-8.

   For sale by the Superintendent of Documents.

4. Dietary Goals and Guidelines:

   U.S. Department of Agriculture, U.S. Department of Health and Human Services, *Nutrition and Your Health, Dietary Guidelines for Americans,* 1980.

   For sale by the Superintendent of Documents.

5. Journals:

   Nutrition Today

   Nutrition Reviews

   American Journal of Clinical Nutrition

   Journal of the American Dietetic Association

   Journal of Nutrition Education

6. Other sources:

   Local offices of:

   Public Health Department
   Cooperative Extension
   Food and Drug Administration
   American Dietetic Association
   American Heart Association
   American Diabetes Association

   Nutrition departments at local colleges and universities

   Dietitians

   Qualified nurses and physicians

Study Guide

SUMMARY

More and more, people want to know how to choose a diet that will maintain optimal health. We also have become more concerned about the diet of the American population as a whole. On one hand, many poor people in the United States do not have enough to eat; on the other, a great deal of evidence has accumulated that indicates that the dietary pattern typical of most Americans may contribute to several common diseases, including heart disease, obesity, diabetes mellitus, high blood pressure, and certain types of cancer. As a result, the United States Senate issued a set of recommendations in 1977, the U.S. Dietary Goals, for modifying the diet to combat these disorders. The Dietary Goals are a significant step toward a national nutrition policy. Internationally, concern has grown about how to feed the expanding populations of the developing nations. Solving this problem is one of the nutrition challenges for the 1980s.

To make sound decisions about personal nutrition and to better understand national and international food policies, we need a firm grasp of the basic principles of nutrition: how nutrients function in the body, how standards of nutrient intake such as the RDAs are derived and what they mean, how food-composition tables, the basic four food groups, and the Dietary Guidelines for Americans can be used to choose a nutritious diet, what factors influence our food choices, what methods are used to evaluate nutritional status, and what happens if we consume too much or too little of a nutrient. In addition, we need to understand the role of experimentation in testing new information so we can better evaluate both sides of the many controversies currently raging in the nutrition field.

VOCABULARY

anthropometry
balance studies
blind experiment
double-blind experiment
nutrients
nutrition
placebo
Recommended Dietary Allowances (RDAs)
United States Recommended Dietary Allowances (USRDAs)

STUDY QUESTIONS

1. List some factors that influence a person's choice of foods to eat. Give some examples of how each applies to your choice of food.
2. Describe the means by which the RDAs are derived and used:
   a. Briefly describe four types of experiments that generate data about nutritional requirements.
   b. How does the FNB set the RDA so that the recommended level of intake will meet the needs of most healthy people?
   c. Do the RDAs give the nutritional requirements for any particular individual? Why or why not? How can individuals make use of the RDAs in diet planning?
   d. What are some other uses of the RDAs?
3. How can each of the following be used in diet planning? Describe some problems or controversies involving each.
   a. Food-composition tables
   b. Basic Four Food Group Plan
   c. U.S. Dietary Goals

4. Describe the four methods for evaluating nutritional status. What are the shortcomings of each?
5. Why is it risky to rely on hearsay evidence or our own casual observations in drawing valid conclusions about nutrition? How do experimental procedures attempt to control these problems?

FURTHER READING

1. The Food and Nutrition Board's own explanation of how the RDAs have been derived, as well as complete tables of their recommendations.

   Food and Nutrition Board: *Recommended Dietary Allowances,* 9th ed., National Academy of Sciences, Washington, DC, 1980.

2. A clear and practical explanation of the four food groups, including recipes.

   Davis, C. A., et al.: *Food: The Hassle-Free Guide to a Better Diet,* Home and Garden Bulletin No. 228, USDA, Washington, D.C., 1979.

3. Examples of current arguments in favor of and critical of the U.S. Dietary Goals:

   Hegsted, D. M.: "Dietary Goals—A Progressive View," *Am. J. Clin. Nutr.* **31**: 1504–1509 (1978).

   Harper, A. E.: "Dietary Goals—A Skeptical View," *Am. J. Clin. Nutr.* **31**:310–321 (1978).

   Olson, R. E.: "Are Professionals Jumping the Gun in the Fight Against Chronic Diseases?" *J. Am. Diet. Assoc.* **74**:543–550 (1979).

4. Two interesting and readable accounts about food faddism:

   Deutsch, R.: *The New Nuts Among the Berries,* 2d ed., Bull Publishing, Menlo Park, Calif., 1977.

   Special Supplement, "Nutrition Misinformation and Food Faddism," *Nutr. Rev.* **32**:(July 1974).

Optional Overview of Chemistry and Biology

The human body is a remarkable creation. In many ways it resembles a miniature factory, taking in raw materials in the form of food and transforming it into useful products, including energy, structural components, transport mechanisms, defense systems, and communication systems. At the same time, parts of the body are constantly being torn down, and the body devotes much of its manufacturing capacity to replacing these components. These body processes are collectively called **metabolism**. The building up, or synthetic, processes are called **anabolism**; the breakdown processes are called **catabolism**.

Food contains all the substances required to build, maintain, and fuel the human body. Parents tell their children to consume the proper foods so they will "grow up to be big and strong," and most people are aware of the necessity to "eat right." Few of us, however, understand the specific functions each nutrient performs in the body. These will be described in the next several chapters. However, to increase our understanding of the roles nutrients play, we will first review some basic chemical and biological concepts.

ATOMS AND MOLECULES

Although thousands of chemical substances are found in the human body, they are made up of only about 25 different **elements** (Table 1-3). A basic unit of matter is the **atom**, the smallest particle that can exist alone and still maintain its identity as an element. Atoms can combine with one another to form **molecules**, and the properties of a substance, such as how readily it melts or vaporizes and what chemical reactions it will undergo, depend on its structure: the type, number, and arrangement of the atoms from which its molecules are made. A molecule of ferric chloride, for example, consists of an atom of iron and three atoms of chlorine ($FeCl_3$). Ferric chloride has entirely different properties than carbon tetrachloride, which is composed of an atom of carbon and four atoms of chlorine (CCl_4).

Within a molecule, atoms are joined together by chemical bonds. There are several types of bonds, but the one found most frequently in living matter is the **covalent bond**, in which one or more electrons are shared between two atoms. Two adjacent atoms may be joined by more than one bond. If there is only one bond between atoms, it is called a *single bond*. Two bonds is a *double bond;* three forms a *triple bond* (Figure 1-4). The chemical properties of carbon-carbon double bonds are important in some nutrients, notably fats. The nature of the fat and its effect on the body varies considerably with the number of double bonds it contains (see Chapter 3).

Molecules formed from different types of atoms are called chemical **compounds**. Nearly all the compounds in living systems are based on the element carbon, which occurs in combination with hydrogen, oxygen, nitrogen, and several other elements. An atom of carbon may bind to as many as four other atoms, including other carbon atoms. This capability is responsible for the large number and diversity of chemical substances found in living matter. If a carbon atom joins with four other atoms, each bond is a single bond. Carbon also may bind twice to the same atom, forming a double bond. In this case, carbon joins with fewer than four other atoms, depending on the number of double bonds it forms (Figure 1-3).

Chemists define all carbon compounds except carbon dioxide and carbon salts, such as calcium carbonate ($CaCO_3$), as **organic**, regardless of their origin. Because it contains carbon, vitamin C is an organic substance, whether it is synthesized in the leaf of a plant or in a chemist's test tube. Similarly, the element iron is inorganic, no matter if its source is a tablet or a piece of liver. Some people use the word *organic* to describe substances derived from "natural" plant and animal sources rather than being manufactured commercially. They claim that the "organic," or "natural," compounds are superior to their "artificial," or "synthetic," counterparts. The chemist's definition of organic includes both "natural" and manufactured substances, and as long as both have the same chemical structure, their activity in the body is identical.

FIGURE 1-4
Types of Chemical Bonds. **A** *Single Bonds:* All bonds in these compounds are single bonds. When carbon forms only single bonds, it joins with four other atoms. **B** *Double Bonds:* These compounds contain at least one double bond. When carbon is involved in a double bond, it cannot join with as many other atoms as when it forms only single bonds. **C** *Triple Bonds:* These compounds contain one triple bond. Such compounds are not often found in the human body.

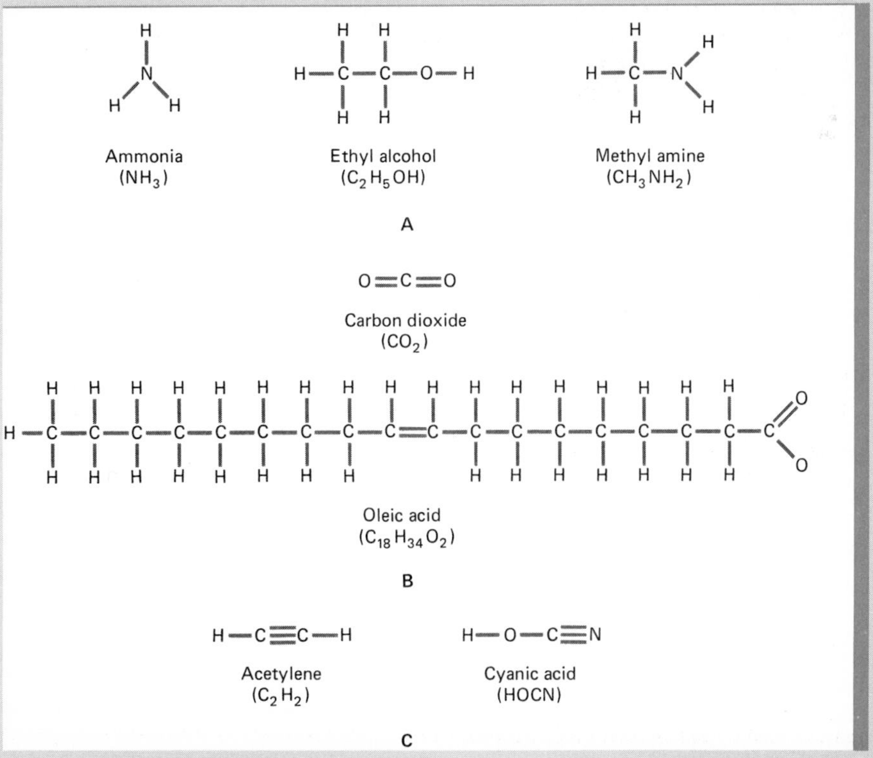

Ammonia
(NH_3)

Ethyl alcohol
(C_2H_5OH)

Methyl amine
(CH_3NH_2)

A

O=C=O

Carbon dioxide
(CO_2)

Oleic acid
($C_{18}H_{34}O_2$)

B

H—C≡C—H

H—O—C≡N

Acetylene
(C_2H_2)

Cyanic acid
(HOCN)

C

FROM CELLS TO ORGAN SYSTEMS

The chemical substances described in the previous section perform their functions as components of a highly organized biological system. The basis of this system is the **cell**, the smallest structural unit of life capable of functioning independently. If we consider any of the body's activities, such as muscle contraction, nerve function, eyesight, defense against infection, and digestion, cells either perform the function directly or provide the means, such as chemical substances, by which the chemical function can be carried out.

The cell is not simply a random collection of chemicals. It is organized into a number of structures called **organelles**, each of which contributes to the functioning of the cell as a whole (Figure 1-5). Some chemical substances are building materials that make up the cell's structure. Others are contained within the organelles or are attached to them and, like workers and machinery, carry out required activities. Still other chemicals are free in solution in the cell and perform their functions there.

Certain organelles are particularly important in nutrition, either because nutrients are involved in their structure and function or because they are involved in the metabolism of nutrients. For instance, the cell is enclosed by a saclike structure called the **plasma membrane**, and this membrane regulates the passage of substances into and out of the cell. Because the plasma membrane does not allow everything to pass through, it is said to be *semipermeable*. Water, oxygen, and many of the nutrients readily cross the membrane; large molecules, such as proteins and nucleic acids, do not.

The inside of the cell is divided into two parts, the nucleus and the

TABLE 1-3

Elements found in the human body

ELEMENT	CHEMICAL SYMBOL	ELEMENT	CHEMICAL SYMBOL
Carbon	C	Selenium	Se
Hydrogen	H	Molybdenum	Mo
Nitrogen	N	Fluorine	F
Oxygen	O	Iodine	I
Phosphorus	P	Manganese	Mn
Sulfur	S	Cobalt	Co
Calcium	Ca	Iron	Fe
Potassium	P	Chromium	Cr
Sodium	Na	Tin	Sn
Magnesium	Mg	Nickel	Ni
Chlorine	Cl	Vanadium	V
Copper	Cu	Silicon	Si
Zinc	Zn		

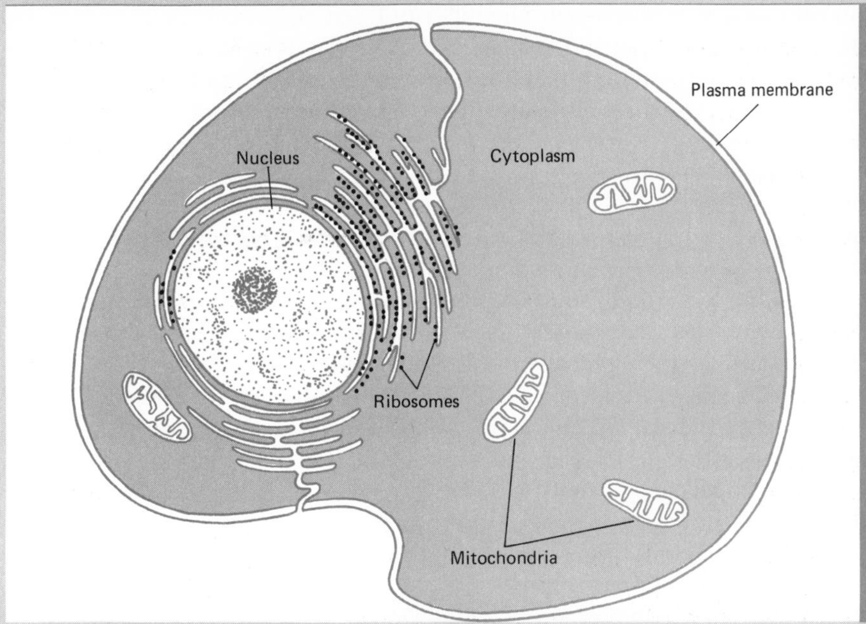

FIGURE 1-5
The Cell. Organelles of particular importance in utilizing nutrients are shown.

cytoplasm. The **nucleus** is the command center; it exerts control by means of the chemical deoxyribonucleic acid (DNA) contained within it. The DNA contains instructions for the synthesis of proteins, which in turn carry out many of the functions of the cell. DNA is also the means by which these instructions are passed on to succeeding generations of cells. This substance is therefore the genetic material responsible for heredity.

The material outside the nucleus, the **cytoplasm**, is a complex mixture of water, proteins, various mineral elements, the sugar glucose, and other substances. The cytoplasm contains many organelles. The **mitochondria** supply energy. Within them the final stages in the breakdown of carbohydrate, fat, and protein occur, and this releases the energy contained in these substances. Unless it were captured in some way, this energy would be lost as heat. The mitochondria trap energy by forming a compound called adenosine triphosphate (ATP) from a related substance, adenosine diphosphate (ADP) (Figure 1-6). Adenosine diphosphate contains two phosphate molecules. When a third phosphate is added, energy is captured in the chemical bond that is formed. Adenosine triphosphate stores the energy until it is needed to drive cell processes, such as muscle contraction, the firing of nerves, and the synthesis of various compounds. Protein synthesis occurs in organelles called **ribosomes**, which are attached to a system of double membranes called the *endoplasmic reticulum.* (The process of protein synthesis is described in detail in Chapter 4.)

Cells are complex and highly organized systems, and each type performs functions that contribute to the well-being of the body as a whole. For example, nerve cells generate and transmit electric impulses, providing a means of monitoring and responding to changes in both the internal and external environments. Movement of the body and maintenance of posture are carried out by muscle cells. Still other cells detoxify foreign compounds, store fat, and provide structural support for the body. To carry out their functions in a coordinated fashion, cells are organized into tissues and organs, which in turn operate as part of elaborate organ systems. **Tissues** are aggregations of cells of a single type. The word *tissue* does not imply any structure; we simply speak of muscle tissue, nerve tissue, adipose (fat) tissue, liver tissue, and so on. **Organs**, however, are structures composed of one or more tissues. The pancreas, for instance, contains one type of tissue that makes digestive enzymes and another that makes certain hormones. The stomach contains muscle tissue, tissue that synthesizes a hormone, and tissue that makes digestive juices. Several organs whose functions are related form an **organ system** (Table 1-4). Thus the stomach, small intestine, and large intestine all participate in the digestion of food and are part of the digestive system.

Within the body, then, a hierarchy of organization exists (Figure 1-7). On one hand, cells group together into tissues, organs, and organ systems to carry out the body's functions in a coordinated manner. The functions of the tissues, organs, and organ systems therefore result from the activities of their component cells. On the other hand, the cell itself is composed of a number of substructures. The functions of the cell and its organelles result from the activity of the chemical substances they contain. The life processes thus have a chemical basis, and it is through their role as chemical substances that the nutrients make their contributions to the body.

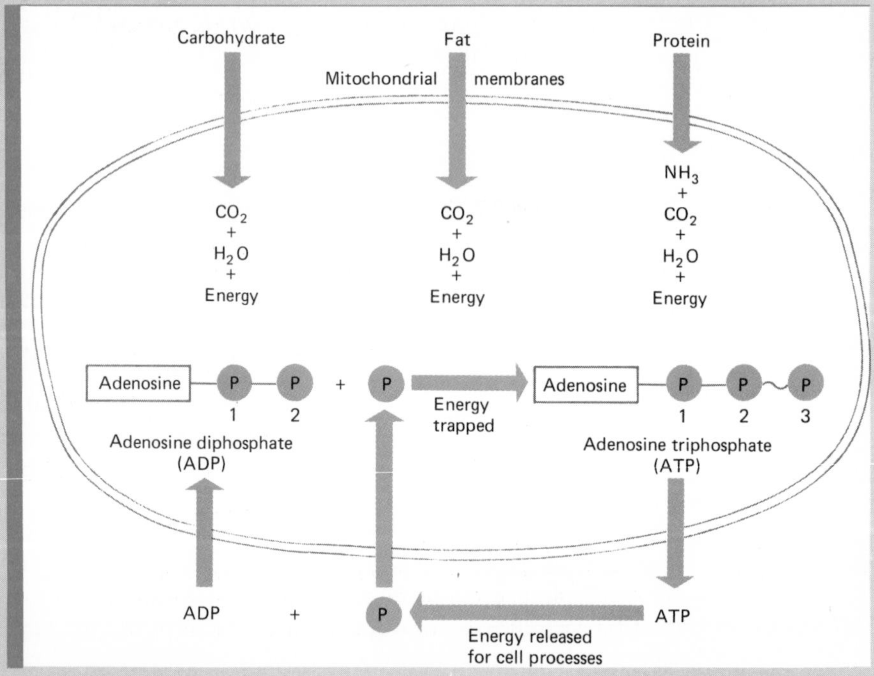

FIGURE 1-6
Energy Production in the Mitochondria. The breakdown of carbohydrate, fat, and protein is completed in the mitochondria. The energy given off is stored by synthesizing ATP. Later ATP can be broken down, releasing the energy for use by the cell.

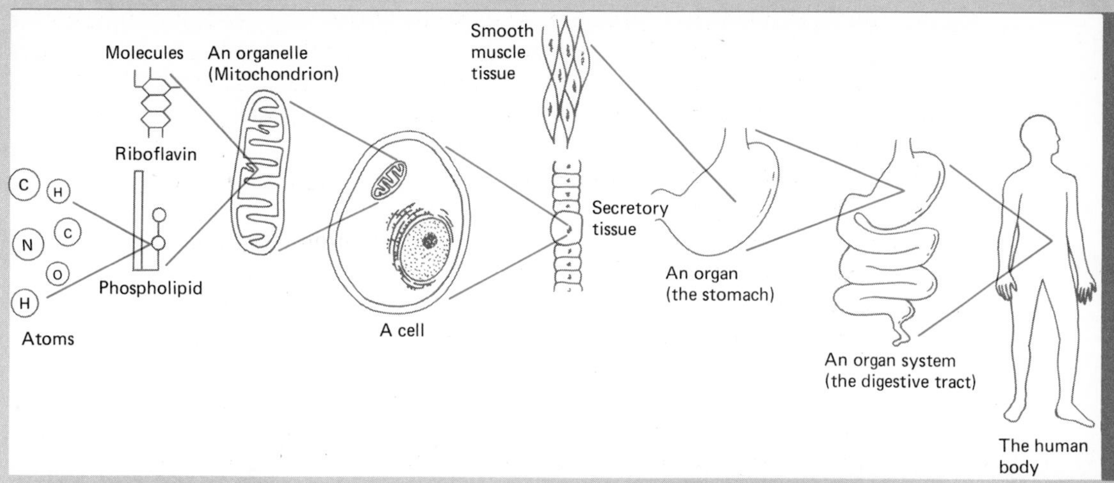

FIGURE 1-7
The Organization of Matter in the Human Body. There are many levels of organization within the body. Each level involves larger and more complex structures than the ones below it.

TABLE **1-4**
Organ systems of the body

ORGAN SYSTEM	ORGANS AND TISSUES INVOLVED	FUNCTIONS
Digestive system	Mouth, esophagus, stomach, small intestine, large intestine, and auxiliary organs (liver, pancreas, salivary glands)	Breakdown of food into simpler components that can be absorbed into the body
Circulatory system	Heart, blood vessels, and blood	Transport of substances throughout the body
Respiratory system	Lungs	Uptake of oxygen, elimination of carbon dioxide
Excretory system	Kidney and urinary bladder	Elimination of waste products from the body, maintenance of acid-base balance and water balance
Musculoskeletal system	Muscles and bones	Body movement, structural support
Nervous system	Brain, spinal cord, and other nervous tissue	Monitoring and responding to changes in internal and external environments, control of many body processes, higher thought processes
Integument	Skin	A protective barrier separating the internal and external environments
Reproductive system	Genital organs	Reproduction
Endocrine system	Pituitary gland, adrenal gland, thyroid gland, and many others	Production of hormones that control many body processes

HOMEOSTASIS: NERVES, HORMONES, AND ENZYMES

The goal of much of the body's activity is to maintain an internal environment that promotes optimal functioning. To do this, the cells in each tissue and organ must operate at the appropriate level of activity, and the concentration of a large number of substances in the body fluids must be maintained within fairly narrow limits. Maintenance of a balanced state within the body is called **homeostasis**. When this equilibrium exists, the body functions properly and generally remains healthy. If homeostasis is disrupted, the unbalanced state may result in the development of an unhealthy condition. Under most circumstances, however, disruption of the status quo brings into play a number of mechanisms that attempt to restore equilibrium and avert trouble.

The body maintains homeostasis by three general means: the nervous system, hormones, and enzymes. The nervous system is composed of the brain, the spinal cord, and thousands of nerves that control tissue and organ functions by means of electric impulses they transmit throughout the body. In this way, the nervous system initiates a response to both internal and external stimuli by activating or deactivating appropriate tissues. **Hormones** are chemical messengers secreted into the blood by endocrine glands (Figure 1-8) in response to stimuli, such as changes in the glucose, sodium, or calcium concentrations in the blood. The hormones are carried throughout the body, and they stimulate or inhibit the activity of one or more tissues or organs in an attempt to restore homeostasis. **Enzymes** are proteins that act as catalysts to speed up the rates of chemical reactions in the cell. Without enzymes, the reactions would proceed too slowly. Enzymes play a part in both the synthesis and breakdown of a

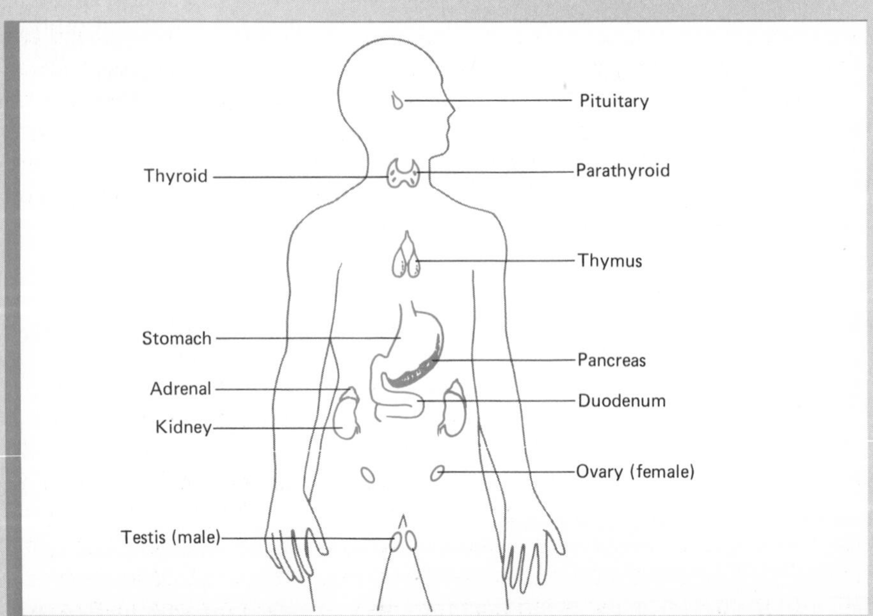

FIGURE 1-8
The Endocrine System. These glands and organs secrete hormones into the blood, which transports them throughout the body. Each hormone acts on specific target tissues to stimulate or inhibit their activity.

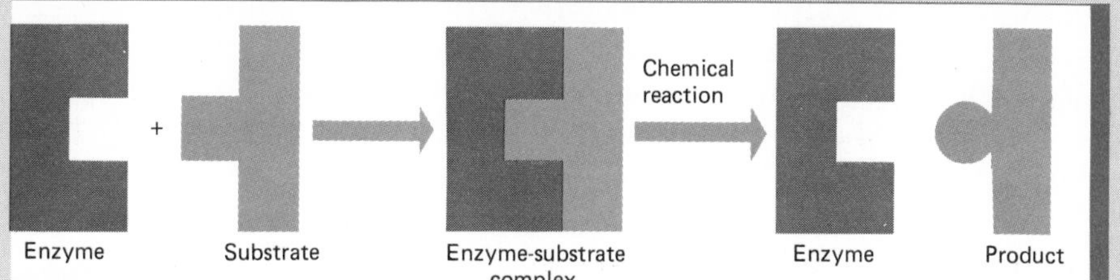

FIGURE 1-9
How Enzymes Work. Each type of enzyme combines with a specific substance (its substrate) and catalyzes a chemical reaction involving the substance. The resulting product is released, and the enzyme can combine with a new substrate molecule to repeat the process.

variety of substances, including fats, carbohydrates, and proteins, and they may be thought of as the "machinery" of the cell. The substance on which an enzyme acts is called its *substrate.* The enzyme and substrate combine to form a complex within which the enzyme carries out the required chemical changes. When the reaction is complete, the enzyme releases the product and is itself unchanged by the reaction. It can combine with another substrate molecule and repeat the cycle (Figure 1-9). Some enzymes can react with thousands of substrate molecules in 1 minute. Enzymes are often organized into biochemical pathways, a series of reactions that transform one substance into another. For example, the conversion of glucose into carbon dioxide and water is a pathway with over 25 steps.

Although nerves, hormones, and enzymes operate in their own particular ways, their mechanisms have some things in common. In each case, the environment within the body is monitored by some means. Changes in this internal environment alter the activity of part of the nervous system, of one or more hormones, or of one or more enzymes, which in turn produce alterations in the activity of particular tissues and organs or in the concentration of certain substances in the blood. This sequence of events is called a **negative feedback system**, because the original stimulus initiates a series of events that counteracts or opposes it, thereby maintaining homeostasis. Negative feedback systems involving nerves, hormones, and enzymes, acting alone or together, govern most body processes. One example is given in Focus 1-3.

FOCUS 1-3 BLOOD GLUCOSE REGULATION: AN EXAMPLE OF NEGATIVE FEEDBACK

An important homeostatic mechanism in the body is the one that maintains the level of glucose in the blood within a fairly narrow range. If blood glucose concentrations drop too low, the functioning of the nervous system is impaired, and the individual might even die. High blood glucose levels indicate the sugar is not being used properly by the body. This condition, called *diabetes mellitus,* results in loss of body weight, excessive urination, and other problems (see Chapter 2).

Blood glucose concentrations are maintained within normal limits by a negative feedback system involving several hormones and a large number of enzymes. In response to high blood glucose levels, the pancreas secretes the hormone insulin, which stimulates a number of tissues, including muscle and adipose (fat) tissue to remove the sugar from the blood. Insulin also stimulates the enzymes within these tissues that break down glucose for energy, store it in the form of glycogen, or convert it to fat. In this way, blood glucose concentration is brought back to normal (Figure 1-10*a*). If blood glucose levels drop too low, the pancreas secretes different hormones: glucagon, epinephrine, and the glucocorticosteroids. They stimulate the release of glucose from storage into the blood, as well as the biochemical pathway that synthesizes glucose from other substances. The net effect of these processes is to raise the blood glucose concentration back to its normal level (Figure 1-10*b*).

Many other negative feedback systems in the body are of nutritional importance. For example, fluid and salt balance and calcium and phosphate balance are controlled in this way. Body weight also appears to be under negative feedback control.

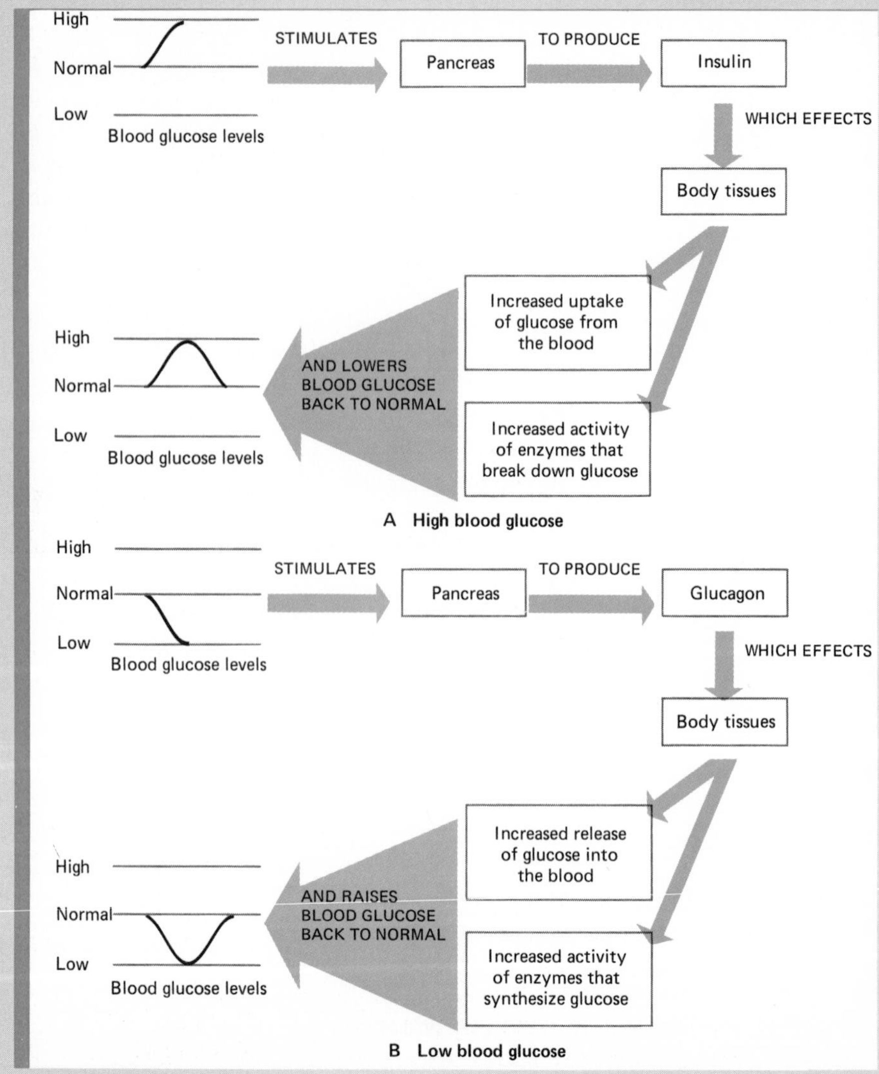

FIGURE 1-10 *Regulation of Blood Glucose Levels.* **A** When blood glucose becomes elevated, the pancreas secretes insulin, a hormone that stimulates clearance of the glucose and returns the blood glucose level to normal. **B** When blood glucose drops too low, the pancreas secretes glucagon, which stimulates release of glucose into the blood and restores normal blood glucose concentration.

Study Guide

SUMMARY

Certain chemical and biological concepts are important to the study of nutrition. The fundamental unit of life, the cell, is made up of chemical compounds, including the nutrients, which form its structure and carry out its functions. In order to operate in a coordinated manner, cells are organized into tissues, organs, and organ systems. The activity of these structures is controlled by nerves, hormones, and enzymes. One type of control mechanism is the negative feedback system, in which a change or stimulus initiates a sequence of events that counteracts the initial stimulus. Negative feedback systems maintain the proper balance of certain nutrients, including glucose, water, salt, calcium, and phosphorus, in the body.

VOCABULARY

anabolism
atom
catabolism
cell
chemical compounds
covalent bond
cytoplasm
element
enzyme
homeostasis
hormone
metabolism
mitochondria
molecule
negative feedback system
nucleus
organ
organelle
organic
organ system
plasma membrane
ribosomes
tissues

STUDY QUESTIONS

1. What is the function of each of the following cell structures?
   a. Plasma membrane
   b. Nucleus
   c. Mitochondria
   d. Ribosomes

   As you read further in this text, determine what roles these organelles play in the metabolism of the nutrients (e.g., ribosomes: protein synthesis) and how nutrients function as components of cells (e.g., folacin: DNA synthesis, cell division).
2. Explain how some hormones and enzymes work as part of negative feedback systems in the body, such as the one that controls blood glucose concentrations.

FURTHER READING

1. General biology:

   Keeton, W. T.: *Biological Science,* 3d ed., Norton, New York, 1979.
2. General chemistry:

   Seager, S. L., and Slabaugh, M. R.: *Introductory Chemistry: General, Organic, Biological,* Scott Foresman, Glenview, Ill., 1979.
3. Biochemistry:

   Lehninger, A. L.: *Biochemistry: The Molecular Basis of All Structure and Function,* 2d ed., Worth, New York, 1975.
4. Physiology:

   Guyton, A. C.: *Physiology of the Human Body,* 5th ed., Saunders, Philadelphia, 1979.
5. Nutrition:

   Guthrie, H. A.: *Introductory Nutrition,* 4th ed., Mosby, St. Louis, 1979.

   Briggs, G. M., and Calloway, D. H.: *Bogert's Nutrition and Physical Fitness,* 10th ed., Saunders, Philadelphia, 1979.

   Pike, R. L., and Brown, M. L.: *Nutrition: An Integrated Approach,* 2d ed., Wiley, New York, 1975.

   Goodhart, R. S., and Shils, M. E.: *Modern Nutrition in Health and Disease,* 6th ed., Lea & Febiger, Philadelphia, 1980.

   Krause, M. V., and Mahan, L. K.: *Food, Nutrition and Diet Therapy,* 6th ed., Saunders, Philadelphia, 1979.

   Nutrition Reviews' Present Knowledge in Nutrition, 4th ed., Nutrition Foundation, Washington, D.C., 1976.

PART 1 THE ENERGY NUTRIENTS

When preschool children are asked "What does food give you?" very often they will answer "Energy!" Even at a young age, they recognize that food supplies the body's fuel. Adults are more specific about the energy value of food. Many know that carbohydrates such as sugar and starch are important sources of energy and that large amounts of energy can be stored as fat. They may have heard that the amount and type of fat in the diet may increase the risk of developing heart disease. Many people have misconceptions about these nutrients as well. Some people believe that sugar is dangerous or that carbohydrates are fattening. Others overemphasize the value of protein as an energy source.

Chapters 2, 3, and 4 will explain the roles of the energy nutrients—carbohydrate, fat, and protein—in the body. We will look at how much of each is needed in the diet and which foods contain them. We will learn what happens when we consume too little or too much. These chapters also will explore some of the current issues and misconceptions about the energy nutrients and present strategies for making wise choices regarding their intake.

2

CARBOHYDRATES

Like many American women today, Joan Smith leads a double life: she teaches at the local high school all day and prepares dinner and helps care for a demanding family at night. By midafternoon, Joan almost always feels irritable and tired, so she heads to the cafeteria for a snack. This usually improves her mood, but since she has little time for exercise, she is gaining weight. These are problems many of us share, and in recent years, many popular books have appeared that claim they can solve them for us. By cutting down drastically on the intake of substances called carbohydrates, advises one, we can lose weight without restricting the intake of favorite foods that lack them (1). Another book blames one carbohydrate, the sugar sucrose, for the fatigue and irritability many of us sometimes experience. It attributes these symptoms to low blood glucose levels (hypoglycemia) caused by overconsumption of sucrose and recommends eliminating this sugar from the diet (2). Still another book claims that increasing the intake of indigestible carbohydrates (fiber) can improve our health (3).

Although it is tempting to follow the advice offered in these books, much of it is misleading. Carbohydrate is important for normal body function, and at a time when food prices are rising rapidly, it provides a relatively inexpensive source of energy. Medical authorities do not believe that sucrose causes hypoglycemia, nor do they believe that the disorder is usually responsible for the fatigue and irritability of which people complain. In addition, the role of fiber in human nutrition is still unclear. Authorities disagree about what actually comprises fiber, and much remains to be discovered about its properties, the amounts needed in the diet, and its content in food.

In this chapter we will examine the different types of carbohydrate in the diet, how the body uses them, the amounts needed by the body, and the foods in which they occur. We also will evaluate the adverse publicity surrounding sucrose and the roles fiber may play in maintaining health.

The Carbohydrates

Carbohydrates are chemical compounds containing carbon, hydrogen, and oxygen arranged in a particular way. They are usually divided into three general classes: monosaccharides, disaccharides, and polysaccharides. The first two groups are the sugars; the third includes starches and fiber.

MONOSACCHARIDES AND DISACCHARIDES: THE SUGARS

Monosaccharides are the simplest carbohydrates; they are single molecules that cannot be subdivided into other carbohydrates. Monosaccharides contain carbon, hydrogen, and oxygen in a ratio of 1:2:1 ($C_nH_{2n}O_n$), where *n* equals the number of carbon atoms in the sugar molecule). The formula for a four-carbon monosaccharide would be $C_4H_8O_4$, and for a six-carbon monosaccharide, $C_6H_{12}O_6$.

Many monosaccharides exist in nature, but only three are of major nutritional importance: glucose, fructose, and galactose, each of which contains six carbon atoms (Figure 2-1). **Glucose**, the primary sugar in the human body, is found in honey and many fruits and vegetables. Another name for glucose is *dextrose*. **Fructose**, also called *fruit sugar* or *levulose,* occurs in honey and many fruits. **Galactose** does not occur freely in nature; it is released by the breakdown of another sugar, lactose, in the intestine.

The joining together of any two monosaccharides forms a **disaccharide**. The bonding of the two sugars causes the release of a water mol-

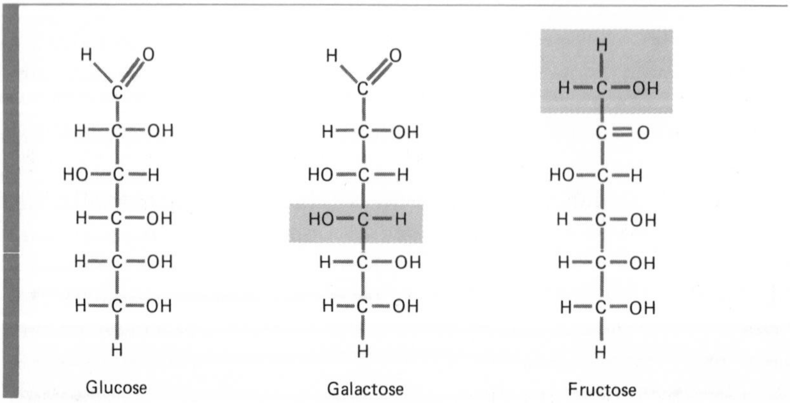

FIGURE 2-1
The Monosaccharides of Nutritional Importance. Each has the same chemical composition, but differs in the arrangement of the oxygen and hydrogen atoms (shaded areas highlight structural differences between glucose and galactose or fructose).

Glucose	Galactose	Fructose
H–C=O	H–C=O	H–C(H)–OH
H–C–OH	H–C–OH	C=O
HO–C–H	HO–C–H	HO–C–H
H–C–OH	HO–C–H	H–C–OH
H–C–OH	H–C–OH	H–C–OH
H–C–OH	H–C–OH	H–C–OH
H	H	H

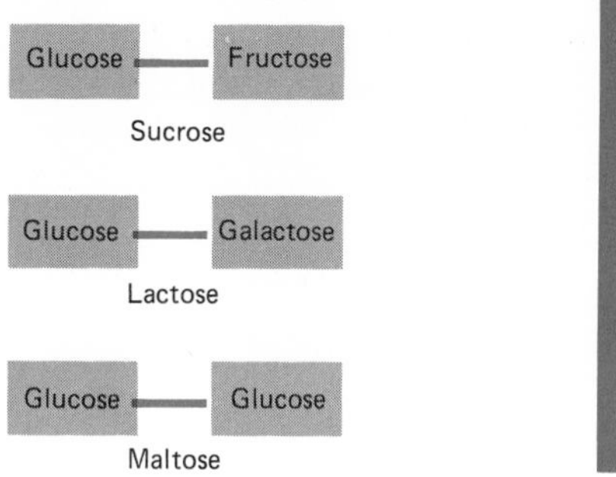

FIGURE 2-2
The Disaccharides of Nutritional Importance. Each is composed of two monosaccharides.

ecule so that the chemical formula of the disaccharide is $C_n(H_2O)_{n-1}$. Three disaccharides are important in nutrition—sucrose, lactose, and maltose—and all have the chemical formula $C_{12}H_{22}O_{11}$. **Sucrose**, common table sugar, contains a molecule of glucose and a molecule of fructose. A molecule of glucose and a molecule of galactose make up the milk sugar **lactose**, while **maltose** is composed of two molecules of glucose (Figure 2-2).

THE STARCHES AND OTHER POLYSACCHARIDES

Monosaccharide molecules can be organized into complex carbohydrates called **polysaccharides**, which may contain hundreds of these subunits (Figure 2-3). An example of a polysaccharide is **starch**, which is found in

FIGURE 2-3
The Polysaccharides of Nutritional Importance. Each is composed of glucose subunits.

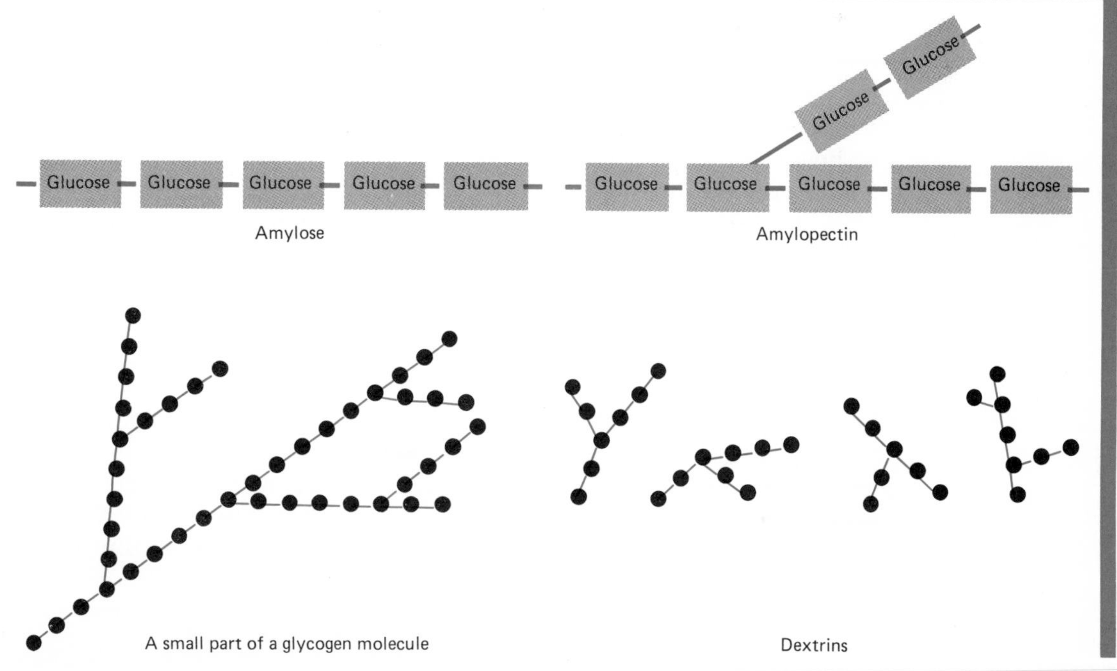

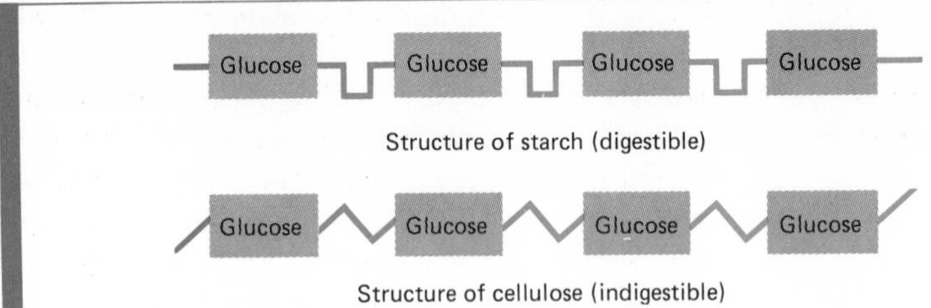

FIGURE 2-4 *Comparison of Starch and Cellulose.* Both are composed of glucose, but differ in the manner in which these subunits are joined together. The bonds in cellulose are resistant to human digestive enzymes.

plants. Starch is composed of glucose subunits arranged into branched chains (amylopectin) and long, unbranched chains (amylose). Starches from different sources, such as potatoes, corn, or soybeans, vary in the proportion of amylose and amylopectin they contain, and this gives them different characteristics.

Glycogen, or animal starch, is similar to plant starch, but much more complex. Glycogen contains many times the number of glucose subunits and is very highly branched (Figure 2-3). The human body can store more than one-third of a kilogram (three-quarters of a pound) of carbohydrate as glycogen in the liver and muscles.

Dextrins are polysaccharide fragments that result from the breakdown of starches (Figure 2-3). Although they contain glucose subunits, dextrins are smaller molecules than starches. They are found in toasted bread and in zwieback, because dry heat breaks down some of the starch in the flour. Dextrins also are used to prevent crystallization of sugar in certain types of candy. Because the body readily digests dextrins and metabolizes the resulting glucose molecules, this food additive is harmless.

Cellulose is another polysaccharide composed of glucose subunits. In cellulose, however, the glucose molecules are joined together in such a way that the body cannot break them down (Figure 2-4), so it remains in the digestive tract as a component of **fiber**. Other polysaccharides, such as hemicellulose and pectin, also contribute to the fiber content of the diet. **Hemicellulose** is a polymer made up of the sugars xylose, arabinose, glucose, mannose, and galactose, while **pectin** contains mainly a galactose derivative, galacturonic acid.

How Carbohydrate Works in the Body

Carbohydrate is a source of energy for the body. Some tissues, such as the nervous system and the red blood cells, cannot use fat for fuel and under normal conditions use only glucose. Carbohydrate contributes to the maintenance of energy balance by providing 4 kilocalories for each gram consumed. The ultimate source of this energy is sunlight, which plants trap by synthesizing glucose from carbon dioxide and water (**photosynthesis**):

$$6CO_2 + 6H_2O + \text{light energy} \xrightarrow{\text{photosynthesis}} C_6H_{12}O_6 + 6O_2$$

The plant then stores the glucose in the form of a sugar or starch, which we consume as food (Figure 2-5).

After carbohydrate is eaten, it must be digested into monosaccharide form to be absorbed into the body (Figure 2-6). Starch, dextrins, and maltose are broken down into their glucose subunits by the small intestine. Lactose is digested into glucose and galactose, while sucrose yields glucose and fructose. These monosaccharides are readily absorbed into the body, but before they can be used for fuel, the galactose and some of the fructose are converted to glucose. Thus glucose is the primary carbohydrate in the body. It is by far the most abundant one in the bloodstream, and when we speak about "blood sugar," we mean glucose.

In cells throughout the body, glucose and the remaining fructose are broken down into carbon dioxide, water, and energy. The energy is trapped in the chemical bonds of adenosine triphosphate (ATP) (see Chapter 1), which can then be used for body processes, such as muscle

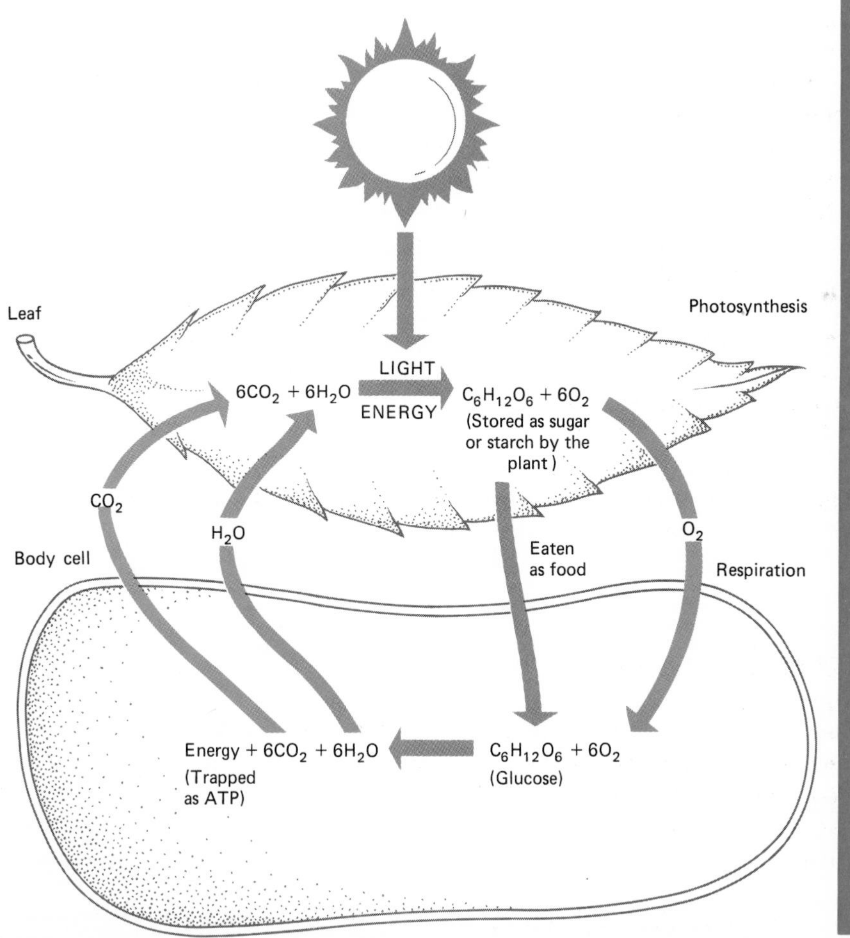

FIGURE 2-5
The Energy Cycle. Plants synthesize carbohydrate from carbon dioxide and water using energy provided by sunlight. Oxygen liberated by photosynthesis is utilized by cells to break down carbohydrate and release the energy to meet the cells' needs. Carbon dioxide and water produced by respiration can eventually be reused for photosynthesis.

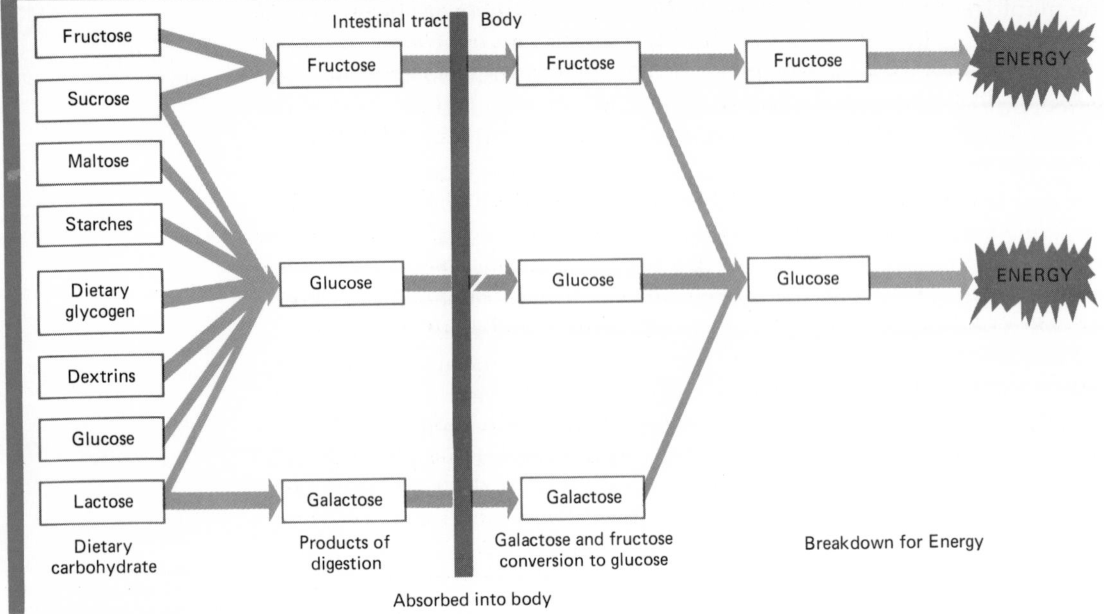

FIGURE 2-6
Metabolism of Dietary Carbohydrate. Dietary carbohydrates are digested into monosaccharide form in the small intestine. After absorption, nearly all of the galactose and most of the fructose are converted to glucose, which is then broken down to release energy. The remaining fructose is also used for energy.

contraction, nerve activity, heart beat, and breathing (Figure 2-5). This process is called **respiration**:

$$C_6H_{12}O_6 + 6O_2 \xrightarrow{\text{respiration}} 6CO_2 + H_2O + \text{energy trapped in ATP}$$

When we consume more carbohydrate than the body can use for energy, some of the excess is stored in the liver and muscles as glycogen. Glucose becomes incorporated into long chains within the glycogen molecule; when it is needed, it can be released back into the bloodstream (Figure 2-7). However, only limited amounts can be stored in this way; as storage sites become filled, the body must dispose of the remaining excess

FIGURE 2-7
Glycogen Metabolism. **A** When excess glucose is available, such as after a meal, some is stored by incorporating it into glycogen in the liver and muscles. **B** In times of need, such as between meals or during physical activity, glucose is released from glycogen to maintain blood glucose levels.

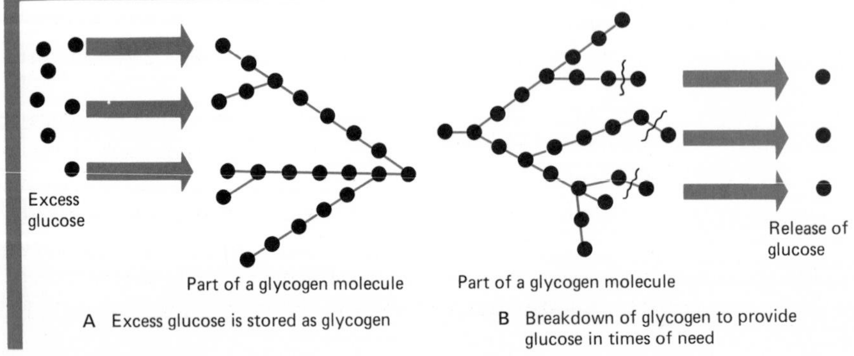

carbohydrate by converting it to fat for storage in adipose tissue. Large amounts of energy can be stored in this way, providing a reserve for use when insufficient food is available. Under these circumstances, the body begins living off its own fat and loses weight.

Carbohydrates also play a part in other body functions. For example, they combine with proteins and other nitrogen-containing compounds to form **glycoproteins** and **mucopolysaccharides**. Some of the structural components of cartilage, skin, bone, certain enzymes and hormones, the antibodies, and the substances responsible for blood type are glycoproteins. Mucopolysaccharides function as structural components of cartilage, skin, and bone, in the joint and eye fluids, and as anticoagulants.

CARBOHYDRATE DEFICIENCY

We need a certain amount of carbohydrate each day; although the body does not need any particular kind, severely restricting the total carbohydrate content of the diet can cause problems. The body as a whole must maintain a proper balance in the utilization of protein, fat, and carbohydrate for fuel. When we cut carbohydrate intake, the fat stored in adipose tissue is broken down at such a rapid rate that the body cannot oxidize all

Severely restricting the total carbohydrate content of the diet can cause problems.

of it to carbon dioxide and water. Some of the product of fat breakdown is then converted to substances called **ketone bodies**. Although the body can use ketone bodies for energy and also excretes them in the urine, production of large amounts causes them to accumulate in the blood, leading to a condition called **ketosis**. Dangerously high levels occur only in disease states, such as uncontrolled diabetes mellitus, but even moderate levels indicate an imbalance in the metabolism of carbohydrate and fat by the body.

The level of dietary carbohydrate also influences the use of protein for energy. When carbohydrate intake is too low, the body breaks down amino acids to supply energy and to synthesize its own glucose, so that tissues requiring this sugar can get enough to function. Because some of the body's own protein may be used for this purpose, too little carbohydrate can lead to the breakdown of lean tissue, such as muscle, to supply energy.

Still other problems occur when the diet lacks carbohydrate: fatigue, dehydration, nausea, vomiting, loss of appetite, and a temporary drop in blood pressure when getting up from a reclining position (4). Adequate dietary carbohydrate also is important in maintaining the glycogen stores needed for prolonged physical activity. Increasing muscle glycogen by the process of carbohydrate loading has been shown to improve performance in activity lasting longer than 30 to 60 minutes (see Chapter 12).

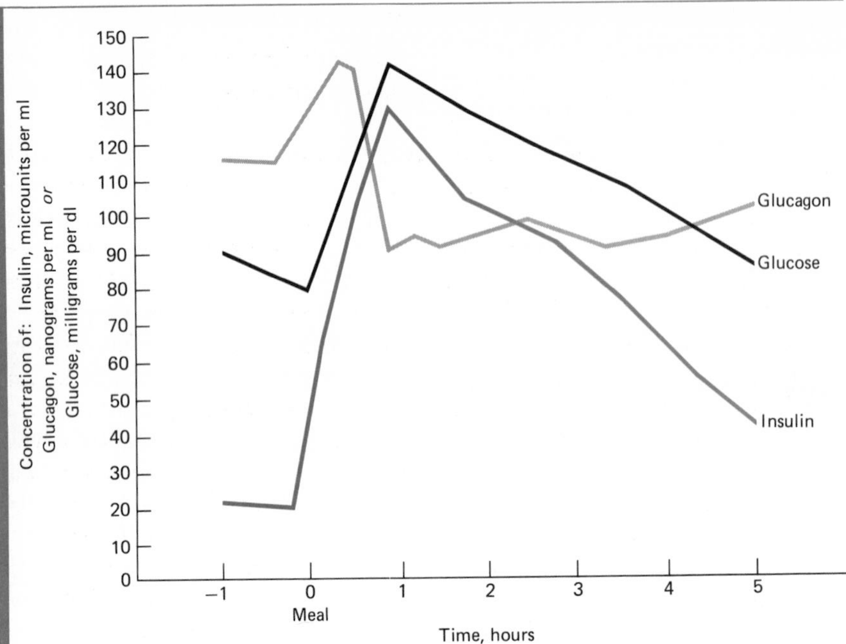

FIGURE 2-8 *Changes in Blood Glucose, Insulin, and Glucagon Levels Before, During and After a Meal Containing Carbohydrate.* Blood insulin concentration rises with that of glucose after a meal and stimulates clearance of glucose from the blood. As blood glucose falls insulin levels decline. Between meals, glucagon concentration rises to prevent blood glucose from dropping too low.

REGULATING BLOOD GLUCOSE

Without the help of hormones, the concentration of glucose in the blood would fluctuate wildly throughout the day. It would rise very high just after a meal as glucose from food floods the body, and during periods of no food intake, it would plunge very low as the body exhausted the sugar consumed at the previous meal. To prevent dangerous fluctuations, the body regulates the level of this sugar mainly through two hormones: insulin and glucagon (Figure 2-8). **Insulin** is secreted by certain cells in the pancreas in response to a high blood glucose concentration (**hyperglycemia**), which generally occurs after a meal. It reduces glucose levels in the blood by stimulating glucose uptake by the tissues and then promoting its breakdown for energy, its storage as glycogen, and its conversion to fat. The result is a lowering of blood glucose levels back to normal within 2 to 2½ hours after a meal. In response to a low blood glucose concentration, other cells in the pancreas secrete **glucagon**, which increases the level of circulating glucose by stimulating the synthesis of glucose from amino acids and causing its release from storage as glycogen in the liver. The activities of insulin and glucagon therefore oppose each other. Several other hormones also help raise blood glucose concentrations. One of the most important is **epinephrine** (**adrenaline**), which stimulates release of glucose from glycogen. Epinephrine, often called the "flight or fight" hormone, is secreted in situations in which the body is under stress or in danger, and its elevation of blood glucose helps prepare the body to fight or run away.

IMBALANCES OF CARBOHYDRATE METABOLISM

When hormonal control of blood glucose concentration does not work properly, diabetes mellitus or hypoglycemia may result.

Diabetes Mellitus

Diabetes mellitus is an imbalance in the body's utilization of carbohydrate, fat, and protein resulting from a reduction or total loss of insulin activity. Blood glucose levels increase, sometimes drastically, because the sugar can no longer be removed from the bloodstream. The body then shifts to fat for fuel, and the breakdown of fat stored in adipose tissue accelerates. Ketosis can develop and become so severe that the body's ability to neutralize acids in the blood is overwhelmed. The increasing acidity of the blood may then cause coma and eventually death. Diabetics also break down their own protein to provide amino acids for energy, causing a gradual reduction in the amount of lean body tissue. A number of symptoms accompany severe, uncontrolled diabetes, including excessive thirst, frequent urination, loss of weight, dehydration, and glucose in the urine. The disease often, but not invariably, leads to secondary complications later in life, including atherosclerosis (which may result in a heart attack, stroke, or gangrene in a limb), eye problems, and damage to the kidney and nervous system. The causes of these complications are largely unknown.

Diabetes is classified into two major types (80). *Insulin-dependent (juvenile-onset) diabetes,* which accounts for about 5 percent of the total number of diabetics, can develop at any time of life, but usually begins in childhood or puberty. It tends to be a more severe form of the disease (5, pages 977–997). Insulin production generally stops, and the diabetic requires regular injections of this hormone, as well as a special diet. Even so, this form of diabetes is difficult to control, because large fluctuations of blood glucose occur in response to even small changes in insulin dose, to exercise, and to infection. *Non-insulin-dependent (maturity-onset) diabetes* generally arises gradually, usually after the age of 35. The body produces insulin, sometimes in larger amounts than in nondiabetics, but it seems to be ineffective in carrying out its functions. Non-insulin-dependent diabetes, which accounts for about 80 percent of all cases, is usually less severe than the insulin-dependent forms, and the individual may not show any symptoms (5, pages 977–997). Non-insulin-dependent diabetes often can be controlled with a proper diet and/or the use of **oral hypoglycemic agents**, such as tolbutamide and phenformin. Non-insulin-dependent diabetes is frequently associated with obesity and tends to decrease in severity with a reduction in weight.

Although diabetes is a major cause of death in the United States today, no one yet knows what causes it. Genetic factors probably play a role. Viruses and an **autoimmune response**, in which the body attacks its own tissues, also have been suggested as causes of the juvenile-onset form, while obesity may lead to the adult-onset type. Many attempts have been made to link diet, especially sucrose consumption, to the incidence of diabetes.

Hypoglycemia At the opposite end of the spectrum from diabetes is **hypoglycemia**, or low blood glucose. Lack of glucose profoundly affects the nervous system, resulting in weakness, fatigue, lightheadedness, shakiness, sweating, irritability, anxiety, and accelerated heart beat. If the hypoglycemia is severe enough, nervous system function can become depressed to the point of coma and even death.

Hypoglycemia is a symptom rather than a disease, and it has many causes. It may result from overproduction of insulin owing to a tumor of the pancreas or from liver disease, defective glycogen metabolism, various hereditary errors of metabolism, the use of certain drugs, fasting, and ethyl alcohol. Most of these conditions are quite specific and occur relatively rarely. Of 250,000 patients seen by the Mayo Clinic annually, fewer than 100 have true hypoglycemia (6). However, many people experience hypoglycemic symptoms now and then during the course of their daily routines, and because of something they have read, they often diagnose themselves as having the disorder. In some cases, the symptoms arise from overproduction of insulin in response to a meal (reactive hypoglycemia). This condition is temporary, since hormones such as glucagon come into play to raise glucose levels back to normal. Frequently, symptoms resembling hypoglycemia result from secretion of epinephrine in response to tension, stress, or anxiety. Because the symptoms are not actually caused by hypoglycemia in this case, the disorder is called *nonhypoglycemia* (6,7).

1. "Natural" sugars (honey and brown sugar) are more nutritious than refined white sugar.
2. White table sugar (sucrose) is a poison.
3. If you are always feeling tired and irritable, you probably are hypoglycemic.

FACT OR FANTASY

To establish a diagnosis of true hypoglycemia, the appearance of symptoms must be shown to coincide with low blood glucose levels. Treatment first requires that any primary causes, such as a pancreatic tumor, be discovered and treated. In those individuals with reactive hypoglycemia, a diet with a relatively high protein and fat and moderate carbohydrate content is generally recommended. The diet is divided into five or six meals per day to help maintain blood glucose concentration at a normal level.

Sources of Carbohydrate

The Dietary Guidelines for Americans suggest eating foods that contain adequate starch (81), but a Recommended Dietary Allowance for starch or for total carbohydrate intake has not been established. The Food and Nutrition Board estimates that 50 to 100 g/day of carbohydrate is sufficient (8). However, 100 grams supplies only 400 kilocalories (less than 20 percent of the body's energy needs), and most adults can consume considerably more with no adverse effects. Since the American Heart Association and the U.S. Dietary Goals recommend restricting fat intake to less than 30 to 35 percent of the total kilocalories (9,10), as much as 50 to 55 percent of a person's caloric intake should be derived from carbohydrate. In addition, the Dietary Guidelines recommend avoiding too much sugar, and the Dietary Goals suggest limiting sugar intake to only 10 percent of the total caloric intake (10,81). To accomplish this, the proportion of complex carbohydrate (starch) in the diet should be increased. Let us see what foods contain each type of carbohydrate.

PLANT SOURCES: STARCHES AND SUGARS

Carbohydrates are found mainly in foods of plant origin. Sources of starch include grains and their products, legumes (beans and peas), and root and

TABLE **2-1**

The carbohydrate content of some foods

FOOD	Serving Size: MEASURE	Serving Size: GRAMS	CARBOHYDRATE, g	FAT, g	PROTEIN, g	KILOCALORIES
Animal Sources						
Sirloin steak (separable fat removed)	3 oz	85	0	6.5	27.4	176
Milk (whole)	1 cup	245	12.5	8.5	8.5	159
Cheddar cheese	1 oz	28	0.6	9.1	7.1	113
Sources Containing Mainly Starch						
Soybeans (mature, cooked)	1 cup	180	19.4	10.3	19.8	234
Peanuts (shelled, roasted)	½ cup	72	14.8	35.0	18.9	469
Cashews (roasted in oil)	½ cup	70	20.5	32.0	12.0	392
Brown rice (long grain, cooked)	1 cup	145	37.0	0.9	3.6	173
Whole wheat bread	2 slices	50	23.8	1.6	5.2	122
Macaroni (cooked)	1 cup	105	24.2	0.4	3.6	117
Potato (baked, skin removed)	1 potato	202	32.8	0.2	4.0	145
Potato (baked, skin removed, 2 pats butter	1 potato	212	32.0	4.3	4.0	181
Carrots	1 carrot	81	7.0	0.1	0.8	30
Sources Containing Mainly Sugar						
Apple	1 medium	150	20.0	0.8	0.3	80
Orange	1 orange	180	16.0	0.3	1.3	64
Strawberries (raw)	1 cup	149	12.5	0.7	1.0	55
Red raspberries (raw)	1 cup	123	16.7	0.6	1.5	70
Grapes	1 cup	160	27.7	0.5	1.0	107
Apricots (dried)	1 cup	130	86.5	0.7	6.5	338
Raisins	1 cup	145	112.2	0.3	3.6	419

Source: C. F. Adams, *Nutritive Value of American Foods in Common Units,* Agriculture Handbook No. 456, USDA, Washington, 1975.

tuber vegetables. The carbohydrate content of foods from these groups is shown in Table 2-1. Note that legumes such as soybeans are fairly good sources of protein, as well as of starch, and do not contain much fat. Grains and their products also provide significant amounts of starch, but somewhat less protein and very little fat. Potatoes, commonly considered fattening, contain relatively few kilocalories; it is the heavy use of butter, margarine, or sour cream that makes them high in kilocalories. Substituting dishes containing grains and legumes for some of the meat and cheese in the diet and making better use of root and tuber vegetables such as potatoes can increase the starch content of the diet, lower kilocalorie and fat consumption, and maintain an adequate intake of protein.

Sugar is the other major source of carbohydrate in the diet. Relatively concentrated sources of sugar include white sugar, brown sugar, molasses, honey, and maple syrup. Many other foods, such as baked goods, jams and jellies, cereals, canned fruits and fruit beverages, candy, cured meats, and ketchup, contain significant amounts of added sugar. Reading the package label will tell you whether or not sugar has been added to a food.

Some people claim that honey, brown sugar, and molasses are more beneficial to the body than white sugar and should be substituted for it. Let us evaluate this claim by comparing these foods. Table 2-2 shows that the nutrient content of honey is only minimally greater than that of white sugar, and brown sugar is significantly superior in calcium and only slightly superior in iron. Compared with white sugar, blackstrap molasses provides significant amounts of calcium and iron and contains small amounts of thiamine, riboflavin, and niacin as well.

However, other factors besides nutrient content must be considered. All these sugar sources contain large amounts of sucrose, and consumption of any one brings the problems associated with this substance. In particular, white sugar, brown sugar, honey, and molasses all can pro-

TABLE **2-2**

Nutrient content of some sources of sugar (per 100 grams)

NUTRIENT	WHITE SUGAR	BROWN SUGAR	HONEY	MOLASSES (BLACKSTRAP)	ADULT RDA
Carbohydrate (g)	99.5	96.4	82.3	55	None
Kilocalories	385	373	304	213	None
Calcium (mg)	0	85	5	684	800 mg
Iron (mg)	0.1	3.4	0.5	16.1	10–18 mg
Thiamine (mg)	0	0.01	Trace	0.11	1.5 mg
Riboflavin (mg)	0	0.03	0.04	0.19	2.0 mg
Niacin (niacin equivalents)	0	0.2	0.3	2.0	13–18 NE
Ascorbic acid (mg)	0	0	1	—	60 mg

Sources: B. K. Watt and A. L. Merrill, *Composition of Foods—Raw, Processed, Prepared,* Agriculture Handbook No. 8, USDA, Washington, 1963.

Food and Nutrition Board, *Recommended Dietary Allowances,* 9th ed., National Academy of Sciences, Washington, 1980.

duce **dental caries**. Furthermore, using brown sugar and blackstrap molasses may be impractical in many situations because of their strong flavor. It is difficult to support the claim that molasses, brown sugar, and honey are significantly superior to white sugar. Each sugar source has its disadvantages, and the choice of one over the others becomes mainly one of personal taste and convenience.

It is difficult to support the claim that molasses, brown sugar, and honey are significantly superior to white sugar.

ANIMAL SOURCES

There are few animal sources of carbohydrate. The most important is lactose, the sugar found in milk; cow's milk contains about 5 percent and human milk about 7 percent lactose by weight. Fermented dairy products, such as yogurt, cheese, and buttermilk, contain less because some of it is broken down by bacteria during the fermentation process.

ISSUE: IS SUCROSE A POISON?

On a recent Saturday morning some children viewing their favorite cartoon show watched animated Dracula and Frankenstein monsters arguing on the television set. The scene was not part of the cartoon show itself; it was an advertisement for two heavily sugared breakfast cereals manufactured by a major cereal company. During the morning the children were to see other commercials for cereals, candy, soft drinks, and a variety of baked goods promoted by cartoon characters, other children, and several celebrities (Figure 2-9). Many children spend a substantial part of their allowances on some of these items, and their parents find it difficult not to include many of them on the weekly grocery list.

Sugar's presence in many foods is not obvious.

Breakfast cereals, candy, soft drinks, and certain baked goods are among the more obvious sources of sucrose in the diet. Sucrose is also found in fruit drinks, some brands of peanut butter, tomato sauce, canned fruit syrups, ketchup, crackers, salad dressings, canned and dehydrated soups, fruit yogurt, bacon and other cured meats, some canned or frozen vegetables, pot pies, and many baby foods (11). It is estimated that sugar consumption in the United States is close to 50 kilograms (110 pounds) per person per year and accounts for almost 20 percent of our caloric intake (12,13).

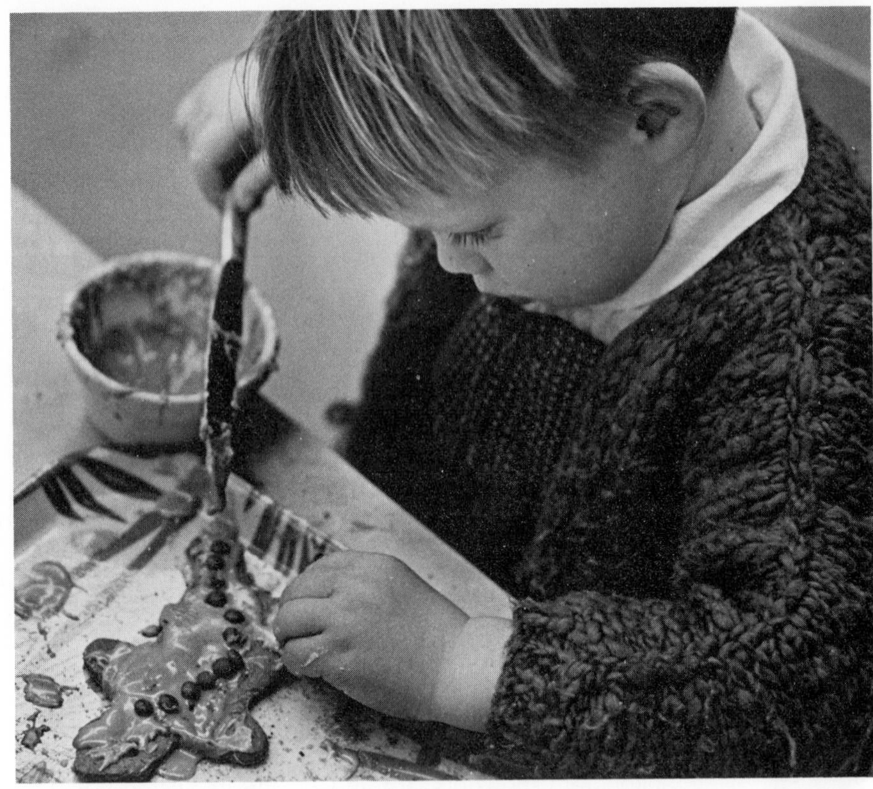

FIGURE 2-9
During early childhood consumption of heavily sweetened foods is often promoted in a variety of ways. Although moderate sugar consumption is not a problem if children are taught proper dental care, they should be encouraged to substitute fruits, vegetables, and dairy products for many of the sweets they consume. (Photograph by Myron Papiz, Courtesy of Photo Researchers, Inc.)

At the same time that sugar is so available in the food supply, heart disease, obesity, and diabetes mellitus are among the most prevalent and persistent American health problems. Heart disease and diabetes rank first and fifth, respectively, as causes of death (excluding accidents), while obesity may affect more than 30 percent of the population (14,15). Unfortunately, despite the expenditure of billions of dollars for research, the specific causes of these disorders and the means by which they can be prevented and cured remain unknown. Over the last 25 years, however, a number of researchers have pointed an accusing finger at sucrose as the major culprit. Excessive sucrose consumption has been blamed for heart disease, diabetes, obesity, dental caries (tooth decay), hypoglycemia, and nutritional deficiencies. One of the U.S. Dietary Goals recommends cutting sugar intake in half, to about 10 percent of the caloric intake. Food faddists have seized the issue and carried it to its logical conclusion: they call sugar a poison. Let us look at this claim by examining sugar's role in these problems and whether or not reducing sugar intake will make you healthier. ”

FOCUS 2-1 LACTOSE INTOLERANCE (68,69)

Milk is a highly nutritious and wholesome food, which supplies generous amounts of protein, calcium, phosphorus, riboflavin, and many other B vitamins, vitamin A, and, if fortified, vitamin D. Its consumption is widely promoted in the United States, and we generally take it for granted as a dietary component. Most humans, however, including many Americans, experience problems when they drink more than a small amount of milk; they suffer from **lactose intolerance**, a deficiency or total lack of the enzyme **lactase** in the small intestine. Lactase is needed to digest lactose (milk sugar) for absorption into the body, and in its absence, lactose remains in the digestive tract. It passes into the large intestine, where it draws water out of the intestinal wall and is fermented by bacteria. The result is a bloated feeling, flatulence, belching, cramps, and a watery diarrhea. If prolonged, the diarrhea can lead to malabsorption of nutrients and fluid imbalance.

Lactose intolerance is widespread (Figure 2-10). Although nearly all infants have lactase (its absence in infancy is a rare genetic defect), at least 70 percent of the world's population partly or totally loses the ability to produce the enzyme during childhood. Up to 80 percent of some Mediterranean populations, such as Greek Cypriots, Arabs, and Ashkenazic Jews, 70 percent of most black populations, including American blacks, and over 90 percent of Oriental populations are intolerant to lactose to some degree (5, page 934). Most Scandinavians, west Europeans, and certain pastoral tribes in Africa, as well as their descendants in the New World, retain the enzyme during adulthood. Some researchers believe that losing lactose is a normal part of human development, and those who retain it do so either be-

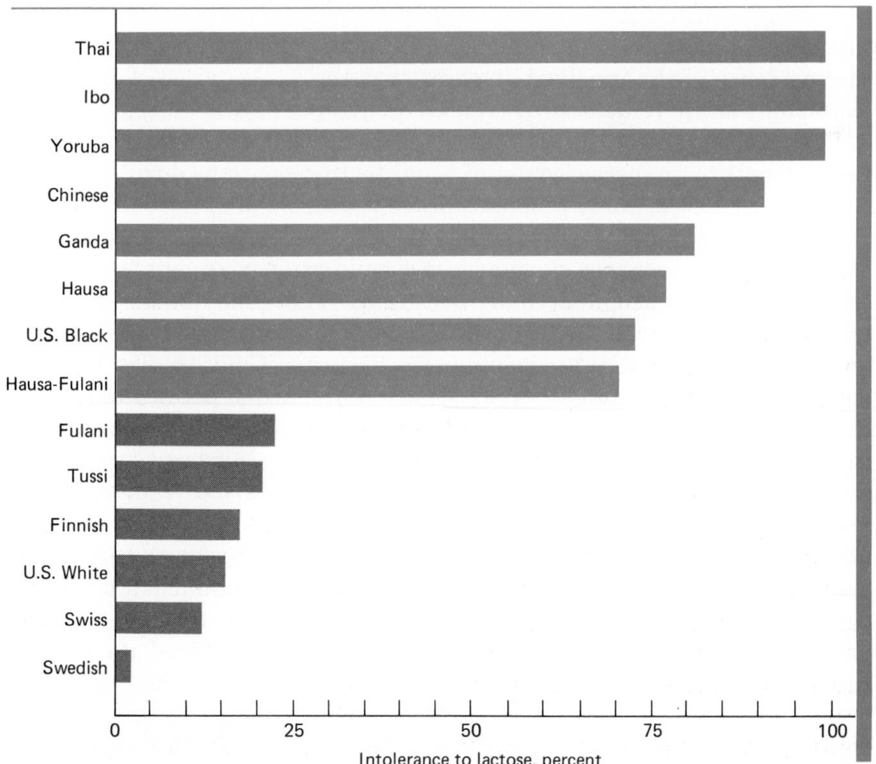

FIGURE 2-10
Prevalence of Lactose Intolerance in Certain Populations. Lactase deficiency occurs more frequently in Asians (Thai and Chinese) and most Blacks (Ibo, Yoruba, Hausa) than among Whites. A Black population with a relatively low rate of lactose intolerance is the Fulani. (*Source:* Kretchmer, N., "Lactose and Lactase," *Scientific American* October 1972, p. 76. Copyright © 1972 by Scientific American, Inc. All rights reserved.)

cause milk in their diets induces intestinal synthesis of the enzyme or because a mutation has allowed them to retain it during adulthood.

Lactose intolerance has important nutritional implications; if the diet does not contain dairy products, particular care must be taken to find other sources of calcium and riboflavin. For example, calcium can be obtained from legumes (especially soybeans) and dark green leafy vegetables, while enriched grain products and dark green leafy vegetables provide riboflavin. In addition, many people with lactose intolerance can consume up to a cup of milk per day without distress. Fermented milk products, such as cheese and yogurt, generally contain less lactose than milk and often can be tolerated. Milk in which the sugar has already been digested by added lactase also has been developed (70).

Because of the high prevalence of lactose intolerance among people of the developing nations, companies promoting milk products in these countries have been severely criticized. However, milk is a good source of kilocalories and protein, as well as calcium and riboflavin, and the American Academy of Pediatrics believes that there is not enough evidence at this time to discourage the distribution of milk to nations where childhood malnutrition is a problem (68). Nevertheless, care must be taken to maintain the sanitary quality of the milk, and children should be monitored for symptoms of lactose intolerance.

A LOOK AT THE EVIDENCE

Sugar-Consumption Patterns and Disease A large part of the evidence implicating sucrose as a cause of disease involves population statistics. These statistics show an increase in sugar consumption and a rise in the incidence of the involved diseases over the same period of time. For example, Yudkin relates the increased occurrence of heart disease and diabetes mellitus in the United States and Great Britain during the last 70 years in part to an increased use of sugar by these nations during that period (16). However, many problems prevent us from drawing solid conclusions from such data. For example, sugar-consumption data show only the rate of disappearance of sugar into consumption channels; they do not tell us how much people actually consumed. There may be a significant difference between the two, and we can only assume that the disappearance figures reflect actual consumption patterns. Caution also must be used when examining data showing the occurrence of heart disease and diabetes during the last 70 years. First of all, diagnostic procedures have improved tremendously since 1910, and part of the apparent increase in deaths from diabetes and heart disease since 1910 may be owing to underestimation of the prevalence of these problems in those earlier years. In addition, death certificates frequently list only the major or immediate cause of death and neglect contributing causes. For example, a review of death certificates in Pennsylvania from May of 1968 to April of 1969 showed that 2639 people died from diabetes, but a check of physician's records revealed that more than 20,000 of the people who died that year actually had the disease (17). In addition, changes in the death rate may not reflect changes in the occurrence of the disease in the population;

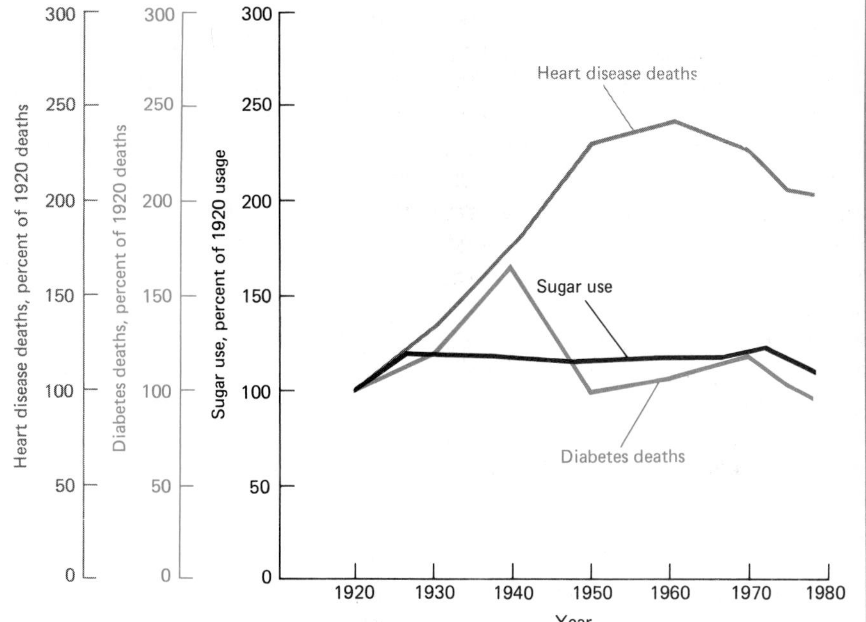

FIGURE 2-11
Trends in sugar consumption and heart disease and diabetes mortality in the United States during the twentieth century. [*Sources:* Bureau of the Census, *Statistical Abstracts of the United States,* 81st, 91st and 101st Editions, Washington, DC.: Dept. of Commerce (1960, 1970, and 1980 respectively); Marsten, R. M., Peterkin, B. B., "Nutrient Content of the National Food Supply," *National Food Review* (NFR-9), Winter 1980, pp. 21–25.

more people may be developing the problem, but fewer die from it because of improved medical care.

Even if we feel that the data are reliable, problems arise in their interpretation. Figure 2-11 shows that although sugar consumption in the United States increased by 30 percent since early in the century, the increase was not a steady one (12). During the Depression and World War II, for example, sugar consumption remained the same or decreased and did not begin to rise again until the late 1960s. We can therefore agree with both Yudkin's contention (16) that sugar consumption has increased since 1910 and with Keys' opposing argument (18) that it remained relatively constant over much of that period. Similarly, the incidence of heart disease and diabetes did not increase uniformly during this period. Thus, stating that sugar consumption and the incidence of heart disease and diabetes are higher now than in 1910 oversimplifies the situation.

Taken as a whole, then, data relating sugar consumption to the occurrence of heart disease and diabetes mellitus in the United States since 1910 do not necessarily show a strong association between the two. Figure 2-11 shows that the pattern for neither disease closely matches that of sugar consumption. In contrast, deaths resulting from both disorders have decreased since 1970, while sugar consumption has increased. This point is underscored by comparing sugar intake and diabetes incidence in several countries (Table 2-3). The three nations with the greatest availability of sugar in the diet (Denmark, the United Kingdom, and New Zealand) had considerably fewer deaths from diabetes than several countries with a much lower availability of sugar (Switzerland, Germany, and

TABLE **2-3**

Sugar intake and diabetes mortality rates in western populations

COUNTRY	Mean Sugar Available: PER CAPITA PER DIEM, g	Mean Sugar Available: PER CAPITA PER ANNUM, kg	DIABETES MORTALITY RATE PER 100,000
Denmark	139	50.4	12.8
United Kingdom	136	49.5	13.3
New Zealand	134	48.5	12.2
United States	134	48.5	19.2
Netherlands	133	48.0	12.6
Sweden	120	43.6	18.5
Switzerland	118	42.6	26.2
Finland	113	40.8	14.0
Germany	91	33.0	27.7
France	88	31.8	16.7
Italy	72	26.3	20.7

Source: A. R. P. Walker, "Sugar Intake and Diabetes Mellitus," *S. Afr. Med. J.* **51**:842–851 (1977). Used with permission.

Italy) (19). Moreover, a large number of population studies performed in all parts of the world show no consistent association between sugar intake and the incidence of diabetes (20).

Despite the amount of data showing no strong relationship between sugar consumption and the occurrence of diabetes and heart disease, some studies have found an association between the two. One example is a population study by Cohen and his colleagues (21). They compared the sugar intake and incidence of diabetes and heart disease in Yemenite Jews who had lived in Israel for a long period of time with those of newly arrived Yemenites, as well as with Yemenite Jews who had remained in Yemen. The longer the Yemenite Jews had lived in Israel, the higher their sugar intake and the higher the incidence of diabetes and heart disease among their population. Sugar intake of Jews who had remained in Yemen was by far the lowest of the three groups, and diabetes and heart disease were virtually unknown in that group of people.

Cohen's studies point toward a role of sugar in causing diabetes and heart disease. However, they do not *prove* that sugar causes them because other factors besides sugar could influence the occurrence of these disorders among the Yemenite Jews. The most important of these is body weight, which increased by an average of 18 pounds in the Yemenites who had lived in Israel the longest (21). Since increased body weight is an important risk factor in diabetes (5, pages 977–997), the heavier weight of the older Yemenite settlers could account for the greater incidence of diabetes in that population. The settlers who had lived in Israel for longer periods of time also had higher caloric intakes than new settlers (21) and might be subjected to other influences, such as increased blood pressure, decreased physical activity, and increased nervous stress, that are characteristic of Western society. All these factors could have contributed to the greater incidence of heart disease in the long-time Yemenite settlers.

Sugar, Diabetes, and Heart Disease: Controlled Experiments Whenever one attempts to associate a factor such as sugar intake with a disease, it is important to determine how that factor could cause the disease by conducting controlled experiments. One way sugar could contribute to the development of heart disease is by increasing the levels of cholesterol and fat (**triglycerides**) in the blood (see Chapter 3). A number of researchers have conducted experiments in which they substituted sucrose for starch in the diet, and some have found an increase in the concentration of blood cholesterol and especially triglyceride in those on the sucrose diet (18,22). However, examination of other experimental data indicates that these results must be interpreted with caution for several reasons. First, large increases in blood triglyceride levels seem to occur in *normal subjects* only when extremely large amounts of sucrose (at least 3 times the average intake of the U.S. population) are included in the diet (23). When the experiments substitute sucrose for starch at levels normally consumed in the United States, the increase in blood triglycerides is either relatively small or does not occur (22,24). In a few individuals who have a genetic predisposition toward elevated blood triglycerides, sucrose can induce a large rise in the level of fat in the blood, and such people are generally advised to reduce their intake (23,24).

Some studies show that blood cholesterol levels increase when sucrose is substituted for starch in the diet, but the increase is small when compared with that induced by increasing the level of saturated fat in the diet (18,22,24). Most researchers therefore consider it unlikely that sucrose has any significant influence on blood cholesterol concentrations. The impact of sucrose on the incidence of heart disease seems to be minor in comparison with that of dietary fat and cholesterol.

A number of studies also have been performed to determine whether excess consumption of sugar impairs the body's ability to metabolize glucose. Some experiments have found that substituting sucrose for starch in the diet results in a greater rise in blood glucose after a meal (25). However, the amount of sucrose consumed in the experiments was three times higher than the average sugar intake in Israel and almost twice the average U.S. intake. Other researchers found no change in the body's ability to handle glucose in people fed sucrose at levels comparable with those found in a typical Western diet (19). So again, there is no clear experimental evidence linking sucrose intake and diabetes.

Hypoglycemia As described earlier, hypoglycemia has many causes, and the symptoms may sometimes be psychological in origin. No studies appear to have been carried out to test whether excess sucrose intake causes hypoglycemia, but prevailing medical opinion indicates that sugar does not play a role (26).

Obesity Many people believe that sucrose causes obesity. It can, but only indirectly. Obesity results from a greater intake of kilocalories than the body can expend, regardless of the source. The tasty nature of many foods that contain sugar could make them more likely to be overconsumed, but the same could be said for foods containing relatively large amounts of fat. No one nutrient "causes" overeating, although overconsumption of one or more does cause obesity (20,27).

Empty Kilocalories Foods containing large amounts of sugar are often referred to as sources of "empty" kilocalories. Pure sucrose itself has almost no nutritional value except for the energy-providing carbohydrate, and foods containing large amounts of sugar, such as candy and soft drinks, frequently lack many nutrients. These foods are therefore considered sources of empty kilocalories. However, yogurt sweetened with preserves and many types of fruit contain significant amounts of sugar, as well as appreciable quantities of other nutrients. Ultimately, the importance of sucrose as a source of empty kilocalories depends on the nutrient content of the rest of the diet. If other foods cannot make up for the nutrients displaced by consuming foods high in sucrose but containing little else of nutritional value, then the individual risks developing a nutritional deficiency.

Dental Caries (Tooth Decay) Although sugar has long been known to cause **dental caries**, it does not do so in all situations. The ability of sugar to produce cavities depends on several factors, including the physical form of the sugar-containing food, the frequency of eating, and the frequency of cleaning the teeth (28). For example, several studies show that the risk of cavities is greater if the sugar is consumed in a form that adheres to the teeth. This allows bacteria plenty of time to produce plaque, which in turn leads to tooth decay (29,30). Sugar in solution, such as soft drinks, does not have such a high potential for producing cavities, since most of the sugar leaves the mouth rapidly and the remainder is readily washed away by saliva. Cavities also increase with increased frequency of eating, correlating particularly with the frequency of between-meal snacks (28–32). This effect may be due in part to a failure to properly clean the teeth at these times.

FOCUS 2-2
NUTRITION AND DENTAL HEALTH
(5, PAGES 852–891)

In our concern with the effect of diet on heart disease, diabetes, obesity, and certain forms of cancer, we tend to neglect the relationship between sound nutrition and dental health. Dental disease, however, is one of the most prevalent and costly health problems in the United States, and proper diet and eating habits can play an important role in preventing it.

The basic structure of a tooth is shown in Figure 2-12. Like bones, teeth are made up of a framework, or matrix (mainly the connective-tissue protein collagen), onto which is deposited crystals of hard minerals. The *enamel* is 97 to 98 percent mineral, containing calcium, phosphorus, magnesium, and fluoride. Although it is very hard, enamel is permeable to mineral ions in saliva. *Dentin* is about 80 percent inorganic matter, mostly calcium and phosphorus. Surrounding dentin below the gum line is a calcified tissue called *cementum,* to which attach the periodontal ligaments that anchor the tooth to the jawbone. The soft, innermost layer, the *pulp,* contains the nerves and blood vessels that supply the tooth.

The permanent teeth begin to calcify during the first 2 years of life, erupt between the ages of 6 and 13 years, and complete their development by about the age of 16. One of the most important factors influencing tooth integrity is nutritional status during this period. Vitamin A is needed for proper development of the enamel and vitamin C for formation of the dentin. Because it facilitates absorption and utilization of calcium and phosphorus by the body, vitamin D is required for proper calcification of the teeth. Fluoride, when incorporated into tooth mineral, makes it more resistant to decay. When development is complete, the tooth does not become totally inert: it is still permeable to mineral ions from the saliva and blood. Thus fluoride may be taken up by teeth during adulthood, although at a slower rate than during their development.

Dental caries (tooth decay) occur when bacteria metabolize food on the teeth, releasing acids that break down the enamel. Food can stick to the teeth or accumulate in pits, fissures, and between teeth. Bacteria convert carbohydrate in the food, particularly sugar, into a sticky polysaccharide called *dextran,* forming dental plaque. Using the glucose released from food or from the dextran, the bacteria produce the acids that destroy the enamel. The cavity can eventually progress through the dentin and destroy the pulp.

To prevent cavities, dentists recommend (28):

1. Avoiding sugar-containing products for between-meal snacks
2. Avoiding sticky forms of sugar
3. Rinsing the mouth with warm water after consuming anything containing sugar
4. Brushing after every meal and flossing daily
5. Fluoridating drinking water
6. Seeing a dentist regularly

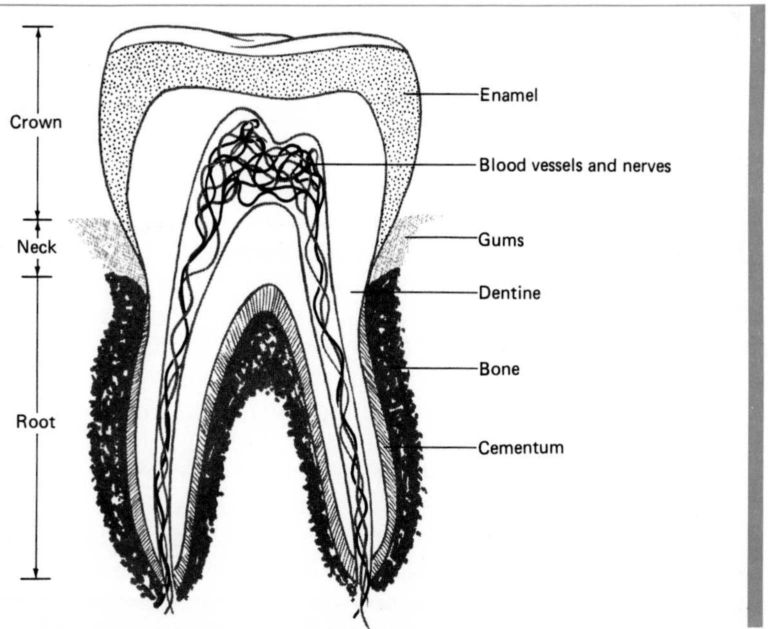

FIGURE 2-12
The Structure of a Tooth.

SHOULD WE CONSUME LESS SUGAR?

Although factors besides sugar intake, such as excess caloric, fat, and cholesterol intakes, heredity, and a lack of physical activity, appear to play major roles in causing heart disease, obesity, and diabetes mellitus, this does not rule out the possibility of some contribution by sugar intake to these disorders. A modest reduction in sugar intake may therefore prove to be beneficial. The U.S. Dietary Goals recommend that sugar intake be restricted to 10 percent or less of the dietary kilocalories. At this level of intake, a person consuming 2500 kcal/day could eat about 63 grams of sugar, about half the current rate of consumption. Here are some suggestions for reducing sucrose intake:

1 Restrict or eliminate the use of sugar or honey in coffee, on fruits, and on breakfast cereals.
2 Restrict or eliminate highly concentrated sources of sugar from the diet. These include candy and heavily sweetened foods, such as some baked goods, certain presweetened breakfast cereals, and most soft drinks.
3 Read food labels and choose foods that contain little or no sugar. For example, buy peaches canned in water rather than in heavy syrup.
4 Substitute foods with lower sugar content and higher nutritional value for those with high sugar content and low nutritional value. For example, substitute fruit for candy or heavily sweetened baked goods.

FOCUS 2-3 SUGAR SUBSTITUTES Scientists have been looking for an acceptable sugar substitute for decades. Although the original aim was to provide a sweetening agent diabetics could use, the potential value of such a substance in weight control and prevention of tooth decay has added impetus to the search. Saccharin has been used as an artificial sweetener since before the turn of the century. However, experiments reported by the Wisconsin Alumni Research Foundation (WARF) in 1971 and the Food and Drug Administration (FDA) in 1973 found that rats fed high levels of saccharin developed bladder cancer. Critics claimed the cancer may have been caused by an impurity, *ortho*-toluenesulfonamide (OTS), in the saccharin, but in the mid-1970s, Canadian scientists conducted a study using saccharin free of OTS, and the results confirmed the earlier research (71).

Many people question the applicability to humans of rat experiments in which saccharin was fed at levels hundreds of times higher than those consumed by humans. In addition, recent population studies show no general increase in the risk of bladder cancer among saccharin users, although some increase in risk occurred in several subgroups, such as cigarette smokers and heavy saccharin users (72–74). However, these studies were not sensitive enough to detect low levels of **carcinogencity**, and their results are compatible with the theory that saccharin is a weak **carcinogen** or may enhance the carcinogenicity of other compounds (74,75). Food and Drug Administration scientists estimate that even the amount of saccharin present in one large soft drink, if ingested regularly over a lifetime, might lead to 1200 additional cases of bladder cancer per year (71), and other authorities find heavy use by pregnant women and children to be cause for worry (75). In March of 1977, the FDA invoked the Delaney Clause (see Chapter 9) and banned saccharin from use in food, drugs, and cosmetics. However, the storm of protest that followed led Congress to pass a law, signed by President Jimmy Carter in November of 1977, preventing the FDA from implementing the ban until May of 1979. During this moratorium period, a warning label was placed on food containing saccharin:

> Use of this product may be hazardous to your health. This product contains saccharin, which has been determined to cause cancer in laboratory animals.

At the present time, the FDA has not attempted to reinstate the ban.

A variety of other sweetening agents have been considered as replacements for saccharin. Cyclamates were banned in 1969 because large amounts were found to cause bladder cancer in rats. The sugar alcohols, xylitol and sorbitol, may benefit diabetics and do not lead to tooth decay, but both provide kilocalories for the body. Found naturally in many fruits and vegetables, they do not have saccharin's bitter aftertaste (76,77). They are absorbed from the intestine more slowly than glucose, and substituting them for sugar may prevent a large increase in blood glucose after a meal. However, there are no long-term studies to show concrete benefits of xylitol or sorbitol for diabetics (76,78). In addition, 20 to 30 g/day of sorbitol or 30 to 40 g/day of xylitol produce diarrhea and flatulence (76,78). Xylitol has been associated with bladder stones and cancer in mice (77,79), and chewing gum manufacturers have voluntarily removed it from their products (78).

Fructose has recently been promoted as a substitute for sucrose. Although it is a sugar and a component of sucrose, by itself it is 15 to 80 percent sweeter than sucrose and is more slowly absorbed from the intestine (76–78). However, fructose's sweetness decreases with a reduction in temperature and acidity. In one test, a taste panel could not distinguish it from sucrose in cookies, cake, or pudding. Fructose also provides the same number of kilocalories as sucrose, and it is considerably more expensive. There is no evidence that substituting it for sucrose will benefit diabetics or obese people; this simply results in exchanging one form of sugar for another (78).

The newest sugar substitute is aspartame, a combination of the amino acid L-aspartate and a derivative of the amino acid phenylalanine. It is 180 times sweeter than sucrose and does not have saccharin's bitter aftertaste. The Food and Drug Administration withheld approval for many years because there were some questions about aspartame's safety. Early in 1981, however, the agency granted approval for its use as a table sweetener and in many food products (82).

ISSUE: SHOULD WE INCREASE FIBER INTAKE?

"Our parents and grandparents called it "roughage" or "bulk" and probably consumed considerably more of it in the diet than we do today. It was known in our grandparents' time to have a laxative effect, but otherwise it was thought to be an inert substance that contributed little nutritionally to the body. Today we call it *fiber,* and it appears to be important for maintaining normal function of the large intestine. Some authorities blame a deficiency of fiber in the American diet for the relatively high prevalence of constipation, diverticulitis, hemorrhoids, colon cancer, and other diseases of the large intestine in the United States. They also believe that low fiber intakes may contribute to the incidence of heart disease, diabetes mellitus, and obesity in this country. For these reasons, some food manufacturers are currently adding fiber to such products as bread and are promoting natural sources of this dietary component, such as whole-grain products and bran.

Considerable controversy surrounds fiber. Because fiber is made up of many chemical compounds and its composition and properties vary depending on its source, authorities disagree about how to define it and have obtained conflicting results when testing its effectiveness in preventing or treating disease. It is therefore difficult to make conclusive recommendations about whether or not to increase the fiber content of the diet. In this section, we will look more closely at fiber, its components, and its properties and examine the evidence for including more high-fiber foods in the diet. ”

WHAT IS FIBER?

Fiber consists of a variety of chemical substances, many but not all of which are carbohydrates. A concrete definition of fiber has not been agreed upon, but a commonly used criterion is that it cannot be broken down by human digestive enzymes. Van Soest suggests that **true fiber** includes only the components of the cell wall in plants: cellulose, hemicellulose, and lignin (33). We have seen that cellulose and hemicellulose are polysaccharides. **Lignin** is a noncarbohydrate polymer. There are other chemical compounds in food that cannot be broken down by human digestive enzymes, and these may be included in a different definition of fiber. **Pectin**, which occurs naturally in some fruits and is used to make jams and jellies, consists largely of a galactose derivative, galacturonic acid. Other examples include indigestible sugars, such as raffinose in soybeans, and vegetable gums, such as carrageenan and guar gum. In addition, certain compounds formed during baking or frying, such as in the browning of breakfast cereals and toast, are resistant to human digestive enzymes and may be included as components of fiber. Van Soest calls all compounds resistant to the digestive enzymes of animals the **total dietary fiber** (33).

For many years, analysis of **crude fiber** has been used to measure the fiber content of foods. However, during the analytical process, about 50 to 90 percent of the lignin, 85 percent of the hemicellulose, and up to 50 percent of the cellulose are lost. Hence crude fiber greatly underestimates the actual fiber content of the food. For example, in wheat bran the value for true fiber is four times that for crude fiber (34). New methods have been developed that more closely estimate the true fiber content of food, but no simple method exists to measure the total dietary fiber complex.

Fiber from different sources has different proportions of the various components. For example, whole-grain products tend to have more hemicellulose and lignin, but less cellulose than raw vegetables (35). These variations result in different properties among fiber types. Hemicellulose, for instance, is more effective than cellulose in increasing stool weight (36,37), while pectin and rolled oats are more effective than wheat bran in reducing blood cholesterol levels (36). Food processing also affects the properties of the fiber. Grinding wheat bran reduces its ability to absorb water and its effects on movement of feces through the large intestine (34,38). Extracted and purified cellulose does not have the same properties that it does when it is found naturally in food (34). The proper-

The properties of the different forms of fiber are still largely unknown, so it is difficult to make blanket statements about fiber's effects on health.

ties of all the different forms of fiber are still largely unknown. It is therefore difficult to make blanket statements about the effects of fiber on health.

The words *indigestible* and *nonnutritive* are often used in connection with fiber, but neither term is completely accurate. Although human digestive enzymes cannot break fiber down, bacteria in the large intestine ferment it to varying degrees. Some of the products, called *volatile fatty acids,* may be absorbed into the body and be used for energy (34). The contribution is slight, however, only accounting for about 3 percent of the total energy intake (39).

FIBER AND DISEASE: IS THERE A CONNECTION?

Although fiber was considered an inert and unimportant component of food for decades, in recent years a dietary deficiency of fiber has been associated with a large variety of medical problems, including many disorders of the large intestine, heart disease, diabetes mellitus, and obesity. Several investigators have observed that these diseases are more common in Western populations than in much of the developing world, such as rural Africa (40–42). A major difference between Western populations and those studied in the developing countries is diet. For example, rural Africans consume as much as 25 g/day of crude fiber, while Western diets provide less than one-quarter of this amount (43). On the basis of such studies, low fiber intake appears to contribute to the high incidence of diseases of the large intestine, heart disease, diabetes, and obesity found in Western society. However, these studies by no means *prove* that low fiber intake causes these problems. Other dietary factors, especially high fat and animal protein intakes in the West, also may play a role or be the major cause (40), while nondietary factors common to the affluent societies, such as less exercise, higher exposure to nervous stress, more cigarette smoking, and higher alcohol intakes, also could contribute. Nevertheless, the association between low fiber intake and many diseases has intrigued nutritionists for over a decade and has stimulated much research in the area. Let us take a closer look at what is known.

Disorders of the Large Intestine Population studies by Burkitt and others show that disorders of the large intestine, including constipation, diverticular disease, hemorrhoids, and colon cancer, are less common in groups with a high fiber intake than in those with a low intake (42). The first three problems can be related to difficulty in moving feces through the large intestine; constipation refers to infrequent defecation; diverticular disease may result from increased pressure in the colon because of difficulty moving feces; and hemorrhoids may in some cases result from straining at stool. According to the fiber hypothesis, a number of properties of fiber may be helpful in treating and perhaps preventing these problems. Since fiber reaches the large intestine virtually intact, it provides bulk in the feces. Many types of fiber also absorb or hold water, increasing bulk and softening the stools. The increased bulk stimulates peristaltic contractions of the wall of the large intestine to move the material along, while the softening effect eases the passage of the feces.

Some population studies support the fiber hypothesis (42,44). Groups with higher dietary fiber intakes defecate more frequently, have greater stool volumes, and require a shorter time for food to pass through the digestive tract than those consuming less fiber. In addition, their stools are generally unformed, soft and passed with ease, whereas those of people with low fiber intakes tend to be small, hard, segmented, and often voided with discomfort (44).

The results of controlled laboratory experiments, however, are less clear. While most show an increase in stool bulk and water content on high-fiber diets (39,45), the effect on transit time varies (36,39,45,46). Differences may be because of the type of fiber used; a recent study, for example, found that cellulose increases stool volume and reduces transit time, whereas pectin's influence was negligible (48). It may be that fiber "normalizes" transit time, speeding it up when it is too slow and slowing it down when it is too fast, but having little influence when it is normal (46,47). Fiber also has proven useful clinically in treating constipation and diverticulitis (37). In some cases, however, it is suspected that the improvement is a placebo effect (46,47).

Cancer of the large intestine is another disease that may in part be owing to low fiber intakes (36,37,43,44). Its geographic distribution generally follows that of economic development and modern Western culture, and one of the most important differences between affluent societies and the developing world is in fiber intake. Similarly, the incidence of this disease is lower among Seventh Day Adventists than other Americans, in northern India than in southern India, and among rural Finns than among Danes. One of the differences between these populations is the higher fiber intakes of the Seventh Day Adventists, northern Indians, and rural Finns (43,49).

Colon cancer is probably caused by contact of **carcinogenic** (cancer-causing) substances with the wall of the large intestine. In addition to carcinogens present in food, gut bacteria may convert certain substances, such as urea, bile acids, and cholesterol, into cancer-causing derivatives. Some proponents of fiber hypothesize that it might minimize these effects by favoring growth of bacterial species that do not produce carcinogens (37,43). However, most studies show that diet, including fiber content, has little influence on the types of bacteria that grow in the intestine (50). Others theorize that by decreasing transit time of material through the colon, fiber reduces the opportunity for bacteria to synthesize carcinogens and reduces the time that any such chemicals can act on the intestinal wall (37,43). However, the evidence does not wholly support this hypothesis either; the rate of colon cancer is no higher in constipated people than in nonconstipated people (39), and there was no difference in transit times between two Scandinavian populations that have a fourfold difference in the rate of colon cancer (51). A third hypothesis proposes that by increasing fecal bulk and water content, fiber dilutes the concentration of carcinogens in the digestive tract, thereby minimizing their cancer-causing potential. Some evidence supports this theory: rural Finns with a lower incidence of colon cancer had greater fecal bulk than Danes, who had a higher colon-cancer rate (51).

Although some evidence points toward low-fiber diets as a cause of colon cancer, the association is tenuous at the present time. Other dietary factors, such as excessive protein and fat intakes, also may play a role. Red meat, especially beef, has been associated with an increase in colon cancer in a population (51–53). Raising the level of protein in the diet increases the amount of ammonia produced by bacteria in the large intestine, and ammonia is a suspected carcinogen (54). In addition, some population studies implicate high-fat diets as a cause of colon cancer (55,56). Fats stimulate the secretion of bile acids into the digestive tract, and bacteria may convert them into cancer-causing substances. Burkitt points out that fat, protein, and fiber are not mutually exclusive causes of colon cancer. Low-fiber diets are generally high in fat and animal protein, so increasing fiber also will lead to a reduction in fat and animal protein intakes (43).

Heart Disease Many population studies show that the incidence of heart disease is higher in affluent Western societies than in the developing countries (42). In addition, Seventh Day Adventists who are **lacto-ovo-vegetarians** (eat dairy products and eggs in addition to plant products) have a lower risk of dying from heart disease than nonvegetarian Seventh Day Adventists or the rest of the population of California (49). Since dietary fiber intakes are higher in the populations with a lower risk of heart disease, increasing the fiber content of the diet may be useful in reducing the occurrence of this problem.

Elevated blood cholesterol concentrations are a major risk factor in atherosclerosis and heart disease, and fiber may reduce this risk by lowering the level of blood cholesterol. Some authorities believe that fiber increases the excretion of both cholesterol and bile acids in the feces. Because bile acids are made from cholesterol, their loss means that more cholesterol must be broken down to make new ones, reducing the body cholesterol pool and lowering blood cholesterol (37,57). Not all types of fiber are effective in this capacity, however; cellulose and bran appear to have little influence on blood cholesterol levels in humans, whereas pectin, guar gum, rolled oats, and a mixed diet of fruits, vegetables, and legumes lower them (36,57). Moreover, because of the controversy surrounding the value of dietary manipulations in lowering blood cholesterol levels (see Chapter 3), it is not certain to what degree increasing dietary fiber will be protective.

Obesity Increasing the fiber content of the diet may help in the treatment of another disease of affluence: obesity (58). Because it provides bulk but very few kilocalories, fiber decreases the caloric content of the diet at the same time it promotes satiety by allowing the individual to consume a larger volume of food. High-fiber foods also must be chewed more extensively, thereby increasing the effort of eating and slowing down the rate of ingestion. Fiber also may interfere slightly with the efficiency with which protein, fat, and carbohydrate are absorbed.

Few studies have been performed to test these hypotheses. Some show that the obese will eat less than the nonobese when forced to work to obtain food, such as shelling nuts or drinking a thick milkshake through a narrow straw. Other studies show that teaching the obese to eat more slowly may help them lose weight. In some experiments, synthetic bulking agents had virtually no effect on nonobese subjects, but induced a substantial weight loss in obese individuals. It may be that the nonobese compensate for the dilution of kilocalories in high-fiber diets by eating more food, whereas the obese do not. More experiments are needed before concrete conclusions regarding fiber and obesity can be drawn.

Diabetes Mellitus Trowell has suggested that fiber-depleted, starchy foods are conducive to the development of diabetes in genetically predisposed individuals (59). The disorder is rare in rural Africans who consume a diet high in fiber, but it has become more common among urban Africans as their fiber intakes have decreased. In addition, the death rates from diabetes in England and Wales fell between 1941 and 1954, coinciding with an increase in the fiber content of the country's flour.

There have been few controlled experiments to test these observations. In one study, pectin and guar flour reduced the rise in blood glucose and insulin concentrations that occurs after a carbohydrate meal in both diabetic and nondiabetic individuals (59). Other experiments have found that the need for insulin injections and oral hypoglycemic agents could be reduced in many mild diabetics by feeding them a high-carbohydrate, high-fiber diet (59,60). The practical significance of these results, however, remains to be established.

INCREASING DIETARY FIBER: IS THERE A HAZARD?

The promise of beneficial effects has led many people to increase their consumption of fiber. However, this practice is not without its potential hazards. It increases nitrogen excretion, indicating that it may interfere with the digestion and absorption of protein (45,62). Fiber may retard the absorption of minerals, such as iron, calcium, copper, magnesium, zinc, and silicon (62–64). However, some data conflict with this hypothesis, and the influence of fiber on mineral balance is still uncertain. In view of the fact that many of the benefits are not firmly established, that only certain types of fiber may affect certain diseases, and that there may be adverse effects, some authorities believe caution must be exercised in raising the fiber content of the diet.

INCREASING DIETARY FIBER: STRATEGY

The Dietary Guidelines for Americans recommend consuming adequate fiber, and increasing the amount of fiber in the American diet may have many beneficial effects on health. However, how much should we consume? The average American currently ingests about 4 g/day of crude fiber (66), and the recommendations range from raising it slightly to increasing it fivefold or more (66,67). Because much remains to be learned about fiber, a moderate increase to about 6 to 8 g/day of crude fiber seems reasonable at this time (67).

Adding fiber to the diet does not mean one should begin adding bran indiscriminantly to foods or taking bran tablets. Bran is only one of many sources of fiber, and it has been shown that different types of fiber have different effects on the body. Consuming a balanced diet containing whole grains and their products, legumes, fruits, and vegetables is probably the best approach (Table 2-4). This will provide some variety in the types of fiber consumed and will ensure an adequate intake of vitamins and minerals as well.

TABLE **2-4**

Fiber content of some foods

FOOD	CRUDE FIBER, g/100 g	TOTAL DIETARY FIBER, g/100 g
Grain Products:		
White flour	0.3	3.1
Whole wheat flour	2.3	7.9
Vegetables (raw):		
Broccoli	1.5	4.1
Cabbage	0.8	2.8
Peas	2.0	7.7
Carrots	1.0	3.7
Potato	0.5	3.5
Fruits:		
Apple (flesh only)	0.6	1.4
Banana	0.5	1.8
Peach (with skin)	0.6	2.3
Pear	1.4	2.4
Strawberry	1.3	2.1
Tomato	0.5	1.4

Sources: B. K. Watt and A. L. Merrill, *Composition of Foods: Raw, Processed, and Prepared,* Handbook No. 8, USDA, Washington, 1963.

D. A. T. Southgate, B. Bailey, E. Collinson, and A. F. Walker, "A Guide to Calculating Intakes of Dietary Fiber," *J. Human Nutr.* **30**:303–313 (1976). Reprinted with permission of D.A.T. Southgate.

Study Guide

SUMMARY

1. Carbohydrates may be grouped into three categories:
   a. *Monosaccharides:* glucose, galactose, and fructose
   b. *Disaccharides:* sucrose, lactose, and maltose
   c. *Polysaccharides:* starch, glycogen, dextrins, and cellulose
2. Glucose is the primary carbohydrate used by the body; almost all the digestible carbohydrate consumed in the diet is converted to this sugar before it is metabolized further.
3. Carbohydrate provides 4 kcal/g. If more is consumed than can be utilized for energy, the body stores it as glycogen or converts it to fat.
4. A negative feedback system regulates blood glucose levels. If they rise, the pancreas secretes insulin, which acts to clear glucose from the blood. If they fall, the pancreas secretes glucagon, which works to increase blood glucose concentration.
5. Imbalances of this regulatory mechanism include diabetes mellitus (hyperglycemia caused by a lack of insulin activity) and hypoglycemia. Another disorder of carbohydrate metabolism, lactose intolerance, results from reduced production of lactase, the enzyme that digests milk sugar in the small intestine.
6. Some nutritionists believe that excess sucrose consumption plays an important role in causing heart disease, diabetes mellitus, obesity, hypoglycemia, and tooth decay. Food faddists have called this sugar a poison. Most studies, however, indicate that fat and cholesterol intakes and a lack of physical activity probably contribute more to the development of heart disease and that obesity is more closely associated with diabetes. Current medical opinion also suggests there is no link between sucrose and hypoglycemia. Obesity can be caused by excess consumption of kilocalories, regardless of their source. Sucrose, particularly in forms that stick to the teeth, has been shown to cause tooth decay.
7. Despite the bad publicity it has received, carbohydrate is an important part of a balanced diet. A minimum of 50 to 100 g/day is needed by the body to maintain a proper balance in the utilization of carbohydrate, protein, and fat for energy. The U.S. Dietary Goals recommend that about 50 percent or more of the total caloric intake come from carbohydrate, with sucrose contributing less than 10 percent. Carbohydrate deficiency may result in ketosis, breakdown of lean body tissue, fatigue, dehydration, and other symptoms. In addition, carbohydrate-containing foods generally are less expensive sources of kilocalories than those high in protein and fat.
8. Grains, legumes, and root and tuber vegetables provide much of the starch in the diet. Sugars are found naturally in fruits, honey, molasses, white and brown sugar, and maple syrup. Sucrose is also added to a large variety of manufactured products.
9. In recent years, fiber has attracted a great deal of attention in both the scientific and popular media. Proponents claim that it can prevent or treat many diseases of the large intestine, including constipation, diverticular disease, colon cancer, and hemorrhoids, as well as heart disease, obesity, and diabetes mellitus. While beneficial effects on digestive tract function are fairly well documented, less experimental evidence exists to link fiber-depleted diets with colon cancer, heart disease, obesity, and diabetes. In addition, authorities have not yet agreed on a concrete definition of fiber, and there are many different types of fiber, many of which vary in their properties. Much re-

search remains to be done before a conclusive recommendation on daily fiber intake can be made. Increasing intake of whole-grain products, legumes, fruits, and vegetables from many sources appears to be the best approach at this time.

VOCABULARY

autoimmune response
carcinogenic
cellulose
crude fiber
dental caries
dextrins
diabetes mellitus
disaccharide
epinephrine (adrenaline)
fiber
fructose
galactose
glucagon
glucose
glycogen
glycoprotein
hemicellulose
hyperglycemia
hypoglycemia
insulin
ketone bodies
ketosis
lactase
lacto-ovo-vegetarian
lactose
lactose intolerance
lignin
maltose
monosaccharide
mucopoly saccharide
oral hypoglycemic agents
pectin
photosynthesis
polysaccharide
respiration
starch
sucrose
total dietary fiber
triglyceride
true fiber

STUDY QUESTIONS

1. List the monosaccharides that comprise each of the following:
   a. Sucrose e. Glycogen
   b. Lactose f. Cellulose
   c. Maltose g. Hemicellulose
   d. Starch

   What distinguishes starch, glycogen, and cellulose?
2. What is the ultimate source of energy in carbohydrate? By what process is the energy trapped in the carbohydrate? How is the energy released for use by the body? What happens to excess carbohydrate consumed in the diet?
3. Explain why the body requires a certain amount of dietary carbohydrate each day.
4. Describe the hormonal mechanism that regulates blood glucose concentrations. How is this mechanism altered in diabetes mellitus? In hypoglycemia?
5. If a person has lactose intolerance, what nutrients must he or she be particularly careful to obtain from the rest of the diet? (You may wish to consult Chapters 7 and 8 for help with this question.)
6. What are the U.S. Dietary Goals regarding carbohydrate consumption? To meet these goals, intake of which foods should be increased? Which should be reduced? Will this guarantee freedom from heart disease, diabetes, or obesity? Why or why not?
7. If a population study shows an association between two factors, such as high sugar intake and high rates of heart disease or low fiber intake and high rates of colon disease, does this necessarily prove that one causes the other? Why or why not?
8. Are brown sugar and honey nutritionally superior to white sugar? Defend your answer.
9. Explain the role of sucrose in causing dental caries. How can the occurrence of caries be reduced?
10. Why is it currently difficult to make a blanket statement about the role of fiber intake in certain disease processes? By how

much should the fiber intake of Americans probably be increased? What foods should you consume if you wish to increase your fiber intake?

SELF-TEST

Multiple choice: Select the best answer.

1. The sugar around which body carbohydrate metabolism revolves is
   a. Fructose
   b. Glucose
   c. Sucrose
   d. Galactose
2. The sugar found in milk is
   a. Maltose
   b. Glucose
   c. Fructose
   d. Lactose
3. Under normal conditions, which tissue can only use glucose for energy?
   a. Liver
   b. Muscle
   c. Brain and nervous system
   d. Kidney
4. Which hormone is secreted during "fight or flight" situations and elevates blood glucose levels?
   a. Insulin
   b. Glucagon
   c. Estrogen
   d. Epinephrine
5. Which of the following would improve the nutritional quality of the diet?
   a. Drink fruit juice or milk instead of soda pop.
   b. Substitute honey for sucrose.
   c. Substitute saccharin for sucrose.
   d. All of the above.
6. Which of the following would help increase the starch content of the diet?
   a. Honey
   b. Grapes
   c. Grains
   d. Molasses
7. Which of the following carbohydrate sources is also a good source of protein?
   a. Cornstarch
   b. Honey
   c. Soybeans
   d. Molasses
8. Lactose intolerance is
   a. An allergy to lactose
   b. An inability to digest lactose
   c. A very rare condition
   d. Found only in infants
9. Which of the following has most conclusively been linked to excess sucrose consumption?
   a. Dental caries
   b. Heart disease
   c. Diabetes mellitus
   d. Hypoglycemia
10. Which of the following would help increase the fiber content of the diet?
    a. Whole wheat bread
    b. Eating the skin of a baked potato
    c. Eating a salad
    d. All of the above

True-False

1. Controlling obesity can help treat adult-onset diabetes.
2. People who feel weak, tired, irritable, and anxious much of the time usually have hypoglycemia.
3. Sucrose occurs naturally in many foods and is easily metabolized by the body.
4. Potatoes and macaroni are carbohydrate sources that are high in kilocalories.
5. Sucrose consumption invariably makes you fat.
6. The chemical composition and properties of fiber vary depending on its source.
7. Measuring crude fiber accurately represents the actual fiber content of a food.
8. People with lactose intolerance must eliminate all dairy products from their diets.
9. A disadvantage of fructose, xylitol, and sorbitol as artificial sweeteners is that they provide kilocalories.
10. Current studies have conclusively shown that saccharin does not cause bladder cancer.

SUGGESTED ACTIVITIES

1. The following activities require completion

of a diet record as instructed in Activity 10-1.

a. How does the percent of your daily caloric intake contributed by carbohydrate compare with that recommended by the U.S. Dietary Goals?
b. Identify those foods in your diet in which the carbohydrate is refined sugar (sucrose). What are some low-sugar foods you can substitute for foods in your diet that are high in sugar?
c. Does your diet contain any foods that are good sources of fiber? What are some foods you enjoy that would help increase the fiber content of your diet?

2. Make a list of foods you enjoy eating that would help you increase the consumption of starch in your diet. Be sure to select foods that are also good sources of such other nutrients as protein, vitamins, and minerals.
3. Make a trip to the grocery store and check the ingredient listing on the labels of a variety of foods. The ingredients are listed in order of decreasing abundance in the food (the ingredient present in largest amount first, next largest amount second, and so on). Make a list of foods in which sugar is the most abundant ingredient and a list in which sugar is one of the first four ingredients named. Are there suitable substitutes containing little or no sugar for any of these foods?

FURTHER READING

1. Kretchmer, N.: "Lactose and Lactase," *Sci. Am.* **227:**70–78 (October 1972).

2. An excellent review on the causes, diagnosis, and treatment of hypoglycemia:

   Permutt, M. A.: "Is It Really Hypoglycemia? If So, What Should You Do?" *Med. Times* **108:**35–43 (1980).

3. A book by one of the leading proponents of the theory that sucrose is harmful to health:

   Yudkin, J.: *Sweet and Dangerous,* Wyden, New York, 1972.

4. A series of articles that dispute Yudkin's hypothesis regarding sucrose and heart disease, diabetes, hypoglycemia, and obesity; includes a good review of the effects of sugar on tooth decay:

   Stare, F. J., (ed.): "Sugar in the Diet of Man," *World Rev. Nutr. Diet.* **22**:237–326 (1975).

5. An article critiquing the hypothesis that sucrose causes diabetes:

   Walker, A. R. P.: "Sugar Intake and Diabetes Mellitus," *S. Afr. Med. J.* **51**:842–851 (1977).

6. A readable and thorough summary of fiber's role in the diet:

   National Dairy Council: "The Role of Fiber in the Diet," *Dairy Council Digest* **46**(1) (1975).

7. A more technical treatment of current fiber research:

   Roth, H. P., and Mehlman, M. A. (chairpersons): "Symposium on the Role of Dietary Fiber in Health and Disease," *Am. J. Clin. Nutr.* **31**:S1–S291 (1978).

LIPIDS

Fats, Steroids, and Phospholipids

Issue: Diet and Atherosclerosis

Steve Jones is typical of many middle-aged Americans today. He likes to have meat in some form nearly every night for dinner and often for lunch as well. He loads his potatoes with butter and salts many of his foods heavily. He is about 20 pounds overweight. His overeating and his two-pack-per-day cigarette habit are part of his way of coping with the stress of his office job. He drives to work and most evenings settles down to watch television until he falls asleep. Steve's idea of exercise is his bowling night or a weekend game of golf.

Unknown to him, some insidious changes are occurring inside his body. His blood pressure and the level of cholesterol and fat in his blood are abnormally high. The walls of several major arteries, including one that feeds part of his heart, are in a well-progressed stage of atherosclerosis; they have thickened tremendously and are laden with cholesterol. If the coronary artery becomes totally blocked, Steve Jones will suffer a heart attack.

Fat and cholesterol, the chemical substances so often associated with the development of atherosclerosis and heart disease, belong to a class of chemical compounds called **lipids**. The property that distinguishes lipids from other compounds is their insolubility in water. If you try to mix vegetable oil and water, the vegetable oil reunites into a layer above the water. However, lipids dissolve readily in organic solvents such as ether, chloroform, and benzene. Vegetable oil mixed with one of these disappears, much the way sugar dissolves in water.

Like carbohydrates, lipids have received a great deal of bad publicity. However, they are important for the normal functioning of the body. In addition, not all authorities agree that fat and cholesterol are the real villains behind heart disease. Let us take a close look at these substances, their importance to the body, and their suspected role in causing heart attacks.

Fats, Steroids, and Phospholipids

Most lipids belong to one of three general categories: fats, steroids, and phospholipids. Their structures and properties vary, but they all belong to the lipid group by virtue of their relative insolubility in an aqueous medium.

IMPORTANCE OF FATS IN NUTRITION

Fats are a particular combination of carbon, hydrogen, and oxygen (Figure 3-1). They consist of a molecule of glycerol, to which is attached one, two, or three fatty acids. If the fat contains glycerol and one fatty acid, it is called a **monoglyceride**. Glycerol and two fatty acids form a **diglyceride**, while glycerol combined with three fatty acids is referred to as a **triglyceride**.

Only small amounts of the mono- and diglycerides are found in food. Food manufacturers frequently add them as **emulsifying agents** to facilitate the mixing of other lipids in the food (Figure 3-2). They can play this role because part of their molecular structure is soluble in water and part is soluble in the lipid. When the lipid is mixed in the food or with water, the mono- and diglycerides arrange themselves so that their water-soluble parts face the water and the lipid-soluble parts face the lipid. In this way, they form a barrier on the surface of the lipid droplets that prevents them from clumping together into one large mass. Because they are readily broken down by the body, mono- and diglycerides appear to be relatively safe food additives.

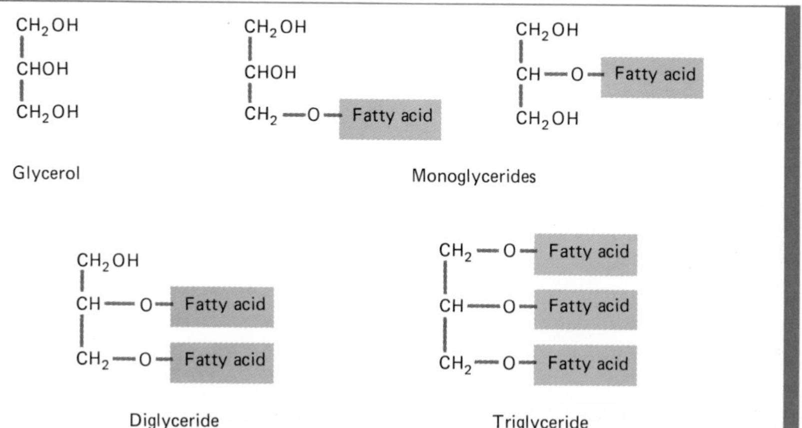

FIGURE 3-1
The Fats. Fats are combinations of glycerol with one, two, or three fatty acids.

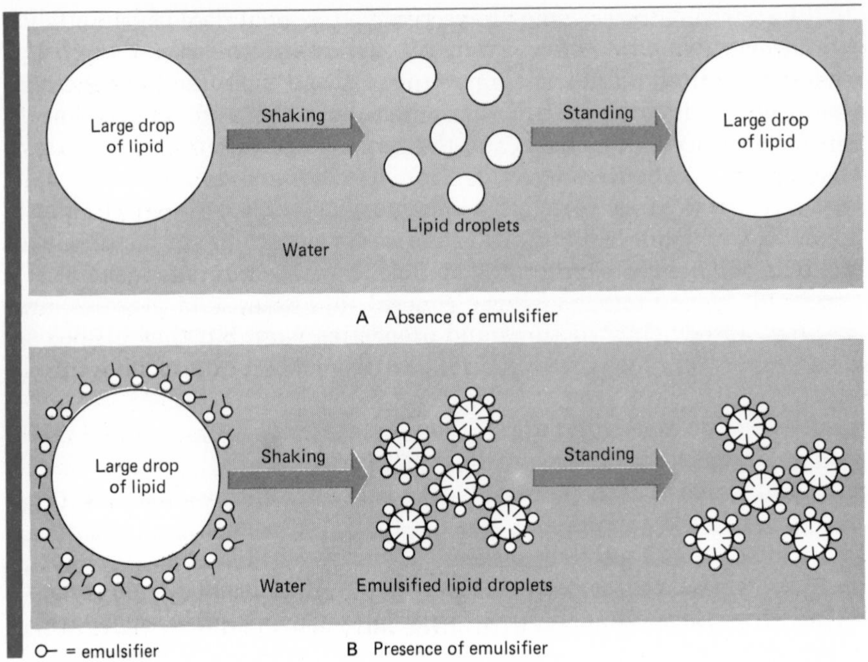

FIGURE 3-2
Emulsification. **A** In the absence of an emulsifier, lipid droplets aggregate back into a single mass after dispersion. **B** An emulsifier forms a barrier on the surface of lipid droplets, which allows them to remain dispersed.

Triglycerides comprise most of the fat in food and nearly all the fat in the body. However, there are many kinds of triglycerides, and they differ in the types of fatty acids that comprise them. **Fatty acids** are chains of carbon atoms with hydrogens attached and an acid group (COOH) at one end. They differ from one another according to the number of carbon atoms and the number of double bonds in the chain (Figure 3-3). Most of those commonly found in food contain 16 to 20 carbons and sometimes carbon-carbon double bonds. If the fatty acid contains no double bonds, all carbons in the chain are bound to the maximum number of hydrogen atoms possible, and the molecule is referred to as **saturated**. If one double bond is present, two of the carbon atoms lack one hydrogen atom apiece, and we call the fatty acid **monounsaturated**. **Polyunsaturated** fatty acids contain two or more double bonds, indicating that several pairs of carbon atoms are not bound to the maximum possible number of hydrogen atoms.

The length of the carbon chain and the degree of saturation (number of double bonds) determine the properties of each type of fatty acid. For example, fatty acids with longer chains and no double bonds tend to have higher melting points, whereas shorter-chain fatty acids and those with one or more double bonds tend to have lower melting points. Triglycerides are generally mixtures of several types of fatty acids, and the relative proportion of each type determines the overall nature of the fat. Let us look at some of the fatty acids found most frequently in food (Figure 3-3).

Palmitic acid and **stearic acid** are saturated fatty acids that contain 16 and 18 carbon atoms, respectively, and occur predominantly in animal fat. Because of the relative length and saturation of these fatty acids, triglycerides containing large amounts of them tend to be solid at room temperature. Triglycerides containing saturated fatty acids of shorter length are found in foods such as milk and dairy products, coconut oil, and palm oil. Although these fats are solid at room temperature, they have lower melting points than those containing stearic or palmitic acid. One monounsaturated fatty acid, **oleic acid**, is the major constituent of triglycerides found in peanut and olive oils and can be found in a variety of other foods. Olive and peanut oils are liquid because of their unsaturated fat content. Three polyunsaturated fatty acids commonly occur in food: **linoleic acid** (18 carbon atoms and two double bonds), **linolenic acid** (18 carbons and three double bonds), and **arachidonic acid** (20 carbon atoms and four double bonds). Triglycerides composed mainly of these fatty acids are liquid because of their highly unsaturated nature and are found in safflower oil, sunflower oil, corn oil, soybean oil, cottonseed oil, and wheat germ oil.

Fat in the Body Fat is a concentrated and storable source of energy. It contains 9 kcal/g, more than twice the energy value of carbohydrate or protein. When the body consumes energy in amounts greater than it needs, it stores most of it in the form of fat in adipose tissue. Besides providing a storable form of energy that can be used when food is scarce, fat

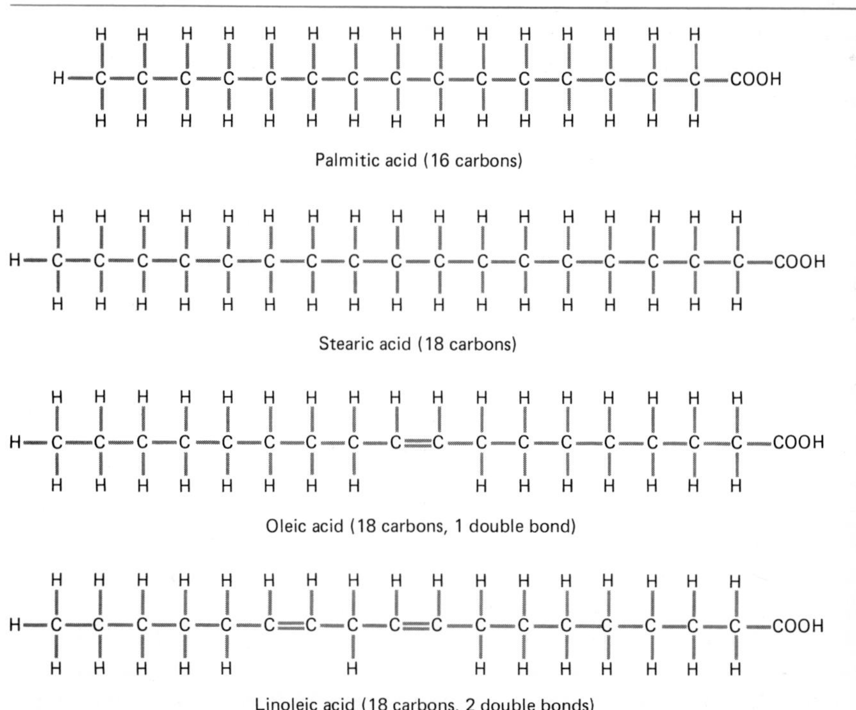

FIGURE 3-3
Some of the Fatty Acids of Nutritional Importance. The fatty acids differ in the number of carbon atoms and the number of double bonds they contain.

insulates the body and prevents excessive heat loss. It pads certain vital organs, such as the heart and kidneys, protecting them from physical injury. Vitamins A, D, E, and K are fat-soluble, so fat is required in the diet in order for them to be absorbed efficiently from the digestive tract. Fat also contributes to the taste and satiety value of food. Many of the flavors in food are fat-soluble, while the slower rate at which fat leaves the stomach contributes to a longer period of satiety following a meal.

Linoleic acid, which promotes growth and healthy skin, cannot be synthesized by the body and must be obtained from the diet. It is therefore called an **essential fatty acid**. Arachidonic acid also contributes to healthy skin, but since the body can synthesize it from linoleic acid, arachidonic acid is not considered essential. Arachidonic acid and certain other derivatives of linoleic acid also are involved in the synthesis of hormonelike compounds called **prostaglandins**. The effects of these substances on the body vary, depending on the type of prostaglandin, and include both contraction and relaxation of smooth muscles in the walls of the blood vessels, raising and lowering of blood pressure, and proper functioning of the nervous, digestive, and reproductive systems. The other polyunsaturated fatty acid of nutritional importance, linolenic acid, promotes growth, although it is not yet clear whether linolenic acid is actually required in the diet.

Fat in Food The National Academy of Science has not set an RDA for fat, although it is estimated that the intake of essential fatty acids (especially linoleic acid) should represent about 2 percent of the daily kilocalories. Moreover, a certain amount of dietary fat is needed to promote the absorption of the fat-soluble vitamins. A daily intake of 15 to 25 grams of appropriate food fats can meet these needs (1). In view of the role of saturated fat in causing high blood lipid levels, which may contribute to the development of atherosclerosis, the Dietary Guidelines for Americans recommend that Americans avoid too much fat and saturated fat (42). The American Heart Association and the U.S. Dietary Goals make the more specific recommendation that fat contribute no more than 30 to 35 percent of the daily caloric intake. Of this, about a third should be polyunsaturated, a third saturated, and the remainder monounsaturated (2–4).

Except for vegetable oils and products made from them, most of the fat in the American diet occurs in foods from animal sources (Table 3-1) and is mainly saturated. Many cuts of red meat, such as choice-grade steak, contain particularly large amounts of fat. Even when the meat is trimmed, some remains in the **marbling** (Figure 3-4). Lean cuts of meat, such as beef round, contain somewhat less fat and can be substituted for the richer cuts.

Another source of fat is whole-milk dairy products. Although it makes up only 3.5 percent of the total weight of whole milk, fat constitutes 28 percent of the dry weight and 48 percent of the kilocalories. In addition, more than 80 percent of the caloric value of some cheeses consists of fat, and nearly all the kilocalories in butter occur in this form.

TABLE **3-1**

Total fat content of some representative foods

FOOD	Fat Content: PERCENT BY WEIGHT	PERCENT DRY WEIGHT	PERCENT kcal
Porterhouse steak (choice grade)			
Broiled (total edible)	42.2	67	82
Broiled (separable fat removed)	10.5	25	42
Hamburger (cooked)			
Lean	11.3	28	46
Regular	20.3	44	64
Beef round (choice grade)			
Broiled (total edible)	15.4	34	50
Broiled (separable fat removed)	6.1	16	29
Lamb chops (choice grade)			
Broiled (total edible)	29.4	55	74
Broiled (separable fat removed)	7.5	20	36
Milk			
Whole	3.5	28	48
Skim	0.1	1	Insignificant
2% Milk	2.0	18	33
Buttermilk (from skim milk)	0.1	1	Insignificant
Cheddar cheese	32.2	51	73
Chicken (flesh and skin)			
Fryer (fried)	11.9	26	43
Roaster (roasted)	14.7	34	53
Chicken (flesh only)			
Fryer (fried)	7.8	19	34
Roaster (roasted)	6.3	17	31
Haddock (fried)	6.4	19	35
Cod (broiled)	5.3	15	28
Tuna fish (drained solids)			
Packed in water	0.8	3	6
Packed in vegetable oil	8.2	21	37
Soybeans (cooked)	5.7	20	31
Peanuts (roasted)	49.0	51	76
Whole wheat flour	2.0	23	6

Source: B. K. Watt and A. L. Merrill, *Composition of Foods—Raw, Processed, and Prepared,* Agriculture Handbook No. 8, USDA, Washington, 1963.

FIGURE 3-4
Fat in Meat. Separable fat, the thick layers bordering the muscle, can be removed before cooking or eating. Marbling, the thin wisps of fat scattered throughout the muscle, contributes to the juiciness and flavor of the meat. (Photograph by Martha N. Solonche.)

Some foods from animal sources contain relatively little fat. Skim milk has virtually none, while products made from it differ depending on the proportion of skim milk in them. For example, some of the milk used in the manufacture of cheese and yogurt can be skim milk, thereby reducing the fat content of these foods. Despite its name, most buttermilk is also a low-fat product, since it is usually made by fermenting skim milk. Your grandmother may remember making it from the milk remaining after butter was removed by churning, however.

Poultry and fish are other good examples of foods with relatively low fat content. Fat comprises about 30 percent of the dry weight and contributes 43 to 53 percent of the kilocalories in chicken, but the values are far less when the skin is removed. In fish such as haddock or cod, fat makes up 15 to 19 percent of the dry weight and about one-third of the caloric value. Tuna fish packed in water contains less than 1 percent fat, but when packed in vegetable oil, its fat content increases to over 8 percent.

Most foods from plant sources contain relatively little fat (Table 3-1); the exceptions are avocados (fat provides over 90 percent of the kilocalories) and nuts (up to 85 percent). Beans, grains, and seeds contain small amounts of fat, but good use is made of this fat by pressing the seed to yield vegetable oils such as corn oil, safflower oil, sunflower oil, wheat germ oil, soybean oil, and cottonseed oil. With the exception of coconut oil and palm oil, which are about 90 percent saturated fat, vegetable fat is predominantly unsaturated. The fat in peanut oil, olive oil, and avocados consists largely of the monounsaturated oleic acid, while the triglycerides in soybean oil, cottonseed oil, wheat germ oil, corn oil, sunflower oil, and safflower oil contain mainly linoleic acid.

Many food labels contain the words *hydrogenated oil* or *hardened vegetable oil*. This indicates that the oils have been subjected to **hydrogenation**, a process that involves the addition of hydrogen to the double bonds of their fatty acids. As a result, the fatty acids become saturated, and the fat is transformed from a liquid to a solid (Figure 3-5). Margarine, which was originally invented as an inexpensive substitute for butter, contains vegetable oil. Because vegetable oils are liquid, the oil is partially hydrogenated to solidify it to the desired consistency. Another technique is to hydrogenate the oil completely and mix it with liquid vegetable oil until the required degree of solidity is attained. Further processing yields a food that can be used in much the same way as butter. Hydrogenation is also used in the manufacture of peanut butter and vegetable shortening. Solidifying some of the peanut oil and mixing it thoroughly into the peanut butter prevents separation of the oil when the product sits on a shelf for a long period of time. Vegetable shortenings, which are composed of hydrogenated vegetable oils, are a substitute for lard or butter in baking.

In recent years, researchers have found that the consumption of polyunsaturated fat may reduce blood cholesterol levels and thus may help in the prevention of heart disease. This has implications for the use of hydrogenation in the manufacture of foods (Table 3-2). Margarine contains more unsaturated fat than butter and no cholesterol, so it may serve as a

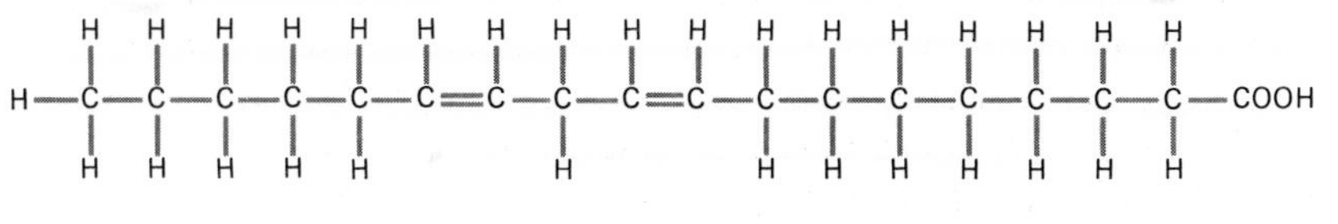
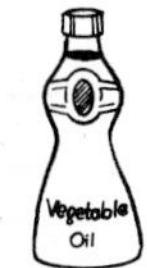

Linoleic acid
A polyunsaturated fatty acid. Liquid at room temperature.

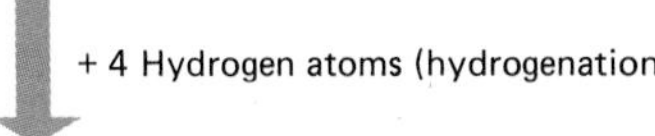

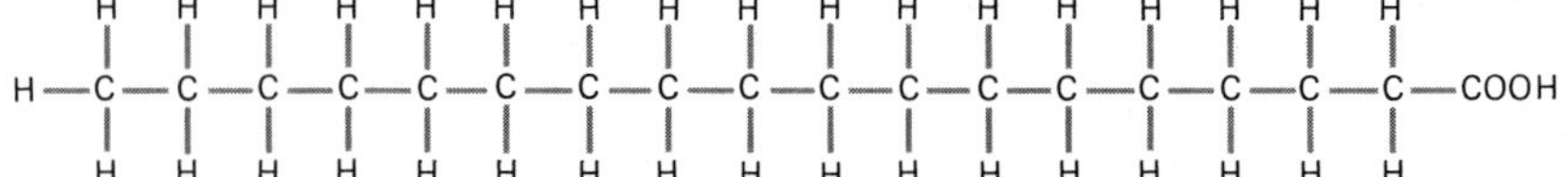
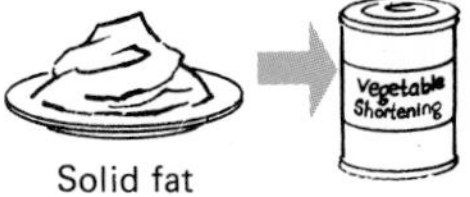

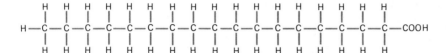

Stearic acid
A saturated fatty acid. Solid at room temperature.

+

Color, flavor, water, and emulsifiers

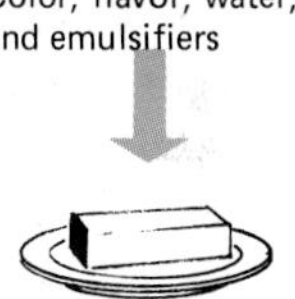

FIGURE 3-5
Hydrogenation. Adding hydrogen atoms to an unsaturated fatty acid fills the double bonds and saturates it. Complete hydrogenation transforms the fat from a liquid into a solid.

TABLE **3-2**

Comparison of margarine, butter, corn oil, vegetable shortening, and lard

LIPID	BUTTER	LARD	CORN OIL	STICK MARGARINE FROM VEGETABLE OIL (HARD)	TUB MARGARINE (SOFT)	VEGETABLE SHORTENING
Total fat (percent of total weight)	81	100	100	81	81	100
Saturated fat (percent of total weight)	46	38	10	15	15	23
Monounsaturated fat (oleic acid) (percent of total weight)	27	25	28	40	30	65
Polyunsaturated fat (linoleic acid) (percent of total weight)	2	2	53	22	30	7
Cholesterol (mg/100 g)	250	95	0	0	0	0

Source: B. K. Watt and A. L. Merrill, *Composition of Foods—Raw, Processed, and Prepared,* Agriculture Handbook No. 8, USDA, Washington, 1963.

substitute for butter for people who wish to reduce blood cholesterol concentrations. However, hydrogenation has certain disadvantages. Because it reduces the unsaturated fat content, neither margarine, hardened peanut oil, nor vegetable shortening contains as much polyunsaturated fat as the vegetable oils from which they are made. Hydrogenation also transforms some fatty acids into a form different from that normally used by the body, and no one yet knows whether this has any effect on human health.

THE ROLE OF STEROIDS

The **steroids**, which include the sex hormones, the hormones of the adrenal cortex, vitamin D, bile acids, and cholesterol, are an important group of lipids. All these substances share a similar structure, with minor variations that confer unique properties on each. Cholesterol is probably the most important steroid in the diet because the body synthesizes all the other steroids from it (Figure 3-6). In addition, excessive cholesterol intake and the elevation of its concentration in the blood have been associated with the development of atherosclerosis.

The body synthesizes two to three times the amount of cholesterol it obtains from an average diet and uses this substance in a variety of ways. Cholesterol is a structural component of cell membranes. The body also uses it to make vitamin D, bile acids, and the steroid hormones. Vitamin D is synthesized in the skin upon exposure to sunlight and plays a role in the absorption of calcium and phosphorus. Bile acids aid in the digestion and absorption of lipids from the intestine. The steroid hormones, which include the sex hormones and the adrenocortical hormones, regulate many body processes.

The Dietary Guideline recommending that Americans avoid too much cholesterol is based on an American Heart Association and U.S. Dietary Goal recommendation that cholesterol intake be limited to 300 mg/day (2–4,42). As Table 3-3 shows, this requires restricting consumption of certain foods, including eggs, organ meats (such as liver, kidney, and brain), fish eggs (caviar), meat, whole milk and dairy products, and other foods from animal sources. (Cholesterol is not found in foods from plant sources.) This recommendation is controversial, as we shall see later in this chapter.

FIGURE 3-6
Cholesterol Structure.

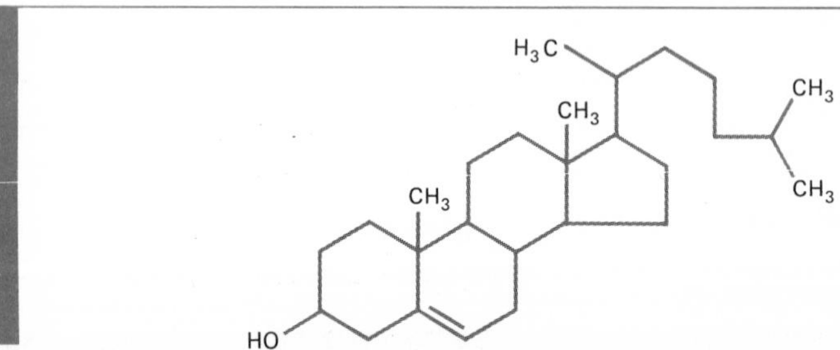

TABLE **3-3**

Cholesterol content of some foods*

FOOD	SERVING SIZE	CHOLESTEROL CONTENT, mg
Beef (cooked)†	3 oz	80
Butter	1 tbsp	35
Cheese		
Cheddar	1 oz	28
Cottage (4% fat)	1 cup	48
Mozzarella (low moisture-part skim)	1 oz	18
Chicken (flesh and skin, cooked)	3 oz	75
Whole egg	1 large	252
Haddock fillet (raw)	3 oz	51
Liver (cooked)	3 oz	372
Margarine		
All vegetable fat	1 tbsp	0
2/3 animal fat, 1/3 vegetable fat	1 tbsp	7
Milk		
Whole	1 cup	34
Skim	1 cup	5
Yogurt (plain, nonfat)	1 cup	17

* Plant products do not contain cholesterol.
† Cholesterol content of lamb and pork is similar.

Source: R. M. Feeley, P. E. Criner, and B. K. Watt, "Cholesterol Content of Foods", *J. Am. Dietetic Assoc.* **61**:134–149 (1972). Cholesterol data used with permission.

HOW PHOSPHOLIPIDS WORK

A third general group of lipids is the **phospholipids**. These consist of a diglyceride, a phosphate group, and a third molecule (X) joined as shown in Figure 3-7. Depending on what the third molecule is, different phospholipids can be formed. For example, if X is choline, the phospholipid is **lecithin** (phosphatidyl choline); if X is ethanolamine, the phospholipid is **cephalin** (phosphatidyl ethanolamine); if X is inositol, the phospholipid is **lipositol** (phosphatidyl inositol); and so on.

Like cholesterol, the phospholipids are structural components of cell membranes. In addition, because part of the phospholipid molecule is soluble in water and part in lipid, they are powerful emulsifying agents that help disperse or make soluble other lipids in the digestive tract and the

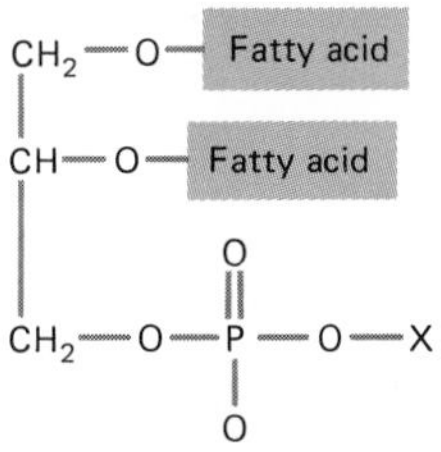

FIGURE 3-7
Phospholipid Structure. Phospholipids are made up of a diglyceride, a phosphate molecule, and a third chemical group (X) which can be any one of a number of compounds.

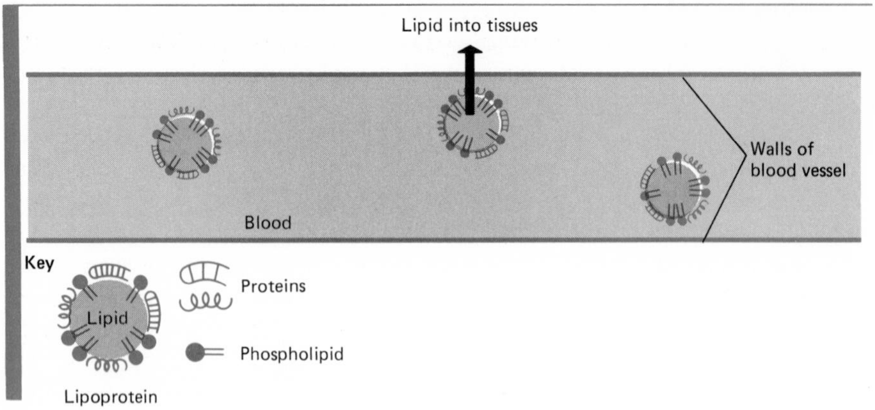

Lipid into tissues
Walls of blood vessel
Blood
Key
Lipid
Lipoprotein
Proteins
Phospholipid

FIGURE 3-8
Blood Lipid Transport. Lipids in the blood are emulsified by proteins and phospholipids to form lipoproteins which transport the lipids throughout the body.

bloodstream. The fact that most lipids tend to clump together when mixed with water would interfere with their digestion and absorption. However, bile acids, with the help of phospholipids, disperse the lipids into small droplets so that they can be digested and absorbed more efficiently.

The function of phospholipids in the bloodstream is very similar. Without an emulsifying agent, lipids in the blood would clump together and clog the blood vessels. To prevent this, lipids are combined with proteins to form **lipoproteins**. With the help of phospholipids, the lipoproteins facilitate the movement of lipids in the bloodstream (Figure 3-8). There are several types of lipoproteins in the body, and as we will see later in this chapter, some of them may be important in accelerating or preventing the development of atherosclerosis.

FOCUS 3-1 LECITHIN Probably the most widely known phospholipid is lecithin. Some people promote lecithin as a dietary supplement to prevent or treat several disorders, including atherosclerosis. Lecithin is often said to mobilize triglyceride and cholesterol, thereby preventing or reversing their accumulation in the walls of the arteries. It is true that lecithin participates in the transport of other lipids in the blood, and it is also known to play a role in the metabolism of cholesterol (41). However, there is no experimental evidence to support the idea that taking lecithin supplements will prevent or reverse the atherosclerotic process. First of all, the body synthesizes its own lecithin, although a certain amount is supplied by the diet (41), and moreover, lecithin forms only a part of the lipoprotein structure by which blood lipids are transported. Consequently, there is no evidence thus far to suggest that supplements have any significant impact on this mechanism.

Phospholipids play important roles in other body processes, including nervous tissue function and the clotting of blood. They are therefore vital body components, but because the body synthesizes them, they are not required in the diet. They do occur in many foods, such as eggs, meats, legumes, and grains, and most people consume relatively large amounts (1 gram or more) each day.

ISSUE: DIET AND ATHEROSCLEROSIS

For thousands of years, infectious diseases were the scourge of humanity. The Bible tells of plagues that ravaged ancient civilizations; in the fourteenth century, bubonic plague decimated the population of Europe. Smallpox, pneumonia, tuberculosis, and typhoid were major contributors to the high human death rate in the past. During the last century, however, these diseases have largely been brought under control by improved public sanitation and the use of vaccines and antibiotics, and other disorders have taken their place as major causes of death. Previously overlooked because many people did not live long enough to develop them and because diagnostic techniques were primitive, heart disease, cancer, stroke, and diabetes mellitus have become the modern scourges. Their causes remain unknown, and each may in fact have a number of origins.

FACT OR FANTASY

1. Lecithin is a dietary essential and will help prevent or treat atherosclerosis.
2. Cholesterol has been proven to cause heart attacks.

Coronary heart disease, which includes heart attacks, is the single greatest cause of death in the United States today. It was responsible for 642,000 fatalities in 1978, 34 percent of all deaths reported. The second leading cause of death is cancer, followed by **cerebrovascular disease (stroke)**. Strokes killed 176,000 people in 1978, 10 percent of the total (5). Both coronary heart disease and stroke are manifestations of a disease of the arteries called *atherosclerosis:* one disorder thus lies at the root of almost 1 million deaths each year in the United States.

The term **arteriosclerosis** was coined to describe any disease involving hardening of the arteries. **Atherosclerosis**, a particular type of arteriosclerosis, is a thickening of the walls of the large and medium arteries characterized by growth of tissue and an accumulation of lipids, particularly cholesterol. This thickening can become so severe that it actually blocks blood flow through the artery, causing death of the tissue it nourishes.

PREVALENCE

Atherosclerosis and heart disease appear to be diseases of affluence; their rate of occurrence is particularly high in the United States and other industrialized nations. They are also more common among those in higher socioeconomic classes than among the lower classes (6). The severity of atherosclerosis and the incidence of heart disease increase with age, and they are both less prevalent among women during the childbearing years than among men of the same age. After menopause, however, the difference narrows considerably (6).

The incidence of death from heart disease has shown a steady decline in the United States during the last 10 years, but it is still high. Moreover, in many industrialized nations, the death rate from heart disease is still increasing, making it a major health problem (7).

DEVELOPMENT

The atherosclerotic process begins in infancy and early childhood (8). Deposits of lipid called *fatty streaks* can be found in the innermost layer of many of the large arteries from infancy onward. These often spontaneously disappear, and many authorities no longer believe they always become atherosclerosis in adults (9). Even so, infancy and childhood may have a profound effect on the development of the disease because it is then that food-consumption patterns and other relevant habits such as physical activity are set.

It is thought that the atherosclerotic process begins with damage to the innermost layer of the artery (the **intima**), which allows cholesterol-bearing lipoproteins to infiltrate the arterial wall (Figure 3-9). The injury may result from turbulent blood flow in the affected part of the artery, from exposure to chemical agents, and from other causes (10). The artery responds to the damage by growing new tissue, which traps cholesterol and other lipids. Some researchers believe that a single cell multiplies, much like a cancer cell, to produce this new tissue (11). The result is a thickening of the arterial wall, called **atherosclerotic plaque**. If there is no further injury, healing can occur. If the damage is sustained, the plaque may develop into more advanced atherosclerosis (6,10).

In most people, arterial damage apparently continues, because atherosclerosis is often quite pronounced by the early twenties. Autopsies performed on American soldiers killed in action in Korea and Vietnam showed a high prevalence of atherosclerosis in their arteries. Of those killed in the Korean conflict, 77 percent had some evidence of atherosclerosis, and in 15.3 percent, the arterial "tubes" had narrowed to about half their normal size (12). The arteries of American soldiers killed in Vietnam were less affected. Forty-five percent of those examined showed some evidence of atherosclerosis, and in only 5 percent was the disease characterized as severe (13). The average age of the men in both studies, however, was only 22.1 years.

As a person ages, the atherosclerotic process may continue until the thickening becomes great enough to block blood flow through the artery. In many instances, the plaque provides a rough surface that is ideal for blood clotting (**thrombosis**). The clot may then obstruct the artery in which it is formed, or it may break off and travel in the bloodstream until it lodges in another artery (Figure 3-9) (14).

In advanced atherosclerosis, blood flow through one or more arteries may be obstructed. The tissue normally receiving that blood no longer obtains the oxygen it needs, and it dies. If a coronary artery becomes blocked, part of the heart tissue dies and the person suffers a heart attack. Stroke results from obstruction of blood flow to the brain; restriction of blood to the kidney can lead to kidney failure. Atherosclerosis or the resulting blood clots also may block arteries supplying the limbs and

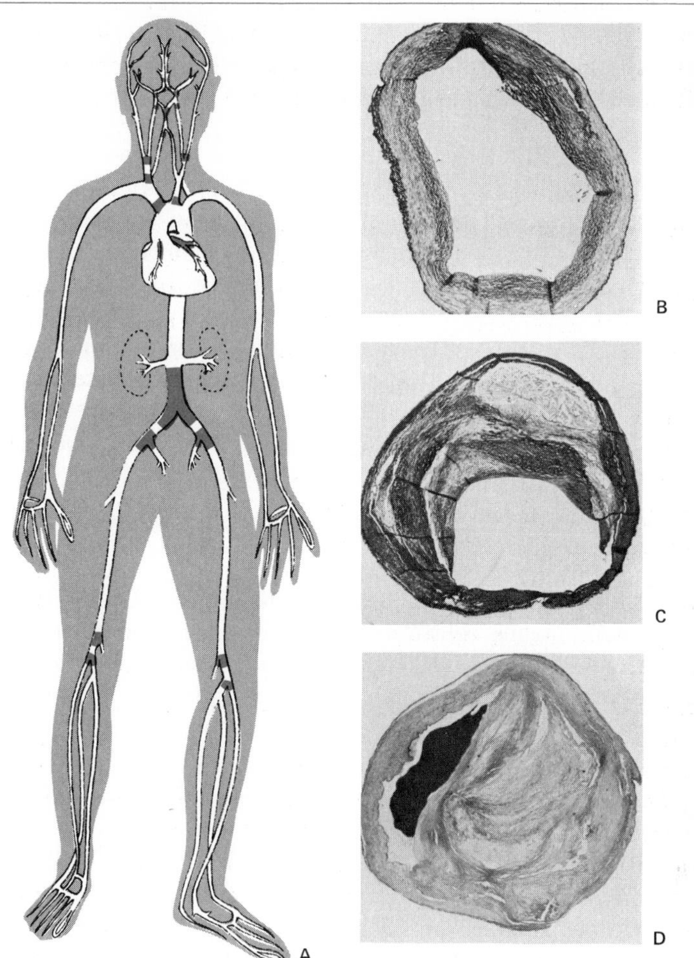

FIGURE 3-9
The Progression of Atherosclerosis. **A** The shaded areas show the sites at which atherosclerosis is most likely to occur. (Adapted from Spain, D.M., "Atherosclerosis", *Scientific American,* August 1966, p. 50. Copyright © 1966 by Scientific American, Inc. All rights reserved.) **B–D** The passageway of the artery gradually fills up with atherosclerotic plaque. (Photographs courtesy of the American Heart Association.)

cause gangrene. Atherosclerosis can lead to still other problems. Sometimes the wall of the artery becomes weakened by the disease and expands like a balloon. This is called an **aneurysm**, and it may burst. This can be instantly fatal if a large artery is involved (14).

CAUSES AND RISK FACTORS

Despite the expediture of billions of dollars and millions of research hours, no specific cause for atherosclerosis has yet been found. The increasingly clear picture that has emerged, however, has given us an image of a typical individual who is at risk of developing the disorder and its manifestations. Some of the evidence has come from **epidemiologic studies** in which large groups of people have been monitored for as long as 30 years. One example is the Framingham Study, in which several thousand individuals in Framingham, Massachusetts have been followed since 1949. In addition, considerable experimental evidence has accumulated to support and extend the results of these population studies.

FOCUS 3-2
RISK FACTORS FOR HEART DISEASE

One result of all the research into the causes of heart disease has been the identification of a number of factors that are more commonly found in people who develop the disorder. These characteristics are called **risk factors**, and they include the following:

1. Elevated blood cholesterol and triglyceride concentrations
2. High blood pressure
3. Cigarette smoking
4. Diabetes mellitus
5. Obesity
6. Lack of physical activity
7. Nervous stress
8. Family history of the disease (genetic)

The presence of any one of these factors in an individual may increase the risk of heart disease. When two or more factors are operating at once, the risk multiplies accordingly. A typical American who is overweight, has high blood lipid levels, smokes cigarettes, does not exercise, and is subject to a great deal of nervous stress stands a good chance of suffering a heart attack. Remember, however, that the connection between these risk factors and heart disease does not mean that any one of them *causes* the disorder; they merely occur in association with it.

High blood cholesterol levels have long been associated with an increased risk of developing heart disease (6,15). The Framingham Study has shown a strong relationship between elevated blood cholesterol concentrations and increased risk of heart disease in men less than 50 years old, although the relationship becomes progressively less striking in older men (16). In recent years, high blood triglyceride concentrations also have been associated with increased risk of heart disease (15,17). A major influence on blood lipids appears to be diet, a subject we will look at a little later in this chapter.

In addition to level of cholesterol in the blood, the means by which it is transported is important. Two kinds of lipoproteins carry most of the cholesterol, **low-density lipoproteins (LDL)** and **high-density lipoproteins (HDL)**. Elevated levels of LDL have been associated with increased risk of developing atherosclerosis and heart disease, while the HDLs appear to have a protective effect (16,18). Cholesterol in LDL has thus been called "bad" cholesterol, and that in HDL, "good" cholesterol. Many factors, including diet and physical activity, influence the levels of LDL and HDL in the blood, and any factor that increases LDL and/or reduces HDL concentrations increases the risk of atherosclerosis and heart disease (19–21).

High blood pressure is a second risk factor associated with atherosclerosis and heart disease. The Framingham Study showed that both men and women with high blood pressure had a much greater risk of developing heart disease than those with normal blood pressure (6,22). One way high blood pressure might contribute to the formation of atherosclerosis is by the mechanical stress of pressure on the arterial wall.

Several studies have associated cigarette smoking with atherosclerosis and heart disease (23). The risk is greater in smokers who inhale than in those who do not. When a person quits smoking, the risk of heart disease declines, and after 10 years it reaches a level close to that of nonsmokers. Some studies show that it may be carbon monoxide rather than nicotine that is the culprit in cigarette smoke.

Diabetes mellitus and obesity are two other risk factors in atherosclerosis and heart disease (6,22). The incidence of coronary heart disease is at least two times greater in diabetics than in nondiabetics. Obesity may not contribute directly to the occurrence of heart disease, but evidence indicates that it may aggravate the effects of other risk factors.

The incidence of heart disease in sedentary societies is high. In the United States, most of us drive to and from school or work, use elevators and escalators rather than climb stairs, and spend much of our day sitting in classrooms, libraries, offices, theaters, and in front of our television sets. Heart disease kills more of us than any other cause. In contrast, a study of Masai warriors, who walk a great deal each day, found that they were in as good condition as a well-trained athlete, and heart disease was virtually unknown in their society, despite high cholesterol and saturated fat intakes (24). Overall, active people experience half as many heart attacks and die from them one-third as often as less-active individuals (25). Several studies show that moderate to vigorous physical activity can have a beneficial effect on blood lipid levels, as well as increasing HDL and lowering LDL concentrations (19,26).

Another aspect of industrialized life, nervous tension, also may be a contributing factor for heart disease. One study showed that compulsive, aggressive, striving individuals (type A personalities) experienced almost three times as many heart attacks as their more easygoing and passive colleagues (type B personalities) (6,27). However, other studies do not support these results, so the overall importance of this risk factor remains to be determined (6,22).

Heredity also may play a role, because heart disease appears to run in families. Certain risk factors, such as blood lipid levels, obesity, blood pressure, and diabetes mellitus, may be in part under genetic control (28). For example, certain genetic disorders lead to high blood cholesterol and/or triglyceride concentrations and, in some cases, to premature atherosclerosis. However, the same risk factors are also in part environmentally determined, and the environment within a family unit tends to be very similar for all members. It is difficult to determine whether the high blood cholesterol levels found in all members of the Jones family are hereditary or result from their high consumption of meat, whole milk, cheese, and eggs.

DIET, BLOOD LIPIDS, AND ATHEROSCLEROSIS

An intense controversy surrounds the relationship among diet, blood lipid concentrations, and atherosclerosis. As we saw earlier, epidemiologic studies have found a positive association between elevated blood cholesterol and triglyceride concentrations and an increased risk of developing heart disease (6,15–17,29). In addition, many experiments in humans and in experimental animals have shown that diet can modify blood cholesterol and triglyceride concentrations. Increased levels of saturated fat, cholesterol, and animal protein in the diet tend to raise blood cholesterol concentrations, whereas lower levels of these substances and increased intake of vegetable proteins and polyunsaturated fatty acids tend to reduce them (6,22,29,30). Certain types of fiber also may lower blood cholesterol concentrations (see Chapter 2). High caloric intake and sometimes high sucrose intake tend to increase the concentration of triglycerides in the blood (see Chapter 2) (17). The Intersociety Commission for Heart Disease Resources (ICHDR) of the American Heart Association and the United States Dietary Goals issued by the U.S. Senate have therefore recommended that the American diet be modified to reduce the incidence of atherosclerosis and heart disease (2–4).

However, is there evidence that dietary modifications will really work? In the United States, a decrease in saturated fat and an increase in polyunsaturated fat intake during the last decade has coincided with a reduction in the number of deaths from heart disease (Figure 3-10) (5,31).

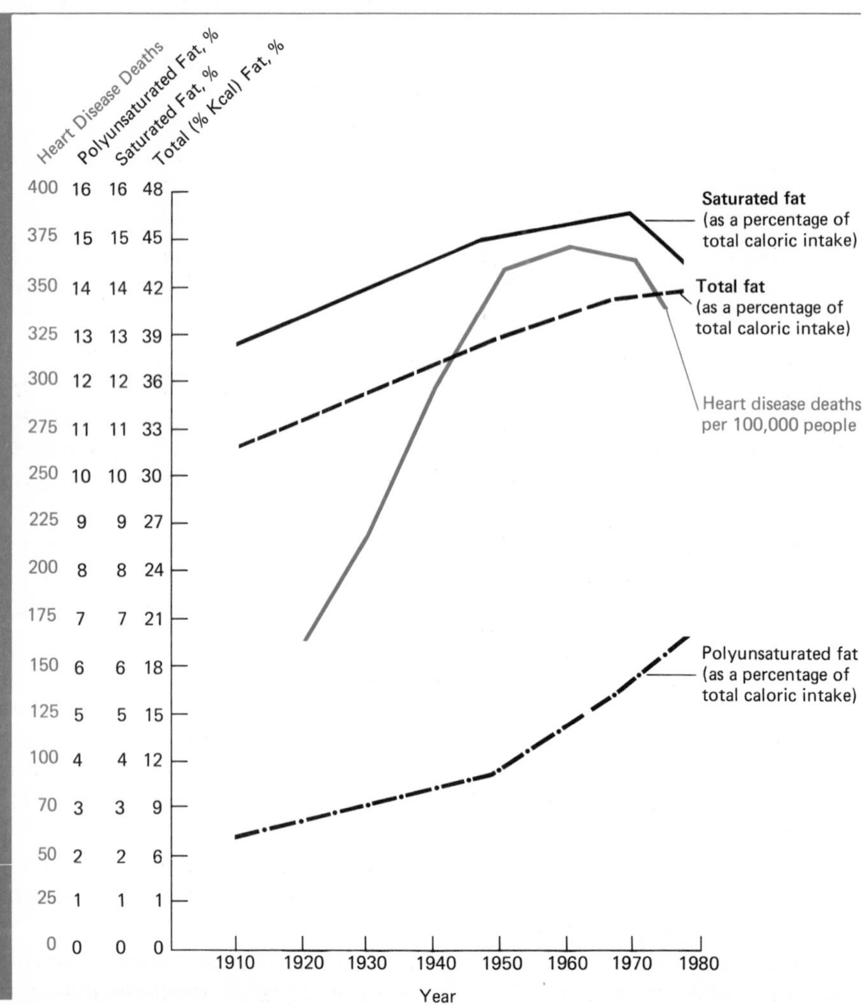

FIGURE 3-10 *Changes in Fat Intake and the Incidence of Heart Disease.* The reduction in heart disease mortality during the last 20 years has coincided with a decline in saturated fat and an increase in polyunsaturated fat intakes. Whether the changes in fat intake have actually contributed to the decline in heart disease mortality has not been established. (Sources: Bureau of the Census, *Statistical Abstracts of the United States*, 99th edition, Washington, DC, Dept. of Commerce (1978); Marston, R., Page, L., Nutrient Content of the National Food Supply", *National Food Review No. 5*, December 1978.)

Northern Belgians, who have a higher polyunsaturated fat and lower saturated fat intake than southern Belgians, also have lower plasma cholesterol levels and incidence of heart disease (32). However, these data must be interpreted with caution. Did the change in fat intake cause the reduction in heart disease fatalities or is the association purely coincidental? Many other factors, such as differences in blood pressure, smoking habits, physical activity, and exposure to nervous stress and the improvement of treatment for heart attack victims, could have contributed to the decline. In addition, a number of clinical experiments have been unable to show any striking reduction in the incidence of heart disease as a result of dietary modifications (22,33). The Framingham Study did not find any relationship between diet and blood cholesterol levels or diet and the development of heart disease, despite finding that blood cholesterol concentrations are a risk factor for the disease (34). Other population studies also have found no relationship between diet and blood cholesterol levels (35–37), and several experiments adding one or two eggs a day to normal diets produced no significant changes in blood cholesterol concentrations (38).

Whether or not most Americans should change their diets to prevent atherosclerosis and heart disease is still an unsettled issue.

PREVENTION

Whether or not most Americans should change their diets to prevent atherosclerosis and heart disease, therefore, is still an unsettled issue. One authority estimates that a maximum of 30 percent of the U.S. population could benefit from dietary changes (38). Another believes that because identifying this group would be difficult, we should try to modify everybody's diet (29). In spite of the controversy, the ICHDR and the U.S. Dietary Goals have made the following list of recommendations. Controlling the risk factors is no guarantee that you will avoid a heart attack, but your chances of doing so may be improved, along with your chances of survival should one occur.

1 Reduce cholesterol intake to no more than 300 mg/day, perferably less. This can be accomplished by restricting eggs in the diet and reducing intake of meat and whole-milk dairy products. Vegetable margarine and other sources of vegetable fat should be substituted for animal fat whenever possible.

2 Reduce total fat intake to less than 30 to 35 percent of the total caloric intake. Substituting low-fat products for those high in fat, as described earlier in this chapter, will help.

3 Reduce saturated fat intake and increase consumption of polyunsaturated fat. Ideally these should be consumed in equal proportions in the diet

(P:S ratio = 1). In general, use fat from vegetable rather than animal sources; for example, substitute margarine for butter or vegetable shortening or oils for lard.

4 The U.S. Dietary Goals recommend cutting intake of refined sugars to about 10 percent of the dietary kilocalories and increasing consumption of complex carbohydrate (starches) and natural sugars to about 48 percent of the total caloric intake.

5 Detect and control high blood pressure. The U.S. Dietary Goals recommend reducing salt intake by one-half or more.

Other authorities add the following recommendations:

1 Substitute protein from vegetable sources, such as legumes, grains, nuts, and seeds, for that from animal sources (meat, milk and dairy products, and eggs) (30,39).

2 Increase the fiber content of the diet.

3 Maintain desirable body weight (3).

4 Quit smoking (3).

5 Detect blood lipid abnormalities early (10).

6 Engage in moderate to vigorous physical activity, such as running, swimming, cycling, and skating. The aim is to increase breathing and heart rates significantly during the period of exercise. The physical activity should be carried out for 1/2 to 1 hour daily, three to four times a week.

Study Guide

SUMMARY

1. Lipids, which include fats, steroids, and phospholipids, are substances that are relatively insoluble in water.
2. Fats are a combination of glycerol and one (monoglyceride), two (diglyceride), or three (triglyceride) fatty acids. Mono- and diglycerides are used as emulsifying agents and are found only in small amounts in food. Triglycerides are the fats found in food and in the body.
3. Depending on the fatty acids from which they are made, triglycerides differ from one another. Triglycerides containing saturated fatty acids, such as palmitic and stearic acid, are predominant in animal fat and tend to be solid at room temperature. Triglycerides containing monounsaturated fatty acids, such as oleic acid, and polyunsaturated fatty acids, such as linoleic, linolenic, and arachidonic acids, occur in large amounts in vegetable oils and tend to be liquid at room temperature.
4. In addition to supplying a concentrated (9 kcal/g) and highly storable source of energy, fat insulates the body, protects the vital organs from injury, aids in the absorption of fat-soluble vitamins, and contributes to the flavor and satiety value of food.
5. One fatty acid, linoleic acid, promotes growth and healthy skin. Because the body cannot synthesize this fatty acid and it must be obtained in the diet, linoleic acid is called an *essential fatty acid*. Linolenic acid and arachidonic acid are sometimes classified as essential, but if sufficient linoleic acid is provided, they are not needed in the diet.
6. The National Academy of Science has not set an RDA for fat, but 15 to 25 grams of appropriate fats will meet the body's need for linoleic acid and promote absorption of the fat-soluble vitamins. Most Americans consume too much fat, and the U.S. Dietary Goals recommend limiting intake to no more than 30 percent of the daily caloric intake. The proportion of saturated fat, monounsaturated fat, and polyunsaturated fat should be 1:1:1.
7. Foods from animal sources, such as meat and whole-milk dairy products, tend to be relatively high in saturated fat. Fish, poultry, and skim-milk dairy products are relatively low in fat. Most foods from plant sources contain little fat, and what they do contain is usually polyunsaturated. *Hydrogenation* is a process that converts unsaturated fats to more saturated forms used in the manufacture of margarine, peanut butter, and vegetable shortening.
8. Although cholesterol has been associated with the development of atherosclerosis, it has many important functions in the body, for example, as a component of cell membranes and as a precursor for bile acids, vitamin D, and the steroid hormones. Cholesterol is made by the body and is found only in foods of animal origin. The U.S. Dietary Goals recommend limiting intake to less than 300 mg/day.
9. Phospholipids, which include lecithin, cephalin, and lipositol, are structural components of membranes, help emulsify lipids in the digestive tract and in the blood, and function in nervous tissue and blood coagulation. Lecithin, which is widely promoted as a dietary supplement, is synthesized by the body and occurs in many foods; there is no evidence of any benefit from supplements.
10. *Atherosclerosis* is a thickening of the walls of the large and medium arteries characterized by an accumulation of lipids, especially cholesterol. Heart disease and stroke, two manifestations of atherosclerosis, are the first and third leading causes of death in the United States today. Many studies have found that elevated triglyceride and cholesterol levels in the blood

increase the risk of developing heart disease. Some indicate that reducing intake of saturated fat and cholesterol and increasing polyunsaturated fat may reduce cholesterol concentration. Lowering calorie intake and, in some cases, sucrose consumption may help control high blood triglyceride levels. However, considerable controversy exists about whether such dietary modifications are of any benefit in preventing atherosclerosis. Many factors besides elevated blood lipid levels, including high blood pressure, cigarette smoking, obesity, diabetes mellitus, lack of physical activity, nervous stress, and heredity, may increase the risk of developing the disease.

VOCABULARY

aneurysm
arachidonic acid
arteriosclerosis
atherosclerosis
atherosclerotic plaque
cephalin
cerebrovascular disease (stroke)
diglyceride
emulsifying agents
epidemiologic studies
essential fatty acids
fatty acid
high-density lipoprotein (HDL)
hydrogenation (hardening)
intima
lecithin
linoleic acid
linolenic acid
lipid
lipoprotein
lipositol
low-density lipoprotein (LDL)
marbling
monoglyceride
monounsaturated fatty acid
oleic acid
palmitic acid
phospholipids
polyunsaturated fatty acids
prostaglandins
risk factors
saturated fatty acids
stearic acid
steroids
thrombosis
triglycerides

STUDY QUESTIONS

1. List the major fatty acids of nutritional importance and describe the differences among them. Which ones form triglycerides that are solid at room temperature? Liquid at room temperature? What use is made of these properties in food processing?
2. Even though no RDA has been established for fat, a certain amount must be included in the diet each day. Why?
3. What are the U.S. Dietary Goals regarding fat and cholesterol consumption? List some ways of changing the diet so it conforms to the goals.
4. What are the functions of cholesterol and phospholipids in the body? Why is neither essential in the diet?
5. Describe briefly the process by which atherosclerosis develops. How does it result in a heart attack? A stroke?
6. List eight factors that increase the risk of developing heart disease. What is the suspected role of dietary lipids in the development of atherosclerosis?
7. What dietary modifications are recommended to reduce blood cholesterol levels? If these are followed, is there any guarantee that the individual will not develop heart disease?

SELF-TEST

Multiple choice: Pick the one best answer.

1. Most of the fat in food and in the body is in the form of
   a. Monoglycerides
   b. Diglycerides
   c. Triglycerides
2. If you eliminated all fat from food:
   a. Absorption of fat-soluble vitamins

would be impaired.
b. Food would not be as flavorful.
c. You could still synthesize fat in the body.
d. All of the above.

3. Which of the following is needed for growth and a healthy skin, but cannot be synthesized by the body?
a. Arachidonic acid
b. Palmitic acid
c. Oleic acid
d. Linoleic acid

4. Which of the following is most common in animal fat?
a. Linoleic acid
b. Stearic acid
c. Linolenic acid
d. Arachidonic acid

5. Of the following, which is the best source of polyunsaturated fat?
a. Soybean oil
b. Animal fat
c. Olive oil
d. Hydrogenated vegetable oil

6. Which of the following will help reduce the fat content of the diet?
a. Substitute whole-milk cheese for meat
b. Substitute meat for fish and poultry
c. Substitute skim milk for whole milk
d. All of the above

7. Which of the following does not contain cholesterol?
a. Cheese
b. Fish
c. Round steak
d. Peanut butter

8. Lecithin:
a. Is synthesized by the body.
b. Does not perform any important body functions.
c. Is not found in very many foods.
d. Supplements will help prevent heart disease.

9. Atherosclerosis:
a. Can occur in any blood vessel in the body.
b. Can lead to a heart attack, stroke, kidney failure, or gangrene.
c. Occurs only in middle or old age.
d. All of the above.

10. Which of the following might help reduce the risk of heart disease?
a. Swimming for 1/2 hour three times a week
b. Archery
c. Bowling
d. Lifting weights occasionally

True-False

1. Fat is a more concentrated form of energy than carbohydrate or protein.
2. All vegetable oils are high in polyunsaturated fat.
3. Mono- and diglycerides are dangerous food additives and should be avoided.
4. Removing the skin from poultry reduces the fat content of the poultry.
5. A meal containing fat will satisfy you longer than one that is low in fat.
6. Cholesterol is a dangerous substance that plays no role in the body.
7. The means by which cholesterol is transported in the blood may influence its ability to cause atherosclerosis.
8. The specific cause of atherosclerosis is not known.
9. Studies so far have found drastic reductions in the occurrence of heart disease among subjects who reduced dietary cholesterol intake.
10. Quitting smoking may reduce your risk of heart disease even if you have been smoking for many years.

SUGGESTED ACTIVITIES

1. The following will require completion of a diet record (Activity 10-1):
   a. What percent of your caloric intake is derived from fat? What proportion is saturated fat? Polyunsaturated fat?
   b. List some foods you enjoy that can be substituted in your diet to reduce total fat and saturated fat and increase polyunsaturated fat intake.
2. Compare the fat contents of commercial products. By examining their labels, compare the polyunsaturated and saturated fat

contents and cholesterol content of each of the following:

a. Vegetable oils from different sources, such as soybean oil, corn oil, safflower oil, sunflower oil, and peanut oil.
b. Stick margarine with soft tub margarine and liquid margarine. Compare these with butter.
c. Mayonnaise with imitation salad dressings.
d. Nondairy coffee creamers with cream or "half-and-half."
e. Eggs with egg substitutes.

3. Which of the heart disease risk factors apply to you? What steps can you take to minimize each of these risks?

FURTHER READING

1. A graphic description of the causes, results, and treatment of atherosclerosis:

   Stare, F. J. (ed.): *Atherosclerosis,* CPC International, Best Foods Division, Englewood Cliffs, N.J., 1974.

2. Two books about diet and heart disease:

   Bennett, I.: *The Prudent Diet,* David White, New York, 1973.

   Mayer, J.: *Fats, Diet, and Your Heart,* Newspaperbooks, Norwood, N.J., 1976.

3. Two articles that explore the pros and cons of the value of modifying the diet to prevent heart disease:

   Glueck, C. J., and Connor, W. E.: "Diet-Coronary Heart Disease Relationships Reconnoitered," *Am. J. Clin. Nutr.* **31**:727–737 (1978).

   Reiser, R.: "Oversimplification of Diet: Coronary Heart Disease Relationships and Exaggerated Diet Recommendations," *Am. J. Clin. Nutr.* **31**:865–875 (1978).

PROTEIN

Americans today are involved in a great love affair with protein. Most of us enjoy the taste of meat, fish, poultry, eggs, and dairy products; most of us also believe that if a certain amount of protein is good for building healthy bodies, more must be even better. Steve Jones, for example, likes to think of himself as a "meat and potatoes man." He eats meat in some form for dinner nearly every night and for lunch several times a week. Frequently, Steve enjoys an omelet or scrambled eggs for breakfast and a snack of cheese and crackers late in the afternoon. He believes that the protein will help strengthen his muscles, even though he does not get much exercise.

American protein consumption is among the highest in the world, with the U.S. food supply providing each American with more than twice as much protein as his or her body requires (1,2). A single meal of a quarter pound of meat and a pint of milk, for instance, provides about 75 percent of a day's protein allowance for a 70-kilogram male. What are the consequences of the high rate of consumption by the United States and other affluent nations? What does protein actually do in the body? How much do humans, in fact, require, and how can these needs best be met? These questions are particularly important now, because much of the population of the developing world faces a shortage of energy-providing nutrients, including protein. Avoiding global malnutrition in the future depends in part on our ability to measure the protein and caloric needs of a population and to provide for a better distribution of food. In this chapter, we will describe the roles and needs for protein in human nutrition. We will also look at what happens when these needs are not met and the many factors that contribute to protein-energy malnutrition.

What Are Proteins?

A **protein** is a chain composed of subunits called *amino acids*. Much like the links in a steel chain, the amino acids join together to form a long, unbranched structure (Figure 4-1). Since the chain often contains as many as 300 amino acids, proteins are rather large and complex molecules. **Amino acids** are particular combinations of carbon, hydrogen, nitrogen, oxygen, and in some cases, sulfur. Figure 4-2 shows the basic structure of an amino acid. At the center is a carbon atom to which four other chemical groups may attach. An amino ($—NH_2$) group, a carboxylic acid (—COOH) group, and a hydrogen atom (H) occupy three of the positions. The fourth position, designated by the letter R, may contain any one of a number of chemical groups (Ready Reference 11). For example, the amino acid glycine has a hydrogen atom in the R position, while alanine has a methyl ($—CH_3$) group.

Human proteins are combinations of 22 amino acids (Ready Reference 11) and differ one from another in three ways:

1 Total number of amino acids in the chain
2 Proportion of each amino acid in the chain
3 Sequence or order of the amino acids in the chain

For example, consider two proteins, the hormone **insulin** and the enzyme **ribonuclease** (Figure 4-1). The protein chain of ribonuclease is considerably longer than that of insulin, containing 124 amino acids to insulin's 51. The two proteins are also composed of different amounts of each of the amino acids; insulin contains more leucine, while ribonuclease has more threonine, and so on. Finally, the order or sequence of the amino acids in insulin differs from that of ribonuclease. Even if the amino acid composition of the two proteins were identical, they could still differ in the order in which the amino acids were arranged.

Amino acids provide the raw material for the synthesis of a variety of nitrogen-containing substances besides proteins (Table 4-1). For instance, the deoxyribonucleic acid (DNA) and ribonucleic acid (RNA) are derived in part from amino acids. Amino acids also contribute to the formation of *heme,* an iron-containing compound that is one of the components of hemoglobin. Creatine, a compound that stores small amounts of energy in muscle, is another example.

How the Body Uses Protein

Over a thousand different proteins have been identified in the human body alone, and they perform a variety of functions: they carry out chemi-

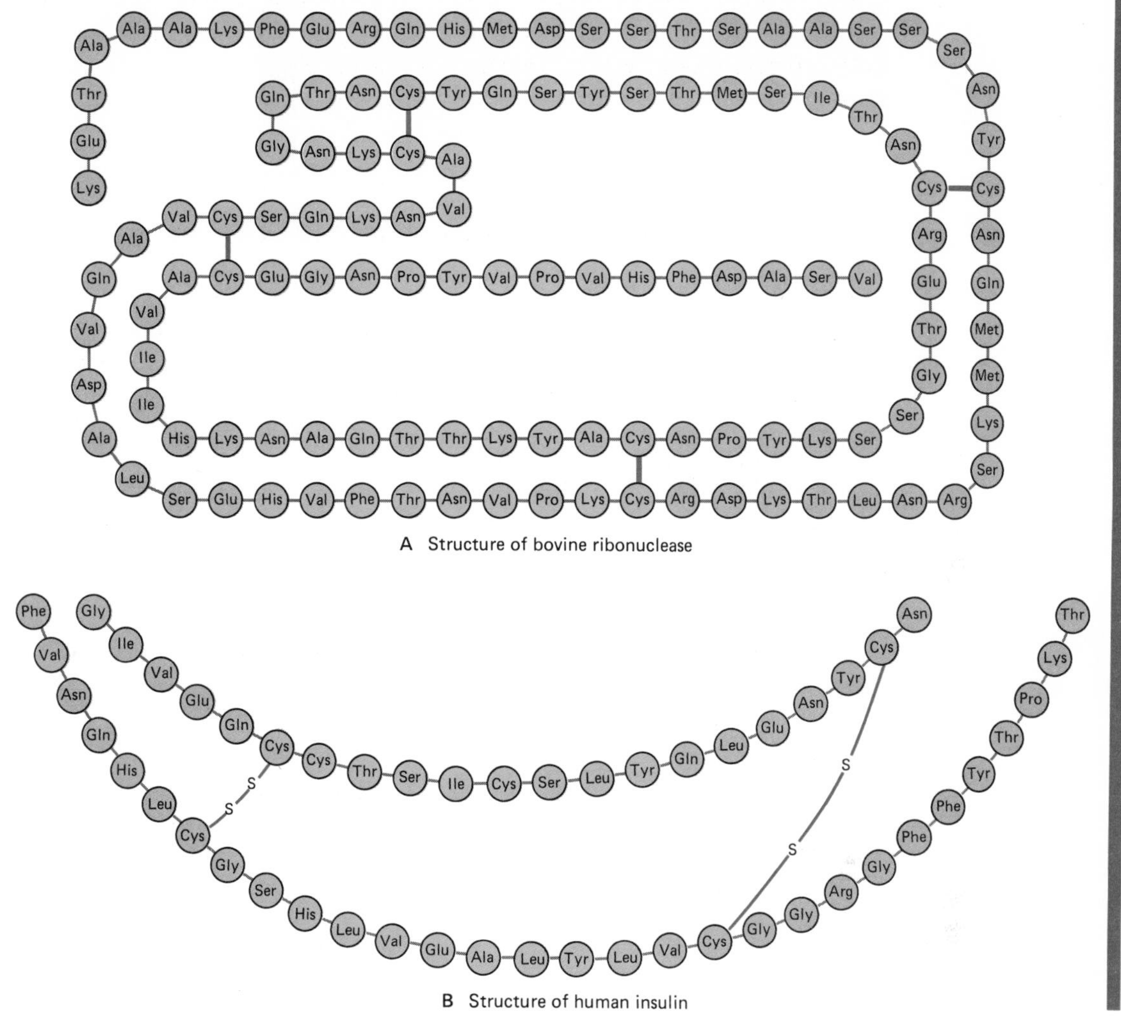

A Structure of bovine ribonuclease

B Structure of human insulin

FIGURE 4-1
Two Examples of Proteins. Proteins differ in the total number of amino acids, the proportion of each amino acid, and the sequence of amino acids in their chains.

cal reactions, transport substances, regulate **metabolism**, and provide structural support. Body proteins themselves undergo a dynamic process involving synthesis (**anabolism**) and degradation (**catabolism**) (3). The body synthesizes certain amino acids and uses them, along with amino acids obtained from the diet, to make the proteins it needs. At the same time, it also breaks down its own proteins, releasing amino acids that may be recycled for protein synthesis or used to provide energy. Keeping a proper balance between synthesis and degradation is crucial to the maintenance of a healthy body. Let us look at the various processes involved in protein metabolism, as well as some of the factors, including diet, that may cause imbalances to occur.

FIGURE 4-2
The General Structure of an Amino Acid. The amino group, carboxylic acid group, and hydrogen atom are common to all amino acids. The R group may be any one of 20 different chemical groups.

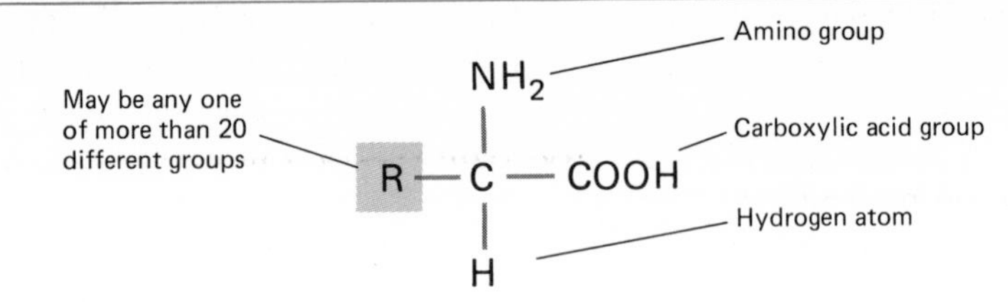

PROTEIN SYNTHESIS

How does the body convert the proteins found in food into those which can perform the functions needed to maintain life? The process begins in the stomach and the small intestine. Here the protein we eat is broken down or digested into its component amino acids (Figure 4-3). These amino acids are then absorbed into the body and pass into the bloodstream, which transports them to every cell. Within each cell, structures called **ribosomes** use the amino acids to build body protein. Digestion, absorption, and some aspects of metabolism will be discussed in detail in Chapter 6. Here we will describe how the amino acids are assembled into proteins once they reach the cell.

For protein synthesis to proceed normally, 20 of the amino acids must be present in the cell in sufficient amounts and at the same time. (The other two, hydroxyproline and hydroxylysine, are found in only a few proteins and are made from proline and lysine, respectively, after the

TABLE **4-1**

Nitrogen-containing compounds synthesized using amino acids

COMPOUND	AMINO ACIDS USED	FUNCTIONS IN BODY
Deoxyribonucleic acid (DNA)	Aspartic acid, glycine, glutamine	Carries the genetic code required for protein synthesis and to transmit traits to succeeding generations
Ribonucleic acid (RNA)	Aspartic acid, glycine, glutamine	Required to carry the genetic code to the ribosome (mRNA), transport amino acids to the ribosome (tRNA), and aid in protein synthesis (rRNA)
Heme	Glycine	Component of hemoglobin, which transports oxygen in the blood
Creatine	Arginine, glycine, methionine	A means of storing small amounts of energy in the muscles
Serotonin	Tryptophan	Important in nervous system functioning—stimulates the brain
Thyroxine	Tyrosine	A hormone that stimulates growth and development and metabolism
Adrenaline (epinephrine)	Tyrosine	The fight-or-flight hormone that prepares the body for stress situations

protein has been assembled.) If any of the 20 amino acids is deficient or missing, synthesis can continue only until the supply of this amino acid becomes exhausted. Much as the construction of a building stops when the contractor runs out of bricks, the synthesis of a protein ceases when one of the amino acids is missing.

Dietary protein is an important source of amino acids, but it is not the only source. They are also provided by recycling of some amino acids released by the breakdown of the body's own protein. In addition, the human body can synthesize 13 of the amino acids itself. They are called **nonessential amino acids**. Diet, however, is important for their synthe-

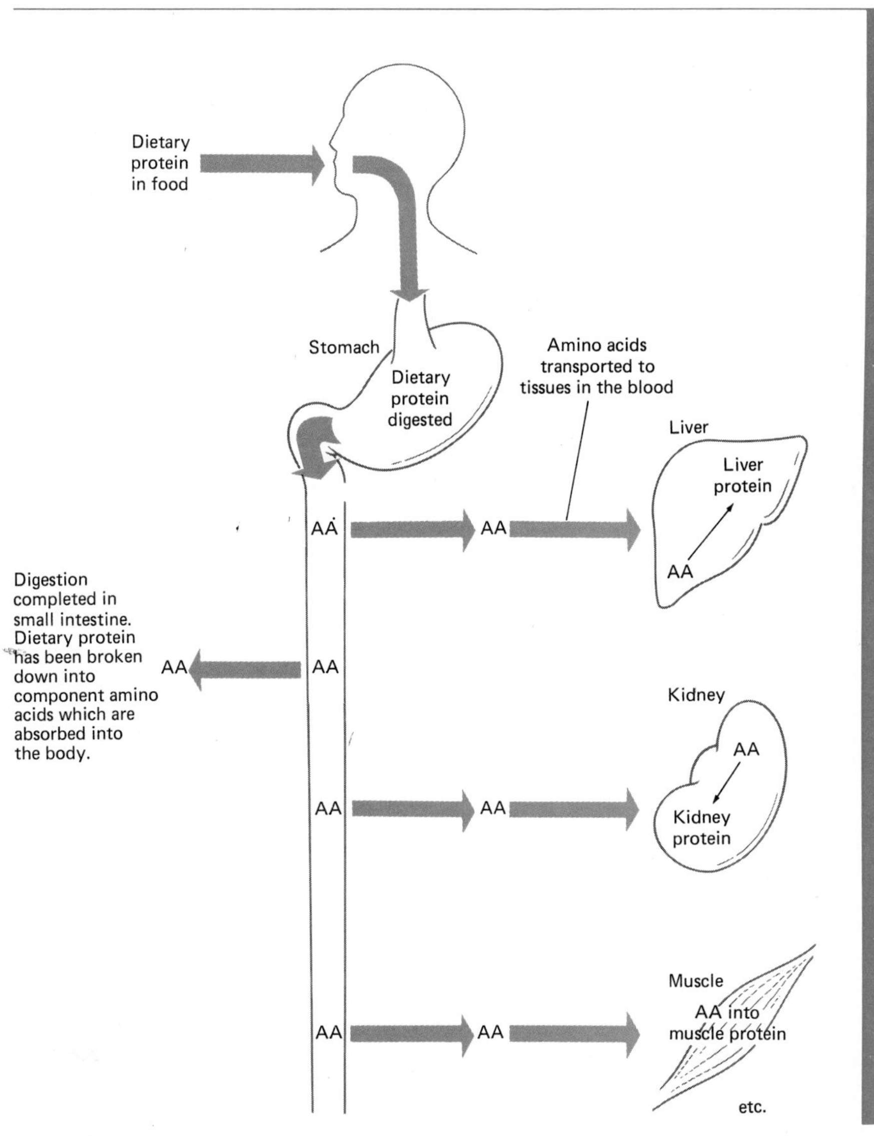

FIGURE 4-3
How Food Protein Becomes Body Protein. Food protein is digested into its component amino acids (AA), which are absorbed into the blood and carried to all tissues of the body. Cells in each tissue use the amino acids to synthesize their own proteins according to their needs.

sis because it provides the necessary raw materials, particularly the amino (—NH_2) group characteristic of amino acids. The nine **essential amino acids** the body cannot synthesize in amounts great enough to meet its needs must be obtained from the diet (see Table 4-3). If dietary protein supplies these simultaneously and in sufficient quantities, as well as enough raw materials to allow the body to make the nonessential amino acids, protein synthesis can proceed normally.

The steps involved in protein synthesis are shown in Figure 4-4. The ribosome assembles a protein using a set of instructions found in the nucleus of the cell in the form of **deoxyribonucleic acid (DNA)**. Along a segment of the DNA molecule, the total number, the proportion, and the sequence of amino acids needed to synthesize a particular protein are spelled out. Each segment that contains instructions for a whole protein is called a **gene**, and the instructions themselves are called the **genetic code**. Since DNA cannot leave the nucleus, the cell needs a messenger to carry the coded instructions to the ribosome. A substance called **messenger RNA (mRNA)** fills this role. Using the appropriate segment of DNA as a guide or pattern, a molecule of mRNA containing the coded instructions in that segment is synthesized. Biochemists say the code in DNA

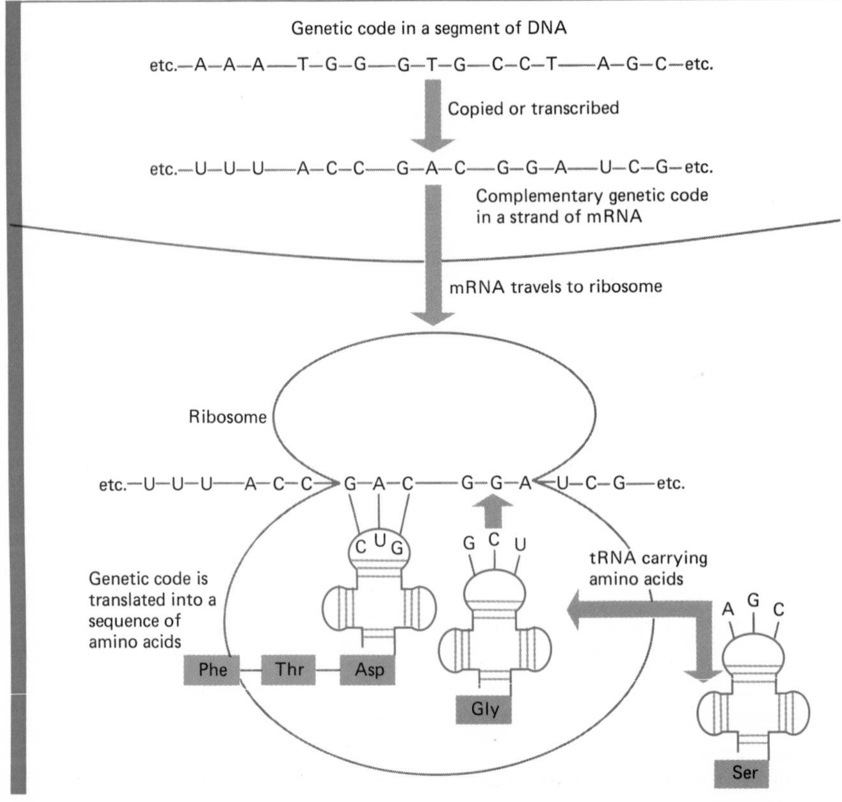

FIGURE 4-4
Protein Synthesis in the Cell. Instructions for protein synthesis are contained in the genetic code in a segment of a DNA molecule. The instructions are copied into a complementary code in messenger RNA, which then travels to the ribosome. There, transfer RNA molecules read the code and bring their specific amino acids into place at the correct spot in the growing protein chain.

B Globular protein

FIGURE 4-5
Examples of Protein Folding. As they are made, proteins fold into long, fibrous shapes or spherical (globular) conformations. The function the protein carries out depends on its shape.

has been copied, or **transcribed**, into the mRNA molecule. The mRNA then travels to the ribosome, where it directs the synthesis of a particular protein.

Amino acids are transported to the ribosome by a second type of RNA, called **transfer RNA (tRNA)**. Each of the amino acids has at least one specific tRNA molecule to carry it. Beginning at one end of the mRNA, the tRNAs "read" the code, and with the aid of the ribosome, each brings its amino acid into position at the right time to be incorporated into the protein chain. As each amino acid is brought into place, it becomes attached to the growing chain by a **peptide bond**. This process continues until the protein is completed. At this point, biochemists say that the code on the mRNA has been "**translated**" into the sequence of amino acids that make up a specific protein.

As the ribosome synthesizes the protein, the chain folds into a characteristic shape, or **conformation**. This shape results from interactions between amino acids and is determined by the sequence of amino acids in the chain. The conformation dictates what functions the protein will perform. Some proteins, for example, are fibrous in shape; they wind into long strands (Figure 4-5). Muscle proteins have this structure, and it is partly responsible for the ability of the muscle to contract. Other proteins, such as enzymes, fold into spherical or globular shapes. The ability of an enzyme to act as a catalyst in chemical reactions within the cell depends on the specific nature of its globular shape. In addition to folding, proteins often associate themselves with other molecules. If they do not do so, or if they combine only with other proteins, they are called **simple proteins**. Simple proteins yield only amino acids when they are broken down. If the protein associates with a nonprotein molecule, it is called a **conjugated protein**. The substance with which the protein combines usually plays a critical role in the functioning of that protein. (Table 4-2 gives several examples of conjugated proteins and their functions.)

When we look at protein synthesis as a whole, we can see that DNA, by controlling the process, exerts ultimate control over cellular and body functions (Figure 4-6). What a protein does depends on its structure, which in turn is determined by the order of amino acids in the protein chain. DNA, through its mRNA messenger, dictates the sequence of

DNA, by controlling protein synthesis, exerts ultimate control over cellular and body function.

amino acids. In so doing it plays the pivotal role in directing the processes of life.

CATABOLISM

Just as the body continuously synthesizes new proteins, it constantly breaks down old ones. Proteins are first split into their component amino acids by enzymes. Some of the amino acids may be recycled to synthesize new body protein. The remainder undergo further degradation and ultimately provide energy for the body.

The catabolism of amino acids for energy begins with the removal of the amino (—NH_2) group, which is ultimately converted to the waste product **urea** by the liver and excreted from the body in the urine. The so-called carbon skeleton left behind by the removal of the amino group is used in several ways (Figure 4-7). Many tissues use it directly for energy. The liver, however, can convert the carbon skeletons of some amino acids, known as **glucogenic amino acids**, into glucose and the carbon skeletons of others, called **ketogenic amino acids**, into fatty acids. The glucose may be stored temporarily as glycogen and the fatty acids as triglycerides.

PROTEIN BALANCE

In a healthy person there is normally a balance between the synthesis of new proteins and the breakdown of old ones. A number of situations, however, can influence this equilibrium. Growth, pregnancy, and lactation

TABLE **4-2**

Examples of conjugated proteins containing nutrients

PROTEIN PART	NONPROTEIN PART	CONJUGATED PROTEIN	FUNCTION
Apoenzyme (inactive enzyme)	Coenzyme (made from a B vitamin)	Holoenzyme (active enzyme)	Catalysis
Globin	Heme	Hemoglobin	Oxygen transport in blood
Opsins	Retinaldehyde (vitamin A)	Visual pigments (e.g., rhodopson)	Eyesight
Apolipoprotein	Lipids	Lipoprotein	Lipid transport in blood
Apoferritin	Iron	Ferritin	Iron storage in liver

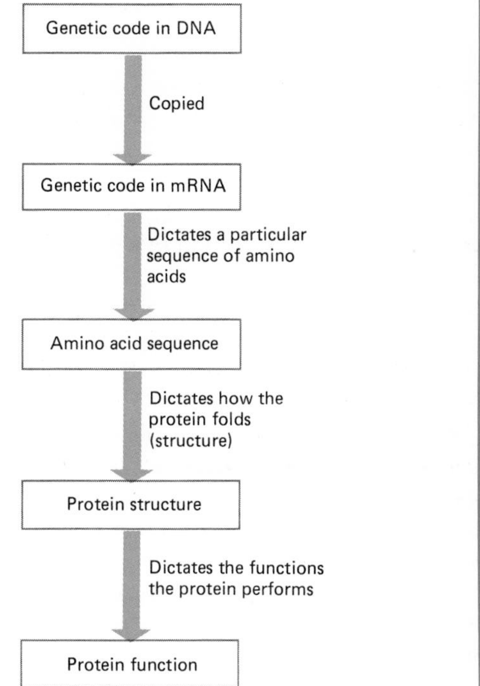

FIGURE 4-6
How DNA Controls Cell and Body Function. Most cell and body functions are performed by proteins. A protein's function is determined by its structure, which in turn depends on the sequence of amino acids in its chain. This sequence is ultimately dictated by the genetic code contained in DNA.

shift the balance in favor of protein synthesis to promote tissue development or the synthesis of milk. Several factors, including a deficiency of energy and the quantity or quality of protein in the diet, can displace the equilibrium in favor of breakdown. A starving person lacks energy and protein in the diet. Particularly in the initial stages, protein catabolism increases to supply amino acids for both glucose synthesis and energy production. The body then begins to consume itself and break down its own protein. Increased protein catabolism also can result from other conditions, including surgery, injury, diabetes mellitus, and infectious dis-

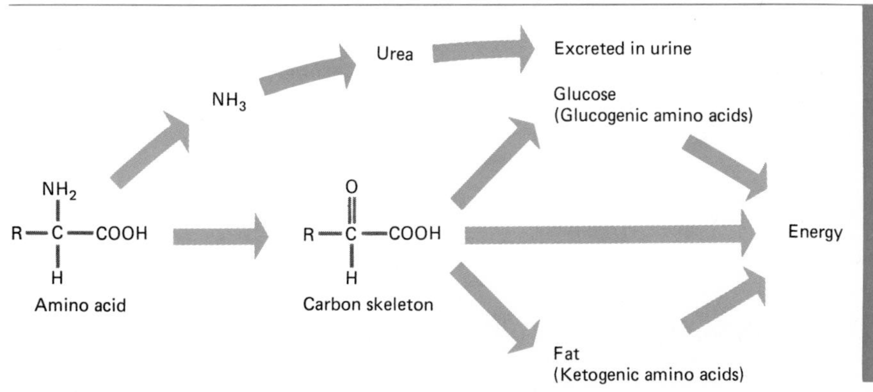

FIGURE 4-7
Catabolism of Amino Acids. The amino group is removed and ultimately converted to urea for excretion in the urine. The remaining carbon, hydrogen, and oxygen form a "carbon skeleton" that can be used directly for energy or converted first into glucose or fat, depending on the amino acid.

eases. In these cases, the breakdown of protein may be caused by an increase in the body's need for energy or by hormonal imbalances.

Eating low-quality protein is another situation in which the balance between synthesis and breakdown is disrupted. In order for protein synthesis to proceed normally, the diet must provide the nine essential amino acids simultaneously and in sufficient quantities, as well as enough nitrogen to allow for the production of nonessential amino acids. A low-quality protein, however, is deficient in one or more of the essential amino acids. When the supply of one of these amino acids becomes exhausted, protein synthesis in the cell stops, but all the unused amino acids remain. Since they can no longer be used to make protein, the body diverts them to energy production. A long-term deficiency of an essential amino acid can interfere with the body's ability to grow and maintain itself.

The cycle of synthesis and breakdown of body proteins is called **turnover**. Proteins in the liver, pancreas, and small intestine turn over rapidly. In circumstances such as starvation, in which the body breaks down its own proteins to provide amino acids for energy or for glucose synthesis, these tissues are particularly affected (3,5–7). Muscle protein turns over much more slowly, but because of the large amount of muscle in the body, it is the greatest contributor of amino acids during starvation. The turnover of protein in the brain and nervous system is negligible, and the body does not rely on them to supply amino acids (3,5–7). Thus, while the body does not store protein as it does carbohydrate and fat, it can draw on functional proteins to supply amino acids (5–7). In cases of extreme malnutrition, this can have severe consequences, as we will see later in this chapter.

WHAT PROTEIN DOES

What do proteins do? Many of us might say they build muscles because of a long-standing, if not entirely accurate, association of protein intake with athletic ability. Protein's function in hair and skin or as a component of blood might be mentioned by others. Yet proteins play many other vital roles in the body.

FOCUS 4-1 PHENYLKETONURIA (PKU)

Like most babies in the United States today, Jimmy Smith was tested for high blood levels of the essential amino acid phenylalanine soon after he was born. The results were positive, and subsequent tests confirmed Jimmy has phenylketonuria (PKU), a genetic disorder that afflicts 1 out of every 15,000 newborn infants. Normally, an enzyme called *phenylalanine hydroxylase* converts a certain amount of phenylalanine into another amino acid, tyrosine. In phenylketonuric infants, however, the enzyme is defective, and phenylalanine and related compounds, the phenylketo acids, accumulate in the blood and urine. If untreated, the disorder leads to severe mental retardation.

Phenylketonuria is treated by providing a diet from which most but not all of the phenylalanine has been removed (small amounts are required to support protein synthesis). A phenylalanine-deficient formula, Lofenalac, has been developed for this purpose. As the child grows older, new foods are introduced into the diet, and blood phenylalanine concentration must be monitored so that it does not increase to dangerous levels. Usually the child will attain normal or near normal mental development. The age at which the special diet can be terminated is not known, but studies in which subjects began consuming a normal diet between $4^1/_2$ and 6 years of age found no adverse effects. However, women with PKU who wish to have children may need to resume the diet before becoming pregnant. Otherwise, the high phenylalanine levels in their blood may cause mental retardation in their children.

Every minute, for example, thousands of chemical reactions take place in the body. Some release energy, others break down various substances, and still others synthesize new compounds. Without the aid of **enzymes** acting as catalysts, most of these reactions would proceed too slowly to be useful. With an enzyme present, reactions that would take hours, days, or even longer are completed in a matter of minutes. (How enzymes work is discussed in Chapter 1.) Other proteins play a more passive role. Keratin, for example, is a major constituent of hair, finger and toe nails, and the outer layer of skin. Bones, cartilage, blood vessels, the skin, and other tissues contain collagen, which is extremely important in maintaining their structural integrity.

Whenever you suffer a cut or abrasion, proteins come to the rescue. First, they participate in the blood-clotting process that seals the wound. Any bacteria, virus, or foreign particle that enters the body through the wound is attacked by white blood cells and a group of proteins called **antibodies**. Antibodies play a role in a variety of **immunologic** processes: they protect the body from bacterial- and viral-borne diseases and produce allergic responses to foreign substances in the body. Each foreign agent, or **antigen**, stimulates the production of a specific type of antibody, which then attacks and neutralizes the invader. Antibodies remain in the body long after their initial job is done, and they will protect the body against future exposure to the antigen (Figure 4-8). Finally, as the wound begins to heal, collagen and other proteins help form the scar tissue.

Proteins also maintain the water balance between the bloodstream and the fluid surrounding the blood vessel (Figure 4-9). A number of proteins, the most abundant of which is serum albumin, circulate in the blood. Because they cannot diffuse out of the blood vessels, they act to "hold" water within it. During a protein deficiency, blood albumin levels fall. Less water can be held within the blood vessels, and it diffuses into the surrounding tissues. Often enough water accumulates in the tissue to cause a swelling that is called **edema**, a common symptom of severe protein deficiency. Proteins also help maintain another type of balance in the body, the acid-base balance. Acidity and alkalinity are measured by the **pH**: a pH of 7.0 is neutral; a pH lower than 7.0 is acidic; and a pH above 7.0 is basic, or alkaline. In order for body processes to operate at optimal levels, the pH of the body fluids must be maintained within rather narrow limits. Blood pH may range as low as 7.0 and as high as 7.8 without

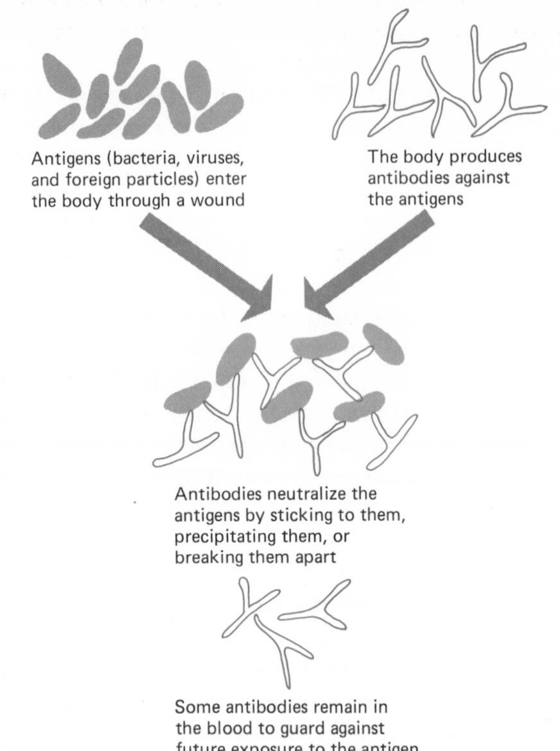
Antigens (bacteria, viruses, and foreign particles) enter the body through a wound
The body produces antibodies against the antigens
Antibodies neutralize the antigens by sticking to them, precipitating them, or breaking them apart
Some antibodies remain in the blood to guard against future exposure to the antigen

FIGURE 4-8
How Antibodies Protect the Body. Each antigen that enters the body stimulates the production of specific antibodies that can neutralize it. The antibodies remaining after the antigens have been destroyed confer an immunity against future attack.

FIGURE 4-9
The Role of Protein in Maintaining Fluid Balance. **A** When plasma albumin concentration is normal, it holds water in the bloodstream. **B** When plasma albumin concentration is low, as in kwashiorkor, water diffuses from the blood vessel into the surrounding tissues.

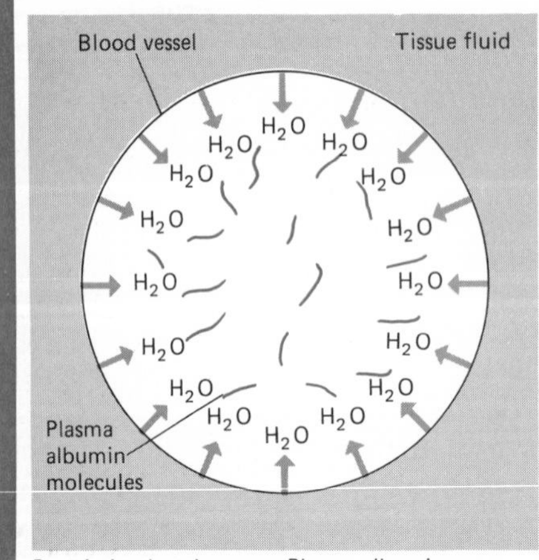
Blood vessel
Tissue fluid
H_2O
Plasma albumin molecules

Protein intake adequate: Plasma albumin concentration high — water held in the blood vessel

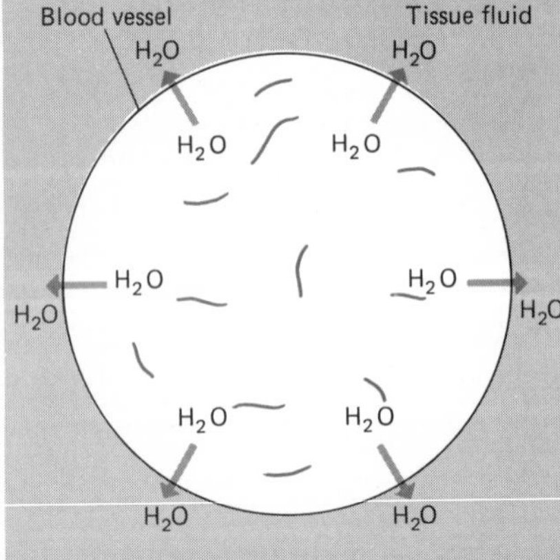
Blood vessel
Tissue fluid
H_2O

Protein deficiency: Plasma albumin concentration low — water diffuses from blood vessel into surrounding tissues

causing death, but ideally it should be about 7.4. Since proteins are buffers that can neutralize both acids and bases, they contribute to the maintenance of pH within the normal range.

Many proteins are transport mechanisms. Some carry molecules across membranes, such as the plasma membrane and the mitochondrial membranes of the cell. Hemoglobin, an iron-containing protein, transports oxygen in the blood, while the lipids are carried in the blood by lipoproteins. Other substances, including iron, copper, drugs, and some hormones, attach to proteins for transport in the bloodstream.

Proteins play still other roles. One group, called the *opsins,* combine with vitamin A to form the eye pigments involved in both black-and-white and color vision. Yet another function of protein is to provide energy; each gram supplies the body with 4 kilocalories. Proteins contribute to the regulation of body activities as well. Many of the **hormones** are either proteins, peptides (small chains of amino acids), or amino acid derivatives. They act to control blood glucose concentrations, energy expenditure, growth, and many other processes. (Hormones were described in detail in Chapter 1.)

Nitrogen Balance

We have been looking at what proteins and amino acids do *within* the body. Another way of looking at protein metabolism is to focus on the nature and quantity of what enters and leaves the body—on the inputs and outputs of the system as a whole. Because protein metabolism involves nitrogen-containing compounds other than proteins and amino acids, including a number of important body substances and waste products, it is more convenient to look at nitrogen metabolism and to measure nitrogen rather than protein input and output.

NITROGEN OUTPUT (LOSSES)

The body loses nitrogen in three ways: through the urine, through the feces, and through the skin. Because urea, the major nitrogenous waste in the urine, results from the catabolism of amino acids, the quantity excreted varies with changing circumstances in the body. Any condition that leads to the breakdown of amino acids, including diabetes mellitus, injury, immobilization, and consumption of a diet containing excess protein or inadequate amounts of carbohydrate, kilocalories, or essential amino acids, increases the output of urea. When amino acids are used for growth, pregnancy, or lactation, urea loss is lower. Small amounts of ammonia, creatinine, and uric acid also are excreted in the urine. Ammonia results from the catabolism of amino acids, uric acid from the breakdown of DNA and RNA, and creatinine from the breakdown of creatine in muscle.

The feces are another way by which the body loses nitrogen. An average of 8 percent of the protein consumed at each meal simply passes through the digestive tract for excretion in the feces. Fecal nitrogen arises from digestive enzymes that break down food, as well as protein from cells that fall off the inner wall of the digestive tract. Although the enzymes and proteins mix with food and are partially digested and reabsorbed into the body, a considerable proportion is lost. Relatively small amounts of nitrogen are lost through the skin. These losses take the form of skin cells that flake off from the body, proteins in hair and nails, and a small amount of urea in sweat. As might be expected, skin losses increase under conditions that induce sweating.

Much of the nitrogen lost from the body represents a loss of the body's own protein. Because the source of the nitrogen is within the body, these are called **endogenous** nitrogen losses. Some of the urea in urine comes from the catabolism of excess dietary amino acids, and some of the nitrogen lost in the feces comes from undigested and unabsorbed dietary protein. Since this nitrogen originates outside the body, it is called **exogenous** nitrogen.

NITROGEN INPUT (INTAKE)

If endogenous nitrogen losses are not replaced, the body will waste away. To maintain a balance, the body must obtain nitrogen in the form of protein in the diet. The amino acids provided by dietary protein are used to synthesize new body proteins to replace those broken down and lost as urea. The body also uses these amino acids to synthesize new digestive enzymes, proteins of the wall of the digestive tract, and new skin, hair, and nails. However, as we pointed out earlier, some of the protein in food is lost before the body can use it, so our intake must be increased to account for exogenous as well as endogenous nitrogen losses.

EQUILIBRIUM AND IMBALANCES

A person attains a state of **nitrogen equilibrium**, or **zero nitrogen balance**, when nitrogen intake equals nitrogen losses. Because body proteins and amino acids are replaced at the same rate at which they are broken down, an equilibrium-level protein intake is sufficient to meet an individual's needs. Nitrogen equilibrium is therefore the desired state in a healthy, nonpregnant, nonlactating adult.

In certain situations, such as growth, pregnancy, and lactation, nitrogen intake exceeds output, and there is a **positive nitrogen balance**. This is a highly desirable situation, because in each case, the body uses the nitrogen for a synthetic process, such as tissue development or milk production. The retained nitrogen in pregnancy or lactation is ultimately lost when the mother gives birth or nurses her child; at these times she returns to a state of nitrogen equilibrium.

Negative nitrogen balance occurs when nitrogen output is greater than intake. This happens when the body breaks down its tissue proteins faster than it replaces them. During starvation, for instance, dietary protein intake is insufficient to balance the losses resulting from the breakdown of tissue proteins. Injury, prolonged immobilization, and certain diseases, such as diabetes mellitus, also speed up the catabolism of tissue proteins. Consuming low-quality protein may reduce the body's ability to replace its own proteins to the point where it cannot keep pace with protein breakdown in the tissues.

Protein Requirements (2)

As we have seen, the body normally requires protein in the diet to balance nitrogen losses and maintain itself, as well as to provide the additional protein needed for growth, pregnancy, and lactation. Consumption of protein meets these needs in two ways:

1 It provides the nonessential amino acids or sufficient amino groups to allow the body to synthesize the nonessential amino acids.
2 It supplies the nine essential amino acids the body cannot synthesize itself.

Nutritionists use the Recommended Dietary Allowances (RDAs) established by the Food and Nutrition Board (FNB) as the basis for estimating the protein needs of Americans. The RDAs, in turn, are based on the results of careful research. Let us take a closer look at how this is done.

DETERMINING REQUIREMENTS: THE ADULT ALLOWANCE

Protein requirements for adults are determined by first estimating the amount of protein needed to balance nitrogen losses when the diet does not contain any protein. Daily nitrogen output under these circumstances has been measured in adults, and calculations show that 0.45 grams of a high-quality standard protein (egg protein) per kilogram of normal body weight will offset losses in most people. When the egg protein is actually fed to subjects at levels high enough to meet requirements, however, only about 70 percent of it is used by the body, so an additional 30 percent must be added to the allowance. In addition, not all food proteins are of as high a quality as egg protein. On the average, the body uses other dietary proteins only about 75 percent as efficiently as egg protein, so the protein allowance must be increased by another 33 percent. The FNB has therefore established a Recommended Dietary Allowance of 0.8 g of food protein/kg of body weight/day, for adults. The allowance for a 70-kilogram male, for example, would be $70 \times 0.8 = 56$ g/day of protein.

THE ALLOWANCE FOR GROWTH, PREGNANCY, AND LACTATION

Because growth, pregnancy, and lactation involve synthetic processes in addition to maintenance, they increase the requirement for protein. To meet growth needs in infants, for instance, the Recommended Dietary Allowance ranges as high as 2.2 g of protein/kg of body weight/day. This amount gradually declines until it reaches adult levels at maturity. The body also requires more protein to support tissue development during pregnancy. The additional 30 g/day recommended by the FNB is thought

TABLE **4-3**

Estimated requirements for essential amino acids

AMINO ACID	Requirement, mg/kg of body weight/day INFANT (3–6 MONTHS)	CHILD (10–12 YRS)	ADULT
Isoleucine	80	28	12
Leucine	128	42	16
Lysine	97	44	12
Total sulfur-containing (methionine + cysteine)	45	22	10
Total aromatic (phenylalanine + tyrosine)	132	22	16
Threonine	63	28	8
Tryptophan	19	4	3
Valine	89	25	14
Histidine*	33	?	?

* Originally thought to be essential only for infants, histidine is now thought to be essential for adults as well. According to the 1980 edition of the RDAs, arginine is not essential for healthy humans.

Source: Food and Nutrition Board, *Recommended Dietary Allowances,* 9th ed., National Academy of Sciences, Washington, 1980, p. 43.

to be sufficient to meet the increased requirements of most pregnant women. Because protein is an important component of milk, lactating women need an additional 20 g/day above the maintenance allowance.

THE REQUIREMENTS FOR ESSENTIAL AMINO ACIDS

Requirements for essential amino acids have been determined largely by studies in which all the essential amino acids, except for the one in question, are fed to subjects in relatively large amounts. The experimenters then vary the quantity of the amino acid in question until the level of intake needed to maintain equilibrium in adults or satisfactory growth in infants and children is found. Table 4-3 lists the estimated essential amino acid requirements for humans. Because histidine has been identified only recently as essential for adults, an adult requirement has not yet been established.

Protein in Food

Nearly all foods contain some protein, but certain ones are particularly important sources: meat, fish, poultry, eggs, milk and dairy products, legumes (peas and beans), nuts and seeds, and grains. So all the food groups except the vegetable-fruit group contribute significant amounts of protein to the diet. Meeting protein requirements, however, is more than a matter of consuming a particular quantity of food from one of these groups. In choosing a protein source, we need to consider:

1 The quantity of the protein.
2 The quality of the protein.
3 The amount of energy, saturated and polyunsaturated fat, and cholesterol.
4 The presence of other nutrients.
5 The cost.

The quantity of protein in a food may be found by consulting a food-composition table such as that in Ready Reference 1. Some examples are shown in Table 4-4, which lists the protein content of representative foods from each food group.

TABLE **4-4**

The quantity and quality of protein in selected foods

FOOD	PERCENT PROTEIN BY WEIGHT, g Protein/100 g FOOD	NPU, PERCENT	SERVING SIZE	USABLE PROTEIN PER SERVING, g
Eggs	13.8	94	1 egg (46 g)	5.9
Whole milk	3.5	82	1 cup (244 g)	7.0
Cheddar cheese	25.0	70	1 oz (28 g)	4.9
Sirloin steak (choice grade, separable fat removed, cooked)	32.2	67	3 oz (85 g)	18.4
Hamburger (regular, cooked)	24.2	67	3 oz (85 g)	13.8
Haddock (breaded, fried)	19.6	83	4-oz fillet (110 g)	17.9
Chicken (flesh only, fried)	31.2	73	3 oz (85 g)	19.4
Soybeans (mature seeds, cooked)	11.0	61	1 cup (180 g)	12.1
White beans (average of several types of mature seeds, cooked)	7.8	38	1 cup (180 g)	5.3
Pecans (halves)	3.2	42	1/2 cup (59 g)	0.7
Cashews (whole)	17.2	58	1/2 cup (70 g)	4.8
Peanuts (shelled, roasted)	26.2	43	1/2 cup (72 g)	8.1
Whole wheat bread	10.0	60	2 slices (50 g)	3.0
White rice (cooked and cooled)	2.0	57	1 cup (145 g)	2.2
Rolled oats (oatmeal, cooked)	2.0	66	1 cup (240 g)	3.2
Sesame seeds	18.6	53	1/2 cup (75 g)	7.4
Sunflower seeds (kernels)	24.0	58	1/2 cup (72 g)	10.0
Cabbage (coarsely shredded)	1.3	35	1 cup (70 g)	0.3
Potato (baked in skin)	2.6	60	1 potato (202 g)	3.1
Mushrooms (raw)	2.7	72	1 cup (70 g)	0.9
Corn (cooked)	3.5	51	1 cup (165 g)	2.8

Sources: C. F. Adams, *Nutritive Value of Foods in Common Units,* Agriculture Handbook No. 456, USDA, Washington, 1975.

Food and Agriculture Organization, *Amino Acid Content of Foods and Biological Data on Proteins,* FAO, Rome, 1970. (NPU data used with permission.)

QUALITY

Even if two foods contain the same amount of protein, one might be a superior source because of its higher quality. Quality depends on the amounts of the essential amino acids a protein contains. The more closely the protein can match the body's requirements for essential amino acids, the higher its quality. Compare, for example, the milk and wheat protein shown in Figure 4-10. The black line in the figure represents the human requirement for six of the essential amino acids, while the colored line indicates the amount of these amino acids found in 25 grams of each protein. Twenty-five grams of milk protein, the amount in about three cups of milk, easily matches the body's requirement for each of the essential amino acids. However, an equal amount of wheat protein, which is contained in about 10 slices of whole wheat bread, does not, because the amino acid lysine is deficient. When the body exhausts its supply of lysine, what remains of the other essential amino acids (shaded area) can no longer be used for protein synthesis and is used for energy. The body uses the wheat protein less efficiently than the milk protein, so the wheat protein is said to be of lower quality. Nutritionists call the amino acid present in the least amount relative to the body's need for it the **limiting amino acid**. For example, lysine is the limiting amino acid in wheat protein and methionine is the limiting amino acid in soybeans.

The quality of a protein may be measured in several ways. We can chemically analyze its essential amino acid content or we can evaluate its ability to support growth. The most useful method, however, is **net protein utilization (NPU)**. Experimenters feed a protein to subjects and measure the proportion of nitrogen retained by the body:

$$\text{NPU} = \frac{\text{grams nitrogen retained}}{\text{grams nitrogen ingested}} \times 100$$

The higher the quality of the protein, the more of it the body uses for synthetic purposes. Therefore, a greater proportion of the protein's nitrogen

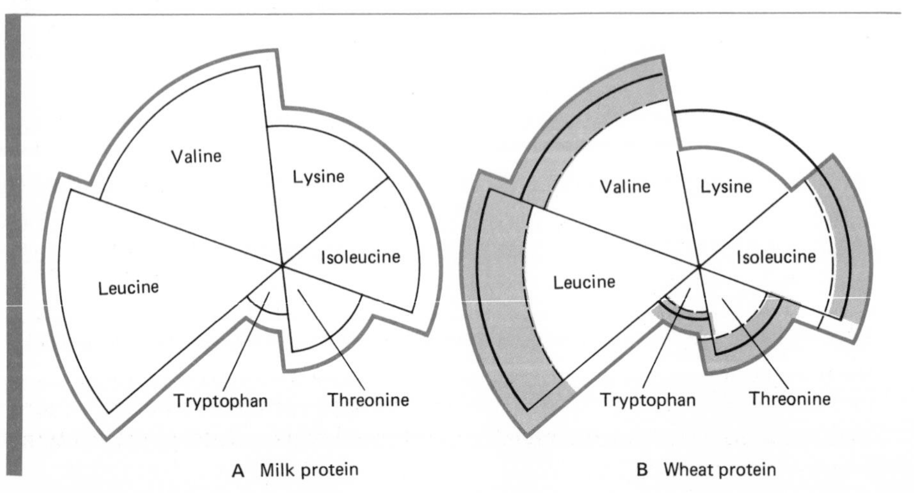

FIGURE 4-10 *Comparison of the Quality of Two Food Proteins.* **A** Milk protein: 25 grams exceeds the body's need for essential amino acids in all cases. **B** Wheat protein: 25 grams lacks sufficient lysine to meet the body's need, and the body cannot make full use of the other amino acids. The leftover amino acids (shaded areas) are catabolized for energy.

will be retained by the body, and it will have a higher NPU. For example, the body retains about 94 percent of the nitrogen in an egg, but only 61 percent of that in soybeans. Since the body uses a greater proportion of the egg protein for synthetic purposes, it is thus a higher-quality protein. The NPUs of other proteins are listed in Table 4-4.

Animal proteins are generally of higher quality than those from plants. Because they contain sufficient amounts of all the essential amino acids, they are called **complete proteins**. Most plant proteins are deficient in one or more essential amino acids and are therefore called **incomplete proteins**. Suppose you have a friend who is a strict vegetarian who relies solely on plant sources to meet the protein requirement. At first glance you might think this person's diet is inadequate. However, sufficient quality can be attained by using a technique called **mutual supplementation**, or **complementation**, in which the strengths of some proteins make up for the weaknesses of others. Consider, for instance, the proteins in wheat and beans. Alone, both are incomplete proteins, since wheat is deficient in lysine and, beans are deficient in methionine. When they are combined, however, the lysine content of the bean protein makes up for the deficiency in the wheat, while the methionine content of the wheat complements that of the soybeans. The result is a protein of higher quality than either one by itself.

ENERGY, FAT, AND CHOLESTEROL

Because of our concern with obesity and heart disease in the United States, Americans may need to consider the energy, fat, and cholesterol contents of protein sources (see the U.S. Dietary Goals in Chapter 1). To reduce caloric intake, for example, an obese person can substitute protein sources containing fewer kilocalories for sources with higher energy content (Table 4-5). Skim milk, tuna packed in water, and uncreamed cottage cheese can replace whole milk, tuna packed in oil, and creamed cottage cheese in a weight-loss diet. The obese person also may prefer to eat chicken without the skin and use methods other than frying to cook food. Nuts and seeds are unsuitable as protein sources for the dieter because of their high fat content. Grains and vegetables also have a large number of kilocalories per gram of usable protein. They are needed in the diet to provide vitamins and minerals, but they must be used with sources that provide more protein and less energy.

The association of elevated blood cholesterol concentrations with increased risk of heart disease makes the fat and cholesterol content of a protein source an important consideration. Protein from animal sources generally will be accompanied by varying amounts of saturated fat and cholesterol, which may lead to a rise in blood cholesterol levels. This effect can be reduced somewhat by eating low-fat animal products, such as skim-milk products. Plant sources lack cholesterol and provide relatively more polyunsaturated fat or very little fat at all. Consumption of protein from these sources may help reduce the cholesterol concentrations in the blood. In addition, the type of protein itself appears to be important; animal proteins can elevate blood cholesterol levels, while plant proteins tend to lower them (8).

TABLE **4-5**

Energy, fat, and cholesterol in various protein sources

FOOD	ENERGY, kcal/g USABLE PROTEIN	FAT, g/g USABLE PROTEIN*	CHOLESTEROL, mg/SERVING
Whole milk	22.5	1.2	34/cup
Skim milk	12.2	0.03	5/cup
Tuna (drained)			
Packed in vegetable oil	8.5	0.35	60/3 oz
Packed in water	5.6	0.035	60/3 oz
Steak (separable fat removed, broiled)			
Sirloin (choice grade)	9.5	0.35	approx. 80/3 oz
Sirloin (good grade)	8.6	0.25	approx. 80/3 oz
Round (choice grade)	8.9	0.28	approx. 80/3 oz
Fish			
Haddock (breaded and fried)	10.5	0.41	51/3 oz
Halibut (broiled)	8.5	0.35	43/3 oz
Eggs			
Fried	16.0	1.3	250/egg
Hard boiled	13.2	0.96	250/egg
Chicken			
With skin	11.3	0.54	approx. 68/3 oz
Without skin	9.2	0.34	approx. 67/3 oz
Cottage cheese			
Creamed (4% fat)	7.6	0.31	48/cup
Uncreamed	5.1	0.018	14/cup
Cheddar cheese	22.8	1.9	28/oz
Peanuts (roasted)	52.1	4.4	0
Soybeans (cooked)	19.3	0.8	0
Cashews	56.9	4.7	0
White rice (cooked)	94.7	0.09	0
Macaroni (cooked tender)	55.0	0.2	0
Sesame seeds	56.6	4.9	0
Mushrooms (raw)	14.3	0.15	0
Potato (baked in skin)	59.5	0.06	0

* Animal fats tend to be higher in saturated fatty acids; plant fats tend to be higher in polyunsaturated fatty acids.

Sources: B. K. Watt and A. L. Merrill, *Composition of Foods—Raw, Processed, Prepared,* Agriculture Handbook No. 8, USDA, Washington, 1963.

Food and Agriculture Organization, *Amino Acid Content of Foods and Biological Data on Proteins,* FAO Nutritional Series No. 24, Rome, 1970. (NPU data used with permission.)

R. M. Feeley, P. E. Criner, and B. K. Watt, "Cholesterol Content of Foods," *J. Am. Diet. Assoc.* **61**:134–149 (1972). (Used with permission.)

PATTERNS OF PROTEIN CONSUMPTION

Throughout the 1960s, much attention was focused on the "protein gap" between the affluent and the developing nations. Agricultural research since that time has attempted to close the gap by increasing the amount and quality of protein available to the world's hungry. During the 1970s, however, reports began to appear indicating that the deficiency of protein in the developing nations was secondary to a shortage of energy and food in general. Many authorities called for a reassessment of our priorities in agricultural research and in providing food aid. In the following sections, we will look more closely at this issue. Do the industrialized nations consume more protein than the developing nations? What are the effects of this practice? What can be done to solve the problem of protein-energy malnutrition among the world's hungry?

1. You must eat meat to obtain enough protein.

2. A "protein gap" exists between the industrialized and the developing nations.

FACT OR FANTASY

ISSUE: CAN WE CONSUME TOO MUCH PROTEIN?

In 1978 the amount of protein available to each person in the United States was estimated to be about 103 g/day, almost twice the Recommended Dietary Allowance for a 70-kilogram adult male and $2^1/_4$ times that recommended for a 55-kilogram adult female (Figure 4-11) (1,2). Since certain segments of the population

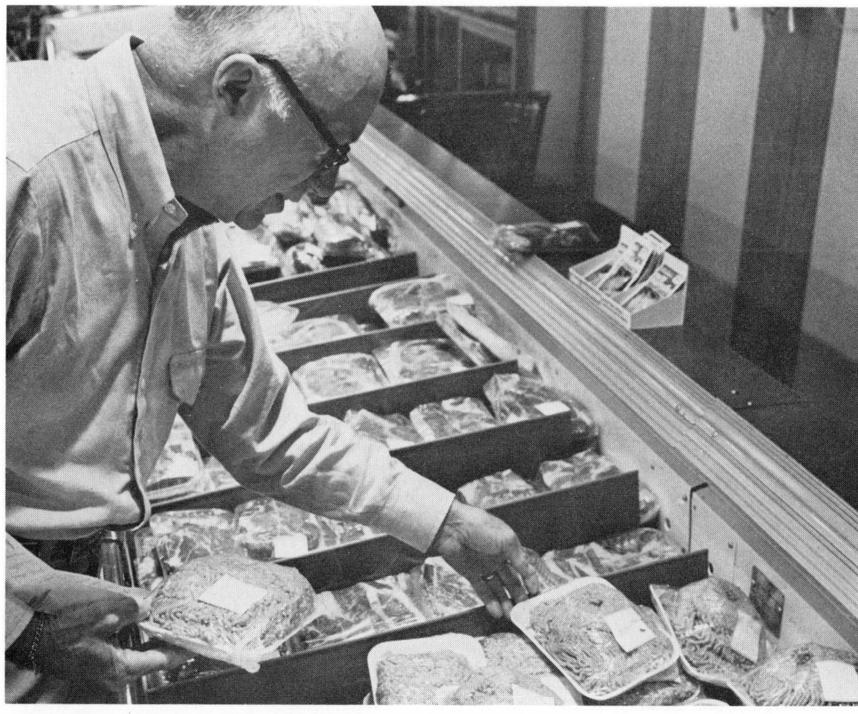

FIGURE 4-11
A Scene from an American Supermarket. Protein-rich foods are readily available to most Americans. (Photograph by Jim Goodwin, Courtesy of Photo Researchers, Inc.).

consume only subsistence levels, a significant number of Americans are eating far more than their bodies need. The so-called HANES survey, for example, found that 90 percent of the white males between 18 and 44 years of age with incomes above the poverty level met or exceeded the RDA for protein for a 70-kilogram adult male, while 45 percent twice exceeded the RDA and 10 percent exceeded the RDA by three times. Protein intakes exceeded the RDA for the majority of the people in all populations studied (9).

Consumption of protein in amounts two to three times the RDA has been thought to be harmless to healthy adults (2). Eskimos have traditionally consumed diets providing up to 200 g/day of protein without any apparent ill effects (10). However, recent studies have shown that high protein consumption increases the excretion of calcium in the urine (2,11). The effects of this are unknown, but it may contribute to the formation of kidney stones and to progressive loss of bone mineral (12). In addition, the higher prevalence of colon and breast cancer in the wealthier countries has been associated with their high intake of protein, especially from animal sources (13,14). However, the association does not prove that protein causes either type of cancer, and other factors, such as high fat and low fiber intakes, may be more important. American protein consumption patterns also may play a role in heart disease: roughly two-thirds of our dietary protein is derived from animal sources (1), which contain saturated fat and cholesterol and may increase blood cholesterol levels (8,15). ”

FOCUS 4-2
GETTING THE MOST FOR YOUR MONEY

As inflation eats away at everyone's food budget, it becomes important to obtain the most nutrition for our money. Table 4-6 compares the cost of various sources of protein in December of 1980, and Activity 4-3 shows you how to calculate these values yourself. Making wise choices of protein sources can greatly stretch your food dollar. In addition, reducing the protein and increasing the carbohydrate content of the diet can save money. Most of us consume far more protein than our bodies need, and the excess is simply broken down for energy. Since both carbohydrate and protein provide 4 kcal/g and protein costs more to produce and to buy, we are paying high prices for energy that could be obtained more cheaply from carbohydrate (Table 4-7).

The quality of a food depends on the presence of nutrients beside protein. Milk, for instance, is also a valuable source of calcium, riboflavin, and, if fortified, vitamins A and D. Nonfat dry milk, particularly if fortified with vitamins A and D, is thus an inexpensive source of many key nutrients. Meat contains iron, zinc, and many of the B vitamins; soybeans supply some B vitamins, calcium, and iron. Grains provide some iron and many B vitamins, and if they are whole grains, they contain significant amounts of fiber. In general, it is best to obtain protein from a variety of sources in each of the food groups. Not only will this increase the likelihood of meeting vitamin and mineral needs, it also will help improve the quality of the protein through mutual supplementation. We will discuss vitamins and minerals in more detail in Chapters 7 and 8.

TABLE **4-6**

Cost comparison: protein sources

FOOD	COST/GRAM OF USABLE PROTEIN, CENTS*	FOOD	COST/GRAM OF USABLE PROTEIN, CENTS*
Hamburger (raw)	2.8	Peanuts	3.4
Sirloin steak (raw, choice, boneless)	6.8	Peanut butter	2.4
Frankfurters	3.1	Nonfat dry milk	1.0
Chicken breasts (with ribs)	3.1	Cashews	8.0
Fresh haddock	4.1	White rice (long grain)	1.6
Eggs (large)	1.4	Whole wheat bread	2.8
Whole milk	2.1	Rolled Oats	1.3
Sharp cheddar cheese	3.4	Spaghetti	1.6
Cottage cheese (4% fat)	2.4	Mushrooms	19.6
Soybeans	0.3	Cabbage	11.0
Great Northern beans	1.4	Potatoes	5.6

* Prices for December 1980, Buffalo, New York; largest containers available were surveyed.

Sources: C. F. Adams, *Nutritive Value of American Foods in Common Units,* Agriculture Handbook No. 456, USDA, Washington, 1975.

B. K. Watt and A. L. Merrill, *Composition of Food—Raw, Processed, Prepared,* Agriculture Handbook No. 8, USDA, Washington, 1963.

Food and Agriculture Organization, *Amino Acid Content of Foods and Biological Data on Proteins,* FAO Nutrition Series No. 24, Rome, 1970. (NPU data used with permission.)

TABLE **4-7**

Cost comparison: carbohydrate vs. protein

SOURCES	COST/GRAM, CENTS*
Protein	
Soybeans (lowest cost)	0.3
Mushrooms (highest cost)	19.6
Average, all sources (Table 4.6)	4.1
Carbohydrate	
Soybeans	0.22
Rice	0.07
Spaghetti	0.15
Whole wheat bread	0.38
Potatoes	0.41
Average	0.25

* Prices for Buffalo, New York, December 1980.

Source: B. K. Watt and A. L. Merrill, *Composition of Food—Raw, processed, Prepared,* Agriculture Handbook No. 8, USDA, Washington, 1963.

ISSUE: THE COSTS OF MALNUTRITION

The abundance of food in the affluent nations contrasts sharply with the situation elsewhere in the world. In the developing countries of Africa, Asia, and Latin America, millions of children live in poverty, and in many areas, they receive little to eat. Measles, malaria, and digestive tract infections are common. Combined with poor diet, these diseases often leave the children wasted and apathetic, victims of protein-energy malnutrition (PEM) (Figure 4-12), the most widespread and urgent nutritional problem facing the world today (Table 4-8). The severe forms of PEM may affect more than 10 million children under 5 years of age, and it is estimated that PEM may be directly or indirectly responsible for more than half the infant deaths in the developing nations. Yet this is only the tip of the iceberg, since milder forms of PEM, recognizable only by a moderate reduction in stature or body weight, afflict an additional 90 million children in the 5 years old and under age group (16, pages 23–54).

In many regions, emaciated children resembling wizened old people suffer from a type of PEM called **marasmus**, which results from a severe deficiency of energy, including protein (17). The problem commonly begins during the first year of life, when the child is weaned onto a diet providing insufficient food. Often the child may receive little more than overdiluted milk, sweetened water, or water in which other foods have been cooked (18). Such a deprivation of energy and other nutrients at this stage of the life cycle drastically limits the child's growth, and the resultant severe muscle wasting and loss of body fat leads to a "skin and bones" appearance (16, pages 23–54).

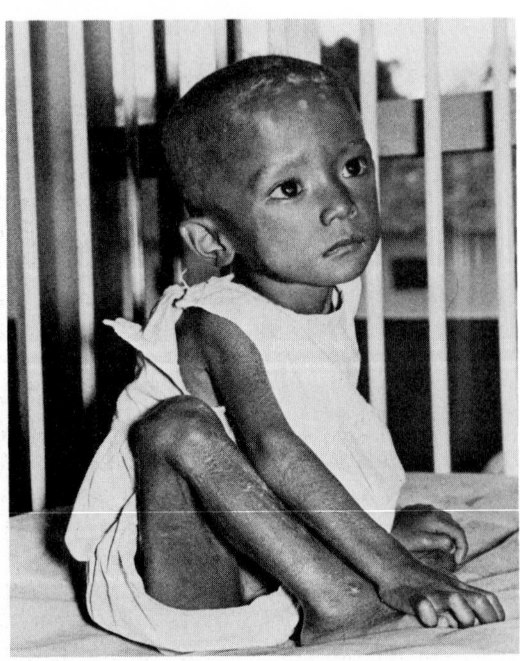

FIGURE 4-12 *Malnutrition.* Suffering from malnutrition, a young boy sits quietly on his hospital bed. His "skin and bones" appearance is characteristic of marasmus. (Photograph by Jack Ling, courtesy of UNICEF.)

TABLE **4-8**

Prevalence of protein-energy malnutrition in the underdeveloped world

AREA	0–5 YEAR OLD POPULATION, MILLIONS	NUMBER WITH SEVERE PEM, MILLIONS	NUMBER WITH MODERATE PEM, MILLIONS	TOTAL, MILLIONS
Latin America	46	0.7	8.8	9.5
Africa	61	2.7	16.3	19.0
Asia	206	6.6	64.4	71.0
Total	314	10.0	89.5	99.5

Source: G. H. Beaton and J. M. Bengoa (eds.), "Nutrition in Preventive Medicine—The Major Deficiency Syndromes, Epidemiology, and Approaches to Control," *WHO Monogr. Ser.* **62**:23–54, 1976. Reprinted with permission.

Another manifestation of PEM is **kwashiorkor**, which usually occurs in children 2 to 5 years old and has historically been associated with a severe protein deficiency. Energy intake also may be deficient, but caloric deprivation is not as severe as that which produces marasmus (17). Kwashiorkor generally seems to result when the child is weaned onto a starchy, low-protein diet, such as one consisting mainly of **cassava**, **plantain**, maize, or rice (18). Swelling (edema) of the legs, face, and sometimes arms is one of the striking characteristics of this disease (16, *pages* 23–54). The protein deficiency reduces albumin concentrations in the blood, allowing fluid to diffuse from the blood vessels into the surrounding tissues, where it accumulates to cause the swelling. Body fat is often present in children with kwashiorkor and, coupled with the edema, gives them a bloated look despite their malnutrition (19, pages 697–720). Growth impairment and muscle wasting are often not as severe as in marasmus. In addition, hair often becomes sparse and lighter in color, while the skin may show both light and dark discoloration. Children with kwashiorkor exhibit many behavioral changes; they become irritable, listless, and apathetic (20, page 3).

In many instances, a victim will exhibit characteristics of both diseases, depending on the relative severity of the protein and caloric deficits. For example, the severe stunting of growth in marasmus and the edema of kwashiorkor may be observed in the same child. These intermediate forms of severe PEM are often referred to as *marasmic kwashiorkor* (20, page 5). Kwashiorkor and marasmus, the most severe forms of PEM, are the most visible and therefore attract the most attention. A far greater number of children in the developing nations suffer from mild or moderate forms of PEM characterized by a low height and weight for their age or a low body weight for their height (16, pages 23–54).

FINDING THE ROOTS

Historically, marasmus has been linked with a deprivation of food in general, while kwashiorkor has been associated more with a deficiency of protein (21). Some recent dietary studies, however, have led certain experts to reconsider this view. A study in India found no difference in the proportion of energy and protein in the diets of victims of kwashiorkor and marasmus (22). In kwashiorkor, as well as in marasmus, the intake of both energy and protein was low. Similar observations have been made in other countries (20, pages 11–14; 21).

Some researchers now hypothesize that marasmus and kwashiorkor may actually be two facets of the same problem. They believe marasmus to be a normal adaptation to food deprivation in which various hormonal mechanisms protect organ functions at the expense of the muscles (20, pages 11–14). Severe wasting of the muscles occurs, but liver function remains near normal. Blood albumin concentrations do not drop and tissue swelling (edema) does not develop. Kwashiorkor may result from a breakdown of this adaptive system, perhaps caused by certain types of infection, such as measles (20, page 17; 23, pages 353–367). This "dysadaptation" produces liver changes, a decrease in blood albumin concentrations, edema, and the other symptoms characteristic of kwashiorkor.

The underdeveloped world faces a "food gap" rather than a "protein gap."

Further studies must be performed before we will understand the biochemical and physiological basis of kwashiorkor. However, the issue may be of little practical importance; in most cereal-based diets, providing sufficient kilocalories will ensure an adequate protein intake. The underdeveloped world faces a "food gap" rather than a "protein gap," and future aid programs should be geared toward increasing the total amount of food available to these people. To accomplish this, many factors, including a low level of socioeconomic and agricultural development, uneven distribution of food, high birth rates, poor sanitation, the prevalence of infectious diseases, and the lack of education, must be dealt with. Let us examine how each contributes to malnutrition.

Right now, the worldwide availability of agricultural resources to produce enough food does not appear to be the problem (see Chapter 14). Because of the low degree of economic development and the backwardness of their agricultural technology, many nations with the potential to produce large quantities of food never approach their capabilities. In many underdeveloped countries, rich soil is used to grow coffee, tea, cocoa beans, and other export items. Many developing nations also export foods rich in energy and protein, including peanuts, cottonseed, sunflower seed, sesame seed, and meat to the affluent countries (26). The money obtained from the sale of these products to the industrialized nations usually does not reach the poor, but is used to finance industrial development or buy weapons.

Even if more food were grown, the problem would not be solved, because poor distribution of existing supplies is a major factor in malnutrition (Figure 4-13). Within a given country, an uneven distribution of wealth and inadequate storage and marketing systems often prevent food from reaching needy segments of the population (16, pages 389–405). Food distribution is inequitable even within families. Moreover, this problem is complicated by high birth rates in the developing nations. In many cultures, the adult male has the first choice of a limited supply of food, and the mother and children divide the remainder (26). Often the youngest children receive little more than mush made from rice or maize or the water in which other foods have been cooked (18). Except when there is war, natural disaster, or outright famine, PEM in the underdeveloped world is primarily a disease of children (27). One authority estimated that reducing family size in India to three children could in itself reduce malnutrition in that country by 60 percent (20, pages 21–22).

One of the most important factors contributing to PEM in the developing nations is the prevalence of infectious diseases, including infections of the digestive tract and the respiratory system, parasitic infections, malaria, and a variety of childhood diseases, such as measles, chickenpox, German measles, and whooping cough. As a result of disease, a child may lose his or her appetite, or the food consumed may be only partially digested and absorbed. In addition, caloric expenditure increases during a fever, and infection may induce breakdown of tissue protein, leading to

FIGURE 4-13
A Market Scene in a Developing Nation. In most developing countries, protein is provided largely by plant sources. (Photograph by C. Sanchez, courtesy of the World Food Program/FAO.)

negative nitrogen balance (16, pages 23–54). Infection may be partly responsible for the breakdown of the body's normal adaptive response to starvation. Kwashiorkor, for example, generally occurs after an acute infection in children whose diets may have been marginal if infection had not adversely influenced the intake and absorption of protein (20, pages 181–182). The relationship between malnutrition and infection can become a vicious cycle. Disease contributes to the occurrence of PEM, and malnutrition lowers resistance to infection. Thus a cycle of periodic infection and progressively worsening malnutrition may be established.

Ignorance, superstition, and lack of education compound the effects of other causes of PEM. This is particularly true with regard to breast-feeding practices. Breast milk alone is usually the optimum means of feeding an infant up to 4 to 6 months of age. Supplementing breast milk with the gradual addition of locally available foods is then necessary. However, the mother may not know when to begin supplementing her breast milk, with what foods her milk should be supplemented, when to wean the child, and onto what foods the child should be weaned. The mother also may be unaware of proper sanitary procedures to be used in preparing the infant's food. In many underdeveloped areas, urbanization and modernization have encouraged mothers to bottle feed their children or to wean them from the breast to a bottle by 6 months of age (16, pages 23–54, 18). They may do so because they believe bottle feeding is better for the child or because they must work outside the home (16, pages 23–54; 20, pages 181–182). Often the bottle contains overdiluted cow's milk or formula prepared under poor sanitary conditions. In addition to the dietary deficiency, the child may contract a gastrointestinal infection and develop diarrhea (18). In other situations, the child may be fed sweetened water or water left over from cooking other foods (28). In either case, marasmus is a likely result. Even if the child is not weaned, the mother may not recognize that she may need to supplement her breast milk as early as the third or fourth month. As the child continues to grow, its demands for protein and energy may not be met by milk alone, and it becomes progressively marasmic (28).

In many areas of the world, when a child is weaned after 2 to 3 years, it is often given high-carbohydrate, low-protein foods. These include cassava, plantain, and sweet potatoes in Africa, maize in Latin America, and rice in Asia. Ignorance and superstition play a role here. Foods that contain more protein of a higher quality, such as meat, eggs, dairy products, and legumes, may be thought unnecessary (28). In a few parts of Kenya it is believed that feeding a child eggs causes convulsions (26), while in other cultures, feeding a child meat is thought to make it greedy (28). In addition, as pointed out earlier, the youngest children in the family often receive food that is left over after the parents and older siblings have made their choices. This late weaning onto a high-carbohydrate, low-protein diet is one of the factors associated with development of kwashiorkor.

Thus, in each region, a variety of factors interact to produce the circumstances of energy and/or protein deficiency that lead to marasmus or kwashiorkor. Eliminating PEM is therefore far more than a nutritional problem. It also requires changes in the economic, agricultural, public health, and educational systems of a nation.

SOLVING THE PROBLEM: TREATMENT AND PREVENTION

The aim in treating severe cases of PEM is to produce rapid recovery. To accomplish this, physicians and nutritionists feed patients therapeutic diets high in protein and energy, correct any fluid and mineral imbalances that may have occurred, and attempt to control any accompanying infections (20, page 104). Milk is the most frequently used protein source in the therapeutic diets, although other sources, such as vegetable-protein mixtures, may be used. The diets are often supplemented with potassium, since this mineral may become depleted during PEM. Depending on the severity of the PEM, the child may recover within 6 to 12 weeks (19, pages 697–720; 20, page 121).

In recent years, experts in the field have become increasingly concerned with the long-term effects of PEM on growth and mental development. Unfortunately, because of the complexity of the problem, these influences are difficult to trace. A child who has recovered from an episode of PEM often returns to a nutritionally and educationally deprived situation, and adverse effects on growth and mental development can be attributed to this as well as to the initial PEM (20, page 123). Evidence is accumulating, however, that PEM early in life, especially if prolonged, may permanently retard both physical growth and mental development (20, pages 122–132; 30).

Treating PEM is not the answer, therefore; only through prevention can the problem be eradicated. From a nutritionist's point of view, prevention means providing a diet adequate in protein and energy content. One important aspect of this is to promote breast feeding and the proper supplementation of breast milk with other foods after the fifth to sixth month of life (23, pages 435–452). Many experts consider it vital to reverse the present trend toward bottle feeding in the underdeveloped nations. Breast feeding is a relatively inexpensive way for poor mothers to nourish their infants, and they do not have to worry about preparing the milk and proper sanitation procedures.

FOCUS 4-3
PEM AND MENTAL DEVELOPMENT

Considerable evidence has been accumulated showing that PEM impairs mental as well as physical development (20, pages 126–132; 29–31; 36). General reasoning, spatial perception, and motor function seem to be most adversely influenced, while short-term memory and learning ability are less severely affected (20, pages 126–132). Some of these disturbances may slow the development of reading and writing skills.

It appears that at least some of these problems result from the adverse effect of PEM on the brain's growth and development (36, 37). Brain growth in humans continues well into the second year of life, and it may be particularly vulnerable to PEM during this critical period (see Chapter 12) (36, 37). PEM also may influence mental development in other ways (31, 37). For example, the malnourished child often does not interact with the environment to the same extent as a healthy child and may therefore be deprived of valuable learning experiences at a critical stage of development (31). An apathetic child often generates apathy from its parents, reducing the parent-child interactions that are vital to proper development (31). Cravioto and others have stressed that PEM is only one aspect of an environment that stifles mental growth (31). Infectious diseases, as well as PEM, reduce a child's interactions with her or his surroundings, while a low level of parental education limits the nature and variety of the experiences to which parents can expose their children.

The extent and nature of PEM's influence on mental development is thus unclear. In addition, the question of whether or not the mental impairment is permanent is highly controversial (37). Much probably depends on the severity, timing, and duration of the malnutrition; severe deprivation within the first 2 years of life may have long-lasting or even permanent consequences.

Providing foods adequate in protein and energy to supplement breast milk or to feed a child after weaning can be accomplished in several ways. The most obvious is to increase the availability of food. This was the aim of the genetic research that improved grain yields and sparked the so-called Green Revolution (see Chapter 14). The protein content and quality, as well as the yields per acre, of grains have been increased. Efforts also are being made to improve the yields and usability of legumes. These include increasing yields per acre, increasing the quantity and quality of the protein they contain, improving digestibility, and removing various toxic or annoying substances (32). Since the proteins of grains and legumes complement each other, increasing the production of both sources is particularly beneficial.

The quality of food can be improved by other methods. Using the principle of mutual supplementation, researchers have developed a variety of mixtures of vegetable proteins. One of the most famous is Incaparina, a combination of maize, cottonseed, and defatted soya flours (16, pages 389–405). However, such mixtures have made little impact on the incidence of PEM. Most developing nations have not had a social welfare structure capable of distributing the mixtures widely, and efforts at retail marketing have generally been unsuccessful (33). Another way of improving the quality of vegetable proteins is to fortify them with their limiting amino acids. For instance, lysine can be added to wheat and methionine can be added to legumes (27). However, this has not been a useful means of preventing PEM: it is practical only when the grains are milled at a central facility; it is often difficult to determine the ideal level of supplementation; and it is possible to create an imbalance by adding too much of the limiting amino acid.

Single-cell proteins (SCP) and fish meal also have been considered as protein sources. Single-cell protein is made from yeast, algae, bacteria, or fungi grown on petroleum derivatives, potato starch wastes, methyl alcohol, and molasses. Their use for human consumption has not yet been feasible: they are more expensive to produce than grains and legumes, contain large amounts of the nucleic acids DNA and RNA (which can aggravate gout and cause kidney stones), and, if grown on petroleum derivatives, may contain other harmful chemicals (34). Fish meal, which is derived from whole fish, also has made little impact on the world food situation. It requires a large input of capital, energy, and expertise, all of which are lacking in the developing nations. In addition, a means of transforming it into a food palatable to humans has not been developed (35).

The practical significance of increasing the availability of protein is questionable. First, the assumption that protein is deficient is increasingly under attack (24,25). Moreover, these programs require efficient distribution systems for their products to reach the needy. For these reasons, many experts argue that government resources might be put to better use by investing in agricultural, economic, and educational development. More efficient distributing and marketing systems will help. Educational programs can teach proper breast-feeding techniques, what foods to buy, and safe methods of preparing food. Sanitation must be improved and programs established to control infectious diseases. Finally, because the earth's capacity to produce food is finite, at some point, population growth must be controlled. Without family planning and birth control, all the other measures are only postponing a nutritional catastrophe.

Study Guide

SUMMARY

1. Proteins are chains composed of simpler subunits called *amino acids.* The human body contains over a thousand different proteins, each one a different combination of these subunits. Twenty-two amino acids occur in human protein. Some, the nonessential amino acids, the body makes itself. Others, the essential amino acids, must be obtained in the diet.
2. The amino acids are assembled into proteins by cellular structures called *ribosomes.* The instructions are provided by the genetic code contained in DNA, and it is by controlling protein synthesis that DNA controls many functions of the cell. Once synthesized, the proteins assume particular shapes and combine with other molecules to become functional proteins.
3. Proteins perform a variety of functions in the body, including catalysis (enzymes), structural roles, maintaining fluid and acid-base balances, fighting infections, blood clotting, transporting substances in the blood, muscle contraction, eyesight, providing energy, and as hormones.
4. Body proteins are in a constant state of turnover—being broken down and replaced. This occurs faster in some tissues than in others. Under certain circumstances, such as growth, pregnancy, and lactation, protein synthesis exceeds the rate of degradation. In other situations, such as starvation, low quality of protein in the diet, disease, injury, and prolonged immobilization, degradation proceeds faster than synthesis. These situations are reflected on the whole-body level by changes in nitrogen balance. When synthesis predominates, nitrogen input exceeds output (*positive nitrogen balance*), while when degradation predominates, nitrogen output exceeds input (*negative nitrogen balance*).
5. Nitrogen balance also is used to determine protein requirements. The amount of protein required to maintain nitrogen equilibrium in adults or promote proper weight gain in children and pregnant women serves as the basis for the Recommended Dietary Allowances. The RDA for the adult is 0.8 g of protein/kg of body weight/day, with greater amounts required for growth, pregnancy, and lactation.
6. Many foods can serve as sources of protein: eggs, milk and dairy products, meat, fish, poultry, legumes, nuts and seeds, grains, and some vegetables. However, several factors must be considered in choosing a protein source, including quantity and quality of the protein; caloric, fat, and cholesterol content of the food; presence of other nutrients; and cost.
7. Americans tend to consume far more protein than their bodies can use. This may have some harmful effects, including increasing risk of colon cancer, breast cancer, and kidney stones. It is also expensive because the excess protein is simply used for energy, and carbohydrates provide a less-expensive source of an equal amount of energy. In addition, millions of children in the underdeveloped nations suffer from a lack of energy and protein. This produces the deficiency diseases of marasmus and kwashiorkor. A variety of factors, including the socioeconomic and agricultural status of the nation, high birth rates, high incidence of infection, and poor education, interact to create the malnutrition situation. In addition to an increase in food production, these factors must be controlled if protein-energy malnutrition is to be eradicated.

VOCABULARY

amino acids
anabolism
antibodies

antigen
cassava
catabolism
complete protein
conformation
conjugated protein
deoxyribonucleic acid (DNA)
edema
endogenous
enzyme
essential amino acids
exogenous
gene
genetic code
glucogenic amino acids
hormone
immunologic
incomplete protein
insulin
ketogenic amino acids
kwashiorkor
limiting amino acid
marasmus
messenger RNA (mRNA)
metabolism
mutual supplementation (complementation)
negative nitrogen balance
net protein utilization (NPU)
nitrogen equilibrium (zero nitrogen balance)
nonessential amino acids
peptide bond
pH
plantain
positive nitrogen balance
proteins
ribonuclease
ribosome
simple proteins
transcription
transfer RNA (tRNA)
translation
turnover
urea

STUDY QUESTIONS

1. Why is it not necessary for the diet to contain sufficient amounts of the *nonessential* amino acids? What happens to protein synthesis when the diet does not supply enough of the *essential* amino acids? Why does this lead to a state of negative nitrogen balance?
2. What are some situations in which protein breakdown exceeds protein synthesis? When protein synthesis exceeds breakdown? What state of nitrogen balance is associated with these situations? Why?
3. List the functions performed by proteins in the body. What substance ultimately determines the functions a protein carries out?
4. What is the adult RDA for protein, and how is it determined? Why does it increase during growth, pregnancy, and lactation?
5. What are the major sources of protein in the diet? Which tend to be lower in caloric content? Saturated fat and cholesterol content? Less costly?
6. What determines the quality of a food protein? Why does the body retain more nitrogen from a high-quality protein than from a low-quality protein? What effect does this have on the net protein utilization (NPU) of the protein? Describe a method by which the quality of incomplete proteins can be improved.
7. What are the economic, sociocultural, and other factors that lead to malnutrition, and how can they be alleviated to provide a long-lasting solution to the problem?

SELF-TEST

Multiple choice: Choose the one best answer.

1. Amino acids are assembled into proteins in cell structures called
   a. Mitochondria
   b. Lysozomes
   c. Nuclei
   d. Ribosomes
2. Excess dietary protein is
   a. Broken down for energy or used to synthesize glucose and fat
   b. Excreted directly in the urine
   c. Stored in the body
   d. All of the above
3. Under which of the following circum-

stances is the body in a state of positive nitrogen balance?
   a. Starvation
   b. Consumption of a low-quality protein
   c. Growth
   d. Diabetes mellitus
4. Which of the following proteins does the body use most efficiently?
   a. Chicken (NPU = 73)
   b. Milk (NPU = 82)
   c. Peanuts (NPU = 43)
   d. Soybeans (NPU = 61)
5. Which of the following protein sources does not contain cholesterol?
   a. Roast beef
   b. Tunafish
   c. Rice
   d. Cheese
6. Combination of the protein opsin with vitamin A to form a visual pigment is an example of
   a. Conjugated protein
   b. Complemented protein
   c. Condensed protein
   d. Complete protein
7. Phenylketonuria results from
   a. An inability to absorb phenylalanine from the diet
   b. A defective enzyme
   c. A kidney disorder
   d. A vitamin deficiency
8. The amount of protein in the average American's diet
   a. Is generally far more than the body needs to maintain itself
   b. Is totally harmless
   c. Barely meets the RDA
   d. Is a relatively inexpensive way of obtaining energy
9. Which of the following does not contribute to PEM at the present time?
   a. Poor distribution of food supplies
   b. Infectious diseases
   c. Ignorance
   d. A worldwide scarcity of land and other agricultural resources
10. Which of the following is the most effective way of eliminating PEM?
   a. Amino acid supplementation of plant proteins
   b. Improving the agricultural, economic, and educational status of developing nations
   c. Developing single-cell proteins
   d. Developing fish-meal products

True-False:

1. It is impossible to meet protein requirements if animal products are excluded from the diet.
2. The quality of a protein depends on its ability to meet the body's needs for essential amino acids.
3. If dietary protein is deficient, the body breaks down functioning proteins to provide amino acids.
4. Promotion of bottle feeding has led to a decline in PEM in the developing nations.
5. PEM in the first 2 years of life can permanently impair mental and physical development.

SUGGESTED ACTIVITIES

1. This activity requires completion of a diet record as given in Activity 10-1.
   a. How does your percent of kilocalories obtained from protein compare with the recommendation of 10 to 15 percent?
   b. Which protein sources in your diet are high-quality and which are low-quality?
2. Compute your RDA for protein:
   a. Multiply your body weight in kilograms by 0.8.
   b. Compare the number of grams of protein you consumed in one day (Activity 4-1) with your RDA.
3. Calculate the cost of protein from various sources:
   a. Using the food's label or a food composition table, determine the number of grams of protein in one retail unit (package, pound, quart, etc.) of the food.
   b. Multiply the protein content by the NPU for that food. [NPU values can be found in *Diet for a Small Planet,* (Further

Reading 1).] This will give the grams of usable protein in the food.

c. Divide the cost of the retail unit by the grams of usable protein to give the cost per gram of usable protein.

4. Compare the cost of food protein with that of a protein supplement sold in a health-food store:

a. Divide the cost of a retail unit of a protein supplement by the number of grams of protein it contains.

b. Compare this cost with those of food proteins in Activity 4-3.

FURTHER READING

1. An easy-to-read and practical guide to meeting protein needs from plant sources:

   Lappe, F. M.: *Diet for A Small Planet,* 2d ed., Ballantine, New York, 1975.

2. A detailed discussion of protein-energy malnutrition:

   Olson, R. E.: *Protein-Calorie Malnutrition,* Academic, New York, 1975.

3. An overview of the world food problem:

   The entire September 1976 issue of *Scientific American.*

PART 2

ENERGY AND THE BODY: AN OVERVIEW

In order for the energy nutrients to perform their functions, they must be liberated from food and absorbed into the body. Even inside the body, however, their fates remain strongly intertwined. With the exception of the nitrogen in protein, they are converted to the same end products: carbon dioxide, water, and energy. During their metabolism, they sometimes follow the same pathways, and interconversions among some of them take place. Utilization of the energy nutrients is coordinated by hormones and certain enzymes. In this way, the body can maintain balance in spite of changes in the availability of carbohydrate, fat, and protein, such as after a meal or during a fast. The total amount of energy taken into and expended by the body, regardless of the source, is also of great importance. A balance between intake and expenditure must be maintained to avoid underweight or obesity.

This part of the book examines the concept of energy as a whole. In Chapter 5 we will discuss energy intake and expenditure and the causes and results of imbalances between them. In Chapter 6 we will explore more deeply the body's utilization of the energy nutrients and learn how they are digested, absorbed, and metabolized. Particular attention will be paid to the coordination of their metabolism to meet the body's changing needs.

ENERGY BALANCE AND WEIGHT CONTROL

As anyone who has recently taken up jogging can tell you, physical activity requires a great deal of energy. Although much of it is used by the muscles, other tissues demand energy too. The nervous system, for instance, coordinates the muscles to perform the act of running, and each impulse transmitted by a nerve fiber requires the expenditure of a small amount of energy. Several muscles work to fill and empty the lungs, while the heart pumps blood throughout the body. Supplying the tissues with oxygen and nutrients and removing carbon dioxide and other wastes expends energy. In a race, the adrenal glands secrete epinephrine, the hormone that prepares the body for "fight or flight." The kidneys and the digestive tract are also working: while the individual runs, the kidneys produce urine, and if there is any food in the digestive tract, digestion and absorption are occurring as well.

To balance this expenditure of energy, the body must take in new supplies. Three nutrients—protein, carbohydrate, and fat—provide energy, and many vitamins and minerals take part in or facilitate the processes by which energy is produced. In this chapter we will examine overall energy balance and the results of imbalance: underweight and obesity. The specific roles of the nutrients in energy production are discussed in their respective chapters.

The Energy Equation

Chemists describe the energy content of a substance in terms of units called **calories**. One *calorie* is the energy required to raise the temperature of one gram of water one degree Celsius. This unit is too small to describe energy expenditure in living systems, so we generally talk about energy in terms of larger units called **kilocalories**. One *kilocalorie* equals 1000 calories and thus is the energy required to raise the temperature of one kilogram of water (slightly more than one quart) one degree Celsius. About 300 kilocalories are required to heat a gallon of water from room temperature (20°C) to the boiling point (100°C). This amount of energy is released by the complete combustion of 2 1/2 tablespoons of corn oil or 7 1/2 tablespoons (2/5 cup) of sugar (Figure 5-1). In everyday conversation, a kilocalorie is often called a *Calorie*:* a friend who is trying to lose weight, for example, may speak about "counting Calories." To avoid confusion when we discuss energy, we use *kilocalorie* to distinguish between the larger and smaller energy units.

In the near future, another unit of energy will come increasingly into use. This is the **kilojoule**, a unit in the metric system: 1 kilocalorie equals 4.18 kilojoules, and 1 kilojoule is equivalent to 0.239 kilocalories.

If energy expenditure is not offset by the intake of an equivalent number of kilocalories, the body must rely on stored energy. As this becomes depleted, body function becomes impaired, and death eventually results. However, a person may consume more energy than necessary, in which case the excess is stored as fat. The state in which energy intake from food equals energy expenditure is called **energy balance**, and it is a state consistent with maintaining good health (Figure 5-2). We will look now at how this balance is maintained, beginning with the process of using energy.

* When it signifies a kilocalorie, the word *calorie* is spelled with a capital C.

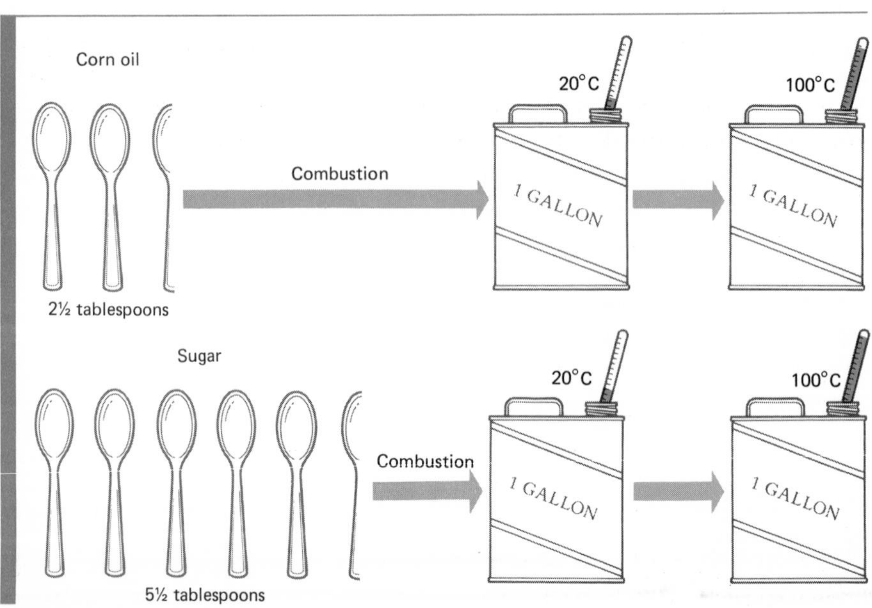

FIGURE 5-1
The Energy Content of Kilocalories. About 300 kilocalories are needed to heat 1 gallon of water from 20 to 100° Celsius. This amount of energy is contained in 2 1/2 tablespoons of corn oil or 5 1/2 tablespoons of sugar.

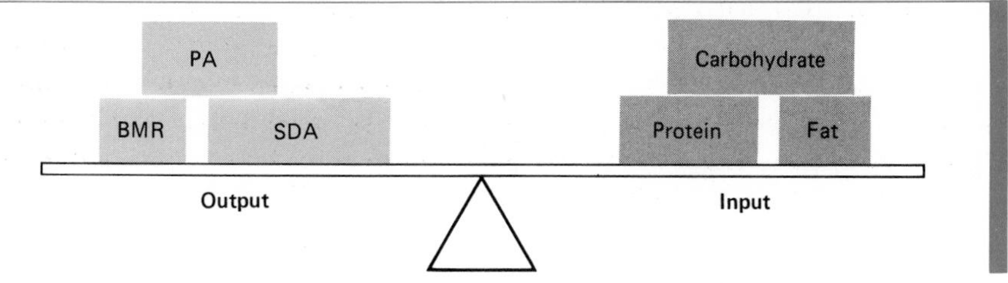

FIGURE 5-2
Energy Balance. To maintain body weight, energy expended must equal energy consumed.

ENERGY EXPENDITURE

The body uses energy in three general ways: to maintain the basal metabolic rate (BMR), in physical activity (PA), and for specific dynamic action (SDA). Total energy expenditure is the sum of these three components.

Basal Metabolic Rate

The **basal metabolic rate (BMR)** is the energy required to maintain life when the body is at complete rest, but awake, and the person has not eaten in 12 hours. It includes the energy expended to sustain heartbeat, breathing, nerve activity, kidney function, glandular activity, body temperature, and other basic functions. The BMR also includes the energy required to meet the maintenance needs of tissues, such as muscles and the digestive organs, which are relatively inactive under basal conditions. The whole concept of BMR thus revolves around *maintenance,* the amount of energy required just to stay alive.

The BMR may be determined in two general ways. In the first, *direct calorimetry* measures the heat given off by the body (Figure 5-3). The subject lies within an insulated chamber (respiration chamber), through which run pipes carrying water. Body heat is absorbed by the water, raising its temperature. By knowing the volume of water in the pipes and measuring the increase in its temperature, we can calculate energy expenditure. However, this is an expensive and difficult procedure. Basal metabolic rate can be measured much more easily by measuring oxygen consumption (*indirect calorimetry*) (Figure 5-4). The body uses oxygen to "burn" carbohydrate, fat, and protein for energy, and the oxygen con-

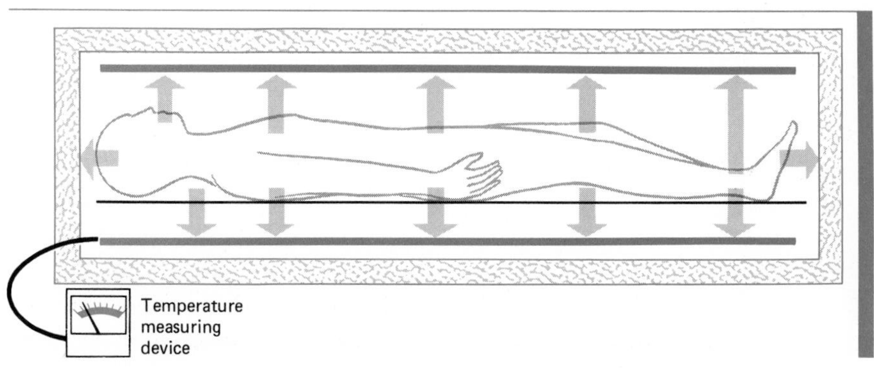

FIGURE 5-3
Direct Measurement of Energy Expenditure. The subject is placed in a respiratory chamber, and the heat released is determined by measuring the increase in temperature of water surrounding the chamber.

FIGURE 5-4
Indirect Measurement of Energy Expenditure. The subject breathes into a device that measures oxygen consumption, which is then used to calculate energy expenditure.

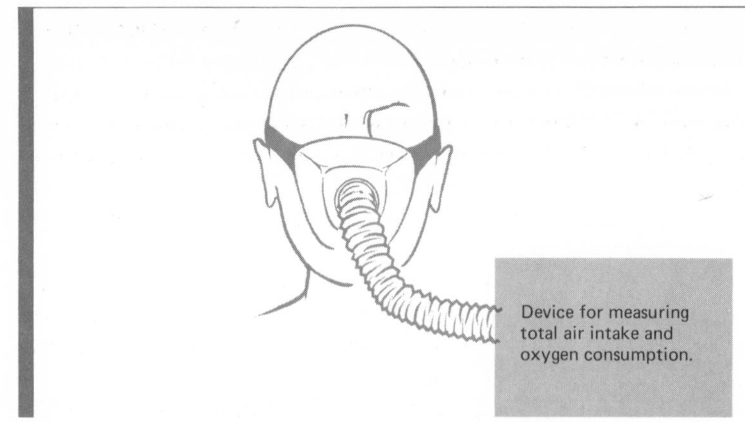

sumed is related to the energy given off by the breakdown of these nutrients. On the average, consumption of 1 liter of oxygen by the body represents an expenditure of 4.82 kilocalories of energy. For example, under basal conditions, a person might consume 1.5 liters of oxygen during a 6-minute test period, a rate of 15 liters/h of oxygen. The person's BMR is therefore about 72.3 kcal/h, or 1735 kcal/day.

Basal energy expenditure varies from person to person and is influenced by hereditary and environmental factors. One such factor is body composition, which includes body size and the relative proportion of lean to fatty tissue (Figure 5-5). As you would expect, a large person re-

FIGURE 5-5
The Influence of Body Composition on BMR. **A** On a whole-body basis, BMR is greater for a large person than for a small one. **B** Obese people do not have as large a BMR as would be expected from their body weight; fat is metabolically less active, so an obese person's BMR is lower than for a person of the same weight who has more lean tissue. (Photograph **A** by David S. Strickler, Monkmeyer Press Photo Service. Photograph **B** by Ray Ellis, Rapho/Photo Researchers, Inc.)

A

B

quires more kilocalories overall than a smaller person. In addition, an individual with a relatively lean body (a low proportion of fatty tissue) needs more energy than a person of the same weight who has a higher proportion of body fat (1). This is so because lean tissue, which includes muscles, nerves, liver, and kidneys, is relatively more active than adipose (fatty) tissue. Muscles maintain a certain degree of contraction, even at rest, nerves generate and conduct electric impulses, the kidneys filter blood, and so on, whereas most of the adipose tissue is devoted to the storage of fat. Women tend to have a lower basal metabolism than men of the same age and body size. This reflects differences in body composition between the two sexes, since a woman's body contains a proportionally larger amount of adipose tissue than a man's.

Hormone secretions are probably the single most important factor affecting BMR. In particular, **thyroxine**, an iodine-containing hormone produced by the thyroid gland, increases energy expenditure. Elevated thyroxine production (**hyperthyroidism**) may increase the BMR by as much as 80 percent, whereas low thyroxine production (**hypothyroidism**) may reduce it by as much as 30 percent. In hospitals and clinics, testing thyroid gland function has replaced indirect calorimetry as a means of evaluating the BMR. For example, the protein-bound iodine (PBI) test and the T_4 test reflect the amount of thyroxine circulating in the blood. Although these tests cannot quantitatively measure the BMR, they do indicate whether the patient's BMR is higher or lower than normal.

Age also influences BMR (2). Basal energy expenditure increases up to the age of 5 years and then decreases as the person grows older, except for a slight rise during adolescence (Figure 5-6). This decrease, coupled with a reduction in physical activity, results in lower energy requirements in the elderly.

Many other factors also affect the rate of basal metabolism. It in-

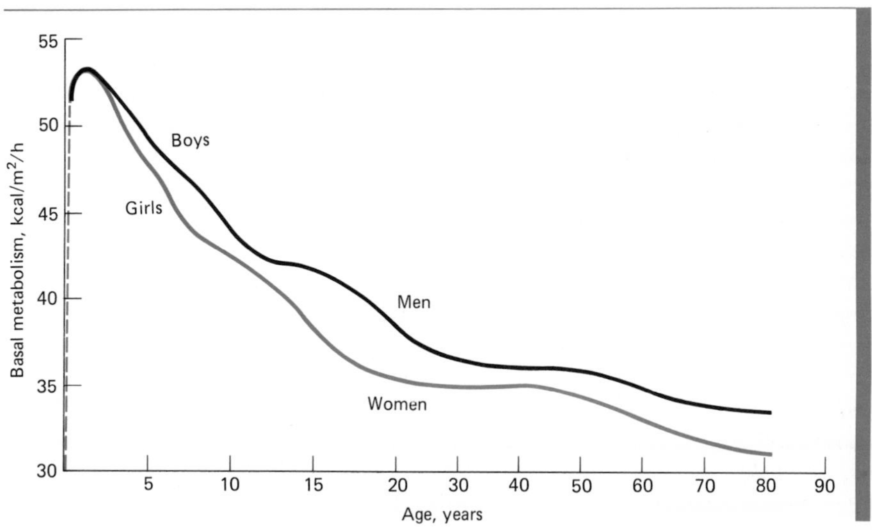

FIGURE 5-6
The Influence of Age on BMR. Basal metabolism per unit of surface area peaks within the first year or two of life and gradually declines thereafter. (Source: Adapted from H. H. Mitchell, *Comparative Nutrition of Man and Domestic Animals,* Vol. 1, Academic Press, New York (1962), p. 43. Reprinted with permission.)

creases during certain diseases and with an increase in body temperature and decreases during starvation. Pregnancy causes the mother's BMR to increase. Basal energy needs are lowest at an environmental temperature of about 78°F (26°C) and increase as the temperature rises or falls. Because each person experiences all these factors to a different extent, basal energy requirements vary markedly from individual to individual. Furthermore, when a person grows older, experiences an extreme change in climate, or in other ways alters one of the factors influencing BMR, his or her basal energy needs will change accordingly. Nancy, for example, weighed 20 pounds more on her fiftieth than she did on her twentieth birthday, partly because she did not adjust her food intake to compensate for the reduction in BMR over that period.

Physical Activity The basal metabolic rate represents only the energy expended to maintain life processes while a person is resting and has not eaten in 12 hours. Humans also expend a great deal of energy carrying out a variety of physical activities (Ready Reference 5). Running requires about 7.0 kcal/kg of body weight/h, whereas walking at a speed of 3 mi/h expends only 2.0 kcal/kg/h. Activity that is predominantly mental in nature, such as sitting quietly or writing, requires a minimal amount of energy (0.4 kcal/kg/h) (3). How much physical activity a person engages in plays a major role in determining total energy needs. Jerry, who plays two hours of basketball after school almost every day, requires more energy in his diet than his classmate Fred, who bowls once a week.

Specific Dynamic Action The third general means by which the body uses energy is for **specific dynamic action (SDA)**, the energy required to digest, absorb, transport, and metabolize food. This is the energy that must be expended to make the energy in food available to the body, and it is sometimes called the *thermogenic effect* of food. The SDA of the average diet is equivalent to about 10 percent of the sum of the BMR and physical activity (6, page 596). For example, a person who expends 2500 kcal/day for BMR and physical activity requires an additional 250 kcal/day for SDA. His or her total energy expenditure is therefore 2750 kcal/day.

Protein, carbohydrate, and fat each influence specific dynamic action differently. Protein has by far the greatest specific dynamic effect of the three energy nutrients (4, page 600). The large amount of energy needed to utilize the protein in food is the reason high-protein diets are sometimes used to lose weight. If more of the energy in the food is expended just to utilize it, less should be available for storage as fat. In practice, however, this hypothesis does not work: although the SDA for pure protein is high, when protein is mixed with fat and carbohydrate, even in small amounts, the dynamic effect is greatly reduced. It seems to be difficult to alter the SDA much from its 10 percent value by changing the proportion of protein, carbohydrate, and fat in a mixed diet (5). Furthermore, in the United States, high-protein diets tend to contain large amounts of fat, because the principle sources of protein are meat, dairy products, and eggs. Since fat contains more than twice the kilocalories of either carbohydrate or protein, any advantage gained by increasing the protein content of the diet may be offset by the high caloric value of the extra fat that comes with it.

ESTIMATING TOTAL ENERGY REQUIREMENTS

Measuring energy requirements by direct or indirect calorimetry requires special equipment that most people do not have. One simple way to estimate energy expenditure is to calculate it using tables that show the energy required by the average person to perform various activities. The methods given here are fairly accurate for people who are not subject to extremes of the factors that influence energy expenditure (Table 5-1).

JoAnn is a 5 ft, 6 in, 132-lb (61-kg), 18-year-old female. She determined that she spent the following amounts of time performing the activities listed below in 1 day:

Sitting	8 h
Walking (3 mi/h)	3 h
Cooking	2 h
Swimming	1/2 h
Standing relaxed	1 h
Cleaning	1 h

The first step in method 1 is to calculate the BMR using Ready References 6 and 7. Drawing a line from JoAnn's height in the left column of Ready Reference 6 to her weight in the right column, we find that her surface area (the middle column) is 1.69 m^2. Ready Reference 7 gives her hourly caloric expenditure as 35.7 kcal/m^2/h. Multiplying her surface area by the caloric expenditure per hour yields the BMR per hour, and multiplying this number by 24 gives the BMR per day. Next, the energy expended by physical activity must be determined. The number of hours spent at each activity is multiplied by JoAnn's body weight in kilograms and by the amount of energy required to perform the activity (Ready Reference 5). The results are added to obtain the total number of kilocalories expended by physical activity. Last, we calculate the SDA by taking 10 percent of the sum of the BMR and physical activity. Adding the values obtained for the BMR, physical activity, and SDA yields JoAnn's total energy expenditure.

Method 2 is simpler but less precise. First, we determine energy expenditure while the person is asleep: calculate the BMR as in method 1 and multiply by 0.9 and the fraction of the day spent sleeping. To calculate other energy used during the day, classify all activities into one of the categories in Ready Reference 8. Multiply the number of hours spent at each level of activity by the appropriate factor from Ready Reference 8 and by body weight in kilograms. The sum of these numbers should be added to the energy expended while asleep to obtain the total caloric expenditure.

TABLE **5-1**

Estimating energy expenditure

I. Method 1

A. Calculate BMR:

1. Surface area (Ready Reference 6): 1.69 m^2
2. Hourly energy expenditure (Ready Reference 7): 35.7 $kcal/m^2/h$
3. BMR = surface area × hourly energy expenditure × 24
   = 1.69 × 35.7 × 24
   = 1447 kcal/day

B. Calculate energy expended via physical activity (PA):

ACTIVITY	HOURS SPENT	ENERGY EXPENDED, kcal/kg OF BODY WEIGHT/h (READY REFERENCE 5)	BODY WEIGHT kg	TOTAL
Sitting	8	0.4	61	195
Walking (3 mi/h)	3	2.0	61	366
Cooking	2	About 1.0	61	122
Swimming	$^1/_2$	7.9	61	241
Standing relaxed	1	0.5	61	31
Cleaning	1	About 1.2	61	73
			Total energy expended =	1028 kcal

C. Calculate specific dynamic action (SDA):
(1447 + 1028) × 0.1 = 247 kcal

D. Calculate total daily expenditure (TDE):
Total daily expenditure = BMR + PA + SDA
= 1447 + 1028 + 247
= 2722 kcal

II. Method 2

A. Calculate energy expended while asleep:

1. Multiply surface area (Ready Reference 6) by hourly energy expenditure (Ready Reference 7):
   1.69 m^2 × 35.7 $kcal/m^2/h$ = 60.7 kcal/h
2. Multiply result by hours spent sleeping and 0.9:
   60.7 × 8$^1/_2$ × 0.9 = 464 kcal

B. Calculate energy expended while awake:
Group each activity into one of the categories in Ready Reference 8 and multiply the hours spent by the appropriate factor and body weight in kilograms.

CATEGORY	HOURS	FACTOR, kcal/kg OF BODY WEIGHT	BODY WEIGHT kg	TOTAL
Very light (sitting, standing)	9	1.3	61	714
Light (walking, cooking, cleaning)	6	2.6	61	952
Heavy (swimming)	$^1/_2$	8.0	61	244
			Total expenditure =	1910 kcal

C. Add together the energies expended while asleep and awake:
Total daily expenditure = 464 + 1910
= 2374 kcal

Note that in JoAnn's case there is a 348-kilocalorie difference between the two methods. Because of the imprecision involved in estimating time spent performing various activities and the fact that the energy expenditure in Ready References 5 and 8 are subject to variation from person to person, this difference is not considered significant; these calculations provide a "ballpark" figure of an individual's energy needs.

THE RECOMMENDED DIETARY ALLOWANCE (8)

Calculating energy expenditure by these methods provides a reasonable estimate of the caloric needs of most people, but the methods are not always practical. When planning diets for large groups of people, such as for the residents of a nursing home or for a school lunch program, we cannot calculate energy requirements for every person in the group. Some general standard of intake that applies to most of the population must be used. The Recommended Dietary Allowances (RDAs) established by the Food and Nutrition Board in 1980 give a level of caloric intake (Ready Reference 3) that will cover the energy needs of the average healthy American engaged in light activity as defined in Ready Reference 8. The RDA must be adjusted to meet individual needs: a moderately active person may need as much as 300 kcal/day and a very active person may need 600 to 900 kcal/day more than average. Very large or very small people may need as much as 10 to 15 percent more or less energy than average (8). Requirements are also higher during growth, pregnancy, and lactation. The RDAs do not apply to people subject to extreme environmental conditions, people who have metabolic disorders, people who are ill, or those who in some other way differ from the general population.

As shown by Ready Reference 3, the average 70-kilogram adult male requires about 2700 kcal/day, while the average 55-kilogram adult female needs only about 2000 kcal/day. In order to maintain energy balance within the body, these caloric losses must be replaced by an equal number of kilocalories from food.

ENERGY INTAKE

Measuring Food Energy The energy content of food may be determined in ways similar to those for estimating energy expenditure. Direct calorimetry measures the heat given off by the complete combustion of a food in an atmosphere of oxygen. Inside an instrument called a **bomb calorimeter** (Figure 5-7), the food is placed in a small chamber contain-

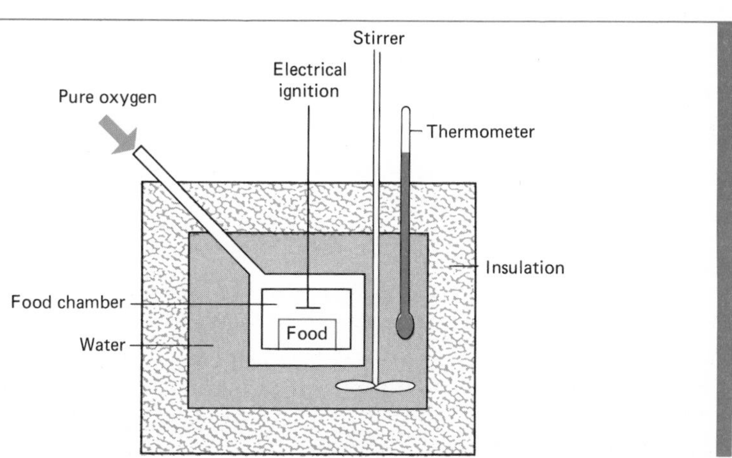

FIGURE 5-7
A Bomb Calorimeter. The heat given off when the food is completely burned is determined by measuring the increase in temperature of the water in the calorimeter.

ing pure oxygen. Igniting the food causes it to burn completely, and the heat released is absorbed by a water bath surrounding the chamber. Since 1 kilocalorie represents the heat required to raise the temperature of 1 kilogram of water 1°C, knowing the volume of the water in the calorimeter and the increase in its temperature allows us to calculate the energy value of the food. An indirect method, called *oxycalorimetry,* also may be used. In this case, the instrument measures the oxygen required for complete combustion. Although the values of both methods compare well, oxycalorimetry is seldom used.

When 1 gram of pure protein is completely burned in a bomb calorimeter, it gives off 5.65 kilocalories. Carbohydrate and fat yield 4.1 and 9.45 kcal/g, respectively. These values, called the **heat of combustion**, represent the total amount of energy contained in these substances (4, page 596). However, not all the energy present in a food is available to the body. To begin with, the body does not digest and absorb all the food it takes in: only about 98 percent of the carbohydrate, 95 percent of the fat, and 92 percent of the protein is digested and absorbed. In addition, protein is not completely burned when the body uses it for fuel, and part of its caloric value is excreted in the urine.

The energy actually available to the body from a food is called its **physiological fuel value**. Thus 1 gram of protein provides 4 kilocalories for the body, while carbohydrate and fat contribute 4 kcal/g and 9 kcal/g, respectively. Alcohol supplies 7.0 kcal/g (4, page 596). The physiological fuel value of a food can be calculated by determining the number of grams of protein, carbohydrate, and fat it contains and multiplying them by 4, 4, and 9 kcal/g, respectively. The sum of the caloric values indicates how much energy the food provides for the body. For example, a cup of whole milk contains 8 grams of protein, 11 grams of carbohydrate, and 8 grams of fat. Thus protein provides 32 kilocalories, carbohydrate 44 kilocalories, and fat 72 kilocalories, for a total of 148 kcal/cup.

Estimating Caloric Intake The relative proportion of protein, carbohydrate, and fat determines the energy value of a food. For example, cheddar cheese, which has a high fat and protein content, a moderate amount of water, and virtually no carbohydrate or fiber, contains more kilocalories than an equivalent amount of potato, which contains a great deal of water and carbohydrate, some fiber and protein, and essentially no fat (Figure 5-8).

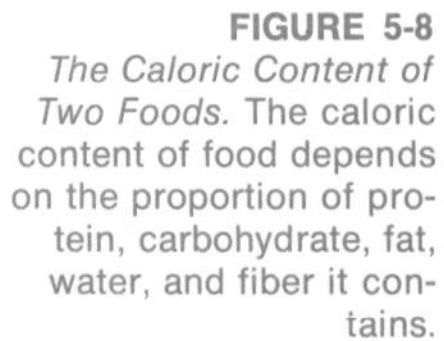

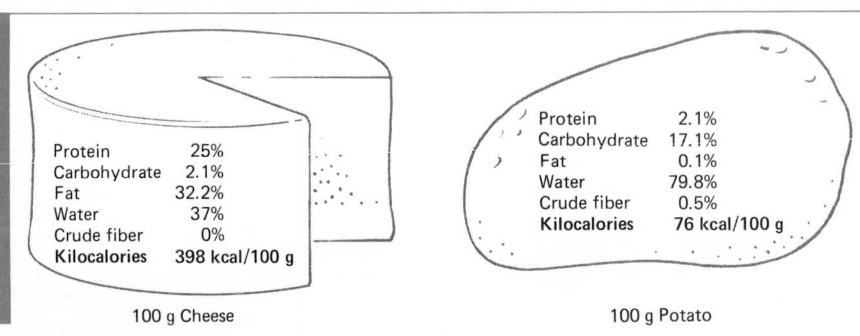

FIGURE 5-8 *The Caloric Content of Two Foods.* The caloric content of food depends on the proportion of protein, carbohydrate, fat, water, and fiber it contains.

The caloric values of many common foods are given in Ready Reference 1. By keeping a record of the types and amounts of food he or she eats, we can determine the number of kilocalories a person consumes. For example, a meal consisting of one peanut butter sandwich (2 slices of whole wheat bread and 2 tablespoons of peanut butter), a cup of whole milk, and a medium-size apple contains 480 kilocalories:

2 slices of whole wheat bread	=	60 kcal
2 tablespoons of peanut butter	=	190 kcal
1 cup of whole milk	=	150 kcal
1 medium-size apple	=	80 kcal
Total		480 kcal

Imbalances: Underweight and Obesity

When energy expenditure equals intake, body weight remains steady. Consuming too few kilocalories to meet the body's needs leads to loss of weight. If prolonged, this **negative energy balance** results in *underweight.* When the body takes in more kilocalories than it can use, the excess is stored as fat. If prolonged, this **positive energy balance** leads to a condition called *obesity.*

NEGATIVE ENERGY BALANCE: UNDERWEIGHT

Underweight is defined as a body weight 15 percent less than ideal and results when expenditure of energy chronically exceeds intake. Slight to moderate underweight is common in the affluent nations, and in its severest forms, underweight is widespread in the developing countries (see Chapter 4).

The most obvious cause of underweight is inadequate consumption of food. This may be because of the unavailability of food, a fast-moving, tension-filled lifestyle, or psychological disturbances, such as anorexia nervosa. Parasites, infectious diseases, metabolic disorders such as hyperthyroidism, and diseases that interfere with the digestion and absorption of food also produce underweight. Because underweight is frequently a complication of other problems, treatment must relieve the primary disorder as well as increase food intake.

1. Carbohydrates, not kilocalories, make you fat.
2. Fasting, liquid protein diets, or drugs are safe and effective ways to lose weight.
3. Spot reducing devices will allow you to remove fat selectively from specific parts of the body.
4. Since you can consume energy so much faster than you can expend it, exercise is of little value in weight control.

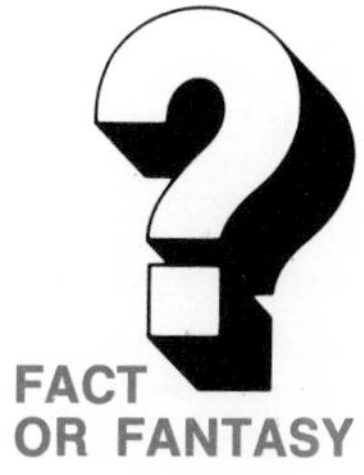

FACT
OR FANTASY

Underweight has a variety of effects on the body, depending on its severity and duration. Being slightly underweight may actually reduce the risk of certain diseases and prolong life. In its severe forms, however, it impairs growth and mental development in children (see Chapters 4 and 12), decreases resistance to infection, reduces work capacity, sexual functioning, and neuromuscular performance, and interferes with the activity of tissues such as those of the digestive tract and the heart (9,10).

The first step in correcting underweight is to eliminate any underlying causes. Then the person should follow a diet that provides 500 to 1000 more kilocalories than are expended to produce a weight gain of 1 lb/week or more (11). The diet should supply at least 100 grams of protein and increased amounts of carbohydrate and fat, but large quantities of fat should be avoided because its high satiety value will dull the appetite. Care must be taken to consume foods that will provide adequate amounts of vitamins and minerals. Some practical suggestions for increasing caloric content include using whole milk instead of skim milk, adding powdered milk or ice cream to milk products, including an egg with cereal, juice, and toast for breakfast, using butter, sour cream, or gravy on potatoes, and eating nutritious, high-kilocalorie foods, such as nuts and dried fruits. Regular exercise is necessary so that some of the weight gained will be lean tissue instead of fat, and periods of relaxation should be taken to reduce tension.

Anorexia Nervosa **Anorexia nervosa** (12–14) is a cause of underweight that is becoming more common in our society. It generally occurs in adolescent women and is believed to be a psychological disorder. The individual is usually a healthy and obedient child; she excels academically and is held in high esteem by parents and teachers. The refusal to eat appears to be triggered by a traumatic event, such as the first real separation from her parents, onset of menstruation, or starting high school or college. In some cases, the person's reaction is an attempt to exert control over some aspect of her life, a struggle for identity or independence from overprotective and overambitious parents. Other individuals appear to be afraid of growing up and the onset of adulthood, and still others appear to be simply obsessed with a desire to be slim. An anorexic person may go to great lengths to avoid food intake, including inducing vomiting. She is totally unconcerned about her progressing emaciation and often perceives herself as being fat. Some victims literally starve themselves to death.

Treatment of anorexia nervosa is difficult; some patients must be force-fed. However, unless the underlying psychological problems are treated, the condition will reappear. Psychotherapy is supportive at first, but gradually transfers more responsibility to the patient. The majority of patients show improvement or even recover, although some have eventually died from the disease.

POSITIVE ENERGY BALANCE: OBESITY

Of all nutritional problems, probably none is more prominent in America than obesity (Figure 5-9). Our preoccupation with the young, slender, and beautiful, coupled with the health hazards known to be associated with obesity, has spawned a multibillion-dollar industry to deal with one of the more unfortunate by-products of an affluent society (15). Dozens of books on dieting crowd the health section of bookstores. Newspapers and magazines constantly carry articles and advertisements describing ways to lose weight quickly. There are special foods, diet aids, exercise aids, and organizations whose sole purpose is to facilitate weight loss. Let us take a closer look at this disease, for which neither the cause nor the cure is known.

Defining the Problem We usually refer to an obese person as being "overweight." The method we most often use to determine a person's status is to compare body weight with a table of ideal or desirable weights (Ready Reference 9). A body weight greater than 10 percent above the ideal for a person of a given height and body frame is considered **overweight**; exceeding the ideal by 15 to 20 percent is defined as **obesity** (16, pages 7–10). However, high body weight does not always mean the individual is obese. Some people, such as weightlifters and other athletes, possess an unusually large mass of muscle, which makes them overweight for their height and body frame. A sedentary person could have more than the normal amount of fat and still fall within the ideal range on the height-weight tables. *Obesity* is more precisely defined as an accumulation of body fat. If fat comprises more than 20 percent of the body weight of an 18-year-old male or more than 30 percent of the body weight of an 18-year-old female, he or she is said to be obese. Fat content of the body increases with age, so the standards change as one grows older (16, page 157).

FIGURE 5-9
About 25 to 30 percent of the adults and at least 10 percent of the children in the United States are overweight or obese. (Photograph by Peter Menzel, Stock, Boston, Inc.)

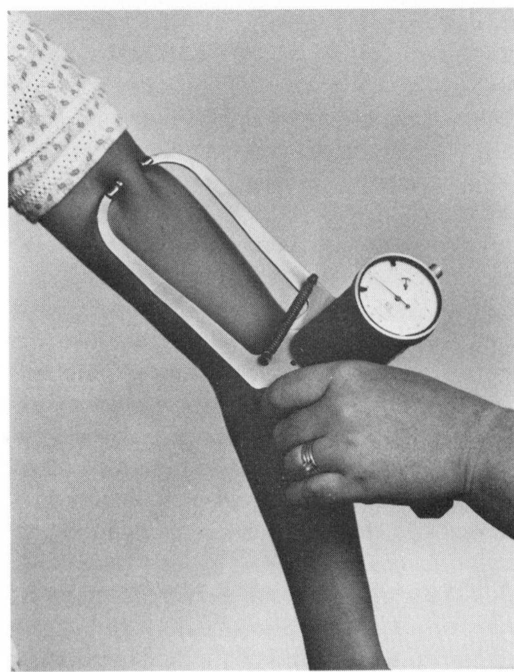

FIGURE 5-10 *Triceps Skinfold Measurement.* Calipers are used to measure the thickness of the skin and underlying fat on the back of the upper arm. (Courtesy of *Morse Hemco Corporation.*)

We often determine the amount of body fat by means of skinfold calipers, which measure the thickness of a piece of skin lifted away from the underlying muscle (Figure 5-10), usually on the back of the upper arm. Obesity also may be established by underwater weighing to measure body density, by measurement of body water using radioactive deuterium oxide, and by determining the amount of lean tissue by measuring the amount of radioactive potassium 40 in the body. However, these methods are time-consuming and require sophisticated equipment, which makes them more suited to research than clinical use.

Depending on the criteria used, it has been estimated that 25 to 30 percent of the adults and at least 10 percent of the children in the United States are either overweight or obese (17). The Ten-State Survey and the HANES preliminary survey indicate that the disorder is especially prevalent among certain population groups (18,19). For example, obesity appears to be more common among women than among men. White men are more likely to be obese than black men, but the reverse is true when comparing white and black women. In addition, the incidence of obesity is higher among women from lower socioeconomic classes than among women from higher income groups (18–21). Most recent studies have found the opposite to be generally true of men (18,19,21).

Examining the Causes Obesity results from the consumption of more kilocalories than the body can expend. In the nonobese person, a mechanism seems to regulate food intake to maintain energy balance. The exact nature of this mechanism and the reason it fails to function properly in some people is not known, but in the obese individual its operation seems to be affected by a number of physiological, environmental, and psychological factors. Obesity is thus not a single disease, but the manifestation of one or more underlying problems.

The Hunger Mechanism People normally eat in response to the sensation of hunger, which appears to be controlled by a part of the brain called the **hypothalamus**. When the body is in need of food, one part of the hypothalamus sends signals to the stomach, causing the feeling we call "hunger." After food has been consumed, a different part of the hypothalamus depresses the sensation of hunger.

The question that intrigues nutritionists is this: How does the hypothalamus know the body needs food? Many theories have been proposed. One of the most widely known is the "glucostatic" theory suggested by Jean Mayer (16, pages 70–73; pages 560–577), which postulates that the hunger-control center responds to its own rate of glucose utilization. If plenty of glucose is available in the blood, the hunger-control center uses it rapidly and represses the hunger sensation. As glucose availability declines, utilization decreases and the hypothalamus triggers a hungry feeling.

Another factor that may influence the hunger-control center is the amount of fat stored in the body (the lipostatic theory) (16, pages 70–73; 23). A low level of fat may be interpreted as a need for food, and the hunger mechanism may be stimulated under these conditions. A high level of fat, which indicates excessive food intake, may repress the hunger mechanism. Some scientists believe that the level of fat stored in the body provides for long-term regulation of food intake, whereas the glucostatic mechanism controls intake on a short-term, hour-by-hour basis. Still other mechanisms may play a role: for example, certain compounds produced by nervous tissue, called **neurotransmitter substances**, are capable of activating the hunger and satiety mechanisms (24).

Physiological Influences What causes the mechanism to fail in the obese person is not clear. In some cases, the hunger-control mechanism may be "set" to maintain a greater body weight than in others. There is also evidence that metabolic abnormalities, such as differences in the utilization of carbohydrate and fat for energy, occur in some obese people. They may use these nutrients more efficiently than the nonobese, losing less of their energy value as heat and trapping more as ATP. They therefore require less carbohydrate and fat to make a given amount of energy (ATP) available to the body and divert relatively more of a meal to storage as fat (25). This may account for the commonsense observation that two people can consume the same amount of food, but one will be obese and the other thin. In some, such a situation may arise from hypothyroidism; in others, the cause is not clear.

Obesity may be determined in part by heredity; obese parents have a 73 percent chance of producing an obese child. If only one parent is obese, the odds drop to about 40 percent. If both parents are lean, there is only a

9 percent chance they will produce an obese child (26). In some studies, as many as 80 percent of the obese subjects had one or both parents who were obese (16, page 173). A relationship between obesity in parents and in their children also was found in the Ten-State Survey (18). However, can the fact that obesity "runs in the family" be caused by environmental factors rather than heredity? Studies of twins and of parents and their children indicate that genetic factors may predispose an individual toward obesity, but the extent of their influence and the mechanism by which they work remain to be discovered (22, pages 721–740).

One environmental factor, feeding patterns in infancy, may cause physiological changes leading to obesity later in life (27). Some researchers believe that the excessive number of fat cells found in many obese people result from overfeeding in infancy. Once adulthood is reached, these fat cells are established and supposedly cannot be lost. Weight loss in adults only reduces the amount of fat in them, which then creates a drive to regain the lost fat. As a result, the person with an excess number of fat cells finds it very difficult to maintain a normal body weight. Other authorities disagree (28,29). Although the obese individual has excess numbers of fat-filled cells, there is no evidence indicating when they came into being. They may have existed at birth and only become visible later. Moreover, although obese infants and children *tend* to become fat adults (29,30), many do not (29,31). Only one-third of the obese adults in one study could trace their obesity back to childhood (30). Other research indicates that the number as well as the size of fat cells can be increased by overfeeding during adulthood as well as infancy.

Environmental Influences A variety of environmental factors may influence the body's ability to control its own weight, and they seem to do so by overcoming the influence of the hunger-control center in some way. Attitudes toward food developed during infancy and childhood may play a greater role in determining obesity later in life than changes in fat-cell number (29). Some studies show that the obese respond to external cues, such as the taste, appearance, or smell of food, apparently ignoring the signals generated by their internal regulatory system (33). In one experiment, obese subjects drank more of a vanilla milkshake than nonobese subjects when the milkshake tasted good, but consumed less than the nonobese when the milkshake had been laced with quinine. Obese people also have been shown to eat more than the nonobese in response to the time of day (belief that it was lunchtime or dinnertime) and to the sight of food. However, several recent studies have failed to confirm these observations (32). Although not all studies agree (36), some also have found that the obese eat faster, take fewer bites, chew less, and finish a meal sooner than the nonobese (34,35). Thus the obese may respond more to the external cues and desire for oral gratification than to internal feelings of hunger. Parents sometimes encourage this type of behavior by making their children eat all the food given to them and by using food as a reward for good behavior.

Psychological Influences Eating to satisfy needs other than hunger forms the basis for the psychological influences on food intake. Many people overeat as a response to or compensation for frustration, tension, anxiety, and other emotional stresses (14,37,38). For some, these stresses are the usual pressures of everyday life, and the person simply needs to find another means of adjusting to them. In others, overeating reflects deep emotional conflicts, and treatment may require intensive psychotherapy. In either case, the individual again ignores internal cues. Bruch and others believe that psychological influences are among the most important in governing food intake and that most cases of obesity that cannot be traced to a specific physiological disorder have psychological origins (14).

Physical Activity Levels Rate of energy expenditure also plays a part in controlling body weight. Some studies show that the obese do not consume any more food than the nonobese, which suggests that lack of physical activity may be another factor in obesity. Both basal metabolic rate and physical activity decrease with age, so the reduced expenditure of calories can result in a gradual weight gain unless intake is adjusted. Americans' increasingly sedentary lifestyle reduces the need for energy, yet food is easily available and can be consumed in large quantities. Studies of overweight children indicate that the obese may lack the inclination to engage in physical activity. Not only did obese individuals participate in fewer vigorous activities than the nonobese, but they moved much less than their thinner counterparts (39).

The influence of caloric expenditure on energy expenditure can be very subtle. A person may expend only 100 to 200 fewer kcal/day at age 50 than at age 20 or in going from a moderately active occupation to a more sedentary one. The effects of this positive energy balance, however, accumulate with time, producing striking changes in body fat after a period of months or years.

Examining the Results Obesity is associated with an increased risk of developing a variety of problems, and it may lead to premature death. Premature death rates among the obese run higher than among the nonobese (Table 5-2) (40), although the effects on mortality do not become significant until body weight reaches 30 percent above desirable or ideal weight. At this point there is a sharp increase in the premature death rate with increasing obesity (41). In addition, obesity has been associated with increased risk of developing high blood pressure, diseases of the heart and circulatory system, gall bladder disease, diabetes mellitus, respiratory difficulties, and complications during pregnancy and surgery (16, pages 215–243; 17). Obesity does not necessarily cause these disorders; it appears more to hasten their development or increase their impact on the body. In particular, although obesity increases the severity of certain traits that lead to heart disease, such as high blood pressure and diabetes mellitus, weight gain itself contributes only a small part to the total risk of developing a heart attack (17).

TABLE **5-2**

Effect of obesity on the death rate

AGE	Increase in Death Rate above that Expected for the Population, percent	
	MALE	FEMALE
All ages	50	47
20–29	80	34
30–39	69	52
40–49	52	50
50–64	31	38
Degree of Overweight		
Moderate obesity	42	42
Marked obesity	79	61

Source: D. B. Armstrong, L. I. Dublin, G. M. Wheatley, and H. H. Marks, "Obesity and Its Relation to Health and Disease," *J.A.M.A.* **147**:1007–1114, (1951). (Copyright 1951, American Medical Association. Used with permission.)

Despite the health advantages connected with losing weight, for most people the motivation to reduce seems to revolve around appearance—a desire for a flatter stomach, smaller thighs, and a trimmer waistline. This is not as silly as it might seem, because an obese body image is a negative one in the eyes of both the American public and obese people themselves.

An obese body image is a negative one in the eyes of the American public. **!**

The obese in America suffer a number of social, economic, and psychological disadvantages (15). In one experiment, both children and adults, when shown pictures of a child with no disability, a child with crutches and a left leg brace, a child in a wheelchair with covered legs, a child with a left hand missing, a child disfigured around the left side of the mouth, and an obese child, liked the obese child the least of all (42). Physical attractiveness was found to be the most important factor in dating behavior among college students (43), and obesity may reduce a person's chances of being hired or promoted in a job.

Given the social stigma that seems to be attached to obesity, it is no wonder that the obese frequently develop psychological problems. They often have a distorted body image, seeing themselves as grotesque and loathsome, and believe that others look at them with contempt and hostility (44). Adults who have been fat since childhood cannot relate to themselves as being thin when they lose weight (45). Monello and Mayer found that obese adolescent girls are obsessively aware of their condition and in many ways behave like a minority group (46). Obese individuals often feel excluded and excessively criticized because of their condition. Since emotional stress helps bring on overeating, these feelings may serve to perpetuate the problem.

ISSUE: DIETS AND DANGERS

The need for many people to lose weight and the great difficulty in doing so has provided a golden opportunity for some people to earn quick profits by playing on the desires and fears of an unwary public. The job is made easier by the American love of gimmicks, as well as the desire that lurks within everyone to obtain as much as possible while sacrificing as little as possible. Most diets and diet aids are expensive and nearly always do not provide lasting results. Some are even dangerous. There are, however, a number of methods for reducing weight that are safe and at least somewhat effective. Although they require discipline and commitment, they are the best means for achieving permanent weight loss. Before we look at how to lose weight safely, let us examine a number of current fad diets. ”

LOW-CARBOHYDRATE DIETS

The high-fat, high-protein, low-carbohydrate diet has been reincarnated several times as the Pennington diet (1953), the Air Force diet (1960), the "Calories Don't Count" diet (1961), the "Drinking Man's" diet (1964), the Stillman diet (1967), and most recently as the Atkins diet (1972). It involves keeping the body in a state of **ketosis**, in which abnormally large amounts of substances called **ketone bodies** are circulating in the blood (see Chapter 2). To accomplish this, carbohydrate intake must be restricted. Most low-carbohydrate diets limit intake to 50 to 60 g/day; the most extreme, the Atkins diet, recommends total abstinence from carbohydrate for the first week, with gradual additions of small amounts thereafter until a level just low enough to maintain ketosis is reached.

Proponents claim low-carbohydrate diets work better than conventional diets because they increase the body's breakdown of fat for energy. Atkins even suggests that there is a special fat-mobilizing hormone (FMH) that accelerates the process (47). In addition, when the ketone body level in the blood increases sufficiently, the excess is excreted in the urine. Since ketone bodies are incompletely utilized fat and contain 4.5 kcal/g, their excretion means that kilocalories are being lost from the body. The weight losses reported are impressive: Dr. Atkins claims up to 8 pounds can be lost in the first week, and he cites examples in which hundreds of pounds were lost without the feelings of deprivation experienced on other diets. The dieters supposedly ate as much as they wanted and still lost weight as long as they restricted carbohydrate intake according to instructions.

The American Medical Association and most nutritionists have criticized low-carbohydrate diets and the Atkins diet in particular (48). We can analyze the Atkins diet using the criteria presented in Focus 5-1:

FOCUS 5-1 EVALUATING A FAD DIET We cannot possibly examine all the diets and reducing aids that promise quick, easy results, but there are several criteria we can use to evaluate a weight-reduction program:

1. *Does it have any real advantages over existing or conventional diets?* Most fad diets have a gimmick, such as eating grapefruit or using liquid-protein supplements. Do these gimmicks work, or are they only a means of attracting attention to the diet?
2. *Is the diet easy to follow?* Fasting, for instance, produces a weight loss, but it requires a great deal of will power. Most people cannot keep it up for very long.
3. *Does the diet provide any long-term modification of eating habits that will allow the weight loss to be maintained after the diet is over?* Many diets, such as liquid-protein diets and fasting, and diet aids, such as drugs, can produce a weight loss. However, because eating behavior is not changed, the person usually regains the weight.
4. *Does the diet present any hazard to health?* Very restrictive diets may lead to malnutrition; others, such as liquid-protein diets, have caused injury and even death.
5. *How much does it cost?* Often the dieter is enticed into buying expensive equipment or overpriced "special" foods. Seldom are these items of any value.
6. *Does the diet promise quick results in return for little effort on the part of the dieter?* This is one of the hallmarks of a fad diet. Many of these claims simply are not true. Rapid weight losses observed on some diets, such as the low-carbohydrate diet, are because of loss of water.
7. *Are there any inconsistencies with established knowledge?* Examples include the assertion that carbohydrates rather than excess kilocalories are fattening and that grapefruit possesses some magical weight-reducing property.

1 *Advantages* Most studies indicate that a low-carbohydrate diet does not possess any inherent advantages over other diets (49,50). The dramatic weight loss experienced during the first week on the Atkins diet seems to be the result of salt and water loss from the body (51). To lose body fat, caloric intake *must* be lower than caloric expenditure, regardless of the composition of the diet. Thus any further weight reduction attained on a low-carbohydrate diet results from a deficiency of kilocalories, just like any other diet (52).

The claim that excretion of ketone bodies in the urine represents a significant loss of kilocalories is untrue. On this diet, ketone body losses amount to 0.5 to 10 g/day, a maximum of about 50 kcal/day (48). In addition, although a fat-mobilizing substance has been isolated from the urine of people deprived of carbohydrate, little is known about its activity in the body or of any role it may play in weight reduction (48,53).

2 *Ease of Adherence* Because the person can consume unlimited quantities of foods containing little or no carbohydrate, the diet appears to be relatively easy to keep to over the short term. However, no one would want to consume such small quantities of carbohydrate for long. In addition, some of the symptoms described under item 4, such as nausea, dehydration, and postural hypotension, might mean the diet could not be used long enough to accomplish its goal.

3 *Modification of Food Habits* Although the low-carbohydrate diet provides for modification of dietary patterns to maintain the weight loss, it is doubtful that a person would want to restrict carbohydrate intake for a lifetime, even if such restriction had any tangible benefits.

4 *Hazards to Health* The state of mild ketosis generated by a low-carbohydrate diet does not pose a serious hazard to health, except to a fetus. However, a number of other aspects of the diet give cause for concern (48). Low carbohydrate intake has been associated with complaints of fatigue within 2 to 3 days, as well as nausea and postural hypotension (a sudden fall in blood pressure when the person stands up from a reclining position). In addition, ingestion of large amounts of fat may raise the levels of fat and cholesterol in the blood, increasing the risk of heart disease. Elevated uric acid concentrations in the blood, which may aggravate gout, also have been observed in people on a low-carbohydrate diet. Restriction of carbohydrate increases the use of protein for energy and can cause a loss of lean tissue, such as muscle. The Food and Nutrition Board recommends an intake of at least 50 to 60 g/day of carbohydrate to prevent these problems (8).

5 *Cost* Foods containing carbohydrate tend to be less expensive than those containing large amounts of protein and fat (see Chapter 4). A low-carbohydrate diet could conceivably cost more than a conventional diet of equivalent nutritional value.

6 *Quick Results* One of the major attractions of the low-carbohydrate diet is the ability to eat unlimited amounts of certain types of food, while at the same time losing weight. However, carbohydrate contains fewer kilocalories per gram than fat (4 as compared with 9), so substituting fat for carbohydrate would seem to make the job of losing weight that much more difficult. Maintaining this diet for any length of time is not easy, and the promise of quick results is unwarranted.

7 *Inconsistencies with Established Knowledge* Many statements made by Dr. Atkins are untrue or at least highly controversial. He attempts to link **hypoglycemia** with obesity, which runs contrary to experimental evidence. In many obese people, insulin does not function properly, and they tend to be **hyperglycemic** rather than vice versa. Moreover, the link between high carbohydrate intake and an increased incidence of hypoglycemia and diabetes is highly controversial (see Chapter 2).

Low-carbohydrate diets provide no particular benefits that cannot be attained with other diets and carry certain potential health hazards. They are by no means the easy way to successful, permanent weight loss.

FASTING

Fasting is another widely used method of weight reduction. Fasts may last longer than 200 days and result in a weight loss of 150 pounds or more, depending on the initial body weight (16, page 334). However, several factors make this method undesirable for a general weight-reduction program. In the first place, the diet is difficult to follow, for obvious reasons. A number of physiological problems occur, including high blood uric acid levels (which may aggravate gout and precipitate kidney stones), fatigue and lassitude, ketosis, nausea, impaired mental and physical functioning, loss of body fluids, and postural hypotension (54,55). There is also an increase in nitrogen in the urine, which reflects the breakdown of body protein for energy (54). The fasting person thus loses lean as well as fatty tissue.

A fast longer than a day should not be undertaken except under the supervision of a physician. During long-term fasts, the person is usually hospitalized, both to remove access to food and to deal with any complications that may arise. Another serious drawback to fasting is that no permanent changes in food-consumption patterns occur, and people who fast often regain the lost weight within a year or two (56,57).

FOCUS 5-2 THE PROTEIN-SUPPLEMENTED FAST

In an effort to prevent the loss of lean tissue such as muscle while fasting, a number of researchers began feeding their patients protein, salts, and sometimes carbohydrate. In one regimen, the subjects were given a dietary supplement containing 45 grams of protein (180 kilocalories), 30 grams of glucose (120 kilocalories), and potassium. Weight loss was high, and the breakdown of lean body tissue was reduced. Unfortunately, the success of this diet, which is still experimental, brought publicity, a book, and then commercial products (61). The protein supplements are sold in liquid, powder, and tablet form at high prices, with the claim that a fast supplemented with these products will change body chemistry and bring about weight loss.

Evidence is accumulating that these diets are very hazardous (62,63). By the middle of 1978, the Food and Drug Administration had received reports of over 45 people who died and 100 more who became ill while on very low-calorie protein diets. Symptoms included nausea, vomiting, diarrhea (with the liquid products), constipation (with the dry products), faintness, muscle cramps, and weakness. The deaths resulted from rapid and uncoordinated heart contractions. In addition, the diet is expensive and does not bring about any long-term changes in food-consumption patterns: the lost weight will be regained after a period of time. The diet therefore poses a distinct health hazard without any tangible long-term benefits for the individual and should not be used.

OTHER INEFFECTIVE OR HAZARDOUS METHODS

Many easy weight-loss methods have been advocated over the years. Some are simply ridiculous, ineffective, and overpriced; others pose real hazards to health. For example, certain foods, such as grapefruit, have been reputed to possess the ability to induce weight loss, although no food is known to be effective in this way.

Appetite depressants, ranging from preparations that contain sugar to drugs such as amphetamines, also have been used in weight control. The sugar preparations act by increasing blood sugar concentrations, thereby depressing the appetite at meal time. Although harmless, they are greatly overpriced; a piece of candy will have the same effect. Drugs such as amphetamines carry the risk of addiction and psychological changes and can be obtained legally only by a physician's prescription. Because of their side effects, many are no longer used in appetite control (16, pages 369–380).

Diuretics are another class of drugs sometimes recommended for weight loss. They act by stimulating urination and thus lead to loss of body water rather than fat. To maintain fluid balance, the body must replace the water, so that any weight loss is temporary. These drugs are not without their hazards too, because prolonged use can result in excessive potassium excretion from the body. Steam baths, sauna baths, and plastic clothing worn while exercising produce a loss in weight by increasing the loss of body water through sweating. As with diuretics, the effects are temporary.

Hormones also have been used in the treatment of obesity. Because of their stimulatory effect on energy expenditure, physicians have been prescribing thyroid hormones for several decades. However, a number of side effects, such as increased breakdown of body protein and heart problems, accompany the use of these hormones, and the weight is usually regained after the therapy is discontinued (16, pages 381–390). Thyroid preparations also depress the body's ability to synthesize its own hormones. Since this depression is slow to reverse, the body's production of thyroid hormones will be lower after the therapy is over, contributing to the regaining of weight. Another hormone of questionable benefit is human chorionic gonadotropin (HCG), which is found in the urine of pregnant women. Some researchers have found HCG to be beneficial in controlling appetite in patients on a 500-kilocalorie diet (58). Other studies show that injections of HCG are of no benefit in achieving weight loss, and the diet used with it can produce malnutrition (16, pages 391–394; 59).

The only way to lose body fat is to reduce caloric intake below expenditure. !

Probably one of the most widely advertised weight-control methods is spot reducing, in which the individual attempts to lose fat from one part of the body but not another by means of massage, sauna belts, or a wide variety of exercise machines. None of these methods has been shown to be effective (16, pages 391–394).

Losing Weight Safely

The only way a person can lose body fat is to reduce caloric intake below expenditure. Any diet that works conforms to this rule. The aim of a sound weight-loss program is to achieve the desired state of negative energy balance in a safe, pleasant, and effective manner and to initiate changes in attitude, habits, and lifestyle that enable the dieter to maintain a lower body weight long after the original reducing diet has ended.

DESIGNING AN EFFECTIVE PROGRAM

The first step is to establish a reasonable goal. By comparing an individual's weight with the ideal or desirable weight on a height-weight table

(Ready Reference 9), an estimate of the number of pounds he or she needs to lose can be obtained. For example, the charts indicate that Joe, who is 5 feet 11 inches tall with a medium frame and weighs 200 pounds, needs to lose from 35 to 50 pounds to attain his ideal weight of 150 to 165 pounds.

Next, the person should determine the extent to which the energy-balance equation must be altered to attain the desired weight loss. Nutritionists recommended trying to lose no more than 2 lb/week. Since 1 pound of fat represents roughly 3500 kilocalories, caloric expenditure must exceed intake by 7000 kcal/week or 1000 kcal/day. At this rate it will take Joe between 17 and 25 weeks to achieve his goal. This seems like a long time, but it avoids drastic restrictions in food intake that may be difficult to tolerate for a prolonged period.

The required change in the energy-balance equation may be accomplished by decreasing caloric intake, increasing caloric expenditure, or both (Figure 5-11). Suppose Joe, using one of the methods outlined earlier in this chapter, found that he expends about 2800 kcal/day. By keeping track of his food intake, he determined that he consumes about 3000

FIGURE 5-11 *How Joe Calculated His Energy Needs to Lose Weight.* By reducing intake, increasing expenditure, or both, Joe's energy expenditure must exceed energy intake by 1000 kilocalories per day to lose 2 pounds of weight per week.

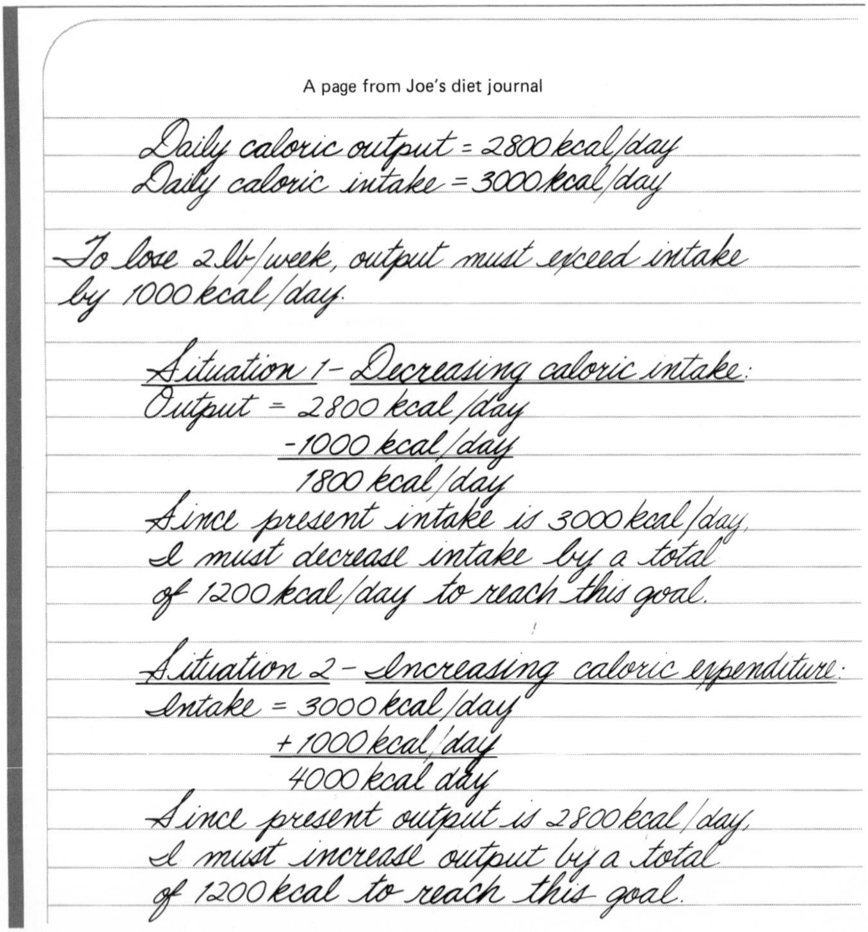

A page from Joe's diet journal

Daily caloric output = 2800 kcal/day
Daily caloric intake = 3000 kcal/day

To lose 2 lb/week, output must exceed intake by 1000 kcal/day.

Situation 1 – Decreasing caloric intake:
Output = 2800 kcal/day
-1000 kcal/day
1800 kcal/day
Since present intake is 3000 kcal/day, I must decrease intake by a total of 1200 kcal/day to reach this goal.

Situation 2 – Increasing caloric expenditure:
Intake = 3000 kcal/day
+1000 kcal/day
4000 kcal/day
Since present output is 2800 kcal/day, I must increase output by a total of 1200 kcal to reach this goal.

kcal/day. To attain his objective, Joe must lower caloric intake to 1000 kilocalories *below his present 2800 kcal/day output,* a total reduction in caloric intake of 1200 kilocalories, or he must raise his caloric expenditure to 1000 kilocalories *above his present 3000 kcal/day intake,* a total increase in output of 1200 kilocalories. This will result in a daily intake of 1800 kilocalories *or* an expenditure of 4000 kilocalories, depending on which method is used.

Joe decided to use a combination of the two methods. He raised his daily energy expenditure 400 kilocalories by walking more and taking up swimming, and at the same time he decreased his caloric intake by 800 kcal/day. He is now consuming 2200 kcal/day and expending 3200 kcal/day, thereby attaining the 1000 kcal/day difference necessary to reach his weight-loss goal. Any combination of increase in expenditure and decrease in intake can be used, as long as the difference is maintained.

After levels of caloric intake and expenditure have been decided upon, the weight-reduction program should be set up in a pleasant and practical way. One good technique is to reduce portion sizes throughout the diet rather than eliminate all foods high in kilocalories. In this way the dieter may still enjoy the taste of favorite foods, and retaining a variety will ensure an adequate intake of vitamins and minerals. A second technique is to substitute low-calorie foods. For example, skim milk, which contains 90 kcal/cup, can be substituted for whole milk, which contains 160 kcal/cup. Lean meats, poultry without the skin, fish (especially when baked rather than fried), macaroni products, and bean dishes using little fat provide good substitutes for cuts of meat high in fat (Table 5-3). It is important not to eliminate fat entirely, because it contributes to the satiety value of a meal. Retaining some fat may delay the onset of hunger before the next meal.

It may be desirable to reduce the intake of some foods greatly or eliminate them altogether. Joe might avoid putting sugar on breakfast cereal, in coffee and tea, or on fruit (sugar contains 40 kcal/tablespoon). Vinegar,

TABLE **5-3**

Some low-calorie substitutes for high-calorie foods

HIGH-CALORIE FOOD	kcal/100 g	LOW-CALORIE SUBSTITUTE	kcal/100 g
Whole milk	66	Skim milk	36
Beef (sirloin steak, separable fat removed)	207	Fish:	
		Fried haddock	165
		Tunafish (in water)	127
Beef (sirloin steak)	207	Chicken (white meat only)	166
Hamburger (lean, cooked)	219	Soybeans (cooked)	118
Tuna fish (in oil, drained)	197	Tuna fish (in water)	127

Source: B. K. Watt, and A. L. Merrill, *The Composition of Foods—Raw, Processed, Prepared,* Agriculture Handbook No. 8, USDA, Washington, 1963.

lemon juice, or spices can be substituted for butter or margarine on vegetables (butter and margarine contain 100 kcal/tablespoon). The use of butter and margarine on bread and potatoes should be curtailed. Because alcohol contains 7.0 kcal/g, reducing its consumption can significantly decrease caloric intake (12 oz of beer contains 150 kcal; 3 1/2 oz of wine has 140 kcal; and 1 1/2 oz of 80 proof whiskey contains 100 kcal).

Increasing the fiber content of the diet is another way to reduce caloric intake (see Chapter 2) (60). Fiber is the nondigestible component of food. It provides bulk, but has virtually no energy value. Including foods high in fiber may increase the diet's satiety value without contributing kilocalories. It also requires greater time and effort to chew and digest high-fiber foods, giving the satiety center time to be activated before too much food is consumed. Examples of foods high in fiber are whole-grain products, bran, most vegetables, and many fruits. Many of these foods also contain valuable vitamins and minerals.

The objective of a sound weight-loss diet, then, is not to cut food intake drastically; the person must be able to use the diet comfortably for a long period of time. Much of the trauma of a restrictive diet can be avoided, and the dieter has a better chance of developing consumption patterns that he or she can continue to use to maintain weight after the desired reduction has been achieved. Such a diet also allows the individual to eat many of the same foods the family consumes. This prevents disruption of family eating patterns and may bring support rather than criticism from other family members.

It is vital for the dieter not to become discouraged or feel guilty should he or she occasionally succumb to temptation and overeat. A successful diet is not made or broken by a single day's activity. However, many people, even with the best of intentions, cannot follow any diet for very long without some kind of outside help. For this reason, a number of psychological techniques have been developed to aid the dieter.

PSYCHOLOGICAL AIDS

Behavior modification techniques are based on evidence that many obese people ignore internal appetite controls in favor of environmental and psychological cues. The tendency of the obese to overeat in response to the taste, sight, and smell of food is one example; overeating to compensate for emotional stress is another. Because such behavior appears to be a "learned" response to a given set of environmental conditions, the aim of the therapist is to create a new environment that will elicit new responses with regard to food (32). To accomplish this, eating behavior is studied in relation to its immediate causes and consequences. Analysis of the causes provides insights into the stimuli that promote eating, while analysis of the consequences reveals rewards or punishments that can be used to increase desired behavior and reduce undesired behavior.

Most behavior therapy for weight control consists of these four steps:

1 *Describing Eating Behavior* The obese individual is required to keep careful records of what foods are eaten, how much is consumed, when and

where eating takes place, and the environmental situation associated with the eating. These records provide clues concerning what prompts a person to overeat, and they also increase the individual's awareness of her or his eating behavior.

2 *Controlling the Stimuli Associated with Eating* Next, the therapist tries to decrease the effects of the stimuli that initiate the eating behavior. For example, many people eat constantly while watching television. Such techniques as limiting the availability of food in the house, reducing the amount of small change that is carried (to discourage use of vending machines), eating low-kilocalorie foods when resistance breaks down, and confining all eating to one place (usually the kitchen) are used.

3 *Controlling the Act of Eating* These techniques include decreasing the speed of eating by counting mouthfuls of food or placing utensils back on the table after each bite, not pairing eating with other activities such as watching television or reading, and savoring food, thereby eating less and enjoying it more. The goal is to make eating a pure experience and remove it from association with various environmental stimuli.

4 *Modifying the Consequences of Eating* This involves a system of formal awards and punishments for desirable and undesirable behavior. Rewards may include money, relief from chores, or anything else the person values. An unpleasant consequence for undesirable behavior, such as having to pay money, serves as punishment. The rewards and punishment can be tailored to the person's particular situation.

Although behavioral techniques for weight control are fairly new, they are more effective than other methods of weight reduction and seem to hold great promise for the future.

Another psychological technique is the use of peer support. This is the basis for such groups as Weight Watchers, Inc., and Take Off Pounds Sensibly (TOPS). Dieters attend weekly meetings to evaluate progress, support success, and educate themselves. Although dropout rates are high, the evidence so far indicates that these groups can be successful.

PHYSICAL ACTIVITY

Reducing food intake is only one means of controlling body weight. The person also can increase physical activity, which not only increases caloric expenditure, but has many other benefits as well. Climbing stairs instead of using an elevator, walking instead of riding, and performing tasks by hand instead of with a machine are all familiar ways of increasing physical activity. Each dieter also should engage in some vigorous physical activity, such as running, swimming, bicycling, and skating, on a regular basis. Although the impact on body weight may not seem to be great in proportion to the exertion (one must swim for almost $1/2$ hour to burn the 260 kilocalories in an ice cream soda), the continued expenditure of 200 to 300 kcal/day adds up to a considerable weight loss over a long period of time. In addition, strenuous exercise is beneficial to the heart, lungs, and circulatory system, as well as contributing to a general feeling of well-being.

Study Guide

SUMMARY

1. All life processes require energy. Total energy expenditure, which is expressed in terms of kilocalories, can be divided into three categories:
   a. *Basal Metabolic Rate* (*BMR*)—the energy needed to maintain life processes when at rest and in the fasting state.
   b. *Physical Activity*
   c. *Specific Dynamic Action* (*SDA*)—the energy required to digest, absorb, and utilize food.
2. Since many factors, including body composition, sex, hormones, age, climate, body temperature, pregnancy, and starvation, influence BMR and each individual engages in a different amount of physical activity, energy requirements vary from person to person.
3. Energy expenditure must be balanced by the intake of food; protein, carbohydrate, fat, and alcohol provide kilocalories.
4. Energy expenditure can be determined by measuring the heat given off or the oxygen consumed by the body. The caloric content of a food can be found by similar methods.
5. If energy intake equals energy output, the person is in a state of energy balance and will maintain the same body weight.
6. If energy intake is less than energy expenditure, the person is in a state of negative energy balance and will lose weight. Moderate or severe underweight can impair growth and development, increase risk of infection, reduce work capacity, and impair the function of certain organs.
7. Underweight may be a secondary complication of many disorders, including parasitic infections, infectious diseases, metabolic disorders, and diseases of the digestive tract. Treating the primary cause is an important part of treating underweight.
8. Regular rest, exercise, and a nutritious diet high in kilocalories will facilitate weight gain.
9. Anorexia nervosa, a psychological disorder found mainly among adolescent women, is a cause of underweight that is becoming more common in our society. Psychotherapy and dietary intervention can improve or cure the condition in most cases.
10. If intake exceeds output, the person is in a state of positive energy balance and will gain weight.
11. Normally, food intake is controlled by a physiological mechanism in the hypothalamus of the brain, but a number of physiological, environmental, and psychological factors appear to modify or overcome this mechanism in obese individuals.
12. Obesity can be a hazard to health, increasing the risk of premature death and aggravating or precipitating high blood pressure, diseases of the heart and circulatory system, gall bladder disease, respiratory problems, diabetes mellitus, and complications during pregnancy and surgery. Obesity is also a social disadvantage.
13. Many fad diets and diet aids promise quick results in return for little input on the part of the dieter. Some are expensive; others, including low-carbohydrate diets, fasting, protein-supplemented fasts, and the use of drugs and hormones, can be dangerous.
14. To lose weight safely, the dieter must first establish a reasonable goal of 1 to 2 lb/week. Caloric intake should be reduced in a pleasant manner that also will lead to permanent changes in eating habits. Behavior modification and weight-loss groups, such as Weight Watchers, Inc., can be helpful. Physical activity is an important addition to any weight-loss regimen.

VOCABULARY

anorexia nervosa
basal metabolic rate (BMR)
bomb calorimeter
calorie
energy balance
heat of combustion
hyperglycemia
hyperthyroidism
hypoglycemia
hypothalamus
hypothyroidism
ketone bodies
ketosis
kilocalorie (kcal)
kilojoule (kJ)
negative energy balance
neurotransmitter substances
obesity
overweight
physiological fuel value
positive energy balance
specific dynamic action (SDA)
thyroxine
underweight

STUDY QUESTIONS

1. List as many body processes as you can that contribute to the basal metabolic rate.
2. List as many factors as you can that would make one person's *total energy expenditure* different from another's.
3. Why can oxygen consumption be used as a method for measuring BMR (i.e., why is oxygen consumption a measure of energy output)?
4. Why is the energy available to the body from a food lower than its energy content as determined by bomb calorimetry?
5. List four causes of underweight. What can an underweight individual do to gain weight?
6. Explain briefly how the hypothalamus controls food intake. What physiological, environmental, and psychological factors can modify the hunger-control mechanism in an obese person and how does each work?
7. For each of the following methods of inducing a weight loss, tell whether it works better than a conventional, nutritionally balanced regimen, whether it provides any long-term modification of eating habits, and whether it poses any hazards to health:
   a. Low-carbohydrate diets
   b. Fasting
   c. Protein-supplemented fast (liquid-protein diet)
   d. Amphetamines
   e. Diuretics
   f. Thyroid hormone
   g. Human chorionic gonadotropin (HCG)
   h. Spot reducing devices
8. Explain how physical activity can contribute to maintaining a desirable body weight.
9. What is the basic principle behind the use of behavioral modification in the treatment of obesity? Describe the four steps that are used.

SELF-TEST

Multiple choice: Choose the one best answer.

1. In a 1-hour period, John's body released enough energy to raise the temperature of 100 kilograms of water 0.75°C. His basal metabolic rate in kilocalories is
   a. 750
   b. 1.3
   c. 75
   d. 13
2. Testing Marsha's basal metabolic rate by indirect calorimetry showed it was about 40 percent above normal. You would expect the results of a protein-bound iodine (PBI) test to be
   a. Above normal
   b. Below normal
   c. Approximately normal
3. One cup of whole milk contains 9 grams of protein, 9 grams of fat, and 12 grams of carbohydrate. It provides the body with

a. 165 kcal
b. 180 kcal
c. 210 kcal
d. 225 kcal

4. Which of the following is a *practical* suggestion for helping a person gain weight?
a. Substitute skim milk for whole milk.
b. Do not exercise at all.
c. Avoid salad dressings containing oil, mayonnaise, or yogurt.
d. Add powdered milk to milk products.

5. Studies show that
a. Obese people always consume more food than nonobese people.
b. Obese people almost always have obese parents.
c. Obese children tend to engage in less physical activity than nonobese children.
d. Obese infants almost always become obese adults.

6. Obese people with a body weight greater than 30 percent above ideal have a greater risk of
a. Diabetes mellitus
b. High blood pressure
c. Heart disease
d. All of the above

7. The rapid weight loss experienced during the first week on a low-carbohydrate diet is because of
a. Accelerated energy expenditure
b. Loss of ketone bodies in the urine
c. Increased mobilization of body fat
d. Water loss

8. Which of the following is true regarding a protein-supplement fast (liquid-protein diet)?
a. It alters eating behavior so the weight loss can be maintained.
b. It is safe.
c. It prevents the breakdown of body protein that occurs during a total fast.
d. It is enjoyable and can be adhered to for a long period of time.

9. Which of the following situations will allow Roger to lose 20 pounds in 20 weeks?
a. Intake of 2100 and expenditure of 2600 kcal/day
b. Intake of 2600 and expenditure of 2100 kcal/day
c. Intake of 1500 and expenditure of 2500 kcal/day
d. Intake of 2500 and expenditure of 1500 kcal/day

10. Which of the following would be most helpful for losing weight (see Ready Reference 5)?
a. Running 20 minutes twice a week
b. Riding a bicycle to work 5 days a week (10-minute round trip)
c. Swimming 20 minutes twice a week
d. Taking a brisk walk (about 4 mi/h) for 20 minutes every day

True-False

1. The high specific dynamic action of protein is of practical use in losing weight.
2. The amount of energy contained in a food is greater than the amount it provides for the body.
3. A person can be overweight but not obese.
4. A low-carbohydrate diet providing 1500 kcal is more effective in inducing a permanent weight loss than a conventional diet containing 1500 kcal.
5. Because it is easier to consume kilocalories than to expend them through physical activity, exercise is of no value in losing weight.

SUGGESTED ACTIVITIES

1. Determine your energy balance:
a. Estimate your daily caloric intake. Instructions are given in Activity 10-1 as part of the diet-record exercise.
b. Using either of the methods given in this chapter, determine your energy expenditure for 1 day.
c. Compare your energy intake and expenditure. According to your calculations, should you be gaining or losing weight? Differences of 100 to 200 kilocalories between intake and expenditure are not significant because of

inaccuracies in estimating duration of physical activity and portion sizes.

2. Set up a diet and exercise program that would allow you to lose 2 lb/week.
   a. Determine a caloric intake and expenditure schedule that will create the necessary energy deficit. Do not choose a diet providing less than 1200 kcal/day.
   b. For one day, plan a diet and select some physical activities that will meet the specifications calculated in part 2*a*.
3. Using Ready Reference 1 or food labels, make a list of low-calorie foods that can be substituted for foods high in kilocalories.
4. Using the seven criteria presented in this chapter and appropriate references, including the Consumer Guide *Rating the Diets,* analyze any new diets that have appeared in the last 2 years.
5. Collect advertisements promoting weight-reduction diets and devices. Analyze them using the seven criteria presented in this chapter.

FURTHER READING

1. For a comprehensive look at all aspects of obesity:

   Bray, G. A.: *Major Problems in Internal Medicine,* vol. 9: *The Obese Patient,* Saunders, Philadelphia, 1976.

2. A highly readable analysis of current weight-loss diets:

   Berland, T., and the editors of Consumer Guide: *Rating the Diets,* Signet, New York, 1979.

3. An example of a critique of a fad diet:

   Council on Foods and Nutrition (AMA: "A Critique of Low Carbohydrate Ketogenic Weight Reduction Regimens—A Review of *Dr. Atkins' Diet Revolution,*" *J.A.M.A.* **224**:1415–1419 (1973).

4. An account of what happens to the body during a fast:

   Young, V. R., and Scrimshaw, N. S.: "The Physiology of Starvation," *Sci. Am.* **225**: 14–21 (October 1971).

5. A guide to behavior modification techniques for the dieter:

   Stuart, R. B., and Davis, B.: *Slim Chance in a Fat World: Behavioral Control of Obesity,* Research Press, Champaign, Ill., 1977.

6. Accounts of the psychological aspects of obesity and anorexia nervosa:

   Bruch, H.: *Eating Disorders; Obesity, Anorexia Nervosa and the Person Within,* Basic Books, New York, 1973.

   Bruch, H.: *The Golden Cage—The Enigma of Anorexia Nervosa,* Harvard University Press, Cambridge, Mass., 1978.

7. An interesting description of some environmental influences on food intake:

   Schachter, S.: "Some Extraordinary Facts about Humans and Rats," *Am. Psychol.* **26**:129–144 (1971).

DIGESTION, ABSORPTION, AND METABOLISM

Americans seem to be particularly preoccupied with their digestive tracts. Many people, encouraged by advertising, believe that they must have a bowel movement every day, while others frequently complain of "heartburn" after eating certain foods or large meals. The image of a harried business executive nursing a chronic ulcer has almost become a caricature of upper-middle-class urban society. Every drugstore or supermarket contains a long row of shelves devoted to products designed to treat these problems. Some products, such as Alka-Seltzer, are almost institutions. In recent years, the type of food we eat has come into focus in relation to digestive problems; some people now claim that fiber can treat or even prevent many common disorders of the large intestine and rectum, including constipation, hemorrhoids, diverticulitis, and colon cancer.

The digestive tract is responsible for breaking down food and making its nutrients available to the body. That we can control what we put into it is probably a major reason we have so many problems with it and spend so much money trying to alter its functioning. Like other body systems, the digestive system is composed of tissues and organs that normally perform their roles in a balanced and coordinated manner. Let us look first at how the digestive tract normally operates and then at how its balance is disrupted in certain situations.

The Digestive System

Food in the digestive tract still lies outside the body proper. Nutrients cannot pass into the body without first being released from food. **Diges-**

tion mechanically and chemically breaks food down into a form that can cross into the body; the nutrients freed by this process are then **absorbed** from the digestive tract for transport to all tissues.

The digestive tract is like a 26-foot-long tube through the center of the body (Figure 6-1). In successive stages along its length it forms the mouth, pharynx, esophagus, stomach, small intestine, and large intestine. The structure of each organ is specialized to carry out a particular part of the digestive process. Other organs, such as the salivary glands, the liver, and the pancreas, are connected to the digestive tract by ducts. These organs secrete a variety of substances, including saliva, bile, and enzymes, which are needed for digestion. The body coordinates the activity of the digestive tract by means of hormones and a system of nerves that regulate both the movement of food and the secretion of substances needed to digest it. By looking at what happens when we eat a meal, we can examine the roles each organ plays and the way the entire process is coordinated.

FROM THE MOUTH TO THE STOMACH

Both the mechanical and chemical breakdown of food begins in the mouth. The teeth grind food into progressively smaller particles and, with the help of the tongue and cheek muscles, mix it with saliva. Fluid and mucus in saliva moisten and lubricate the food. An enzyme, **salivary**

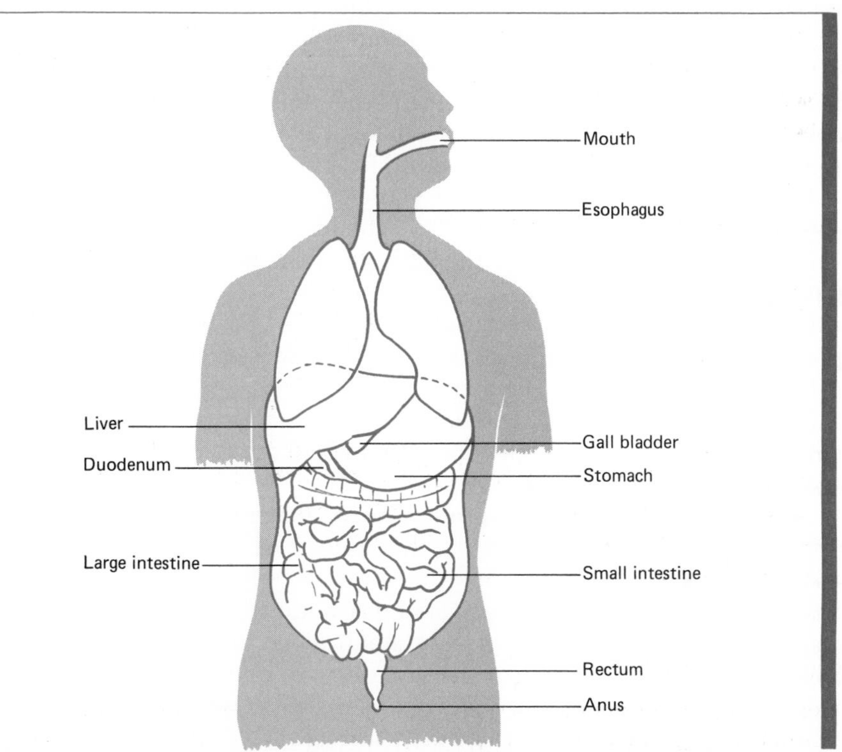

FIGURE 6-1
The digestive system.

amylase, or ptyalin, begins the chemical breakdown of starch. If you drop a small amount of saliva into pudding, you can see the action of salivary amylase. The pudding becomes increasingly watery as the starch in it is digested. As a result of the activity in the mouth, food is formed into a soft mass called a **bolus**, which can then be maneuvered to the back of the mouth for swallowing.

As the bolus moves into the back of the mouth, the muscles of the pharynx initiate the swallowing reflex. The tongue pushes upward against the roof of the mouth so that the food cannot be expelled; muscles in the pharynx and the roof of the mouth block the nose passage; the vocal cords and a small flap of cartilage called the **epiglottis** prevent food from going down the windpipe; and the pharynx muscles contract to force food into the esophagus. This muscular tube conveys food into the stomach. The presence of the bolus stimulates a small segment of the esophagus just behind the bolus to constrict, and as the constriction moves down the esophagus, it pushes the food in front of it in much the same way that squeezing the bottom end of a tube of toothpaste forces the contents toward the open end (Figure 6-2). This process, called **peristalsis**, occurs throughout the digestive tract and keeps the digesting food moving.

In the stomach, the digestive tract assumes the shape of a muscular pouch that can stretch to accommodate large amounts of food. The presence of food in the stomach stimulates glands in its walls to secrete a hormone, **gastrin**, into the blood. Gastrin causes other cells in the stomach to produce **gastric juice**, which contains hydrochloric acid, digestive enzymes, and mucus. Secretion of gastric juice also can be induced by nerve activity: anticipation of food or the presence of food in the stomach causes the brain to send electric impulses to the stomach, where they stimulate production of the juice. Gastric juice is then mixed with the food by contractions of the stomach wall. A ring of muscle, the *cardiac sphincter,* prevents these contractions from pushing food back into the esophagus.

The mixture of food and gastric juice is called **chyme**. In the stomach, chyme is extremely acidic. This condition, which deactivates salivary amylase, is essential for the activity of the major stomach enzyme, **pepsin**. Pepsin begins the digestion of proteins by breaking them into smaller fragments called **polypeptides**. Since pepsin would digest the proteins in the cells that make it, it must be synthesized in an inactive form called **pepsinogen**. Pepsinogen is converted to pepsin by hydrochloric acid after secretion into the stomach. Pepsin then activates other pepsinogen molecules. Mucus protects the wall of the stomach from the action of the acid and pepsin.

The partial breakdown of proteins is the major digestive activity that occurs in the stomach; only small amounts of carbohydrate and fat are digested there. Of greater importance for the whole process is the fact that the stomach can hold relatively large quantities of food. By contrast, the small intestine can accept only small amounts of chyme at a time. The chyme is held in the stomach by a ring of muscle called the *pyloric sphincter,* which opens only when a peristaltic wave pushes a small amount of the partially digested food through it.

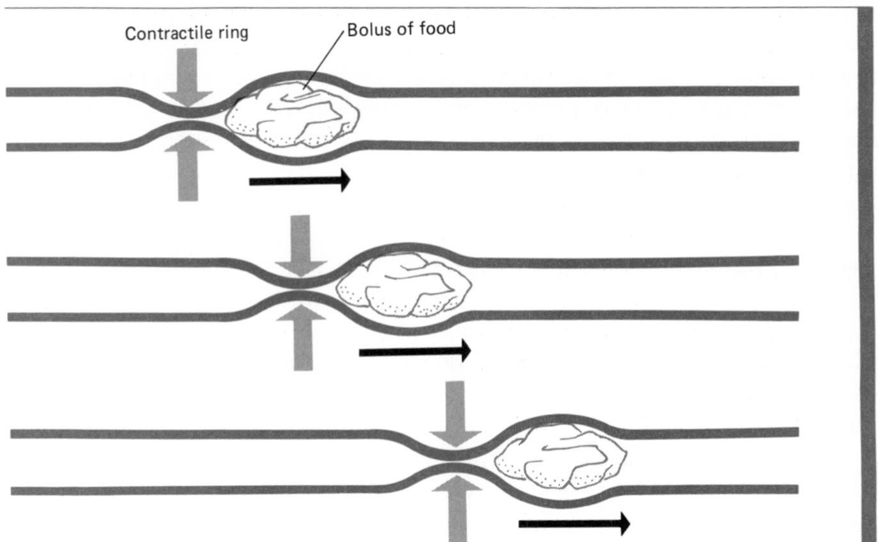

FIGURE 6-2
Peristalsis. The segment of the digestive tract just behind the food contracts, and as the contraction moves it pushes the food ahead of it.

THE SMALL INTESTINE

The stomach gradually releases its contents into the small intestine, the major site of digestion and absorption. The small intestine is specialized to carry out these activities efficiently. Its great length provides a great deal of time for digestion and absorption to take place. The inner wall of the small intestine has large folds covered with millions of smaller protrusions called **villi**. The villi themselves have an irregular contour; hundreds of **microvilli** extend from each cell on their surface. This extensive folding increases the absorptive area of the small intestine by 600 times over what it would be if it were a smooth cylinder (Figure 6-3).

As chyme passes from the stomach into the intestine, it stimulates the intestinal wall to secrete two hormones that promote digestion into the blood. **Secretin** causes the pancreas to secrete a juice rich in bicarbonate, which neutralizes the chyme, protecting the intestinal wall from attack by the acid and providing a favorable environment for digestive enzymes. At the same time, **cholecystokinin-pancreozymin (CCK-PZ)** stimulates the pancreas to secrete an enzyme-rich juice and the gall bladder to release bile. The pancreatic juice and bile, mixed into the chyme by the contractions of the intestinal wall, function directly in the digestion of carbohydrate, protein, and fat (Figure 6-4).

Carbohydrate Digestion Because salivary amylase is made inactive by stomach acid, carbohydrates reach the intestine nearly intact. In the small intestine, **pancreatic amylase** breaks down starch and dextrins into maltose, while enzymes located in the microvilli of the intestinal wall digest the disaccharides into their component monosaccharides: **maltase** splits maltose into two glucose molecules; **sucrase** breaks down sucrose into glucose and fructose; and **lactase** digests lactose into glucose and galactose. The monosaccharide subunits are then readily absorbed into the bloodstream. Absence or low activity of lactase can cause varying degrees of milk intolerance (see Chapter 4).

Protein Digestion Much of the protein digestion in the intestine is carried out by two pancreatic enzymes, **trypsin** and **chymotrypsin**. Like pepsin, they must be synthesized in inactive forms, **trypsinogen** and **chymotrypsinogen**, so they will not digest proteins in the cells that make them. **Enterokinase**, an enzyme synthesized by the intestine, activates trypsin, which in turn activates chymotrypsin. Both enzymes then continue the breakdown of proteins and large polypeptides into free amino acids, dipeptides (two amino acids joined together), and tripeptides (three amino acids joined together). Dipeptides and tripeptides undergo further digestion by the enzymes in the microvilli, and the free amino acids thereby released are absorbed into the bloodstream.

Fat Digestion Fat in chyme tends to clump together into large globules that present a relatively small surface area on which digestive enzymes can act. To make the digestion of fat more efficient, the globules must first be dispersed or emulsified into much smaller droplets. The emulsification process is carried out by **bile acids**, which are synthesized from cholesterol in the liver, stored in the gall bladder, and released into the intestine with the bile. Like the mono- and diglycerides described in Chapter 3, bile acids have a charged part that faces the water and an uncharged part that faces the fat. When the contractions of the intestinal wall break the fat globules into small droplets, the bile acids prevent them from clumping back together again. This increases the surface area on which the digestive enzyme can work.

1. It is important to have a bowel movement every day.
2. Regular use of laxatives is a safe and effective way to prevent or treat constipation.
3. Regular use of antacids is a safe and effective way to treat heartburn and acid indigestion.

FACT OR FANTASY

Fat is digested in the intestine by **pancreatic lipase** to produce a monoglyceride and two fatty acids. Once these are absorbed into the cells in the intestinal wall, they are reassembled into triglycerides. Along with a small amount of cholesterol, phospholipid, and fat-soluble vitamins, the

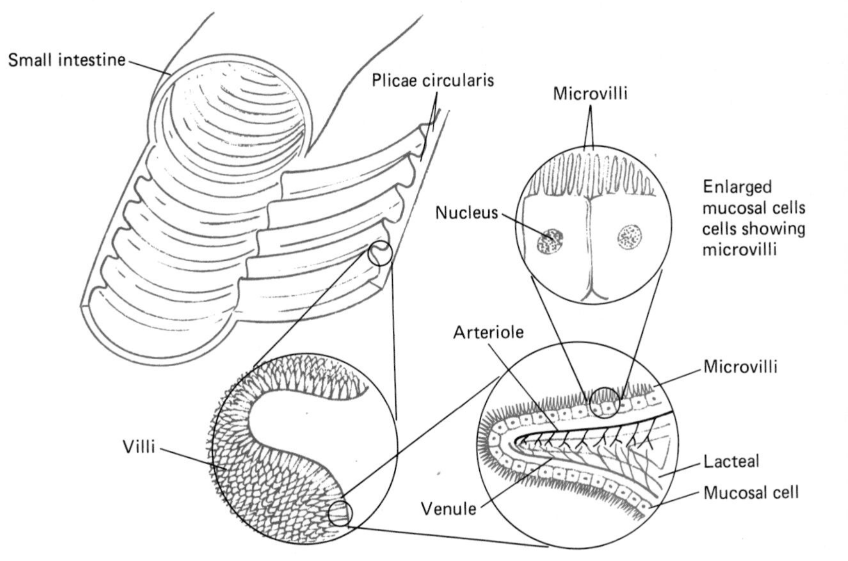

FIGURE 6-3
Folding Increases the Surface Area of the Small Intestine. The inner lining of the small intestine is extensively folded; microvilli protrude from the villi, which in turn protrude from large folds called plicae circulares. This increases the surface area to 600 times that of a smooth cylinder of the same diameter.

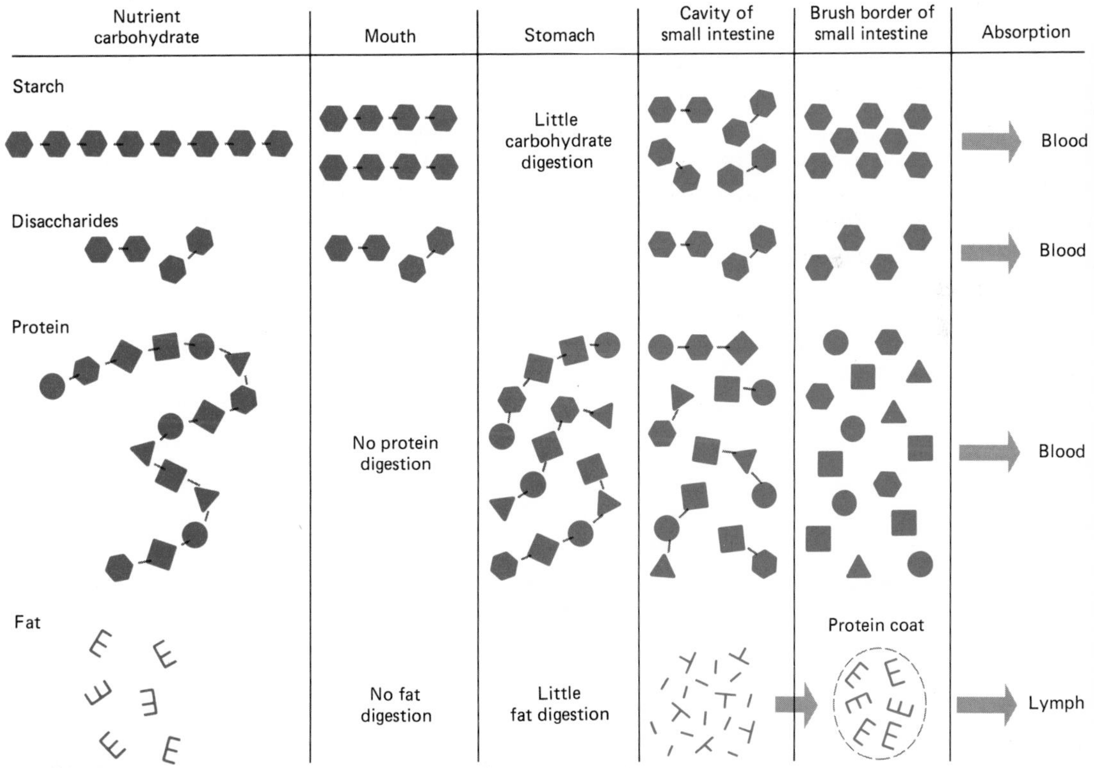

Nutrient carbohydrate	Mouth	Stomach	Cavity of small intestine	Brush border of small intestine	Absorption
Starch		Little carbohydrate digestion			Blood
Disaccharides					Blood
Protein	No protein digestion				Blood
Fat	No fat digestion	Little fat digestion		Protein coat	Lymph

FIGURE 6-4
Digestion and Absorption of the Energy Nutrients. Some starch is digested in the mouth, and some protein is digested in the stomach. But most digestion of the energy nutrients is carried out in the small intestine. Water soluble substances, such as monosaccharide sugars and amino acids are then absorbed into the blood. Lipids are combined with protein and are released into the lymph, which carries them into the bloodstream.

triglyceride is then combined with protein to form a lipoprotein that is released into the lymph system.

Absorption in the Small Intestine Most of the nutrients released by digestion are absorbed in the intestine. Water-soluble substances, such as amino acids, the monosaccharide sugars, water-soluble vitamins, and minerals, are absorbed directly into the bloodstream, which carries them first to the liver and then throughout the body. Triglycerides, cholesterol, phospholipids, and the fat-soluble vitamins are combined with protein to suspend them in water and are then released into the lymph system. Eventually the lymph system transports these substances into the blood for distribution throughout the body.

THE LARGE INTESTINE (COLON)

The large intestine, or colon, which is shorter in length but greater in diameter than the small intestine, prepares what is left of the chyme for elimination from the body. As the chyme moves through the large intestine, water is absorbed, leaving the **feces**, which are then excreted from the body via the anus. Many kinds of bacteria inhabit the large intestine; they break down small amounts of otherwise undigestible fiber, ferment sugars, and decompose proteins that were not digested and absorbed by the small intestine. Certain bacteria also synthesize vitamin K and B vitamins. Although it is not clear how much of the B vitamins can be absorbed from the large intestine, as much as half the human requirement for vitamin K may be of bacterial origin (1).

The discussion so far has described the way the digestive process normally works. Many influences, including diet, nervous stress, infection, and exposure to toxic chemicals, can upset normal functioning and lead to disease. Unlike most other diseases, however, those of the digestive tract are treated by modifying the diet as well as with medicine.

Common Digestive Tract Disorders (2,3)

HEARTBURN

At one time or another, most of us have experienced the burning sensation in our upper chest and throat called *heartburn*. It generally occurs within an hour after eating, especially if we have had a large meal. In most people, heartburn is caused by regurgitation of acidic stomach contents into the esophagus. Normally, the cardiac sphincter prevents this from happening, but if enough pressure builds up in the stomach, chyme can be forced into the esophagus. In addition, high-fat meals, alcohol, certain spices (such as peppermint), and cigarette smoking cause the sphincter to relax, making reflux more likely. Coffee, orange juice, and tomato juice will irritate an esophagus that is already inflamed. To prevent heartburn, smaller, more frequent meals are advised. High-protein, low-fat meals and avoiding foods that cause irritation also will help. For many people, loss of excess body weight is accompanied by a reduction in the occurrence of heartburn (4).

FOCUS 6-1 DRUGS AND THE DIGESTIVE TRACT (6,7)

A significant part of the advertising aimed at adults today promotes nonprescription drugs. Without consulting a physician, we can choose from thousands of products designed to relieve headaches, heartburn, indigestion, muscle pain, and arthritis, stimulate or inhibit defecation, soothe itches and burns, and alleviate symptoms of colds and flu. Although some of these drugs have a place in medical practice, they are often abused when they are self-prescribed. Several of the most widely used, including antacids, laxatives, and aspirin, are of concern in nutrition because they affect the digestive tract.

Antacids, which neutralize stomach acid, are frequently prescribed by physicians to treat peptic ulcer. They also are promoted in the media for relief of heartburn and indigestion resulting from consuming too much food too quickly, and over $140 million worth are sold in the United States annually (7). Although there is little harm in taking antacids occasionally, it should not become a habit. The problems that accompany overindulgence in food are more properly treated by eating less, eating more slowly, and relaxing during the meal. In addition, long-term use of some commonly available antacids can produce undesirable side effects. For example, if taken with milk or some other source of calcium, chronic use of sodium bicarbonate can lead to milk-alkali syndrome, in which body pH becomes markedly alkaline, blood calcium levels rise, kidney function is disrupted, and the risk of kidney stones is increased. Calcium carbonate, alone or in combination with milk, has a similar effect. Sodium bicarbonate and calcium carbonate also stimulate the stomach to secrete more acid, a phenomenon known as "acid rebound." Another commonly used antacid, magnesium hydroxide, or milk of magnesia, has a laxative as well as antacid effect. Aluminum hydroxide binds phosphate and fluoride, preventing their absorption from the digestive tract. Long-term use of aluminum hydroxide has resulted in depletion of body phosphate, bone pains, fragile bones, muscle weakness, and fatigue (8). Many antacids also contain large amounts of sodium, which is thought to increase the risk of high blood pressure.

Preoccupation with regular bowel habits has induced many people to use **laxatives** and **cathartics** to stimulate a bowel movement. In 1975, Americans spent about $130 million on these drugs (7). However, there are few legitimate medical reasons for using laxatives, and physicians seldom prescribe them (9). Most cases of constipation not requiring medical attention are better treated by increasing the amount of fiber in the diet, exercising regularly, and establishing proper habits. Laxatives should not be given to treat lower bowel pain, because the pain may be owing to appendicitis and the laxative will aggravate the problem. These drugs also have undesirable side effects. Many people become psychologically dependent on them. Chronic abuse causes diarrhea, abdominal discomfort, depletion of body potassium, and dehydration. In some cases, the natural motility of the large intestine becomes impaired, worsening the constipation (10).

Aspirin has been widely used for decades to relieve pain, reduce fever, and treat rheumatoid arthritis. However, chronic use leads to erosion of the inner wall of the stomach and bleeding into the digestive tract. The drug thus can aggravate peptic ulcers (11).

PEPTIC ULCER

The complaint "My ulcer is bothering me!" is a common one in our society, particularly among people subjected to a great deal of nervous stress. Although we may laugh at the television shows in which the harried corporate executive's ulcer acts up every time something goes wrong, the condition can be a painful and sometimes dangerous one. A **peptic ulcer** is a localized erosion or loss of the tissue lining the inner wall of the digestive tract (Figure 6-5). It appears that hydrochloric acid and pepsin in gastric juice literally eat away the digestive tract lining; in severe cases, it may wear a hole completely through the wall. Ulcers occur most frequently in the first few centimeters of the small intestine, but they are also common in the stomach. In rare instances, they develop in the esophagus.

Anything that increases the production of gastric juice or reduces the activity of the mechanisms that normally protect the digestive tract lining can lead to an ulcer. The problem occurs more often in people with tension-filled and anxiety-producing occupations, probably because nervous stress increases the stomach's secretion of hydrochloric acid. Intestinal ulcers develop more frequently in people with blood type O than in those with type A, B, or AB, but the reason for this has not been determined. Hereditary factors and certain hormonal disturbances also increase the risk of ulcers, while aspirin, alcohol, and caffeine aggravate them.

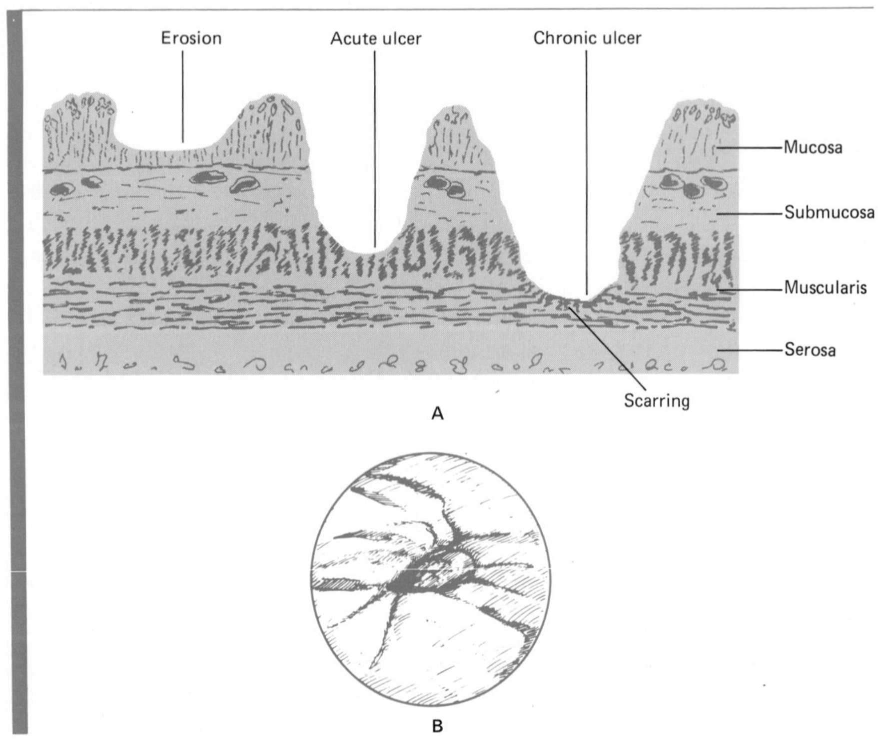

FIGURE 6-5 **A** Cross-sectional view of an ulcer. **B** An ulcer as it would appear in the stomach wall. (Adapted from S. Price and L. Wilson, *Pathophysiology: Clinical Concepts of Disease Processes,* McGraw-Hill, New York (1978), pages 212 and 215 respectively).

Many types of dietary modification have been tried in the treatment of peptic ulcers, but few have had any effect. There is no conclusive evidence that coarse or spicy foods aggravate the problem or that a soft or a bland diet will speed healing. High-fat diets are sometimes used, but these may raise blood cholesterol levels and increase the risk of heart disease. Because many foods are alkaline and can help neutralize stomach acid, frequent meals (five to six small meals per day) are usually advised. Foods containing caffeine or alcohol should be avoided, and antacids are usually taken to neutralize stomach acid. Although recurrences of ulcers are common, the condition generally responds to intelligent medical care.

DIARRHEA

Diarrhea refers to the rapid movement of feces through the large intestine, resulting in the passage of loose, watery stools. It is really a symptom rather than a disease in itself. In some cases, the wall of the large intestine is irritated by a bacterial or viral infection or by a chemical in the diet. It responds by secreting fluids and increasing contractions to flush out the irritant. Nervous tension can do the same thing.

Because little fluid can be absorbed and large quantities may be secreted, diarrhea can lead to a considerable loss of water, sodium, potassium, chloride, and bicarbonate. If it is severe or prolonged, the absorption of other nutrients, such as proteins, fat, vitamins, and minerals, may be impaired. So prompt treatment, as well as finding and treating the primary cause, is important. Drugs may be used to slow the movement of feces through the large intestine. In some cases, water, minerals, and energy may be given orally or intravenously. Warm, salty broths and weak teas can help replace fluid and salt losses, while thin, cooked cereals can provide some energy.

CONSTIPATION

Constipation, the reverse of diarrhea, results from the slow movement of feces through the large intestine. Because there is plenty of time for water to be absorbed, the individual passes hard, dry stools. Although constipation can be caused by blockage of the bowel, it usually results from a failure of the lower colon and rectum to respond to the presence of feces. This can happen because of major changes in one's pattern of living (such as travel, going to school, or changing jobs), as a result of illness or

It is not necessary to have a bowel movement every day.

emotional stress, or simply by resisting the urge to defecate. Some authorities believe constipation results from a diet low in fiber.

The goal of treating constipation is to restore normal bowel habits. It is not necessary to have a bowel movement every day. Because the bowel habits of healthy people vary widely, frequency should be dictated by what is comfortable for the individual. Laxatives are not recommended unless prescribed by a physician, because the individual may begin to depend on them to stimulate a bowel movement.

DIVERTICULAR DISEASE

Diverticular disease is characterized by the formation of pouches called *diverticula* in the wall of the large intestine (Figure 6-6). These are believed to result from high pressure within the colon generated by the slow or difficult movement of feces. Sometimes feces accumulate in the pouches and produce an infection called *diverticulitis*. Because it improves the movement of feces through the large intestine, increasing the fiber content of the diet is a treatment often used for diverticular disease.

HEMORRHOIDS

Hemorrhoids are swollen veins in the rectum. They may occur during pregnancy, with chronic liver disease, from straining at stool, and from sudden increases in intraabdominal pressure. Most respond to sitz baths, suppositories, and medication; sometimes, however, surgery is necessary.

FLATULENCE

Excessive production of gas by the large intestine can be uncomfortable as well as socially undesirable. The source of the gas varies from person to person. In some, most of it is swallowed air, but in others, bacteria produce large quantities of hydrogen, methane, and carbon dioxide by

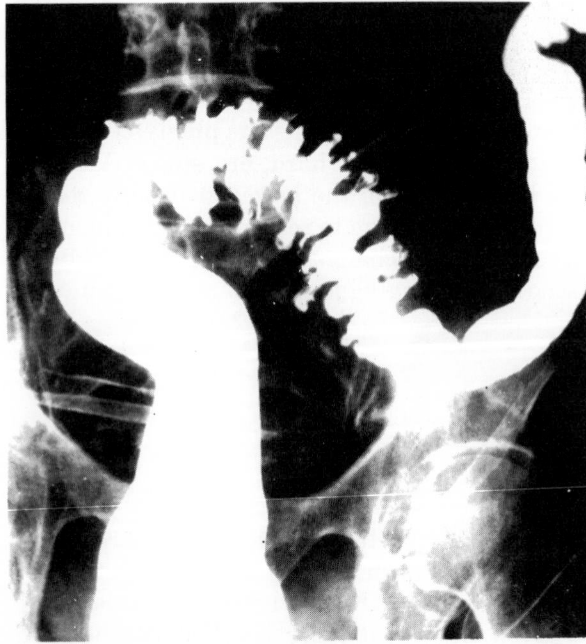

FIGURE 6-6
Diverticula in the colon. (From G. W. Thurn et al., *Harrison's Principles of Internal Medicine* McGraw-Hill, New York (1979), page 1421.)

metabolizing undigested and unabsorbed food (5). Particularly well-known offenders are raffinose and stachyose, which are indigestible sugars found in legumes such as soybeans. Much intestinal gas is normally absorbed by the intestines, but nervous anxiety and other conditions can speed up peristalsis so that these gases are expelled instead.

Metabolism: The Molecular Level

In Chapters 2 through 5, we looked at the nutritional importance of carbohydrate, fat, and protein. We discussed in a general way how the body uses them for energy and, in the case of protein, for the synthesis of many vital components. Life, however, has a chemical basis: carbohydrate, fat, and protein **metabolism** can be described at the molecular level as well. What happens to these substances after they have been digested, absorbed, and transported to every cell? How are the biochemical processes coordinated to meet body needs at any given moment? This section provides an overview of metabolism of the energy nutrients. A more detailed discussion can be found in the biochemistry text listed at the end of the chapter.

FOLLOWING THE METABOLIC MAP

Figure 6-7 shows the major biochemical pathways involved in the breakdown (**catabolism**), synthesis (**anabolism**), and interconversion of the energy nutrients. It can be thought of as a metabolic map. Each process requires a substance to follow a particular route. There are several points

FIGURE 6-7
A metabolic map of carbohydrate, fat, and protein metabolism.

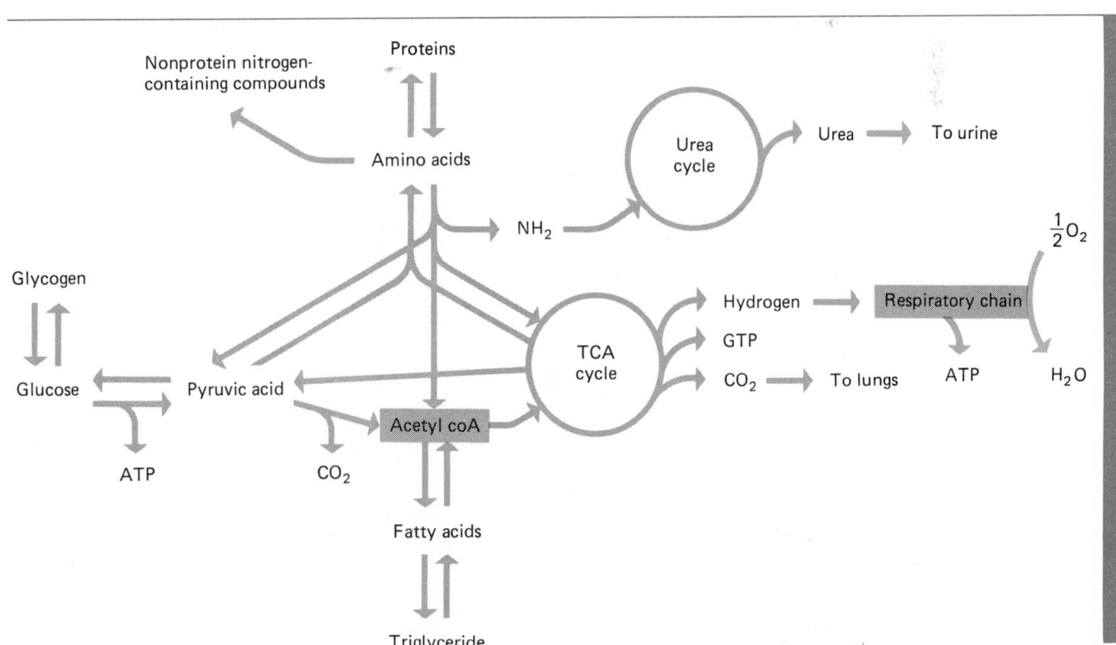

at which pathways intersect, as well as points at which they follow the same route or run in opposite directions. How does a substance follow the proper route? Much like traffic lights, **control enzymes** regulate the flow of metabolic traffic. Under a given set of body conditions, certain control enzymes are active and others are inactive, causing material to travel through particular pathways. When conditions change, some control enzymes become inactivated and others are stimulated so that the flow of material is diverted into other routes.

The Catabolic Pathways The biochemical pathways that catabolize carbohydrate, fat, and protein have the common goal of breaking these substances down into carbon dioxide, water, and, in the case of protein, urea. Breakdown of these nutrients occurs in a series of small steps that allows some of their energy to be trapped in ATP, a form the body can use. The process begins differently for each nutrient, but in each case, the pathway leads to the formation of the same **intermediate compounds**: acetyl coenzyme A (acetyl CoA) or certain components of the tricarboxylic acid (TCA) cycle (Figure 6-7). Glucose breakdown produces pyruvic acid, which is then converted into acetyl CoA; fatty acids directly yield acetyl CoA. Amino acid catabolism begins with the removal of the amino ($-NH_2$) group, which ultimately is converted to urea for excretion in the urine. The remainder of **ketogenic amino acids** produces acetyl CoA; **glucogenic amino acids** yield pyruvic acid or one of the TCA cycle compounds.

Acetyl CoA is further broken down by being incorporated into the TCA cycle. This sequence of reactions results in the release of carbon dioxide and hydrogen. Carbon dioxide passes into the blood and is carried to the lungs, where it is released. The hydrogen atoms enter the **respiratory chain**, a series of enzymes that extract their energy to form ATP, which is used to carry out a variety of processes. Ultimately, the hydrogen is combined with oxygen to form water, which the body can use or excrete.

The Anabolic Pathways The human body can synthesize glucose, fat, and 13 of the amino acids from intermediate compounds. Glucose is synthesized from pyruvic acid and TCA cycle compounds derived from the glucogenic amino acids. Lactic acid, which is produced during strenuous physical activity, and glycerol released by triglyceride breakdown also serve as substrates. The glucose may be released into the blood or stored as glycogen until needed. Fatty acids are assembled from acetyl CoA molecules joining together and then combining with glycerol to form triglycerides, the body's major form of stored energy. The 13 amino acids can be formed from other amino acids or by adding an amino group to pyruvic acid or to certain TCA cycle compounds. These amino acids can then be assembled into proteins if the other nine essential amino acids are available from the diet.

Interconversions of the Energy Nutrients The processes described so far are also the means by which carbohydrate, fat, and protein are interconverted: the intermediate compounds produced by one pathway serve as raw materials for others (Figure 6-8). For example, acetyl CoA generated by glucose and ketogenic amino acid catabolism can be used to synthesize fat. In addition, pyruvic acid and TCA cycle compounds produced by the breakdown of glucose can be converted into amino acids, and amino acids can be converted into these intermediates for use in glucose synthesis. One interconversion that cannot take place, however, is the synthesis of glucose from fatty acids. The product of fatty acid catabolism, acetyl CoA, cannot be converted back to pyruvic acid; instead, it enters the TCA cycle, where it is completely broken down.

COORDINATION OF THE METABOLIC PATHWAYS

In the cell, the biochemical pathways operate as part of a coordinated system: control enzymes activate and deactivate each pathway at the appropriate times. The control enzymes themselves are regulated by certain hormones and by the presence or absence of the substrates and products of the pathways. Insulin and glucagon are among the most important hormones that influence control enzymes. Insulin stimulates pathway control enzymes that catabolize glucose and synthesize glycogen, fat, and protein; glucagon generally has the opposite effect. There are several mechanisms by which substrates and products influence control enzymes, but the results are similar: the presence of large amounts of a raw material tends to stimulate a pathway, while the presence of large amounts of product tends to inhibit it. This is an example of negative feedback control of body processes.

We can see how this works by tracing the metabolism of the energy nutrients before and shortly after a meal. When a person has not eaten in several hours, the concentration of glucose and free amino acids in the

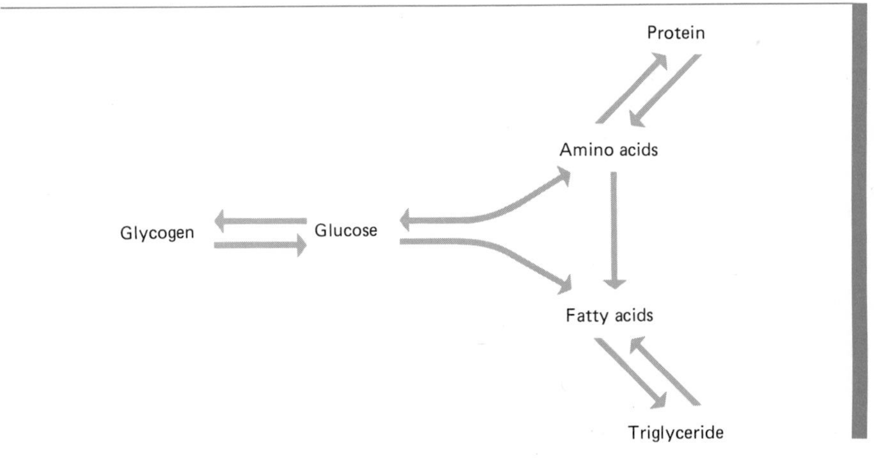

FIGURE 6-8
Interconversions of the Energy Nutrients. Carbohydrate and protein are interconvertible, and both can be converted to fat. But fat cannot be converted into protein or carbohydrate.

blood and tissues is relatively low. In addition, relatively little triglyceride is found in the blood; most of it is in storage in adipose tissue. The pancreas is secreting glucagon at this time. As a result of this metabolic situation, the control enzymes of glycogen breakdown, glucose synthesis, fat catabolism, and protein breakdown are stimulated. Those of glycogen synthesis, glucose catabolism, fat synthesis, and protein synthesis are inhibited. Fat catabolism provides the fatty acids used by most body tissues for energy, while glycogen breakdown and glucose synthesis supply glucose for tissues that cannot use fat, such as the nervous system. Protein breakdown is accelerated to provide amino acids for glucose synthesis.

Now suppose this individual eats a fairly large meal. Glucose, fat, and amino acids flow into the blood, and the pancreas secretes insulin in response. The control enzymes of glucose catabolism and glycogen, fat, and protein synthesis are stimulated; those of glucose synthesis, glycogen breakdown, fat catabolism, and protein breakdown are inhibited. As a result, glucose is removed from the blood and catabolized for energy, stored as glycogen, or converted to fat. Fat is removed from the blood and stored in adipose tissue, while amino acids are used for protein synthesis. Any excess amino acids are converted to fat or used for energy. Within a couple of hours, the energy nutrients in the meal are metabolized and the situation returns to what it was before the meal.

Study Guide

SUMMARY

1. The process of digestion mechanically and chemically breaks down food, releasing the nutrients, which are absorbed into the body.
2. The structure of each organ in the digestive tract is specialized to carry out its role in this process. The muscles and teeth in the mouth chew the food and mix it with saliva, and the muscles of the pharynx and esophagus convey the food into the stomach. The stomach is a muscular pouch that stores food, gradually releasing it into the small intestine. Because of its great length and large surface area, the small intestine is ideally suited for its role as the major site of digestion and absorption. The large intestine completes the process by converting the undigested and unabsorbed food into feces and eliminating them from the body.
3. Carbohydrate digestion begins in the mouth with the partial breakdown of starch by salivary amylase (ptyalin). Carbohydrate digestion is interrupted by the acidic conditions of the stomach, but is completed by the action of sucrase, lactase, maltase, and pancreatic amylase in the small intestine. The resulting monosaccharides are absorbed into the blood.
4. The stomach enzyme pepsin begins the digestion of protein. Trypsin, chymotrypsin, and other enzymes finish the process in the small intestine, and the amino acids released are absorbed into the blood. Because they would digest proteins in the cells that make them, pepsin, trypsin, and chymotrypsin are synthesized in an inactive form. They are activated once they have been secreted into the digestive tract.
5. Most fat digestion occurs in the small intestine. Bile acids increase the efficiency of digestion by dispersing the fat, and pancreatic lipase breaks down the triglycerides into monoglycerides and free fatty acids. In the intestinal wall, the monoglycerides and fatty acids are reassembled into triglycerides and are packaged with cholesterol, phospholipids, and fat-soluble vitamins inside a protein coat. The resulting lipoproteins are released into the lymph system, which eventually carries them into the bloodstream.
6. Disorders of the digestive tract are relatively common in the United States and other affluent nations. They include peptic ulcers, diarrhea, constipation, diverticular disease, hemorrhoids, and flatulence.
7. Antacids, laxatives, and aspirin are the most widely used nonprescription drugs that affect the digestive tract. Although each has legitimate medical uses, many people abuse them, resulting in undesirable side effects.
8. At the molecular level, the metabolism of the energy nutrients is carried out by biochemical pathways. The flow of material through these pathways is regulated by control enzymes so that the appropriate ones are active or inactive depending on the body's needs.

VOCABULARY

absorption
anabolism
antacids
bile acids
bolus
catabolism
cholecystokinin-pancreozymin (CCK-PZ)
chyme
chymotrypsin
chymotrypsinogen
constipation
control enzymes
diarrhea
digestion
diverticular disease
enterokinase

epiglottis
feces
gastric juice
gastrin
glucogenic amino acids
hemorrhoids
intermediate compounds
ketogenic amino acids
lactase
laxatives and cathartics
maltase
metabolism
microvilli
pancreatic amylase
pancreatic lipase
pepsin
pepsinogen
peptic ulcer
peristalsis
polypeptides
respiratory chain
salivary amylase (ptyalin)
secretin
sucrase
trypsin
trypsinogen
villi

STUDY QUESTIONS

1. Briefly describe the function of each of the following parts of the digestive system:
   a. Mouth
   b. Salivary glands
   c. Pharynx
   d. Esophagus
   e. Stomach
   f. Liver
   g. Pancreas
   h. Small intestine
   i. Large intestine
2. How are the structures of the stomach and small intestine specialized to carry out their respective functions?
3. List the enzymes that digest carbohydrate, fat, and protein. What are the end products of the digestion of each of these nutrients? Which are absorbed directly into the blood and which are first absorbed into the lymph system?
4. For each of the following hormones, give the stimulus that causes it to be secreted, organ(s) on which the hormone acts, and the result of the hormone's activity.
   a. Gastrin
   b. Secretin
   c. Cholecystokinin-pancreozymin (CCK-PZ)
5. List the probable causes of the following disorders of the digestive tract. What are some ways these disorders are treated?
   a. Heartburn
   b. Peptic ulcer
   c. Diarrhea
   d. Constipation
   e. Diverticular disease
   f. Hemorrhoids
   g. Flatulence
6. What adverse effects accompany the long-term use of each of the following?
   a. Antacids
   b. Laxatives
   c. Aspirin
7. Which of the following pathways would be operating at or near full capacity within an hour or so after a large meal? Justify your answer.
   a. Glucose catabolism–TCA cycle–respiratory chain sequence
   b. Glycogen synthesis
   c. Glycogen breakdown
   d. Fat synthesis
   e. Fat breakdown
   f. Incorporation of amino acids into protein
   g. Protein breakdown

SELF-TEST

Multiple choice: Select the one best answer.

1. To prevent pepsin, trypsin, and chymotrypsin from breaking down proteins in digestive tract tissues, these enzymes are
   a. Synthesized outside of cells
   b. Activated by coenzymes in food
   c. Activated when mixed with other digestive secretions
   d. Activated by food proteins
2. The role of the villi and microvilli in the small intestine is to
   a. Increase the surface area for nutrient absorption
   b. Slow the movement of food

c. Produce all the enzymes needed for digestion
d. Secrete water into the chyme

3. Which of the following carbohydrates must be further digested before it can be absorbed into the blood?
a. Galactose c. Glucose
b. Sucrose d. Fructose

4. An inability to release bile into the small intestine would impair digestion and absorption of
a. Carbohydrate c. Fat
b. Protein d. Minerals

5. Before they are released into the lymph system, lipids are combined with
a. Protein c. Bile acids
b. Carbohydrate d. Secretin

6. Severe or prolonged diarrhea could lead to
a. Diverticulitis c. Heartburn
b. Hemorrhoids d. Dehydration

7. Products of the complete catabolism of carbohydrate, fat, and protein include
a. Carbon dioxide
b. Water
c. ATP
d. All of the above

8. Which of the following cannot be used by the body to synthesize glucose?
a. Glucogenic amino acids c. Fatty acids
b. Glycerol d. Lactic acid

9. Which of the following occurs when blood insulin levels are high?
a. Glycogen breakdown
b. Fat synthesis
c. Glucose synthesis
d. Protein breakdown

10. In the fasting state, which of the following occurs?
a. Glycogen breakdown
b. Protein synthesis
c. Fat synthesis
d. Glycogen synthesis

True-False

1. Most of the digestion of carbohydrate, fat, and protein occurs in the stomach.
2. Proteins are broken down into their component amino acids before they are released into the bloodstream.
3. The best treatment for heartburn and indigestion is to take an antacid.
4. It is necessary to have a bowel movement every day.
5. Most cases of constipation do not require the use of laxatives.

FURTHER READING

1. Any physiology textbook will enhance your understanding of digestive tract function. One good example is

Guyton, A. C.: *Physiology of the Human Body,* 5th ed., Saunders, Philadelphia, 1979.

2. Diet-therapy textbooks contain discussion of dietary treatments for digestive tract disorders. One good example is

Krause, M. V., and Mahan, L. K.: *Food, Nutrition and Diet Therapy,* 6th ed., Saunders, Philadelphia, 1979.

3. A good overview of nonprescription drugs of all types:

American Pharmaceutical Association: *Handbook of Nonprescription Drugs,* 5th ed., American Pharmaceutical Association, Washington, 1977.

4. One of the many good biochemistry books available:

Lehninger, A.: *Biochemistry: The Molecular Basis of All Structure and Function,* 2d ed., Worth, New York, 1975.

PART 3

THE SUPPORTING NUTRIENTS

We have seen how the energy nutrients form a major part of the body's structure and carry out many important functions, as well as providing energy. However, like most complex and highly organized systems, the body requires other components, often in minute amounts, in order to operate. These are the vitamins and minerals, and they work closely with each other and with other substances, such as protein, to facilitate body processes. The magnitude of their effects often seems out of proportion to the body's requirements for them, and this has helped surround the vitamins and some of the minerals with a certain mystique. They have been widely promoted as a means of improving physical and mental performance, retarding the aging process, and achieving "superhealth."

What are these substances, and what can they really do for us? How much do we need? What is the truth behind all the claims made for them? In Chapters 7 and 8 we will look at these questions, as well as how the body's vitamin and mineral needs can be met by intelligent food choices. We also will look at another supporting element without which the body cannot function—water.

7

THE VITAMINS

The value of food in the prevention and treatment of certain diseases has been recognized for centuries. Night blindness, a symptom of vitamin A deficiency, was known to the ancient Egyptians and Greeks, and the Greek philosopher Hippocrates prescribed raw ox liver to treat the problem. During the winter of 1535–1536, Indians in Newfoundland showed explorer Jacques Cartier how to cure scurvy with a tea brewed from the bark and leaves of a spruce tree. In the mid-1700s, the British physician James Lind demonstrated that the juice of citrus fruits also could control scurvy. However, it was not until the early part of the twentieth century that the substances responsible for these cures were discovered and isolated. In 1914, the Polish-American biochemist Casimir Funk summarized the current knowledge about vitamins in his book *The Vitamines* (the word is a contraction of the phrase *vital amines;* the *e* was later dropped because not all vitamins are amines) and proposed that beriberi, pellagra, scurvy, and rickets were caused by deficiencies of these substances. In the following decades, other vitamins were discovered, and since then their "magical" properties have captured the imaginations of people throughout the world.

Nevertheless, vitamins are much misunderstood and frequently overrated. Vitamin supplements will not necessarily provide extra energy, clear up skin problems, improve sexual performance, and prevent or cure diseases such as the common cold, heart disease, and cancer. These problems, unlike scurvy or pellagra, are usually not the result of a vitamin deficiency. Ensuring an intake of vitamins that will maintain health requires an understanding of the relationship of these substances with the human body. How do the vitamins function? What amounts should be obtained in the diet each day, and how have scientists determined these requirements? What foods are the best sources of each vitamin? Is it possible to overdose on vitamins? Coupled with knowledge of appropriate experimental data, the answers to these questions will allow us to make intelligent evaluations of the claims for vitamins and aid us in making sound nutritional choices.

What Are Vitamins?

Vitamins have traditionally been defined as organic compounds required in small amounts in the diet for growth, maintenance, and reproduction. However, there is more to this simple definition than meets the eye. For example, the word *organic* refers to the fact that the vitamins contain carbon, and it is used here to distinguish them from the minerals. The definition also excludes proteins, carbohydrates, and lipids, since these substances are required in relatively large amounts (40 to 100 g/day or more), and the body's need for vitamins ranges from several micrograms to 60 mg/day.

Not all the compounds commonly called vitamins are always required in the diet. The body can synthesize niacin, vitamin A, and vitamin D if the appropriate raw materials (**provitamins**) and environmental conditions are provided. However, because the absence of the vitamin, its provitamin, and the appropriate environmental conditions leads to a distinct deficiency disease in each case, we include these substances among the vitamins. Sometimes a compound that is a vitamin for one organism may not be a vitamin for another. For example, most animals synthesize their own ascorbic acid. Humans, other primates, and guinea pigs do not; they must obtain it from the diet.

Today 13 vitamins are known to be required by human beings: vitamin A, vitamin D, vitamin E, vitamin K, thiamine, riboflavin, niacin, biotin, folacin, pantothenic acid, vitamin B_6, vitamin B_{12}, and vitamin C. Vitamin A was discovered independently by McCollum and Davis at the University of Wisconsin and Osborne and Mendel at the Connecticut Experiment Station in 1913. Subsequent discoveries were labeled B, C, D, and so on. After several years, it became apparent that vitamin B actually contained two factors, which were then called B_1 and B_2. Other vitamins were later grouped in the B complex because of their solubility in water and the similarity of their functions. Only two, vitamins B_6 and B_{12} are still given their B numbers in ordinary usage.

The vitamins are classified into two general groupings: fat-soluble and water-soluble. The fat-soluble vitamins (A, D, E, and K) dissolve only in fat or other organic solvents. A certain amount of fat is required in the diet to facilitate their absorption, and anything that interferes with fat absorption also retards the movement of these vitamins into the body. Because the body stores the fat-soluble vitamins in the liver and adipose tissue, they need not be obtained in the diet every day. The water-soluble vitamins, the B vitamins and vitamin C, may be lost from food that is soaked, boiled, or in other ways brought into contact with large amounts of water. The body does not store these vitamins and generally excretes much of any dietary excess in the urine. Therefore, sufficient quantities should be obtained in the diet nearly every day.

How Vitamins Work in the Body

In the most general sense, vitamins may be thought of as helpers in carrying out body processes. For example, although vitamins do not themselves provide energy, they help promote the processes by which protein, carbohydrate, and fat do. In the same way, vitamins participate in such diverse processes as cell division, eyesight, growth, wound healing, and blood clotting. In this section we will look at how each vitamin functions, paying special attention to how it plays this helping or facilitating role.

THE B VITAMINS

The B vitamins (thiamine, riboflavin, niacin, vitamin B_6, pantothenic acid, biotin, folacin, and vitamin B_{12}) facilitate the activity of many enzymes in the body (Figure 7-1). When these enzymes are synthesized in the ribosome of the cell, they are incomplete. In order to function, they must combine with a molecule called **coenzyme**, which in most cases is derived from one of the B vitamins (Table 7-1). The combination forms an active enzyme, which can then perform its function. For example, enzymes containing the thiamine coenzyme participate in several reactions that help break down glucose for energy. In another form, thiamine aids in the transmission of nerve impulses.

The combination of a riboflavin coenzyme with its enzyme is called a **flavoprotein**. Enzymes containing either of the riboflavin coenzymes participate in **oxidation-reduction reactions** in the body. Chemists define *oxidation* as the removal of an electron or a hydrogen atom from a

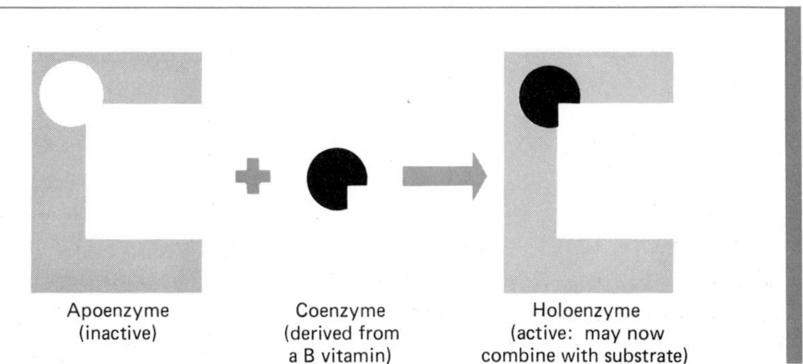

FIGURE 7-1
B Vitamins Facilitate the Activity of Some Enzymes. The vitamin is converted into a coenzyme, which combines with the enzyme molecule and activates it.

TABLE **7-1**

The coenzyme forms of the B vitamins

VITAMIN	COENZYME FORMS
Thiamine	Thiamine pyrophosphate (TPP)
Riboflavin	Flavin mononucleotide (FMN) Flavin adenine dinucleotide (FAD)
Niacin	Nicotinamide adenine dinucleotide (NAD) Nicotinamide adenine dinucleotide phosphate (NADP)
Vitamin B_6	Pyridoxal phosphate (PALP) Pyridoxamine phosphate (PAMP)
Pantothenic acid	Coenzyme A (CoA) Acyl carrier protein (ACP)
Biotin	None—vitamin attaches directly to enzyme
Folacin	Tetrahydrofolic acid (THF)
Vitamin B_{12}	Cobamide coenzymes

molecule; *reduction* is the gain of an electron or a hydrogen atom. Oxidation-reduction reactions involve the transfer of electrons or hydrogen from one molecule to another (Figure 7-2), and they are necessary to metabolize protein, carbohydrate, and fat for energy.

Niacin is made up of either of two substances, nicotinic acid or nicotinamide. Enzymes containing either of the niacin coenzymes function in certain oxidation-reduction reactions that facilitate the body's use of carbohydrate, fat, and protein for energy. The body can synthesize niacin from the essential amino acid tryptophan, which is found in sources of high-quality protein. About 60 milligrams of dietary tryptophan are equivalent to 1 milligram of niacin, and a diet containing sufficient high-quality protein may provide several hundred milligrams of tryptophan a day.

Pyridoxine, pyridoxal, and pyridoxamine are the three forms of vitamin B_6. The body converts them into a coenzyme that participates in the synthesis and breakdown of amino acids and their conversion into other

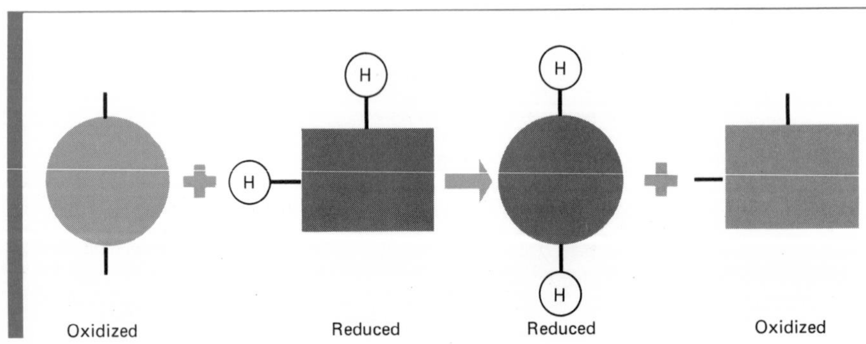

FIGURE 7-2 *Oxidation-Reduction Reactions.* The square containing two hydrogen atoms and their associated electrons is reduced. By transferring the hydrogen and electrons, it reduces the circle and itself becomes oxidized.

substances. In this capacity, vitamin B_6 is important for proper protein synthesis, the synthesis of heme (the iron-containing part of the hemoglobin molecule), some substances important in the functioning of the nervous system, such as serotonin, and other substances. The vitamin B_6 coenzyme also participates in other reactions, including one by which glucose is released from storage as glycogen (see Chapter 2) and another by which the essential fatty acid linoleic acid is converted into arachidonic acid (see Chapter 3).

Biotin combines directly with its enzymes, which catalyze **carboxylation** reactions, which involve the addition of carbon dioxide to a molecule. In this capacity, biotin is important in the synthesis of fatty acids, glucose, and nucleic acids.

Enzymes containing either of the pantothenic acid coenzymes participate in the transfer of certain molecules from one substance or another. For example, they will combine with acetyl groups generated by the breakdown of carbohydrate, fat, and amino acids and later donate them for energy production or to synthesize fatty acids, cholesterol, and other substances (Figure 7-3).

Folacin is also called *folic acid,* or *pterylmonoglutamic acid.* Enzymes containing the folacin coenzyme function in the transfer of molecules containing only one carbon atom (**single-carbon groups**). In this capacity, folacin is important for the synthesis of the nucleic acids DNA and RNA and thus for DNA replication and proper cell division. It is also vital in the metabolism of certain amino acids and in the synthesis of choline, an important body compound described later in this chapter.

Vitamin B_{12} is unique among the vitamins in that a mineral (cobalt) forms part of its structure. Vitamin B_{12}, which is also known as *cobalamin,* exists in several forms, depending on what type of chemical group attaches to it. For example, cyanocobalamin, the form often found in vitamin supplements, contains a cyanide (CN) group. The body converts vitamin B_{12} into its coenzyme forms, which work with the folacin coenzyme to help it carry out some of its functions. In this capacity, vitamin B_{12} is particularly important for the synthesis of DNA and proper cell division. Vitamin B_{12} also participates in the breakdown of certain amino acids and in the metabolism of fatty acids containing an odd number of carbon atoms. Perhaps as a result of its roles in amino acid and lipid metabolism, vitamin B_{12} is needed for the maintenance of the nervous system.

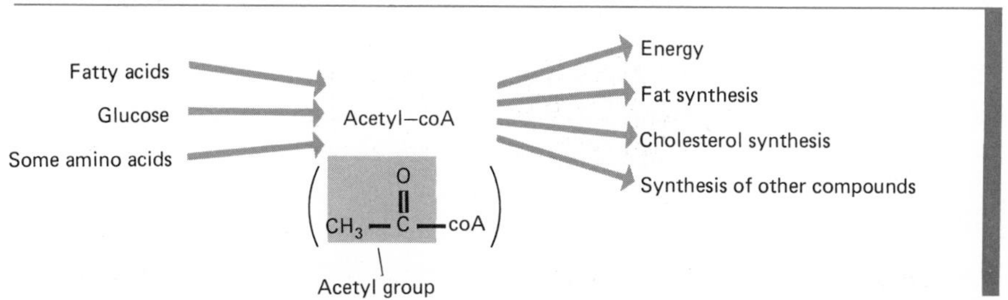

FIGURE 7-3
Metabolism of Acetyl coA. Acetyl groups are derived from the breakdown of fatty acids, glucose, and some amino acids. They attach to coenzyme A, which donates them for use in energy production, fatty acid synthesis, cholesterol synthesis, and synthesis of other compounds.

VITAMIN C

Despite all the controversy about vitamin C in recent years, the roles this substance plays in the human body are not completely known. Two forms of vitamin C function in the body. *Ascorbic acid,* the reduced form, is capable of donating electrons or hydrogen atoms. The oxidized form, *dehydroascorbic acid,* can accept electrons or hydrogen atoms. This capacity for oxidation-reduction is believed to lie at the root of many of vitamin C's functions in the body.

Probably the most extensively studied role of vitamin C is its participation in the synthesis of collagen, the major protein found in the connective tissue of bones, cartilage, tendons, teeth, blood vessels, and skin. The fact that vitamin C facilitates the proper healing of wounds appears to be related to its function in collagen synthesis. In addition, vitamin C functions in the metabolism of some of the amino acids, and this accounts for its role in collagen synthesis. Vitamin C is also vital for the conversion of the essential amino acid tryptophan into serotonin and for the formation of norepinephrine from tyrosine. Since serotonin and norepinephrine function in the nervous system, vitamin C may be important for the normal operation of this tissue. Another important role of vitamin C is in iron metabolism. It promotes the absorption of iron from the diet, as well as its storage as ferritin in the liver. In addition, vitamin C appears to function in maintaining the integrity of the capillaries, in the metabolism of folacin, in the metabolism of cholesterol, and in the breakdown of certain drugs, such as phenobarbitol, and pesticides, such as DDT (1,2).

VITAMIN A

Vitamin A occurs in animal tissues in three forms: *retinol, retinal* (*retinaldehyde*), and *retinoic acid.* A number of other substances, including alpha-, beta-, and gamma-carotene and cryptoxanthin, also provide vitamin A for the body because they can be converted into the vitamin. They are called the *provitamins A* and belong to a group of chemical substances called **carotenoid pigments**, which are responsible for the yellow–orange color of certain fruits and vegetables. The most important is beta-carotene; about one-sixth of the dietary intake of this substance becomes usable vitamin A for the body. Vitamin A functions in four general ways: to facilitate eyesight, to maintain epithelial tissue, to promote growth, especially of the bones, and to facilitate normal reproduction.

The mechanism by which vitamin A functions in eyesight is fairly clear (Figure 7-4). In the back of the eye, on the **retina**, are thousands of structures called *rods* and *cones*. The rods are responsible for the ability to see in dim light, while the cones function in the perception of colors. The rods are packed with a visual pigment called **rhodopsin**, which is composed of vitamin A (retinal) and a protein (opsin). When light strikes the rod, the rhodopsin splits into its component parts, generating a nerve impulse that travels to the visual center of the brain. The more intense the light striking the rod, the stronger the impulse it generates. By receiving these impulses from the entire eye, the brain can put them to-

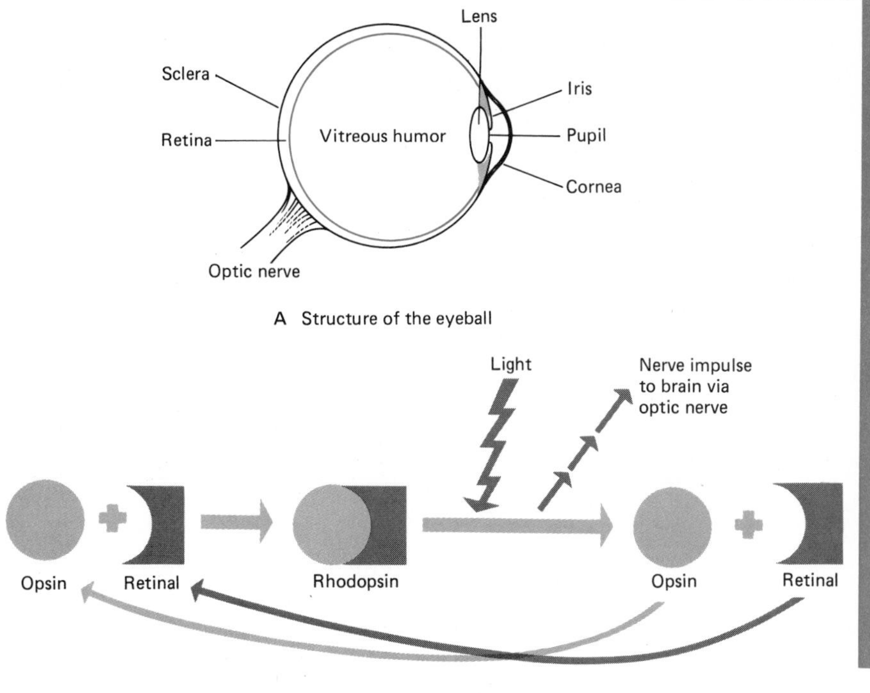

FIGURE 7-4
The Visual Process. **A** The eyeball. The lens focuses incoming light on the retina. **B** Light striking rods in the retina breaks down rhodopsin into opsin and retinal, releasing nerve impulses that travel to the brain. The brain interprets the pattern of impulses coming from the entire retina to form a picture. A similar process involving cones results in color vision.

gether into a visual picture. The cones contain different visual pigments composed of retinal and one of several different opsins.

Epithelial tissue covers all body surfaces exposed to or connected to the exterior of the body, including the lining of the digestive tract, the urinary tract, the uterus, various ducts, such as the pancreatic duct and the bile duct, and the skin. Vitamin A is essential for maintaining this tissue and promoting the normal secretion of mucus by some of its cells. Thus the barrier that protects the body from invasion by bacteria and viruses depends on an adequate supply of vitamin A in the diet.

Vitamin A also influences the size and shape of the bones. In reproduction, vitamin A promotes normal functioning of the testes in males and normal pregnancy in females.

VITAMIN D

Two forms of vitamin D function in the body: *ergocalciferol* (vitamin D_2) and *cholecalciferol* (vitamin D_3). Ergocalciferol is made by exposing ergosterol, a substance found in plants, to ultraviolet light. Similarly, cholecalciferol is synthesized in the skin when 7-dehydrocholesterol, a cholesterol derivative, is exposed to ultraviolet rays from the sun (Figure 7-5). Ergosterol and 7-dehydrocholesterol are thus vitamin D provitamins, because the vitamin can be made from them.

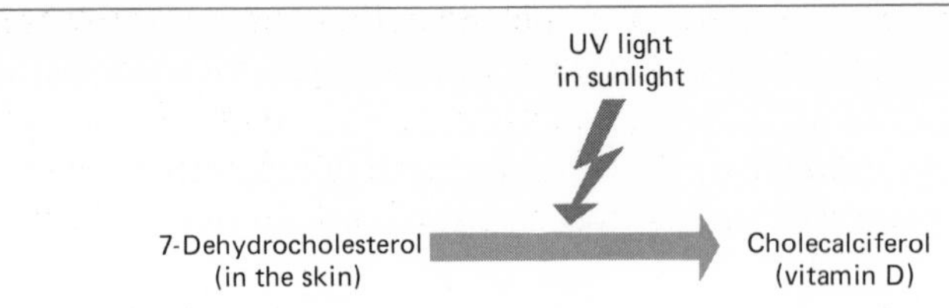

FIGURE 7-5 *Vitamin D Synthesis.* Ultraviolet light striking the skin converts 7-dehydrocholesterol into cholecalciferol, a form of vitamin D.

In the body, the vitamins must be activated before they can work. The activated forms facilitate the maintenance of calcium and phosphorus concentrations in the blood by promoting their absorption from the intestine and their release from bone, thus playing an essential role in the development and maintenance of bones.

VITAMIN E

Two general groups of chemical compounds, the *tocopherols* and the *tocotrienols,* can carry out the functions of vitamin E. Within each group are several substances, called *alpha, beta, gamma,* and *delta.* Alpha-tocopherol, the most potent form of vitamin E, is widely distributed in food and therefore provides a major portion of the vitamin E in the diet. Although gamma-tocopherol has only about one-tenth the potency of the alpha form, the diet of most Americans contains about twice as much gamma- as alpha-tocopherol (4). The potency of the other forms of vitamin E ranges from 1 to 60 percent of that of alpha-tocopherol, but the small amounts found in most foods makes them of relatively minor importance (5).

Like vitamin C, vitamin E has been widely regarded as a "miracle vitamin." It has been promoted as preventing or curing heart disease, improving sexual performance, and enhancing athletic performance. Yet, despite all these claims, vitamin E's functions in the human body have not been clearly determined. **In vitro** (in an artificial environment, such as a test tube) vitamin E acts as an antioxidant, preventing the alteration or destruction of certain compounds by the process of oxidation. Most scientists believe that at least part, if not all, of vitamin E's function in the body revolves around its antioxidant properties. In this way, it appears to be vital in protecting the cell and its components. For example, vitamin E may neutralize **peroxides** formed from polyunsaturated fatty acids, preventing them from destroying cell membranes and inactivating enzymes. It can increase both the utilization and storage of vitamin A, thereby enhancing its activity in the body. Vitamin E also may protect the lungs from damage by certain air pollutants, such as ozone and nitrogen oxide.

It is suspected that vitamin E plays other roles in the body. One of these seems to be in the synthesis of heme, the iron-containing component of hemoglobin. However, the exact nature of vitamin E's role in this process and other body functions is not yet known.

VITAMIN K

In the early 1930s, Henrik Dam discovered a fat-soluble factor that cured a hemorrhagic disease in chickens. He called the substance "vitamin K" for the Danish word *Koagulation,* which describes the vitamin's function. Two forms of vitamin K have been found in nature: vitamin K_1 (*phylloquinone*), which occurs in plants, and vitamin K_2 (*menaquinone*), which is produced by certain bacteria. A synthetic form of vitamin K, *menadione,* has sometimes been used in the treatment of certain hemorrhagic disorders.

Vitamin K facilitates the proper clotting of blood by functioning in the synthesis of several of the proteins needed for this process, including prothrombin. With a vitamin K deficiency, the level of these protein factors in the blood decreases, and proper coagulation cannot occur. *Hemophilia,* a genetic disorder in which the blood fails to clot, does not respond to vitamin K because the defect does not involve vitamin K's role in the synthesis of the clotting factors.

1. Vitamin and mineral supplements are needed by most people.

2. Massive doses of appropriate vitamins will prevent or cure many diseases, such as the common cold, heart disease, cancer, schizophrenia, and acne.

3. Choline, inositol, *para*-aminobenzoic acid (PABA), bioflavonoids, pangamic acid (vitamin B_{15}), and amygdalin (vitamin B_{17}, laetrile) are dietary essentials.

4. Natural vitamins are superior to synthetic ones.

FACT OR FANTASY

Vitamin Requirements and Sources (3)

Part of the mystique surrounding the vitamins is the idea that if a little is good, more must be even better. Many Americans consume far more vitamins than they really need, occasionally hundreds of times the recommended amounts. Taking such large doses, however, can be costly; in the case of two of them, vitamin A and vitamin D, it can be dangerous. Let us look at how much is enough and where the right amounts can be obtained.

The Recommended Dietary Allowance for each of the vitamins is listed in Ready Reference 3. These RDAs are the levels of intake thought to be sufficient to meet the needs of nearly all healthy Americans. So, ex-

Taking large doses of vitamins can be costly; in the case of two of them, vitamin A and vitamin D, it can be dangerous.

cept for unusual circumstances, consumption of larger amounts is unnecessary.

THE WATER-SOLUBLE VITAMINS

The allowances for three of the vitamins, thiamine, riboflavin, and niacin, depend on the individual's caloric intake, since these vitamins are intimately involved in the release of energy from carbohydrate, protein, and fat. The Food and Nutrition Board (FNB) recommends that adults consume 0.5 milligrams of thiamine 0.6 milligrams of riboflavin, and 6.6 niacin equivalents for every 1000 kilocalories ingested each day. Since niacin needs can be met by consuming either the vitamin or the essential amino acid tryptophan, the RDA is expressed in terms of *niacin equivalents* (NE), with 1 niacin equivalent equalling 1 milligram of niacin or 60 milligrams of tryptophan. Thiamine is found in almost all foods, but pork products, beef liver, legumes, certain nuts, green peas, some green vegetables, and whole or enriched grain products make significant contributions (Figure 7-6). Liver, dairy products, meat, and certain green vegetables are good sources of riboflavin (Figure 7-7). Niacin is found in

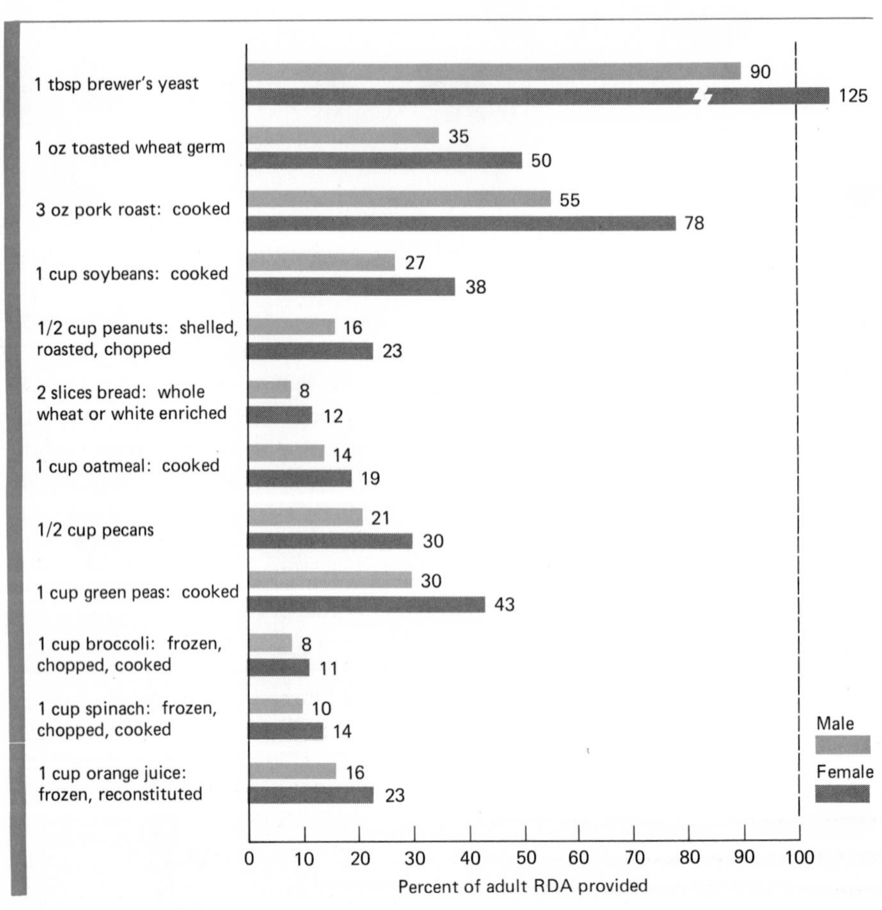

FIGURE 7-6 *Some Good Sources of Thiamine.* [Sources: Food and Nutrition Board, *Recommended Dietary Allowances*, 9th ed., Washington, DC: National Academy of Sciences (1980); C. F. Adams, *Nutritive Value of American Foods in Common Units*, Agriculture Handbook No. 456, Washington, DC: USDA (1975).]

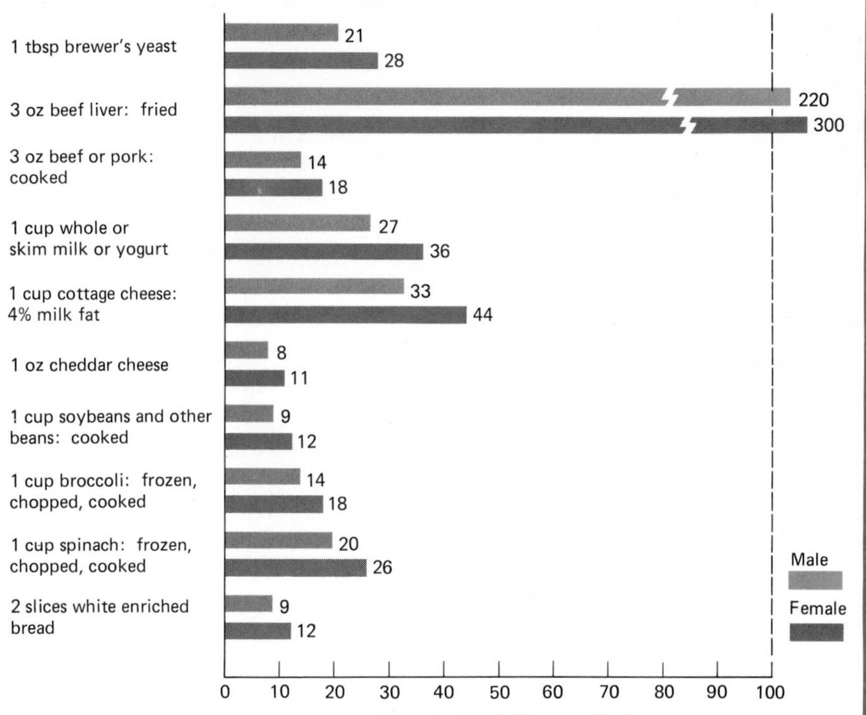

FIGURE 7-7
Some Good Sources of Riboflavin. [Sources: Food and Nutrition Board, *Recommended Dietary Allowances,* 9th ed., Washington, DC: National Academy of Sciences (1980); C. F. Adams, *Nutritive Value of American Foods in Common Units,* Agriculture Handbook No. 456, Washington, DC: USDA (1975).]

significant amounts in a smaller variety of foods. However, the ability to convert tryptophan into niacin means that high-quality protein can help meet the niacin requirement. Thus particularly good sources of niacin equivalents include liver, meat, poultry, fish, some legumes, and nuts and seeds (Figure 7-8).

The human requirement for vitamin B_6 appears to increase when the protein requirement of the diet increases, but an allowance of 2.2 mg/day for males and 2.0 mg/day for females is thought to be adequate for most American adults. Liver, meat, fish, poultry, legumes, whole grains and their products, and certain vegetables are important sources (Table 7-2).

There is evidence that 50 micrograms of folacin will maintain normal blood levels in nondeficient individuals. However, since the body absorbs only part of the folacin it ingests, the adult allowance has been set at 400 μg/day. Folacin occurs in relatively large amounts in liver, legumes, whole grains, certain nuts, green vegetables, and citrus fruits (Figure 7-9). Because food processing destroys folacin, it is good practice to include some raw green vegetables or citrus fruit in the diet every day.

About 1.0 microgram of vitamin B_{12} is adequate to replace the amount lost each day and to cure a deficiency of the vitamin. Since not all the vitamin B_{12} in the diet is absorbed, the adult allowance has been set at 3 μg/day. Vitamin B_{12} is available only in foods from animal sources (Table 7-2). Lacto-ovo-vegetarians and people who consume meat generally obtain sufficient vitamin B_{12} to meet their needs; strict vegetarians do not.

Recommended Dietary Allowances have not been established for pantothenic acid and biotin. The FNB has set an estimated safe and adequate intake for adults of 4 to 7 mg/day for pantothenic acid and 100 to 200 μg/day for biotin. Significant amounts of pantothenic acid occur in liver, meat, fish, poultry, certain legumes, some vegetables, nuts, and grains (Table 7-2). Liver, legumes, eggs, nuts, and some vegetables serve as especially good sources of biotin (Table 7-3).

Less than 10 mg/day of vitamin C relieves the symptoms of vitamin C deficiency (scurvy), while about 30 mg/day is sufficient to replace the amount lost from the body. The FNB believes its recommendation of 60 mg/day will maintain an adequate pool of ascorbic acid and protect against deficiency in adults, even though 100 to 150 mg/day is required to saturate body tissues (6). Consumption of even larger quantities is probably not of any nutritional value because the body excretes any excess. There is some evidence, however, that smokers may require more vitamin C (10). Green vegetables, citrus fruit, potatoes, tomatoes, cauliflower, strawberries, and other fruits and vegetables make significant contributions toward meeting dietary requirements for vitamin C (Figure 7-10).

FIGURE 7-8 *Some Good Sources of Niacin.* [Sources: Food and Nutrition Board, *Recommended Dietary Allowances,* 9th ed., Washington, DC: National Academy of Sciences (1980); C. F. Adams, *Nutritive Value of American Foods in Common Units,* Agriculture Handbook No. 456, Washington, DC: USDA (1975).]

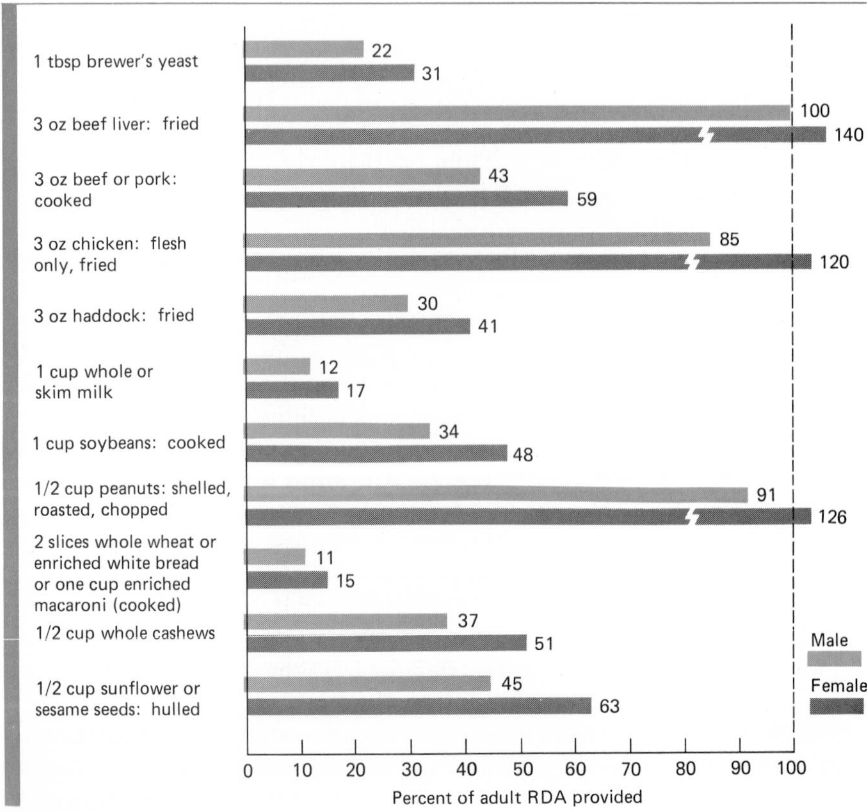

THE FAT-SOLUBLE VITAMINS

Unlike the RDAs for the water-soluble vitamins, those for the fat-soluble vitamins are not usually given in terms of weight. Because each vitamin has several different forms, many of which vary in potency, expressing the RDA in terms of micrograms or milligrams is confusing. For example,

TABLE **7-2**

Some good sources of vitamin B_6, pantothenic acid, and vitamin B_{12}

FOOD	VITAMIN B_6, mg*	PANTOTHENIC ACID, mg*	VITAMIN B_{12}, μg*
Brewer's yeast	2.5	12.0	0
Beef liver (raw)	0.84	7.7	80
Meat, fish, poultry:			
Beef (separable fat removed, averaged all cuts, raw)	0.44	0.6	1.8
Ham (light cure, lean, raw)	0.40	0.68	0.6
Haddock (raw)	0.18	0.13	1.3
Tuna (canned in oil, solids and liquid)	0.43	0.32	2.3
Chicken (no skin, broiled):			
Light meat	0.68	0.80	0.45
Dark meat	0.33	1.00	0.40
Dairy products:			
Whole and skim milk	0.04	0.37	0.4
Cheddar cheese	0.08	0.5	1.0
Cottage cheese (4% fat)	0.04	0.22	1.0
Yogurt (part skim milk)	0.05	0.31	0.11
Legumes:			
White beans (mature, dry)	0.56	0.73	0
Red beans (mature, dry)	0.44	0.5	0
Peanuts (roasted)	0.40	2.1	0
Peanut butter	0.33	—	0
Green vegetables:			
Broccoli spears (frozen, cooked)	0.17	0.53	0
Cabbage (raw, shredded)	0.16	0.21	0
Green peppers (raw)	0.26	0.23	0
Spinach (frozen, cooked)	0.13	0.08	0
Other vegetables:			
Potatoes (baked)	0.23	—	0
Sweet potatoes (raw)	0.22	0.8	0
Cauliflower (frozen, cooked)	0.19	0.54	0
Tomatoes (raw)	0.10	0.33	0
Nuts:			
Cashews	0.21	1.3	0
Pecans	0.18	1.7	0
English walnuts	0.73	0.9	0
Grains and their products:			
Wheat germ (toasted)	1.15	1.2	0
Bread:			
Whole wheat	0.18	0.76	0
White (enriched)	0.04	0.43	0

* All values per 100 grams of food.

Source: M. L. Orr, *Pantothenic Acid, Vitamin B_6, and Vitamin B_{12} in Foods,* Home Economics Research Report No. 36, Washington, DC: USDA (1969).

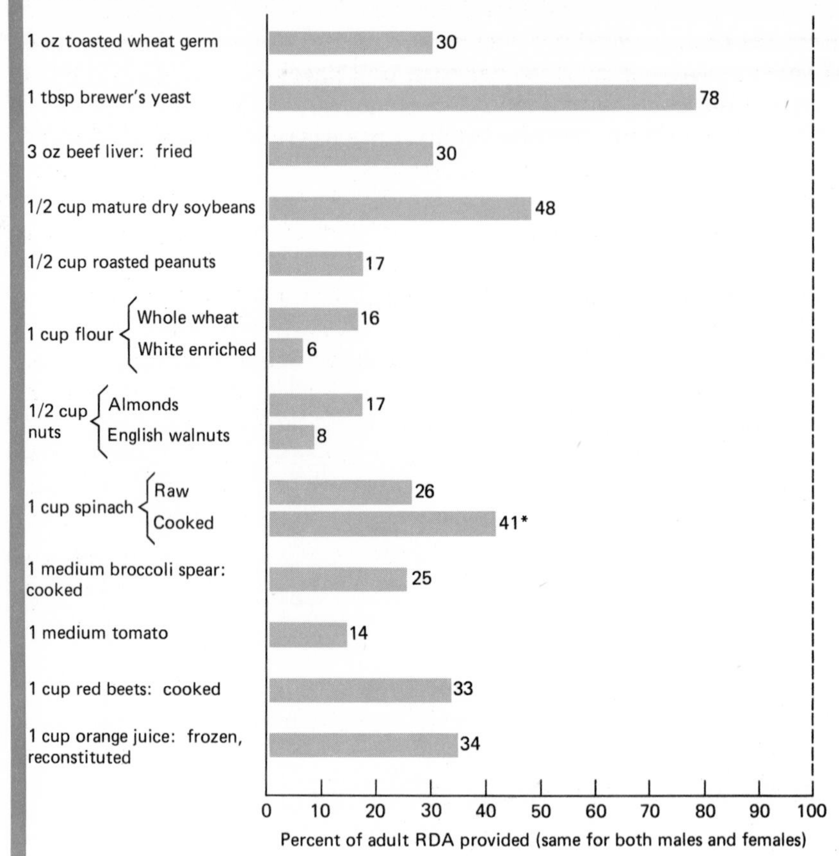

FIGURE 7-9 *Some Good Sources of Folacin.* [Sources: Food and Nutrition Board, *Recommended Dietary Allowances,* 9th ed., Washington, DC: National Academy of Sciences (1980); B. P. Perloff, and R. R. Butrum, "Folacin in Selected Foods," *Journal of the American Dietetic Association* **70**:161–172 (1977). Data from *JADA* used with permission.]

the allowance for vitamin E could be expressed as 15 milligrams of alpha-tocopherol, 45 milligrams of beta-tocopherol, or 150 milligrams of gamma-tocopherol, and so on. Since foods contain a mixture of tocopherols, determining how much to eat to meet the RDA is even more complicated. The RDAs are therefore expressed in terms of standard units of biological activity, to which the potency of all forms of the vitamin can be related. The most common unit is the international unit (IU). One international unit of alpha-tocopherol has the same value to the body as 1 international unit of beta- or gamma-tocopherol.

The Recommended Dietary Allowance for vitamin A is 5000 IU/day for adult males and 4000 IU/day for adult females, where 1 international unit is equivalent to 0.3 micrograms of retinol or 0.6 micrograms of beta-carotene. In recent years, another unit of vitamin A activity has come into use, the retinol equivalent (RE). One retinol equivalent is defined as one microgram of retinol or six micrograms of beta-carotene or twelve micrograms of other vitamin A carotenoids. The RDA in terms of retinol equivalents is 1000 RE/day for adult males and 800 RE/day for adult females. Preformed vitamin A is available only from animal products, but plant sources provide considerable quantities of the provitamin. Good sources are liver, eggs, dairy products, yellow–orange fruits and vegetables (such as carrots, squash, apricots, and peaches), and green vegetables, including spinach, collards, and broccoli (Figure 7-11).

One international unit of vitamin D has been defined as 0.025 micrograms of either ergocalciferol (vitamin D_2) or cholecalciferol (vitamin D_3). Although the precise requirement for adults is not known, it probably can be met simply by exposure to sunlight. If exposure is limited, an intake of 200 IU/day is thought to be adequate. The 1980 edition of the RDAs expresses the vitamin D allowance in terms of weight, listing 5 micrograms of cholecalciferol as sufficient for adults. With the exception of fish-liver oils, vitamin D occurs rarely in foods. Only small amounts are found naturally in, for example, egg yolk, butter, and liver. In many areas, milk is fortified with this vitamin.

The RDA for vitamin E has been set at only 15 IU/day for adult males and 12 IU/day for adult females. The allowance was once twice this amount, but dietary surveys found that the average American diet provided only 10 to 20 IU/day and no deficiency symptoms were evident in

TABLE **7-3**

Some good sources of biotin

FOOD	AMOUNT, μg/100 g
Brewer's yeast	200
Meat, fish, poultry:	
Beef (lean, raw)	3.4
Beef liver	96.0
Pork (raw)	5.2
Chicken: (raw)	
Light meat	11.3
Dark meat	10.0
Tuna (canned)	3.0
Legumes:	
Soybeans (dry)	61.0
Peanuts (roasted)	34.0
Grains and their products:	
Flour:	
Whole wheat	9.0
White (enriched)	1.0
Wheat bran	14.0
Eggs (large)	22.5
Nuts:	
Walnuts	37.0
Almonds	18.0
Pecans	37.0
Vegetables:	
Cauliflower (fresh)	17.0
Green peas	9.4
Mushrooms (fresh)	16.0
Spinach (fresh)	6.9

Source: M. G. Hardinge, and H. Crooks, "Lesser Known Vitamins in Foods," *J. Am. Diet. Assoc.* **38**:240–245 (1961). Copyright © the American Dietetic Association. Reprinted with permission.

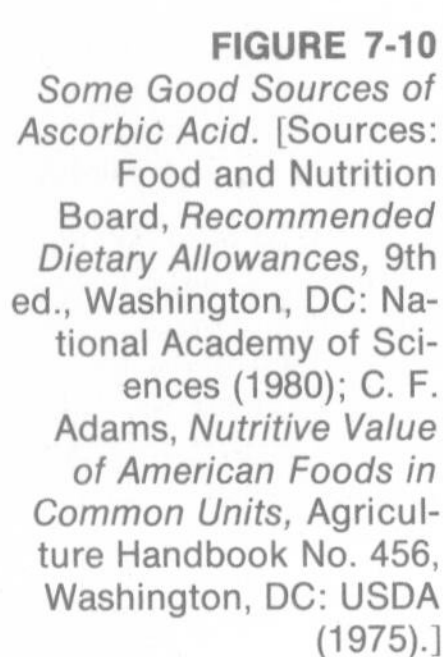

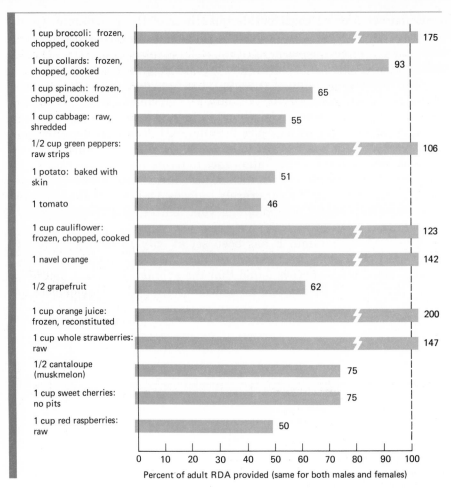

FIGURE 7-10
Some Good Sources of Ascorbic Acid. [Sources: Food and Nutrition Board, *Recommended Dietary Allowances*, 9th ed., Washington, DC: National Academy of Sciences (1980); C. F. Adams, *Nutritive Value of American Foods in Common Units*, Agriculture Handbook No. 456, Washington, DC: USDA (1975).]

the population, so the FNB lowered the allowance. Although vitamin E requirements increase when polyunsaturated fat intake increases, foods high in polyunsaturated fat provide sufficient additional vitamin E to cover this need. In the 1980 edition of the RDAs, the FNB defines the allowances in terms of alpha-tocopherol equivalents, listing 10 alpha-TE as sufficient for adult males and 8 alpha-TE for adult females. Vitamin E occurs fairly widely in food. Vegetable oils and the products made from them are the best sources, but whole grains, nuts, and green vegetables also can make important contributions (Table 7-4).

Because humans absorb the vitamin K produced by bacteria in their intestines and deficiencies are rare in adults, no RDA has been established for this vitamin. However, the FNB has issued an estimated safe and adequate daily intake of 70 to 140 micrograms of vitamin K for adults. Important dietary sources include green leafy vegetables, egg yolk, and liver.

ENSURING AN ADEQUATE INTAKE

Although highly processed foods are proliferating in the American marketplace and many Americans fail to select an adequate diet, we should not be misled into believing that it is impossible to meet vitamin (and mineral) requirements solely from food. Many nutritious foods are available year-round, and by choosing a variety from each food group and preparing them properly, nearly everyone can meet his or her nutritional needs. Table 7-5 shows some foods that are good sources of many vitamins; the effect of processing on vitamin content will be discussed in Chapter 10.

Vitamin Deficiencies

Great strides have been made in controlling vitamin-deficiency diseases, but some still exist in many parts of the world. Severe vitamin deficiencies are rare in the United States, although recent nutrition surveys indicate that moderate or marginal deficiencies do exist in certain population groups. Three general factors usually operate to produce a nutritional de-

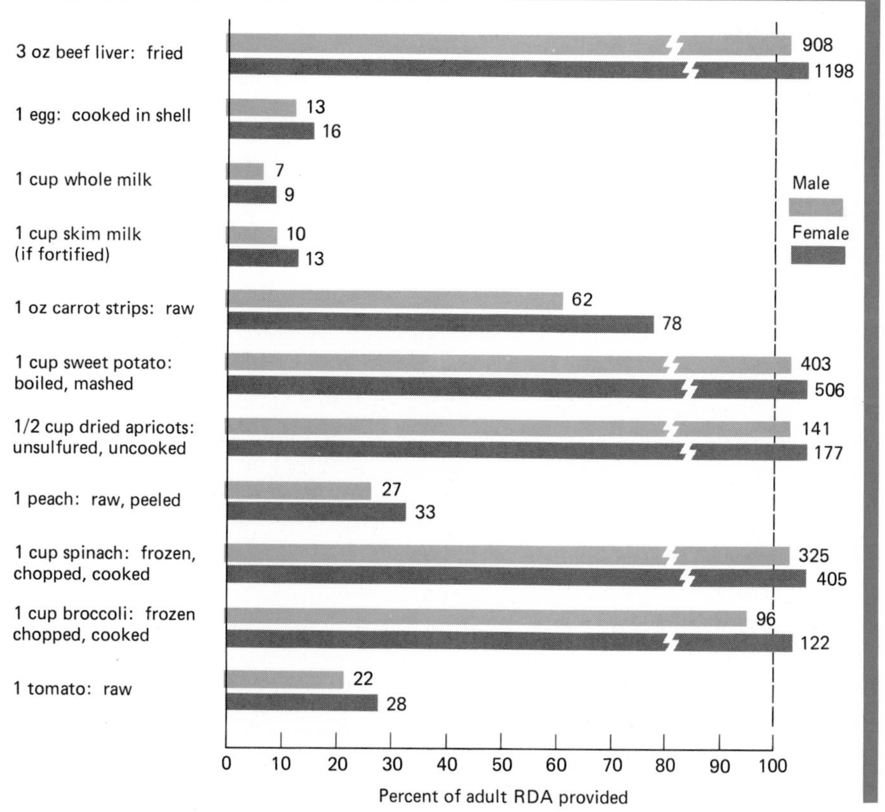

FIGURE 7-11 *Some Good Sources of Vitamin A.* [Sources: Food and Nutrition Board, *Recommended Dietary Allowances,* 9th ed., Washington, DC: National Academy of Sciences (1980); C. F. Adams, *Nutritive Value of American Foods in Common Units,* Agriculture Handbook No. 456, Washington, DC: USDA (1975).]

ficiency: a restriction in the variety and/or amount of food ingested, the absence of the nutrient in question from the foods consumed, or an increase in nutritional requirements, such as in pregnancy and lactation. Vitamin deficiencies also occur as a result of metabolic disorders, alcoholism, and the use of certain drugs.

TABLE **7-4**

Alpha-tocopherol content of some foods

FOOD	ALPHA-TOCOPHEROL CONTENT, mg/100 g
Meat:	
Beef (raw)	0.45*
Beef liver (broiled)	0.63
Haddock (broiled)	0.6
Dairy and Eggs:	
Cheese	0.64
Butter	2.4
Egg (cooked)	0.77
Legumes:	
Navy beans (dry)	0.34†
Soybeans (dry)	0.85†
Peanuts (roasted)	7.8
Grain products:	
Wheat germ	14.1‡
Whole-wheat flour	0.82‡
Bleached-white flour	0.03
Oatmeal (dry)	1.5
Brown rice (dry)	0.68
White rice	0.11
Nuts and Seeds:	
Almonds (shelled, raw)	24.0
Pecans (shelled, raw)	1.2†
Walnuts (shelled, raw)	17.8†
Green vegetables:	
Broccoli (raw)	0.46
Brussels sprouts (cooked)	0.85
Cabbage (raw)	1.7
Mustard greens (raw)	2.0
Spinach (raw)	1.9
Vegetable oils:	
Corn (refined)	14.2
Cottonseed (refined)	35.2
Olive	11.9
Peanut (refined)	11.6
Safflower (refined)	34
Soybean (refined)	11.0†
Sunflower (refined)	59.5
Wheat germ	14.9

* Significant losses occur during cooking.
† Also contains large amounts of gamma-tocopherol.
‡ Also contains large amounts of beta-tocopherol.

Source: P. J. McLaughlin, and J. L. Weihrauch, "Vitamin E Content of Foods," *J. Am. Diet. Assoc.* **75**:647–665 (1979). (Reprinted with permission.)

TABLE **7-5**

Selected foods that are good sources of several vitamins

FOOD	VITAMINS
Brewer's yeast	B vitamins except vitamin B_{12}
Wheat germ	B vitamins (except vitamin B_{12}), vitamin E
Liver	B vitamins, vitamin A
Meat, fish, poultry	Niacin, vitamin B_6, vitamin B_{12}, pantothenic acid (pork is a good source of thiamine)
Dairy products	Riboflavin, vitamin B_{12}, and, if fortified, vitamins A and D
Legumes	B vitamins (except vitamin B_{12}), vitamin E
Citrus fruit	Vitamin C, folacin (orange juice is a good source of thiamine)
Green leafy vegetables	Vitamin A, vitamin C, vitamin E, vitamin K, riboflavin, folacin
Enriched grains	Thiamine, riboflavin, niacin
Whole grains	Thiamine, vitamin B_6, pantothenic acid, vitamin E

THIAMINE: BERIBERI

Thiamine deficiency, or **beriberi**, has been endemic to Oriental cultures for over 4000 years. It is characterized by a variety of problems involving the nervous system, including inflammation and paralysis of certain nerves, as well as fatigue and impaired work capacity, difficulty in walking, and loss of appetite. In moderate thiamine deficiency (*dry beriberi*), the muscles are tender and wasting may occur. A severe deficiency produces tissue swelling, or edema, particularly of the legs, and the condition is referred to as *wet beriberi*. The heart often becomes enlarged and beats abnormally rapidly, even after the slightest exertion. Death may result from heart failure.

Beriberi has traditionally been associated with the rice-consuming cultures of the world because the practice of polishing rice removes the bran and the germ, which contain most of the thiamine. The affluent can obtain thiamine from other sources, but those who cannot afford other sources of the vitamin develop the deficiency. Not all rice cultures have experienced a high prevalence of beriberi, however. In parts of India, for example, rice is parboiled before polishing, and in the process, thiamine is carried into the rice kernel. Handmilling also preserves some of the thiamine content, because it does not remove all the bran. The spread of machine milling in the Orient was accompanied by a greater incidence of beriberi (8).

The effects of the different methods of processing rice are illustrated by the situation in Malaya in the late nineteenth century. Chinese laborers who worked the tin mines consumed large quantities of highly polished rice, whereas the native Malayans either hand milled it or parboiled it before milling. The Indians who worked the rubber plantations also parboiled their rice. Large numbers of the Chinese died from beriberi, whereas the Malayans and Indians were unaffected (8).

Despite the availability of synthetic thiamine, beriberi, particularly in its milder forms, still exists in parts of south and southeast Asia. It is rare in the United States and other developed nations, but is sometimes seen in alcoholics.

NIACIN: PELLAGRA

A deficiency of niacin produces **pellagra**, a disease that became epidemic in parts of Europe during the eighteenth and nineteenth centuries and in the southeastern United States about 1900. Pellagra begins with such symptoms as diarrhea, abdominal pain, flatulence, headache, and dizziness and progresses to a characteristic inflammation of the skin when exposed to sunlight. As the deficiency worsens, disturbances of the nervous system occur, including itchy hands and feet, a burning sensation in the stomach, shoulder, feet, hands, and arms, headache, confusion, mild depression, and apathy. Later, paralysis may occur, and the victim experiences profound depressions, delusions of persecution, and suicidal tendencies. The later stages involve severe wasting of the body, and death may result from a weakened heart or tuberculosis.

In the same way that beriberi is associated with reliance on polished rice as a dietary staple, pellagra has been linked with the heavy consumption of corn. During the mid-1700s, the disease was reported in Spain among peasants who subsisted on a maize diet, to which only turnips, chestnuts, cabbage, beans, nuts, and apples were added. In the southeastern United States, pellagra appeared in poverty-ridden areas where salt pork, corn meal, molasses, and boiled vegetables formed the major part of the diet. Ironically, corn contains niacin, but the vitamin is bound to a protein and is not available to the body. In addition, the protein of corn contains little tryptophan from which the body can synthesize niacin. Pellagra, however, is rare among the Indians of Mexico and Central America, despite their dependence on corn. In utilizing the corn to make tortillas and other products, the Indians treat it with lime (calcium hydroxide), which releases the niacin and makes it available to the body.

Even when niacin was administered to those suffering from pellagra, not all symptoms of the disorder disappeared. Pellagra was subsequently found to be associated with a deficiency of riboflavin as well, largely because of the absence of dairy products in the diet of these people. Since many food products are now commonly fortified with riboflavin, deficiency of this vitamin in the United States has decreased. However, the Ten-State Survey found low blood levels in certain population groups, such as among Spanish-Americans and blacks in low-income areas, and among the young (9). The symptoms are rather nonspecific and may be found in other disorders, including vitamin B_6 and iron deficiencies; they include fissures at the corners of the mouth, a swollen, purple tongue, an oily inflammation of the skin, especially around the nose and in the genital area of males, and sometimes behavioral changes.

FOLACIN AND VITAMIN B_{12}

Because vitamin B_{12} and folacin function together in promoting cell divi-

FOCUS 7-1 HERBS As part of the "back-to-nature" movement, many people have returned to using herbs for their medicinal as well as nutritional properties. They often attempt to diagnose their own ills and prescribe what they believe will cure them. However, this can be dangerous and costly. Here are some points to remember about herbs:

1. Although many plants have pharmacologic properties, it is not wise to treat yourself with them. Lacking medical training, chances are good you will make the wrong diagnosis. You also may poison yourself: if you pick your own, it is easy to misidentify a plant. In addition, the drug content of any given herb varies from area to area, and you will be unable to determine how much of a dose you are taking. It is better to rely on physicians, who are trained in the diagnosis and treatment of disease. Although the drugs they prescribe are more potent than herbs and carry their own risks, they have been clinically tested and produced under carefully controlled conditions; at least you know what you are getting.
2. Many herbs contain appreciable amounts of vitamins and minerals. However, so do foods. Why buy herbs, which are more expensive?
3. Inclusion of herbs in vitamin and mineral supplements is of no value because the small amounts present will not add significantly to the nutritional or medicinal value of the supplement. However, they will make the supplement more expensive.
4. Some herbs are valuable in cooking. They add flavor to food, and the small amounts used are harmless.

---

sion, many of the deficiency symptoms for the two vitamins are similar. Both result in a type of anemia in which the red blood cells are fewer in number, larger in size, and contain less hemoglobin than normal. In addition, many large, immature red cells with nuclei are released into the bloodstream, and the number of white blood cells and platelets is also reduced. This condition is believed to result from the role of folacin and vitamin B_{12} in cell division. During a deficiency of either vitamin, DNA cannot **replicate** properly and cell division slows down. The tissues most severely affected are those which divide rapidly, including those from which blood cells and epithelial tissues are made. In addition, vitamin B_{12} deficiency leads to a degeneration of the nervous system that may eventually be fatal.

Folacin deficiency appears to be the most widespread vitamin deficiency in the United States today, probably because of the rather limited distribution of significant amounts of the vitamin in food, as well as its instability when subjected to processing. Deficiency also may result from alcoholism, from therapy with certain drugs, such as some anticancer agents, and from malabsorption disorders. Because of their high requirements, pregnant and lactating women, young infants, and adolescents are particularly likely to become deficient.

A population group that runs a particular risk of vitamin B_{12} deficiency is strict vegetarians, who consume no animal products. Since only foods from animal sources contain vitamin B_{12}, strict vegetarians may eventually become deficient, and in fact, serum vitamin B_{12} levels are low in strict vegetarians who do not take supplements of the vitamin (10,11). Another type of vitamin B_{12} deficiency is called **pernicious anemia**. In order for vitamin B_{12} to be absorbed into the body from the intestine, it must attach to a substance produced by the stomach called **intrinsic factor**. Intrinsic factor then facilitates vitamin B_{12} absorption. In pernicious anemia, the stomach no longer produces intrinsic factor because a genetic defect or an **autoimmune response** destroys the cells that synthesize it. The absorption of vitamin B_{12} is therefore blocked. Unless treated by intramuscular injections of the vitamin, pernicious anemia is fatal. Other ways vitamin B_{12} deficiency can occur are surgical removal of the stomach or the last foot or so of the small intestine (where vitamin B_{12} is absorbed).

VITAMIN C: SCURVY

For thousands of years, the vitamin C deficiency disease, **scurvy**, ravaged the populations in which it occurred. Since fruits and vegetables are the only significant sources of the vitamin, the incidence of scurvy rose whenever fruits and vegetables became unavailable—on long sea voyages, during the winter, and in prisons, asylums, and homes for the poor. Scurvy hampered many explorations on land and sea and probably resulted in the failure of some of the medieval crusades. During Vasco da Gama's circumnavigation of the globe, most of his crew was stricken with scurvy and many died. The disease also plagued the explorations of Jacques Cartier in Newfoundland during the winter of 1535–1536.

The first controlled experiments involving scurvy were performed by James Lind, a British naval physician, in the mid-1700s. He demonstrated conclusively that citrus fruit could cure and prevent the disease and published his results as *A Treatise on Scurvy* in 1753. Over 40 years later, the British Navy began to follow his advice and stock citrus fruit

FIGURE 7-12
Scurvy. Dr. James Lind, the Scottish physician who discovered the cure for scurvy, is shown distributing oranges and lemons to British sailors suffering from this deficiency disease. (The Bettman Archive, Inc.).

aboard its ships, a practice that may have contributed to the British victory over Napoleon (12). Today scurvy is rare in most parts of the world and usually occurs as a result of poverty, alcoholism, famine, and nutritional ignorance.

Early symptoms include lack of appetite, weakness, and aching of the joints and muscles. Small hemorrhages appear around the hair follicles. The gums swell and bleed, and hemorrhages may occur in the muscles, around the joints, in the digestive tract, on the eye, and elsewhere in the body. The person cannot perform physical tasks, and emotional changes occur. Untreated, scurvy is fatal. In infants, in addition to the other symptoms, there is failure to grow properly. The child is irritable, its body tender to the touch, and it shows a great deal of apprehension when it is being handled.

VITAMIN A: KERATINIZATION AND BLINDNESS

Vitamin A deficiency has been epidemic in certain parts of the world for hundreds of years. Even today it is a major public health problem in most of south and southeast Asia, parts of Africa and South America, and in some areas of the Middle East (13). Like protein-energy malnutrition, with which it is often associated, vitamin A deficiency is a disease of poverty and is most prevalent among young children of the developing nations. More than 100,000 new cases of blindness stemming from vitamin A deficiency occur yearly worldwide, and most of the victims are children between 2 and 5 years of age (14).

In many developing nations, restricted consumption of food from animal sources results in a low intake of preformed vitamin A, while green leafy vegetables, which are often plentiful in the environment, are frequently ignored. Intake of fats and oils may be low, retarding the absorption of any vitamin A in the diet (13,15). The child generally remains healthy while breast feeding, since human milk provides adequate vitamin A, but when it is weaned, vitamin A deficiency often develops. The situation is aggravated by PEM and infections, and since these children are seldom seen by physicians, the deficiency may go untreated until it is too late (15).

An early sign of vitamin A deficiency is *night blindness,* an inability to see in dim light. As the deficiency worsens, normal secretion of mucus is impaired, and epithelial tissue throughout the body dries out. This process, known as **keratinization**, results in a dry, hardened epithelial tissue, which presents a less effective barrier to bacterial and viral invasion. Keratinization also occurs in parts of the eye, including the **cornea**, the transparent coat that covers the lens. The cornea turns opaque, and unless treated with massive doses of vitamin A within a day or two, the victim will become permanently blind. The disease, called **xerophthalmia**, is a major cause of blindness in the developing nations. In severe and prolonged vitamin A deficiency, the cornea liquefies and the structure of the entire eyeball may deteriorate.

Vitamin A deficiency also impairs growth and reproduction. The development of the bones is affected before that of the soft tissues, and because the brain and spinal cord continue to grow within the confines of a skull and vertebral column that have stopped developing, mechanical damage to these parts of the nervous system may occur. Disruption of reproductive processes results from an inability to produce sperm in males and to maintain a normal pregnancy in females.

Treatment with vitamin A will reverse the deficiency symptoms if the vitamin is administered in time, but the true solution to the problem is prevention. Because the body stores vitamin A in the liver, a single, large dose of 100,000 to 200,000 international units in the diet twice yearly will protect most children. Another preventive measure is fortifying widely used foods, such as sugar, nonfat dry milk, cereals, tea, and monosodium glutamate (MSG), with vitamin A. Finally, promoting the use of green vegetables can help increase the vitamin A content of the diet.

VITAMIN D: RICKETS AND OSTEOMALACIA

Because of vitamin D's role in maintaining proper calcium and phosphate concentrations in the blood, deficiency of this vitamin has profound effects on the mineralization of bone. In children the condition is called **rickets**, and it is shown by soft bones that readily become deformed; bowed legs, knockknees, curved spine, enlarged joints, and a protruding chest are common. Vitamin D deficiency in adults eventually leads to **osteomalacia**, a progressive demineralization of the bones that increases their susceptibility to fracture.

Two general factors usually interact to produce a vitamin D deficiency: dietary lack of the vitamin and low exposure to sunlight. Rickets

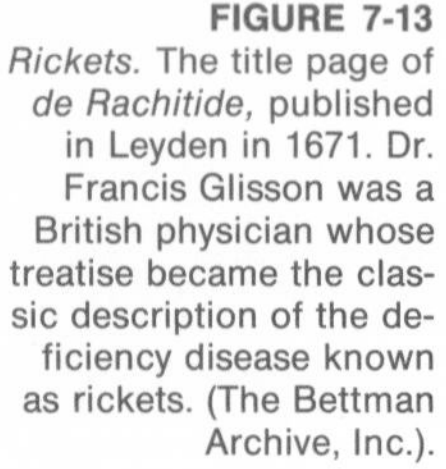

FIGURE 7-13
Rickets. The title page of *de Rachitide,* published in Leyden in 1671. Dr. Francis Glisson was a British physician whose treatise became the classic description of the deficiency disease known as rickets. (The Bettman Archive, Inc.).

was widespread in more northerly regions, such as the British Isles and Scandinavia, particularly after the industrial revolution. In the major industrial and coal mining areas of Britain, air pollution screened out ultraviolet radiation that normally reached the ground, and the disease became virtually epidemic by the late 1800s. Rickets also was found among the affluent classes during the sixteenth and seventeenth centuries, because the wealthy dressed their children in heavy clothing and kept them in relatively dark and poorly ventilated houses. The children of the poor, free to run about in the sunlight and fresh air, were less likely to contract the disease.

VITAMIN E AND VITAMIN K

Vitamin E and vitamin K deficiencies are rare in humans. Vitamin E is plentiful in plant sources and can be stored in the body; deficiency is occasionally seen in formula-fed premature infants because their body stores are low at birth. It results in breakage of red cells in the bloodstream. Adults obtain considerable amounts of vitamin K from the bacteria in their intestines. However, the vitamin does not transfer well to a fetus from its mother and an infant's intestines contain no bacteria at birth. To prevent hemorrhage, the infant's diet is supplemented with vitamin K.

Can We Obtain Too Much?

Most people who consume large quantities of vitamins do so under the impression that because they are essential body substances and natural components of food, they cannot be toxic. Two vitamins in particular, vitamin A and vitamin D, are toxic enough that their dosages should be limited by people taking vitamin supplements.

Many cases of vitamin A toxicity have been reported in the medical literature over the years, often in connection with the treatment of acne. The levels necessary to produce adverse effects vary depending on the person's age, body size, and the duration of the overconsumption, but as little as 25,000 IU/day may cause symptoms (16). Commonly, symptoms of overdose are seen in people who take 50,000 to 100,000 IU/day or more for a period of months or years. The carotenoids, a vitamin A provitamin, are nontoxic because the body cannot convert them into vitamin A rapidly enough to cause trouble. However, they do accumulate in the body, producing a yellow skin tone that disappears when the excess intake is discontinued.

In adults, fatigue, lethargy, insomnia, headache, nausea, vomiting, loss of appetite, and weight loss are common. In addition, the individual may experience bone or joint pains; loss of hair; dry, scaly, itchy skin; severe headaches; constipation; and irregular menstruation in women. Excess vitamin A often causes an increased amount of fluid within the skull, leading to a rise in intracranial pressure and symptoms that mimic a brain tumor. Overdose in children produces many of the same symptoms and also can affect bone growth and development. In some cases, one leg has been seen to grow 1 to 2 inches longer than the other (17). Except for bone changes, the symptoms reverse themselves once excessive intake ceases.

A second vitamin that produces toxic symptoms when consumed in excessive amounts is vitamin D. Levels as low as 2000 to 3000 IU/day have produced high blood calcium concentrations, one symptom of the problem, in infants. Generally, however, ingestion of 1000 to 3000 IU/kg of body weight/day for several months is necessary to produce severe symptoms in adults. These include loss of appetite, nausea, vomiting, fatigue, headache, diarrhea or constipation, excessive thirst, excessive urination, and failure to grow. Blood calcium and phosphate levels increase, and calcium may be deposited in soft tissues, such as the large blood vessels, heart, lungs, and kidney. These calcium deposits sometimes produce irreversible kidney damage, but most adverse effects can usually be alleviated if intake is stopped in time.

So far we have dealt with basic concepts about the vitamins: what they do for the body, how much of each is required in the diet, how these requirements may be met, and the effects of deficiency and excess (see Table 7-6). It should be clear that vitamins do not possess any miraculous properties, and consuming amounts in excess of those recommended provides no additional benefits. Yet, ever since the vitamins were first discovered, they have been prescribed and promoted for a variety of disorders that span the whole range of human afflictions. What is the basis for these claims, and are they valid?

ISSUE: ARE VITAMIN SUPPLEMENTS NECESSARY?

“Advocates of vitamin supplements promote them to combat stress and cure all sorts of disorders, but a comparison of the vitamin contents of foods with the Recommended Dietary Allowances shows that vitamin needs can be met by the diet. An individual who consumes a variety of foods from each of the food groups and prepares them properly will generally not require a vitamin supplement.

In addition to promoting unnecessarily large amounts of vitamins, some advocates push substances that are not known to be required in the diet. Two of these, *choline* and *inositol,* perform important functions in the body, and some scientists do consider them vitamins. Choline forms one part of the phospholipid lecithin and thus functions as a major component of cell membranes and in the transport of lipids in the bloodstream. It also forms a part of the structure of acetylcholine and sphingomyelin, both of which are important in the functioning of the nervous system. Another function of choline is to supply methyl groups, which are important in the synthesis of other substances. Inositol is a component of a phospholipid, lipositol. Both lipositol and lecithin in some way prevent the abnormal

A vitamin can only cure the diseases that result from a deficiency of that vitamin.

accumulation of fat in the liver. However, choline and inositol are not required in the diet because the body synthesizes them, and a deficiency of either has never been observed in humans. Even so, they are widely distributed in food, with the average diet providing 400 to 900 mg/day of choline and at least as much inositol (18, pages 282–291).

A variety of other substances, including *para*-aminobenzoic acid (PABA), bioflavonoids, pangamic acid (vitamin B_{15}), and amygdalin (laetrile, vitamin B_{17}), are often promoted as vitamins, but they have no known role in the body and perform no functions that cannot be adequately performed by other substances. None of these substances is considered indispensable for human beings, and deficiency states have never been observed in humans (19–23). ”

ISSUE: MEGAVITAMIN THERAPY

“ Many of the claims made for vitamins arise from the almost miraculous cures these substances effect in people with severe deficiencies. If vitamins can cure certain types of mental disorders or clear up certain skin diseases, why not try them on others? And if small amounts promote a healthy skin or aid the body in resisting infection, maybe larger amounts can cure acne or prevent colds. Another source of misleading claims for the vitamins are the deficiency states observed in experimental animals. If vitamin E deficiency produces sterility and reproductive failure in rats that can be cured by administering the vitamin, maybe large amounts increase sexual potency in humans? Personal observations made on oneself or on one's family and friends also add to the list of vitamin claims. An athlete may pop a handful of vitamin pills before a race, break the record in that event, and believe that it was the vitamins that made the difference. Some people find they have more energy or just feel better when they take vitamins.

To make sound nutritional choices, we need to keep several things in mind. First, a vitamin can cure only the diseases that result from a deficiency of that vitamin, and deficiency symptoms usually can be prevented by consuming the recommended levels in the diet. In some instances, vitamins have been used in very high doses in the treatment of certain diseases that are not nutritional in origin. In these cases, the vitamin is functioning as a drug, not a nutrient. Prescription of vitamins for this purpose belongs in the hands of qualified physicians who can monitor the treatment and deal with any side effects.

The best sources of nutrition information are professionals trained in the field, including nutritionists in the academic world, dietitians, and some nurses and physicians. Textbooks, reputable journals, such as *The American Journal of Clinical Nutrition,* the *Journal of the American Dietetic Association,* and *Nutrition Reviews,* and such organizations as a county cooperative extension office also provide sound information. Let us look now at some of the most popular vitamin fads and how to go about making intelligent nutritional choices regarding them. ”

TABLE **7-6** Summary of the vitamins

VITAMIN	FUNCTIONS	ADULT RDA	Sources: FOOD GROUPS	Sources: IMPORTANT EXAMPLES	DEFICIENCY	TOXICITY
Thiamine	Coenzyme, involved mainly in carbohydrate metabolism	Male: 1.4 mg/day Female: 1.0 mg/day	Meat, grains, vegetables	Pork, legumes, green peas, some green vegetables, whole and enriched grains	Beriberi—impairment of nerve-tissue function, edema, and/or wasting	Very low
Riboflavin	Coenzyme, involved in oxidation-reduction reactions	Male: 1.6 mg/day Female: 1.2 mg/day	Meat, milk, vegetables	Liver, meat, most dairy products, broccoli, spinach, enriched grains	Ariboflavinosis—fissures in corner of mouth, swollen purple tongue, dermatitis	Very low
Niacin	Coenzyme, involved in oxidation-reduction reactions in metabolism of many substances	Male: 18 mg/day Female: 13 mg/day	Meat, milk	Sources of high-quality protein, including mutually supplemented legumes; nuts and seeds; enriched grains	Pellagra—diarrhea, dermatitis, impairment of nervous system function, psychoses	Flushing and stinging face and hands, digestive tract disturbances, arrhythmic heartbeat
Vitamin B_6 (pyridoxine, pyridoxal, pyridoxamine)	Coenzyme, involved in amino acid, glycogen, and essential fatty acid metabolism	Male: 2.2 mg/day Female: 2.0 mg/day	Meat, vegetables	Liver, meat, legumes, green peppers, potatoes, other vegetables	Fissures in corner of mouth, anemia, impairment of nervous system and immune system function	Very low
Pantothenic acid	Coenzyme, involved in release of energy from carbohydrate, fat, and protein and in other metabolic pathways	Estimated safe intake: 4 to 7 mg/day	Meat, vegetables, grains*	Liver, meat, legumes, some vegetables, nuts, whole grains	Very rare in humans	Very low
Biotin	Coenzyme, involved in carboxylation reactions in the synthesis of glucose, fatty acids, and nucleic acids	Estimated safe intake: 100 to 200 μg/day	Meat,† vegetables	Liver, chicken, eggs, nuts, some vegetables	Flaky dermatitis, loss of appetite, apathy, depression, hallucinations	Very low
Folacin	Coenzyme, involved in transfer of single-carbon groups in synthesis of nucleic acids and metabolism of amino acids and choline	400 μg/day	Meat,† fruits and vegetables, grain*	Liver, legumes, some nuts, green vegetables, citrus fruits, whole grains, wheat germ	Megaloblastic, macrocytic anemia, skin changes	Very low

Vitamin B_{12}	Coenzyme, involved in transfer of methyl groups in nucleic acid synthesis and amino acid metabolism	3 μg/day	Meat, milk	Found in animal products only	Megaloblastic, macrocytic anemia, deterioration of nervous system	Very low
Vitamin C (ascorbic acid)	Collagen synthesis, amino acid metabolism, iron metabolism, capillary integrity, and other functions	60 mg/day	Fruits and vegetables	Citrus fruit, strawberries, green vegetables, tomatoes, potatoes, other fruits and vegetables	Scurvy—weakness, aching of joints and muscles, bleeding gums, bruise easily, mental changes	Increased oxalic and uric acid excretion, digestive tract disturbances, increased tolerance to the vitamin, destruction of vitamin B_{12}
Vitamin A (retinol, retinaldehyde, retinoic acid)	Eyesight, maintenance of epithelial tissue, growth (especially of bones), reproduction	Male: 1000 RE/day (5000 IU/day) Female: 800 RE (4000 IU/day)	Meat,† milk, fruits and vegetables	Liver, eggs, whole-milk products, yellow–orange and dark green leafy vegetables	Mild—night blindness Severe—xerophthalmia, keratinization of the eye, keratinization of epithelial tissues, impaired bone growth and reproduction	Fatigue, lethargy, nausea, weight loss, loss of hair, dermatitis, constipation, irregular menstruation, increased intracranial pressure, impaired bone growth
Vitamin D (cholecalciferol, ergocalciferol)	Maintain calcium and phosphate levels in the blood, thus facilitating formation and maintenance of bone mineral	5 μg/day (200 IU/day)	Rare in food except fortified milk; body synthesizes some of its own	Small amounts in egg yolk, butter, liver; fish-liver oil and fortified milk are only reliable food sources	Children: Rickets, abnormal bone development Adults: Osteomalacia, loss of bone mineral, reducing density of the bones	Loss of appetite, nausea, fatigue, headache, failure to grow, elevated blood calcium levels
Vitamin E (the tocopherols and tocotrienols)	Antioxidant, protects vitamins A and C as well as polyunsaturated fatty acids from oxidative damage	Male: 10 α-TE/day (15 IU/day) Female: 8 α-TE/day (12 IU/day)	Vegetables, grain*	Vegetable oils, nuts, whole grains, green vegetables	Rare in adults; produces a type of anemia in premature infants	Nausea, abdominal distress, interference with blood clotting
Vitamin K (phylloquinone or menaquinone)	Blood clotting	Estimated safe intake: 70 to 140 μg/day	Meat, vegetables; also synthesized by bacteria and absorbed from the intestines	Green leafy vegetables, liver, egg yolk	Rare in adults; bleeding episodes in some infants	Synthetic form, menadione, produced jaundice in infants

* Whole grains only.
† Not found in red meat, fish, or poultry unless specified.

FOCUS 7-2 LAETRILE Amygdalin (vitamin B_{17}) is a substance found in apricot pits, apple and cherry seeds, bitter almonds, and other sources. It contains glucose, benzaldehyde, and cyanide and has been widely promoted as a preventive and cure for cancer, most recently under the name *laetrile.* Its proponents claim that amygdalin, or laetrile, can be broken down by an enzyme, beta-glucosidase, found abundantly in cancer tissue, but not in normal body tissue. As a result, cyanide will be released into the tumor, killing it and leaving the rest of the body unaffected. Any cyanide released into normal tissue is supposedly detoxified by an enzyme called *rhodanese,* which converts it into the less harmful thiocyaniate (cancer tissue is supposed to contain less rhodanese than normal tissue) (58). In fact, beta-glucosidase is found only in small amounts in animal tissue and occurs in smaller amounts in tumor tissue than in the liver or kidney. Further, there is no evidence that the rhodanese concentration of tumors is any lower than in noncancerous tissues. It appears that the body itself breaks down relatively little laetrile into cyanide, and both cancer and noncancer cells should be equally affected. In experiments with rodents exposed to atmospheres containing varying amounts of cyanide, the dosages effective against the tumors were too close to the lethal human dose to be of any practical use (58). Furthermore, clinical trials in humans in which laetrile was used to treat cancer failed to show any benefit from the drug. Its ineffectiveness is also shown by the experiences of people who have given up conventional treatments to undergo laetrile therapy. In one highly publicized case, the parents of a 3-year-old leukemia victim took their child to Mexico for laetrile treatments. He died 3 months later (62).

Aside from the fact that it does not work, the use of laetrile is potentially hazardous. Many common foods, including some of the sources of laetrile itself, contain beta-glucosidase. Examples include almonds, peaches, plums, green peppers, mushrooms, lettuce, carrots, celery, and bean sprouts, as well as peach and apricot pits and apple seeds. Consuming these with laetrile causes the drug to be broken down in the intestine, and the free cyanide can then be absorbed into the body. Since 200 milligrams of cyanide is toxic and 1 gram of laetrile releases 60 milligrams of the substance, potentially lethal doses of cyanide may be absorbed from the intestine. Several deaths related to amygdalin, or laetrile, consumption have been reported (59–61).

NIACIN AND SCHIZOPHRENIA

Despite the fact that mental diseases have plagued the human race throughout history, their causes and the means for curing them have been elusive. Linus Pauling and others have recently proposed orthomolecular psychiatry as one possibility (24). These researchers point out that the normal function of the brain and nervous system involves hundreds of different chemical reactions. Reaction rates depend in part on heredity, but also on the proper concentration of essential substances, including thiamine, niacin, vitamin B_6, vitamin B_{12}, biotin, folacin, and vitamin C. Pauling hypothesizes that in some people the nervous system requires such large amounts of one or more of these vitamins that the diet cannot meet the need, and the deficiency results in impairment of mental function. If optimal amounts of the deficient substances could be provided, significant improvement of mental health might be achieved. For example, Pauling believes schizophrenia is a genetic disease that does not express itself when adequate amounts of essential substances, including vitamins, are present. Deficiency allows expression of the gene and leads to the disease. Thus part of the treatment is large doses of niacin, often accompanied by pyridoxine, ascorbic acid, and vitamin B_{12}.

Experimental evidence regarding the orthomolecular hypothesis appears to be contradictory. On one hand, Osmond and Hoffer and Denison observed positive results when they treated schizophrenics with massive doses of niacin (25,26). Denison found that schizophrenics who received the vitamin spent an average of 10 fewer weeks in the hospital during the year following admission than those not receiving niacin. Similarly, in several trials, Osmond and Hoffer observed that patients receiving niacin spent a longer time out of the hospital, had a lower rate of readmission, and were "well" a greater part of the time than those in the control group. On the other hand, several studies have found no effect of niacin on schizophrenia (27–29). In fact, a series of experiments called the Canadian Mental Health Association Collaborative Study found that niacin had *negative* effects on schizophrenic patients (28).

In 1973, the Task Force on Vitamin Therapy in Psychiatry of the American Psychiatric Association published a review of the effectiveness of megavitamin therapy and concluded that there is no solid evidence to support its use (30). Several groups of qualified psychiatrists and psychologists have obtained negative results in carefully controlled experiments, and the Task Force questions the validity of experiments that obtained favorable results, citing improper methods of diagnosing patients and evaluating treatment response. Some of the best results may have been obtained in patients who were not truly schizophrenic and for whom the rate of spontaneous recovery is high.

Although the evidence surrounding the orthomolecular theory is decidedly pessimistic, the issue of its success or failure is in many ways not a nutritional one. In this case, the vitamins are clearly being used as drugs rather than as nutrients. The amounts are far greater than can be obtained from the diet and are high enough that adverse effects from niacin, such as digestive-tract disturbances, arrhythmic heart beat, high blood glucose and uric acid levels, and flushing of the face and hands, may occur. For this reason, people considering this type of treatment for themselves or loved ones should consult a qualified psychiatrist; self-treatment is not recommended.

VITAMIN C AND COLDS

Since publication of *Vitamin C and the Common Cold* (revised as *Vitamin C, the Common Cold, and the Flu* in 1976) by Linus Pauling in 1970, many people have consumed large amounts of ascorbic acid to prevent or alleviate cold symptoms (31,32). Others have suggested that vitamin C has value in the prevention or treatment of a variety of other disorders, including cancer, mental illness, and heart disease (33). Despite the accumulation of considerable evidence that massive doses of vitamin C confer no additional benefits over recommended intakes of the vitamin and may produce side effects, many people continue to consume large amounts of this substance.

Proponents of vitamin C recommend an intake of 2 to 10 g/day or more to ensure optimum health (31–33). A cornerstone of this theory is Stone's estimate that based on the amount of ascorbic acid a rat synthesizes, humans need 2 to 4 g/day, depending on the amount of stress to which they are subjected. In addition, Pauling contends that millions of years ago, our ancestral primates obtained between 2.3 and 9.4 g/day of ascorbic acid from fruits and vegetables.

These arguments are totally speculative. Determining the amount of vitamin C another animal synthesizes or how much an evolutionary ancestor *might* have consumed may or may not have any bearing on the amount presently required by humans. In the first place, it is not clear how much of the ascorbic acid an animal synthesizes or the ancestral primate consumed is or was actually used by their bodies. Experiments show that large doses of ascorbic acid may stimulate the body's ability to catabolize the vitamin, while doses in excess of those required to saturate body tissues (100 to 150 mg/day) are rapidly excreted in the urine. Thus a considerable proportion of the vitamin synthesized or consumed by an animal could be metabolized by its body or lost in its urine. In fact, experiments have shown that farm animals that synthesize their own vitamin C have blood concentrations comparable with those of humans consuming 30 to 35 mg/day of the vitamin (34).

The major claim made for vitamin C is that it can prevent and treat the common cold. Pauling states that consumption of 1 to 2 g/day of ascorbic acid is the optimal level for the prevention of colds in most people, while the dosage should be increased to 4 to 10 g/day when a cold strikes. The bulk of the experimental evidence available at this time, however, indicates that ascorbic acid has no effect on the incidence of colds and only a minor effect on their severity (35,36).

Some of the more convincing studies were performed by T. W. Anderson and his colleagues at the University of Toronto (37). In the first of three **double-blind** trials, subjects were divided into two groups, one receiving 1 gram of vitamin C daily, the other a **placebo**. At the onset of a cold, the subjects were to increase the dosage to 4 g/day of vitamin C (or placebo) for the first 3 days. The groups were well matched for certain characteristics, such as previous history of exposure to colds, number of smokers, amount of fruit juice consumed, and so on, in an effort to control these influences as much as possible. The experimenters found that vitamin C did not influence the number of colds contracted during the course of the study and had only a minor effect on their severity. The vitamin C group spent 30 percent fewer days out of work or confined to the house than did the placebo group. However, the second and third trials did not repeat the results of the first, despite the fact that larger doses of vitamin C were used in the second trial and time-release capsules were employed in the third trial.

Other investigators have obtained similar results (38–40). In addition, vitamin C produces side effects, including nausea, abdominal cramps, diarrhea, and increased risk of kidney stones in some people (41). It also can increase breakdown of red blood cells in genetically predisposed individuals, such as some Orientals, some American blacks, and some people of Mediterranean extraction (42). Excessive intakes of ascorbic acid may induce a tolerance to the vitamin (36,41). It appears that the body's ability to break down vitamin C increases with higher dosages, and when the individual stops taking excess ascorbic acid, the body still breaks it down at this rapid rate for a period of time, thereby inducing a deficiency. In two cases, infants born to women who had taken large doses of vitamin C while they were pregnant showed symptoms of scurvy (36). In view of these potential risks, the minor effect of vitamin C on colds does not appear worthwhile.

Proponents of vitamin C also claim that it can prevent or treat heart disease, cancer, and mental illness. Experiments show that ascorbic acid is probably involved in the metabolism of cholesterol and triglycerides in the body (43). However, there is no experimental evidence to show that large doses can prevent or cure atherosclerosis or heart disease (34). Although some cancer and mental patients show slightly favorable responses to the administration of large doses of vitamin C, most of the evidence does not support the claim that the vitamin will significantly alter the outcome of either disorder (34,44).

VITAMIN E: A PANACEA

Even more than vitamin C, vitamin E has been promoted as a miracle vitamin. One of the most widely publicized uses has been in the prevention and treatment of heart disease. Its major proponents have been Wilfred and Evan Shute, both physicians in London, Ontario. Wilfred's book, *Vitamin E for Ailing and Healthy Hearts,* described how large doses have benefited patients with heart disease, as well as those with other disorders of the circulatory system (45). Significantly, however, the Shutes and their colleagues have never performed controlled experiments to test their observations. We therefore do not know whether the benefits were because of the vitamin or would have occurred whether it was administered or not. Several controlled experiments have shown no beneficial effect on heart disease, and a number of uncontrolled trials also have failed to produce a favorable effect (46–48). More and better-controlled studies need to be carried out, but the bulk of the evidence at present indicates that vitamin E is of no use in preventing or treating heart disease.

Vitamin E is also widely touted as improving sexual performance. This claim results from the observation that reproductive functions in rats deteriorate during vitamin E deficiency. These observations, however, in no way imply that large doses of vitamin E will improve sexual performance in humans. Furthermore, even if vitamin E were found to be necessary for normal functioning in humans, this does not mean that doses in excess of recommended amounts will have any additional beneficial effect on performance (49,50).

The theory that vitamin E can be used to treat muscular dystrophy also came from animal experiments, since deficiency of the vitamin produces a disorder in rabbits and other animals that is very similar to muscular dystrophy in humans. Again, the hazard of drawing conclusions from animal experiments must be emphasized, because the disease in humans is of different origin and does not respond to vitamin E (18, pages 282–291).

Still another claim made for vitamin E is that it can slow the aging process. Although it does prevent the formation of certain skin pigments that seem to arise as part of aging, vitamin E has no effect on the process itself: it cannot reverse or retard the deterioration of body function that occurs (49,51). There is also no evidence that vitamin E can prevent or cure cancer or treat skin disorders—in fact, some people develop a severe rash when the vitamin is rubbed on the skin (50). Other side effects, including nausea, intestinal distress, interference with blood clotting, and elevated blood triglyceride and cholesterol concentrations, have been observed in some people consuming more than 300 IU/day (52–54).

VITAMIN A AND ACNE

Acne is a source of anguish for many adolescents. Although the disease is no threat to health, the problem occurs at a time in life when the individual is particularly concerned about appearance and highly sensitive to criticism about it. Acne results from an accumulation of dead cells and an oily substance called **sebum** in the passageway leading from oil glands in the skin to its surface. This plugs the passageway, forming a **comedone**, or blackhead. Eventually the lining of the passageway may break, allowing sebum and bacteria to leak into the surrounding skin tissue. As a result, inflammation may occur, leading to the formation of a pimple. Exactly why acne occurs is unknown. It appears to be related to hormonal changes that take place during adolescence and may be affected by a variety of other factors, including heredity and stress (55). The problem usually decreases in severity as the person grows older.

Over the years, many myths have arisen regarding diet and acne. However, there is no well-documented evidence that any food, including chocolate, sweets, and fatty foods, aggravates the condition (56). Since vitamin A functions to maintain healthy epithelial tissues, including the skin, large doses often have been prescribed or promoted to cure acne. Common acne, however, does not result from a vitamin A deficiency, and numerous experiments show that it does not respond to treatment with the vitamin (56). In addition, toxicity symptoms have been reported in some patients.

One form of vitamin A, retinoic acid, has proved useful in treating acne. When applied topically in a cream, retinoic acid helps loosen comedones and facilitates the normal flow of sebum to the surface of the skin. However, retinoic acid burns the skin and precipitates the formation of pimples when it is first applied (57). Further, it is being used as a drug in this instance and therefore should be used only under the direction of a physician.

Study Guide

SUMMARY

1. Vitamins are organic compounds required in small amounts to facilitate body processes. Their functions, recommended intakes, food sources, and the results of deficiency and excess are summarized in Table 7-6.
2. Except in extraordinary circumstances, the body's needs for vitamins can be more than satisfied by consuming a variety of foods from each of the food groups and preparing them properly.
3. Although vitamin deficiencies still occur in certain parts of the world, they are rare in the United States and other affluent nations. A major factor causing vitamin deficiencies is restriction of the quantity or variety of foods in the diet, with the foods consumed lacking one or more vitamins. Vitamin deficiencies also may result from an inability to absorb the vitamin or from factors that increase requirements, such as pregnancy or lactation.
4. Contrary to common belief, vitamins are not harmless. Vitamin A and vitamin D are particularly toxic.
5. Many claims are made for vitamins. Vitamin C is promoted for the prevention and treatment of colds, heart disease, and cancer; vitamin E is supposedly effective against heart disease, cancer, muscular dystrophy, sexual impotence, and aging. Other claims include the treatment of schizophrenia with niacin, acne with vitamin A, and the promotion of choline, inositol, PABA, bioflavonoids, pangamic acid (vitamin B_{15}), and amygdalin (laetrile, vitamin B_{17}) as nutrients. Experimental evidence does not substantiate any of these claims.

VOCABULARY

autoimmune response
beriberi
carboxylation
carotenoid pigments
coenzyme
comedone
cornea
double-blind experiment
flavoprotein
intrinsic factor
in vitro
keratinization
osteomalacia
oxidation-reduction reactions
pellagra
pernicious anemia
peroxide
placebo
provitamin
replicate
retina
rhodopsin
rickets
scurvy
sebum
single-carbon groups
vitamins
xerophthalmia

STUDY QUESTIONS

1. For each of the vitamins describe the body process it facilitates and the means by which it does so.
2. Why are the RDAs and food contents of the fat-soluble vitamins usually expressed in units of biological activity, such as international units, retinol equivalents, and alpha-tocopherol equivalents, rather than weight (micrograms and milligrams)?
3. By what general means can nearly everyone meet his or her vitamin needs from food? For each of the following, give two foods commonly found in your diet that supply significant amounts of the vitamin:
   a. Thiamine
   b. Riboflavin
   c. Niacin
   d. Folacin
   e. Vitamin B_{12}
   f. Ascorbic acid
   g. Vitamin A
   h. Vitamin D (one food)
   i. Vitamin E
4. For each of the following, give the name of the disease that results from a deficiency of the vitamin. Describe the circumstances that have historically resulted in the deficiency.
   a. Thiamine
   b. Niacin
   c. Vitamin B_{12}
   d. Vitamin C
   e. Vitamin A
   f. Vitamin D
5. Can you think of any situations that could potentially occur in the United States today in which the quantity or variety of food might be restricted to the point of producing a vitamin deficiency?
6. Mary bought a supplement that included the following quantities of vitamins:

Thiamine: 10 mg
Riboflavin: 10 mg
Niacin: 100 mg
Vitamin B_6: 10 mg
Vitamin B_{12}: 10 μg
Vitamin C: 250 mg
Vitamin A: 10,000 IU (2000 RE)
Vitamin E: 200 IU (133 alpha-TE)
Can you explain why Mary wasted her money?

7. For each of the following, give the reason that it is not required in the diet. Which is potentially toxic, even at relatively low levels of intake? Why?
   a. Choline
   b. Inositol
   c. PABA
   d. Bioflavonoids
   e. Pangamic acid (vitamin B_{15})
   f. Amygdalin (laetrile, vitamin B_{17})
8. For each of the following, state the claims made by its proponents and briefly describe the current consensus of opinion among nutritionists regarding these claims:
   a. Vitamin C and the common cold
   b. Vitamin E and heart disease
   c. Orthomolecular psychiatry
   d. Vitamin A and acne

SELF-TEST

Multiple choice: For each of the following, choose the best answer.

1. Which of the following *cannot* be synthesized by the body from a provitamin?
   a. Thiamine c. Vitamin A
   b. Niacin d. Vitamin D
2. The RDAs for which of the following depend on caloric intake?
   a. Folacin, vitamin B_{12}, vitamin C
   b. Vitamin B_6, biotin, folacin
   c. Thiamine, riboflavin, niacin
   d. Vitamin B_{12}, vitamin A, vitamin D
3. The body's need for which of the following can partly be met by consuming high-quality protein?
   a. Folacin c. Riboflavin
   b. Vitamin B_6 d. Niacin
4. Which of the following does the body obtain in significant amounts from bacteria in the large intestine?
   a. Vitamin C c. Vitamin D
   b. Vitamin A d. Vitamin K
5. Women in parts of the Middle East clothe themselves from head to toe when they go outside. You would expect them to develop a deficiency of what vitamin?
   a. Vitamin C c. Vitamin D
   b. Vitamin A d. Vitamin K
6. Which two vitamins are particularly toxic in large amounts?
   a. Thiamine and vitamin B_6
   b. Vitamin A and vitamin D
   c. Riboflavin and vitamin B_{12}
   d. Thiamine and vitamin C
7. A deficiency of either of which two vitamins leads to an anemia characterized by large, immature, and fragile red blood cells?
   a. Thiamine and vitamin B_6
   b. Riboflavin and niacin
   c. Vitamin A and vitamin D
   d. Folacin and vitamin B_{12}
8. Eliminating animal products from the diet will eventually lead to a deficiency of
   a. Vitamin A c. Biotin
   b. Vitamin B_{12} d. Pantothenic acid
9. Taking an appropriate vitamin supplement will help cure
   a. Scurvy c. Colds
   b. Cancer d. Heart disease
10. Mary cooked some broccoli in water. Large amounts of which of the following were lost when she threw away the water?
    a. Vitamin A c. Vitamin E
    b. Vitamin C d. Vitamin K

True-False

1. Because of modern processing methods, it is no longer possible to meet most people's vitamin needs solely from food.
2. Vitamins have pharmacologic properties that are useful in the treatment of certain problems.
3. One hundred international units of natural vitamin E are more potent than 100 international units of synthetic vitamin E.

4. Excess water-soluble vitamins are stored in the body.
5. Severe vitamin deficiencies are rare in the United States and other affluent nations.

SUGGESTED ACTIVITIES

1. Visit a health food store or drugstore.
   a. For each of the following, determine the highest and lowest potency available and compare their cost.
      (1) Multivitamin preparations
      (2) Vitamin C
      (3) Vitamin E
   b. For each of the following, compare the cost of different brand names. Compare the costs of the items in the health food store with those available in supermarkets or drug stores. Compare the cost of products promoted as "natural" with that of products not promoted in that way.
      (1) Vitamin C, 100-tablet bottle, 500 mg/tablet
      (2) Vitamin E, 100-capsule bottle, 100 IU/capsule
   c. Talk to the proprietor and/or collect literature available in the store. What claims are made for the vitamins?
2. Make a list of nonnutrient items and the claims made for them. Can you substantiate or refute any of these claims?
3. Keep a diet record as described in Activity 10-1, and using Ready Reference 1, estimate your intake of the following:
   a. Thiamine
   b. Riboflavin
   c. Niacin
   d. Vitamin C
   e. Vitamin A

   Does your intake meet the RDA for each vitamin? If not, add or substitute some foods in your diet that will help you meet the RDA.

FURTHER READING

1. For a more detailed look at the vitamins:

   Goodhart, R. S., and Shils, M. E.: *Modern Nutrition in Health and Disease,* 6th ed., Lea & Febiger, Philadelphia, 1980.

   Nutrition Reviews: *Present Knowledge in Nutrition,* 4th ed., The Nutrition Foundation, Washington, 1976.

2. An interesting and readable account of pellagra and its conquest:

   Roe, D. A.: *A Plague of Corn—The Social History of Pellagra,* Cornell University Press, Ithaca, N.Y., 1973.

3. Recent and readable reviews on vitamin C and vitamin E:

   Anderson, T. W.: "New Horizons for Vitamin C," *Nutrition Today* **12:**6–13 (January/February 1977).

   Tappel, A. L.: "Vitamin E," *Nutrition Today* **8:**4–12 (July/August 1973).

4. A discussion of food fads, including vitamin C, vitamin E, and orthomolecular psychiatry:

   The entire supplement issue of *Nutrition Reviews* **32** (July Supplement 1974).

5. Up-to-date information on pangamic acid (vitamin B_{15}) and amygdalin (laetrile, vitamin B_{17}):

   Herbert, V.: "Pangamic Acid (Vitamin B_{15}): A Review," *Am. J. Clin. Nutr.* **32:**1534–1540 (1979).

   Herbert, V.: "The Nutritionally and Metabolically Destructive 'Nutritional and Metabolic Antineoplastic Diet' of Laetrile Proponents," *Am. J. Clin. Nutr.* **32:**96–98 (1979).

   Herbert, V.: "Laetrile: The Cult of Cyanide," *Am. J. Clin. Nutr.* **32:**1121–1158 (1979).

WATER AND MINERALS

The nutrients discussed so far in this book are chemical compounds synthesized by living organisms. The human body, however, also requires a number of substances that were present on earth long before life appeared: mineral elements and water.

Life began in the oceans, and single-celled and other small organisms still depend on the water that surrounds their bodies to provide an appropriate environment in which to live. Humans do not live in the water; they carry their "ocean" within them. The body fluids bathe each cell, providing the proper environment for cellular function. Our internal environment remains remarkably constant, even in the face of drastic changes in our surroundings. We can step from an air-conditioned room into the heat of a summer's day, climb to the rarefied atmosphere on top of a mountain, and eat foods of widely varying composition—in each case a number of mechanisms work to maintain a constant environment within the body. However, loss of 10 percent of the body's water can seriously disrupt the internal environment; loss of 20 percent is nearly always fatal. As a result, humans can survive for weeks without food; without water they die within days.

Many people are aware of the importance of certain minerals to the body: they know calcium and phosphorus are needed for strong bones and teeth and iron helps build blood. Another 14 minerals are essential in the diet, and unlike the vitamins, the last of which (vitamin B_{12}) was discovered in 1948, the number continues to grow. Elements such as chromium and molybdenum, familiar because of their industrial uses, were added to the list in the 1950s, and today nickel, tin, vanadium, and silicon await confirmation of their essential role. It is possible that there will be more, for we are still learning about the work of these substances in the body.

Water, Electrolytes, Acid-Base Balance

Water is the single most abundant substance in the body: it makes up 50 to 60 percent of an adult's body weight (1, pages 355–394). It is the medium in which all body processes occur. Nutrients, enzymes, hormones, and other substances are dissolved in the body fluids, and such diverse processes as chemical reactions, muscle contraction, and nerve-impulse transmission depend on water. The blood and lymph, composed mainly of water, transport oxygen and nutrients to the cells and carry carbon dioxide and other waste products away. Water also participates in the movement of substances into and out of the body; it is the medium in which digestion and absorption occur, as well as the means by which waste products are eliminated.

However, water functions are more than a solvent and a transport medium. Since a large amount of energy (600 kcal/g) is needed to vaporize it, water provides an excellent means of dissipating body heat. When the body overheats, sweat glands secrete large amounts of sweat onto the skin. Heat is absorbed by the water as it vaporizes, thereby cooling the body. Water participates in many chemical reactions. **Metabolic water**, the water released by the breakdown of carbohydrate, fat, and protein for energy, accounts for about 13 percent of the water retained by the body each day. Water also provides structural support for the body and functions as a lubricant in the joint fluids, saliva, and around the eyeballs.

Humans can survive for weeks without food; without water they die within days.

THE FLUID COMPARTMENTS

All the water in the body, or the **total body water (TBW)**, is found in two main compartments, the **intracellular fluid (ICF)** and the **extracellular fluid (ECF)** (Figure 8-1). The intracellular fluid, which consists of all the water within the cells, comprises 55 percent of the total body water in the average young adult male; the water outside the cells, the extracellular fluid, accounts for 45 percent. In females, water tends to be more evenly distributed between the two compartments (1, pages 355–394). The ECF itself may be subdivided into the blood plasma, the **interstitial fluid (IF)**, which is the fluid lying between the cells, and other fluids, such as the cerebrospinal fluid and the fluid in the eyes. Plasma and the interstitial fluid make up 7.5 and 20 percent, respectively, of the TBW; the remaining body fluids account for 17.5 percent (1, pages 355–394).

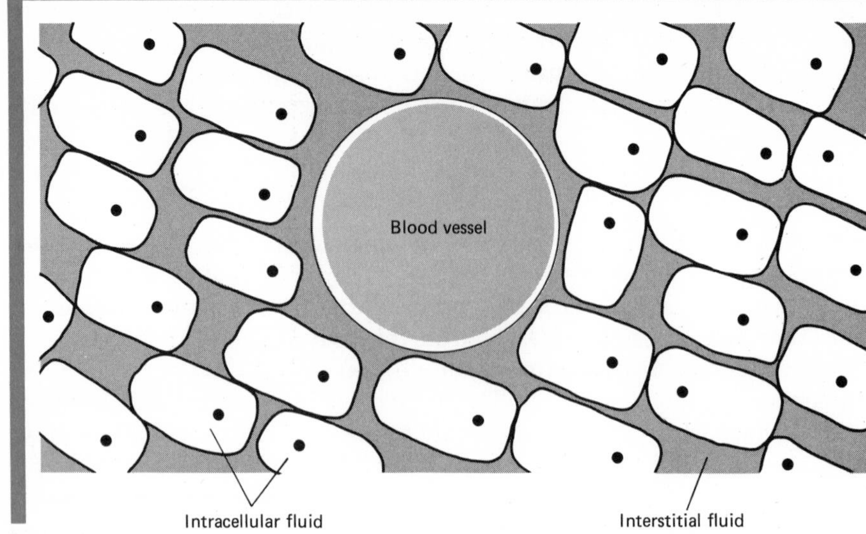

FIGURE 8-1 *The Fluid Compartments.* The extracellular fluid includes the blood plasma and the fluid between cells (interstitial fluid). Intracellular fluid is that contained within cells.

Maintaining water balance between fluid compartments depends largely on the concentration of dissolved material, or **solute**, in each compartment. Because of their great abundance, the minerals sodium, potassium, and chloride (the negative ion of chlorine) are the most important solutes. These three elements belong to a group of substances called **electrolytes** because of their ability to conduct an electric current when they are in solution. Sodium and chloride are found mainly in the extracellular fluid; potassium occurs largely in the intracellular fluid. Although sodium and potassium can cross the cell membrane, a special "pump" works to keep potassium inside the cell and sodium outside. Protein also plays an important role as a solute; it helps keep the plasma fluid in the blood vessels from moving out into the interstitial fluid (see Chapter 4).

Fluid balance within the body is maintained largely by the shifting of water from one compartment to another in response to changes in the concentration of solute (Figure 8-2). When solute concentration is equal on both sides of the cell membrane, water passes across the membrane in equal amounts in both directions. If the solute concentration on one side becomes greater than that on the other side, a net movement of water occurs from the area of lower concentration toward that of higher concentration. This movement of water across the cell membrane, called **osmosis**, keeps the solute concentrations on both sides of the membrane equal.

Suppose, for example, that Jane works for several hours on a hot day without drinking much water. As she sweats, she loses water more rapidly than solute from her ECF. The concentration of solute (sodium and chloride) in the ECF becomes greater than the concentration of solute (potassium and others) in the ICF, and water moves from the cells into the ECF. A similar situation occurs in kwashiorkor. The protein content of the plasma drops, and the solute concentration of the plasma therefore becomes lower than that of the surrounding interstitial fluid. Water then

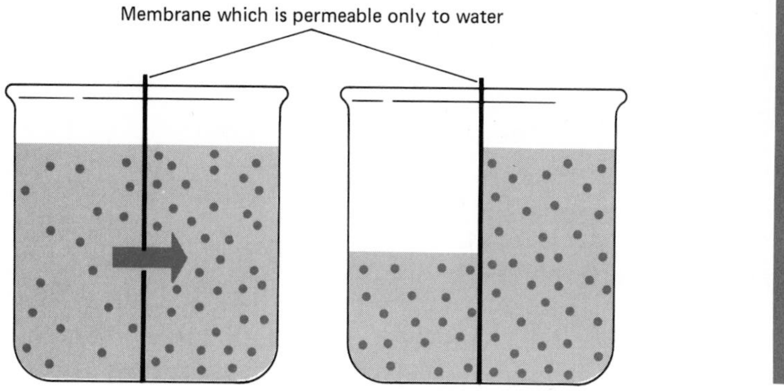

FIGURE 8-2
Osmosis. The membrane allows water to pass through it from an area of low solute concentration to one of higher solute concentration. The process continues until solute concentrations on both sides of the membrane are equal.

moves from the bloodstream into the interstitial fluid, causing the swelling known as **edema**.

WHOLE-BODY WATER BALANCE

Alterations in the water balance between fluid compartments normally reflect some change in the water balance of the body as a whole. To maintain equilibrium, the water lost each day must be replaced (Figure 8-3). The body loses water via the urine, feces, skin, and the lungs, and the amount lost varies with physical activity, body and environmental temperature, humidity, and wind velocity. The kidneys normally produce 1 to 1.5 liters/day of urine, less when the person is dehydrated, and more when too much water has been consumed or when excess solute must be excreted (1, pages 355–394). About 100 to 200 milliliters of water is lost in the feces, and the amount increases with diarrhea (1, pages 355–394). **Insensible water losses**, which include water vapor exhaled from the lungs and invisible perspiration, adds another 600 to 1000 ml/day (1, pages 355–394). During physical activity or in a warm climate, the body perspires visibly, and between 1 and 10 liters/day of water may be lost in this way (2, pages 166–177). So a total of about 2 to 2.5 liters of water may be lost each day by a sedentary individual in a temperate climate and considerably more by an active person or one living in a warm climate (2, pages 166–177). Water is replaced by food (770 to 1000 ml/day), drink (1200 to 1500 ml/day), and the metabolic water released by oxida-

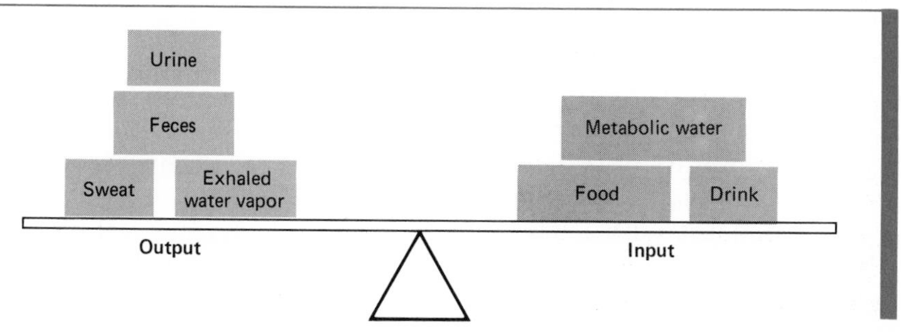

FIGURE 8-3
Water Balance. Daily losses must be balanced by an equivalent intake.

tion of carbohydrate, fat, and protein for energy (200 to 300 ml/day) (3, page 569). When input equals output, the body is in a state of water balance.

Dehydration occurs when the body loses water faster than it replaces it, because of, for example, diarrhea, vomiting, or excessive sweating. Generally, the rate of water loss exceeds that of electrolyte loss, leading to a higher solute concentration in the extracellular fluid. Because water passes from the cells into the ECF to equalize the solute concentrations in the two compartments, the volume of both the ECF and ICF is reduced. The person may feel nauseous, weak, hot, and dry and may lose muscular coordination. The thirst center in the brain responds to the situation by stimulating the individual to drink fluids. In addition, the body secretes two hormones, aldosterone and antidiuretic hormone. **Aldosterone** stimulates the kidney to reabsorb more sodium from the urine, while **antidiuretic hormone** stimulates it to retain more water. In this way, the body conserves both sodium and water to maintain fluid volume.

If the water consumed by a dehydrated person contains enough sodium (equivalent to about 0.2 percent NaCl by weight), the balance is restored. If the person drinks sufficient water but does not take in enough salt, he or she may become overhydrated. The influx of water into the ECF creates a lower solute concentration there than in the ICF, and water moves into the cells. ECF volume falls with a consequent drop in blood pressure, and the individual feels weak or faint. Stimulated by aldosterone, the kidneys increase their retention of sodium in an attempt to restore balance. Consuming small amounts of salt when replacing lost water will help prevent this situation (see Recommended Water Intake).

ACID-BASE BALANCE

Water and certain minerals are involved in another important balancing mechanism: maintaining the body's *acid-base balance* (pH), the relative proportion of hydrogen (H^+) and hydroxide ions (OH^-) in the body fluids. In pure water, a very small number of water molecules dissociate into hydrogen and hydroxide ions:

$$H_2O \rightleftharpoons H^+ + OH^-$$

Since the concentrations of the two ions are equal, pure water is neutral. The presence of a larger amount of hydrogen ions makes the solution acidic, while the presence of a larger quantity of hydroxide ions makes it basic or alkaline.

Acidity and alkalinity of a solution are expressed in terms of **pH**, which is a measure of hydrogen ion concentration. The pH is based on a scale of 1 to 14, with a pH of 1 denoting a high concentration of hydrogen ions (high acidity) and a pH of 14 representing the reverse situation (high alkalinity). The pH of pure water is 7.0, which shows that it is neutral.

For normal body function, the pH of the body fluids must be maintained within very narrow limits. Normal pH is 7.4; the upper limit is 7.8, and the lower limit is 7.0. Exceeding either limit alters the activity of various enzymes in the body to the point where life is no longer possible.

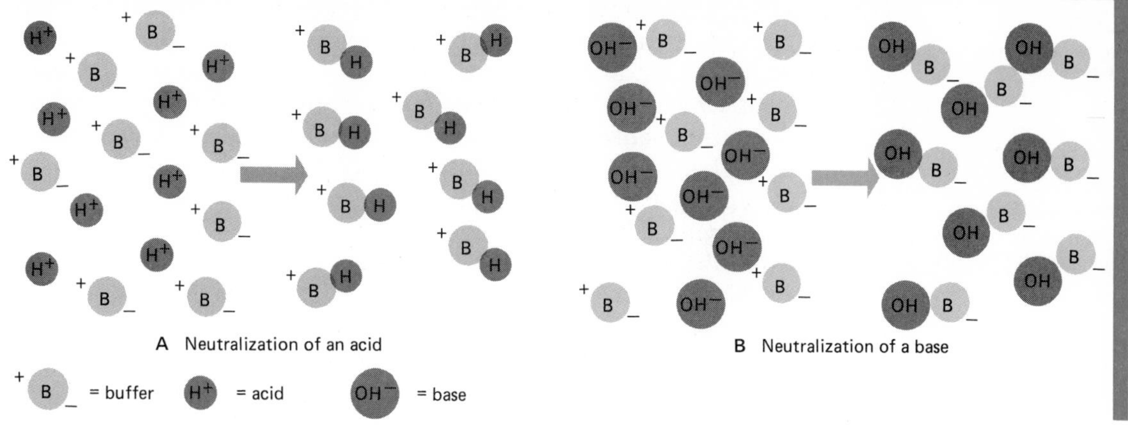

FIGURE 8-4
Buffers. Buffers neutralize both acids and bases. **A** Negative charges in the buffer system neutralize acid-forming protons. **B** Positive charges in the buffer system neutralize base-forming hydroxide (OH) ions.

Three general mechanisms control acid-base balance: buffer systems, the lungs, and the kidneys. **Buffers** are substances that resist changes in the pH of a solution. They can both donate and receive hydrogen ions and can therefore neutralize both acids and bases (Figure 8-4). Buffered aspirin products contain chemicals that neutralize the excess stomach acid resulting from the use of aspirin. Important buffers in the body fluids include bicarbonate, phosphate, and proteins. The lungs also help regulate pH. Breathing faster eliminates carbon dioxide from the blood, which reduces its acidity; slower breathing results in an accumulation of carbon dioxide and an increase in the blood's acidity.* The most potent system for maintaining acid-base balance is the kidney, which excretes hydrogen ions and retains bicarbonate (a buffer) when the body fluids are too acidic and does the reverse when they become too alkaline. Sodium, chloride, and phosphate ions play an important role in these processes.

Several elements found in food, especially chloride, phosphorus, and sulfur, are called *acid-forming substances* because they create a more acidic condition in the body. Meat, fish, poultry, eggs, cereals, and some nuts, such as peanuts and walnuts, contain relatively large amounts of these substances and are therefore called *acid-forming foods*. Foods that contain relatively large quantities of sodium, potassium, calcium, and magnesium are *alkaline-* or *base-forming foods* because these minerals form bases in the body. Fruits and vegetables are generally base-forming foods. Citrus fruits, which we commonly think of as acidic, produce an alkaline reaction in the body. The body breaks down the organic acids in these fruits into carbon dioxide and water, leaving behind the alkaline

* Carbon dioxide in the blood forms carbonic acid and the bicarbonate buffer as follows:

$$H_2O + CO_2 \rightleftharpoons \underset{\text{(carbonic acid)}}{H_2CO_3} \rightleftharpoons H^+ + \underset{\text{(bicarbonate)}}{HCO_3^-}$$

minerals. Some fruits, however, such as plums, prunes, and cranberries, contain organic acids which the body cannot break down and which produce an acid reaction. Milk, pure carbohydrate, and pure fat produce neither an acidic nor an alkaline reaction in the body. The acid-forming phosphate in milk offsets the effects of the alkaline-forming calcium, while pure carbohydrate and fat contain no minerals. Under normal conditions, the degree of acidity or alkalinity contributed by a mixed diet can easily be neutralized by the three body systems that regulate pH.

RECOMMENDED WATER INTAKE (2, pages 166–177)

A Recommended Dietary Allowance (RDA) for water has not been set because physical activity and environmental conditions vary greatly among individuals. However, the Food and Nutrition Board recommends that adults obtain 1 liter of water from food, drink, and metabolic activity for each 1000 kilocalories consumed, while infants should take in about 1.5 liters/1000 kcal. Thus the average adult should consume the equivalent of six to ten 10-ounce glasses of water per day. Adjustments should be made for strenuous physical activity, a hot climate, diarrhea, vomiting, and other situations of high water loss. Although the mechanisms described earlier work to maintain fluid balance, anyone who engages in strenuous physical activity or who lives in a hot climate can help the body to stay in balance by consuming small amounts of water frequently. Sodium losses can be replaced by salting foods or by consuming a slightly salty beverage made by dissolving about 2 grams, or 1/2 teaspoon, of salt in a quart of water.

The Minerals: Functions, Needs, Deficiencies

Minerals are elements required by the body in relatively small amounts for growth, maintenance, and reproduction. Like the vitamins, they generally function along with or as parts of other compounds. They are distinguished from the vitamins, however, by the fact that they are single elements: they contain no carbon and are therefore called **inorganic** substances.

The amount of a particular mineral present in the body varies greatly (Table 8-1). The body of a 70-kilogram male contains about 1.2 kilograms (2.6 pounds) of calcium, but only 9 milligrams (0.0003 ounce) of molybdenum. The 105 grams of sodium in his body are equivalent to that contained in 201 grams (7 ounces) of table salt, while the iron content would be sufficient to make at least three 1 1/2-inch standard nails. Those minerals present in the body in amounts greater than 0.005 percent of body weight are called the **macronutrient elements**. They include calcium, phosphorus, sodium, potassium, chloride, sulfur, and magnesium and are required in the diet in quantities greater than 100 mg/day. The **micronutrient**, or **trace elements**, are found in the body in amounts less than 0.005 percent of the body weight and include iron, io-

TABLE **8-1**

The body content of certain minerals

MINERAL	AMOUNT IN A 70-kg PERSON, g
Calcium	1200
Phosphorus	750
Potassium	245
Sulfur	175
Sodium	105
Chlorine	105
Magnesium	35
Iron	2.8
Manganese	0.21
Copper	0.105
Iodine	0.024

Source: H. C. Sherman, *Chemistry of Food and Nutrition,* 8th ed., Macmillan, New York, 1952, p. 227. (Copyright 1952 by Macmillan Publishing Co., Inc. Used with permission.)

dine, zinc, copper, chromium, selenium, cobalt, molybdenum, manganese, and fluorine—and possibly nickel, vanadium, tin, and silicon.

Let us look now at how the minerals function in the body. How much of each do we need daily? What foods provide them? What are the results of deficiency and excess? Our discussion will include several current issues, such as the superenrichment debate involving iron and the effects of fluoridating water.

HOW MINERALS WORK IN THE BODY

Minerals help carry out a variety of body processes. Sodium, potassium, and chloride, as we have seen, help maintain fluid-electrolyte balance and acid-base balance. Minerals facilitate the activity of hundreds of enzymes, are components of other body substances, play a structural role, and participate in such other processes as blood formation, growth, reproduction, and nerve and muscle function. These functions are summarized in Table 8-4.

Enzymes Like the B vitamins, minerals are required for the activity of a large number of enzymes. In some cases, minerals are incorporated into the enzyme in such a way that they cannot be removed without destroying the enzyme. For example, iron functions in the body in two forms, heme iron and nonheme iron. Heme iron is that contained within a complex organic molecule called **heme** (Figure 8-5). In this form, the iron is a structural component of many enzymes, including several that participate in the release of energy from carbohydrate, fat, and protein. The iron cannot be removed from the heme without destroying the enzyme. In other instances, minerals are bound to enzymes with varying degrees of tightness, but can be removed without breaking down the enzyme. These

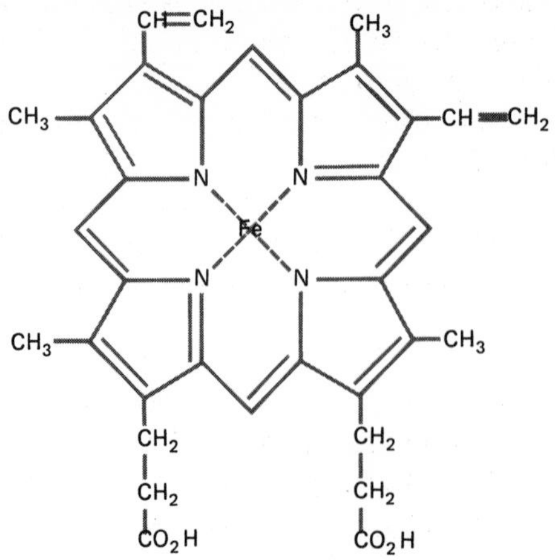

FIGURE 8-5
The Heme Molecule.
Heme is found in hemoglobin, myoglobin, and a variety of enzymes.

removable minerals are often called **cofactors** for the enzymes. **Nonheme iron**, for instance, is iron in its elemental form, and it functions as a cofactor for several enzymes. Calcium, potassium, magnesium, zinc, copper, selenium, manganese, and molybdenum are among the other minerals that participate in enzyme function.

Structural Components Of the many minerals that help form the structural components of the body, calcium and phosphorus are probably the most important. Together they form the hard-mineral **hydroxyapatite** of bones and teeth. Connective tissue, containing collagen and other organic substances, makes up the matrix, or framework, of the bone, much like steel girders provide a framework for a building. The hydroxyapatite is deposited in this framework to harden it so it can support the body. At one time it was thought that once this mineral was deposited, it became relatively inactive. Now we know that bone is a dynamic tissue and that hydroxyapatite is continually being broken down and re-formed to allow the bone to adjust to stress. For example, bones thicken when subjected to heavy loads and generally remodel themselves to provide maximum support at stress points. Bone also performs other functions. For example, the skull and spinal column protect the brain and spinal cord from injury. Bone serves as an anchor point for muscles and as the place where blood cells form. It stores minerals such as calcium, magnesium, sodium, and iron and releases them in times of need. Hydroxyapatite also forms the hard mineral of teeth, but its crystals are much more densely packed and its rate of turnover is considerably slower than in the bones. Teeth change very little once they have erupted into the mouth and have completed their mineralization.

Fluoride (the negative ion of fluorine) also plays an important structural role by strengthening bones and teeth. It substitutes for some of the hydroxide (OH^-) ions in hydroxyapatite, forming *fluorapatite,* which has a more perfect crystal structure and is more resistant to breakdown. The incidence of tooth decay and the bone disease osteoporosis, for example, are lower in areas where fluoride intake is relatively high (see Issue: Fluoridation at the end of this chapter).

Several minerals, including zinc, copper, and manganese, are essential for the formation of connective tissue, which is an important structural component of cartilage, skin, blood vessels, and other tissues besides bone. This may explain why zinc is important for normal wound healing and why copper deficiency in animals leads to weakened bones and blood vessels.

Blood Formation and Function Iron, copper, sodium, chloride, phosphorus, and calcium are among the minerals that play a role in the formation and functioning of the blood. Heme iron is a component of *hemoglobin,* the oxygen-carrying substance packed into every red blood cell. Copper, which plays an important role in mobilizing iron for hemoglobin synthesis by facilitating iron absorption from the intestine and its release from storage in the liver, is vital for red blood cell formation. Sodium and chloride help maintain fluid and electrolyte balance; phosphate is a buffer that aids in maintaining acid-base balance; and calcium is required for blood clotting.

Metabolism of the Energy Nutrients A variety of minerals function in the biochemical pathways by which carbohydrate, fat, and protein are metabolized. Phosphorus, for example, participates in the synthesis and breakdown of glucose and is a component of many coenzymes and the energy-storage compound ATP. Magnesium is a cofactor for enzyme reactions in which phosphate groups are transferred from one molecule to another, including all reactions in which ATP is synthesized or broken down, and is therefore vital for the release of energy from food. Other minerals, such as potassium, calcium, iron, zinc, copper, and manganese, are cofactors for enzymes that participate in the synthesis or the breakdown of carbohydrate, fat, and protein.

Components of Other Body Compounds Minerals are components of or are required for the functioning of a variety of other body compounds. Phosphorus is found in phospholipids and in the nucleic acids DNA and RNA, while chloride forms a part of the hydrochloric acid secreted by the stomach. Myoglobin is a heme-containing compound found in muscle tissue. It accepts oxygen from the blood and passes it to the muscle cells. Zinc is needed for the proper functioning of insulin in regulating carbohydrate metabolism, and copper is a cofactor for one of the enzymes involved in the synthesis of **melanin**, the pigment responsible for suntans and for the dark skin of black people.

The functions of iodine, chromium, and selenium are highly specialized. Iodine is a component of thyroid hormones, which strongly influence the growth and development of the body, its rate of metabolism, and its ability to reproduce. These hormones stimulate a variety of body processes, including the rate of energy release from carbohydrate, fat, and protein and protein synthesis. As a component of a substance called the **glucose tolerance factor (GTF)**, chromium is essential for the utilization of glucose by the body. (It appears that GTF in some way facilitates the activity of insulin, possibly by promoting its binding to cell membranes.) Selenium functions in the body as part of an enzyme that helps neutralize the hydrogen peroxide produced by certain metabolic reactions, as well as the peroxides of polyunsaturated fatty acids. Like vitamin E, it thus helps to protect cell membranes from damage.

Sulfur and cobalt enter the body as components of the substances in which they function. Sulfur is found in the amino acids methionine and cysteine and in several vitamins, while cobalt is part of the vitamin B_{12} molecule.

Growth and Reproduction As a result of the functions they perform, all the minerals are needed in some way for growth and reproduction. Zinc and iodine, however, appear to be particularly important. The iodine-containing thyroid hormones stimulate growth and development and are needed for normal reproduction. The actual mechanism by which zinc participates in these two processes is still unknown, but because zinc deficiency results in impaired growth and underdeveloped sex organs, we know it plays a significant role.

Nerve and Muscle Function Sodium, potassium, calcium, magnesium, and copper play a role in the function of the nervous system and muscles. The maintenance of a relatively high concentration of sodium in the extracellular fluid and potassium in the intracellular fluid is important for the generation and conduction of electric impulses along both nerve and muscle fibers (Figure 8-6). When an appropriate stimulus is applied to a nerve or muscle fiber, sodium and potassium rapidly change places. During this process, a nerve impulse is generated or a muscle contraction is initiated. Continued function of the nerve or muscle cell depends on its ability to pump sodium back out of the cell and potassium back in so that the exchange can occur again. Calcium and magnesium both play a role in the generation and transmission of electric impulses, perhaps by influencing the ability of sodium and/or potassium to pass through the cell membrane. In addition, calcium plays a direct role in the contraction of muscle fibers. Copper is important in nervous system functioning because it is needed for the synthesis of the phospholipids that are components of the **myelin sheath** surrounding the nerve fibers.

Membrane Transport Calcium and sodium facilitate the movement of various substances across cell membranes. Calcium is needed for the absorption of vitamin B_{12}, and sodium is needed for the absorption of glucose and amino acids from the intestine.

MEETING MINERAL NEEDS (2, pages 125–178)

The human requirement for a mineral is generally determined by estimating the amount lost to the body each day and adjusting this value to account for the part of a given intake that the body does not absorb from

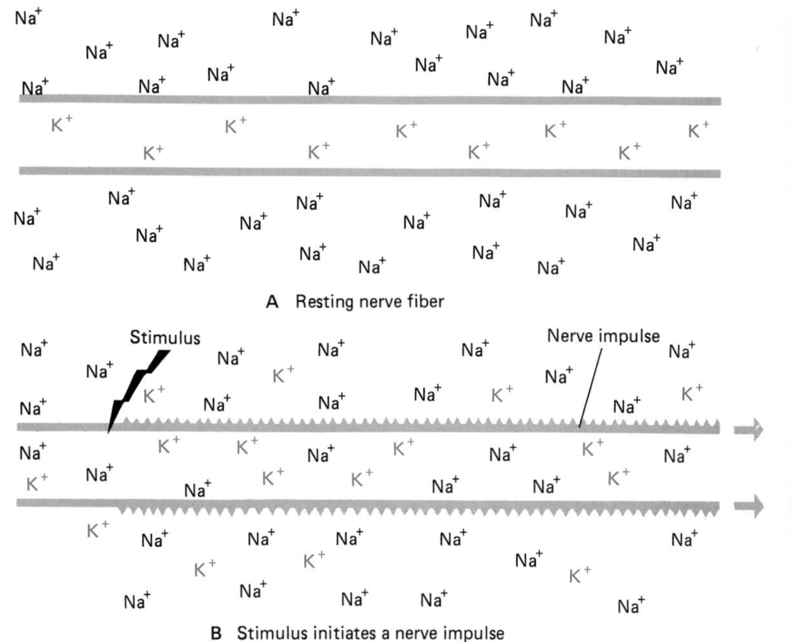

FIGURE 8-6
Nerve Impulse Generation. **A** In a resting nerve fiber, sodium is found mainly outside and potassium mainly inside of the fiber. **B** A stimulus, such as physical contact, heat, or cold, results in an exchange of sodium and potassium across the nerve cell membrane, which generates an electrical impulse. As the area of sodium-potassium exchange progresses along the fiber, so does the nerve impulse.

food. Another source of data is studies of the intake of various population groups. If no deficiency symptoms are observed in a population, the intake of the mineral is probably adequate. The Recommended Dietary Allowances (RDA) for calcium, phosphorus, magnesium, iron, zinc, and iodine are listed in Ready Reference 3. Because we do not have enough data to establish RDAs for the other minerals, the Food and Nutrition Board (FNB) has expressed these requirements in terms of estimated safe and adequate daily dietary intakes. These give a range of intakes thought to be adequate for most Americans and are also listed in Ready Reference 3.

In meeting the body's needs for minerals, a general rule of thumb is to consume a variety of foods from each of the food groups. What is not present in one food will probably be found elsewhere in the diet. Some foods are particularly good sources of specific minerals; others contain substances that inhibit the absorption of minerals. Let us take a closer look.

Macronutrient Elements The Food and Nutrition Board recommends an allowance of 800 mg/day of calcium for adults. The Food and Agriculture Organization of the United Nations has suggested that a more practical allowance for adults is between 400 and 500 mg/day, because there appears to be no evidence of calcium deficiency in countries where intakes are of this order (4). The demands of growth, pregnancy, and lactation greatly increase the requirement for calcium. Ingestion of large amounts of protein increases the excretion of the mineral in the urine, so people with high protein intakes may have somewhat higher calcium requirements (2, pages 125–178).

Some good food sources of calcium are shown in Figure 8-7. Milk and dairy products are by far the best sources of this mineral, and meeting the RDA becomes difficult if they are excluded from the diet. Certain green vegetables, such as broccoli, collards, mustard greens, and turnip greens, also provide significant amounts of calcium. Spinach, chard, and beet greens are *not* good sources despite their high calcium content because they contain oxalic acid, which binds the mineral and prevents its absorption. Other good sources include fish eaten with their bones, legumes (especially soybeans), almonds, sesame seeds, dried fruit, and molasses. Bread can be a fairly good source of calcium if it contains nonfat dry milk or molasses. In some areas of the world, drinking water supplies significant amounts of calcium.

Many factors influence the availability of calcium from food. Among the most important is the body's need for the mineral. Normally, adequately nourished individuals absorb 25 to 30 percent of the calcium they ingest, but someone who is deficient may retain as much as 60 percent. Similarly, pregnant and lactating women, infants, and children, all of whom have high calcium requirements, tend to absorb two and even three times more calcium than the nonpregnant, nonlactating adult (5, pages 38, 54–56). Vitamin D facilitates calcium absorption and is partly responsible for a person's ability to adapt to a relatively low calcium in-

FIGURE 8-7 *Some Good Sources of Calcium.* [*Sources:* Food and Nutrition Board, *Recommended Dietary Allowances,* 9th ed., Washington, DC, National Academy of Sciences (1980); C. F. Adams, *Nutritive Value of American Foods in Common Units,* Agriculture Handbook No. 456, Washington, DC, USDA (1975).]

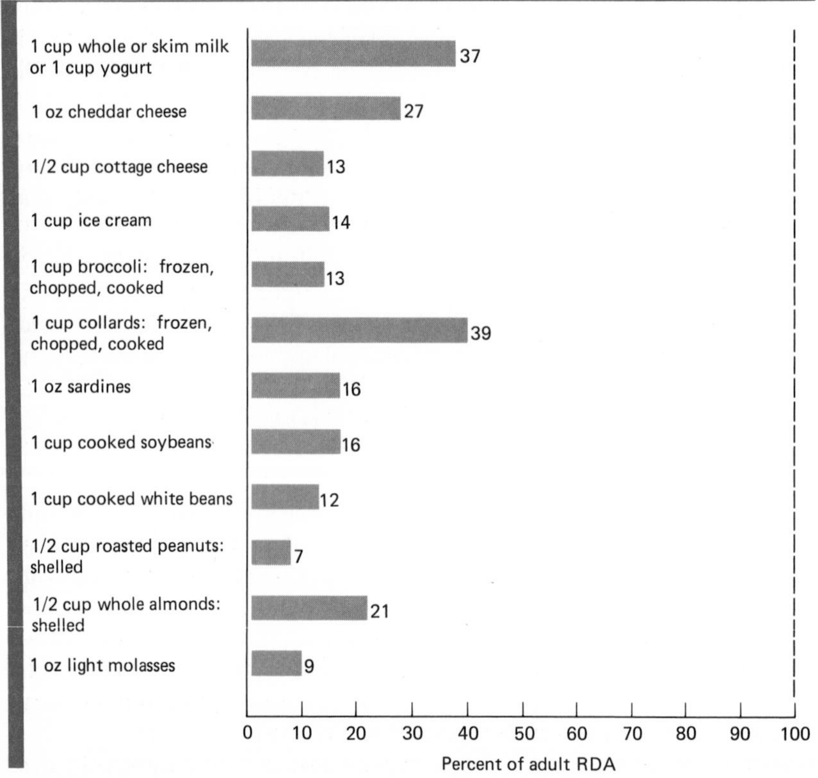

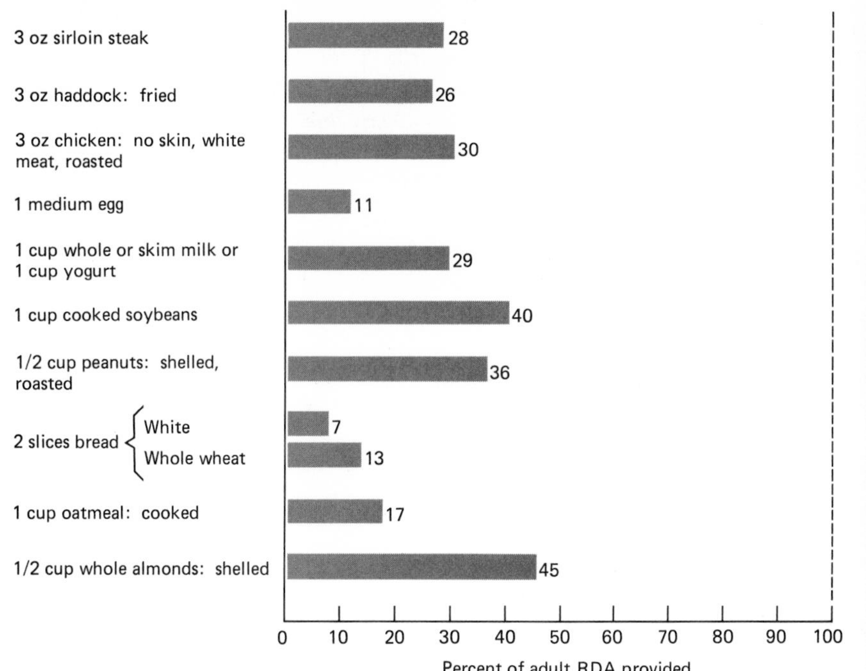

FIGURE 8-8
Some Good Sources of Phosphorus. [*Sources:* Food and Nutrition Board, *Recommended Dietary Allowances*, 9th ed., Washington, DC, National Academy of Sciences (1980); C. F. Adams, *Nutritive Value of American Foods in Common Units*, Agriculture Handbook No. 456, Washington, DC, USDA (1975).]

take. Another factor that increases calcium absorption is lactose, the sugar found in milk. Since milk contains generous amounts of calcium and lactose and frequently is fortified with vitamin D, it is a particularly good source of this mineral. An acid medium, ascorbic acid, and certain amino acids also improve calcium absorption. The oxalic acid found in certain vegetables, the phytic acid found in whole grains, and fiber bind calcium in the digestive tract and prevent its absorption. The ratio of calcium to phosphorus may play a role in maintaining calcium balance. It is thought that the two should be present in equal amounts in the adult diet (Ca:P ratio of 1:1) and in a ratio of 1.5:1 in the diets of infants. However, a rather wide variation in the ratio can be tolerated if there is enough vitamin D in the diet (2, pages 125–178).

The adult RDA for phosphorus of 800 mg/day reflects the 1:1 ratio of dietary calcium and phosphorus recommended by the FNB. Among the best sources of phosphorus in the diet are foods that supply animal protein, such as meat, fish, poultry, eggs, and dairy products (Figure 8-8). Legumes, cereals, and nuts also supply generous amounts.

The magnesium allowance for adult males is 350 mg/day; that for adult females is 300 mg/day. Plants and their products—legumes, nuts, whole grains, and green leafy vegetables—supply the largest amounts (Figure 8-9). Vitamin D enhances magnesium absorption; calcium, phosphate, phytic acid, and oxalic acid reduce its availability. Thus spinach, beet greens, and chard, which contain considerable amounts of magnesium, may not contribute much to the dietary intake.

Because sodium requirements vary considerably from person to per-

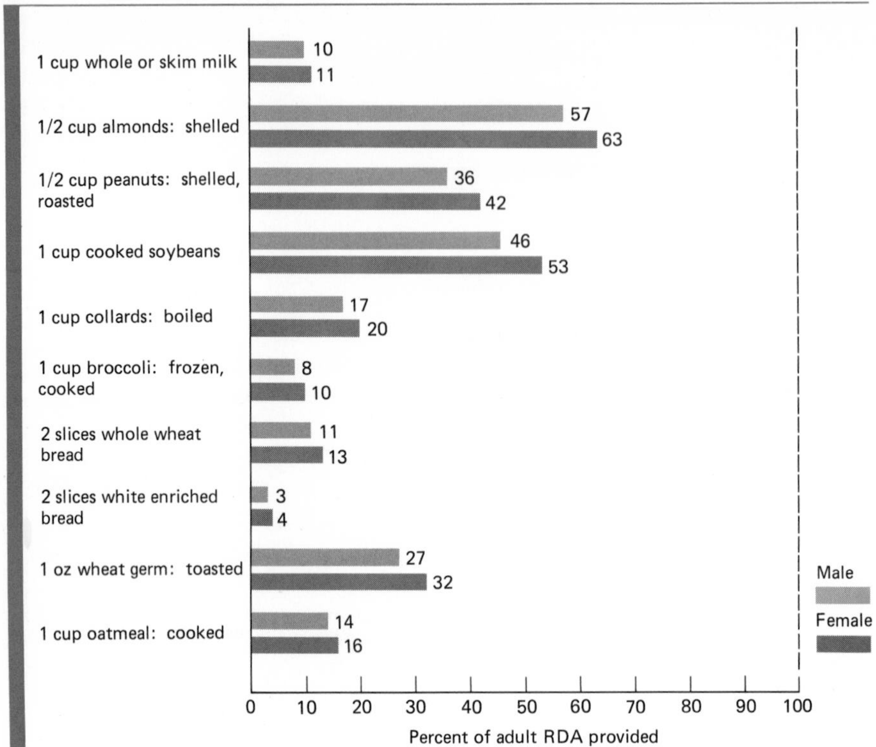

FIGURE 8-9
Some Good Sources of Magnesium. [*Sources:* Food and Nutrition Board, *Recommended Dietary Allowances,* 9th ed., Washington, DC, National Academy of Sciences (1980); B. K. Watt, and A. L. Merrill, *Composition of Foods, Raw, Processed, Prepared,* Washington, DC, USDA (1963).]

son, there is no Recommended Dietary Allowance for it. People with intakes of 500 mg/day or less have been able to maintain sodium balance, and estimates of the requirement range as low as 200 mg/day (2, pages 125–178; 3, page 579). The estimated safe and adequate dietary intake for adults is 1.1 to 3.3 g/day. Dietary intakes in the United States range between 2.3 and 6.9 g/day (equivalent to 6 to 18 grams of salt), a level clearly in excess of the body's needs (2, pages 125–178). Since prolonged high intake has been associated with high blood pressure, the Dietary Guidelines for Americans suggest avoiding too much sodium (43). The U.S. Dietary Goals established by the Senate in 1977 more specifically recommend limiting salt consumption to 5 g/day or less (6).

Sodium requirements depend a great deal on physical activity and exposure to high temperatures, since considerable quantities of the mineral can be lost in sweat. Under conditions of heavy fluid loss, salt as well as water should be replaced, as described under Recommended Water Intake.

Sodium is naturally present in a variety of foods, generally of animal origin (Table 8-2). Meat, fish, poultry, dairy products, and eggs contain relatively large amounts; legumes, grains, nuts, fruits, and vegetables do not. Considerable quantities are added during food processing in the form of salt and food additives such as sodium bicarbonate, monosodium glutamate (MSG), sodium propionate, and sodium benzoate. Canned goods, cured meat products, salted nuts, bread, Oriental foods, sauerkraut, and many breakfast cereals contain large quantities of added sodium. In addition, many recipes call for salt, and people commonly sprinkle it on food before eating. Drinking water, particularly if it is softened by certain types of ion-exchange units, also adds sodium to the diet. Drastically reducing sodium intake would lead to major changes in the diet, but a simple way to curtail consumption is to use less in cooking and to restrict or eliminate salt added to food at the table.

An RDA also has not been established for potassium. However, the estimated safe intake for adults is 1875 to 5625 mg/day. Prolonged or frequent heavy sweating, such as may be experienced during physical activity in hot climates, increases potassium requirements, as does the use of diuretics (7). These drugs stimulate urination and increase the excretion of potassium from the body. The amount of potassium generally provided by the American diet is between 1950 and 5900 mg/day. As Table 8-3 shows, many foods contain generous amounts of potassium. Individuals who need to lower sodium consumption but not that of potassium should obtain much of their potassium from plant sources such as nuts, legumes, fruits, and vegetables.

The estimated safe intake of chloride is between 1.7 and 5.2 g/day. Needs increase under the same circumstances as those for sodium, and as a component of table salt, chloride frequently accompanies sodium in food.

Micronutrient Elements The RDAs for iron in adults are based on the amount lost by the body each day and the body's ability to absorb this mineral from the diet. Adult males and postmenopausal females lose about 1.0 mg/day of iron via the urine, feces, and skin. If adequately nourished, these adults absorb about 10 percent of the iron in the diet. The allowance for these two groups of people has therefore been set at 10 mg/day. Women during the childbearing years lose an additional 0.5 to 1.0 mg/day if menstrual losses are averaged out over a whole month, so their allowance is 18 mg/day. The needs of many pregnant and lactating women exceed 18 mg/day. During the childbearing years many women experience difficulty satisfying their iron requirements through diet alone, and iron supplements may be recommended by their physicians.

A major problem in maintaining iron balance is obtaining sufficient amounts of the mineral from food (Figure 8-10). Diets adequate in other respects provide about 6 mg of iron/1000 kcal, a level that meets the RDA for males and postmenopausal women, but not menstruating, pregnant, or lactating women. Liver is the best source, since animals store iron in this organ. Meat also provides reasonable amounts in a form that is readily available to the body. Legumes, nuts, grains, dried fruits, and certain vegetables, such as broccoli, collards, and mustard greens, contain generous quantities of iron. However, legumes and dried fruits are not consumed in large amounts by Americans, and the iron in whole grains, legumes other than soybeans, and many vegetables is not readily available. For example, although 1 cup of cooked frozen spinach contains 4.3 milli-

TABLE **8-2** The sodium content of some foods

FOOD	SODIUM CONTENT, mg/100 g	Serving: MEASURE	Serving: GRAMS	SODIUM CONTENT, mg/SERVING
Meat, Poultry, Fish				
Sirloin steak (separable fat removed, cooked)	79	3 oz	85	67
Hamburger (regular, cooked)	59	3 oz	85	50
Ham (light cure, separable fat removed, cooked)	909	3 oz	85	770
Pork chop (separable fat removed, cooked)	74	3 oz	85	63
Haddock (breaded, fried)	177	3 oz	85	150
Chicken (no skin, white meat, fried)	73	3 oz	85	62
Milk and Dairy Products				
Milk (whole and skim)	51	1 cup	244	125
Cheddar cheese	711	1 oz	28	199
Cottage cheese (4.2% milk fat)	229	1 cup	225	515
Yogurt (part skim milk)	51	1 cup	245	125
Egg	108	1 medium	50	54
Legumes				
Soybeans (cooked)	2	1 cup	180	4
White beans (cooked)	7	1 cup	185	13
Peanuts (roasted)				
Salted	418	1/2 cup	72	301
Unsalted	10	1/2 cup	72	7

FOOD	SODIUM CONTENT, mg/100 g	Serving: MEASURE	Serving: GRAMS	SODIUM CONTENT, mg/SERVING
Grains and Their Products				
Bread:				
Whole wheat	528	2 slices	50	264
White enriched	496	2 slices	54	268
Spaghetti (enriched, cooked tender in unsalted water)	0.7	1 cup	140	1
Oatmeal (cooked):				
No salt added to water	0	1 cup	240	0
Salt added	218	1 cup	240	523
Rice (white enriched long grain, cooked, cooled):				
Unsalted water	0	1 cup	145	0
Salted water	374	1 cup	145	542
Vegetables				
Spinach (frozen, chopped, cooked):				
Unsalted water	49	1 cup	190	93
Salted water	285	1 cup	190	541
Spinach (canned)	236	1 cup	205	484
Broccoli (frozen, chopped, cooked):				
Unsalted water	15	1 cup	185	28
Salted water	253	1 cup	185	468
Fruits				
Apples	0.7	1 apple	150	1
Oranges	0.6	1 orange	180	1
Grapes	2.0	1 cup	153	3

Source: C. F. Adams. *Nutritive Value of American Foods in Common Units,* Agriculture Handbook No. 456, USDA, Washington, 1975.

TABLE **8-3** Some good sources of potassium

FOOD	POTASSIUM CONTENT, mg/100 g	Serving: MEASURE	Serving: GRAMS	POTASSIUM CONTENT, mg/SERVING	FOOD	POTASSIUM CONTENT, mg/100 g	Serving: MEASURE	Serving: GRAMS	POTASSIUM CONTENT, mg/SERVING
Meat, Fish, Poultry					*Fruit*				
Sirloin steak (separable fat removed, cooked)	362	3 oz	85	307	Apples	101	1 medium	150	152
Hamburger (regular, cooked)	261	3 oz	85	221	Cherries (sweet, stems and pits removed)	191	1 cup	145	277
Ham (light cure, separable fat removed, cooked)	284	3 oz	85	241	Bananas	251	1 medium	175	440
Haddock (breaded, fried)	350	3 oz	85	297	Oranges	146	1 orange	180	263
Chicken (no skin, white meat, fried)	465	3 oz	85	394	Orange juice (frozen re-constituted 1:3)	202	1 cup	249	503
Milk and Dairy Products					Apricots:				
Milk (whole and skim)	145	1 cup	244	353	Raw halves	281	1 cup	155	436
Cheddar cheese	82	1 oz	28	23	Dried, sulfured	979	1 cup	130	1273
Cottage cheese (4.2% milk fat)	85	1 cup	225	191	Raisins	763	1 cup	145	1106
Yogurt (part skim milk)	143	1 cup	245	350	*Vegetables*				
Egg	114	1 medium	50	57	Broccoli (frozen, chopped, cooked)	212	1 cup	185	392
Legumes					Spinach (frozen, chopped, cooked)	333	1 cup	205	683
Soybeans (cooked)	540	1 cup	180	972	Potato:				
White beans (cooked)	416	1 cup	185	770	Baked in skin (skin not eaten)	387	1 potato	202	782
Peanuts (roasted, salted, whole	675	1/2 cup	72	486	Mashed (milk added)	261	1 cup	210	548
					Potato chips	1142	1 oz	28	320
Nuts					Tomato	222	1 tomato	135	300
Almonds (shelled, whole)	773	1/2 cup	71	549					
Cashews (whole)	464	1/2 cup	70	325					
Pecans (shelled, halves)	602	1/2 cup	54	325					

Source: C. F. Adams, *Nutritive Value of American Foods in Common Units,* Agriculture Handbook No. 456, USDA, Washington, 1975.

grams of iron, the body can absorb only about 1 to 2 percent of that amount (8).

Many factors influence the availability of iron in the diet. The most important is the person's need for the mineral: if the body needs more, it will absorb a greater percentage. Thus children and iron-deficient individuals, both of whom require relatively more iron, absorb as much as twice the iron absorbed by nondeficient adults (9, page 27). The form in which the iron occurs also influences its absorption. The body absorbs heme iron more readily than nonheme iron, and iron in the reduced state (**ferrous**) also is absorbed more efficiently than iron in the oxidized state (**ferric**). An acid medium, such as the stomach, and organic acids, such as ascorbic acid, promote iron absorption by converting it to the ferrous form. An alkaline medium reduces availability. Ascorbic acid and some amino acids form complexes with iron that render it more available; oxalic acid, phytic acid, phosphate, and fiber bind iron in the digestive tract and make it less available.

Meeting iron needs with food therefore becomes a complicated affair. It is made simpler by consuming liver and meat. If you omit meat, it is important to include some alternate sources, such as soybeans, dried

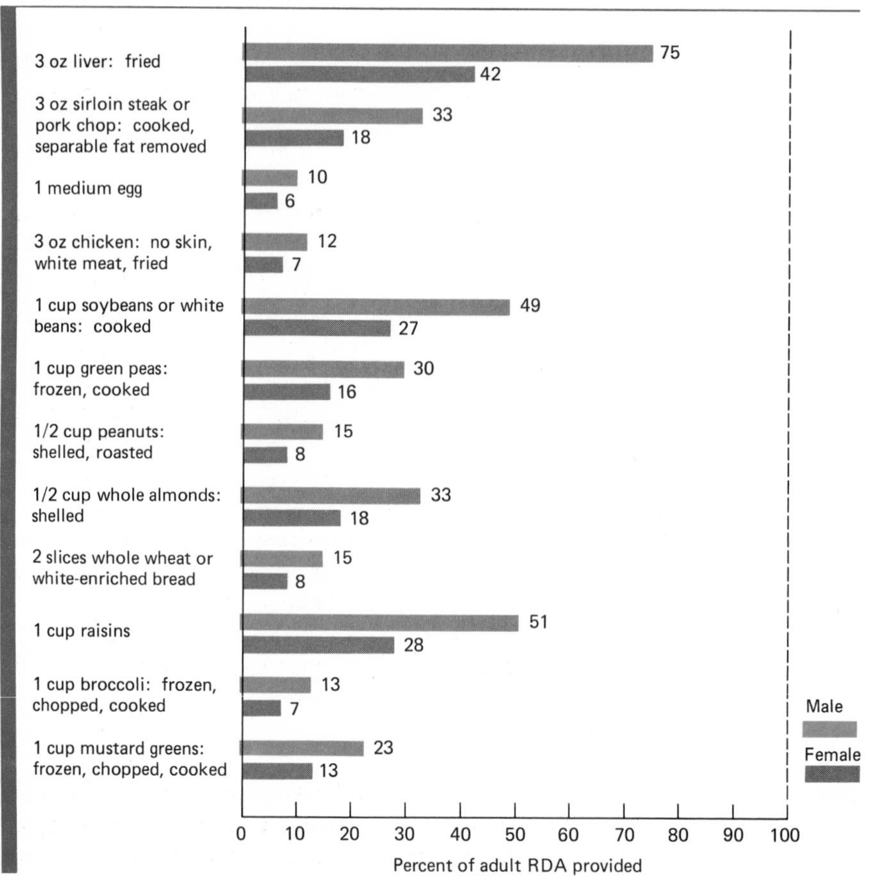

FIGURE 8-10 *Some Good Sources of Iron.* [*Sources:* Food and Nutrition Board, *Recommended Dietary Allowances*, 9th ed., Washington, DC, National Academy of Sciences (1980); C. F. Adams, *Nutritive Value of American Foods in Common Units*, Agriculture Handbook No. 456, Washington, DC, USDA (1975)].

fruit, enriched grain products, and such green vegetables as broccoli, collards, and mustard greens. Consuming some source of vitamin C with food sources of iron will promote absorption.

The Food and Nutrition Board recommends 150 μg/day of iodine for adults, with greater allowances during pregnancy and lactation. Seafood and seaweed are the best sources, because saltwater organisms acquire it from the water. The iodine content of other foods depends on the region in which they are grown, because the amount of this element in the soil varies greatly from area to area. Addition of iodine to table salt has proven to be an effective public health measure to decrease the incidence of iodine deficiency. However, not all salt is iodized, and you must read the label on the salt container to determine whether or not it contains iodine.

Not all salt is iodized; check the container label.

Certain foods contain substances called **goitrogens**, which interfere with the body's ability to utilize iodine. One such chemical is found in cabbage, cauliflower, brussels sprouts, broccoli, kale, kohlrabi, turnips, and rutabaga. Although most people in the United States do not consume these foods in large enough quantities to cause an iodine deficiency, goitrogens of various kinds appear to be responsible for this problem in certain areas of the world.

The adult RDA for zinc is 15 mg/day, with additional amounts needed during pregnancy and lactation. Good sources of zinc include meat, liver, eggs, seafood, milk and dairy products, whole-grain products, and legumes (Figure 8-11). The zinc in animal sources tends to be more readily available to the body, while fiber and phytic acid in some plant sources reduce absorption (11, pages 155–180). Enriched white flour is a poor source of zinc, because much is lost during the milling process and the zinc is not replaced (9, page 232).

Estimated safe and adequate daily dietary intakes have been established for copper, manganese, fluoride, chromium, selenium, and molybdenum and are listed in Ready Reference 3. Data on the amounts of these minerals and their availability from foods are still not complete, but choosing a variety of foods from all the food groups should result in an adequate intake. Some important sources are listed in Table 8-4, which is a summary of the minerals.

Ensuring Adequate Mineral Intake Following the Four Food Group Plan is a practical way of meeting mineral needs as long as a variety of foods from each group are chosen. During the childbearing years, how-

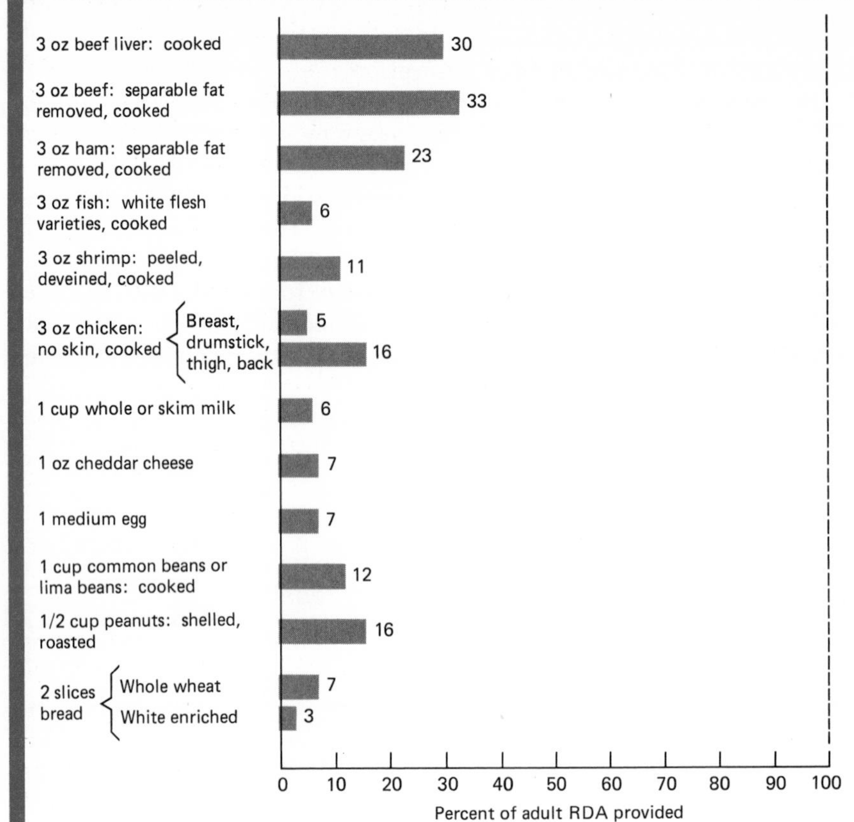

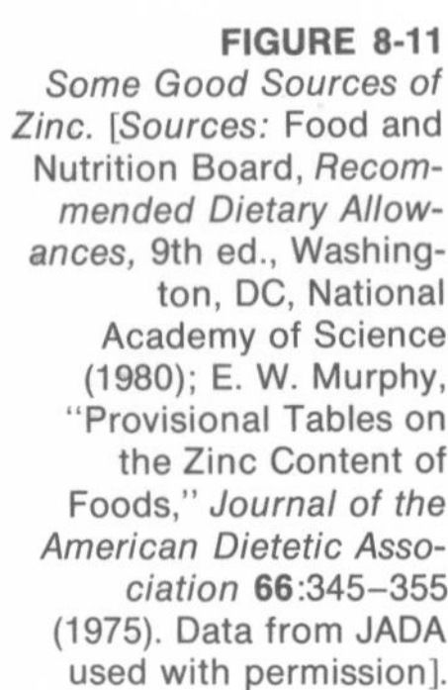

FIGURE 8-11 *Some Good Sources of Zinc.* [*Sources:* Food and Nutrition Board, *Recommended Dietary Allowances*, 9th ed., Washington, DC, National Academy of Science (1980); E. W. Murphy, "Provisional Tables on the Zinc Content of Foods," *Journal of the American Dietetic Association* **66**:345–355 (1975). Data from JADA used with permission].

ever, many women cannot fulfill their iron requirements with food alone and should consult their physicians about taking an iron supplement.

Minerals in animal products are generally more easily absorbed by the body than those from plant sources; many plants contain chemical substances that combine with the minerals and reduce their availability. For example, the oxalic acid in spinach and certain other vegetables makes them a poor source of iron, calcium, and magnesium, even though they contain appreciable amounts of these elements. Because broccoli, collards, mustard greens, and turnip greens contain little oxalate, they are better sources. Similarly, the phytic acid in whole grains can prevent the absorption of iron, zinc, calcium, and perhaps other minerals, but yeast fermentation, as in bread making, breaks down the phytate, making the minerals more available (12,13). There is evidence that fiber also can reduce mineral absorption (14).

MINERAL DEFICIENCIES

Mineral deficiencies, like those of the vitamins, arise from an interplay of many factors. Low income, personal preferences, and cultural practices may reduce the amount or variety of food consumed, thereby restricting intake of certain minerals. In addition, some elements, such as iron, zinc, calcium, and iodine, are abundant in only a few foods. Furthermore, most minerals are inefficiently absorbed: in well-nourished individuals, about 25 to 30 percent of the calcium, 10 percent of the iron, up to 40 percent of the zinc, and 40 percent of the magnesium are absorbed from the diet. Deficient people absorb somewhat more, and the presence of substances that promote or retard absorption, the pH of the intestine, and other factors can influence absorption. In this section, we will look at several of the more important mineral deficiencies and their effect on health.

Calcium Because blood calcium concentration is under hormonal control, it is not appreciably influenced by dietary calcium intake: the mineral is deposited in or mobilized from the bones in order to maintain balance. Two bone disorders, rickets and osteomalacia, appear most often to result from a lack of vitamin D rather than calcium (see Chapter 7) (4). There is evidence, however, that inadequate calcium intake over a long period of time may result in **osteoporosis**. In contrast to osteomalacia, in which the bone remains the same size but decreases in density, osteoporosis is characterized by a decrease in size and maintenance of normal density. In this condition, the bones become increasingly fragile and more susceptible to fracture.

Some experimental evidence indicates that osteoporosis is not simply a calcium-deficiency disease (2, pages 125–178). It appears that by the fifth decade of life, loss of calcium from the bones is normal in most humans, and high intake of the mineral will not prevent the problem. Some experts believe that the amount of calcium found in the bones when an individual reaches old age depends on the amount of calcium present in early adulthood and not on subsequent calcium intake. Other studies show that taking calcium supplements improves retention and relieves the symptoms of osteoporosis (2, pages 125–178). In addition, high protein and phosphorus intakes increase the mobilization of calcium from bone and its excretion in the urine, and the efficiency with which calcium is absorbed from food decreases with age. For these reasons, the Food and Nutrition Board recommends 800 mg/day of calcium and 400 IU/day of vitamin D throughout adulthood. Because it strengthens the bones, dietary fluoride is also recommended (2, pages 125–178).

1. If you are always feeling tired, you probably have "iron-poor blood."

2. Fluoridation of public water supplies has been shown to cause mongolism, heart disease, and cancer.

Electrolyte Depletion With the exception of potassium deficiency during severe protein-energy malnutrition and sodium depletion resulting from prolonged restriction in the treatment of heart, liver, or kidney disease, dietary deficiencies of the major electrolytes are seldom found in

TABLE **8-4**

Summary of the minerals

MINERAL	FUNCTIONS	ADULT RDA	Sources: FOOD GROUPS	Sources: IMPORTANT EXAMPLES	DEFICIENCY	TOXICITY
Calcium	Structural mineral in bones and teeth, blood clotting, nerve and muscle function, permeability of membranes, cofactor for enzymes	800 mg/day	Milk, vegetable-fruit, meat*	Most dairy products, some green, leafy vegetables, legumes, almonds, dried fruit	No clear-cut dietary deficiency in humans except possibly osteoporosis	Low: Several grams per day appear to have no effect
Phosphorus	Structural mineral in bones and teeth, component of other body substances (e.g., ATP, DNA, RNA, phospholipids), also needed for glucose catabolism, acid-base balance	800 mg/day	Milk, meat, cereal-bread	Meat, fish, poultry, eggs, dairy products, legumes, grains, nuts	Rare	May interfere with calcium absorption
Sodium	Fluid-electrolyte balance, acid-base balance, nerve and muscle function, absorption of glucose and amino acids from the intestine	Estimated safe intake: 1.1 to 3.3 g/day	Naturally found in meat and milk; may be added to others	Meat, fish, poultry, dairy products, eggs, salted foods, bread, canned goods, Oriental foods	Dietary deficiency rare; can lose in sweat; leads to nausea, weakness, cramps	Longterm; may lead to high blood pressure
Potassium	Fluid-electrolyte balance, acid-base balance, nerve and muscle function, cofactor for enzymes	Estimated safe intake: 1875 to 5625 mg/day	Meat, milk, vegetable-fruit	Meat, fish, poultry, dairy products, nuts, legumes, many fruits and vegetables	Dietary deficiency associated with PEM; can lose in sweat; diuretics promote loss in urine; leads to nausea, weakness, rapid and arrhythmic heartbeat	Dietary excess unlikely in healthy individuals
Chloride	Fluid-electrolyte balance, acid-base balance, component of stomach acid	Estimated safe intake: 1.7 to 5.1 g/day	Same as sodium	Same as sodium	Sometimes with prolonged vomiting	Dietary excess unlikely
Magnesium	Cofactor for many enzymes involved in energy metabolism; also needed for protein synthesis, nerve and muscle function, and in bone structure	Males: 350 mg/day Females: 300 mg/day	Meat,* vegetables, and cereal-bread†	Legumes, nuts, whole grains, and green, leafy vegetables	Dietary deficiency found in starvation; leads to uncontrolled neuromuscular activity leading to convulsions	Dietary excess unlikely in healthy individuals

Sulfur	Component of the vitamins thiamine, biotin, and pantothenic acid, the amino acids methionine and cysteine, and other compounds	None	All groups	Any good source of protein or the three sulfur-containing vitamins	Associated with deficiency of specific sulfur-containing substances	Unlikely
Iron	Heme: Hemoglobin for O_2 transport in blood, myoglobin for O_2 transfer in muscle, and in certain enzymes; nonheme: cofactor for enzymes	Males: 10 mg/day Females: Premenopausal: 18 mg/day Postmenopausal: 10 mg/day	Meat,‡ vegetable-fruit, cereal-bread	Liver, red meat, legumes, nuts, dried fruit, some green, leafy vegetables, whole and enriched grain products	Anemia; small pale red blood cells, fatigue, pallor, reduced work capacity	Hemochromatosis, siderosis (accumulation of iron in liver, heart, and pancreas)
Iodine	Component of thyroid hormones, which stimulate growth, development, and metabolism	150 μg/day	Meat,§ vegetable-fruit	Seafood, vegetables grown in soils with high iodine content, and iodized salt	Adults: simple goiter Infants and children born to deficient mothers: Cretinism	In sensitive individuals, may depress thyroid function
Zinc	Cofactor for many enzymes; also needed for growth, reproduction, wound healing, taste acuity, and insulin function	15 mg/day	Meat, milk, cereal-bread†	Meat, liver, eggs, seafood, dairy products, whole grains, legumes	Reduced growth, loss of taste, underdeveloped sex organs, poor wound healing	Low: Dietary excess unlikely unless excess supplement is ingested
Copper	Cofactor for many enzymes, including some involved in connective tissue, skin pigment, and myelin synthesis, facilitates iron metabolism	Estimated safe intake: 2.0 to 3.0 mg/day	Meat, vegetable-fruit, cereal-bread	Nuts, legumes, shellfish, dried fruit, mushrooms, whole grains	Rare except during starvation; produces anemia similar to iron deficiency, low white cell count, and bone disease	Low–moderate: Can occur with excess supplement intake; preparing acid foods in copper utensils; leads to nausea and vomiting
Fluoride	Integrity of teeth and bones; prevents tooth decay	Estimated safe intake: 1.5 to 4.0 mg/day	Meat,§ vegetable-fruit	Seafood, vegetables grown in areas with high soil content; most reliable source is if added to drinking water	Tooth decay; may increase risk of osteoporosis	2 to 8 mg/day: mottling of teeth; 20 to 80 mg/day: bone changes
Manganese	Cofactor for several enzymes, including some involved in connective-tissue synthesis, carbohydrate and lipid metabolism; also needed for growth, reproduction, and blood clotting	Estimated safe intake: 2.5 to 5.0 mg/day	Meat,* cereal-bread,† vegetables	Nuts, legumes, whole-grain cereals, green vegetables	Dietary deficiency is rare	Dietary excess unlikely

(*Table continues on page 238.*)

TABLE **8-4** *(Continued)*

Summary of the minerals

			Sources			
MINERAL	FUNCTIONS	ADULT RDA	FOOD GROUPS	IMPORTANT EXAMPLES	DEFICIENCY	TOXICITY
Selenium	Cofactor for an enzyme that neutralizes peroxides	Estimated safe intake: 0.05 to 0.2 mg/day	Meat, cereal-bread	Meat, seafood, grains grown in soil high in selenium	Low blood levels seen in PEM; effect unknown	Rare; sometimes found in areas with high soil content; leads to discolored teeth, tooth decay, loss of hair, and other problems
Chromium	Component of glucose tolerance factor, which aids in metabolism of glucose	Estimated safe intake: 0.05 to 0.2 mg/day	Meat, milk, cereal-bread†	Meat, cheese, whole-grain products, brewer's yeast	A diabeteslike condition	Excess dietary intake unlikely
Molybdenum	Cofactor for a few enzymes	Estimated safe intake: 0.15 to 0.5 mg/day	Meat, cereal-bread†	Meat, legumes, whole grains; food content greatly influenced by soil content	Dietary deficiency unlikely	Interferes with copper metabolism
Cobalt	Component of vitamin B_{12}	None	Same as vitamin B_{12}	Same as vitamin B_{12}	Same as vitamin B_{12}	Dietary excess unlikely

Note: Vanadium, silicon, nickel, and tin are suspected as being essential for humans, but little is yet known about their functions, requirements, and distribution in food.

* Legumes and nuts only.
† Whole grains only.
‡ Excludes poultry and fish.
§ Seafood only.

humans. Electrolyte depletion can occur in situations in which large amounts of fluid are lost to the body, such as profuse sweating, diarrhea, and vomiting. Vomiting particularly can result in chloride loss, because of the presence of this element in stomach acid. Cirrhosis of the liver, burns, certain kidney diseases, and the use of diuretics also can lead to excess losses of potassium. General symptoms of electrolyte depletion include nausea, vomiting, weakness, and lethargy. Sodium deficiency also produces abdominal cramps, and potassium loss can lead to a rapid and arrhythmic heart beat. To prevent electrolyte depletion, sodium, potassium, and chloride must be replaced frequently. All three elements are abundant in food, and additional sodium and chloride can be obtained by salting foods more heavily. During situations producing excess sweating, a 0.2 to 0.7% salt solution taken intermittently can help replace sodium and chloride losses. When potassium, but not sodium, is required, such as in the treatment of high blood pressure, foods such as bananas, citrus fruit, legumes (cooked in unsalted water), and dried fruits can be eaten. Some people also take a potassium salt supplement.

Iron: Anemia Iron deficiency is the most widespread nutritional deficiency in the United States. The Ten-State Nutrition Survey (1968–1970) found a high prevalence of low hemoglobin levels in all population groups studied and particularly among blacks (15). The deficiency in most groups appeared to be largely because of inadequate dietary intake, but there is evidence that the lower hemoglobin concentrations found in blacks may be genetic in origin (16). In addition, the preliminary results of the First Health and Nutrition Examination Survey (HANES; 1971–1972) found a higher percentage of low hemoglobin values among 12- to 17-year-old males than in females of the same age, while in the 18–44 age group, the problem was more prevalent in women. The very young and the elderly are other age groups at risk (17).

Two means for determining whether a person is iron deficient or not are to measure the **hemoglobin concentration** and the **hematocrit**. Hemoglobin concentration is measured by taking a blood sample and chemically determining the amount of hemoglobin in 100 milliliters (1 deciliter) of blood. The average hemoglobin concentration in females is 12 to 16 g/dl, while that in males is 14 to 18 g/dl (18). Levels less than 11 g/dl in females and 13 g/dl in males are considered **anemic**. Hematocrit measures the percentage of the blood volume occupied by red blood cells. A blood sample in a capillary tube is centrifuged to separate the red cells from the plasma, and the volume of the red cells is compared with the total blood volume (Figure 8-12). Normal hematocrits in women range between 37 and 47 percent, while those in men range between 45 and 52 percent (18).

A change in hemoglobin and hematocrit is the last stage in iron deficiency. First, the iron stored in the body and that circulating in the plasma outside the red blood cells must be nearly depleted. Excess dietary iron is normally stored in the form of two compounds, **ferritin** and **hemosiderin**, primarily in the liver, spleen, and bone marrow. It can be

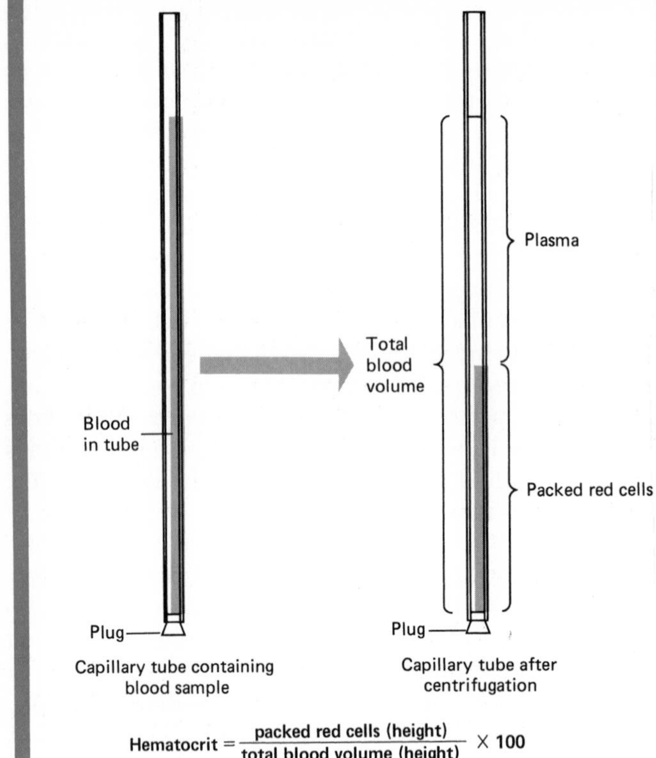

$$\text{Hematocrit} = \frac{\text{packed red cells (height)}}{\text{total blood volume (height)}} \times 100$$

FIGURE 8-12
Measuring Hematocrit. Blood is drawn into a small, thin glass tube, the end of which is then plugged. The sample is centrifuged, and the height of the red cells is expressed as a percent of the height of the total blood sample.

released during iron deficiency, and the stores must become almost empty before changes in the blood occur. Iron circulating in the blood outside the red cells is bound to the transport protein **transferrin**, and this iron also must be nearly depleted before changes in the hemoglobin and hematocrit occur.

The deficiency finally manifests itself in the red blood cells as an anemia characterized by small, pale-colored cells. The red cells tend to be fewer in number as well. A variety of symptoms have been observed, including fatigue, abnormally rapid heartbeat and breathing on exertion, reduced work capacity, pale skin, inflamed tongue, and cracks in the corner of the mouth, along with irritability, headaches, and dizziness.

The blood changes and symptoms that result from iron deficiency are commonly called **anemia**, although the term has a more general meaning: the reduction of the oxygen-carrying capacity of the blood. Anemias of various types also may result from a deficiency of folacin, vitamin B_{12}, protein, vitamin B_6, and copper. **Hemolytic anemia**, in which the red blood cells break, results from exposure to certain drugs in genetically predisposed individuals and also may be found in vitamin E–deficient premature infants. A genetic disorder prevalent in black populations, **sickle-cell anemia**, occurs because of the presence in the red cells of a hemoglobin slightly different in structure than normal. The use of certain drugs, such as the antibiotic chloramphenicol, leads to an inability to

Self-prescription may cure a mineral deficiency, but mask or delay discovery of the primary problem.

produce red blood cells (**aplastic anemia**). Anemia also may result from blood loss, or **hemorrhage** (giving one pint of blood, for example, means a loss of 250 milligrams of iron from the body).

One reason iron deficiency occurs in the United States is that the mineral is present in significant amounts in a relatively small number of foods and only 5 to 10 percent is absorbed by the body. The iron needs of adolescents and women during the childbearing years are often high enough that the iron in the food they consume is not sufficient. However, a physician should be consulted before taking an iron supplement, because iron deficiency may be caused by circumstances other than diet, such as bleeding ulcers, parasites, or certain types of cancer. A self-prescription may cure the deficiency, but delay discovery of the primary problem.

Iodine: Goiter and Cretinism Iodine deficiency results in reduced production of thyroid hormone, and in adults this leads to **simple goiter**. The thyroid gland enlarges in an attempt to compensate for the lack of iodine, producing a swelling of the neck that may become as large as a softball. Although goiter is painless and does not pose any significant hazard to health in adults, children born to iodine-deficient women are profoundly affected (Figure 8-13). Their failure to develop properly results in **cretinism**, both mental and physical retardation. Prompt treatment with iodine or thyroxine after birth may reverse the symptoms of this disorder.

Iodine deficiency occurs in areas of the world in which the soil content of this mineral is low. The region around the Great Lakes and north central United States was once known as the "Goiter Belt" for this reason. The use of iodized salt has greatly reduced the incidence of iodine deficiency throughout the United States.

Zinc: Underdevelopment Severe zinc deficiency has been observed in Egypt and Iran in association with diets high in unleavened whole-grain products and containing negligible amounts of animal protein (11, pages 1–20). The lack of animal products eliminates the most important sources of easily absorbed zinc from the diet, and the phytic acid and fiber of the whole grains inhibits the absorption of the small amounts of zinc available. Parasitic infections aggravate the situation in Egypt, while geophagia, the practice of eating clay, appears to contribute to the situation in Iran (11, pages 1–20). The deficiencies result in dwarfism and underdeveloped gonads, both of which respond to the administration of zinc.

Zinc deficiency also has been found in association with protein-energy malnutrition in several parts of the world, including Egypt, South

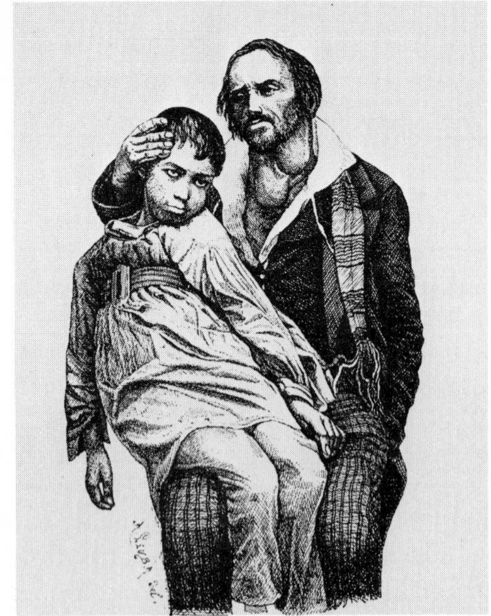

FIGURE 8-13
Simple Goiter. This nineteenth-century engraving of a man with goiter and his cretinous son shows clearly the connection between the two. (Courtesy of the World Health Organization.)

Africa, and India (11, pages 21–32). A moderate lack of the mineral has been reported in the United States (19). A survey of apparently healthy children in Denver, Colorado showed low zinc concentrations in the hair, an impaired sense of taste, poor appetite, and suboptimal growth. Hair levels and taste returned to normal with the administration of zinc. There is some evidence that zinc deficiency may be prevalent in the United States and may affect women and alcoholics as well as children (10, pages 290–295).

Toxicity

OBTAINING TOO MUCH

In general, minerals are more toxic than most vitamins; the margin of safety between the amount required to meet nutritional needs and that which produces toxicity symptoms is smaller. For example, a person can consume more than 1000 times the RDA of thiamine, riboflavin, pantothenic acid, vitamin B_6, folacin, or vitamin B_{12}, at least 20 times the RDA of vitamin C, and at least 20 to 50 times the RDA of vitamin E before symptoms are observed. In addition, the results of vitamin C and vitamin E overdose are relatively mild and seldom life-threatening. In contrast, chronic consumption of iron at a level 10 to 20 times the RDA has produced toxicity symptoms in healthy people. Fluoride produces adverse effects at intakes 2 to 8 times and copper at 10 to 20 times the estimated safe amount. Exceeding the upper limit of the estimated safe intakes for selenium and molybdenum is not recommended. Dietary overconsumption of minerals is rare; more often mineral toxicity results from occupa-

FOCUS 8-1 PICA Most of us have heard about the cravings for strange foods experienced by some pregnant women; the story of a mother-to-be sending her husband to the store in the middle of the night for a jar of pickles is almost a cliché. However, pregnant women in all parts of the world also have been observed to eat a variety of nonfoods, including laundry starch, chalk, clay, ashes, and ice. This practice is called **pica**, and it is not confined to pregnant women. It has been observed in other segments of certain populations, particularly among young children.

The cause of pica is not known. Some authorities believe it results from iron deficiency. A craving for ice (pagophagia) appears to be common among iron-deficient women, and the craving disappears when iron therapy is begun (35). Iron therapy is also effective in breaking a habit of eating sand, dirt, and clay (geophagia) in iron-deficient children (35). Culture and tradition also probably contribute to pica. In many areas of the southern United States, it is believed that eating clay, cornstarch, or baking soda will relieve nausea, headaches, and dizziness, prevent vomiting, and ensure healthy and beautiful children (35). Some people even consider certain types of clay a delicacy, while others mail packages of clay to kinfolk who have moved north (35,36). Pica in young children may be linked to emotional factors: in many areas, mothers give a crying child clay to eat (36).

Pica may have important effects on nutritional status, particularly for trace minerals. It has been associated with iron deficiency in many parts of the world and with zinc deficiency in Iran (35,37–39). Certain types of clay may bind iron and zinc, and consumption of many of these substances may displace foods that could provide the minerals (35). An additional concern among young children is consumption of toxic substances. Lead poisoning has been reported in many children who ate paint off the walls in old houses.

tional exposure, as a result of disease, and by accident, such as during medical therapy and in drinking water.

Iron, Sodium, Fluoride, Copper Excess iron may accumulate in the body from prolonged supplementation and from alcoholism. For instance, the Bantu, a tribe in South Africa, brew beer in iron pots. The iron leaches from the pots into the beer, so that consumption may exceed 100 mg/day in adult males. The iron accumulates in abnormal amounts, especially in the liver, heart, and pancreas, and disruption of liver and pancreatic function have been reported in many Bantus (1, pages 297–323). Iron overload from normal intakes also may occur in genetically predisposed individuals. In this disorder, called **hemochromatosis**, the body absorbs an unusually large proportion of the iron in the diet, and since the mineral is poorly excreted, it accumulates in soft tissues. Impairment of liver, pancreatic, and heart function often occur. One out of every 10,000 patients admitted to the hospital in the United States has hemochromatosis, and the problem usually is not diagnosed until tissue damage has occurred (20).

A number of population studies have associated long-term consumption of large amounts of sodium with the development of hypertension (high blood pressure) (1, pages 1007–1018; 21). In addition, rats fed large amounts of sodium for prolonged periods develop high blood pressure, particularly if they are genetically predisposed to do so (1, pages 1007–1018). For this reason the Dietary Guidelines for Americans recommend reducing salt intake, and the U.S. Dietary Goals make the more specific recommendation of limiting it to 5 g/day or less (6,43) (see the discussion of sodium under Meeting Mineral Needs).

Two parts per million of fluoride in the drinking water produce a mottling of the teeth with brown stains, which is not attractive, but nevertheless is not harmful (32). Prolonged consumption of 20 to 80 mg/day may cause skeletal deformities, but this level is far in excess of that likely to be ingested from fluoridated water. The claim that fluoride causes cancer has been refuted by the National Cancer Institute, which found no increase in the malignancy rate in high-fluoride areas (22).

Copper toxicity is rare in humans, but it can result from consumption of acidic food or drink that has been in prolonged contact with the metal. Whiskey sours mixed in copper cocktail shakers may have toxic amounts of the metal, and overnight contact of carbonated water with copper check valves of drink-dispensing machines has increased the copper content of the first drink to toxic levels (11, pages 415–438). Usually, nausea and vomiting protect the individual from more serious effects, such as liver damage, breakage of red blood cells, bleeding in the digestive tract, convulsions, coma, or death. *Wilson's disease* is a genetic disorder in which blood levels of copper are low, but the mineral accumulates in the liver, nervous system, kidney, and other tissues to the point of disrupting their function. Patients are treated with penicillamine, which increases the output of copper in the urine and prevents accumulation in the body.

Other Essential Minerals The other minerals are toxic at some level of intake, but these amounts are seldom exceeded in the diets of healthy humans. Sensitive individuals experience a depression of thyroid function (iodine goiter) after consuming foods high in iodine, such as kelp (23). Ingestion of as little as 150 mg/day of zinc has been shown to interfere with copper and iron metabolism, but oversupplementation or accidental exposure are needed to obtain this much (9, page 232). High blood potassium levels may result from kidney failure, severe dehydration, and hormonal imbalances (1, pages 355–394). The condition produces muscle weakness, abnormal heart function, and a tingling sensation in the scalp, face, tongue, and extremities. Magnesium overdose has occurred from accidental administration of large doses and from kidney failure. It can cause depression of nervous system function as well as coma or death (24, pages 13–15). Toxicity symptoms from selenium and molybdenum have been frequently observed in farm animals consuming forage or grain grown in soil with high contents of these minerals, but evidence of diet-related toxicity in humans is scanty. High dietary selenium levels may contribute to tooth decay, since children raised in areas where the soil has a high selenium content have a greater incidence of dental caries and gum inflammation (gingivitis) than those in low-selenium areas (25).

NONESSENTIAL TOXIC MINERALS

Of the many minerals not known to perform any useful function in the body, three have attracted considerable attention: lead, mercury, and cadmium. As a result of ignorance, occupational contact, and accidents, a relatively large number of people have been exposed to toxic levels of these elements, sometimes with disastrous results.

Lead People may come into contact with lead simply by breathing; as a component of a gasoline additive, considerable quantities of this element are released into the atmosphere by automobiles. Dust and plants growing near highways contain high concentrations of lead. At one time lead was used in housepaint, and children who ate paint chips, especially in older houses, received toxic levels of the element over a period of time. Dust from these houses, as well as lead-containing junk that may be nearby (such as batteries and various items painted with lead-containing paints), may contribute significantly to a child's exposure to lead. Other sources include lead solder used on cans, particularly if the food inside is acidic, lead-lined water pipes, occupational exposure, and lead glaze used in certain types of pottery (24, pages 443–452).

Lead interferes with the production of red blood cells by inhibiting heme synthesis and by promoting the release of immature cells into the blood. It also damages the nervous system and the kidney. Toxicity symptoms include anemia, headache, dizziness, muscular weakness, irritability, behavioral changes, loss of memory, and intellectual impairment (9, pages 418–419; 24, pages 443–452).

In an attempt to reduce exposure to lead, lead pipes and lead-containing paints are no longer used inside homes; automobile engines that use lead-free gasoline have been developed, and lead glazes are no longer used in pottery. In addition, screening methods to detect lead poisoning have been developed. Nevertheless, many older buildings and some pottery still contain lead, providing a potential for exposure.

Mercury Mercury occurs naturally in small amounts in soil and water. These levels have now increased as a result of the release of mercury-containing industrial wastes into the environment. Mercury poisoning results in different problems depending on the type of mercury consumed. Inorganic salts of mercury affect the liver and the kidneys, while the organic compound methyl mercury produces degeneration of the nervous system, including progressive loss of coordination, loss of vision and hearing, and mental deterioration. Infants born to women who have consumed large amounts of methyl mercury show severe birth defects. One recent large-scale instance of mercury poisoning occurred in Japan as a result of the release of mercury wastes into Minamata Bay; it produced severe damage to a whole population and caused a nationwide uproar.

Cadmium Although the human body contains practically no cadmium at birth, the element accumulates throughout life. In addition to its natural occurrence in soil and water, cadmium enters the environment as a

FOCUS 8-2 MERCURY IN FISH In the early 1950s, many people living around Minamata Bay in Japan were stricken with a mysterious disease that resulted in blindness, deafness, loss of coordination, and mental deterioration. Japanese investigators discovered that the problem was due to high concentrations of methyl mercury in fish and shellfish taken from the bay and soon traced the contamination to its source in a local factory. Between 1953 and 1960, 121 people developed the disorder, and 46 died. Twenty-three infants developed "Minamata disease," (Figure 8-14) having received the methyl mercury from their mothers through the placenta (1, pages 485–486).

Such flagrant examples of mercury poisoning are rare and are confined to relatively small areas. However, in the late 1960s and early 1970s, scientists became concerned about mercury contamination in fish taken from certain lakes and streams in Sweden, Canada, and the United States, as well as from the open sea. Some tuna and swordfish marketed in the United States contained mercury in excess of the Food and Drug Administration's 0.5 parts per million tolerance level, and the resulting publicity precipitated a mercury scare.

We now know that mercury occurs naturally in water. It is converted to methyl mercury by bacteria living in the muck on the bottom. Methyl mercury becomes more concentrated in many aquatic organisms because they absorb it from the water and excrete it slowly. Organisms that are high on the food chain, such as tuna and swordfish, accumulate particularly large amounts. However, the amount in recently caught tuna is no greater than in specimens caught 100 years ago, indicating that these concentrations are probably normal (40).

Most scientists believe that at current levels of consumption in the United States, the mercury concentration in fish taken from most waters is not hazardous. One authority estimates we would have to eat 3 lb/week of fish to reach a potentially toxic methyl mercury intake (40). However, individuals with exceptionally large fish intakes could risk mercury poisoning over the long term, and fish from water known to be polluted with mercury compounds should be avoided (1, pages 485–486).

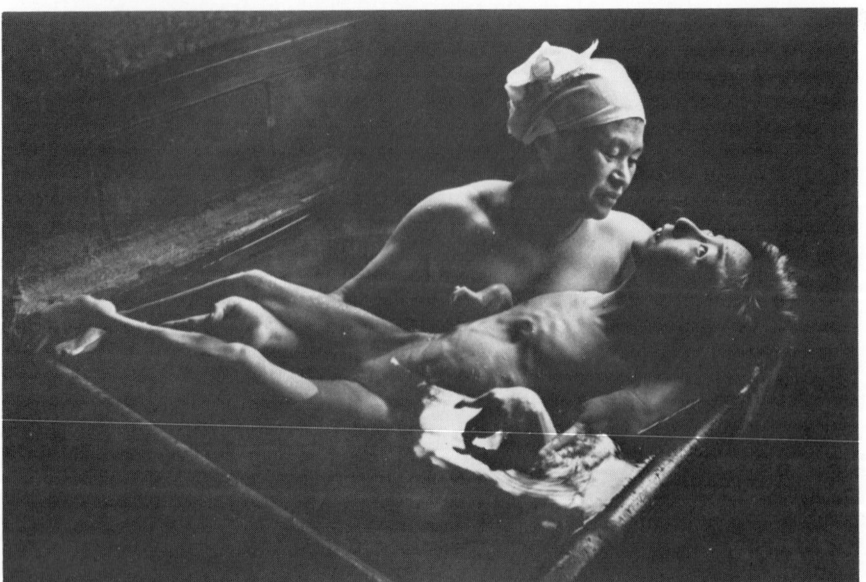

FIGURE 8-14 *Mercury Poisoning at Minamata Bay, Japan.* (Photograph by W. Eugene Smith, © 1972 by W. Eugene Smith and Aileen M. Smith.)

result of its use in batteries, paints, plastics, and other materials and as a contaminant in phosphate fertilizers and sewage sludge. Cadmium is present in cigarette smoke, and heavy smokers may obtain significant amounts from this source. The diet may provide up to 100 μg/day (9, pages 243–257).

Cadmium is toxic to most body tissues. Accidental exposure produces disorders of the kidney, digestive tract, and bones. It has resulted in other symptoms, including high blood pressure, in experimental animals, but its relationship to hypertension in humans is unknown.

Aluminum Another element some people are concerned about is aluminum, because of its use in aluminum cookware. Despite the fact that aluminum does wear from the utensils into food, the amounts obtained in the diet are small and poorly absorbed by the body. As far as we know now, aluminum in cookware does not pose a hazard to health (9, pages 418–419).

ISSUE: ADDING IRON TO THE FOOD SUPPLY

A familiar sight to anyone who regularly watches television is the advertisement for a certain iron-containing tonic that implies that an iron supplement is important for women. The claims are rather overdone, but the advertisement touches on an important health issue. Several surveys have found that iron deficiency is widespread in the United States, not only among women, but among other population groups as well. As a result, the Food and Drug Administration (FDA) proposed in 1971 to increase the levels at which iron is added to enriched-grain products. Many authorities opposed the measure, arguing that the point at which iron deficiency results in physical disability or poses a hazard to health has not been determined. In addition, the supplementation may be dangerous to people who, because of a genetic defect, accumulate abnormally large amounts of iron in their bodies. Let us take a closer look at the evidence presented by both sides and the conclusion the FDA finally reached regarding its proposal.

Enactment of the FDA's proposal would undoubtedly raise the hemoglobin concentrations and hematocrits of many people to the average or satisfactory level. However, some researchers argue that the current standards for classifying people as anemic are inaccurate. Their studies show that the symptoms described earlier do not occur in all iron-deficient individuals, and the severity of these symptoms often does not correlate with the severity of the anemia (26–28). Although a woman with a hemoglobin concentration of 11 g/dl may be considered anemic, symptoms often do not appear until the level drops below 8 g/dl (20). In one study, Elwood and colleagues observed no significant difference in the improvement of six symptoms of iron deficiency in women taking an iron supplement compared with women not receiving the supplement (26). However, many authorities point out that a change in hemoglobin concentration and hematocrit is the last stage of iron deficiency. It is preceded by near depletion of storage iron and significant decreases in plasma iron and the iron in tissues. Gardner and colleagues found that even moderate iron deficiency (hemoglobin concentrations of 11.0 to 11.9 g/dl) produced a reduction in work performance, and severely anemic subjects were most seriously affected (29). Other studies have obtained similar results (30). The conflicting data make it difficult to define iron-deficiency anemia clearly.

Certain risks accompany superenrichment of grain products with iron. It would increase the iron load of people with the genetic disorder hemochromatosis and might accelerate tissue damage in their bodies. In addition, there is the possibility of masking a primary disorder that might otherwise be discovered because of the anemia it produced. Because of the potential risks and the uncertainty about the benefits, the FDA withdrew its proposal for superenrichment in November of 1977 (31). Obtaining sufficient iron has been left to the individual, who must choose foods wisely to be sure of meeting the daily requirement.

ISSUE: FLUORIDATION

The practice of fluoridating public drinking water has been a controversial and highly emotional issue for decades. In the early 1930s it was observed that people living in regions with a high natural fluoride content in the drinking water had brown-stained, but highly decay-resistant teeth. By 1942 the relationship between the fluoride content in the water and the low rate of tooth decay had been confirmed, and by 1950 several studies had begun to test the effects of arti-

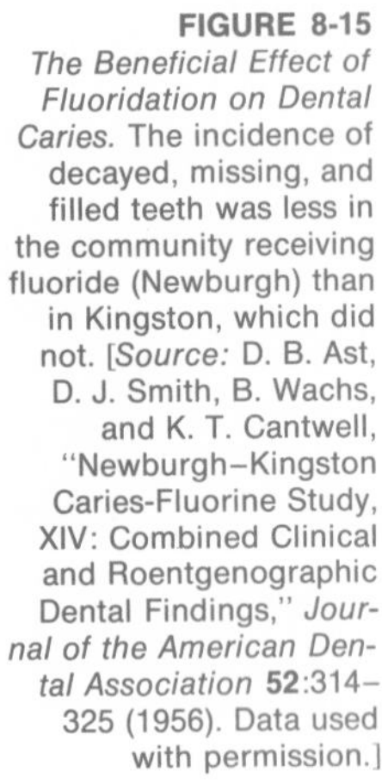

FIGURE 8-15 *The Beneficial Effect of Fluoridation on Dental Caries.* The incidence of decayed, missing, and filled teeth was less in the community receiving fluoride (Newburgh) than in Kingston, which did not. [*Source:* D. B. Ast, D. J. Smith, B. Wachs, and K. T. Cantwell, "Newburgh–Kingston Caries-Fluorine Study, XIV: Combined Clinical and Roentgenographic Dental Findings," *Journal of the American Dental Association* **52**:314–325 (1956). Data used with permission.]

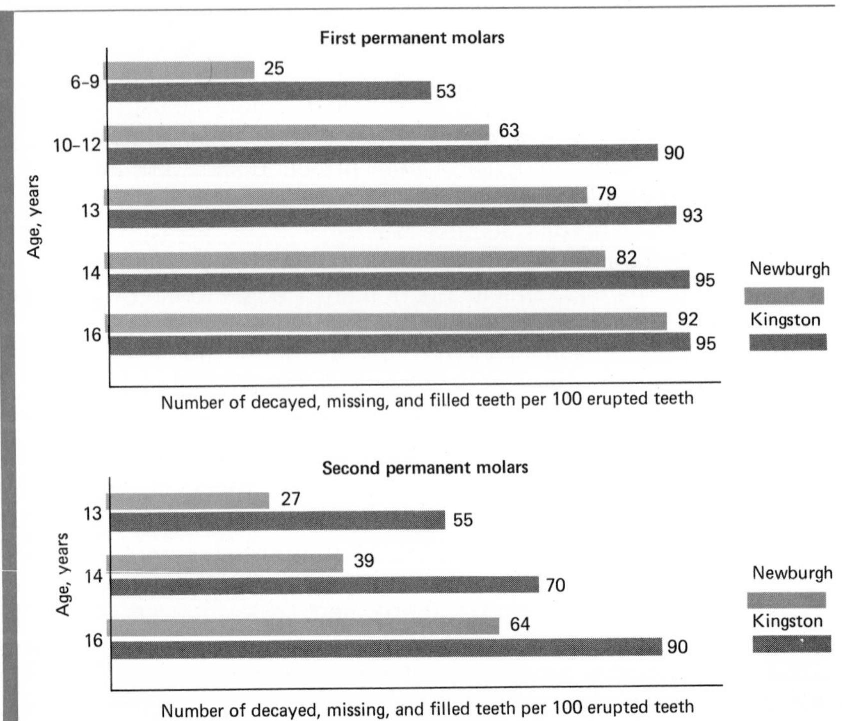

ficially fluoridating drinking water. One of the most impressive experiments was carried out in upstate New York beginning in 1945 (32). The residents of Newburgh received fluoride in their drinking water, while those in nearby Kingston did not. After 10 years, the results indicated that fluoride has a highly beneficial effect in preventing tooth decay (Figure 8-15). Many other studies have confirmed these findings (33). Today, more than 100 million people in the United States drink either naturally or artificially fluoridated water (34).

The arguments against fluoridation have thus far appealed largely to people's emotions. A major issue is freedom of choice, which takes the question of fluoridation out of the realm of science and into that of philosophy, religion, and politics. In recent years, opponents of fluoridation have claimed that it causes Down's syndrome (mongolism), heart disease, and cancer. Experimental work has not supported any of these claims (34). In particular, a study conducted by the National Cancer Institute found no increase in the cancer rate in high-fluoride as compared with low-fluoride areas (22). However, despite the evidence supporting fluoride's safety, as well as its effectiveness in reducing tooth decay, fluoridation programs are still often defeated in public referenda. ”

Study Guide

SUMMARY

1. The life processes require water and mineral elements in addition to organic substances. Water is the most abundant substance in the body and provides the milieu in which body processes occur. It transports substances to and from cells and into and out of the body. Water also functions in the dissipation of body heat, in many chemical reactions, as a structural component of the body, and as a lubricant in the joints and other locations. Total body water can be divided into the intracellular fluid and extracellular fluid. The extracellular fluid may be divided into the blood plasma, the fluid surrounding the cells (interstitial fluid), and other compartments.
2. Balance between fluid compartments is maintained by the movement of water in response to the concentrations of solutes in each compartment. Water balance between fluid compartments reflects water balance in the body as a whole. The body loses water via the urine, feces, skin, and lungs, and these losses must be balanced by water obtained in food and drink and from metabolic reactions in the body. The kidneys respond to imbalances, such as dehydration and overhydration, by either retaining or excreting solute and water.
3. Water and certain minerals, such as sodium, potassium, chloride, sulfur, and phosphorus, function to maintain acid-base balance. Maintenance of proper pH is essential for body processes to continue normally, and the body uses buffer systems, the lungs, and the kidneys to keep the pH in the normal range. Because of these mechanisms, acidity and alkalinity contributed by food do not have any appreciable effect on body pH.
4. Minerals are inorganic elements required by the body in relatively small amounts for growth, maintenance, and reproduction. Like the vitamins, they facilitate the activity of other substances or body processes. The functions, RDAs, food sources, and results of deficiency and excess for each mineral are summarized in Table 8-4.
5. Lead, mercury, and cadmium are toxic minerals with no known function in the body. Lead can cause anemia and damages the nervous system and the kidneys, while a form of mercury (methyl mercury) produces nervous system damage and serious birth defects. Cadmium is toxic to a variety of body tissues. Exposure to these elements is most often accidental or a result of industrial pollution. Efforts are being made to reduce the release of these elements into the environment.

VOCABULARY

aldosterone
anemia
antidiuretic hormone (ADH)
aplastic anemia
buffer
cofactor
cretinism
edema
electrolytes
extracellular fluid (ECF)
ferric iron
ferritin
ferrous iron
glucose tolerance factor (GTF)
goitrogens
hematocrit
heme
hemochromatosis
hemoglobin concentration
hemolytic anemia
hemorrhage
hemosiderin
hydroxyapatite
inorganic
insensible water loss
interstitial fluid
intracellular fluid (ICF)
macronutrient elements

by all levels of government into their lives. Using fluoridation (or the banning of food additives; see Chapter 10) as an example, debate the following question: Is it best for the government to impose measures such as fluoridation for the public welfare, or should such decisions be left to the individual?

2. Keep a diet record as described in Suggested Activity 10-1, and using Ready Reference 1, estimate your intake of calcium and iron. Do they meet your RDA? If not, what foods could be added to or substituted in your diet to increase your intake?

3. a. Using Ready Reference 1 and Agriculture Handbook No. 456 (reference 41), make a list of foods that can provide significant amounts of calcium (10 percent or more of the RDA per serving) if dairy products are omitted from the diet.
   b. Using Ready Reference 1 and Agriculture Handbook No. 456, make a list of foods that can provide significant amounts of iron (10 percent or more of the adult male RDA per serving) if meat and liver are omitted from the diet.

4. a. Check food labels and make a list of foods containing sodium or salt as an ingredient. Using the label or Agriculture Handbook No. 456, determine the sodium content of these foods.
   b. Using Agriculture Handbook No. 456, make a list of foods that naturally contain large amounts of sodium.

FURTHER READING

1. For more detailed information on the minerals:
Nutrition Reviews' Present Knowledge in Nutrition, 4th ed. New York: The Nutrition Foundation, Inc., 1976.
Goodhart, R. S., and Shils, M. E.: *Modern Nutrition in Health and Disease,* 6th ed. Philadelphia: Lea and Febiger, 1980.
Underwood, E. J.: *Trace Elements in Human and Animal Nutrition,* 4th ed. New York: Academic, 1977.

2. Two articles describing the iron superenrichment controversy:
Elwood, P. C.: "The Enrichment Debate," *Nutrition Today* **12:**18–24 (July/August 1977).
Anonymous: "Anatomy of a Decision," *Nutrition Today* **13:**6–8, 28–29 (January/February 1978).

3. Two readable articles about toxic minerals:
Goldwater, L. J.: "Mercury in the Environment," *Sci. Am.* **224:**15–21 (May 1971).
Chisholm, J. J.: "Lead Poisoning," *Sci. Am.* **224:**15–23 (February 1971).

PART 4

NUTRITION DURING THE LIFE CYCLE

For some people, planning a diet is relatively simple: they need only think about themselves and perhaps a spouse and one or two children. Other people may have to prepare food for extended families that include elderly parents and children of different ages. Because each family member may be in a different stage of the life cycle, each may have special nutritional needs. In addition, physiological, psychological, and environmental factors, including dental health, adequacy of digestive secretions, taste preferences, advertising, and peer influences, will affect what foods they consume. Feeding ourselves thus involves far more than knowing what the nutrients are, why we need them, and what foods contain them. We need to combine foods into a diet that will meet the diverse nutritional needs of a family and prepare them in an appetizing manner.

In the following chapters, we will look at how an American family might tackle these challenges. Chapter 9 describes the many principles involved in providing a safe and nutritious diet. In Chapter 10 we will show how to apply them to meet the nutritional needs of healthy, nonpregnant, nonlactating adults. In Chapters 11 through 13 we will look at how nutrient requirements are altered by pregnancy, lactation, growth, and old age; and how the typical diet should be modified to suit these situations.

THE BASIS FOR AN ADEQUATE DIET

Tom and Meg Gerard are an "average" American couple: they have two children at home, and they have elderly parents who live independently but with whom they maintain close ties. Moreover, like many average Americans in the 1980s, they have become aware that their health and that of their family depends a great deal on proper nutrition. To improve their nutrition knowledge, the Gerards decided to take a nutrition course at their local university. For several weeks they attended classes, and they learned a great deal. However, they still have questions. They are not sure which is the best way to choose a nutritious diet. Like many Americans, they have become skeptical about the safety and nutritional quality of the food supply. Can foods currently available in the local supermarket provide enough of all the nutrients? Are food additives dangerous? Are "organic," or "natural," foods better?

With a certain amount of care and planning, it is possible to choose a safe and nutritious diet. By selecting foods wisely and preparing them in a manner that minimizes nutrient losses, nearly everyone can obtain more than enough of each nutrient to meet daily needs. In this chapter we will look at some guidelines that can help accomplish this goal. After reviewing the roles the RDAs, the Basic Four Food Plan, and the Dietary Guidelines for Americans can play in selecting an adequate diet, we will look at the effects of food processing on the safety and nutritional quality of food. We also will evaluate "organic" and "natural" foods and then explore current thinking on the role of diet in the prevention and treatment of cancer.

Some Helpful Tools

In previous chapters we discussed standards for nutrient intake and guidelines for choosing an adequate diet. Let us briefly review some important points.

RECOMMENDED DIETARY ALLOWANCES (RDAs) (1)

As part of planning an adequate diet for themselves, Tom and Meg should know how much of each nutrient they need every day. The **Recommended Dietary Allowances (RDAs)** provide one guideline against which they can compare their nutrient intake (see Chapter 1). The RDAs for all nutrients except energy are generous enough that nearly anyone consuming the recommended amounts will meet or exceed his or her own particular needs. However, the situation is different for energy; its RDA is the caloric requirement of an average individual in the United States population engaged in light activity. Energy intakes of other people must be modified to meet their own particular needs.

The Recommended Dietary Allowances may be thought of as goals for good nutrition, and one way in which they could be used is to plan an adequate diet. The nutrient content of each food can be determined from a **food-composition table**, such as Ready Reference 1, and the total nutrient content of the diet can then be compared with the RDAs. However, this is complex and time-consuming to do every day. In addition, failure to meet the RDAs does not necessarily mean a diet is inadequate; the RDAs provide a margin of safety for most people. For routine diet planning, the usefulness of the RDAs and food-composition tables is limited to determining the contribution of selected foods to meeting nutritional needs. For example, an orange provides about 1½ times the adult RDA for vitamin C, while a 3-ounce serving of fried liver contributes over 40 percent of one day's allowance for iron.

THE FOUR FOOD GROUPS (2,3)

The need for a simple method of choosing an adequate diet has spawned several food plans over the years. The most widely used at present is the Basic Four Food Groups Plan developed by the United States Department of Agriculture in 1957 (2). The plan divides food into four categories: the milk group, the meat group, the vegetable-fruit group, and the bread-cereal group (Table 9-1). Let us take a closer look at how the Basic Four Food Groups Plan can best be used to meet nutritional needs.

The Milk Group The Basic Four Food Plan recommends that adults consume 2 or more cups of milk every day. Cheese, ice cream, or yogurt can replace part of the milk, as shown in Table 9-1. Of the foods commonly consumed by most Americans, milk and dairy products are by far the major source of calcium. Individuals who omit dairy products from the diet must obtain this mineral from other sources. The milk group also provides relatively large quantities of riboflavin and high-quality protein, as well as significant amounts of vitamin B_{12}. If whole-milk products are used, they contribute some vitamin A. Dairy products from which the fat has been removed, such as skim milk, most buttermilk, nonfat dry milk, and products made from them, contain little vitamin A. However, fluid and nonfat dry milks are frequently fortified with vitamin A and vitamin D, making them dependable sources of both nutrients.

Nonfat dry milk can be an inexpensive means of adding the nutrients found in milk to the diet. Like fluid milk, it is an excellent source of calcium, protein, and riboflavin, and if fortified, of vitamin A and vitamin D. In addition to being reconstituted and consumed as a beverage, nonfat dry milk can be added when making milkshakes, yogurt, and many types of bread.

The Meat Group The meat group includes meat, fish, poultry, eggs, legumes (dry beans and peas), and nuts. Two or more servings, defined as 2 to 3 ounces of meat, fish, or poultry, are recommended daily. Eggs, legumes, and nuts may be substituted for some or all of the meat (Table 9-1). The meat group contributes a major portion of the protein to the diet; not only is protein abundant in these foods, but it is generally of high quality. Although the protein quality of legumes and nuts is somewhat lower

TABLE **9-1**

The basic four food groups plan

FOOD GROUP	SERVINGS PER DAY FOR ADULTS	EXAMPLES OF SERVING SIZES	NUTRIENTS PROVIDED IN SIGNIFICANT AMOUNTS
Milk	2	1 cup milk 1/2 ounce cheese 1 cup ice cream 8 ounces yogurt	Protein, calcium, riboflavin, vitamin B_{12}, vitamin A,* vitamin D†
Meat	2	2–3 ounces meat 1 egg 1/2 cup cooked beans 2 tablespoon peanut butter	Protein, iron, niacin, vitamin B_{12}, zinc
Vegetable-fruit: Vitamin A–rich foods Vitamin C–rich foods	4 1 every other day 1	1/2 cup juice (cooked fruit or vegetable) 1 medium fruit or whole vegetable 1/2 large fruit or whole vegetable	Vitamin A, vitamin C, folacin, vitamin E, vitamin K, trace minerals, fiber
Bread-cereal‡	4	1 slice bread 1/2 cup cooked cereal, rice, or pasta 1 ounce ready-to-eat cereal	Thiamine, iron, niacin, some protein
A fifth group: Fats, sweets, and alcohol	Not defined	Not defined	Kilocalories; vegetable oils also supply vitamin E and essential fatty acids

* If made from whole milk or fortified.
† If fortified.
‡ Should be whole- or enriched-grain products.

Source: C. A. Davis, L. H. Fulton, L. Light, D. D. Oldland, L. Page, N. R. Raper, and R. S. Vettel, *Food—The Hassle-Free Guide to a Better Diet,* Home and Garden Bulletin No. 228, USDA, Washington, 1979, p. 2A.

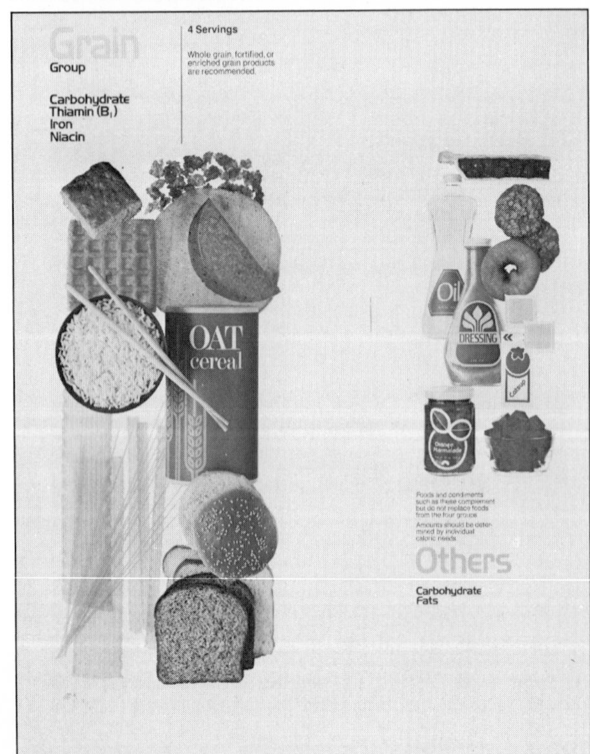

THE BASIC FOUR FOOD GROUPS
Nutrient needs can usually be met by intelligent choices of foods from each of the Four Food Groups. A fifth group, including sweets, fats, and alcohol has been defined, but these foods should be consumed only after the recommended number of servings have been obtained from the other groups. (Courtesy, National Dairy Council.)

than that from the animal sources, supplementation with animal protein or appropriate plant proteins will improve it considerably (see Chapter 4). Depending on which choices are made, another important contribution of the meat group is iron. Liver is the richest source, followed by the muscle meats. Eggs, legumes, and nuts also can provide significant amounts of iron. Legumes and pork are good sources of thiamine, and the meat group supplies many of the other B vitamins, including vitamin B_{12}. Meats also are a major source of zinc.

The Vegetable-Fruit Group Adults should consume at least four servings from the vegetable-fruit group each day. A serving might consist of ½ cup of chopped or cooked greens, carrots, strawberries, or fruit juice, a medium-sized apple, orange, potato, or tomato, or an equivalent amount of another fruit or vegetable (Table 9-1). At least one serving every other day should be a good source of vitamin A, such as a dark-green leafy vegetable or a yellow–orange fruit or vegetable, while a serving of a fruit or vegetable high in vitamin C, including citrus fruits and their juices, cantaloupe, strawberries, and many green vegetables, should be consumed no less than once each day.

In addition to vitamin A and vitamin C, the vegetable-fruit group supplies significant amounts of vitamin E, vitamin K, folacin, certain other B vitamins, iron, other trace minerals, and fiber. Because nutrient content varies widely among these foods, a variety of fruits and vegetables must be selected to take advantage of this group. In particular, Americans need to make better use of green vegetables such as broccoli, brussel sprouts, spinach, collard greens, mustard greens, kale, and watercress. These vegetables can be used in raw form in salads, and most are also available in frozen form, ready for cooking.

The Bread-Cereal Group A minimum of four servings from the bread-cereal group should be consumed daily. A slice of bread, 1 ounce of ready-to-eat cereal, or ½ to ¾ cup of cooked cereal, rice, or macaroni counts as a serving. Maximum benefit will be obtained from this group if whole or enriched grains are used. Grains and their products provide protein, but because the protein is incomplete, they must be combined with beans or sources of high-quality protein, such as meat, eggs, and dairy products, to provide the deficient amino acids. Whole-grain products are reliable sources of thiamine and iron and provide significant amounts of riboflavin, niacin, vitamin B_6, vitamin E, and some trace minerals. The milling process, however, removes a large proportion of these nutrients, and only thiamine, riboflavin, niacin, and iron are replaced in enriched products to levels comparable with or greater than in their whole-grain counterparts. An exception is many of the breakfast cereals, to which most of the vitamins, calcium, and iron are often added, in some instances to levels that meet the adult allowances for these nutrients. Whole grain-products also are good sources of fiber, although the fiber and chemicals called phytates may retard absorption of iron and other trace minerals.

Recently, a fifth food group, the fats, sweets, and alcohol group, has been defined (3). It includes such foods as butter, margarine, mayonnaise, salad dressings, candy, sugar, jams and jellies, syrups, soft drinks, and alcoholic beverages. No serving sizes or basic number of servings has been defined for this group; they should be used in moderation and only in a diet in which nutrient needs have already been met from other sources.

Making the Most of the Basic Four The Basic Four Food Plan provides a foundation for an adequate diet. However, following it does not mean the diet will automatically supply sufficient amounts of all the nutrients; the food plan must be used intelligently to be sure of meeting all nutritional needs. It is easy to defeat the system by consistently choosing poorer-quality foods from within each group, by not making the serving sizes large enough, and by preparing foods in ways that result in significant nutrient losses. Highly processed foods and substitute foods that outwardly resemble other foods, such as fruit juice, egg, and cheese substitutes, may be of inferior nutritional quality. For example, many commercial citrus-based beverages look and taste similar to natural juices and are fortified with vitamin C, but they often lack several other nutrients, such as folacin, thiamine, and trace minerals found in natural juices (Figure 9-1).

Another problem with the Basic Four Food Plan is that it was developed around the need for energy and only eight other nutrients: protein, calcium, iron, vitamin A, vitamin C, thiamine, riboflavin, and niacin. It was hoped that if appropriate foods were chosen, sufficient amounts of the other nutrients would be obtained. However, some nutrients, such as folacin, vitamin B_6, vitamin E, magnesium, zinc, and iron, could be deficient in a diet based on the four food groups, and a modified Basic Four Foods Plan has been proposed to ensure an adequate intake of these nutrients (4) (see Table 9-2). In addition, vitamin B_{12} can be obtained only from animal sources, so strict vegetarians will require supplements of this vitamin. Iodine may be deficient in diets lacking seafood, but the use of iodized salt will ensure an adequate intake.

THE DIETARY GUIDELINES FOR AMERICANS AND THE U.S. DIETARY GOALS (5,50)

Providing a proper balance of protein, vitamins, and minerals is not the only objective of a nutritious diet. In earlier chapters we saw how the proportion of carbohydrate, fat, and protein, the type of fat, and the caloric, cholesterol, sugar, and salt contents of the diet may be important to good health. We also discussed the potential benefits of changing our intake of these dietary components to conform to the Dietary Guidelines for Americans and the U.S. Dietary Goals (see Chapter 1). Although they are controversial at this time, the Dietary Guidelines for Americans and the U.S. Dietary Goals can be used in conjunction with the four food groups to choose an adequate diet: a person can select foods from each group that conform to them. For example, to lower saturated fat and cholesterol intakes, skimmed milk and products made from it can be substituted for whole-milk products, especially if the skimmed milk is fortified with vita-

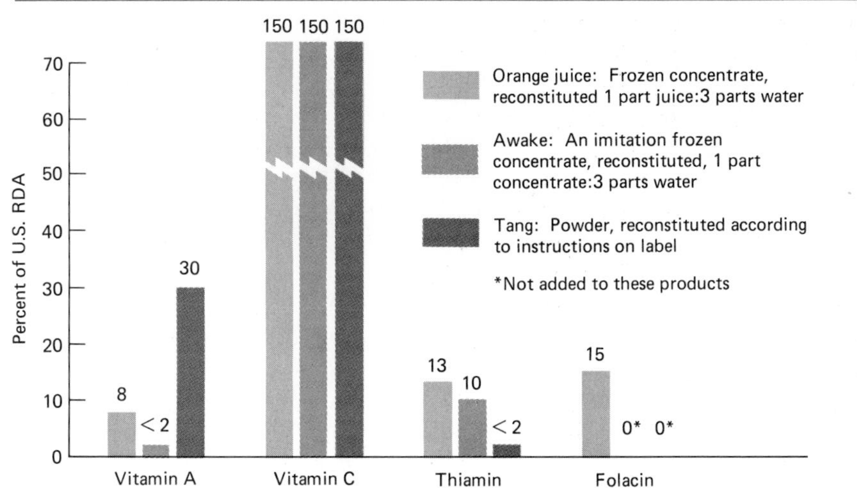

FIGURE 9-1
A Comparison of Orange Juice with Imitation Products. Imitation products sometimes lack nutrients found in the original foods [*Sources:* Product labels; C. F. Adams, *Nutritive Value of American Foods in Common Units,* Agriculture Handbook No. 456, Washington, DC, USDA (1975); B. P. Perloff, and R. R. Bantrum, "Folacin in Selected Foods," *Journal of the American Dietetic Association* **70**:161–172 (1977). Data from *JADA* used with permission.]

mins A and D. Fish, poultry, and appropriate combinations of legumes, beans, and whole grains can replace some meat in the diet, while polyunsaturated fat can be substituted for some of the saturated fat. Heavily sugared breakfast cereals and baked goods, fruits packed in syrup, and other foods with added sugar can be replaced by corresponding foods with lower sugar contents. Foods containing sodium need not be avoided by most people; reducing salt consumption can be accomplished by not adding salt to foods at the table and by avoiding foods on which the salt is visible. Implementing the U.S. Dietary Goals and the Dietary Guidelines for Americans also requires an increased intake of fruits, vegetables, and whole grains. This can be facilitated by using the basic four food groups in dietary planning.

TABLE **9-2**

A modified basic four foods plan

Two servings of milk and milk products

Four servings of protein foods:
- Two servings of animal protein
- Two servings of legumes and/or nuts

Four servings of fruits and vegetables:
- One serving of vitamin C–rich vegetables or fruits
- One serving of dark-green, leafy vegetables
- Two servings of other vegetables or fruits

Four servings of whole-grain cereal products

One serving of fat and/or oil (to ensure adequate vitamin E)

Source: J. C. King, S. H. Lohenour, C. G. Corruccini, and D. Schneeman, "Evaluation and Modification of the Basic Four Food Groups," *J. Nutr. Ed.* **10**:27–29 (1978). (Copyright, Society for Nutrition Education. Used with permission.)

THE EXCHANGE LISTS

Because of health problems, some people must plan their diets on a daily basis. **Exchange lists**, in which foods are grouped together according to the nutrients they contain, simplify dietary calculations. Because the content of the specified nutrients is the same within each exchange group, members of a group can be substituted for each other without significantly altering the composition of the diet with respect to those nutrients.

One of the most widely used systems is the American Dietetic Association (ADA) Food Exchange System, which was originally developed for diabetics. Because diabetics must control their caloric intake and the proportion of carbohydrate, fat, and protein in their diets, the ADA system categorizes foods according to these nutrients. There are six groups: milk, vegetables, fruit, bread, meat, and fat. Nearly every food normally consumed by Americans fits into one of these groups, except those containing large amounts of sugar, such as cookies, cakes, candies, soda, and alcoholic beverages, which are usually prohibited for diabetics. Each list gives its component foods in terms of quantities that provide the same amount of protein, carbohydrate, fat, and kilocalories. For instance, in the fruit list, ½ cup of blackberries, ½ grapefruit, and a small apple each contain about 10 grams of carbohydrate, 40 kilocalories, and negligible amounts of protein and fat. Thus they can be substituted for one another in the diet. The ADA exchange lists and more details about their use are found in Ready Reference 2.

The Issue of Food Processing

A major weakness of the Basic Four Food Plan is that it does not take into account the effects of commercial processing and home preparation on the nutritional quality of food. Yet today, foods are subject to more physical and chemical treatment than ever before. In addition, many people do not know the best ways to prepare food in the home. Let us look at why we process foods and how processing influences the safety and nutritional quality of foods.

WHY PROCESS FOOD?

The surge of interest in nutrition during the last decade has coincided with a "back to nature" movement. Central to this movement has been disillusionment with the intrusion of technology into all areas of our lives, including the food we eat. Nevertheless, commercial food processing has played an important role in maintaining a safe, abundant, and nutritious food supply. For example, canning and freezing allow the storage of food for long periods of time and also prevent the growth of harmful organisms. Pasteurization kills disease-producing bacteria in milk, while certain food additives, such as the propionates, retard the growth of mold in baked goods. In addition to improving the safety and storage life of foods, commercial processing provides other desirable, if not entirely essential, benefits. Appropriate combinations of foods and the use of flavors and colors can enhance the aesthetic appeal of a prod-

Commercial food processing has many benefits; it also has many costs.

uct. Other processes make food more convenient to use; we can buy "minute" rice, "ready-to-eat" cereals, "heat-and-serve" dinners, and baked goods that are ready to "pop into the oven."

The many benefits of commercial food processing are not without their costs; processing almost invariably alters nutritional quality. Moderate heat improves the nutritional value of many proteins, including those in egg white and legumes, but higher temperatures reduce the availability of other proteins, such as those in meat (6, pages 167–177). Considerable quantities of the mineral elements can be lost in processes in which the food comes into contact with water, such as in cooking or **blanching** (6, page 144). However, the presence of calcium in processing water can increase the content of this mineral in the food (6, page 144). Extensive losses of vitamins also occur during food processing (6, pages 47–95; 7, pages 1–4, 16–18). For example, the water-soluble vitamins leach out of foods brought into contact with water. Oxygen destroys vitamin C, thiamine, folacin, vitamin A, and vitamin E. Heat leads to the loss of vitamin C, thiamine, folacin, pantothenic acid, and one form of vitamin B_6. Thiamine is unstable to alkali; riboflavin and vitamin A, to sunlight; and vitamin C and vitamin E, to the presence of iron and copper.

A major concern for most of us is the comparative quality of fresh, frozen, and canned products. Much depends on season of the year and geographic location. Ripe, fresh-picked fruits and vegetables undoubtedly are of the highest nutritional quality, but fresh produce in supermarkets in the northeast United States during the winter spends several days in transit from grower to the market, providing ample time for nutrient losses to occur. During this period, frozen vegetables might be a better choice. The vegetables are generally quick-frozen almost immediately after harvest, and although blanching with steam or hot water before freezing destroys some nutrients, the process also inactivates enzymes that might spoil the food or break down certain vitamins, such as vitamin C. Freezing generally results in lower losses of nutrients than canning, during which the food may be subjected to temperatures of 250°F or more for periods of 20 to 30 minutes or longer (Table 9-3).

Drying and microwave cooking are two processes that are coming increasingly into use. Nutrient losses during drying vary with the method used, but with the exception of vitamin C and beta-carotene, generally they are low. Freeze-drying results in the highest nutrient retention of all (7, pages 289–323). Little work has been done on nutrient retention with the microwave oven, but so far, vitamin retention in meat and vegetables is generally comparable with that of conventional cooking methods using the same amount of water (7, pages 491–493, 508–513).

TABLE **9-3**

Comparison of fresh, frozen, and canned vegetables

VEGETABLE AND NUTRIENTS	FRESH (BOILED AND DRAINED)	FROZEN (BOILED AND DRAINED)	CANNED (DRAINED SOLIDS)
Spinach (per 100 grams):			
Iron, mg	2.2	2.5	2.6
Vitamin A, IU	8100	8100	8000
Thiamine, mg	.07	.08	.02
Riboflavin, mg	.14	.14	.12
Niacin, mg	.5	.5	.3
Ascorbic acid, mg	28	28	14
Green peas:			
Iron, mg	1.8	1.9	1.7
Vitamin A, IU	540	600	690
Thiamine, mg	.28	.27	.11
Riboflavin, mg	.11	.09	.06
Niacin, mg	2.3	1.7	1.0
Ascorbic acid, mg	20	13	8

Note: Some values for frozen and canned foods are greater than for fresh because the food becomes more concentrated during processing.

Source: B. K. Watt, and A. L. Merrill, *Composition of Foods: Raw, Processed, Prepared,* USDA Handbook No. 8, USDA, Washington, 1963.

FIGURE 9-2

Loss of Nutrients in Refined Wheat Flour. Significant amounts of many nutrients are lost during milling, but only thiamine, riboflavin, niacin, and iron are replaced by enrichment. [*Sources* C. F. Adams, *Nutritive Value of American Foods in Common Units,* Agriculture Handbook No. 456, Washington, DC: USDA, (1975); M. L. Orr, *Pantothenic Acid, Vitamin B_6, and Vitamin B_{12} in Foods,* Home Economics Research Report No. 36, Washington, DC: USDA, (1969); B. K. Watt, and A. L. Merrill, *Composition of Foods—Raw, Processed, and Prepared,* Agriculture Handbook No. 8, Washington, DC: USDA, (1963); B. P. Perloff, and R. R. Bantrum, Folacin in Selected Foods," *J. Am. Diet. Assoc.* **70**:161–172 (1977); P. J. McLaughlin, and J. L. Weihrauch. "Vitamin E Content of Foods," *J. Am. Diet. Assoc.* **75**:647–665 (1979).; E. W. Murphy, B. W. Willis, and B. K. Watt, "Provisional Tables on the Zinc Content of Foods," *J. Am. Diet. Assoc.* **66**:345–355 (1975). Data from *JADA* used with permission.]

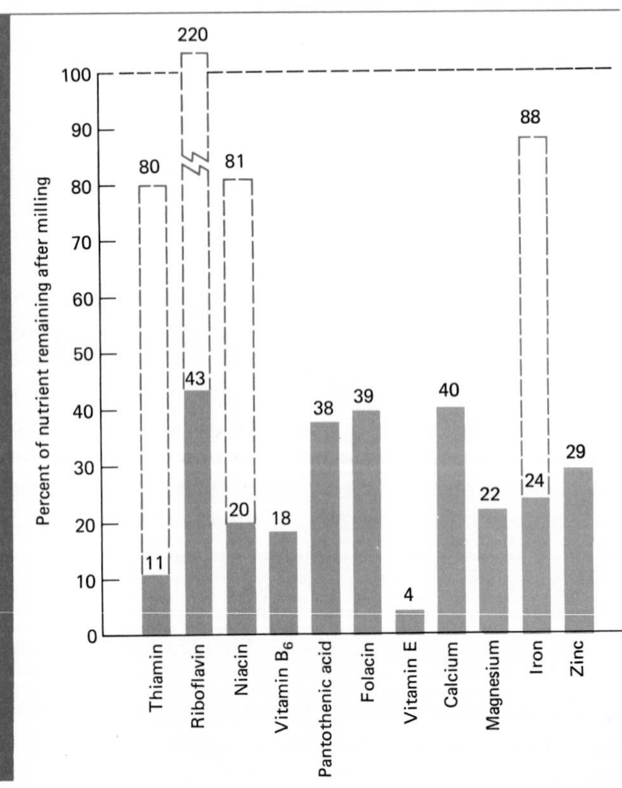

The milling of wheat is another process that substantially alters nutritional quality. As shown in Figure 9-2, white flour has lost a major proportion of most of the nutrients, as well as fiber, contained in whole-wheat flour. This results from the removal of two parts of the wheat berry, the bran and the germ, during the milling process (Figure 9-3). Only thiamine, riboflavin, niacin, and iron are replaced by enrichment in most products.

ENRICHMENT AND FORTIFICATION

During the manufacture of many foods, nutrients are added. **Enrichment** is the practice of adding nutrients back to a refined food at levels established by the government. It generally applies to grain products to which thiamine, riboflavin, niacin, and iron are added. **Fortified** foods are those to which nutrients are added that were not present or were present in small amounts before processing. Examples include milk fortified with vitamin D, iodized salt, margerine fortified with vitamin A, and soft drinks fortified with vitamin C.

In many instances, adding nutrients to foods has been an important public health measure; the virtual disappearance of pellagra, riboflavin deficiency, rickets, and simple goiter in the United States can be attributed to enrichment and fortification procedures. However, these methods also can be abused. Cereals fortified to 100 percent of the U.S.RDA for all the vitamins and several minerals and soft drinks to which vitamin C has been added may lead many consumers to exaggerate the importance of these foods and neglect others in the diet.

HOME FOOD PREPARATION

Preparing foods properly at home is an important part of providing a safe and nutritious diet. Everyone appreciates a home-cooked meal made

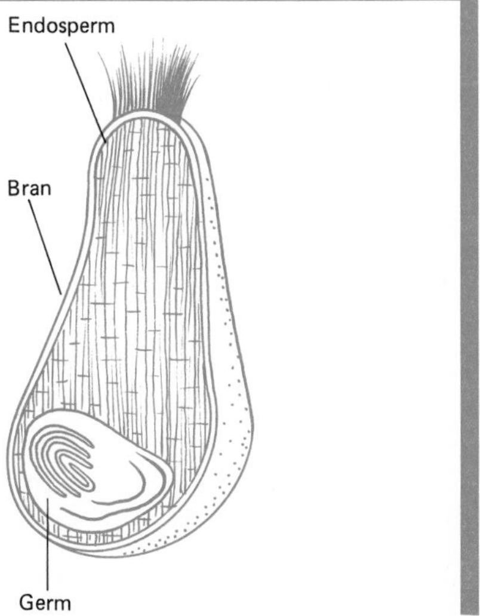

FIGURE 9-3
The wheat berry.

FOCUS 9-1
FOOD-BORNE ILLNESSES

DISEASE NAME/ORGANISM INVOLVED	FOODS INVOLVED	INCUBATION PERIOD/SYMPTOMS	PREVENTION
Botulism: *Clostridium botulinum*	Improperly canned low-acid foods, smoked fish.	Toxin usually requires 12 to 36 hours to work; nausea, abdominal pain, diarrhea, double vision, dizziness, weakness, incoordination; can be fatal in 3 to 10 days.	Canned foods must be thoroughly cleaned and subjected to high temperature under pressure for recommended times; acidification and curing in salt also help.
Clostridium perfringens	Cooked meat and poultry that has stayed at room temperature for several hours or was cooled slowly; gravy, stew, meat pies.	Usually 8 to 12 hours; abdominal pain, diarrhea, occasional dehydration; lasts 1 day or less.	Chill foods rapidly; thaw rapidly or in refrigerator; reheat leftovers to 165°F (60°C).
Salmonella: *Salmonella enteridis, Salmonella choleraesuis*	Meat, poultry, eggs, and their products; also coconut, yeast, smoked fish, dry milk.	Usually 12 to 36 hours; diarrhea, abdominal pain, vomiting, dehydration, fever, headache; duration of several days.	Use sanitary preparation practices; chill foods rapidly; thaw rapidly or in refrigerator; cook thoroughly; avoid cross-contamination; use shallow containers for rapid chilling and thawing.
Staphylococcus aureus	Meat, poultry and dressings, sauces and gravies, cream-filled pastries, potatoes, ham, poultry, and fish salads, hollandaise sauce.	Usually 2 to 4 hours; sudden onset of nausea, salivation, vomiting, diarrhea, abdominal cramps, weakness, dehydration.	Same as for salmonella; avoid food contact with infected cuts.

Source: F. L. Bryan, *Diseases Transmitted by Foods,* DHEW Center for Disease Control, Atlanta, 1973.

"from scratch." In addition, more people are canning and freezing their own fruits and vegetables, baking their own bread, and making a variety of foods ranging from jams and jellies to ice cream and beer and wine. However, more cases of food-borne illness (Focus 9-1) result from home preparation than from commercial processing. Following recommended procedures for home canning and other preservation methods, keeping foods frozen or refrigerated if necessary, thawing frozen foods in the refrigerator, cooking foods thoroughly, and following proper sanitary practices in all phases of food preparation will help prevent these problems. At the same time, many of the factors that influence the nutritional quality of manufactured foods also must be considered when preparing foods at home: water, heat, light, oxygen, and pH. Focus 9-2 gives some practical tips for cooking foods properly and maintaining the highest possible nutrient content.

WHAT ABOUT FOOD ADDITIVES?

An important part of the current concern with commercial food processing revolves around the use of **food additives**; at present more than 3000 chemicals are intentionally added to food during manufacture, and thousands more find their way into food as a result of pollution from food-contact surfaces, migration from packaging, and other sources (6, pages 284–287). Many of these substances are found naturally in the body in small amounts or not at all, and many questions have been raised about their safety.

Safety, however, is not easy to quantify, and absolute safety, or zero risk, simply does not exist. Every human activity, whether it is crossing a street, eating a piece of meat, participating in a sport, or sitting on the porch, entails some risk of injury or even death. We engage in most activities because we have made a decision that our desire to do so or the benefits obtained far outweigh the risks involved. Regulatory agencies, such as the Food and Drug Administration (FDA), use a similar type of **benefit-risk analysis** in decision-making processes. Let us see how the benefit-risk analysis can be applied to food additives.

Benefits of Food Additives Food additives perform a variety of functions (Table 9-4), and their benefits range from ensuring the safety of the food and prolonging its shelf life to making it look more appetizing. For example, the nitrite used in cured meats prevents the growth of *Clostridium botulinum,* a type of bacteria that produces one of the deadliest toxins known. The growth of bread mold is retarded by chemicals called *propionates,* while sorbates are used as mold inhibitors in cheese. Flavors and colors improve the taste and appearance of food, but the FDA and other regulatory agencies must check continually to see that they are not used to mask inferior quality.

FOCUS 9-2 COOKING TO PRESERVE NUTRIENT CONTENT Here are some hints for cooking foods properly and maintaining the highest possible nutrient content:

1. Use as little water as possible. This prevents water-soluble nutrients from leaching out of the food. Wash foods quickly in cold water; do not soak. If possible, do not boil vegetables. Methods such as pressure-cooking, steaming, using a double boiler, and stir-frying in oil require little or no water. Any leftover water, as well as drippings from cooking meat, can be used to make soups and gravies.
2. Do not overcook—some of the vitamins are unstable to heat. An additional advantage of pressure-cooking and stir-frying is that the food is cooked in a shorter time than with other methods.
3. Do not cut fruits and vegetables until just before use, and do not cut them into small pieces. This reduces their exposure to oxygen, which destroys certain vitamins.
4. Refrigerate or freeze leftovers immediately after use. Leaving them out accelerates nutrient losses, provides an opportunity for disease bacteria to grow, and increases the rate of spoilage.
5. Thaw foods in the refrigerator. This reduces nutrient losses and slows down growth of spoilage and disease-producing organisms in the parts of the food that thaw first.
6. Try to prepare only as much food as will be consumed. This will avoid leftovers that will need to be heated a second time.
7. Include some raw fruits and vegetables in the diet.

TABLE **9-4**

Uses of food additives

1. To preserve food:
   Mold inhibitors
   Curing agents
   Antioxidants
2. To improve consistency:
   Emulsifiers
   Stabilizers and thickeners
   Acids and bases
3. To improve flavor:
   Flavors
   Flavor enhancers
4. To add color
5. Miscellaneous purposes:
   Leavening agents—for baked goods
   Maturing and bleaching agents—for flour
   Anticaking agents—for mixes and powders
   Humectants—to retain moisture
   Clarifying agents—for liquids
   Foaming agents
   Foam inhibitors
   Nonnutritive sweeteners
6. To improve nutritional quality
   Vitamins and minerals

Potential Risks Many consumers are concerned about the risks that may accompany the use of food additives. One of the major fears is that some additives may be **carcinogens** (cancer-causing agents). Other additives are suspected **teratogens** (causing birth defects), or **mutagens** (causing mutations), while still other additives may damage tissues or lead to sterility.

The 1958 Food Additive Amendment to the Food, Drug, and Cosmetic Act requires all new additives to be tested for safety before they are used in food (8). Several types of experiments can be performed on animals to assess the safety of a food additive, although not all are carried out for each new additive (9). For example, *acute toxicity studies* test the effects produced by the substance when administered in a single dose and may give information regarding a lethal dose, intoxication levels, and effects on tissues and organs. *Long-term experiments,* in which the additive is fed to animals for up to 2 years or for a lifetime, are required to detect carcinogens. Feeding the additive to pregnant animals helps assess teratogenicity and effects on fertility. Several other tests can be carried out to determine how the chemical is metabolized, as well as to evaluate its safety.

At the time the Food Additive Amendment was passed, many additives were exempted from safety testing. These chemicals had been in use before 1958 and are, in the opinion of scientists qualified to evaluate them, generally recognized as safe (**GRAS**). The so-called GRAS list has been questioned, and in 1969 the FDA began a thorough review of the safety of GRAS substances that it expects to complete in the early 1980s.

As of 1978, 351 additives had been reviewed and only 4 percent showed evidence of adverse effects at the levels currently used in food (10).

Despite the animal studies, questions and difficulties arise in assessing risk. For example, can the results of animal experiments be applied to humans? Experimental animals differ physiologically and biochemically from humans, and their responses to food additives may be different. However, studies have shown that all chemicals proved to be carcinogenic in humans, except for benzene and arsenic, have ultimately been found to cause cancer in animals as well (11).

Threshold Doses One aspect of toxicologic research that puzzles many people is the use of very high doses of food additives in the animal experiments. For example, the dose of saccharin that produced bladder cancer in rats in one experiment is the equivalent of a human drinking eight hundred 12-ounce cans of diet soft drink per day for an entire lifetime. What relevance does such a procedure have to the real-life situation of long-term exposure to much lower levels of the substance? Central to this issue is the concept of a **threshold dose**; does a level of exposure exist above which there is a hazard, but below which the consumer is safe? In other words, if feeding an additive to experimental animals at a level of 5 percent of the diet (50 parts per thousand) causes adverse effects, will feeding it at lower levels also be hazardous? If a threshold exists, feeding large doses of a chemical to animals is meaningless. We could simply set a tolerance for the additive at a much lower level and be confident that no adverse effects will result. However, if no threshold can be found, consumption of any amount of the additive carries some risk, and the results of feeding large doses of the substance can be extrapolated to any level of use. In this case, the risks must be weighed against the benefits of using the chemical.

We do not know whether or not a threshold dose exists for most food additives. This is unfortunate, because it is impossible to test the effects of long-term, low-level exposure. The rate at which extremely small amounts of an additive might cause cancer is so low (1 case out of 20,000 or more subjects) that vast numbers of animals would be needed to show any adverse effect. No laboratory in the world has the money or the facilities to conduct experiments on this scale. As a result, much higher doses of the additive must be used to "force the issue" and produce an effect.

Another problem is that as analytical capabilities have improved, scientists have been able to detect the presence of progressively smaller amounts of a chemical in food. For example, in 1962 the methods available could not detect less than 50 parts per billion of diethylstilbestrol (DES), a synthetic hormone used to promote the growth of livestock. By 1973, however, the technology existed to detect parts per trillion of this compound, the equivalent of one grain of sugar in an Olympic-sized swimming pool (12,13). Because we do not know whether a threshold dose exists, the ability to detect such minute amounts of an additive in food has far outstripped our ability to evaluate its significance.

Although we do not know whether or not a threshold dose exists for most food additives, the most controversial part of the Food Additive Amendment, the Delaney clause, assumes that one does not exist for carcinogenic substances:

> No additive shall be deemed to be safe if it is found to induce cancer when ingested by man or animal (14).

Thus if an additive has been found to cause cancer in a laboratory experiment, it cannot be used in food at all, even though the dose that produced the cancer was thousands of times greater than the level that would be used in food. Some authorities believe threshold doses exist for many food additives, and if added to food at levels well below threshold, these chemicals pose no hazard to humans (13).

At the present time, there is still a question as to whether or not the results of current experiments can be applied to humans. For carcinogenic substances, the answer is dictated by law; the Delaney clause does not allow any amount of these chemicals in the food supply. In regulating potentially teratogenic, mutagenic, and other toxic substances, the FDA can set a tolerance level. Generally, this level is 1/100 of the largest dose that does not produce any adverse effects. In the future, dose-response curves may be used to establish tolerances (Figure 9-4). The incidence of adverse effects for a large number of doses of a substance is plotted on a graph. The tolerance level may then be set at a dose that carries a predefined, but acceptably small, risk of adverse effects.

RISK-BENEFIT: SOME CURRENT EXAMPLES

Toxicologic tests indicate that most food additives in current use are probably harmless at the levels normally encountered in the diet. Let us apply a risk-benefit analysis to some of the more controversial ones.

Monosodium Glutamate (MSG) Monosodium glutamate has been used for centuries in Oriental cooking as a flavor enhancer, and it is currently added to many foods during commercial processing. Glutamate is also one of the amino acids found in human protein. It does not appear to be harmful to most adults, even in large doses (16). Monosodium glutamate is therefore classified as a GRAS substance by the FDA. However, in susceptible individuals, MSG produces headaches, burning sensations on the skin, tightening of the face, and chest pains, a complex of symptoms known as Chinese restaurant syndrome (CRS). The threshold dose varies, but as little as 3 grams of MSG taken on an empty stomach produces CRS in some people (16,17). However, the problem is temporary and does not appear to have any permanent effects.

In 1969, J. W. Olney reported that MSG injected into newborn mice caused brain damage, stunted skeletal development, marked obesity, and sterility (18). Further studies by Olney and others confirmed these results and also found that oral administration of MSG could cause brain

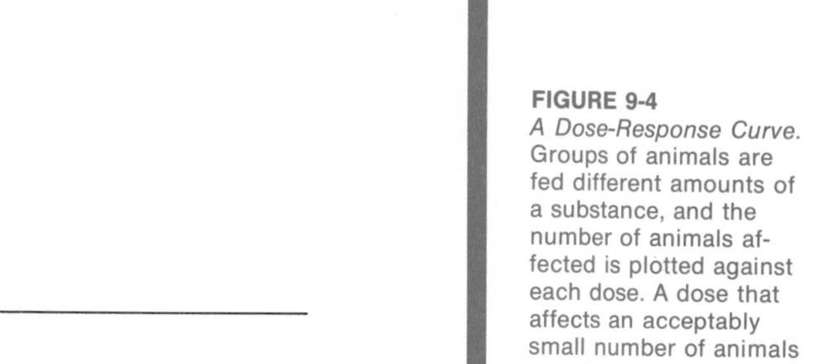

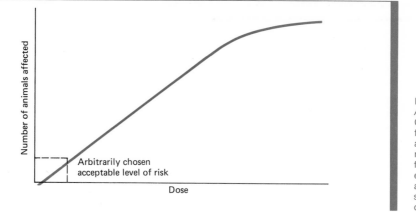

FIGURE 9-4
A Dose-Response Curve. Groups of animals are fed different amounts of a substance, and the number of animals affected is plotted against each dose. A dose that affects an acceptably small number of animals can then be chosen.

damage in infant mice and rhesus monkeys (19). Although these findings conflict with those of some other experiments, they suggest that infants may not be able to handle glutamate in doses beyond those normally found in the diet (19,20). Since the function of MSG is purely aesthetic, the potential risks outweigh the benefits of its use in baby foods, and manufacturers have voluntarily abandoned its use in these products.

Nitrites Nitrites are among the ingredients used in curing meats and in smoked fish. They maintain the red color of meat, help give it the characteristic flavor, and prevent the growth of deadly botulism bacteria (6, pages 374–377). However, they also can combine with substances called *amines,* including certain amino acids, to form *nitrosamines,* which are potent carcinogens (6, page 285). Nitrosamines may be formed in the stomach and have been found in smoked fish and cured meats treated with nitrite (6, pages 374–377). The highest concentrations (108 parts per billion) were found in fried bacon (21). Vitamin C and sodium erythorbate, both of which can be used in curing meat, prevent nitrosamine formation (21).

Cured meat and smoked fish are not the only sources of nitrite in the diet. Humans are exposed to it because of the presence of related substances called *nitrates* in drinking water and in leafy and root-tuber vegetables (22). Some of this nitrate is converted to nitrite by microorganisms in the food, in the intestine, and in the saliva (22). More than two-thirds

1. "Organic," or "natural," foods are superior to those produced by conventional production methods.

2. All food additives are dangerous and should be avoided.

3. Diet can prevent or cure cancer.

FACT OR FANTASY

of the nitrite entering the stomach arrives in the saliva; the other third comes from cured meat products (23).

In October of 1977, the United States Department of Agriculture notified the producers of cured meats that their products could not contain nitrosamines. In May of 1978, the USDA also reduced the amount of nitrite that can be added to bacon to a level that should not produce nitrosamines. The FDA is currently collecting data on nitrite carcinogenicity and may ultimately ban the substance, despite its usefulness in preventing the growth of the botulism organism. Efforts are being made to find a suitable substitute (24).

Color Additives Food colors perform the aesthetic function of improving the appearance of food. They are added to soft drinks, candy, gelatin and other desserts, fruit, sausage casings, and certain dairy products and baked goods. Although some, such as the carotenes, can be derived from plant sources and others, such as titanium dioxide, are mineral salts, most color additives are synthetic substances. Before it is approved for food use, each color must be tested for safety. Once it is in use, the FDA tests and certifies each batch of synthetic color for purity.

In 1938, 15 colors were listed as acceptable for food use, and 4 more were added between 1939 and 1950. However, as toxicologic data have accumulated, many of these have been delisted, leaving 3 synthetic colors permanently listed for use in food and 6 provisionally or temporarily listed pending the results of research into their safety (25). The color most recently delisted is Food, Drug, and Cosmetic Color (FD&C) Red No. 2. Although it is suspected to cause cancer and to interfere with reproduction in rats, the data showing these adverse effects are not overwhelming. However, because food manufacturers could not produce any convincing evidence to prove that Red No. 2 is safe, the FDA will not allow its use in food, drugs, or cosmetics (29).

Another color of current interest is FD&C Yellow No. 5 (tartrazine). This compound produces an allergic reaction (hives) in some people (26,27). It is also suspected as a cause of hyperactivity in some children (28) (see Chapter 12).

Diethylstilbestrol and Other Drugs Used in Animal Feed Diethylstilbestrol (DES) is a synthetic estrogen used to promote growth of livestock. Mixed in the animal's feed or implated in a capsule in their bodies, DES results in more rapid weight gain with the consumption of less feed (30). The drug, however, is a known carcinogen; daughters of women who were given the drug to prevent miscarriages have a rate of vaginal cancer considerably higher than normal (31).

However, DES proponents point out that the amount found in meat is exceedingly small, ranging from 2 parts per billion or less to undetectable levels. One authority calculated that, at worst, this level of exposure would result in one additional case of cancer in 8 years. In addition, he noted that the quantity of DES likely to be found in meat is minute in comparison with the level of estrogens produced naturally within the body (32). Nevertheless, owing to the risk of cancer, DES was prohibited in animal feed in 1972 and in implants in 1973. A federal court overturned the ban because the FDA had not conducted appropriate hearings on the issue, but the hormone was permanently banned from use in livestock production in 1979 (31,33).

Many antibiotics also are used in raising food animals. Not only do these antibiotics fight disease, but many promote growth. Although a withdrawal period is required before the animals are slaughtered or their eggs or milk can be used for food, residues sometimes appear. A major worry is that bacteria exposed to these low levels of antibiotics will develop a resistance to them and transfer their resistance to bacteria that cause disease. This would render some antibiotics useless in treating certain diseases. The FDA is currently looking at the use of antibiotics in animal production and may prohibit the use of penicillin, tetracycline, and others in animal feed (34).

PROCESSED FOODS: STRATEGY

For each of the four food groups, the consumer is faced with a variety of choices. Many factors, including cost, appearance, taste preferences, peer influences, and advertising, influence these choices, and food manufacturers pay much attention to them in developing and promoting their products. However, it is important for consumers also to consider the nutritional quality and safety of manufactured foods when they make their selections. In many cases, a consumer can choose nutritionally superior products instead of inferior ones. For example, if cost and personal tastes will allow it, an individual can purchase whole-grain products rather than refined and enriched goods, fruit juices instead of diluted and fortified fruit drinks and soft drinks, and frozen rather than canned fruits and vegetables. In addition, certain unprocessed foods, such as fresh, raw fruits and vegetables, should be consumed on a regular basis. Products with little redeeming nutritional value, such as pastries, candy, and unfortified soft drinks, should be avoided or consumed in small quantities after needs for vitamins and minerals have been met.

People also must make their own benefit-risk decisions about food additives when choosing foods. The risk of adverse effects from most food additives is very small; there is no need to avoid foods containing them. Like any other type of dietary restriction, avoidance could ultimately result in a deficiency of one or more nutrients. In many cases, foods that do not contain additives can be found in the supermarket and substituted for products that do contain them. For example, many manufacturers of vegetable oil do not add preservatives such as BHA (butylated hydroxyanisole) and BHT (butylated hydroxytoluene) to their products, with no apparent effect on the stability of the oil. Bread, ice cream, breakfast cereals, and fruit juices that contain no additives also are widely available. However, the wise consumer will comparison-shop and not pay outrageously high prices for "natural" foods. Certain food additives can be avoided altogether. Foods containing added nitrite or monosodium glutamate can be eliminated from the diet without harm. A consumer need not be exposed to saccharin (see Chapter 2) unless he or she so chooses, and the intake of artificial colors can be reduced by making appropriate choices.

Another Choice: Organic and Natural Foods Concern about the effects of modern processing on the nutritional quality and safety of the food supply has led many people to purchase "organic" and "natural" foods. Although chemists define organic substances as those that contain carbon (see Chapter 1) and therefore classify all foods as organic, in common usage the word is applied to foods grown without the use of any manufactured fertilizers or pesticides and processed without the use of food additives. Natural does not have a precise scientific meaning but in common usage it indicates products that have undergone minimal refinement or processing (35).

There is no evidence that organic and natural foods are in any way superior to foods produced by conventional commercial means. At least three studies (a 10-year trial at the Michigan Experiment Station, a 25-year experiment at the U.S. Plant, Soil, and Nutrition Laboratory in Ithaca, New York, and a 34-year investigation at a British experimental farm) showed no nutritional superiority for food grown "organically" as compared with that produced by conventional farming methods (35,36). The protein and vitamin content of a plant is largely determined by genetics, climate, and stage of maturity when the foods is harvested. Although the content of many minerals in food is influenced by the concentration of these elements in the soil, there is little evidence that organic fertilizers offer any significant advantage over commerical fertilizers in improving the food's mineral content (35).

A great deal of concern also has been expressed about the highly toxic pesticides used in commercial farming. The organochlorine compounds, such as DDT, degrade slowly and persist in the environment for many years. In recent years, environmentalists also have become concerned about such substances as the polychlorinated biphenyls (PCBs) and the polybrominated biphenyls (PBBs), which are chemically related to the organochlorine pesticides. Used in a variety of manufacturing processes, they have many of the properties and adverse effects, including resistance to degradation, that other organochlorine compounds possess. The extent and hazards of human exposure to organochlorides are currently under study (38). These substances have spread to all parts of the earth, accumulate in fatty tissue, and tend to become more concentrated in animals higher in the food chain. Organochlorine compounds have been shown to interfere with reproduction and other body processes in fish, birds, and mammals, and many, including DDT, are suspected carcinogens (38,39). Because of their persistence and adverse effects, a number have been banned, except for use in public health emergencies. Other pesticides, including organophosphorus and carbamate compounds, have been developed to replace the organochlorides. Although many of these substances are more toxic than organochlorides, they break down much more rapidly, often by the time the food is harvested (6, pages 296–305).

A food labeled *organic* may not necessarily have been grown without the use of chemical fertilizers and pesticides.

FOCUS 9-3 NATURALLY OCCURRING FOOD TOXINS

As the use of natural foods has spread, many people have come to believe they are free of harmful substances. However, nature, as well as humans, adds toxic compounds to food. Here are a few examples.

FOOD	TOXIN	EFFECT
Peanuts, grains	Aflatoxin—produced by the fungus *Aspergillus flavus*	Cancer, liver damage
Clams, mussels, scallops, oysters	Toxin produced by a species of algae (the red tide) accumulates in the shellfish	Paralysis, sometimes death
Brassica genus (includes cabbage, turnips, mustard greens, rutabaga, radish, horseradish), soybeans, peanuts	A variety of substances called *goitrogens*	Interference with iodine utilization
Potato	Solanine—found in shoots and skin, especially if green patches are present	Impairment of nervous system and digestive tract disturbances
Almonds, lima beans, cassava, and seeds of apple, apricot, cherry, peach, pear, plum	Cyanide-containing compounds	Inhibits cellular respiration
Mushrooms—of the genera *Amanita* and *Gyromitra,* among others	A variety of toxins	Varies with species; often fatal
Spinach, beet greens, cocoa, rhubarb (especially leaves), chard	Oxalic acid	Acute poisoning leads to diarrhea, vomiting, abdominal pain, collapse, and sometimes convulsions or coma; oxalate also binds minerals, such as calcium, iron, and magnesium, retarding their absorption
Cheese	Tyramine	Elevation of blood pressure to crisis levels in people taking drugs called *monoamine oxidase inhibitors*

In many cases, such as in foods containing goitrogens, potatoes without sprouts or green patches, spinach, beet greens, cocoa, rhubarb stalks, and chard, the toxin is present at low enough levels and the food is not consumed in large enough quantities to cause problems. In other instances, the food can be prepared in a way that reduces or eliminates the toxin. For example, cassava is often grated, soaked, and allowed to ferment for several days to remove cyanide. The plant is then dried and pounded into a flour. At times, some foods must be avoided. Moldy peanuts and grains, shellfish exposed to the red tide, many species of mushrooms, bitter almonds, apricot and peach pits, and some strains of lima beans have produced adverse effects, including death.

The high crop yields obtained by modern monoculture agricultural systems, such as those found in the United States, would be impossible without the use of pesticides; even with their use, about one-third of all food crops is lost to insect pests, disease, and weeds each year (6, pages 296–305). To minimize the consumer's exposure to these compounds, the FDA has established tolerance levels for pesticides in food and continually monitors the food supply for their presence. In addition, traditional methods, such as companion planting (two or more mutually beneficial crop plants interplanted in the same field) and the use of predators can be employed to control pests. Other biological alternatives, such as insect hormones that interfere with their reproduction and parasites are being developed.

So there are no tangible benefits to be gained by eating organically grown foods; they are not nutritionally superior to commercially grown foods and the risk posed by the pesticides currently in use appears to be small. Moreover, the consumer may pay 30 to 100 percent more for organic foods than for commercially grown products. In addition, it is impossible to know whether foods labeled organic were actually grown without the use of chemical fertilizers and pesticides; the consumer must rely on the word and reputation of the grower.

ISSUE: DIET AND CANCER

"Perhaps more than any other common disease, cancer mystifies and frightens modern civilization. For unknown reasons, the nature of the DNA in a body cell changes so that the mechanisms that normally limit its growth and reproduction break down. The cell multiplies rapidly and, in many types of cancer, forms a firm mass called a *tumor.* (Not all tumors are cancerous, however. Some are *benign* and remain at the site in which they originated.) Cancerous, or malignant, tumors invade the surrounding tissues and also release cells that travel to other parts of the body, where they establish new tumors, called *metastases.* Other types of cancer, such as leukemia, do not involve tumor formation; the abnormal cells are released into the bloodstream. Unless treated (and often in spite of treatment), death occurs because the cancer cells disrupt tissue function or because they use up so much of the body's nutrient supply that normal cells starve to death."

Cancer is the second leading cause of death in the United States and was responsible for 387,000 fatalities in 1977 (40). Although its cause is unknown, many factors, including viruses, radiation, environmental chemicals, cigarette smoking, and diet, have been implicated as causative agents.

It has been estimated that up to 50 percent of all cancers in women and 30 percent of all cancers in men are associated in some way with diet (41). Ten to 15 percent of all cancers may be directly traced to carcinogenic chemicals in the diet, such as nitrates and nitrites, residues from food processing and preparation (including components of smoke), and a variety of other manufactured and naturally occurring compounds

(42,43). The remainder may be due to dietary substances that are converted into carcinogens or to nutrient deficiency or excess.

It is suspected that caloric intake is one of the most important dietary influences on the development of cancer (43,44). In animal experiments, chronic restriction of energy intake inhibits the formation of many types of tumors, and population studies in humans have shown an association between obesity and cancers of the small intestine, liver, genitourinary tract, uterus, gall bladder, and breast. Obesity is also associated with colon cancer, but only in men (44). A mechanism by which excess caloric intake might cause cancer is unknown but may involve alterations in hormonal levels in the body (44). In laboratory animals, a few types of cancer, such as liver cancer, are accelerated by caloric restriction (44).

High intakes of fat and protein have been associated with certain types of cancer, such as breast and colon cancer (41,43,44). Populations with high levels of fat in the diet generally have higher rates of these two types of cancer (Figures 9-5 and 9-6). Scientists hypothesize that fat may contribute to colon cancer by increasing production of bile acids, some of which may be converted into carcinogenic substances by bacteria in the large intestine (41,43). (The role of bile acids in fat digestion is described in Chapter 6.) The means by which excess fat might lead to breast cancer is unknown at this time, but it may involve hormonal imbalances in the body (41). Excess dietary protein also may contribute to colon cancer, possibly by increasing ammonia production by bacteria in the colon (45).

Vitamins and minerals have varying effects on the development of tumors. Vitamin A deficiency has been related to the development of some types of cancer in rats, and excess vitamin A intake has been shown

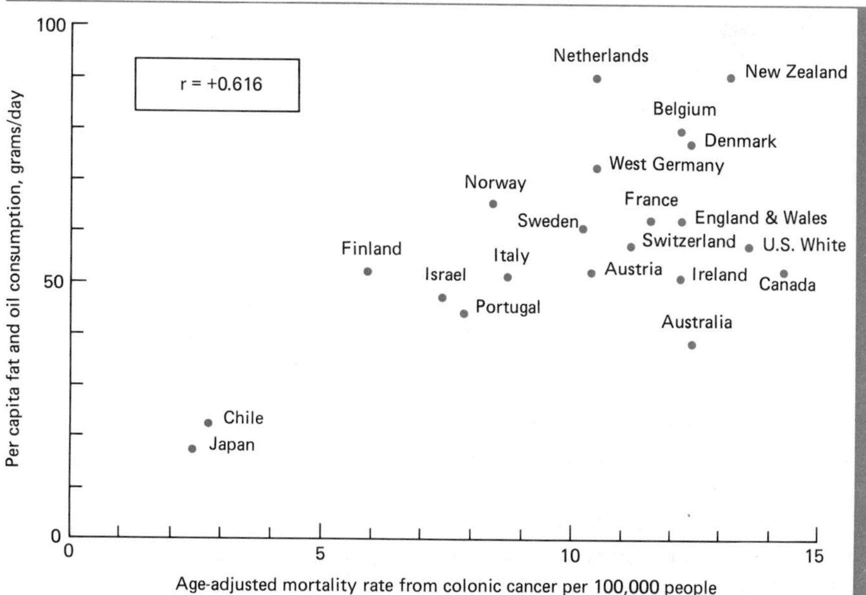

FIGURE 9-5
Fat Consumption and Colon Cancer. High fat intakes tend to be associated with higher rates of colon cancer. [*Source:* Wynder, E. L., "Epidemiology of Large Bowel Cancer", *Cancer Research* **35**:3388–3394 (1975). Used with permission.]

to depress growth of certain tumors. However, because of its toxicity, such large amounts of vitamin A are not recommended as a cancer treatment. Less toxic and more potent synthetic compounds related to vitamin A may prove to be more valuable in tumor therapy (44). Deficiencies of vitamin C, vitamin E, and most of the B vitamins have been shown to increase the susceptibility of experimental animals to certain types of tumors (43). The antioxidant properties of vitamin E neutralize peroxides that may cause cancer (43), and vitamin C prevents the formation of carcinogenic nitrosamines from nitrites in the diet (44). Although not all are nutrients, many minerals found in food affect cancer development (43,44). Deficiency of selenium and iodine and the presence of too much arsenic, beryllium, chromium, radium, lead, nickel, and cadmium may increase the incidence of various types of tumors.

In recent years, fiber has received a great deal of publicity for its possible role in preventing cancer of the large intestine (see Chapter 2). High fiber intakes increase fecal bulk, which may dilute carcinogens in the feces. The greater bulk also may increase movement of feces through the bowel, shortening their contact time with the wall of the colon. The binding of bile acids and changes in bacterial populations in the intestine also have been suggested as mechanisms by which fiber reduces the incidence of colon cancer (43,44).

Thus many relationships may exist between diet and the development of certain types of cancer. However, there is no conclusive evidence that altering the diet will reduce the incidence of cancer. The associations between caloric, fat, and protein intakes and the occurrence of certain

FIGURE 9-6 *Fat Consumption and Breast Cancer.* High fat intakes tend to be associated with higher rates of breast cancer. [*Source:* K. K. Carroll, "Experimental Evidence of Dietary Factors and Hormone Dependent Cancers." *Cancer Research* **35**:3374–3383 (1975). Used with permission.]

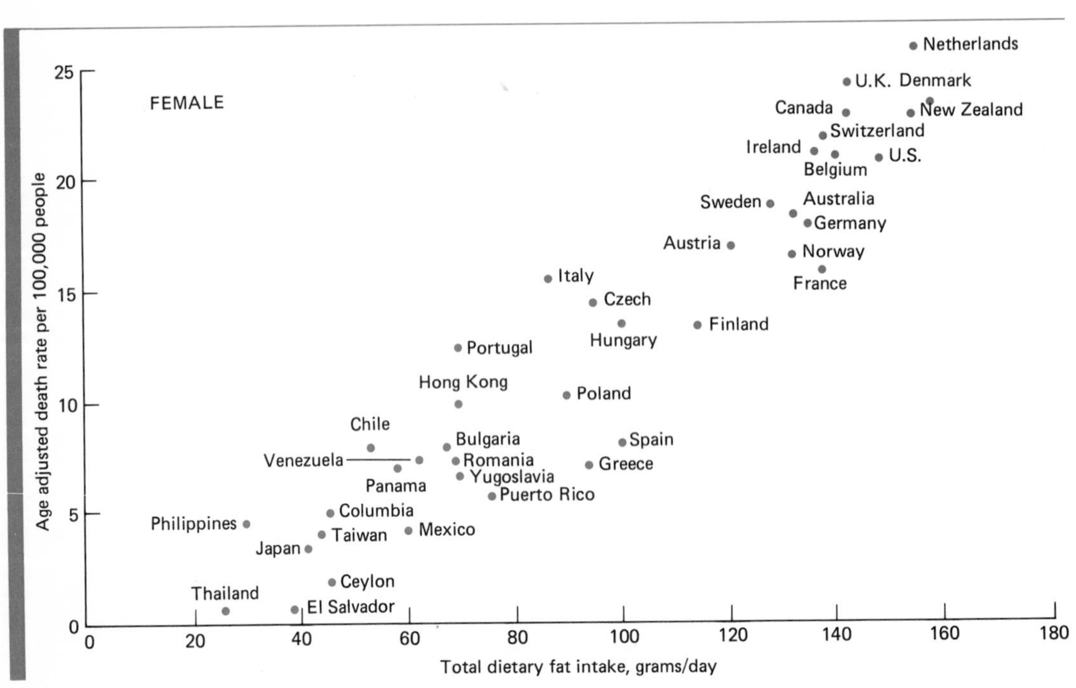

A well-balanced diet is probably the best nutritional defense against cancer.

cancers does not mean that the dietary factors cause the cancers, and there is little evidence that nutrient intakes much above or below the RDAs will protect against cancer. A well-balanced diet that meets all nutrient needs is probably the best nutritional defense against cancer.

Nutrition is also important in the treatment of cancer. Weight loss, severe wasting, and anemia frequently accompany the disease and generally result from impaired digestion and absorption, loss of appetite, increased basal metabolism, and host-tumor competition for nutrients, with the tumor winning over the host (46). Chemotherapy and radiation therapy also affect nutritional status because of their side effects, which often include nausea, vomiting, diarrhea, loss of appetite, and abnormalities in taste (47). When a nutritious diet cannot be consumed by mouth, nutrients must be administered intravenously to improve the person's nutritional status.

Study Guide

SUMMARY

1. The RDAs, the Basic Four Food Plan, and the U.S. Dietary Goals provide the foundation for a nutritious diet.
   a. The RDAs are levels of nutrient intake thought to be sufficient to meet the needs of practically all healthy people.
   b. The Four Food Group Plan shows how to choose a variety of foods to meet protein, vitamin, and mineral needs. Adults should obtain at least two servings from the milk group, two servings from the meat group, four servings from the vegetable-fruit group, and four servings from the bread-cereal group every day. At least one vegetable-fruit serving daily should come from a source rich in vitamin C, and one vegetable-fruit serving every other day should be a source rich in vitamin A. Selecting the higher-quality members of each group and not skimping on portion sizes will help ensure an adequate intake of all nutrients.
   c. The U.S. Dietary Goals and Dietary Guidelines recommend that Americans change the proportion of protein, fat, and carbohydrate, the type of fat, and the caloric, cholesterol, sugar, and salt contents of the diet in order to reduce the risk of heart disease, obesity, diabetes mellitus, high blood pressure, and certain types of cancer. Foods from the four food groups can be chosen to meet the U.S. Dietary Goals.
2. Although commercial and home processing has many benefits, including improving the safety and aesthetic qualities of the food, it can significantly reduce nutrient content. Prolonged storage of produce, canning, milling grains, and exposure to heat, light, oxygen, acid, alkali, and water can alter the nutritional quality of food. Enrichment and fortification improve the nutrient content of the diet, and proper preparation procedures will help minimize losses.
3. The use of chemical additives has become an important part of food manufacture. They help preserve the food, impart desired characteristics to it, and improve its appeal. However, many people believe the use of food additives is accompanied by the risk of cancer, birth defects, mutations, and other hazards. Although food additives must be tested for safety before they can be used in food processing, many problems, including the need to use unusually large doses in the tests, the inability to determine whether a threshold dose exists, and difficulty in applying animal data to humans, make it difficult to accurately assess the degree of risk. The Delaney clause prohibits the use of substances that cause cancer in any amount. In all other cases, the FDA uses a benefit-risk analysis and can set a tolerance level if one is needed. Most additives carry relatively little risk and need not be scrupulously avoided. Several additives, including monosodium glutamate (MSG), nitrites, saccharin, colors, and drugs used in animal feed, have generated a great deal of controversy.
4. As a result of their concerns about modern food-production methods, many people are turning to "organic" and "natural" foods. These foods are generally more expensive than their conventional counterparts, and there is no evidence that they are nutritionally superior. Although pesticides are highly toxic compounds, most of those currently in use degrade fairly quickly, and the FDA monitors the food supply for their presence. It is thought that they pose a minimal risk to humans.
5. Cancer is the second leading cause of death in the United States. Many factors, including viruses, radiation, environmental chemicals, and cigarette smoking,

have been implicated as causes. Diet also may play a role: high intakes of energy, protein, and fat are associated with a higher incidence of certain cancers, such as breast and colon cancer. Vitamin and mineral intakes have a varying effect on the development of tumors, and fiber intake may help prevent cancer of the colon. However, there is little evidence that nutrient intakes much above or below RDA levels will protect against cancer.

VOCABULARY

benefit-risk (cost-benefit) analysis
blanching
carcinogen
enrichment
exchange list
food additives
food composition table
fortification
generally recognized as safe (GRAS)
mutagen
Recommended Dietary Allowance (RDA)
teratogen
threshold dose

STUDY QUESTIONS

1. Examine each of the four food groups and make a list of foods from each group that would help meet the U.S. Dietary Goals and a list that would make it more difficult to meet the goals.
2. What are some precautions to keep in mind in order to make the most of the Basic Four Food Plan?
3. What are some advantages of commercial food processing? List several agents or processes that reduce the nutrient content of a food. What are some ways to minimize nutrient losses in the home?
4. List the benefits or functions of food additives in food processing. In your opinion, which are necessary for a safe and abundant food supply and which simply enhance the sensory characteristics of food? What are some potential hazards of food additives?
5. What are some problems encountered in evaluating the risks of food additives?
6. What is current FDA practice in regulating food additives shown to be carcinogenic in humans or animals? Why do some scientists object to this practice?
7. What is current FDA practice in regulating teratogenic, mutagenic, and other toxic food additives?
8. Is it worthwhile to purchase organic, or natural, foods? Give reasons for your answer.
9. Give some examples of toxic substances that occur naturally in food, and describe how each affects the body.

SELF-TEST

Multiple choice: Select the best answer.

1. The RDAs are useful in diet planning because
   a. They tell you your particular requirements for the nutrients
   b. By meeting the RDAs, you can be reasonably certain you have met your nutritional needs.
   c. They tell you the optimal proportion of protein, fat, and carbohydrate in the diet.
   d. None of the above
2. The recommended number of servings from the fats, sweets, and alcohol group is
   a. One per day
   b. Two per day
   c. Three per day
   d. They should be used in moderation after nutrient needs have been met from the other food groups.
3. To be sure to meet your body's needs for folacin, vitamin B_{12}, vitamin E, magnesium, zinc, and iodine:
   a. Take a vitamin and mineral supplement
   b. Choose organic and natural foods whenever possible
   c. Be careful to choose foods containing these nutrients from the four food groups
   d. Become a vegetarian
4. Which of the following groups of nutrients

are used to enrich grain products?
a. Thiamine, riboflavin, niacin, iron
b. Thiamine, vitamin C, niacin, calcium
c. Vitamin A, vitamin E, vitamin C, iron
d. Thiamine, riboflavin, vitamin B_{12}, calcium

5. According to the Delaney clause, the FDA must ban any food additive that causes
a. Birth defects
b. Mutations
c. Cancer
d. All of the above

6. When testing food additives for safety, very large doses are fed to animals
a. Because animals are more resistant to the additives than humans
b. To be sure the threshold dose is exceeded
c. Because smaller doses would require a huge number of test animals to show an adverse effect
d. All of the above

7. Pesticides currently in use appear to pose little risk to our food supply because
a. They break down rapidly to harmless levels by harvest time
b. They are not toxic to humans
c. They are not very widely used
d. All of the above

8. The best nutritional defense against cancer is probably a diet which
a. Is 5 to 10 times the RDA for each nutrient
b. Restricts caloric intake below expenditure
c. Drastically restricts fat intake
d. Is well-balanced and meets all nutritional needs.

True-False

F 1. John's diet provides 80 percent of the adult RDA for vitamin C, so it is highly likely he will develop scurvy.

T 2. Peanuts, soybeans, and lentils are members of the meat group.

F 3. Following the Basic Four Food Plan will automatically ensure an adequate intake of nutrients.

T 4. Fresh produce is not always nutritionally superior to frozen or canned produce.

F 5. The threshold doses for most food additives are known.

F 6. Organic and natural foods are nutritionally superior to those grown with commercial methods.

F 7. Natural foods do not contain harmful substances.

SUGGESTED ACTIVITIES

1. Using Agriculture Handbook No. 456, *Nutritive Value of American Foods in Common Units* (see Chapter 1), compare the nutrient contents of a variety of frozen foods with their canned counterparts.
2. What cooking methods have traditionally been used in your household? Which could be replaced by methods that would better preserve the vitamin content of foods?
3. Check the labels on foods you buy and make a list of the food additives they contain. Using Jacobsen's *Eater's Digest* (Further Reading 7), textbooks of food science or technology and biochemistry, and magazines or journals such as *FDA Consumer, Food Technology, Nutrition Reviews,* and others, determine the following:
   a. The function of the additive in the food.
   b. Whether or not the additive occurs naturally in any foods or in the body.
   c. What toxic effects may result from ingestion of the additive.
   d. Can the same food without the additive be purchased at the same price?
4. Visit a health food store, food cooperative, or the health food section of a grocery store and compare the prices of foods labeled *natural* or *organic* with the prices of the same foods grown by conventional means.

FURTHER READING

1. A description of the Recommended Dietary Allowances and how they are derived:

Food and Nutrition Board: *Recommended Dietary Allowances,* 9th ed., National Academy of Sciences, Washington, 1980.

2. An up-to-date description of the four food groups, complete with recipes, may be obtained from the Superintendent of Documents, U.S. Government Printing Office, Washington, D.C., 20402:

   Science and Education Administration: *Food: The Hassle-Free Guide to a Better Diet,* Home and Garden Bulletin No. 228, USDA, Washington, 1979.

3. A booklet for consumers based on the U.S. Dietary Goals also may be obtained from the Superintendent of Documents:

   Nutrition and Your Health—Dietary Guidelines for Americans, USDA, DHEW, Washington, 1980.

4. A series of articles discussing the U.S. Dietary Goals:

   American Dietetic Association Commentary: "Dietary Goals for the United States (Second Edition)," *J. Am. Diet. Assoc.* **74**:529–533, (1979).
   Hegsted, D. M.: "Food and Nutrition Policy: Probability and Practicality," *J. Am. Diet. Assoc.* **74**:534–538 (1979).
   Simopoulos, A. P.: "The Scientific Basis of the 'Goals': What Can Be Done Now?" *J. Am. Diet. Assoc.* **74**:539–542 (1979).
   Olson, R. E.: "Are Professionals Jumping the Gun in the Fight Against Chronic Diseases?" *J. Am. Diet. Assoc.* **74**:543–550 (1979).

5. A detailed and technical treatment of the effects of processing on the nutritional quality of food:

   Harris, R. S., and Karmas, E.: *Nutritional Value of Food Processing,* 2d ed. AVI Publishing, Westport, Conn. 1975.

6. Articles dealing with the benefit-risk evaluation of food additives:

   Oser, B. L., Chairman: "Overview—Benefit/Risk: Consideration of Direct Food Additives," *Food Tech.* **32**:54–69, (August 1978).
   Oser, B. L.: "Symposium—Risks Versus Benefits: The Future of Food Safety," *Nutr. Rev.* **38**:33–64 (1980).
   Institute of Food Technologists' Expert Panel on Food Safety and Nutrition: "The Risk/Benefit Concept as Applied to Food," *Food Tech.* **32**:51–56 (March 1978).
   Schmidt, A. M.: "The Benefit-Risk Equation," *FDA Consumer* **8**:27–31 (May 1974).

7. An overview of many of the food additives currently in use:

   Jacobson, M. F.: *Eater's Digest: The Consumer's Factbook of Food Additives,* Doubleday, Garden City, N.Y., 1972.

8. A look at many of the facets of food faddism:

   Special Supplement, "Nutrition Misinformation and Food Faddism," *Nutr. Rev.* **32** (July 1974).

9. Numerous articles in the magazine *FDA Consumer* give the FDA's position and other valuable information on topics such as labeling, food additives, and nutritional supplements.

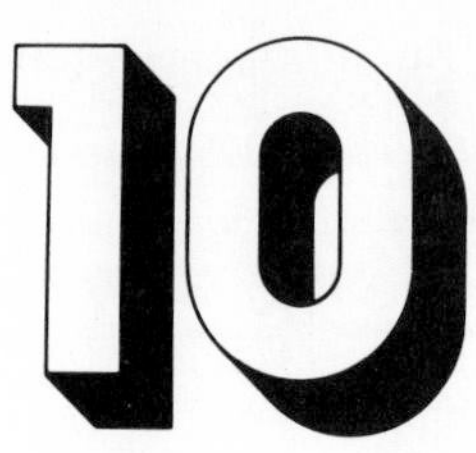

CHOOSING AN ADEQUATE ADULT DIET

So far in our study of nutrition we have looked at each of the nutrients, how our body uses them, our requirements for them, in what foods they occur, and the results of deficiency and excess. We have explored many controversial issues and disproved many myths about nutrition. We also have discussed the effects of commercial processing and home preparation on the safety and nutritional quality of food. But how can we make practical use of this information? Using Tom and Meg Gerard as examples, let us see how we can apply what we have learned to choose a safe, nutritious, and inexpensive diet for adults.

Adult Nutritional Needs

The RDAs for healthy, nonpregnant, nonlactating adults have been given throughout this book as each nutrient was described. They are summarized in Ready Reference 3. Because growth has ceased and the female body is not supporting the development or nurture of an infant, these RDAs, on a per kilogram of body weight basis, are lower than at any other stage of the life cycle except old age (1) (Figure 10-1). For example, during most of adulthood the body requires only enough energy to balance that expended by the basal metabolic rate, physical activity, and the specific dynamic action, so the allowance per kilogram of body weight is lower than during pregnancy, lactation, and the growing years. Furthermore, energy needs decline progressively throughout life because of a gradual reduction in the basal metabolic rate and physical activity (see Chapter 5). If this is not balanced by lowering the caloric intake, the individual gradually gains body fat. This probably accounts for the observation that the proportion of fat tissue in the body increases as people grow older (2). The adult allowances for protein, vitamins, and minerals also reflect the need for these nutrients to maintain the body rather than support growth or reproduction. All this does not mean that adults do not need to pay attention to what they eat: adequate nutrient intake is vital for maintaining good health. For example, progressive loss of bone mineral resulting from inadequate intake of calcium throughout adulthood may be one cause of osteoporosis later in life. Moreover, iron deficiency is prevalent among premenopausal adult women because of menstrual blood losses and depletion of iron reserves during pregnancy.

The Gerards, having recently completed a course in nutrition, want to begin using the Basic Four Food Plan, the Dietary Guidelines for Americans, and other facts they have learned in planning their diet. Let us see how they can apply all this information in a practical way.

PLANNING THE DIET

Although complete records of diet and energy expenditure are impractical to keep on a routine basis, the Gerards decided to do both for 3 days to

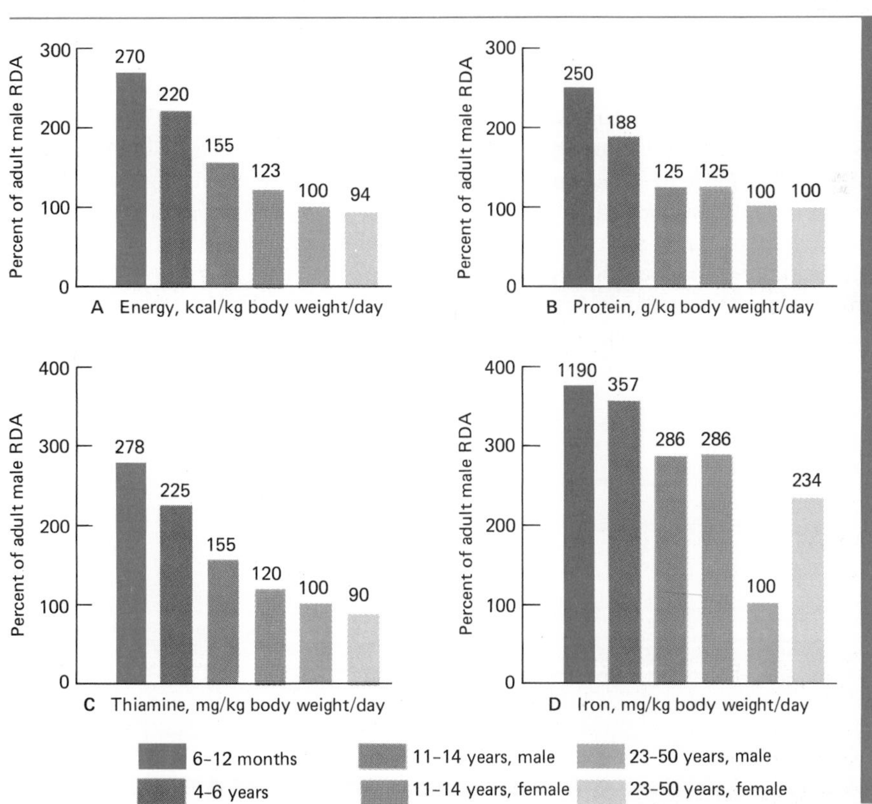

FIGURE 10-1
The Change of RDAs with Age. On a per kilogram of body weight basis, the RDAs generally decline with increasing age. [*Source:* Food and Nutrition Board, *Recommended Dietary Allowances,* 9th ed., Washington, DC, National Academy of Sciences (1980).]

determine what changes they would like to make in their diets. (See Exercise 10-1 for instructions on how to keep these records.) The results of their findings are summarized in Table 10-1.

As a first step, Tom and Meg must determine roughly how many kilocalories their diets should provide. Tom wishes to lose weight, and from his energy-expenditure calculations, he figures a caloric intake of 1500 kcal/day will meet his goal of losing about two lb/week. Since Meg's energy expenditure and intake are roughly equivalent and she has not gained any weight in recent years, she has decided to maintain a caloric intake of about 1800 kcal/day.

Next, Tom and Meg decide to change their diet to conform more closely to the Dietary Guidelines for Americans. They begin looking for ways to reduce their total fat, saturated fat, and cholesterol intakes and increase their consumption of complex carbohydrates and polyunsaturated fat. Their diet records show that they consume large amounts of whole-milk dairy products, beef, and eggs. They decide to replace some of these with skim milk, chicken, fish, and legume and whole-grain dishes. The Gerards also will begin looking for ways to use more polyunsaturated vegetable oil, such as soybean oil and corn oil, in cooking and baking.

Although it does not show on their diet records, both Tom and Meg have observed that they consume large amounts of sugar: they add more than a tablespoon to each cup of coffee, eat heavily sweetened baked goods, and when they consume fruit, it is usually canned varieties packed in heavy syrup. To reduce sugar intake, they will limit themselves to 1 tsp/cup of coffee and replace the baked goods with less sweetened varieties or with fresh fruit. They also have decided to consume fresh fruit or fruit canned in water instead of syrup.

Another change Tom and Meg want to make in their diet is to reduce salt intake. They decide to stop adding salt when preparing foods and instead salt it to taste at the table. They also plan to cut down on heavily salted snacks, such as pretzels, potato chips, and popcorn.

Outside of an occasional salad of iceberg lettuce, carrots, cucumber, and tomato, the Gerards find that their diet is virtually devoid of vegetables. They decide to eat salad nearly every day, and to put some spark

TABLE **10-1**

Results of a diet

	TOM	MEG
Energy expenditure, kcal/day	2500	1800
Energy intake, kcal/day	2800	1750
Kilocalories from protein, percent	20	18
Kilocalories from fat, percent	45	40
Kilocalories from carbohydrate, percent	35	42
Estimated cholesterol intake, mg/day	580	490
Estimated ratio of polyunsaturated to saturated fat (P:S ratio)	1:5	1:5

FOCUS 10-1 REDUCING THE HIGH COST OF EATING*

Like nearly everything else, the cost of food has risen greatly during the last decade. For some people this has meant only paying a higher price to continue eating what they have always eaten, but for increasing numbers of others, it has led to a change in diet as various foods have become too expensive. By shopping carefully, however, we can substantially reduce food costs and still choose a highly nutritious diet. Here are some useful tips.

1. Substitute low-cost foods for similar ones that cost more. For example, a 4-pound box of nonfat dry milk yields liquid skim milk at half the cost of fresh skim milk. Serving a pasta or legume dish is generally less expensive than serving meat.
2. Comparison shop. Store brands generally cost less than major name brands, and generic products (with no brand name) are usually the least expensive of all. In a Buffalo, New York supermarket, for instance, 2 pounds of a name brand white long-grain rice sold for 99 cents, whereas the store's own brand cost 89 cents and a generic label cost 73 cents.
3. Shop the specials. Read the food section of the newspaper to discover which foods are on sale and take advantage of coupons.
4. Join or start a food cooperative. In return for your work, discounts are offered on food. For example, members of a Buffalo cooperative paid 19 ¢/lb for apples, 95 cents for 5 pounds of whole-wheat flour, and $2.40 per pound for sharp cheddar cheese, while the local supermarket charged 33 ¢/lb, $1.39 for 5 pounds, and $2.79 per pound for the same items.
5. Buy in bulk. In many cities, some large food warehouses have "cash-and-carry" outlets from which large quantities of food can be purchased. Food also can be purchased in bulk directly from manufacturers. Often groups of neighbors form "food clubs" that buy the food and divide it among members.

* All prices are for February 1981 in Buffalo, New York.

into it, they include other greens, such as spinach, mustard greens, leaf and Romaine lettuce, cabbage, and watercress, as well as onions, mushrooms, raw broccoli, cauliflower, and bean sprouts. Tom and Meg also purchase a steam rack and a wok to experiment with steamed and stir-fried vegetables.

In changing their diet to conform to the Dietary Guidelines for Americans, the Gerards follow the Basic Four Food Plan pretty closely. The results of a typical day's diet are shown in Tables 10-2 and 10-3. Since Tom is trying to lose weight, fulfilling the requirements of the Basic Four Food Plan brings him almost to his desired caloric intake. The balance is provided by the foods listed at the bottom of the table. After he loses the weight he wants, he will need to add some more food to his diet to maintain a constant weight. By choosing nutritious foods, Tom can raise his intake of vitamins and minerals as well as kilocalories. Meg has fulfilled the requirements of the Basic Four Food Plan with the consumption of about 1054 kilocalories. To make up the rest of her caloric needs, she has chosen the foods listed in the bottom half of Table 10-2. Except for Meg's iron intake, both diets meet or exceed the Recommended Dietary Allowances for the eight key nutrients covered by the Basic Four Food Plan, and the Gerards can therefore be almost certain that their nutrient requirements have been met. Because Meg was found to be anemic after her second pregnancy, she has been taking an iron supplement prescribed by her physician. It is assumed that their wise choice of a variety of foods from each group has enabled the Gerards to meet their needs for other nutrients as well.

Like many people today, Tom and Meg have recognized the value of exercise in maintaining a desirable body weight and good general health. Running, swimming, bicycling, skating, and cross-country skiing are among the most beneficial because they raise the breathing and heart rates. For example 1/2 hour of these or similar activities three or four times per week will result in an adequate level of physical condition in most people. Meg runs about half to three-quarters of an hour four times weekly the year round, while Tom prefers to play a *hard* hour or two of racquetball or tennis several times a week.

TABLE **10-2**

A typical day's diet

	TOM (REDUCING DIET)	MEG (REGULAR DIET)
	Foods Fulfilling the Four Food Group Requirement	
Breakfast:	6 oz orange juice (1 1/2 VF) (frozen, reconstituted) 1 cup oatmeal (2 BC)	6 oz orange juice (1 1/2 VF) (frozen, reconstituted) 1 cup oatmeal (2 BC)
Lunch:	2 slices whole-wheat bread (2 BC) 3 oz turkey (1 Mt) 1 cup skim milk (vitamin A fortified) (1 Mi) 1 medium navel orange (1 VF)	2 slices whole-wheat bread (2 BC) 3 oz tuna fish (packed in water) (1 Mt) 1 cup skim milk (vitamin A fortified) (1 Mi) 1 medium navel orange (1 VF)
Dinner:	1 medium baked potato (1 VF) 3 oz roast beef (1 Mt) 1/2 cup chopped broccoli (1 VF) (frozen, cooked) 1 cup skim milk (vitamin A fortified) (1 Mi)	1 medium baked potato (1 VF) 3 oz roast beef (1 Mt) 1/2 cup chopped broccoli (1 VF) (frozen, cooked) 1 cup skim milk (vitamin A fortified) (1 Mi)
	Extra Foods to Make Up Balance of Caloric Needs	
Breakfast:	1/2 cup skim milk (vitamin A fortified) (1/2 Mi) 1/4 cup raw blueberries (1/2 VF)	1/2 cup skim milk (vitamin A fortified) (1/2 Mi) 1/4 cup raw blueberries (1/2 VF) 1 slice whole-wheat toast (1 BC) 1 tablespoon soft margarine (vitamin A fortified)
Lunch:	1/2 cup iceberg lettuce (1 VF) 1 tablespoon low-calorie mayo-type dressing	1 tablespoon mayonnaise
Dinner:	2 tablespoon soft margarine (vitamin A fortified) 1/2 cup lettuce (1 VF) 1/2 cup chopped spinach (1 VF) 1/4 cup mushrooms (1/2 VF) 2 tablespoons low-calorie Italian dressing 1 slice whole-wheat bread (1 BC)	2 tablespoons soft margarine (vitamin A fortified) 1/2 cup lettuce (1 VF) 1/2 cup chopped spinach (1 VF) 1/4 cup mushrooms (1/2 VF) 2 tablespoons French dressing (regular) 1 cup yogurt, plain (part skim milk) (1 Mi) 1 slice whole-wheat bread (1 BC)

Key: Mi = milk group; Mt = meat group; VF = vegetable-fruit group; BC = bread-cereal group.

TABLE **10-3**

Nutrient content of the typical diets

	TOM	MEG
Kilocalories	1432	1739
Protein, % kcal	29	25
Fat, % kcal	14	21
Carbohydrate, % kcal	57	53
Protein, g	105	113
P:S ratio	1.2:1	1.4:1
Vitamins and minerals, percent of 1980 RDAs		
Vitamin A	151	198
Vitamin C	487	487
Thiamine	94	142
Riboflavin	128	207
Niacin	113	197
Calcium	134	172
Iron	140	82

Sources: FNB, *Recommended Dietary Allowances* 9th ed., National Academy of Sciences, Washington, 1980.

C. F. Adams, and M. Richardson, *Nutritive Value of Foods, Home and Garden Bulletin No. 72,* USDA, Washington, 1977.

USING FOOD LABELS

As a general rule, selecting a wide variety of foods from each of the four food groups and preparing them properly will help ensure an adequate intake of all the nutrients; what is lacking in one food will be provided elsewhere in the diet. However, to obtain maximum benefit from the Basic Four Food Plan, Tom and Meg should make their choices from among the better-quality foods within each group. How can they identify these foods? Food-composition tables give the nutrient content of a large number of foods, but carrying one of these to the store would be inconvenient. An easier way is to study package labels. The labeling on a package is a useful means for determining the nutritional quality of many foods. Nutrition information is required on the label only if a nutrient is added to a food or if a claim that relates to nutrition is made on the label or in advertising. However, many manufacturers voluntarily include this information on their labels. In either case, the label must comply with regulations established by the Food and Drug Administration (FDA) (3,4). Focus 10-2 describes how to read a food label.

FOCUS 10-2 HOW TO READ A FOOD LABEL

The label on a food container provides a great deal of useful information (Figure 10-2). It must identify the food by a commonly used name; if the food is an imitation product, this must be stated. In addition, the net contents of the container, the name and address of the manufacturer, distributor, or repacker, and, unless covered by a standard of identity, a list of ingredients also must appear on the label. Ingredients are listed in descending order of prominence by weight. Thus if

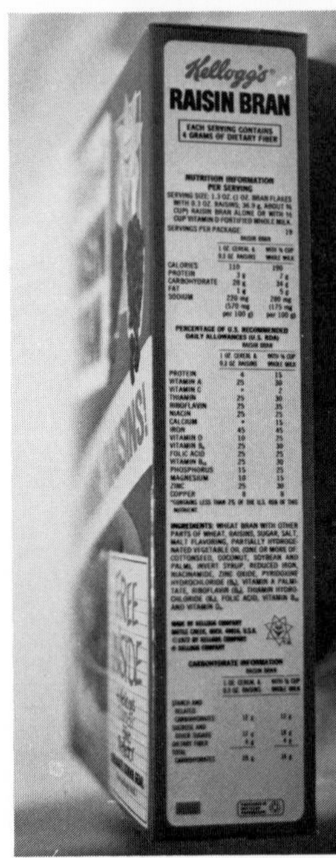

FIGURE 10-2
A Typical Food Label Showing the Principal Display Panel and Nutrition Information. (Photograph © 1981 by Martha N. Solonche. Used by permission of Kellogg Company; © 1972 Kellogg Company.)

water is the most abundant ingredient, it is listed first, followed by whatever ingredient is present in the next greatest amount. In this way, the presence of sugar, salt, hydrogenated fat, and most food additives can be determined. However, flavors, colors, chemical preservatives, and most spices need only be identified by a collective or generic term (flavor, color, etc.); the specific ingredients need not be given.

Manufacturers are not required to list the ingredients for such foods as macaroni and ice cream, for which a **standard of identity** has been established. The standards are published in the Code of Federal Regulations and specify the ingredients that must be used in the manufacture of the food. Required ingredients need not be listed, but some ingredients, those specified as "optional" in the standard of identity, must be listed if they are included in the food.

Many foods carry a grade, such as "U.S. Grade A." These usually refer to aesthetic qualities of the products and do not reflect nutritional content. For example, vegetables may be graded on the basis of size, color, and presence of defects, while meat is evaluated on the basis of the fat marbling it contains, its texture, and its color. Milk products are graded according to the sanitary standards under which they are produced.

Another important item on a label is open dating. Some foods, such as canned goods, may carry a **pack date**, which reveals the day the food was manufactured or packaged. Others provide a **pull or sell date**, after which the food should no longer be sold. Cold cuts, milk, ice cream, and many baked goods have pull dates on their labels. The pull date generally allows some time for storage in the home refrigerator after the date has passed. **Expiration dates** indicate when the food should no longer be eaten. Baby formulas and yeast often carry expiration dates (5,6).

If nutrition information is included on the label, certain information must always appear: serving size, number of servings per container, caloric content per serving, protein, carbohydrate, and fat content per serving, and the amount of vitamin A, vitamin C, thiamine, riboflavin, niacin, calcium, and iron per serving. Certain other vitamins and minerals (vitamin D, vitamin E, vitamin B_6, folacin, vitamin B_{12}, biotin, pantothenic acid, phosphorus, iodine, magnesium, zinc, and copper) may be included on the label if they occur naturally in the food and must be listed if they are added by the manufacturer. The content of protein and each of the vitamins and minerals is expressed as a percentage of its **U.S. Recommended Daily Allowance (U.S.RDA)**, which in most cases is the highest recommended level of intake for any age group (excluding pregnant and lactating women) proposed in the 1968 Recommended Dietary Allowances (see Table 10-4). For example, the U.S.RDA for iron is 18 mg/day, so a food containing 3 mg/serving provides 16 percent of the U.S.RDA. Nutrients present in amounts less than 2 percent of the U.S.RDA may be indicated by a zero or an asterisk, which directs the consumer to a statement at the bottom of the table: "Contains less

TABLE **10-4**

The U.S. RDAs

NUTRIENT	U.S. RDA
Protein	65 g
Vitamin A	5000 IU
Vitamin D	400 IU
Vitamin E	30 IU
Vitamin C	60 mg
Thiamin	1.5 mg
Riboflavin	1.7 mg
Niacin	20.0 mg
Folacin	0.4 mg
Vitamin B_6	2.0 mg
Biotin	0.3 mg
Pantothenic Acid	10.0 mg
Vitamin B_{12}	6.0 μg
Calcium	1.0 g
Iron	18.0 mg
Phosphorus	1.0 g
Magnesium	400 mg
Iodine	150 μg
Zinc	15 mg
Copper	2.0 mg

Source: Code of Federal Regulations, Title 21, Section 101.9 (1981).

than 2 percent of the U.S.RDA for these nutrients."

Because of the widespread concern that diet may contribute to the development of heart disease, optional information about fat, cholesterol, and sodium content may be placed on the labels of foods that can be included in a fat-modified diet recommended by a physician. If this information is given, it must be followed by this statement:

> Information on fat and cholesterol content is provided for individuals who, on the advice of a physician, are modifying their dietary intake of fat and cholesterol.

ISSUE: FAST FOODS

As a result of the rapid pace of modern life, many people find it inconvenient to prepare their own food for every meal. Increasing numbers of people are eating many of their meals at restaurants, and a significant share of them are attracted by fast food establishments. In 1978, fast food sales were expected to total over $18.5 billion, over 34 percent of the restaurant market (5). Fast food chains offer several advantages (6). The food is relatively inexpensive and readily satisfies the appetite. Although it is served quickly, it is generally prepared fresh. Buying and preparation standards are tightly controlled, and the consumer can be sure of uniform quality from one store in a chain to

FIGURE 10-3
Fast food meals are convenient, but most are not nutritionally balanced. Sufficient dairy products, fruits, and vegetables must be obtained elsewhere in the diet. (Photograph by Ed Lettau, Rapho/Photo Researchers, Inc.)

the next. However, the nutritional quality of fast foods has been questioned, and the nutrient content of some representative manufacturers is shown in Ready Reference 4. In general, fast food meals tend to be high in kilocalories, fat, carbohydrate, and salt, but they do provide some protein. If they contain dairy products, such as milk, milkshakes, or cheese on the hamburgers or pizza, they provide calcium. Iron is generally lacking except in hamburgers. Fast foods generally supply enough thiamine, riboflavin, and niacin, but are low in vitamin A, vitamin C, and the other B vitamins (5,6).

Fast foods can be part of a nutritionally sound diet if they are used in moderation and sufficient dairy products, fruits, and vegetables are obtained elsewhere in the diet (6). The consumer also must be wary of the caloric content of the meals. Fast foods should not become a staple in the diet for children; by restricting the choice of foods, they can have adverse effects on the child's developing food preferences. ”

Fast foods can be part of a sound diet if used in moderation.

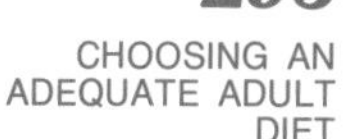

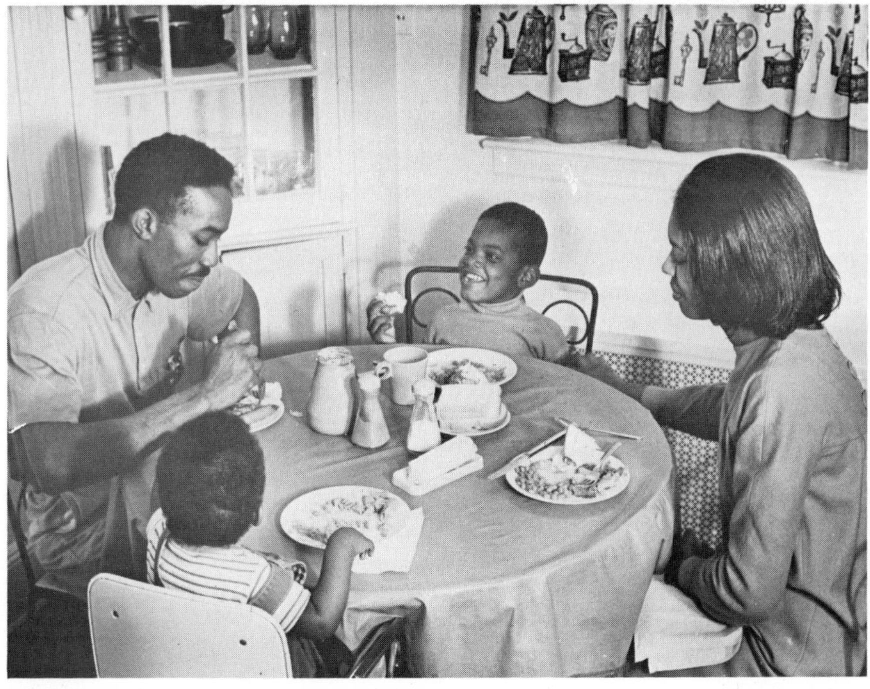

FIGURE 10-4
Meals are times to relax and enjoy food and the company of family and friends. (Photograph by Hanna W. Schreiber, Rapho/Photo Researchers, Inc.)

ISSUE: VEGETARIAN DIETS

When Tom and Meg took their nutrition course, they met many vegetarians. Some turned to vegetarianism for health reasons; they wished to avoid potentially hazardous chemicals present in meat, including saturated fat, cholesterol, uric acid and other metabolic waste products, antibiotics, and hormones. A belief in nonviolence to animals, the desire to achieve spiritual or internal balance, and religious beliefs have led others to eliminate some or all animal products from their diets. Many people feel that meat production is an inefficient use of the world's agricultural resources, and following a vegetarian diet will allow grain normally fed to animals to be eaten directly by humans (7).

There are several types of vegetarian diets (8). A **pure vegetarian**, or **vegan**, consumes only food from plant sources. **Lacto-vegetarians** include dairy products in their diets, while **lacto-ovo-vegetarians** eat eggs and dairy products as well as food from plant sources. A more extreme form of vegetarianism is the **Zen macrobiotic diet**, in which the individual passes through 10 stages, each marked by progressively more restrictive diets. At the highest level, the diet permits only cereal grains.

In light of the controversy surrounding the U.S. Dietary Goals, it is interesting that the vegan and lacto-ovo-vegetarian diets, which conform closely to the goals, provide several health benefits. Serum cholesterol and triglyceride concentrations tend to be lower in vegetarians than in nonvegetarians, with vegans having the lowest cholesterol levels of all (9,10). This may help account for the observation that the mortality rate from heart disease among vegetarian Seventh Day Adventists is about one-third that of Seventh Day Adventists who are not vegetarians (11). Other studies have found that pure vegetarians, or vegans, tend to weigh less and have smaller skinfold measurements than nonvegetarians or lacto-ovo-vegetarians (10,12). Vegetarian diets also provide more fiber than conventional diets, which may have many health benefits (13) (see Chapter 2).

Although vegetarian diets offer certain advantages, nutritional adequacy can be a problem. In general, the more restricted the diet, the more difficult it is to obtain sufficient quantities of all nutrients from it. Except for its iron content, a lacto-ovo-vegetarian diet tends to be nutritionally similar to diets containing meat (8,14). Since liver and muscle meats are omitted, alternative sources of iron, such as legumes (especially soybeans), whole grains, nuts, and dried fruits must be included.

1. The U.S. food supply is so refined and overprocessed that it is difficult to choose an adequate diet from foods available in the supermarket.

2. Meat is necessary to maintain good health.

FACT OR FANTASY

Pure vegetarian diets may be lacking in calcium, riboflavin, iron, zinc, vitamin B_{12}, and, if exposure to the sun is insufficient, vitamin D (14–16). They also can be so high in bulk that they do not meet caloric needs (8,16). Care must be taken to combine plant proteins properly so that all the essential amino acids will be provided. In a pure vegetarian diet, iron can be provided by the same sources as for a lacto-ovo-vegetarian regimen. Green leafy vegetables, such as collards, kale, turnip, and mustard greens, will supply calcium and riboflavin, while additional calcium can be obtained from cabbage, broccoli, cauliflower, legumes (especially soybeans), certain nuts, and dried fruits. Zinc is supplied by legumes, wheat germ, and whole grains, especially whole-grain yeast breads. Since no vitamin B_{12} is found in plant foods, it must be included as a supplement. Failing to do this has resulted in a type of anemia in some cases (17). Vitamin D can be provided by a supplement or by increasing exposure to sunlight.

Because they are so restricted, the higher levels of the Zen macrobiotic diet are nutritionally the most inadequate of the vegetarian regimens. Following them has led to scurvy, anemia, low blood protein and calcium levels, emaciation, and even death (18). In addition, the regimen discourages medical consultation when its adherents are ill; each individual is urged to be his or her own doctor. Because of the hazards involved, this diet is not recommended.

ISSUE: ALCOHOL AND CAFFEINE

Alcohol and caffeine are the two drugs most widely consumed in the diet. Both have a variety of effects on metabolism, and alcohol also may influence nutrition in heavy users. Alcohol is rapidly absorbed into the blood from the stomach and small intestine, although the presence of food in the stomach slows its absorption (20). About 10 percent of the alcohol is lost via the urine, sweat, and lungs; the remainder is broken down by the liver at a rate of about 10 ml/h. Thus it takes about 5 to 6 hours to metabolize the alcohol in 4 ounces of whiskey or in 2½ pints of beer (19). Although physical exercise, vitamin supplements, and caffeine have no effect on the rate of alcohol breakdown, fructose increases its rate of metabolism by 15 to 30 percent (20).

In addition to intoxication, alcohol leads to many nutrition-related problems in chronic alcoholics. For example, chronic alcoholics tend to high blood triglyceride levels and may become severely hypoglycemic after drinking, particularly on an empty stomach (21). Many alcoholics experience multiple nutritional deficiencies. This may arise in part from poor dietary intake; alcoholics sometimes consume as much as one-half their caloric intake as alcohol (23). However, chronic ingestion of alcohol also inhibits the absorption of thiamine, folacin, vitamin B_{12}, and vitamin A; interferes with the metabolism of vitamin B_6, vitamin A, and vitamin D; and leads to reduced blood levels of calcium, magnesium, and zinc (21,23). On the other hand, alcohol enhances iron absorption (21). At one time it was thought that the malnutrition that accompanies alcoholism is responsible for deterioration and cirrhosis of the liver, but alcohol has been found to be toxic to the liver in its own right (24). It also causes birth defects (see Chapter 11) and has been linked to cancer of the mouth and throat.

TABLE **10-5**

Caffeine content of some foods

FOOD	AVERAGE CAFFEINE CONTENT
Cola beverages, mg/12-oz can	
Coca Cola	65
Dr. Pepper	61
Mountain Dew	55
Diet Dr. Pepper	54
TAB	49
Pepsi-Cola	43
RC Cola	34
Diet RC	33
Diet Rite	32
Coffee, mg/cup	
Instant	66
Percolated	110
Dripolated	146
Bagged tea, mg/cup	
Black (5-min brew)	46
Black (1-min brew)	28
Loose tea, mg/cup	
Black (5-min brew)	40
Green (5-min brew)	35
Green (Japan, 5-min brew)	20
Cocoa	13

Source: M. L. Bunker, and M. McWilliams, "Caffeine Content of Common Beverages," *J. Am. Diet. Assoc.* **74**:28–32, 1979. (Copyright © American Dietetic Association, Reprinted with permission.)

In spite of the adverse effects of excessive consumption, small to moderate amounts of alcohol may provide several benefits. Moderate alcohol intake before a meal stimulates appetite and accelerates the digestion of food. Several studies also have found that the incidence of heart disease is lower among men who consume moderate amounts of alcohol than among those who have greater or smaller intakes (25).

The intake of caffeine is prevalent in the United States; the drug is found in coffee and tea, as well as in cola drinks and in chocolate, both of which are heavily consumed by children, and in a variety of over-the-counter drugs (Table 10-5). About 15 percent of a given dose is metabolized per hour (26). One of the most widely recognized properties of caffeine is its stimulation of the nervous system. A dose of 50 to 200 milligrams increases alertness and reduces fatigue, but amounts between 200 and 500 milligrams produce headaches, tremors, insomnia, irritability, and poor motor performance (26). Chronic ingestion of large doses produces symptoms indistinguishable from anxiety neurosis, and for heavy users, sudden withdrawal can produce severe headaches (25). Other effects of caffeine include stimulation of urination, increased heart rate and output, an increase in blood glucose and free fatty acid levels, and an increase in stomach acid secretion (27). Caffeine also has been found to cause birth defects in laboratory animals (28), and pregnant women are advised to reduce their intake. ”

Study Guide

SUMMARY

1. The nutrient requirements of adulthood are based on a need to maintain body tissues. Energy needs decline because of a lower basal metabolic rate and reduced physical activity, while proteins, vitamins, and minerals are needed to replace those broken down and excreted from the body. On a per unit of body weight basis, the RDAs for adults are generally lower than for any other stage of the life cycle.
2. Keeping a record of current food habits provides a basis from which dietary changes can be made. The Basic Four Food Plan and the U.S. Dietary Goals can be used as guidelines for choosing specific foods.
3. Nutritional labeling can help make the best use of the Basic Four Food Plan and the U.S. Dietary Goals in dietary planning. The caloric, protein, carbohydrate, fat, and, in some cases, cholesterol, saturated and polyunsaturated fat, and salt contents of the food are given. Those foods which are good sources of particular vitamins and minerals also can be identified. Other useful information, such as the net contents, name and address of the manufacturer, distributor, or repacker, list of ingredients, food grades, and open dating, are found on the labels.
4. Americans are eating an increasing number of their meals at fast food establishments. These foods tend to be high in kilocalories, fat, and carbohydrate, but provide enough thiamine, riboflavin, and niacin, as well as some protein. They generally lack vitamin A, vitamin C, other B vitamins, and often iron and calcium. Fast foods can be part of a nutritionally sound diet if they are used in moderation and the missing nutrients are provided elsewhere in the diet.
5. For many people, vegetarianism provides a satisfying alternative to the conventional American diet. Vegetarian diets tend to contain less cholesterol and saturated fat and more polyunsaturated fat and fiber than diets containing meat. Strict vegetarian diets also tend to have lower caloric contents. Lacto-ovo-vegetarian diets may lack iron, and strict vegetarian diets may be deficient in calcium, riboflavin, iron, vitamin B_{12}, and vitamin D. Plant proteins also must be appropriately combined to obtain all the essential amino acids. Because they are so restricted, the higher levels of the Zen macrobiotic diet are not recommended.
6. Alcohol and caffeine are the two drugs most widely consumed in the diet. Both have a variety of effects on body metabolism, and overuse can be hazardous.

VOCABULARY

expiration date	standard of identity
lacto-ovo-vegetarian	U.S.RDA
lacto-vegetarian	vegan (strict vegetarian)
pack date	Zen macrobiotic diet
pull date	

STUDY QUESTIONS

1. Why do the RDAs for adulthood tend to be lower than for other stages of the life cycle?
2. What part can fast foods play in a nutritious diet?
3. Under what circumstances must nutrition information be included on a food label? If a manufacturer uses nutrition labeling, what information must appear on the label? What additional information can be listed if so desired?
4. How are the food's ingredients listed on the label? Under what circumstance do the ingredients need not be listed?
5. Describe ways a lacto-ovo-vegetarian diet and a strict vegetarian (vegan) diet conform more closely to the U.S. Dietary Goals than do conventional American diets.

6. What are the precautions which must be taken when using a lacto-ovo-vegetarian diet? A strict vegetarian diet? Why is the Zen macrobiotic diet not recommended?
7. Describe the adverse effects of alcohol and caffeine.

SELF-TEST

Multiple choice: Select the best answer.

1. Food grades, such as U.S. Grade A, are based on the foods
   a. Aesthetic or sanitary qualities
   b. Nutrient content
   c. Freshness
   d. Degree of processing
2. In nutritional labeling, the vitamin and mineral content of a food is expressed
   a. As a percent of the RDAs
   b. By weight
   c. As a percent of the U.S. RDAs
   d. In terms of international units
3. Fast foods
   a. Provide all necessary nutrients
   b. Should be avoided altogether
   c. Can be combined with other foods as part of an adequate diet
   d. Should be included regularly in a child's diet
4. Both lacto-ovo-vegetarians and strict vegetarians (vegans) should be careful to obtain which of the following?
   a. Iron — c. Calcium
   b. Vitamin B_{12} — d. Riboflavin
5. Which of the following may accelerate the breakdown of alcohol?
   a. Fructose — c. Vitamins
   b. Caffeine — d. Strenuous exercise
6. Alcohol may lead to malnutrition by
   a. Displacing nutritious foods
   b. Interfering with nutrient absorption from the intestine
   c. Interfering with utilization of nutrients within the body
   d. All of the above

True-False

1. On a pound of body weight basis, nutrient requirements are lower during adulthood than during any other stage of the life cycle except in the elderly.
2. Nutrient content of a food must be included on all food labels.
3. A list of ingredients must always be included on food labels.
4. The higher levels of a Zen macrobiotic diet can lead to severe nutritional deficiency.

SUGGESTED ACTIVITIES

1. Estimate your intake of kilocalories, protein, carbohydrate, fat, and cholesterol.
   a. Make a form such as the one shown in Ready Reference 14. List every food you consume in 1 day and estimate the serving sizes as closely as possible.
   b. Using Ready Reference 1, determine the caloric, protein, carbohydrate, fat, saturated fat, and linoleic acid contents of each food. Cholesterol content may be found in Table 3-3 (remember, only animal products contain cholesterol). For mixtures of foods, such as salads and casseroles, break food down into its ingredients. For foods not found in the table, use the values for a similar food found in the table or consult a more extensive food-composition table.
   c. For each dietary component, add together the values to obtain the total day's intake.
   d. Determine the percent of your caloric intake derived from protein, carbohydrate, and fat:
      (1) Multiply your protein, carbohydrate, and fat intakes by 4, 4, and 9 kcal/g, respectively.
      (2) Add the kilocalories obtained from protein, carbohydrate, and fat to obtain your total caloric intake.
      (3) Divide the kilocalories obtained from protein, carbohydrate, and fat by the total caloric intake and multiply each result by 100. This yields the percent of your caloric intake derived from each component.

e. Determine the ratio of polyunsaturated to saturated fat (P:S ratio) by dividing the linoleic acid by saturated fat intake.
f. Using Ready Reference 12 and food labels, determine which foods you eat contain significant amounts of sugar.
g. Using Table 8-2 and food labels, determine which foods you eat contain significant amounts of salt.

2. Improving your diet:
   a. What substitutions or eliminations can you make in your diet to bring it more into conformance with the Dietary Guidelines for Americans and the U.S. Dietary Goals?
   b. Are there better choices you could make from any of the four food groups that would improve the nutritional quality of your diet?
3. Do you eat at any of the fast food chains listed in Ready Reference 4? Make a list of a meal you would eat at one of the restaurants. Determine its caloric content; the percentage of kilocalories from carbohydrate, fat, and protein (see Activity 10-1d); and its content of vitamin A, vitamin C, thiamine, riboflavin, niacin, calcium, and iron.
   a. Compare the caloric value of the meal with the total caloric intake determined in your diet record in Activity 10-1. Does the fast food meal contain more than one-third of the caloric intake of a typical day?
   b. How does the percent of caloric intake from carbohydrate, fat, and protein compare with these recommendations:

Carbohydrate:	At least 50 percent
Fat:	Less than 30 percent
Protein:	10 to 15 percent

   c. Does the meal provide less than one-third of your RDA for any nutrient? What are some other sources in your diet that could provide these deficient nutrients?
4. Plan a vegetarian diet for yourself. What substitutions could you make in your diet record (Activity 10-1) that would convert it to a lacto-ovo-vegetarian diet? To a strict vegetarian (vegan) diet?
5. Visit your supermarket and compare the prices on name brands, store brands, and generically labeled foods.
6. Visit a food cooperative and compare its prices with those of your favorite supermarket.

FURTHER READING

1. An easy-to-read and attractively illustrated guide to using the four food groups, including recipes:

   Davis, C. A., Fulton, L. H., Light, L., Oldland, D. D., Page, L., Raper, N. R., and Vettel, R. S.: *Food—The Hassle-Free Guide to a Better Diet,* Home and Garden Bulletin No. 228, USDA, Washington, 1979.

2. Some guides to good vegetarian eating:

   Lappe, F. M.: *Diet for a Small Planet,* revised Edition, Ballantine, New York, 1975.
   Robertson, L., Flinders, C., and Godfrey, B.: *Laurel's Kitchen: A Handbook for Vegetarian Cookery and Nutrition,* Nilgiri, Berkeley, Calif., 1976.

3. These articles discuss alcohol metabolism in the body:

   Iber, F.: "In Alcoholism, the Liver Sets the Pace," *Nutrition Today* **6:**2–9 (January/February 1971).
   Lieber, C. S.: "The Metabolism of Alcohol," *Sci. Am.* **234:**25–33 (1976).

4. Two indepth looks at caffeine:

   Graham, D. M.: "Caffeine—Its Identity, Dietary Sources, Intake and Biological Effects," *Nutr. Rev.* **36:**97–102 (1978).
   Stephenson, P. E.: "Physiologic and Psychotropic Effects of Caffeine on Man," *J. Am. Diet. Assoc.* **71:**240–247 (1977).

PREGNANCY AND LACTATION

Pregnancy and lactation alter a woman's nutritional needs. Not only are the nutrition requirements of the infant her responsibility, but her own body undergoes changes that affect the kind of diet she needs as well. So when Tom and Meg Gerard learned that Meg was pregnant with their third child, they, like most other nutrition-conscious people, became concerned about the type of diet a woman should consume during this critical period. They have asked their obstetrician many questions about what Meg should eat and what, if any, supplements she should take. In addition, they have discussed the pros and cons of breast-feeding, and Meg has decided she will nurse the infant. However, the Gerards are aware that lactation will place an additional nutritional burden on Meg that must be balanced by changes in her diet.

What changes occur in a woman's body during pregnancy and lactation that influence nutrition requirements? To what extent do requirements increase as a result? How must diet be altered to meet these increased needs? Let us take a closer look.

Pregnancy

The Gerard's concern with nutrition during pregnancy is certainly warranted; many studies show that malnutrition impairs fetal growth. At the present time, birth weight is considered to be one of the most important predictors of infant health and future physical and mental development, and researchers have found that nutrition has a major influence on birth weight (1, page 4; 6, pages 76–93). For example, many studies show that an infant's birth weight is directly correlated to its mother's prepregnancy body weight and her weight gain during pregnancy (5, pages 24–27; 7, page 26). Inadequate caloric intake increases the risk of producing a low-birth-weight baby (less than 2.5 kilograms) (8,9), and Burke has observed that the mother's protein intake influences birth weight, length at birth, and the infant's health and well-being (2). In addition, iron and possibly folacin status affect the outcome of pregnancy, because researchers have found a higher rate of low birth weights, birth defects, and infant death among babies born to anemic women than among those born to normal mothers (3). Maternal iodine deficiency leads to mental and physical retardation in offspring, which is a disorder called *cretinism* (see Chapter 8).

The susceptibility of the fetus to malnutrition results from the nature of the physiological processes that occur during pregnancy; taking a closer look at these processes will help us understand why nutrient requirements increase during this period and why it is so important that these needs be met.

PHYSIOLOGICAL CHANGES DURING PREGNANCY

Stages of Fetal Development One of the most miraculous of life's processes begins with the uniting of sperm and ovum. The fertilized egg, or **zygote**, begins to divide, first into two cells, then four, and subsequently into a hollow ball of cells called the **blastocyst**, from which the fetus and its supporting structures will develop (Figure 11-1). During this period,

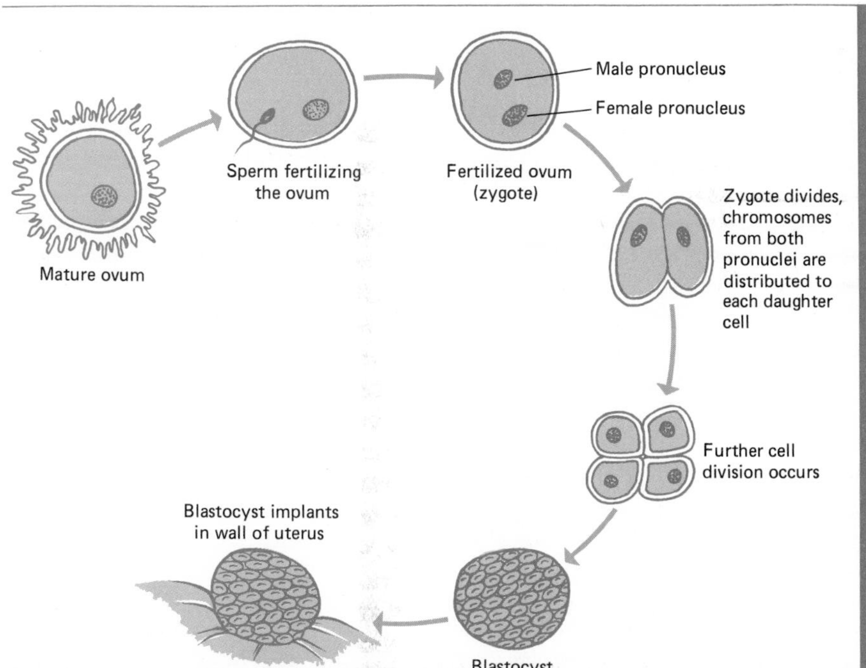

FIGURE 11-1
Fertilization and Implantation of an Ovum. The fertilized ovum divides to form a hollow ball of cells, called a blastocyst, which implants into the wall of the uterus. Cell division continues, forming the fetus and its supporting structures.

the growing mass of cells floats on the surface of the uterus or womb and is nourished by secretions of the uterine lining (6, page 45). About a week or so after fertilization, the blastocyst implants itself into the wall of the uterus, bringing the first stage of pregnancy, the **implantation stage**, to an end.

The next stage, called **organogenesis**, lasts about 6 weeks. During this period, the part of the blastocyst that will become the fetus begins to differentiate into the various organs and tissues; the rudiments of the heart, lungs, nervous system, digestive tract, kidneys, and other organs come into being. In addition, the remainder of the blastocyst, which will enclose the fetus and later provide its nourishment, also begins to develop. At this time, the fetus is sustained largely by cells it digests and blood it releases as it further implants itself into the uterine wall.

The remaining 7 months of pregnancy are the **growth stage**, in which tissues and organs grow until they reach a functional size. First, there is a period during which the number of cells increases rapidly. It is followed by a time in which cells both grow in number and in size. At some point in development, the number of cells in a tissue or organ reaches its maximum, and the organ grows principally by an increase in the size of its cells. However, cell division in some tissues, such as the skin and the blood-cell-producing tissues in the bone marrow, continues throughout life to replace cells that die or are lost from the body.

During the growth stage, the fetus is nourished by the **placenta**, a structure within which oxygen, nutrients, and waste products are exchanged between the mother's blood and that of the fetus. The two circulations do not mix; they simply come into close enough proximity to each other that exchange can occur (Figure 11-2). The placenta is thought to reach full weight by the end of 3 months and takes over hormonal control of pregnancy by producing estrogen, progesterone, and other substances. Malnourished women have a lower placental weight than well-nourished women, and this may contribute to impairment of fetal growth (10).

The period during which cells are rapidly dividing is crucial to development, for it is at this time that the organ receives its full complement of cells. A nutritional deficiency during this **critical period** can reduce the number of cells that are formed and possibly retard the development of the organ. Furthermore, cell division in a few organs and tissues stops forever once a certain stage is reached. So if defects develop during the period of cell division, they are usually permanent unless they are treated before this critical period has ended.

One major example is the brain and nervous system. The neurons themselves are formed from the eighteenth through the twenty-eighth week of gestation, whereas other important cells of nervous tissue, called *glial cells,* proliferate until the child is about 2 years old. Malnutrition during the period of most rapid brain development (the last trimester of pregnancy through the first month or two of life) can cause irreversible brain damage and permanent mental underdevelopment. After the age of 2 years, poor nutrition results in changes in mental development that are more likely to be reversible (1, page 57). Thus the timing as well as the

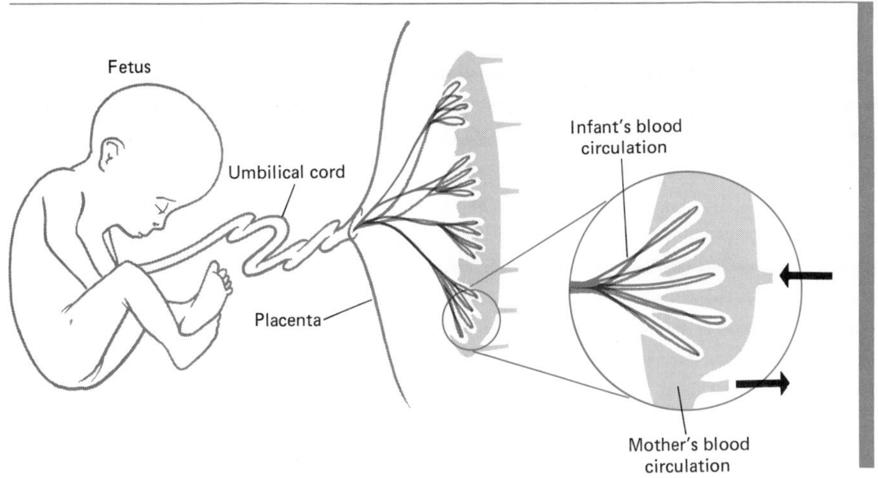

FIGURE 11-2 *Nourishment of the Fetus During the Growth Stage.* The umbilical cord connects the fetus to the placenta which is attached to the wall of the uterus. In the placenta, the fetal and maternal circulations do not actually mix. Fetal blood comes into close proximity to the mother's blood, allowing exchange of nutrients, oxygen, carbon dioxide, waste products, and other substances to occur.

severity, nature, and duration of a nutritional deficiency can have devastating effects on mental performance.

Effects on the Mother's Body During pregnancy, the mother's body undergoes many changes that promote fetal growth and prepare her for birth and lactation. Many of these changes influence nutrition requirements. For example, the mother should gain about 25 to 30 pounds during pregnancy, of which about 6 to 10 pounds is the fetus (4, pages 51–52). The rest includes the weight of the placenta and amniotic fluid, as well as a gain of about 20 pounds by the mother's body itself. The accumulation of body fat for use late in pregnancy and during lactation, the development of the uterus and supporting muscles, and an increase in breast size account for part of this weight gain.

The mother's blood volume increases by as much as 50 percent during pregnancy (4, page 38). Red blood cell production is stimulated, but the increase in the number of circulating red cells usually does not keep pace with the expansion of plasma volume, so that the concentration of red blood cells actually decreases. Another important change during pregnancy is a reduction in the rate at which food moves through the digestive tract. Although many women perceive this change as a kind of constipation, it increases the efficiency with which nutrients are absorbed by lengthening the time they spend in the small intestine. Hormonal changes, including increases in estrogen, progesterone, and thyroxine secretion, also occur during pregnancy, and these promote many of the other changes that occur in the mother's body.

NUTRIENT NEEDS (7)

The growth of the fetus and the changes in the mother's body result in an increase in nutritional requirements during pregnancy. These are reflected by higher Recommended Dietary Allowances (Figure 11-3). Extra energy is needed to support the growth of the fetus and the placenta, to enable the mother to add to her fat reserves, and to balance the increased energy expended by a higher basal metabolic rate and work done in carrying the fetus. The total increase in energy requirements for an entire 9-month pregnancy has been estimated as 80,000 kilocalories, which breaks down to the addition of 300 kcal/day to the energy RDA (7, page 26). Since underweight women and pregnant adolescents will need to gain more weight, their energy needs are somewhat greater. The increase in energy requirements during pregnancy is relatively small in comparison with the increases in protein, vitamin, and mineral needs. A woman does not have to consume very much more food when she becomes pregnant; she must, however, be sure that the foods she chooses are of high nutritional quality.

It is important that pregnant women gain neither too much nor too little weight. Obese, nondiabetic women have an increased risk of complications during delivery and a higher chance of producing an overweight infant. These babies have a higher death rate in the period soon after birth than do normal-weight infants (5, pages 29–30; 6, pages 76–93). However, pregnancy is not a time for starting on a weight-loss diet; doing so may lead to ketosis, which could damage the fetus and deprive it of much needed energy, protein, and other nutrients. Inadequate maternal weight gain increases the risk of delivering a low-birth-weight infant and of developing toxemia, a blood pressure disorder (5, pages 29–30; 6, pages 76–93).

Since protein must be used in the synthesis of new tissue in both the mother and the fetus, a state of positive nitrogen balance must be maintained throughout pregnancy. To meet increased protein needs, the Food and Nutrition Board recommends an additional 30 g/day of protein over the nonpregnant intake. At the same time, adequate intake of kilocalories from carbohydrate and fat must be maintained to facilitate more efficient utilization of the protein.

Mineral needs are also higher in pregnant women. Calcium and phosphorus are required for mineralization of bones and teeth in the fetus. Although the bones are poorly calcified at birth and must gain more mineral early in life, about 30 grams of calcium have accumulated in them by the end of pregnancy. This demand is partly met by increased absorption and decreased excretion of calcium, but the FNB recommends a total allowance of 1200 mg/day because calcium may be stored in the mother's skeleton for use during lactation (7, pages 125–133). The phosphorus allowance is also increased to 1200 mg/day.

The requirement for iron rises during pregnancy because this mineral is needed to synthesize a variety of compounds, including hemoglobin in the fetal red blood cells. In addition, the fetus must store enough iron in its body to last 3 to 6 months after birth. Changes in the mother's body, such as placental development and increased red blood cell production, also raise the iron requirement. Ideally, a woman anticipating pregnancy should increase her iron intake to build up her stores, but it is difficult for many women to do this. Thus, even though the rate of iron absorption doubles or even triples during pregnancy, the FNB recom-

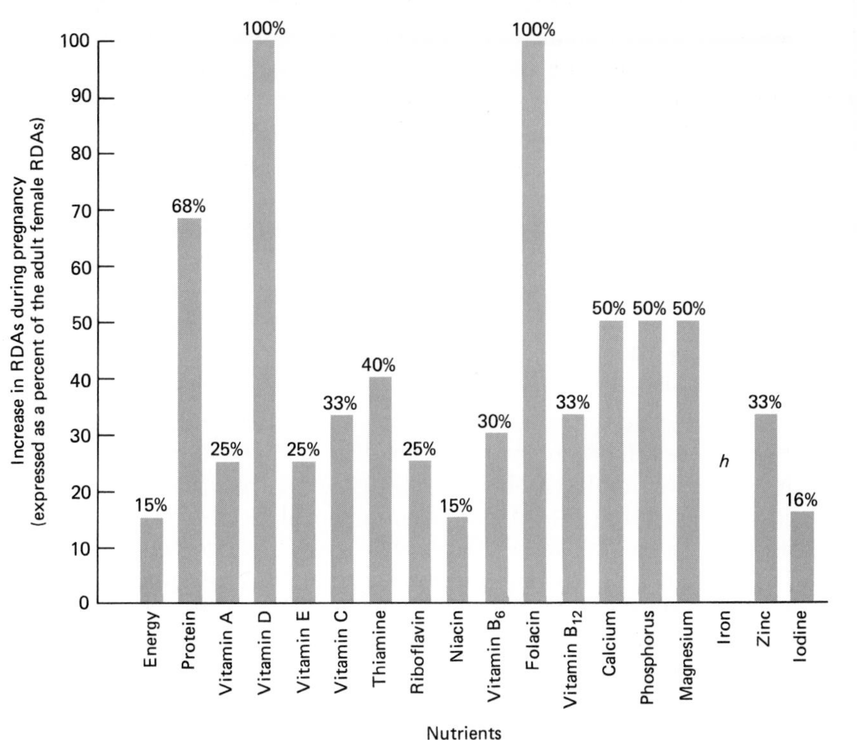

FIGURE 11-3
The Increase of RDAs during Pregnancy. The *h* indicates RDA cannot be met from food sources alone. [*Source:* Food and Nutrition Board, *Recommended Dietary Allowances,* 9th ed., Washington, DC, National Academy of Science (1980).]

mends supplementing the nonpregnant allowance (18 mg/day) with 30 to 60 mg/day of iron.

Because maternal blood and extracellular fluid volumes increase, the need for water and sodium also rises. **Toxemia**, which affects 4 to 5 percent of all pregnant women, is characterized by high blood pressure, **edema** (tissue swelling), and the appearance of protein in the urine (11). It can lead to convulsions and, in some cases, death. Although poor nutrition has been strongly associated with toxemia, a specific nutrient deficiency has not been identified (5, pages 104–107; 12). Sodium restriction and **diuretics** (drugs that stimulate urination) were once used to treat the high blood pressure and edema, but this may make the condition worse and produce other complications (5, pages 104–107). Current recommendations are to consume a well-balanced diet, ingest normal amounts of salt, and avoid diuretics (5, pages 104–107; 12). Edema in the

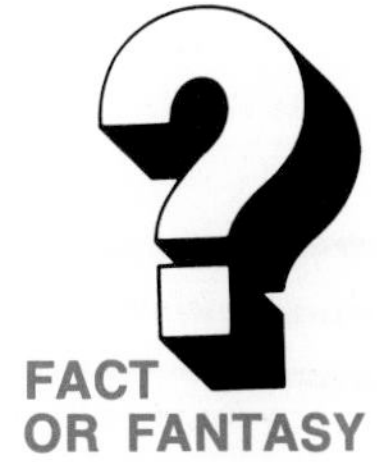

1. Salt restriction and diuretics should be used to treat the water retention (edema) that often occurs during pregnancy.

FACT OR FANTASY

absence of toxemia is common in pregnancy and is usually considered normal. Again, salt restriction and diuretics are not recommended.

Iodine is another important mineral during pregnancy; infants born to iodine-deficient mothers suffer physical and mental retardation. Iodine deficiency need not be a problem if the woman uses iodized salt. If a physician recommends the restriction of salt intake, alternate sources, such as seafood, must be used. The requirements for the other minerals increase during pregnancy as well. For example, studies in rats showed that pregnant females could not withstand even short periods on a zinc-deficient diet without a rise in the incidence of birth defects in their offspring (13). However, much more research must be done to establish specific requirements for zinc and other trace elements during pregnancy.

Vitamin requirements also rise during pregnancy. Since folacin and vitamin B_{12} are needed for cell division, they are important for promoting the growth and development of tissues. Estimates of folacin deficiency among pregnant women in the United States range from 3 to 22 percent, and the incidence is higher in the developing world. Several studies indicate that the incidence of small-for-date infants and malformations is greater in folacin-deficient women than in women with adequate intakes (6, pages 157–160). Although the requirements for vitamins A, D, and C increase during pregnancy, care must be taken not to oversupplement the diet with them. Vitamins A and D are known to be toxic in large doses, and consumption of too much vitamin C may increase fetal need for the vitamin and induce scurvy in the infant after birth (14) (see Chapter 7).

MEETING NUTRITIONAL NEEDS DURING PREGNANCY

When the Gerards began to consider having a third child, they paid a visit to their obstetrician. Among other sound pieces of advice, the obstetrician reminded them that the nutritional status of the mother at the time of conception is as important to the outcome of pregnancy as the diet during pregnancy. During the period prior to conception, Meg paid special attention to selecting an adequate diet. Now that she is carrying the baby, the obstetrician has recommended some modifications in her diet to meet her increased needs. In particular, the obstetrician has pointed out that since the increases in protein, vitamin, and mineral requirements are proportionally greater than the increase in energy needs, Meg should make her choices from among the higher-quality foods in each of the four food groups.

Milk consumption should be increased to four or more servings per

The nutritional status of the mother at conception is as important as diet during pregnancy.

day. One quart of milk will meet this need, but other dairy products, such as cheese and yogurt, can be substituted for some of the milk. Dairy products provide high-quality protein, calcium, riboflavin, vitamin B_{12}, vitamin A, and, if fortified, vitamin D.

Two or more generous servings should be obtained from the meat group each day. This group is a source of high-quality protein, many of the B vitamins, including vitamin B_{12}, and zinc; red meats and liver provide much needed iron. If meat substitutes such as legumes and nuts are used, care must be taken to complement or supplement their proteins.

At least four large servings should be chosen daily from the vegetable-fruit group. It is especially important during pregnancy that the choice of foods from this group be of high nutritional quality. The dark-green, leafy vegetables should make up one of the servings; they are good sources of folacin, vitamin C, vitamin A, vitamin E, and vitamin K. Another serving should come from foods high in vitamin C, such as citrus fruit, melons, cabbage, green peppers, or tomatoes. Orange–yellow fruits and vegetables can be used to provide vitamin A.

A pregnant woman also should choose four servings per day from the bread and cereal group, preferably from whole-grain products. Four slices of bread will meet this need, but ready-to-eat and cooked cereals, macaroni, and rice can be substituted for some of the bread. The grains may be combined with legumes to provide high-quality protein, and they also supply iron and some of the B vitamins. Whole-grain products also are good sources of fiber, which can help prevent the constipation that sometimes occurs in pregnant women.

To fulfill the remainder of the caloric requirements during pregnancy, high-quality foods from each of the groups should be chosen. Normal salt intake should be maintained, and iodized salt should be used to ensure sufficient iodine intake. With the exception of iron and folacin, vitamin and mineral supplements are not necessary during pregnancy (7, pages 106–113, 137–144). If one is taken, its vitamin and mineral content should not exceed RDA levels because of the risk of vitamin A and vitamin D toxicity and vitamin C dependency in the infant. It is best to rely on a physician's advice regarding nutritional supplements.

A carefully selected lacto-ovo-vegetarian diet supplemented with iron and folacin can meet the nutritional needs of pregnancy. However, a strict vegetarian (or vegan) diet is too restrictive and may result in an inadequate intake of vitamin B_{12}, calcium, zinc, iron, folacin, and vitamin D. Such a diet is not recommended during pregnancy.

Unfortunately, many families do not possess the financial resources to provide a diet that will meet the increased needs of a pregnant woman. Because a nutritional diet is so important during this period, the USDA sponsors a supplementation program called *Women, Infants, and Children* (*WIC*) to aid pregnant and lactating women and infants who are at high risk of dietary deficiency. Eligible families may receive supplemental iron-fortified infant formulas; cereals, milk, and juices for infants; and milk, cheese, eggs, cereals, and juices for mothers and other children (15). Nutrition education is also an integral part of the program.

ISSUE: ALCOHOL, SMOKING, DRUGS

"Many of us consume substances besides food that can influence the outcome of pregnancy. Alcohol is probably the most harmful; infants born to alcoholic women have a much higher risk of physical and mental defects than those born to normal women (see Focus 11-1). Even social drinkers have increased risk of producing babies with mild developmental and behavioral defects; average intake of 2 to 3 drinks per day has been associated with reduced birth weights (16).

Smoking also can have adverse effects on the fetus. Infants of smokers tend to be lighter than those of nonsmokers, and the incidence of low-birth-weight infants is greater among smokers (5, pages 113–122). Some researchers think that this results from depressed appetite in smokers, but several studies contradict this view (5, pages 113–122; 17). Others suggest that the carbon monoxide in cigarette smoke combines with hemoglobin in both the mother and the fetus, reducing its oxygen-carrying capacity. In addition, some components of smoke may damage the placenta. Recent population studies indicate that smoking also may result in birth defects. In one case, for example, an association was found between cigarette smoking and cleft lip and cleft palate (18).

A variety of other drugs may be harmful during pregnancy. For instance, caffeine and aspirin have been linked to birth defects, and aspirin also may increase the length of labor and the occurrence of complications during delivery (19,20). It is therefore important for a pregnant woman to avoid all drugs, including over-the-counter preparations, except when recommended by a physician. She also should stop or restrict as much as possible the use of alcohol, tobacco, and caffeine-containing products."

FOCUS 11-1 FETAL ALCOHOL SYNDROME

An association between maternal alcoholism and birth defects has been recognized for centuries, but only recently has it been described in the medical literature as the **fetal alcohol syndrome (FAS)**. This condition, which may include growth retardation, physical deformities, behavioral defects, and mental retardation, has been shown to affect one to two live births out of every 1000 (16,32). As many as one-third to one-half of the infants born to alcoholic mothers exhibit the problem in some degree (33,34). A definitive description of FAS is currently being developed, and it may be found to be a major cause of mental deficiency and, to a lesser extent, congenital abnormalities (35). Because of the widespread social use of alcohol and the sizable number of affected offspring, the potential magnitude of the problem is of national concern.

Although fetal alcohol syndrome is a recognized complication of alcoholism, the effects of smaller and variable doses of alcohol are as yet undetermined (16). However, Hanson and co-workers found that with an intake of 1 to 2 oz/day of pure alcohol, the risk of birth defects approached 10 percent, while an average intake of 2 to 3 oz/day produced abnormalities in 19 percent of the infants. In addition, reduction in birth weight has been found in infants whose mothers consumed as little as two drinks per day (16). Thus risks seem to increase proportionally with alcohol intake (32). Since a safe level of intake has not been defined, total avoidance of alcohol is recommended during pregnancy.

FOCUS 11-2 ORAL CONTRACEPTIVES AND NUTRITIONAL STATUS Today nearly 100 million women all over the world, including 10 to 15 million in the United States, use combination estrogen-progestin oral contraceptive agents (OCA) (30). In recent years, it has become evident that these drugs influence nutritional status by altering blood lipid levels, impairing the metabolism of glucose, and modifying the utilization of vitamins and minerals in the body (30,31). These changes can affect the health of the woman and any future children.

An observation consistently made in OCA users is an increase in blood lipids, especially triglyceride (30). In addition, estrogens increase and progestins decrease the amount of cholesterol carried by high-density lipoproteins (HDL). The effect on HDL depends on the relative proportion of the two hormones in the pill. Since elevated blood lipids and low HDL levels increase the risk of heart disease, long-term use of oral contraceptives could influence the development of atherosclerosis (see Chapter 5). However, blood lipids generally return to normal within 6 months of discontinuing OCA use (30).

In about 10 percent of the women using them, oral contraceptives induce an increase in fasting blood glucose concentrations, indicating a decline in the ability to metabolize this sugar (30). Blood levels of amino acids and some proteins, such as albumin, decrease, but the concentrations of other proteins increase, including transport proteins for iron, copper, thyroxine, vitamin A, lipids, and many proteins involved in blood clotting (30).

Oral contraceptives influence the metabolism of many of the vitamins. For example, they frequently reduce the blood concentrations of vitamin B_6, and administering the vitamin appears to correct the depression that occurs with OCA use in many of these women (30). Although data conflict, experiments show that oral contraceptives also lower the blood levels of folacin, vitamin B_{12}, thiamine, riboflavin, and vitamin C and raise blood concentrations of vitamin A and vitamin E (30,31). It is thought that the elevated vitamin A levels result from a mobilization of the vitamin from body stores rather than an increase of vitamin A in the body (30). Minerals also are affected by oral contraceptive agents. Iron, copper, and protein-bound iodine levels in the blood are increased in OCA users (30,31). Oral contraceptives appear to induce a redistribution of body zinc, since blood levels decline, but the amount in red blood cells increases (30). Estrogens have a beneficial effect on calcium balance by increasing deposition of the mineral in bone (30).

The significance of the effects of oral contraceptives on human health is still unclear (30). Healthy, well-nourished women probably have little cause for concern and do not require supplements (31). However, women who have just had a baby, are planning to have a baby later, have poor dietary habits, already have nutritional deficiencies, have had recent illness or surgery, are still growing, or have a family history of diabetes mellitus or heart disease may be at nutritional risk from OCA use. Diet counseling and supplements may be considered for these women (30).

Lactation

Like most American women, Meg bottle-fed her first two children. However, a revival of interest in breast-feeding in the United States in recent years as well as her own concern about nutrition has led her to consider breast-feeding her third child. In making this decision, she has to consider many factors, including the advantages and disadvantages of each method, the impact of breast-feeding on her nutritional requirements, and the best way of meeting her dietary needs during the lactation period. In the following section we will examine these questions, but first let us look at the physiological basis for lactation: how milk is produced.

HOW IT WORKS (21)

Milk is secreted by mammary glands located in the mother's breasts (Figure 11-4), and its production is controlled by several hormones (Table 11-1). During pregnancy, estrogen, progesterone, and other hormones produced by the placenta promote the development of the breasts, so that later they can produce milk. After the baby is born, **prolactin**, a hormone produced by the anterior pituitary gland, stimulates the secretion of milk. Prolactin synthesis is maintained by the sucking of the infant on the mother's breast; thus the act of nursing itself provides the stimulus for further milk production. As milk is produced, it accumulates in lobules, sinuses, and ducts in the breast. Within 30 to 60 seconds after sucking has begun, a hormone called **oxytocin** causes the lobules to contract. This squeezes milk from them into the ducts, from which it can be sucked by the infant. This **letdown reflex** is vital for obtaining sufficient milk.

The milk secreted during the first few days of lactation is different from the milk produced thereafter. This yellowish, transparent fluid is called **colostrum**, and it contains more protein, less sugar, and much less fat than mature milk. Colostrum also contains antibodies that protect the infant from disease organisms, such as polio virus and *Salmonella* bacteria, that enter the body through the digestive tract. The mother's body begins producing mature milk 2 to 10 days after the infant's birth.

LACTATION AND NUTRITIONAL NEEDS

A lactating woman may produce more than 1.5 liters/day of milk and averages about 850 ml/day over the lactation period (7, page 27). The mother's milk is a rich source of most nutrients for the infant, and be-

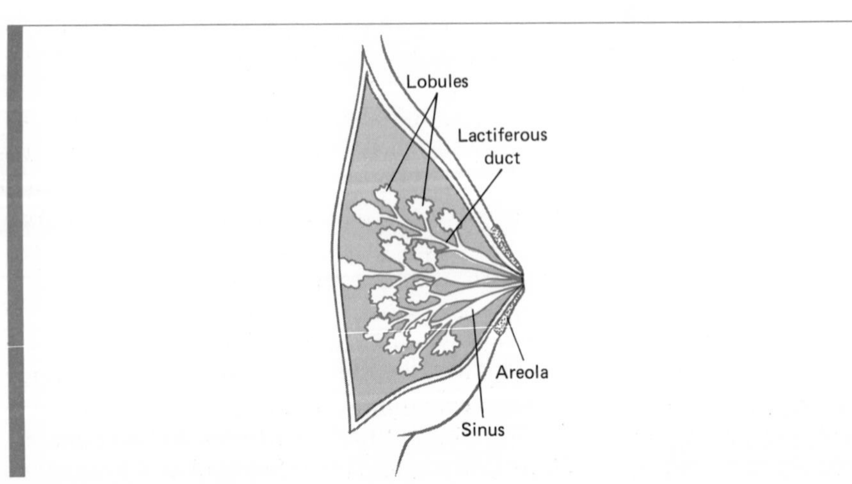

FIGURE 11-4
The human breast.

TABLE **11-1**

Some hormones involved in breast development and lactation

HORMONE	SOURCE	FUNCTION
Estrogen	Ovary and placenta	During pregnancy, stimulates breast development; fall in blood level after birth allows prolactin to stimulate milk secretion
Progesterone	Ovary and placenta	During pregnancy, stimulates breast development; fall in blood level after birth allows prolactin to stimulate milk secretion
Prolactin	Anterior pituitary	Stimulates milk secretion; prolactin synthesis is stimulated by the infant's sucking on the breast
Oxytocin	Posterior pituitary	Causes the letdown reflex, whereby milk is squeezed from the alveoli of the breast into ducts and sinuses and then ejected from the breast

Source: D. Psiaki and C. Olson, *Current Knowledge on Breast Feeding,* Cornell University Cooperative Extension, Ithaca, N.Y., 1977.

cause these nutrients are supplied only by her body, her nutritional requirements increase greatly (Figure 11-5).

The energy cost of producing milk is about 90 kcal/100 ml, of which about 67 to 77 kilocalories is contained in the milk and 13 to 23 kilocalories is expended to produce it. Thus a woman delivering 850 ml/day of milk uses an additional 750 kcal/day above her normal energy expenditure. About one-third of this is provided by fat stored in her body during pregnancy, but the remainder must come from the diet. The Food and Nutrition Board therefore recommends that a lactating woman increase her caloric intake by 500 kcal/day above nonlactating levels. If more than one infant is being nursed or lactation continues longer than 3 months, further increases are necessary (7, page 27). Since the mother's fat is mobilized during lactation, this can be a time to lose some of the weight accumulated during pregnancy. Even if she eats slightly more than usual, a lactating woman can generally lose weight faster than a nonlactating woman can (21).

Allowances for protein, calcium, zinc, vitamin A, and vitamin C increase by 50 percent or more during lactation. For other nutrients, including thiamine, vitamin B_6, and vitamin B_{12}, the increase is more modest. Since little iron is secreted in milk, the RDA for this mineral during lactation is no higher than in the nonlactating state. However, continued supplementation of the mother for 2 to 3 months after birth is advisable to replenish stores depleted during pregnancy (7, pages 137–144).

Nutritional deficiency during lactation can lead to a reduction in either the quantity or the quality of the milk, depending on the nutrient involved. Restricted fluid and caloric intakes reduce the amount of milk produced (21). Some studies have found that low vitamin A, thiamine, riboflavin, vitamin B_6, vitamin C, and iodine intakes lead to a lower concentration of these substances in the milk (6, pages 262–266; 21). The quantity of certain other substances, such as calcium and protein, is relatively unaffected by diet (6, pages 262–266).

Although nutritional requirements are higher during lactation, the nursing mother can meet her needs by choosing the proper foods. Supplements are generally unnecessary unless the intake of one or more specific nutrients is deficient (4, page 150). Increasing milk consumption to at least 5 cups/day is recommended (4, page 150); the milk supplies fluid, kilocalories, high-quality protein, calcium, and riboflavin needed for lactation. To cover increased needs for vitamin C, folacin, vitamin E, and other nutrients, there should be slight increases in the consumption of citrus fruits, green, leafy vegetables, and whole grains. Two generous servings from the meat group also are needed each day. As in pregnancy, choices should be made from the higher-quality members of each food group.

A large variety of drugs and other foreign compounds can be excreted from the mother's body in her milk (a partial list is given in Table 11-2). Some, such as anticoagulants, certain antibiotics, and flagyl, should not be given to lactating women. Others, including sulfonamide, steroids, diuretics, and barbiturates, should be used only under medical supervision (21). Although small amounts of DDT, PBBs, and PCBs are found in human milk, no restrictions on breast-feeding are currently recom-

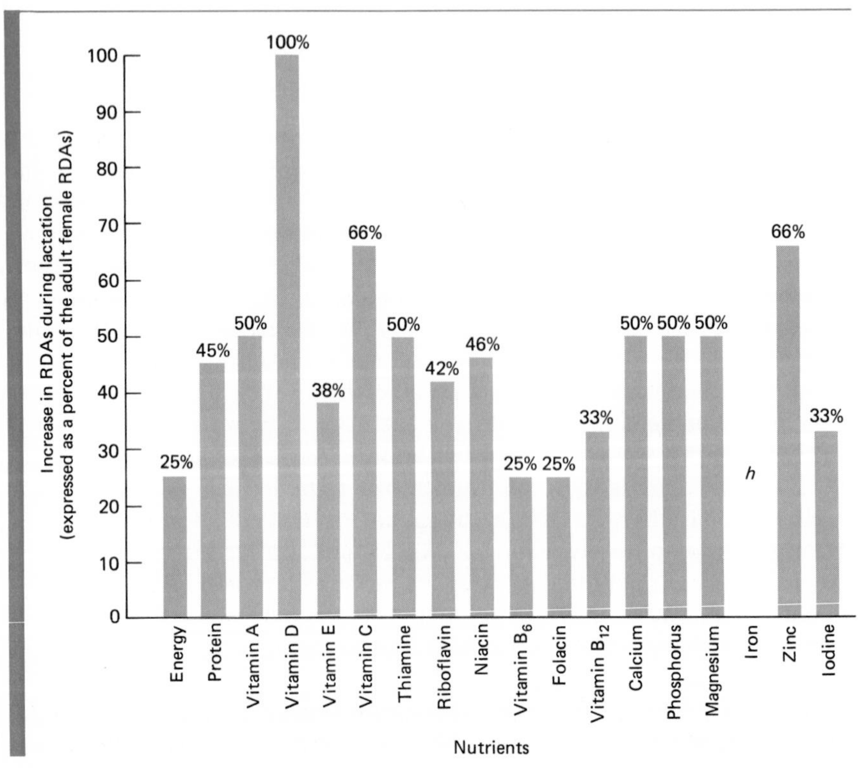

FIGURE 11-5 *The Increase of RDAs during Lactation.* The *h* indicates RDA cannot be met from food sources alone. [*Source:* Food and Nutrition Board, *Recommended Dietary Allowances,* 9th ed., Washington, DC, National Academy of Sciences (1980).]

TABLE **11-2**

A partial list of drugs and foreign compounds transmitted in breast milk

Alcohol	Laxatives and cathartics
Amphetamines	Metals besides nutrients Arsenic Lead Mercury
Aspirin	Methadone
Anesthetics Chloroform Ether	Morphine
Antibiotics Chloramphenical Erythromycin Flagyl Penicillin Streptomycin Sulfonamides Tetracycline	Nicotine
Antihistamines	Phenylbutazone (butazolidine)
Barbiturates	Polybrominated biphenyls (PBBs)
Bromides	Polychlorinated biphenyls (PCBs)
Caffeine	Quinine
Cortisone	Salicylates
DDT	Scopolamine
Dilantin	Sodium chloride
Heroin	Thyroid hormone
	Tranquilizers

Source: J. M. Arena, "Contamination of the Ideal Food," *Nutrition Today* **5**:2–8 (1970). (Used with permission.)

mended. The level of DDT in human milk has been slowly decreasing since DDT was banned in 1972 (22).

ISSUE: BREAST-FEEDING

"After a long period of decline from 1940 to the early 1970s, the number of women who are breast-feeding their babies has begun to increase in the United States (23, pages 7–11, 24) (Figure 11-6). Between 1972 and 1976, the number of women in the Northeast breast-feeding their infants at the time of discharge from the hospital increased from 25 to 45 percent; and on the West Coast, from 40 to 80 percent. At least 37 percent of the West Coast mothers and 20 percent of the Northeastern mothers continued to breast-feed for at least 6 months (24). By examining the benefits of breast- and bottle-feeding, we can see why so many mothers, most of whom were bottle-fed, are turning to human milk to feed their babies."

ADVANTAGES

The milk produced by any species of animal is most suited to feeding the young of that species, and human milk has many nutritional advantages

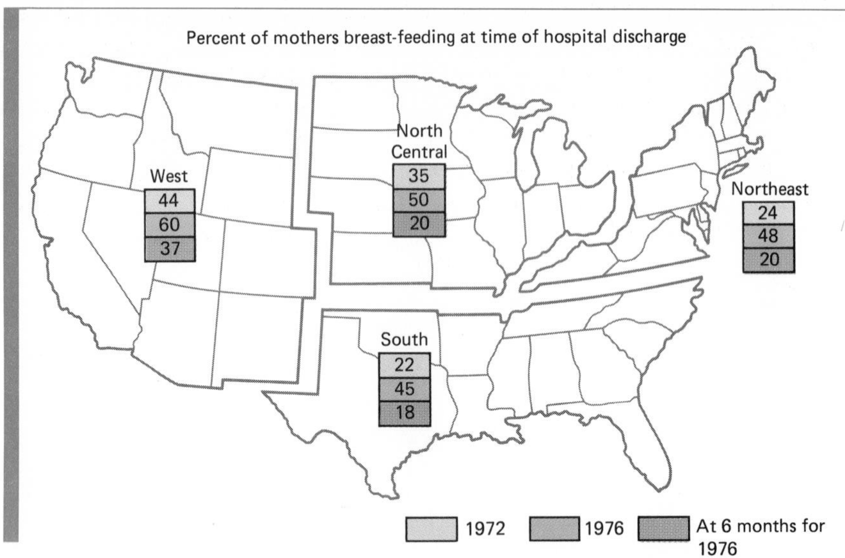

FIGURE 11-6 *The Incidence of Breast-Feeding in the United States.* The percentage of mothers breast-feeding their infants when they left the hospital increased during the early 1970s. [*Source:* L. J. Filer, "Early Nutrition: Its Long-Term Role", *Hospital Practice* **13**:87–95 (February 1978). Used with permission.]

over cow's milk (23, pages 359–382) (Table 11-3). Cow's milk contains three times as much protein as human milk. That protein is predominantly casein, which precipitates into less digestable curds in the infant's stomach. Thus the protein in cow's milk is less available to the infant (21). The proportion of essential amino acids in human milk also is more appropriate for the human infant's needs.

Human milk contains more total fat and a higher proportion of polyunsaturated fat than cow's milk. The fat in human milk also is absorbed more readily, promoting an adequate caloric intake (21). Human milk also is higher in cholesterol, which some authorities believe is necessary to develop the means to metabolize the substance normally (21).

The amount of lactose, vitamin A, vitamin C, and vitamin E is higher in human milk, which also has a more favorable calcium-to-phosphorus ratio than cow's milk. Cow's milk contains the same amount or more of the B vitamins, magnesium, iron, zinc, and iodine. However, the iron and zinc in human milk is much more readily absorbed by the infant (26). The solute load contributed to the body fluids is higher for cow's milk. Because of the immature state of its kidneys, the infant will require more water to excrete this excess solute, thereby increasing the risk of dehydration, especially in hot weather (21).

In commercial infant formulas, cow's milk is modified to more closely resemble human milk. For example, Enfamil and Similac are made from

The milk produced by any species of animal is most suited to feeding the young of that species.

nonfat cow's milk, vegetable oil, and added carbohydrate, usually lactose or corn syrup solids. Others, such as SMA, contain added whey protein (lactalbumin), while a third type, which can be used in instances of milk intolerance or allergy, is made from soybean products. Vitamins and minerals are added to these products to bring their concentrations up to levels more than sufficient to meet an infant's needs.

Both human milk and the iron-fortified commercial formulas available today are generally adequate to meet a baby's nutritional needs for the first 6 months of life (23, pages 359–382; 24,25,27). The formulas con-

TABLE **11-3**

A comparison of the nutrient contents of milks for infants (per 100 ml)

COMPONENT	HUMAN MILK, AMOUNTS VARY	SIMILAC WITH IRON	ISOMIL	EVAPORATED MILK, 1:1 DILUTION	WHOLE COW'S MILK, 3.5% FAT	1980 RDA, INFANT 0–6 MONTHS OLD
Kilocalories	67–75	68	68	69	66	110 kcal/kg
Protein, g	1.1	1.6	2.0*	3.5	3.5	2.2 g/kg
Fat, g	4.5	3.6	3.6	3.8	3.5–3.7	—
Carbohydrate (lactose), g	6.8	7.2	6.8†	4.8	4.9	—
Vitamin A, IU	200	250	250	185	140	2100
Vitamin D, IU	2	40	40	40‡	42‡	400
Vitamin C, mg	4	5.5	5.5	0.5	1	35
Vitamin E, IU	0.2	1.7	1.5	0.04	0.04	4.5
Vitamin K, μg	1.5	—	15	est. 6	0.6	est. 12
Thiamine, mg	0.016	0.07	0.04	0.03	0.04	0.3
Riboflavin, mg	0.036	0.01	0.06	0.19	0.17	0.4
Niacin, mg	0.1	0.7	0.9	0.1	0.1	6
Pyridoxine, mg	0.01	0.04	0.04	0.04	0.06	0.3
Folacin, mg	0.005	0.01	0.01	0.005	0.005	0.03
Vitamin B_{12}, μg	0.03	0.015	0.03	0.08	0.4	0.5
Calcium, mg	34	100	140	126	118	360
Phosphorus, mg	14	77	100	102	92	240
Magnesium, mg	4	8.2	10	12	12	50
Iron, mg	0.05	2.4	2.4	0.05	0.05	10
Copper, mg	40	0.12	0.10	est. 30	30	est. 0.5–0.7
Zinc, mg	0.3–0.5	1.0	1.0	0.3–0.5	0.3–0.5	3
Iodine, μg	3	20	30	5	5	40

* Protein is soy protein isolate.
† Carbohydrate is corn syrup and sucrose with a small amount of modified corn starch.
‡ If milk is fortified with vitamin D.

Sources: Product labels.

S. J. Formon, *Infant Nutrition,* 2d ed., Saunders, Philadelphia, 1974, pp. 362–362, 372. (Used with permission.)

Food and Nutrition Board, *Recommended Dietary Allowances,* 9th ed., National Academy of Sciences, Washington, 1980.

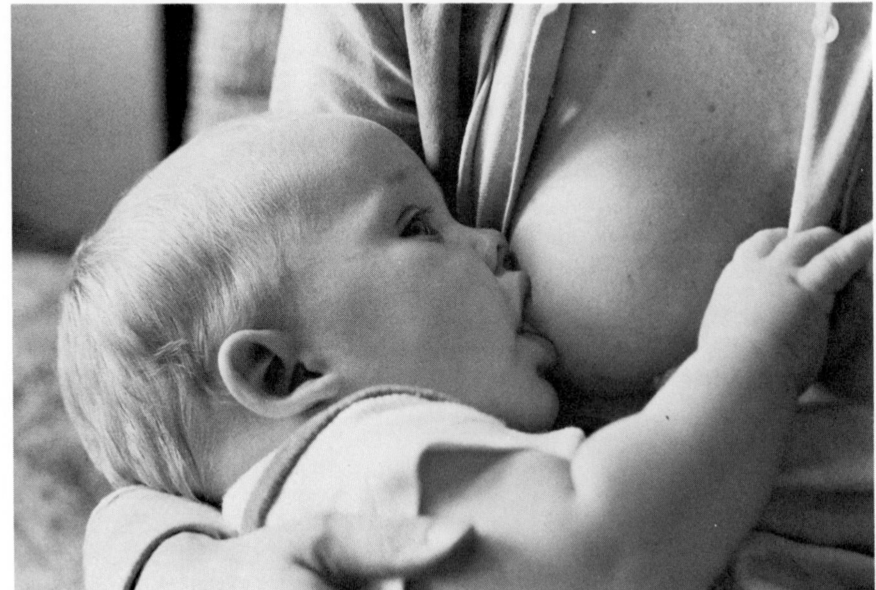

FIGURE 11-7 Breast-feeding can be a rewarding experience for both the mother and her baby. (Photograph by Monique Manceau, Rapho/Photo Researchers, Inc.)

tain sufficient amounts of each of the nutrients (27). Many pediatricians, however, recommend supplementing human milk with iron, vitamin D, and fluorine. Other authorities believe a breast-fed infant does not need supplemental iron until the fifth or sixth month (21,24). Nevertheless, to be on the safe side, these nutrients should be supplemented in a breast-fed baby's diet (27).

Although an infant can thrive on either breast milk or the proper formula, human milk has several other advantages. It contains many agents, including white blood cells, antibodies, and enzymes, that help the baby resist infections, particularly of the digestive tract (21,28). In addition, an iron-binding protein, *lactoferrin,* renders iron unavailable to certain bacteria, thereby inhibiting their growth. *Bifidus factor* promotes the growth of the bacterium *Lactobacillus bifidus,* which produces organic acids that increase the acidity of the digestive tract and prevent growth of certain bacteria and fungi. In addition, the first few days of breast-feeding exposes the infant to colostrum, which contains antibodies that help prevent digestive tract infections.

Another advantage of breast-feeding is that the infant is more likely to regulate its own food intake. Because the mother cannot see how much milk the child has consumed, she generally assumes it is satisfied when it stops sucking. A bottle-fed infant is often forced to finish the bottle. This can lead to overfeeding in bottle-fed babies, and several studies show a lower incidence of infantile obesity with breast-feeding (21). However, breast-feeding cannot ensure that an infant will not become an obese adult. Breast-feeding also reduces the likelihood that the infant will develop an allergy to cow's milk protein (21). The mother does not need to worry about bacterial contamination, and because there are no formulas or bottles to prepare, breast-feeding can be more convenient than bottle-feeding. It also may promote a sense of security and closeness for the infant and satisfaction for the mother (21). Depending on the extra foods chosen to support lactation, breast-feeding also can be less costly (29).

DISADVANTAGES

Certain disadvantages must be weighed when considering breast-feeding. It can be inconvenient, particularly in a social situation. Unless the infant also feeds from a bottle, the job cannot be carried out by someone else, and the responsibility cannot be shared by the father. However, occasional or even once-daily formula feedings probably will not interfere with the success of nursing, and the freedom gained by the mother can be important. Failure to produce enough milk also is a problem for some women, but it often can be avoided by properly educating the mother about breast-feeding techniques. Many commonly prescribed drugs, including tetracycline, atropine, steroids, barbiturates, codeine, and aspirin, as well as ethyl alcohol, nicotine, and heroin, can be transferred in breast milk (21). These substances should be avoided as much as possible.

The choice between breast- and bottle-feeding should be made on the basis of facts, rather than on hearsay from peers. Publications such as those listed at the end of the chapter and organizations such as the La-Leche League provide good information.

EVAPORATED MILK FORMULA

In cases in which the mother does not want to breast-feed and the family cannot afford commercial formulas, evaporated milk is often used as the basis for a homemade formula (27). For example, a typical formula might be 3 ounces of evaporated milk, 4½ ounces of water, and 2 teaspoons of corn syrup. To prevent the growth of undesirable organisms, such formulas should be made one feeding at a time just before use. Infants receiving evaporated milk require supplements of iron and vitamin C.

Study Guide

SUMMARY

1. The rapid growth and development of the infant and changes in the mother's body create a high demand for all nutrients during pregnancy. Failure to provide proper nutrients to the fetus can lead to low birth weight and, in some instances, to permanent mental and physical retardation. Nutritional imbalances also affect the mother and can lead to complications such as toxemia.
2. The timing, as well as the nature, severity, and duration, of a nutritional deficiency is important to the developing fetus. In many tissues, such as the nervous system, the cells stop dividing forever once a certain stage of development is reached. Any factor, such as a nutritional deficiency, that reduces growth during the critical period of cell division can permanently impair the functioning of these tissues.
3. Although adequate caloric intake is critical to optimal weight gain by the mother and to the birth weight of the infant, the increase in the energy requirement during pregnancy is relatively small in comparison with the increased need for protein, vitamins, and minerals. A woman therefore does not have to consume very much more food when she becomes pregnant, but she must be sure that the foods she chooses are of high nutritional quality. Because of the risk of adverse effects, the use of alcohol, caffeine, and most drugs should be restricted or abandoned.
4. Lactation also increases the requirements for most nutrients. Depending on the nutrient involved, nutritional deficiency during lactation can lead to a reduction in either the quantity or quality of the milk produced. Because it supplies many of the components needed for milk production, milk consumption should be increased to at least 5 cups/day. Caution must be exercised in consuming alcohol and most drugs during lactation because many are passed to the infant in the milk.
5. Milk can provide almost all the infant's nutritional needs for the first 6 months of life. Human milk is nutritionally superior to cow's milk. In commercial infant formulas, the milk has been modified to more closely resemble human milk. These formulas are nutritionally adequate for infant feeding. Many pediatricians recommend that human milk be supplemented with vitamin D, iron, and fluorine. Breast-feeding has many advantages over bottle-feeding, including helping the baby resist infection, more reliable sanitary quality, lower risk of allergy, and convenience.
6. Oral contraceptive agents influence nutritional status in a variety of ways, including raising blood lipid levels, impairing metabolism of glucose, and altering the requirements for vitamins and minerals. While this does not appear to be a hazard for healthy, well-nourished women, it may aggravate existing deficiencies or create a deficiency in women with only marginal dietary intakes or in those with high requirements, such as during adolescence, pregnancy, and lactation.

VOCABULARY

blastocyst	implantation stage
colostrum	letdown reflex
critical period	organogenesis
diuretics	oxytocin
edema	placenta
fetal alcohol syndrome (FAS)	prolactin
	toxemia of pregnancy
growth stage	zygote

STUDY QUESTIONS

1. What are the three stages of fetal development? What occurs during each stage? By what means is the fetus nourished during each stage?
2. What changes of nutritional importance

occur in the mother's body during pregnancy, and what is their influence on her nutritional requirements?

3. Refer to Chapters 4, 7, and 8 as well as this chapter and list the functions of each of the following in the development of the fetus.

a. Protein	d. Iodine
b. Calcium and phosphorus	e. Zinc
	f. Folacin
c. Iron	g. Vitamin B_{12}

4. Explain how the Basic Four Food Plan can be used to fulfill the nutritional needs of pregnancy. What two nutrients should be supplemented? Excess intake of which nutrients should be avoided?

5. Can a lacto-ovo-vegetarian diet be adapted to meet the needs of pregnancy? Can a strict vegetarian (vegan) diet? Justify your answer.

6. What are the effects of alcohol on the outcome of pregnancy? What are the effects of smoking? What recommendation can you make regarding the intake of these substances, as well as of drugs such as aspirin and caffeine, during pregnancy?

7. The requirements for which nutrients are particularly affected by lactation? How can the four food groups be used to meet the needs of lactation?

8. List the ways human milk is *nutritionally* superior to cow's milk. In the manufacture of infant formulas, how is cow's milk modified to more closely resemble human milk? What nutrients should be supplemented in a breast-fed infant's diet?

9. Outside of nutritional considerations, what are some advantages of breast-feeding over bottle-feeding? What are some disadvantages of breast-feeding?

10. Is it necessary for a well-nourished woman who uses oral contraceptives to take a vitamin and mineral supplement? In which oral contraceptive users might a supplement be necessary?

SELF-TEST

Multiple choice: Choose the best answer.

1. One of the most reliable predictors of infant health and future development is
   a. Length at birth
   b. Birth weight
   c. Presence of visible birth defects
   d. Milk intake during the first week of life

2. For most mothers, the optimal weight gain (including the fetus) is about
   a. 35 to 40 pounds
   b. 30 to 35 pounds
   c. 25 to 30 pounds
   d. 15 to 20 pounds

3. A pregnant woman should be maintained in a state of
   a. Positive nitrogen balance
   b. Negative nitrogen balance
   c. Nitrogen equilibrium

4. A pregnant woman should take particular care not to oversupplement the diet with
   a. Vitamin A
   b. Vitamin D
   c. Vitamin C
   d. All of the above

5. In comparison with energy needs, the requirements for proteins, vitamins, and minerals in pregnancy:
   a. Increase to a greater extent
   b. Increase to the same extent
   c. Increase to a lesser extent

6. A safe daily level of alcohol intake during pregnancy is equivalent to
   a. About 3 ounces of pure alcohol
   b. About 2 to 3 ounces of pure alcohol
   c. About 1 to 2 ounces of pure alcohol
   d. Is not known

7. Restricting which of the following in the mother's diet will reduce its concentration in her milk?
   a. Fluid
   b. Energy
   c. Protein
   d. Vitamin A

8. During lactation:
   a. No vitamin or mineral supplements are necessary for the mother
   b. Iron supplements should be continued to build up mother's stores
   c. Milk intake should return to prepregnancy levels
   d. Caloric requirements are lower than during pregnancy

True-False

1. The mother's diet prior to conception is as important as that during pregnancy.
2. Because energy needs increase during pregnancy, it is a good time to go on a

weight-loss diet.

3. If a pregnant woman develops edema, she should reduce her salt intake.
4. Iron needs during pregnancy cannot be met solely by food.
5. Some of the body weight gained during pregnancy can be lost during lactation.
6. Commercial infant formulas are inadequate to meet an infant's nutritional needs.
7. Depending on the mother's choice of foods, breast-feeding can be less costly than bottle-feeding.

SUGGESTED ACTIVITIES

1. Compare the cost of breast- and bottle-feeding. For the purposes of this exercise, choose foods for the lactating woman that will meet the following RDAs:

Energy:	An additional 500 kcal/day
Protein:	An additional 20 g/day
Vitamin A:	An additional 400 RE/day (2000 IU/day)
Vitamin C:	An additional 40 mg/day
Thiamine:	An additional 0.5 mg/day
Calcium:	An additional 400 mg/day

   a. Select a variety of more expensive foods to meet these needs (e.g., expensive cuts of meat, milk, cheese, and more expensive grain, fruit, and vegetable products). What is the cost per day?
   b. Select a variety of less expensive foods to meet these needs (e.g., cheaper cuts of meat, powdered milk, meat-substitute dishes, and less expensive grain, fruit, and vegetable products). What is the cost per day?
   c. What is the cost of 850 milliliters of a commercial formula such as Similac or Enfamil? Note that this neglects the cost of bottles. You can add in the cost of three disposable bottles per day as well. How does the cost compare with that of the extra foods chosen for the lactating woman in parts *a* and *b*?

2. Collect myths about food and pregnancy. Refute as many as you can using this Further Reading, and library resources.

FURTHER READING

1. Several more detailed discussions of nutrition during pregnancy and lactation are available:

Worthington, B. S., Vermeersch, J., and Williams, S. R.: *Nutrition in Pregnancy and Lactation,* Mosby, St. Louis, 1977.
Hurley, L. S.: *Developmental Nutrition,* Prentice-Hall, Englewood Cliffs, N.J., 1980.
Luke, B.: *Maternal Nutrition,* Little, Brown, Boston, 1979.

2. A readable description of lactation and breast-feeding:

Psiaki, D., and Olson, C.: *Current Knowledge on Breast-Feeding,* Cornell University Cooperative Extension, Ithaca, N.Y., 1977. Costs $2.50 from Division of Nutritional Sciences, Cornell University, Ithaca, N.Y.

3. An up-to-date summary of the effects of alcohol on the outcome of pregnancy:

Streissguth, A. P., Landesman-Dwyer, S., Martin, J. C., and Smith, D. W.: "Teratogenic Effects of Alcohol in Humans and Laboratory Animals," *Science* **209:**353–361 (1980).

4. A readable survey of the effects of oral contraceptives on nutritional status:

Massey, L. K., and Davison, M. A.: "Effects of Oral Contraceptives on Nutritional Status," *American Family Physician* **19:**119–123 (January 1979).

Infancy, Childhood, Adolescence

After an uneventful pregnancy, Meg Gerard gave birth to a 7-pound 9-ounce girl. The baby, named Kelly, joined two other children in the Gerard family: Kenneth, 13 years old, and Susan, 8 years old. Because each of the children has different nutritional needs and different attitudes toward food, providing an adequate diet for them sometimes becomes a problem. This chapter examines how a family such as the Gerards can tackle the problem of feeding its children. We will look at nutritional requirements at different ages and the factors that influence them, as well as the means by which these needs can be met. We also will consider several questions frequently asked about nutrition during the developing years, such as when to introduce solid food, the effect of food on hyperactivity and allergies, and whether sound nutrition can improve athletic performance.

Infancy: Starting Out

Infancy is a period of intense growth and development; the infant gains both height and weight faster than during any other stage of the life cycle (1) (Figure 12-1). Growth can be monitored by plotting height and weight on charts such as that shown in Figure 12-2. Weight generally doubles by 4 to 6 months and triples by the end of the first year, while height increases by 50 percent in the first year and doubles by the third to fourth year.

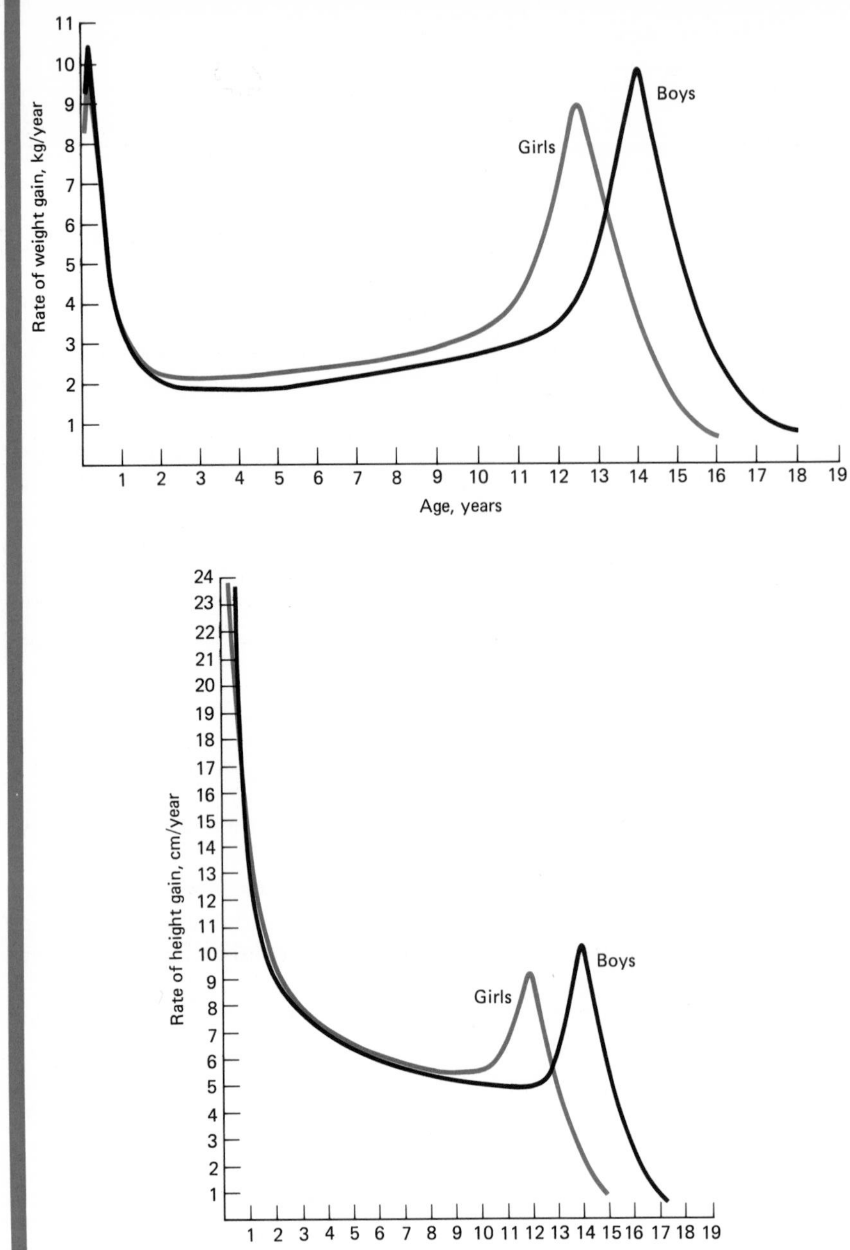

FIGURE 12-1 *Rate of Weight and Height Gain during the Growing Years.* The rate of growth is slower during childhood than during infancy, but it accelerates during adolescence. [*Source:* J. M. Tanner, R. H. Whitehouse, and M. Takaishi, "Standards from Birth to Maturity for Height, Weight, Height Velocity, and Weight Velocity: British Children, 1965" *Archives of Diseases in Children* **41**:454–471 (1966). Used with permission.]

The growth in height and weight are accompanied by changes in tissues and organs within the body. Bones lengthen, and calcium and phosphate are deposited in them. Muscles grow in size and strength. In addition, the brain and nervous system grow until the second year or so (3), while the digestive tract and the kidneys require several months to mature (2, pages 95–108; 4, pages 224–277).

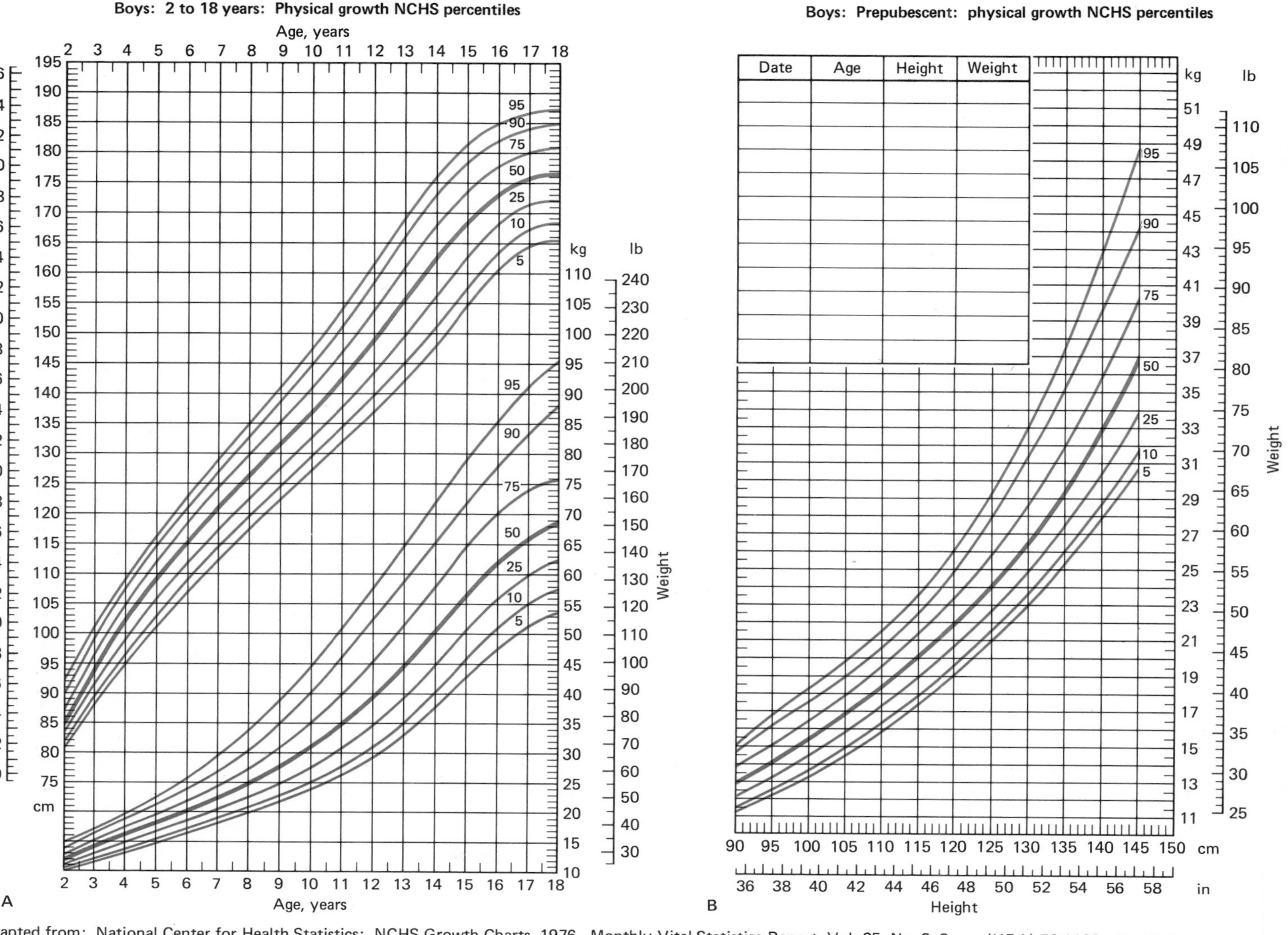

Adapted from: National Center for Health Statistics: NCHS Growth Charts, 1976. Monthly Vital Statistics Report. Vol. 25, No. 3, Supp. (HRA) 76-1120. Health Resources Administration, Rockville, Maryland, June, 1976. Data from the National Center for Health Statistics. © 1976 ROSS LABORATORIES

FIGURE 12-2 *A Growth Chart.* Length and weight are plotted against age as the child grows to compare his or her development with established standards. (Courtesy of Ross Laboratories, Columbus, Ohio.)

The concept of a critical period in which tissue or organ development is particularly susceptible to the effects of malnutrition applies to infancy as well as to gestation. For example, protein-energy malnutrition during early infancy can retard nervous system development, which may in part be responsible for impaired mental capacity later in life (3,5). Some researchers also believe infancy is a critical period for fat-cell development, and overfeeding at this time may lead to a greater number of fat cells than normal.

INFANT GROWTH AND NUTRITIONAL REQUIREMENTS

The rapid growth and development of a healthy baby creates a high demand for nutrients (Ready Reference 3). On a per unit of body weight basis, the nutritional requirements of a 1-year-old are considerably higher than those of an adult (see Figure 10-1). For example, the energy RDA per kilogram of body weight for a 1-year-old is more than 2½ times that of a 23- to 50-year-old male (6). This in part results from a higher basal metabolic rate in infants, which is due to their larger surface area per unit of body weight and larger proportion of metabolically active tissue (7, pages 753–754). Physical activity also contributes to an infant's energy requirement; crying, for example, can almost double a baby's energy needs (7, pages 753–754).

The protein requirement relative to body weight is also high in infancy. This is so because protein is an important building block for growing tissues: during the first year of life, the protein content of the body increases from 11.4 to 14.6 percent and body weight rises by almost 7 kilograms (2, pages 68–69). The Food and Nutrition Board recommends an intake of 2.2 g/kg of body weight of high-quality protein for infants up to 6 months of age and 2.0 g/kg of body weight between the ages of 6 months to 1 year (6). According to another authority, infants should obtain between 7 and 16 percent of their kilocalories from protein (2, page 376). However, it is important not to overdo it, because the excess amino acids are catabolized for energy and the nitrogen contained in them is converted to urea for excretion by the kidney (see Chapter 5). This can accelerate water loss via the urine and increase the chance of dehydration (8, page 29).

Fat and carbohydrate are needed to provide energy for the infant. Fat should contribute 30 to 55 percent of the caloric intake, with carbohydrate making up 40 to 65 percent of the energy needs (2, page 376). Fats also supply the essential fatty acids needed for growth and healthy skin. The American Academy of Pediatrics recommends that linoleic acid contribute at least 2.7 percent of the kilocalories in infant formulas (9).

Infants have relatively high requirements for vitamins (6). The RDA for vitamin A, 400 to 420 RE/day (2000 to 2100 IU/day) can easily be met by the diet. The need for vitamin D depends on the baby's exposure to sunlight. Since infants less than 1 year of age generally do not receive much sun, their entire RDA of 10 μg/day (400 IU/day) should be provided by food (2, page 216). However, care must be taken not to overdose the infant with vitamin D and vitamin A, because excess intake of these vitamins is toxic. The vitamin E allowance is 3 to 4 mg/day of *d*-alpha-tocopherol or the equivalent (4.5 to 6.0 IU/day). Because of the low rate of transfer of vitamin E across the placenta, premature infants may have unusually low blood levels of this vitamin. They require somewhat more in their diet, especially if their intake of polyunsaturated fat is high (8, page 47). A provisional allowance of 10 to 20 μg/day of vitamin K has been established (6). Many infants, particularly those who are breast-fed, develop a moderate vitamin K deficiency 2 to 3 days after birth. An injection of vitamin K prevents this problem (2, page 223).

Except in certain circumstances, the allowances for the water-soluble vitamins can be easily met by the diet. For example, infants born to women who take large doses of vitamin C may become conditioned to a greater need for this vitamin. In two reports, these babies developed scurvy when fed the recommended levels of vitamin C after birth (10). In addition, large doses of vitamin B_6 administered during infancy sometimes reverse the effects of certain hereditary errors of metabolism involving amino acids (7, page 777).

Although the allowances for minerals relative to body weight are generally higher in infancy than in adulthood, certain elements are particularly important. Calcium and phosphorus are needed for the mineralization of bone. The RDAs (Ready Reference 3) reflect a recommended Ca:P ratio of 1.5:1. Expansion of blood volume, as well as tissue growth, requires substantial amounts of iron. Recent surveys indicate that iron-deficiency anemia is relatively common among infants, particularly those from lower socioeconomic groups (11,12). The zinc requirement of the infant is not known precisely, but evidence of zinc deficiency has been uncovered among preschool children in Denver, Colorado (13). Taste perception was impaired in these children, and they had not grown as much as children receiving adequate dietary zinc. The infant's need for iodine reflects this element's role as a component of the thyroid hormone in promoting growth and development. Fluoride is required for the development and maintenance of strong bones and teeth. Because excess sodium may contribute to the development of high blood pressure later in life and the intake of this element by most infants greatly exceeds the requirement, the American Academy of Pediatrics has recommended reducing salt intake (14).

Maintaining water balance is especially important during infancy. Water losses tend to be relatively high because the immature kidneys cannot adequately concentrate the urine and the relatively large surface area of the body allows proportionally more water to evaporate from the skin (8, pages 62–63). Water requirements range as high as 160 g/kg of body weight/day during the first year of life (8, pages 62–63). Thus an infant weighing 15 pounds should obtain more than a quart of water from the diet each day.

MEETING NUTRITIONAL NEEDS

Meg had decided to breast-feed Kelly. Because lactation will increase her nutrient requirements, she must pay close attention to her own diet (see Chapter 11). Breast milk is sufficient to meet her baby's needs during the first 5 to 6 months of life. However, many authorities recommend supplementing it with iron, vitamin D, and fluoride (5). There is no rigid rule for the number of times an infant should be fed each day; feeding the baby on a self-demand schedule promotes milk production, prevents breast engorgement, and results in better weight gain by the infant (16, page 167). Meg has contacted the local chapter of the LaLeche League for other information on breast-feeding techniques as well as diet.

One of Meg's friends, Kathy, has a 2-month-old boy she is bottle-feeding. The formula has been specially prepared to meet the infant's nutritional needs up to about the sixth month of life. Kathy has been careful to dilute the formula properly, sterilize the bottles and formula before use, and keep opened, unused formula covered and refrigerated. Some mothers prefer not to sterilize the formula before use; they thoroughly wash their hands and all equipment to be used, prepare the formula immediately before feeding, and store opened, unused formula in the refrigerator. Any formula remaining in the bottle after feeding is discarded (7, page 765).

FOCUS 12-1 COMMERCIAL VERSUS HOMEMADE BABY FOODS Commercially prepared baby foods can be a part of a healthy diet for an infant. They are convenient, and most are nutritious (Table 12-1). Some commercial baby foods have been criticized because of their relatively high caloric, sugar, and salt contents, as well as the presence of certain food additives, such as **modified starch**, nitrates and nitrites, and monosodium glutamate (MSG). However, foods high in kilocalories, such as desserts, can be avoided, and plain vegetables, which contain fewer kilocalories, can be substituted for creamed vegetables. In addition, manufacturers have reduced the salt and sugar contents of most of their products in recent years (17). Nitrates, nitrites, and monosodium glutamate have been eliminated from commercial baby foods because of potential adverse effects (17) (see Chapter 10). Available evidence on modified food starches indicates no toxicity, even at levels above those currently used in infant food. However, their major benefit is to improve the texture and consistency of the food (79). The product label can be consulted to determine whether sugar is a major ingredient and salt and other undesirable substances have been added.

Many families prefer to make their own baby foods with a blender. Sanitation is an important consideration (78). Use only fresh and wholesome foods; canned varieties usually contain added salt, sugar, or unwanted food additives. Utensils must be washed thoroughly in scalding water, and all foods must be carefully washed and well-cooked. Do not taste the foods and put the spoon back in them. Store prepared baby foods in the freezer; do not keep them longer than 1 month. It is important not to defrost and refreeze the foods. Because of its high nitrate content, fresh spinach should not be fed to infants younger than 3 months of age. When stored for 4 days at room temperature or for a longer period under refrigeration, nitrates in the spinach are converted into nitrites. The nitrites react with hemoglobin in the blood to form methemoglobin, a compound that cannot carry oxygen. In some infants, enough hemoglobin has undergone this transformation to cause serious injury or even death (80).

TABLE **12-1**

Average caloric distribution of commercial infant foods

STRAINED FOODS	ENERGY, kcal/100 g	Percent of Kilocalories from		
		PROTEIN	CARBOHYDRATE	FAT
Egg yolks	192	21	3	76
Meats	106	53	1	46
Desserts and puddings	96	4	89	7
Fruits	85	2	96	2
High-meat dinners	84	29	24	47
Fruit juices	65	2	96	2
Creamed vegetables	63	13	74	13
Soups and dinners	58	16	56	28
Plain vegetables	45	14	80	6

Source: T. A. Anderson, "Commercial Infant Foods: Content and Composition," *Pediatr. Clin. North Am.* **24**:37–47, 1977. (Used with permission.)

INTRODUCING SOLID FOODS

Both Meg and Kathy would like to know when it is best to introduce solid food into their babies' diets. The trend throughout the twentieth century has been to do so at a progressively earlier age; in 1920, solid foods seldom were given before 1 year of age; now many infants receive their first solid foods within the first month of life (17). However, there are no nutritional or psychological benefits to be gained by this practice, and most authorities believe that human milk or commercial formulas are sufficient to meet nutritional needs until about 5 or 6 months of age (2, pages 408–409; 15).

In practice, the time at which the infant will accept solid foods varies from individual to individual. The introduction of solids should be determined by the baby's stage of development rather than by its age (19). By 5 to 6 months, milk can no longer meet the caloric needs of most infants, and iron reserves are being depleted (20). The child's sucking pattern has changed, so it is less likely to expel food from its mouth (19). In addition, the baby can now sit with support, has head and neck control, and can more freely communicate its willingness to accept solid foods (17). The infant will show desire for food by opening its mouth and leaning forward and its disinterest or satiety by leaning back and turning away. Until the infant can express these feelings, feeding it solid foods may be a form of

Introducing solid foods depends on a baby's stage of development rather than on its chronological age.

forced feeding. Hand-to-mouth coordination is also good in many infants this age, so they are able to grasp soft foods and move them to their mouths. By the fifth or sixth month, the digestive tract and kidneys also have matured, and the kidneys can handle the increased solute load created by solid foods (4, pages 245–272). There also is less likelihood of developing a food allergy by this time (2, page 455; 17).

When the introduction of solid foods is delayed until 5 to 6 months of age, the order in which new foods are introduced seems to be of little importance (15). In the United States and western Europe, cereals are generally the first solid foods given to infants (2, pages 408–409). These should be fortified with iron; if not, iron supplements should be given. Fruits, especially applesauce and bananas, and yellow vegetables are generally favored by infants, but spinach, beets, and meats often are not. New foods should be introduced one at a time and in small amounts. Generally, not more than one or two new items should be tried in one week (15). They should never be forced on an infant; if the child rejects a new food at first, the food may be tried again later. If the baby continually rejects a particular item, another can be substituted for it.

Many foods commonly fed to infants, such as cereals, fruits, and mashed potatoes, provide most of their energy in the form of carbohydrate. Infants receiving breast milk and these solid foods need some other sources of protein in the diet, such as meat and egg yolk. If cow's milk or evaporated milk is substituted for human milk or formula at this time, vitamin C should be provided as a supplement or in the form of a fruit or juice containing the vitamin. Fruit juices and other sweet drinks should be fed by cup rather than by bottle, because bottle-feeding these foods can lead to tooth decay (15). Fluoride should be given to all infants at a level dependent on the amount found in the local water supply, and vitamin D supplementation should be continued for babies who are both breast-fed and are receiving solid foods (15).

Vitamin D–fortified whole milk can be fed to infants beginning at about 1 year of life. Prior to that time, whole cow's milk leads to increased loss of blood from the digestive tract, which may result in anemia (15). Feeding skim milk or low-fat (2 percent) milk during infancy is not recommended because neither supplies enough energy to support proper weight gain (15).

TABLE FOODS

Table foods, as well as commercial and homemade infant foods, can be introduced during the first year of life (8, pages 112–115). The time at which these foods are first given to the baby depends on its stage of development. Teeth begin to erupt at about 5 to 7 months of age (4, page 202), and the child can sit up with support, can grasp food, and shows rudimentary chewing movements. Finger-feeding with whole-wheat crackers (without salt) and whole-wheat toast can begin at this time. By 7 to 8 months, the child can sit up without support, its grasp is stronger, and its movements are more coordinated. More table foods can be added: grapefruit and orange sections, other cooked fruits and vegetables, corn bread, and bite-sized pieces of cheese. Raw vegetables, such as carrots or celery, should not be given at this time, because the infant may not chew them sufficiently to avoid choking. However, foods should not be overcooked. By the end of the first year, the child should be eating a variety of foods from the table.

LONG-TERM EFFECTS OF NUTRITION DURING INFANCY

Proper nutrition during infancy plays an important role in the child's health and well-being later in life. Malnutrition can impair growth and mental development, and atherosclerosis and obesity may have their roots in infancy. In addition, an individual's taste preferences and attitudes toward food are in part formed at this time.

Malnutrition, Growth, and Mental Development Malnutrition during infancy profoundly affects physical growth: malnourished children tend to be shorter and lower in weight than well-fed children. Depending on the timing, severity, nature, and duration of the deficiency, the effects may be permanent (24). Often, however, correction of the deficiency results in rapid catch-up growth, and the child may attain its normal height and weight (24).

Many studies show that protein-energy malnutrition during infancy can permanently reduce mental performance, possibly because it interferes with development of the nervous system during a critical period (3,5,21–23). Nutritional deficiency after the first year may affect a child's ability to learn, to pay attention, and to sustain interest in learning activities, but these can be reversed by improving the diet (24). In most cases, however, it is difficult to separate the effects of malnutrition from other factors, such as a lack of environmental and social stimuli and unresponsiveness of the mother (23). A stimulating learning environment can help overcome mental impairment resulting from malnutrition; without it a child cannot live up to its full potential no matter how well-fed that child may be.

Atherosclerosis In recent years it has been recognized that the roots of atherosclerosis may lie in infancy (see Chapter 3). Fatty streaks are found in the arteries of nearly all 3- to 5-month-old infants, but it is not certain if these progress to atherosclerosis later in life (32). More important may be the establishment in infancy of eating patterns that contribute at a later time to the development of atherosclerosis. However, because the effectiveness of dietary intervention in the prevention and treatment of atherosclerosis is still highly controversial (see Chapter 3), the American Academy of Pediatrics recommends against major dietary changes for all infants. Only those with a genetic predisposition toward high blood lipid levels should eat a diet lower in lipids, and then not before 1 year of age (33). However, because of the association of excess sodium intake with high blood pressure, frequent intake of highly salted foods, such as potato chips, should be discouraged, and salt should not be added to infant foods prepared at home. Physical activity, such as crawling and playing, should be encouraged.

FOOD ALLERGIES

Allergies to food are commonly reported in infants and children. Symptoms include vomiting, abdominal pain, diarrhea, malabsorption of nutrients, shock, coughing and other respiratory difficulties, rashes, such as "hives" and eczema, headache, apathy, irritability, other behavioral changes, and retarded growth (2, pages 435–458). The most common offender is milk, but chocolate, cola, corn, wheat, eggs, legumes (especially peanuts), citrus fruits, tomato, cinnamon, and certain food additives such as tartrazine (FD&C yellow No. 5) also produce reactions (34).

Food diaries and elimination diets are frequently used to identify the food producing the allergy. The elimination diet restricts food intake to those items which are known to cause no reaction in most children. If there is a remission of symptoms, new foods are added gradually at intervals of 5 to 7 days and the child is watched for reactions. Because of the restrictive nature of the diet, it should be attempted only under the supervision of a qualified physician. If it lasts for very long, nutrient intake must be monitored.

ISSUE: FAT INFANTS, FAT ADULTS

"One of the major controversies currently involving obesity is whether obese infants grow up to become obese children and obese adults. A number of studies have found this to be true, and a mechanism that postulates an increase in fat-cell number as a result of overfeeding has been proposed (25,26) (see Chapter 5). Bottle-feeding and early introduction of solid foods also have been implicated as contributing factors (35). However, the experimental evidence supporting these hypotheses is far from conclusive, and many authorities regard the "fat-cell hypothesis" as an oversimplification of what actually happens (25,27–29). They contend that there is no evidence that the excess fat cells found in obese adults were formed during infancy and believe that infant obesity is only one of many factors contributing to obesity later in life (25,29).

Some research indicates that breast-feeding for at least 3 months and introducing solid foods no earlier than 4 to 5 months may be useful in preventing obesity (28,85,86). However, other studies show no difference in the amount of food consumed, the incidence of breast-feeding, or the time of introduction of solid foods between obese and nonobese infants (30,31). These researchers suggest that infant obesity may result from a genetic predisposition or because these babies are less active than others (30,31). Even so, an infant should not be forced to finish a bottle or eat more solid food than it wants to (28).

If the infant becomes obese, it should not be placed on a weight-loss diet. Because the child's demand for nutrients is high, dietary restrictions may inhibit growth or produce nutritional deficiencies (28). Slowing the rate of weight gain so that it is more in line with the increase in height is more desirable. This should be done only under the supervision of a qualified physician or dietitian (28)."

Childhood

Susan Gerard is a healthy, active 8-year-old. Like most children her age, she is asserting her independence and is gradually assuming more control over her diet. Susan refuses to eat some foods her parents offer her and often tries to pressure them into buying certain foods when they take her shopping. She also receives a small allowance which she is free to spend on food. At the same time, influences outside the family, including television and other advertising, her friends, and her school, are helping to shape Susan's food habits. Providing an adequate diet for her, therefore, becomes a complicated problem. In this section we will look at the nutritional needs of childhood, some of the factors that influence the ability to meet these needs, and how an adequate diet can be provided for children such as Susan.

GROWTH AND NUTRITIONAL NEEDS DURING CHILDHOOD

Although children between the ages of 2 and 10 to 12 years continue to grow, they do so at a slower rate than during infancy (1) (Figure 12-1). The rate of weight gain declines rapidly during the second year of life and then gradually increases again until the adolescent growth spurt begins at age 10 to 12. The rate of increase in height also drops rapidly until age 2, after which it declines more slowly until adolescence. Most tissues and organs also continue to grow during childhood. For example, the bones lengthen and calcify, muscles grow larger, and blood volume expands. The digestive tract and its associated organs also increase in size.

The pattern of growth during childhood results in nutritional requirements which, on a per kilogram of body weight basis, are lower than during infancy but generally higher than in adulthood (6) (see Figure 10-1). On a whole-body basis, however, nutritional requirements increase during childhood as the body increases in size (6) (Ready Reference 3). Energy needs rise as the child grows and becomes more active. More protein is needed to support a larger body, as well as tissue growth. Vitamins and minerals also are required in larger amounts.

MEETING NUTRITIONAL NEEDS

The first 10 to 12 years of life is a time when children begin to establish themselves as independent people, and the physical and emotional changes through which they go have an important influence on their total food intake and their choice of foods. A majority of parents find that appetite tends to decrease between the ages of 2 and 4 and may remain erratic for several years (35,36) (Figure 12-3). The child may eat well for one meal or for several days and then become finicky and eat poorly for a period of time (36). Many children dawdle and play with their food (35). Loss of appetite and disinterest in food may be because of the reduced growth rate, a greater impact of distractions from the environment, and the efforts of the child to establish an identity (35). Most parents worry that the child is not receiving enough food, but the stage appears to be a normal one for children to go through.

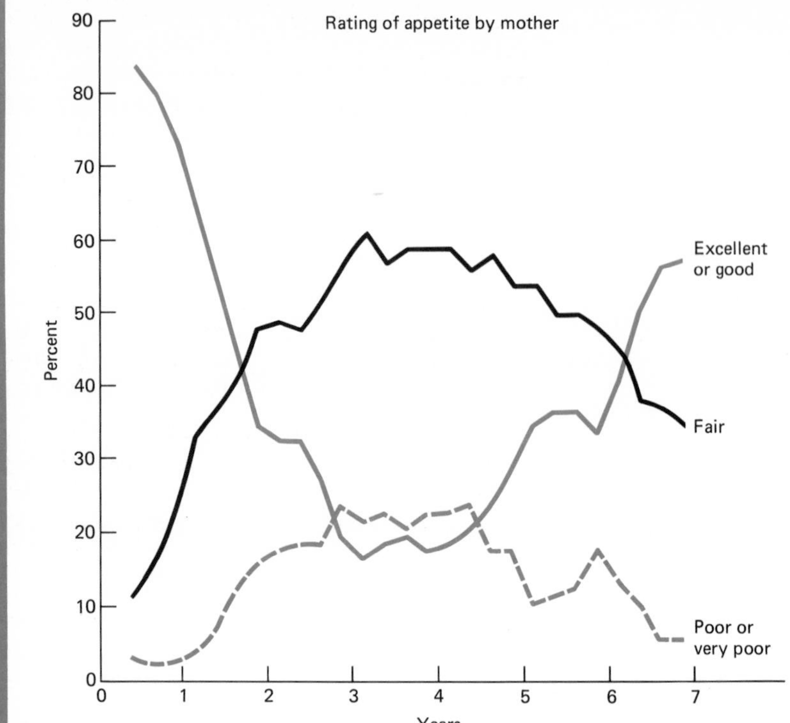

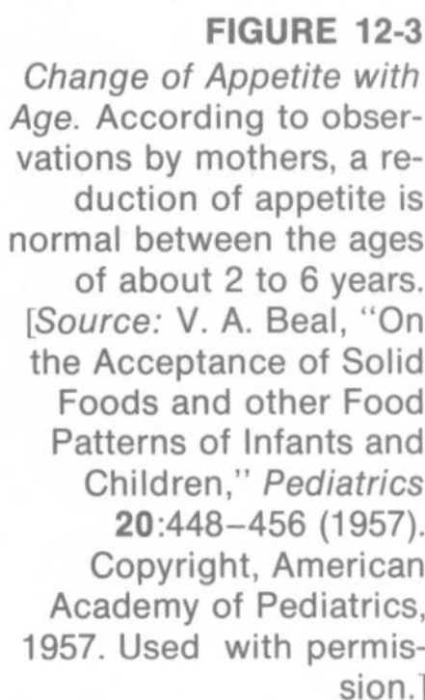

FIGURE 12-3 *Change of Appetite with Age.* According to observations by mothers, a reduction of appetite is normal between the ages of about 2 to 6 years. [*Source:* V. A. Beal, "On the Acceptance of Solid Foods and other Food Patterns of Infants and Children," *Pediatrics* **20**:448–456 (1957). Copyright, American Academy of Pediatrics, 1957. Used with permission.]

A variety of factors, including parents, other children, television, day-care centers, and schools, influence a child's food intake and help shape its food habits as well. Some of these eating patterns are short-lived. Others, however, last a lifetime.

Parents Because children are dependent on their parents for the foods they consume at home, parental influences strongly affect food intake. Many studies have shown that the mother is the "gate-keeper"; in a majority of households, she decides which foods to buy and how they are to be prepared (8, pages 119–131; 35). However, fathers, through their influence on what mothers purchase, also affect what comes into the house (37). In addition, as social values change, men are assuming more of the responsibility for shopping and food preparation. The level of the parent's education is another important influence on providing a nutritious diet. One study found that the better-educated the mother was, the higher the content of calcium, iron, thiamine, riboflavin, and vitamin C in her child's diet (35). Mothers who were less knowledgeable about nutrition were more permissive about what their children consumed, and increased permissiveness was related to a lower content of all nutrients except fat in the child's diet (35).

Parental attitudes also influence eating patterns. Parents who eat a variety of foods and who practice proper eating habits at the table provide a good example for their children to follow. Depending on how the situation is approached, mealtime and eating can take on a positive meaning of love, support, and togetherness, or it can become associated with a fear of punishment and conflict with the parents. Battling with children to clean their plates, drink their milk, or use their utensils in a certain way may establish unfavorable attitudes toward eating that last into adulthood. In addition, rewarding a child's good behavior with food and punishing bad behavior by witholding it may create an association of food with approval and feeling good. This can establish a pattern of turning to eating as a primary source of satisfaction (38).

Other Children Youngsters often model themselves after other children, especially older brothers and sisters, and they often pick up the same likes, dislikes, and food habits. In addition, children may coerce parents into buying a particular food item simply because other children eat it (8, pages 119–131).

Television Children spend a lot of time watching television: nearly every American home has a television set, and according to a Nielsen survey in 1975, preschool children watched about 54 h/week (39). Older children, up to the age of 17, averaged 3 to 4 h/day, and almost 3 hours on Saturday morning (39,40). As a result, commercial programming has a powerful influence on children's eating patterns.

FIGURE 12-4 Brothers and sisters, as well as parents, influence a child's choice of food. (Photograph by Barbara Alper, Stock, Boston, Inc.)

Unfortunately, the impact of television advertisements on children's food habits has been largely negative (41–43). Studies show that breakfast cereals, many of which are highly sweetened, are most frequently advertised, followed by candies and other sweets (41,42). Sugar-containing foods are promoted as a source of quick energy, and little attempt is made to include other foods in the commercials to show that these are important in a nutritious diet. Sensory qualities rather than nutritiousness of foods are emphasized (41,42).

Younger children are the most likely to believe that television advertisements tell the truth (40). Kindergarteners often cannot differentiate commercials from the rest of the program. As they grow older, children become much more suspicious of the advertisements (8, pages 119–131). Nevertheless, one study found that fifth and sixth graders believed 70 percent of the commercials they saw, prompting a statement by the researchers that 70 percent of all health messages on television were not true, but 70 percent of those messages are believed by children (44).

In many cases, television commercials can influence children to buy products with their own money (40). In addition, children exert a strong influence on what their parents buy. One study found that 88 percent of the mothers surveyed yielded to their 5- to 7-year-old children's requests for breakfast cereals, 52 percent yielded to requests for snacks, and about 40 percent gave in on requests for candy and soft drinks (41). Another survey found a strong relationship between the number of requests the child made and the number of times the mother yielded (40).

Many authorities believe food advertising aimed at children is having a negative effect on their nutritional status and their present and future health (42,43). Because the commercials emphasize criteria other than nutritiousness for choosing a food, they distort children's ideas about what is good to eat. Advertising heavily sweetened breakfast cereals fortified with vitamins and minerals and beverages fortified with vitamin C also downplays the importance of obtaining nutrients from a variety of foods. Consuming too many high-kilocalorie foods contributes to obesity, while excess sugar has been shown to cause tooth decay and may contribute to other health problems (see Chapter 2).

Although current television advertising practices are unsound nutritionally, they are an effective marketing device and therefore may be expected to continue. Some concerned educational organizations have developed public service messages to counter these advertisements (45). Consumer pressure has forced some modifications, such as the removal of vitamin-supplement advertisements from children's programming (8, pages 119–131). Parents also can play a role by paying attention to the programs their children watch, pointing out the fallacies in the advertising, and not always yielding to children's requests for advertised products of questionable nutritional value.

School Because they provide meals and snacks outside the home and are involved (or not involved!) in nutrition education, day-care centers and schools contribute to children's food intake and help shape eating

TABLE **12-2**

School lunch pattern—approximate per lunch minimums

COMPONENTS		MINIMUM QUANTITIES				RECOMMENDED QUANTITIES
		GROUP I, AGE 1–2 (PRESCHOOL)	GROUP II, AGE 3–4 (PRESCHOOL)	GROUP III, AGE 5–8 (K–3)	GROUP IV, AGE 9 AND OLDER (4–12)	GROUP V, 12 YEARS AND OLDER (7–12[2])
Milk	Unflavored, fluid lowfat, skim, or buttermilk must be offered[1]	3/4 cup (6 fl oz)	3/4 cup (6 fl oz)	1/2 pint (8 fl oz)	1/2 pint (8 fl oz)	1/2 pint (8 fl oz)
Meat or Meat Alternate (quantity of the edible portion as served)	Lean meat, poultry, or fish	1 oz	1 1/2 oz	1 1/2 oz	2 oz	3 oz
	Cheese	1 oz	1 1/2 oz	1 1/2 oz	2 oz	3 oz
	Large egg	1	1 1/2	1 1/2	2	3
	Cooked dry beans or peas	1/2 cup	3/4 cup	3/4 cup	1 cup	1 1/2 cup
	Peanut butter or an equivalent quantity of any combination of any of above	2 Tbsp	3 Tbsp	3 Tbsp	4 Tbsp	6 Tbsp
Vegetable or Fruit	2 or more servings of vegetable or fruit or both	1/2 cup	1/2 cup	1/2 cup	3/4 cup	3/4 cup
Bread or Bread Alternate (servings per week)	Must be enriched or whole grain—at least 1 1/2 serving[3] for group I or one serving[3] for groups II–V must be served daily	5	8	8	8	10

[1] If a school serves another form of milk (whole or flavored), it must offer its children unflavored fluid lowfat milk, skim milk, or buttermilk as a beverage choice.

[2] The minimum portion sizes for these children are the portion sizes for group IV.

[3] Serving 1 slice of bread or 1/2 cup of cooked rice, macaroni, noodles, other pasta products, other cereal product such as bulgur and corn grits, or as stated in the Food Buying Guide for biscuits, rolls, muffins, and similar products.

Source: Code of Federal Regulations, Title 7, Section 210.10, 1981.

habits. Lunches, which are frequently obtained from the school, supply about one-third of the day's caloric intake (about 800 kilocalories for a 10-year-old child) (46), so it is important that the foods be of high nutritional quality. A federally funded program, the School Lunch Program, provides these foods. Its offerings are shown in Table 12-2, and depending on financial need, students pay full or reduced prices or receive the food free (47). Another federal program, the School Breakfast Program, helps ensure that participants receive a nutritious breakfast. A minimum of 1 cup of milk, ½ cup of fruit, vegetable, or full-strength vegetable or fruit juice, and 1 slice of whole-wheat or enriched bread or 1 ounce of fortified cereal or the equivalent are provided per day (48). Younger children receive smaller amounts of food. Breakfast, lunch, supper, and supplemental foods are supplied to children in day-care centers under the Child-Care Food Program (49).

The federal food programs can serve as a vehicle for nutrition education (50). With teacher support, they can help develop wholesome attitudes toward food as well as proper eating habits. Student involvement in menu planning can increase the acceptability of food items and reduce waste. Some imaginative programs, including introduction of a modified fast-food menu, have met with success.

Attempts by the Reagan administration to reduce federal spending will probably have profound effects on child-feeding programs during the early 1980s. For example, proposed budget cuts will reduce the number of children who qualify for free lunches, raise the prices other students must pay for lunch, and perhaps alter the standards specifying types of foods that must be served.

PROVIDING AN ADEQUATE DIET

By 1 year of age, a child is eating a variety of foods from the family table. New foods can be introduced at home and in day-care centers in many ways. However, in all cases it is important for children to actively participate in the educational experiences. They should be allowed to feed themselves as much as possible, even though they may spill food. Finger-feeding will help introduce children to the size and texture of foods. Introducing new items with the help of pictures, stories, and games may promote more positive attitudes toward food. As children grow older, they can participate in preparing foods. Fruit or vegetable salads, sandwiches, soups, pudding, cookies, and bread are examples of foods young children can help prepare.

During the second year of life, parents can begin using the Basic Four Food Plan as the foundation of an adequate diet for the child. At least 3 cups of milk, 2 servings of meat, 4 servings of fruits and vegetables, and 3 servings of cereals and grains are recommended. Serving sizes must be tailored to the child's size and appetite. New foods should not be forced; it is important that mealtime be relaxed and enjoyable. If the child dislikes a food, a new one can be substituted for it, and it can be reintroduced at a later time. Giving only small amounts at first, such as a teaspoonful, also may increase the chance of acceptance.

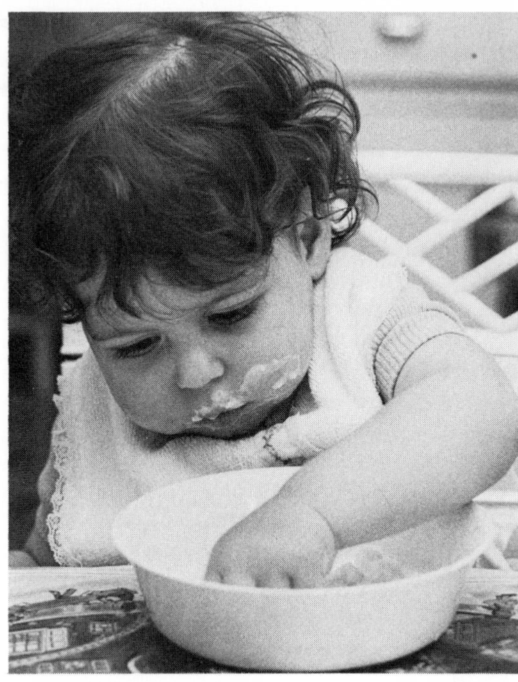

FIGURE 12-5
Finger-feeding is a way young children can be encouraged to feed themselves and to try new foods. (Photograph by Erika Stone, Photo Researchers, Inc.)

As children approach adolescence, they become more independent in their eating behavior. They tend to eat away from home more often. Because they are more active, it is harder to get them to sit down and eat a whole meal. Snacks form a significant part of a school-age child's food intake. Good food habits established earlier in childhood, the providing of nutritious meals by school and parents, and a certain amount of parental patience can help ensure adequate nutrient intake.

It is important that children eat a good breakfast. Studies have shown that omitting breakfast lowers mental and physical efficiency, maximum work rate and output, and scholastic performance in the late-morning hours (51). Breakfast should supply up to one-fifth of the day's caloric intake, and the foods need not be limited to traditional items, such as juice, cereal, eggs, pancakes, or toast. Other nutritious foods, including cheese, peanut butter, and pieces of fruit, can provide an excellent beginning to a day.

Proper snacking is also vital. Since snacks provide 20 percent or more of a child's energy needs, it is important that those kilocalories be accompanied by significant quantities of other nutrients. Nutritious cookies, fruits (including raisins), fruit juices, and peanut butter should be consumed instead of highly sweetened baked goods, candy, and soft drinks.

VEGETARIAN DIETS FOR CHILDREN

As more people have turned to vegetarianism as an alternative to the traditional American diet, questions have arisen about the adequacy of vegetarian diets for growing children (52). In general, the more restrictive the diet, the more difficult it is to meet nutritional needs. Sufficient quantities of most nutrients are supplied by a lacto-ovo-vegetarian diet. For example, dairy products, eggs, and combinations of plant proteins provide protein and the dairy products contain needed calcium, phosphorus, riboflavin, and, if fortified, vitamin A and vitamin D. However, the lack of meat could lead to iron and zinc deficiencies. Legumes, some green, leafy and other vegetables, whole- or enriched-grain products, some nuts, and dried fruit can be used to supply iron. Nuts, beans, wheat germ, and cheese provide zinc (see Chapter 8).

Totally vegetarian diets increase the difficulties of meeting nutritional needs. Mothers should seriously consider breast-feeding their infants to ensure an intake of high-quality protein, but if not, fortified soy-based formulas normally given to infants who cannot handle milk can be used for babies of vegetarian parents. Care must be taken to provide adequate caloric intake and to complement plant proteins for older children. Omission of milk means that calcium and riboflavin must be obtained from alternative sources. Legumes, certain dark-green, leafy vegetables, and some nuts provide calcium (see Chapter 8) and riboflavin is found in legumes, whole grains, and vegetables (see Chapter 7). Since foods from plant sources contain no vitamin B_{12} or vitamin D, these vitamins must be supplemented in the diet. As in the lacto-ovo-vegetarian regimen, strict vegetarians must be careful to obtain foods containing iron and zinc.

Diets that are more restrictive than the strict vegetarian, such as the Zen macrobiotic diet, provide inadequate amounts of many nutrients and often discourage obtaining medical help when the child is sick. Such diets should not be used by adults or children.

LONG-TERM IMPLICATIONS OF CHILDHOOD NUTRITION

Nutrition during childhood plays an important role in determining the child's future health. Improper diet and development of bad food habits at this time can contribute to obesity, atherosclerosis, and poor dental health later in life.

Obesity In contrast to infancy, obesity during childhood has been shown to be strongly associated with obesity in adulthood; the obese child has a high probability of becoming an obese adult (53). Obesity also has a number of direct effects on the child. Clumsiness, shortness of breath on exertion, skin irritation, and heat discomfort are often observed. Obese children are frequently teased, ridiculed, and left out of activities. This can have a devastating effect on their self-image and social behavior (54).

Many of the principles for preventing or treating childhood obesity are the same as for obesity during infancy. Overreacting must be discouraged; children should not be forced to finish their meals and should not receive food as a reward or be denied food as a punishment. Second servings and desserts should be limited. Low-calorie snacks, such as raw fruit, can be substituted for those higher in energy content. Nutritional counseling and behavioral modification techniques (see Chapter 5) may prove helpful. The child also should be encouraged to engage in as much physical activity as possible.

Atherosclerosis Unless the child has a genetic predisposition toward high blood cholesterol levels, experts disagree about the desirability of modifying the diet during childhood in an attempt to prevent heart disease (53). Although the experimental evidence strongly suggests that atherosclerosis originates in infancy or childhood, it is uncertain whether changes in diets will be beneficial. However, a modified diet probably is not hazardous, provided that the decision is made by a physician based on his or her understanding of the particular child and its family (53).

Dental Health By 2½ years of age, the child has received a full set of deciduous, or temporary, teeth. The replacement of these teeth begins at about age 6 and is complete by about 14 years (4, pages 68–69). Establishing good food habits during childhood plays a major role in the prevention of tooth decay and will promote proper dental care throughout life.

The chemical and structural quality of the teeth can be improved by providing adequate amounts of protein, vitamin C, vitamin A, calcium, phosphorus, vitamin D, and fluoride (55). Fluoridation of drinking water and use of fluoridated toothpastes will help maintain the integrity of the teeth throughout life (see Chapter 8). In addition, foods high in sugar, particularly in sticky forms, should be restricted, and if eaten, they should not be consumed between meals (see Chapter 2). Foods containing starch rather than sugar have a much lower potential to produce tooth decay; fibrous foods, such as raw fruits and vegetables, increase saliva flow, which has a detergent action and helps neutralize plaque acidity that leads to cavities. Brushing teeth after meals, flossing the teeth daily, and regular visits to the dentist also help prevent deterioration of the teeth.

ISSUE: DIET AND HYPERACTIVITY

Susan Gerard has a classmate named Kevin, who through much of their first several months together in kindergarten had caused many problems. He seldom spent more than a few minutes at any activity and continually interrupted the other children at theirs. During naptime Kevin never fell asleep and often would get up before the period was over. Attempts by his teacher to discipline him would frequently result in a temper tantrum. Kevin was finally diagnosed as hyperactive, and as a result of therapy with stimulant drugs, now shows more acceptable behavior.

Hyperactivity (hyperkinesis) and its associated learning disabilities are the most common behavioral and developmental problems of childhood, affecting at least 5 percent of all children (56). The disorder is more properly called the *hyperkinetic syndrome,* because it encompasses a variety of symptoms, including excessive activity, short attention span, limited ability to concentrate, impulsiveness, inability to delay gratification, and rejection of disciplinary measures (58). Learning ability, nervous function, and muscle coordination are often impaired; the child may have a normal to high IQ, but may perform poorly in school. Hyperkinetic syndrome is generally treated with stimulant drugs, such as amphetamines and methylphenidate (Ritalin), which calm the child and restore normal behavior. Because of side effects, including loss of appetite, insomnia, growth retardation, and psychological dependence, efforts have been made to find alternative treatments.

Probably the most widely publicized alternative is that proposed by the allergist Ben Feingold (57). Feingold hypothesizes that as many as half the cases of hyperkinetic syndrome result from the child's sensitivity to food flavors and colors and certain naturally occurring food substances. Many of these compounds are related to salicylate, which forms the basis for aspirin, as well as for wintergreen flavor. However, the syndrome is not thought to be an allergic response; Feingold believes it results from a sensitivity brought about by other mechanisms, perhaps found only in genetically susceptible individuals (56). By eliminating the offending chemicals from the diet, Feingold claims that these children will return to normal behavior patterns.

It has been difficult to determine whether or not the Feingold diet really works. First, confusion exists about how to diagnose the syndrome. Most children show one or more of the symptoms at one time or another, and they may result from the child's basic personality, anxiety, or the interpretation of the observer, as well as true hyperkinesis (58). In addition, Feingold's claims are based only on clinical observations rather than on controlled experiments. The results he observed might be because of the increased attention focused on the child as a result of the diet, to a placebo effect, or to bias on the part of the observers, who generally knew that the children were on the diet (58).

Since the publication of Feingold's hypothesis, several experiments have been performed to test its effectiveness (56,59,60). In one (59), the children were randomly assigned to the additive-free diet or the control diet. After 4 weeks, the children were switched to the alternative diet for a second 4-week period. Parents and teachers rated the children's behavior on each diet. Significant improvements in the behavior of children on the additive-free diet were observed by the teachers, but not the parents. However, this study has been criticized because the diets were not well-disguised. In another study in which the diets were more cleverly disguised, no significant changes were observed. In addition, the improvements in the first study may have resulted from the order in which the diets were offered to children; beneficial behavior changes were noted only when the additive-free diet followed the control diet (56).

In a third study, all the children were placed on an additive-free diet and then were fed cookies or candy bars that contained or did not contain food colors (60). The presence of the food colors did not, in most cases, adversely influence the behavior of hyperactive children. Several other challenge-type studies have been performed with similar results. In the few instances in which improvement was observed, children under the age of 5 years tended to respond better than older ones. However, these challenge experiments tested only food colorings. It remains to be seen if similar negative results will occur when food flavors and other offending substances are tested (56).

Despite the generally negative experimental results, it is possible that the Feingold diet will work for some hyperactive children, if only because of a placebo effect or the increased attention they receive (56). The diet should be used only under the supervision of a qualified physician or dietitian. In addition, parents of unruly children should not attempt to diagnose or treat their children; a qualified physician can perform the necessary tests and prescribe the most appropriate treatment for each child.

Adolescence

Like many parents, Tom and Meg Gerard worry about the eating habits of their adolescent son, Kenneth. Thirteen years old, Ken is growing rapidly, and the Gerards realize that his nutrient requirements are high. At the same time, Ken's diet is notoriously lacking in variety. He often eats away from home, and a good part of his diet consists of hamburgers, submarine sandwiches, and pizza. Although these are nourishing foods, they do not provide all the nutrients the body requires. Ken shuns nearly all vegetables and only occasionally grabs an apple or orange from the refrigerator. He has increased his intake of soda, as well as maintaining his normal milk consumption.

The Gerards would like to know the long-term effects of this combination of high nutritional requirements and poor food intakes. How can they ensure that Ken's diet will provide sufficient amounts of all the nutrients he needs? In the following section we will look at the reasons behind the Gerards' concerns and ways to provide adequate diets for teenagers like Ken. In addition, we will see in what ways engaging in athletic competition, as many adolescents do, alters nutritional needs and how these additional needs can be met.

THE ADOLESCENT GROWTH SPURT

Adolescence is the only time after birth in which the child's growth rate accelerates (Figure 12-1). The "growth spurt" begins at age 10 or so in females and at about age 12 in males, reaches a maximum about 2 years

1. Infants and children should be encouraged to finish eating all the foods given to them.

2. It is best to introduce solid foods into a baby's diet as early as possible.

3. Protein, vitamin, and mineral supplements will enhance athletic performance.

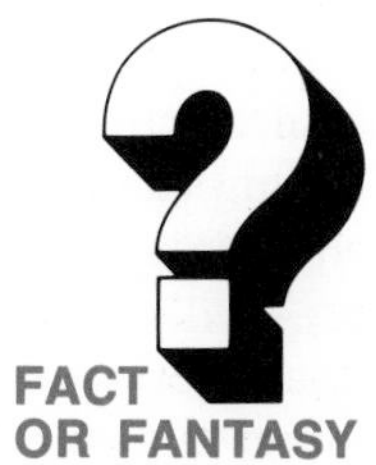

later, and then declines as adulthood approaches. At its peak, the rate of weight gain is almost as rapid as during infancy. The child's body weight doubles by the time it reaches adulthood, and height increases by about 15 percent during adolescence (61).

Growth during adolescence is accompanied by a variety of changes in the body (4, pages 318–371). Males gain proportionally more lean body mass, whereas females gain relatively more adipose tissue. The bones continue to grow; about 45 percent of the adult skeletal mass is formed during adolescence (62). Blood volume expands with increased body size, and the number of red cells and the hemoglobin concentration of the blood rise (4, pages 318–371; 62). Changes also occur in other tissues, including the nervous system (4, pages 318–371). In addition, the period of adolescence known as *puberty* is a time of maturation of the reproductive organs in both sexes and the beginning of menstruation in females. In the last 100 years, sexual maturation has been occurring at a progressively earlier age, a phenomenon that has been attributed in part to better nutrition (63). Studies indicate that females must reach a certain weight and body composition before the onset of *menarche* (beginning of menstruation) (64), and nutrition is one of the factors that influences the time this body weight is reached.

High nutrient requirements and poor food habits can get adolescents in nutritional trouble.

The accelerated growth of adolescence creates a high demand for nutrients (see Ready Reference 3). On a per kilogram of body weight basis, the Recommended Daily Allowances for adolescents are greater than those for adults (6) (see Figure 10-1). Energy and protein are needed to support tissue growth, and the active lifestyles of many adolescents also increase caloric requirements. Proper bone growth requires adequate amounts of vitamin A, vitamin D, calcium, phosphorus, and fluoride. Iron needs are especially high at this time. Not only is iron needed for tissue growth and the production of blood, but it must be provided to balance menstrual blood losses in adolescent females. Folacin and vitamin B_{12} also function in the synthesis of blood cells, and adequate amounts of zinc and iodine must be provided to promote body growth and development.

MEETING NUTRITIONAL NEEDS

Eating patterns among adolescents are highly variable. Vending machines, mobile food vans, fast food restaurants, and grocery stores are among the alternative places at which teenagers eat (62). Mealtimes are often determined by the adolescent's active schedule, and skipping meals, especially breakfast and lunch, is common among this age group (62,65). Teenagers are noted for snacking as well; the Ten-State Nutrition Survey found that many teenagers obtain about a quarter of their kilocalories from foods eaten between meals (62). Food choices are often determined by advertising, peer pressure, and the desire to fit in (8, pages 136–138). Teenagers may select particular foods because they are advertised by respected adults or by celebrities, to lose weight, or to help in a body-building program. A desire to assert their independence may lead them to experiment with vegetarianism and health foods.

The combination of relatively high nutritional requirements and poor food habits sometimes leads to nutrient deficiencies in adolescents. The Ten-State Nutrition Survey reported that the incidence of unsatisfactory nutritional status was higher in 10- to 16-year-olds than in any other age group surveyed (66). Other studies show that vitamin C, folacin, vitamin A, vitamin B_6, iron, and calcium are the nutrients most likely to be deficient (8, pages 136–138; 61; 62). Marginal zinc intakes also may be a problem for adolescents (61,62).

FOCUS 12-2 TEENAGE PREGNANCY Pregnancy during adolescence is an increasingly common occurrence. In the United States between 1950 and 1978, the proportion of babies born to mothers 19 years of age or younger rose from 12 to 17 percent of the total number of births (81,82). In addition, the number of infants born to unwed mothers in this age group has increased (Figure 12-6). This increase is of great concern because there is relatively greater risk of adverse effects on mother and infant in an adolescent pregnancy. Maternal mortality, the occurrence of toxemia, and the incidence of low-birth-weight infants tends to be higher among adolescent mothers than among those between 20 and 40 years of age (16, pages 119–132). More than one pregnancy during the teenage years is especially stressful and may help establish conditions leading to kidney damage and high blood pressure later in life (16, pages 119–132).

In comparison with older women, a pregnant teenager generally is at a physiological, psychological, educational, social, and nutritional disadvantage (83). Her body has not reached full maturity and may not be ready to withstand the stresses of pregnancy. Adolescence is a turbulent time of life, in which the young woman is attempting to establish her identity and independence. Pregnancy adds to this psychological burden. In addition, because the child is generally conceived out of wedlock, society tends to take a punitive attitude toward the mother. It is often difficult for a pregnant adolescent to continue her educa-

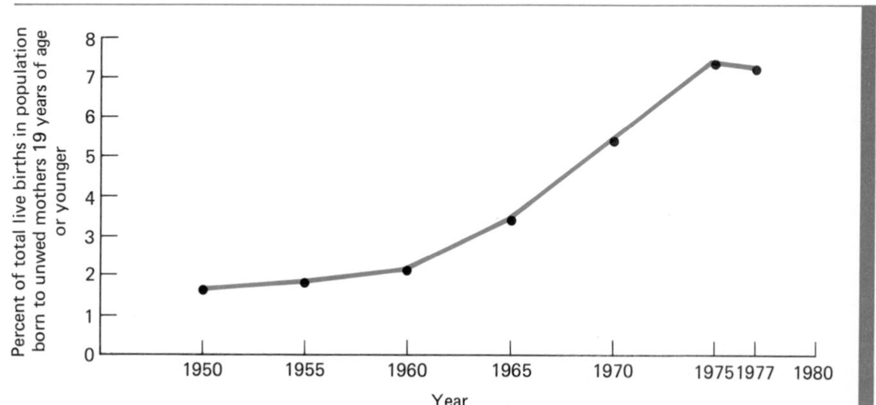

FIGURE 12-6
The Increase in Birth Rate Among Unwed Mothers 19 Years Old or Younger, 1950 to 1975. [*Source:* Bureau of the Census, *Statistical Abstracts of the United States,* 99th edition, Washington, DC, Dept. of Commerce (1978) pp. 59, 65.]

tion. Many teenage mothers belong to a low socioeconomic group and may not have access to adequate medical care.

The nutritional stresses on a pregnant adolescent are particularly great; the already high nutrient requirements of adolescence are further increased by the needs of pregnancy. Adding the RDAs for pregnancy to those for adolescence provides a rough estimate of the nutrient requirements of pregnant teenagers (6) (Table 12-3). The combination of high requirements and the poor eating habits of most teenagers increases the risk of deficiency in pregnant adolescents. One study found that although pregnant teenagers ate more than nonpregnant ones, not one of the nutrients studied was supplied in adequate amounts to all the subjects. The nutritional factors most poorly provided were energy, calcium, iron, and vitamin A (84). Other nutrients that are often deficient in a pregnant teenager's diet include vitamin C, folacin, and, if she is a strict vegetarian, vitamin B_{12} (16, pages 119–132).

The pregnant adolescent must be encouraged to consume an adequate diet to maintain weight gain and prevent nutritional deficiencies. Vitamin and mineral supplements will be needed if the young woman refuses to improve her dietary habits. A pregnant adolescent also should take advantage of community programs that have been designed to help her. With a proper diet and prenatal care, the chances of adverse effects during an adolescent pregnancy can be reduced.

TABLE **12-3**

Nutrient requirements of pregnant teenagers

NUTRIENT	Age: 11 TO 14 YEARS	Age: 15 TO 18 YEARS
Kilocalories	2500	2400
Protein, g/kg of body weight	1.7	1.4
Vitamin A:		
Retinol equivalents	1000	1000
International units	5000	5000
Vitamin D:		
Micrograms	15	15
International units	600	600
Vitamin E, μg of alpha-tocopherol	10	10
Vitamin C, mg	70	80
Thiamine, mg	1.5	1.5
Riboflavin, mg	1.6	1.6
Niacin, mg or niacin equivalents	17	16
Vitamin B_6, mg	2.4	2.6
Folacin, μg	800	800
Vitamin B_{12}, μg	4	4
Calcium, mg	1600	1600
Phosphorus, mg	1600	1600
Magnesium, mg	450	450
Iron, mg	18+	18+
Zinc, mg	20	20
Iodine, μg	175	175

Note: The requirement for iron is more than 18 mg, but the precise amount needed is not known.

Source: Food and Nutrition Board, *Recommended Dietary Allowances*, 9th ed., National Academy of Sciences, Washington, 1980.

With a certain amount of care, nearly all adolescents can consume an adequate diet. They must be encouraged to broaden their choice of foods. Consuming at least 3 to 4 cups/day of milk will add calcium and, if fortified, vitamin A to the diet, as well as ensuring an adequate intake of protein and riboflavin. Citrus fruits and their juices provide vitamin C. Obtaining enough iron is a problem for most age groups, but the high requirements of adolescence (18 mg/day) are particularly difficult to meet. Teenagers generally like meat, and this comprises a major source of iron in their diets. Encouraging them to eat nuts, iron-fortified breads, cereals, baked goods, and raisins will add iron to the diet. Meat, eggs, seafood, and nuts are sources of zinc that adolescents might enjoy.

Since adolescents tend to assert their independence, parental advice or pressure to eat certain foods is not likely to have much impact on their food choices. Parents can exert some control by making nutritious foods available at home. Appealing to some of the teenager's concerns, such as losing or gaining weight, improving complexion, and facilitating athletic training, can help. Role models, such as parents, teachers, respected peers, and celebrities, can create good examples for adolescents to follow.

ADOLESCENT OBESITY

It has been estimated that 10 to 13 percent of the teenagers in the United States are obese (67). Obesity that originates during adolescence is not as common as that beginning in the preadolescent years, and a large proportion of obese teenagers have been overweight since childhood (67). Obese adolescents are particularly difficult to treat. As many as 80 percent will remain obese into adulthood (8, pages 149–152).

In addition to increasing the risk of diabetes, high blood pressure, and other problems later in life (see Chapter 5), obesity has a variety of effects on the teenager. Obese adolescents tend to mature earlier physically and sexually, and menarche generally occurs at an earlier age in obese teenage girls (8, pages 149–152; 67). Because adolescents are so concerned about their appearance, obesity can be a psychological and so-

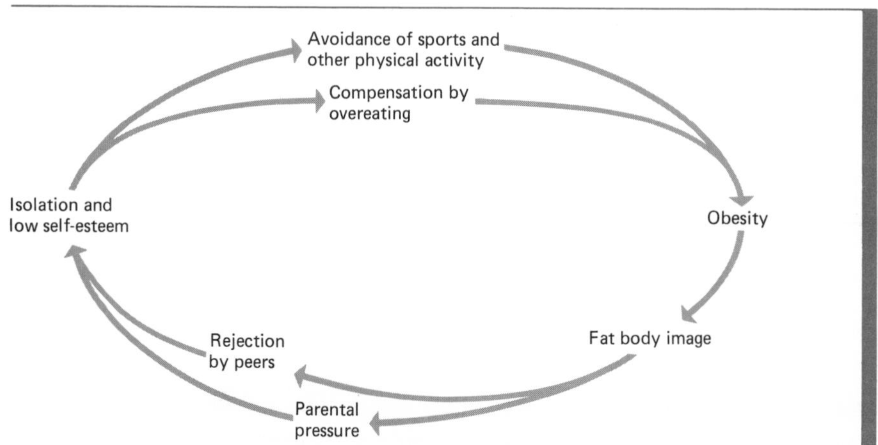

FIGURE 12-7
The Cycle of Teenage Obesity. Obesity can lead to behavior which perpetuates the problem.

cial liability. A distorted body image, poor self-concept, social isolation, and feelings of rejection resulting from obesity can be especially difficult for an adolescent to deal with. Many cope by turning to food. This can establish a vicious cycle, in which eating serves as an outlet for the frustration, isolation, and depression brought on by obesity (Figure 12-7).

Treatment of obese adolescents must aim at more than just reducing food intake. Although caloric intake must be lowered and a balanced diet encouraged, psychological factors contributing to the problem also must be considered. Group and behavior therapy can be helpful in this regard (see Chapter 5). Many obese adolescents also are relatively sedentary: Encouraging them to increase physical activity increases energy expenditure and helps get them involved in something besides eating. It is important that goals be realistic and as much positive reinforcement as possible be given so that the adolescent will not become discouraged and give up.

ISSUE: DIET AND ATHLETIC PERFORMANCE

"Kenneth Gerard is a competitive swimmer. Like many adolescents, he pursues his athletic interest avidly and trains for at least 2 hours almost every day. Ken is interested in anything that will help him swim faster. He has read many advertisements for wheat germ oil, vitamin and mineral supplements, protein supplements, sugar pills, and other products that are supposed to improve athletic performance. Although he has not yet tried any of them, Ken wonders if they actually work.

Like Ken, athletes have always turned to nutrition to improve athletic prowess, and many fads and superstitions have grown from this practice. However, the question of nutrition and athletics is relatively straightforward;

TABLE **12-4**

Energy cost of 1 hour of performing various athletic activities

	Energy Cost, kcal	
ACTIVITY	70-kg MAN	55-kg WOMAN
Bicycle racing	532	418
Fencing	511	402
Playing table tennis	308	242
Rowing in a race	1120	880
Skating	245	193
Swimming (2 mi/h)	553	434
Running	490	385

Note: The energy costs here exclude basal metabolic rate and specific dynamic action.

Source: C. M. Taylor and G. McLeod, *Rose's Handbook for Dietetics,* 5th ed., Macmillan, New York, 1949, p. 18. Copyright 1956 by Macmillan Publishing Co., Inc. Reprinted with permission of Macmillan Co.

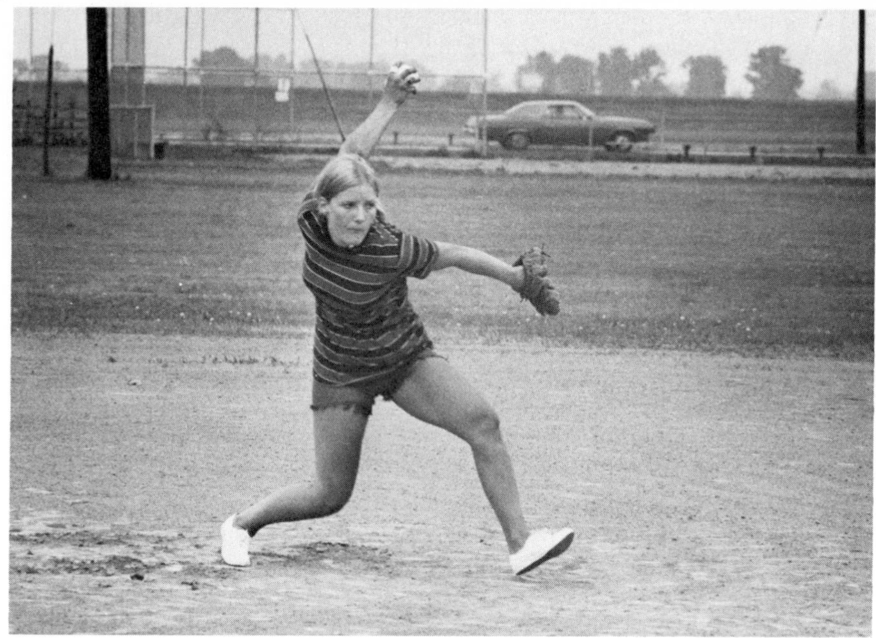

FIGURE 12-8
Athletes have an especially high need for energy and should be careful to replace water and electrolyte losses. A balanced diet will provide sufficient amounts of the other nutrients. (Photograph by Ken Heyman).

the best diet for athletes, like nonathletes, is one that meets the individual's requirements for water, energy, protein, carbohydrate, fat, vitamins, and minerals (68). There is no evidence that any particular food or excess quantities of nutrients will work better than a balanced diet.

Athletes have especially high energy needs. Depending on body size and the sport, an athlete in training may require more than 3000 kcal/day (68) (Table 12-4). Protein, carbohydrate, and fat provide energy for the body as a whole at rest, but working muscles do not use protein as a major source of fuel (68,69). The amount of carbohydrate and fat burned by the muscle for energy depends on the amount of oxygen available. In light to moderate activity, such as walking or long-distance running, plenty of oxygen can be supplied to the muscles and fat provides about 50 to 60 percent of the energy. In moderate activity lasting more than about 3 hours, fat contributes up to 70 percent of the caloric needs.

In contrast to light and moderate exercise, intense short-term physical activity creates a demand for oxygen that cannot be met completely by the lungs, heart, and circulatory system. Under these conditions, the muscles use carbohydrate for fuel. However, because exhaustion results from a lack of oxygen in the muscle and not the unavailability of carbohydrate, **carbohydrate loading** (see Focus 12-3) will not improve performance in this situation.

Large protein intakes have been promoted over the years as a means of improving athletic performance; plenty of meat at the training table and taking protein supplements are familiar rituals for many athletes. As we have seen, however, working muscles do not use protein as a source of energy. In addition, large amounts of protein have little effect on increasing

FOCUS 12-3 CARBOHYDRATE LOADING (GLYCOGEN PACKING)

Although fat provides most of the energy in light to moderate exercise, carbohydrate also plays an important role in maintaining this level of physical activity for an extended period of time. Carbohydrate supplies 30 percent or more of the muscles' energy requirements and virtually all the energy required by the nervous system. Most of the muscles' carbohydrates needs are provided by their own glycogen stores, and by manipulating their diets, athletes can increase the quantity of this stored glycogen and improve endurance in events longer than 30 to 60 minutes. First, about 1 week prior to the competition the muscles are exercised heavily to exhaust glycogen stores. During this and the next 3 days the diet is modified to contain almost exclusively protein and fat. During the last 3 days prior to the competition, a carbohydrate-rich diet is consumed. This technique, called **glycogen packing**, or **carbohydrate loading**, doubles the glycogen content of the muscle (69). However, about 2.7 grams of water are stored with each gram of glycogen. The additional weight can give the muscle a feeling of heaviness and stiffness. Carbohydrate loading also produced heart pains and an abnormal electrocardiogram in an older marathon runner. For this reason, the practice should not be undertaken without advice of a physician or trainer experienced with the technique (68).

muscle size or strength (70,71). Mature athletes should obtain about 1 g/kg of body weight/day of protein, and growing athletes should obtain about twice that amount. The quantity of protein that accompanies the higher caloric intake needed by athletes generally meets their requirements. Protein supplements have no advantages, and they can induce dehydration, loss of appetite, and diarrhea (70).

Although many athletes take vitamin and mineral supplements, there is no conclusive evidence of any benefits to be gained from doing so. Requirements for thiamine, riboflavin, and niacin increase with greater energy intake, but larger amounts of these vitamins are provided from food, along with the extra kilocalories. Studies show that intakes of vitamin C, vitamin E, or vitamin B_{12} above RDA levels have little or no influence on physical performance (72–74).

One of the most important nutritional considerations for athletes is providing enough water and electrolytes (sodium, potassium, and chloride). Failing to do so may lead to dehydration and impairment of the body's ability to regulate its temperature (68,70). Both fluid and salt should be replaced. Water should be taken in small amounts throughout the period of activity. Salt can be replaced during or after the activity by adding it to the water at a rate of 2 g salt/liter water (about $^1/_2$ tsp salt/liter water) or at the end of the day by adding salt to food. Because they can cause stomach and intestinal problems, salt tablets are not recommended (68). During long-distance events, small amounts of glucose can be added to the salt solution. However, it is not certain that this will make a significant contribution of energy to the working muscles; they rely mainly on their glycogen stores for carbohydrate. In addition, too much glucose slows the rate at which the stomach empties into the small intestine and also tends to retain water in the digestive tract. This causes abdominal discomfort during exercise. A 5% solution (50 g glucose/liter water/or 1¾ oz glucose/qt water) appears to work well (76). A number of solutions, such as Gatorade, are sold for this purpose, but there is no evidence that they work better than a homemade water, salt, and glucose solution (68).

For some sports, such as wrestling and boxing, the athlete competes in a particular weight class. In order to attain a lower weight classification, many competitors starve themselves, avoid water, and wear plastic suits to make them sweat. This practice is hazardous because it dehydrates the body and leads to losses of protein, glycogen, vitamins, minerals, and enzymes. Some ways of ensuring the lowest possible weight but maintaining adequate nutrient intake are to reduce water retention by avoiding foods high in sodium and to avoid high-residue foods, which increase fecal weight (77).

A balanced diet will help athletes perform their best. The diet should contain 50 to 60 percent of kilocalories as carbohydrate, 30 percent as fat, and 10 to 20 percent as protein. Vitamin and mineral supplements are generally unnecessary. On the day of the competition, the last big meal should be consumed at least 3 to 4 hours before the event. The meal should not contain large amounts of fat and protein, since these require more time to digest. In some cases, liquid meals have been found to eliminate the nausea, vomiting, and abdominal and localized cramps owing to nervous tension because they are easier to digest (68). ”

Study Guide

SUMMARY

1. The growth that occurs during infancy, childhood, and adolescence results in relatively high nutritional requirements. On a per unit of body weight basis, the RDAs tend to decrease as the child grows older, but because body size increases, the total allowances increase throughout the growing years.
2. Milk is the best food for infants during the first half year of life. Many pediatricians recommend supplementing human milk with iron, vitamin D, and fluoride. Formulas, especially those enriched with iron, are designed to supply adequate amounts of all the nutrients. If evaporated milk is used as a basis, it should be supplemented with vitamin C, iron, and, if unfluoridated water is used, fluoride. When the infant is bottle-fed, care must be taken to maintain the sanitary quality of the milk and utensils.
3. Solid foods are best introduced during the fifth or sixth month. Infant cereals are usually introduced first. Later, soft fingerfoods are given, and by the end of the first year, the child should be eating a variety of foods from the table.
4. As the child grows older, the Basic Four Food Groups can provide the basis for an adequate diet. Serving sizes must be adjusted to the needs of the individual. Childhood and adolescence are periods when children establish their independence, and many factors, including parents, peers, television and other advertising, and school, help shape their food choices. Making nutritious foods available to them and providing sound nutritional education can help children and adolescents make better choices.
5. Failure to supply adequate amounts of nutrients can reduce physical growth and mental development. However, providing too many kilocalories leads to obesity. Although it is not certain whether obese infants usually become obese adults, obesity during childhood and adolescence generally leads to obesity during adulthood. Atherosclerosis also appears to have its roots early in life. Because of the high demand for nutrients, dietary modifications are not recommended during infancy, except on the advice of a physician. However, improving food habits and increasing the amount of physical activity during childhood and adolescence may be beneficial in preventing obesity and atherosclerosis later in life.
6. Many infants and children experience allergies to certain foods. Food diaries and elimination diets are used to identify the offending foods, which can then be avoided.
7. Hyperactivity, or hyperkinesis, is another disorder that has been linked to diet. Feingold believes that it is caused by salicylates and related compounds that occur naturally in foods, as well as by food additives and colors. Although some studies show positive results, most experiments have found little beneficial effect of Feingold's additive-free diet in treating hyperkinesis.
8. Athletes have always turned to nutrition as a means of improving their performance. However, the best diet for athletes, like nonathletes, is one that meets the individual's requirements for water, energy, protein, carbohydrate, fat, vitamins, and minerals. Glycogen packing, or carbohydrate loading, can improve performance during extended physical activity.

VOCABULARY

glycogen packing (carbohydrate loading)
hyperactivity (hyperkinesis, or hyperkinetic syndrome)
modified starch

STUDY QUESTIONS

1. Refer to this and earlier chapters and de-

scribe the role each of the following nutrients plays in growth and development of body tissues:

a. Protein
b. Vitamin A
c. Vitamin D
d. Folacin
e. Vitamin B_{12}
f. Vitamin C
g. Calcium and phosphorus
h. Iron
i. Zinc
j. Fluoride
k. Iodine

2. In general, how does the adult RDA/kg of body weight for each nutrient compare with those of infancy, childhood, and adolescence? List some foods that will help meet the RDA for each nutrient during infancy, childhood, and adolescence.
3. When is the best time to introduce solid foods to an infant's diet? Why? What is the best way to accomplish this?
4. What are the ingredients that should be avoided when choosing commercial baby foods? Why?
5. Describe some general principles to consider when preparing and using homemade baby foods.
6. What are some foods that commonly cause allergies in infants and children? What means are used to identify the allergy? Why should diagnosis and treatment of an allergy be a physician's responsibility?
7. What are some factors that influence food choices in children and adolescents? How can each of these factors be modified or used to have a positive impact on the individual?
8. Describe how a lacto-ovo-vegetarian diet can be adapted to meet the nutritional needs of childhood and adolescence. Do the same for a strict vegetarian diet.
9. What is the current medical opinion regarding the effectiveness of the Feingold diet in treating hyperactivity in children?
10. Why are nutritional requirements especially high for pregnant teenagers? What other problems might a pregnant teenager have?
11. What general statement can you make about the best diet for athletes as compared with nonathletes? Why might an athlete require more of each of the following than a nonathlete? How can the increased need for each be met?
    a. Energy
    b. Thiamine, riboflavin, and niacin
    c. Water
    d. Electrolytes (sodium, potassium, and chloride)
12. Describe the method for carbohydrate loading. Why should this be undertaken only with advice of a qualified physician or trainer?
13. What are some hazards associated with starvation and water loss as a means for attaining a lower weight class in wrestling or boxing?

SELF-TEST

Multiple choice: Select the best answer.

1. If a formula is used to feed an infant, it is important to
    a. Observe proper sanitation and preparation techniques
    b. Give the baby a vitamin supplement
    c. Introduce solid foods as early in life as possible
    d. All of the above
2. By the fifth or sixth month of age, the infant is depleting its stores of
    a. Calcium
    b. Vitamin A
    c. Iron
    d. Fat
3. Introducing whole milk during the first year of life is not recommended because it may lead to
    a. High blood pressure
    b. High blood lipids
    c. Rickets
    d. Bleeding in the digestive tract
4. When whole milk is substituted for human milk or formula in the infant's diet, the infant should also be receiving
    a. A source of iron, such as fortified cereal
    b. A source of vitamin C, such as fruit or juices

c. A source of fluoride, such as drinking water
d. All of the above

5. Severe protein-energy malnutrition during infancy may lead to
   a. An increased number of fat cells
   b. Permanent retardation of growth and mental development
   c. A predisposition toward atherosclerosis later in life
   d. Hyperactivity
6. Between the ages of 2 and 4 years:
   a. A child's appetite increases enormously
   b. A child's eating habits tend to stabilize
   c. A child's appetite tends to decrease
   d. A child will generally try any new food that is offered
7. Obesity during which of the following periods is least conclusively associated with obesity in adulthood?
   a. Infancy
   b. Childhood
   c. Adolescence
   d. They are equally associated with adult obesity
8. Adolescents have a relatively high risk of developing a nutritional deficiency because
   a. Hormonal changes increase excretion of nutrients
   b. They have relatively high requirements and poor food habits
   c. The capacity of the intestine to absorb nutrients does not increase as fast as the body's need for them
   d. An increase in physical activity depletes the body of many nutrients
9. Carbohydrate loading is helpful to a
   a. High jumper
   b. Sprinter
   c. Person running a mile race
   d. Marathon runner
10. The best precompetition diet for an athlete is
   a. A relatively high carbohydrate meal 3 to 4 hours before the event
   b. Steak and eggs for breakfast
   c. Fasting
   d. Protein and vitamin tablets

True-False

1. On a per unit of body weight basis, the nutritional requirements of infancy are higher than for any other stage of the life cycle.
2. Introducing solid foods as early in life as possible is important for an infant's mental development.
3. Bottle-feeding and introducing solid foods before the fifth month of life have been conclusively shown to cause obesity.
4. The American Academy of Pediatrics recommends putting all children on a diet to reduce cholesterol levels within the first 2 years of life.
5. If snacks are chosen properly, they can make a significant contribution toward meeting nutrient needs.
6. Omitting breakfast may have an adverse effect on a child's mental and physical performance in the late morning.
7. Consuming large amounts of protein will accelerate muscle development in athletes.
8. One of the most important nutritional considerations for athletes is to maintain water and electrolyte balance.

SUGGESTED ACTIVITIES

1. Examine the ingredient labels on commercial baby foods. In which is water the first ingredient listed? Which appear to contain significant amounts of sugar or salt? Do any contain food additives? Check Jacobson's *Eater's Digest* (see Further Reading in Chapter 10) to determine the status of these additives.
2. Evaluate nutritional advertising for children by watching television on Saturday morning. How many advertisements did you see for heavily sugared breakfast cereals? For candy? For soft drinks? For other "junk" food? For fast foods? Did any of the commercials for these products convey information about choosing a nutritious diet? How many public service messages did you see regarding choosing an

adequate diet? Were there any advertisements by the producers of nutritious foods, such as dairy products, fruits and fruit juices, vegetables, or nutritious grain products?

3. If a friend or relative has a baby or preschool child, observe the child's eating behavior. How does the child indicate it is hungry? What foods does it like and dislike? How does the child consume food it is given? How much "junk" food does the child consume? Try to note changes in these patterns as the child grows older.
4. Members of your class might enjoy planning and performing some nutrition education experiences for preschool or elementary school children. Some background can be obtained by reading appropriate parts of Further Reading 3. Ideas and materials can be obtained from sources such as those in Further Reading 4 or from local sources familiar to your instructor.
5. Interview coaches and athletes at your school. Make a list of their beliefs about nutrition and athletics. Using this text and Further Reading 5, confirm or refute their beliefs.

FURTHER READING

1. An up-to-date summary of nutrition for infants:

   Fomon, S. J., Filer, L. J., Anderson, T. A., and Ziegler, E. E.: "Recommendations for Feeding Normal Infants," *Pediatrics* **63:** 52–58 (1979).

2. A more extensive treatment of infant nutrition:

   Fomon, S. J.: *Infant Nutrition,* 2d ed., Saunders, Philadelphia 1974.

3. A detailed look at nutrition during the growing years:

   Pipes, P. L.: *Nutrition in Infancy and Childhood,* Mosby, St. Louis; 1977.
   Endres, J. B., and Rockwell, R. E.: *Food, Nutrition, and the Young Child,* Mosby, St. Louis; 1980.

4. Kits with ideas for teaching young children may be obtained from:

   Early Childhood Nutrition Program
   Department of Nutritional Sciences
   Martha Van Rensselaer Hall
   Cornell University
   Ithaca, N.Y. 14853

   National Dairy Council
   6300 N. River Road
   Rosemont, Ill. 60018

5. Two indepth, but readable books about nutrition and athletics:

   Darden, E.: *Nutrition and Athletic Performance,* Athletic Press, Pasadena, Calif., 1976.
   Williams, M. H.: *Nutritional Aspects of Human Physical and Athletic Performance,* Thomas, Springfield, Ill., 1976.

6. A recent review of nutrition during adolescence:

   Greenwood, C. T., and Richardson, D. P.: "Nutrition during Adolescence," *World Rev. Nutr. Diet.* **33:**1–41 1979.

THE LATER YEARS

Tom and Meg Gerard both have parents who are still alive. Meg's father died several years ago, and her 66-year-old mother lives in an apartment on the other side of town. Tom's father and mother are 70 and 68 years old, respectively. They live in their own home in another part of town. Tom's parents are healthy and generally eat well: they have a comfortable income, and because they own a car, they can search for the best food buys in town. For a time, however, the Gerards worried about Meg's mother. After her husband's death, she did not have much desire to bother about making meals; she ate canned soups, sandwiches, and some occasional fruit. Fortunately, a friend introduced her to several other widowed women and men, and the group gets together often for meals and good times. Tom and Meg invite her over for dinner weekly. They also leave the children with her frequently, which motivates her to cook. As a result, Meg's mother feels wanted and useful; she enjoys eating again and looks forward to planning meals and being with people.

Through their own planning and initiative, as well as the love and concern of relatives and friends, the Gerard's parents do well nutritionally. Others are not so fortunate, and they are increasingly becoming a source of national concern. Twenty million Americans were 65 years or older in 1970; the number increases by 3 to 4 million every decade (18). The Census Bureau projects there will be 31.8 million people in this age group by the year 2000 (10). Other data indicate that the proportion of

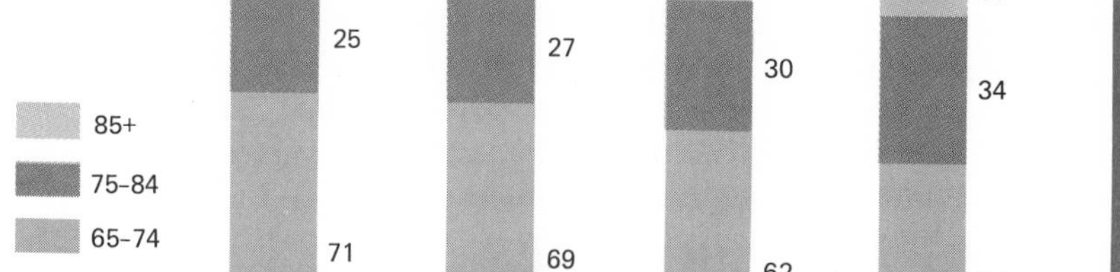

FIGURE 13-1
The Increase of Very Old People among the Elderly in the United States. [*Source:* National Institutes of Health, *Our Future Selves,* Bethesda, MD, Public Health Service (1977), p. 9.]

very old people is increasing among the elderly (19) (Figure 13-1). What are the nutritional needs of this population group? What are the problems they face in meeting these needs? In this chapter we will examine these questions and try to determine how the nutritional requirements of older people can be met.

Why Do People Grow Old?

Since the beginning of recorded history, humans have wondered why they grow old. Despite the advances of modern science, we are not much closer to solving the riddle than were people during Aristotle's time (1, page 408). Many theories have been proposed, and they suggest that aging results from one or a combination of three general processes: loss of cells, decline in function of existing cells, and an impairment of communication between cells.

The loss of cells in body tissues and organs reflects an inability to synthesize new ones as fast as old ones are broken down (Figure 13-2). Some cells, such as neurons, stop dividing early in life, and there is a progressive decline in their number as the individual ages (1, page 502). Others, such as kidney cells, retain the ability to reproduce, but do not divide rapidly enough to offset the losses that occur with age. Many theories attempt to explain why cells die. One proposes that natural radiation, such as cosmic rays, produces mutations in DNA faster than they can be repaired, and the defective DNA leads to the synthesis of defective proteins (5). Another suggests that cell death results from an impairment in the processes by which the genetic code is translated into a functional protein. (For a description of protein synthesis, see Chapter 4.) Some authorities believe that such malfunctions are genetically "programmed" to occur when the cell reaches a certain age (2, pages 49–84).

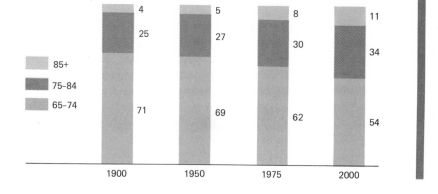

A variety of other changes may lead to a reduction in cell function and ultimately to cell death (2, pages 49–84). Certain cell structures, such as the mitochondria, may stop functioning properly. In addition, the accumulation of substances, including antibodies that act against the body's own tissues, certain types of viruses, and aging (lipofucsin) pigments, in the cell may contribute to loss of cellular function. Deterioration of one function may lead to the impairment of others, creating a "snowball" effect until the cell dies. This makes it impossible to tell which processes are the causes and which are the results of growing old.

Loss of communication between cells also may contribute to aging. Reduced hormone production, changes in the permeability of the plasma membrane, and alterations in the ability of the cell to react to hormones are among the factors that may reduce intercellular communication (2, pages 49–84).

Another factor in aging is an alteration in the structure of collagen. This protein is a major component of connective tissue and is found in bones, cartilage, skin, walls of the blood vessels, and many other parts of the body. As the body grows older, collagen loses its elasticity, which may result in a loss of flexibility and structural integrity of the tissues.

ISSUE: DIET AND AGING

Although no nutrient or particular type of food can retard aging, the diet as a whole can influence longevity. Overeating eventually leads to obesity, which increases the risk of premature death and of developing diabetes mellitus, high blood pressure, and other problems (see Chapter 5). Diet also may influence the develop-

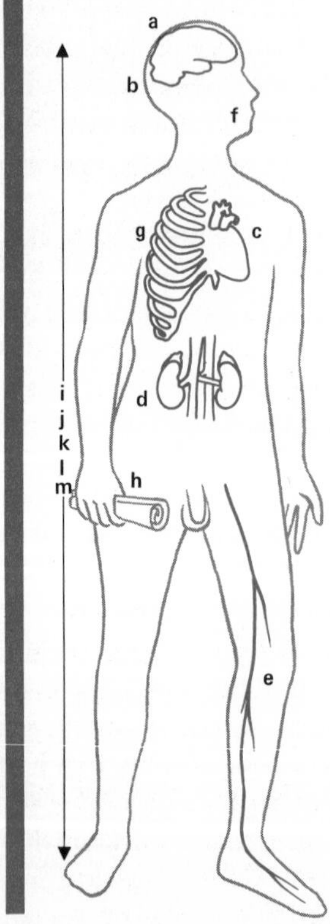

FIGURE 13-2
Loss of Tissue Function with Age. As the body ages, the activities of its tissues decline at different rates. The numbers in parentheses indicate the percent of tissue function remaining in a 75-year-old man as compared to an average 30-year-old man.
a. Brain weight (56);
b. Blood flow to brain (80);
c. Cardiac output at rest (70);
d. Kidney plasma flow (50);
e. Number of Nerve trunk fibers (63);
f. Number of Taste buds (36);
g. Maximum breathing capacity (voluntary) (43);
h. Hand grip (55);
i. Maximum work rate (70);
j. Maximum work rate for short burst (40);
k. Basal Metabolic Rate (84);
l. Body water content (82);
m. Body weight (males) (88);
(Source: N. W. Shock, "The Physiology of Aging," *Scientific American* **206**:100–110 (Jan. 1972). Copyright © 1972 by Scientific American. All rights reserved.)

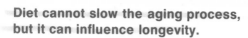

Diet cannot slow the aging process, but it can influence longevity.

ment of atherosclerosis, a major cause of death in the United States (see Chapter 3).

Experiments in rats and mice found that restricting food intake beginning early in life extended their life span, in some cases to an age equivalent to 180 years in humans (4). The incidence of many degenerative diseases, including certain types of cancer, was lower in animals with restricted diets. However, the researchers found that the older the animals when the dietary restrictions were begun, the less striking the beneficial effect on life span. If restrictions were imposed after the animal reached maturity, the life span was actually reduced. However, little work has been done to test this hypothesis in humans, and at this point, the diet used with rats should not be used by humans. It would lead to retarded growth and nutrient deficiencies. Dietary restriction also increases the malignancy of certain types of cancer (4). The best strategy is to use a well-balanced diet that will promote growth and avoid accumulation of excess fat.

Vitamin E has been promoted as an antiaging vitamin. Lipofucsin pigments appear to be derived from lipids in the cell membrane, and vitamin E has been shown to retard their formation. However, the role of these pigments in aging is not known; they may simply be harmless by-products of the aging process. Current evidence indicates that vitamin E plays no role in preventing aging (3,20).

Aging and Nutritional Requirements

The progressive loss of cells and impairment of cellular processes that occur with aging are associated with changes in a variety of body processes. These alterations sometimes influence nutritional requirements. For example, the basal metabolic rate and physical activity both decline as the individual grows older (see Chapter 5). The resulting reduction in caloric requirements is accompanied by a gradual loss of lean body tissue and an accumulation of fat (6). Thus it is important for an older person to reduce caloric intake to maintain energy balance.

Although the RDA for protein is the same for those over the age of 50 as for younger adults, some data suggest that the allowances for the elderly should be somewhat higher. The authors of this report believe that obtaining 12 to 14 percent of the caloric intake from protein will be enough to meet the needs of older people (7). The protein should be of high quality and be easily digested. Excess intake should be avoided because it may put unnecessary stress on the kidneys (8).

Little research has been done to determine the vitamin and mineral requirements of older adults. The Recommended Dietary Allowances for individuals over the age of 50 are generally the same as those for younger adults (see Ready Reference 3). However, iron requirements for elderly women are less than those for younger women because menstruation has stopped. The requirements for some nutrients may be higher in the elderly than is currently recommended. Calcium absorption declines with age, possibly resulting in a greater need for this mineral. Reduced hydrochloric acid and intrinsic factor may retard iron and vitamin B_{12} absorption in the elderly, thereby increasing these requirements (2, pages 32–34; 8).

Adequate dietary fiber also is needed by older people to prevent constipation and diverticular disease. The problem here is that high-fiber foods are more difficult to chew and may be avoided because of bad teeth (21).

Because nutritional requirements generally seem to remain the same as a person ages, it is especially important to provide a nutritious diet for older people. Surveys show that many of the elderly have acceptable levels of nutrient intake. However, a significant proportion of the senior citizens in each study had deficient intakes of one or more nutrients. Calcium, iron, vitamin A, vitamin C, thiamine, riboflavin, and sometimes protein are the nutrients most often reported lacking (9). Caloric intake has frequently been found to be inadequate as well, but the standards against which energy intakes were compared may have been set too high for a sedentary population group such as the elderly.

A variety of physiological, psychological, and environmental factors may restrict food choices or interfere with the body's ability to utilize food, thereby leading to a nutritional deficiency. A major example is the loss of teeth. As many as half the people in the United States over the age of 60 have lost all their teeth, and many more have some missing teeth (9,10,21). Although most people without teeth have dentures, they sometimes fit poorly. As a result, the individual avoids foods that cause discomfort when chewed.

The senses of taste and smell also decline with age. One study found an average of 288 taste buds per papilla (the small bumps on the surface of the tongue) in children, but only 88 in a group of people 74 to 85 years old. In addition, half the taste buds in the elderly group had deteriorated and were probably no longer functional (2, pages 30–31). Another study showed that many older people also have difficulty in smelling anything at all or cannot accurately identify an odor (2, pages 30–31). Because enjoyment of the taste and smell of food is a major motivation to eat, these changes can adversely affect food intake.

Aging impairs the secretion of saliva, stomach acid, digestive enzymes, and bile (2, pages 32–34; 10). In most people, enough are still secreted to digest food normally, but in some cases digestion is impaired. In addition, digestive upset in response to one or more foods often leads to avoidance of certain foods (21).

Loss of muscular strength and coordination is a problem in the elderly. Some become immobilized or cannot travel outside their homes. They depend on food brought to them by friends, relatives, and government-funded agencies. Others experience a loss of control over fine movements and may have problems handling utensils. They may avoid social situations or foods that give them difficulty (21).

Living alone often leads to nutritional problems. Preparing meals for only one person does not seem to be worth the bother for many people,

FOCUS 13-1 BREAKING OUR STEREOTYPES OF OLDER PEOPLE (15)

This chapter looks at a variety of factors that influence the ability of many elderly people to meet their nutritional requirements. However, these factors do not make up a stereotypical picture of most old people; the majority of the elderly are self-sufficient and enjoy life. Most live independently or with relatives. In 1970, only 5 percent of those 65 years of age or older and 9.2 percent of those 75 years of age or older were in extended-care facilities such as nursing homes. Eighty percent of all people over the age of 65 say they continue to engage in their normal activities, and the majority feel just as happy as they were when they were younger. Although some older people have memory problems, such as inability to remember their correct age, birth date, telephone numbers, and addresses, less than 10 percent are seriously demented or disoriented. The majority do not feel lonely or socially isolated.

Older people can make many contributions to society. Those who are able to work are generally as effective as younger people. The older worker tends to have more consistent output, stays with a job longer, has fewer accidents, and has less absenteeism. The elderly are not necessarily set in their ways and unable to change. They must adapt to many new situations, including retirement, children leaving home, widowhood, moving to a new house, and serious illnesses. Their political and social attitudes shift with those of the rest of society, but at a slower rate. Older people can learn as well as younger people; it just takes them a little longer. And they have a lifetime of experience on which to draw in assimilating new knowledge.

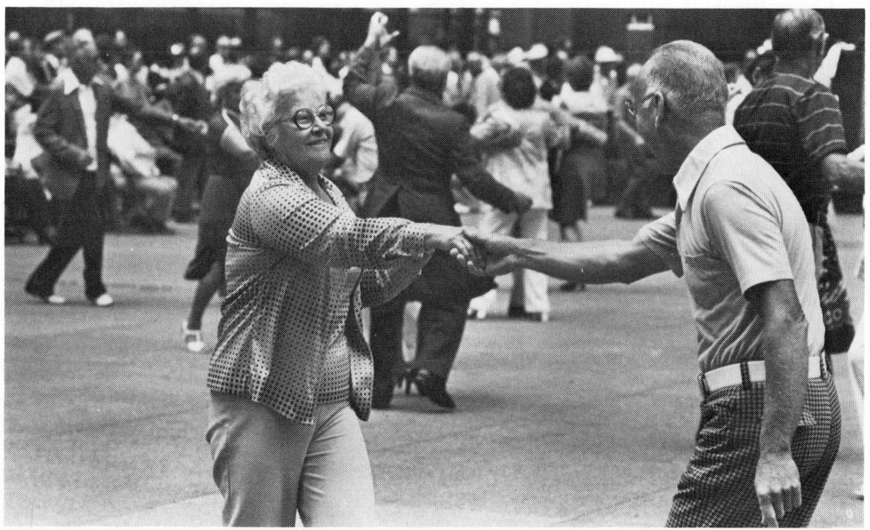

FIGURE 13-3 Most older people remain active and enjoy life. (Photograph by Christopher Brown, Stock, Boston, Inc.)

and they tend to select foods that are convenient to make. This may lead to a restricted diet and can result in deficient nutrient intake (11).

Retirement for most people means a drop in income, and as many as 25 percent of the elderly in America have incomes below the poverty level (22). Most older people live on fixed incomes, and their buying power decreases with continuing inflation. Reduced income limits the quantity and variety of foods that can be purchased; many elderly people buy less expensive, high-carbohydrate foods that are lacking in certain nutrients and pass up meat, milk, and fresh fruits and vegetables (21). A 1965 survey, for instance, found poor diets were four times as frequent among households with incomes less than $3000 as among those with incomes of $10,000 or more (13).

Other factors, including apathy, chronic illness, medication, alcoholism, and lack of nutritional knowledge, also contribute to poor nutrition in older people. Food habits are firmly established by this age, and if they are poor, it is difficult to replace them with better ones (21). Elderly people living in older areas of cities often live in fear of violence and robbery. Many tend to lock themselves in their apartments, which helps restrict the quantity and quality of their diets (23).

Placing the elderly in a nursing home is no guarantee of an adequate diet. In fact, many older people adapt their food habits to the nursing home situation and also have fewer food choices than their free-living counterparts. Their diets are sometimes not as good as those living at home (14).

Providing an adequate diet for the elderly therefore must take into account the particular problems and needs of each individual. The Basic Four Food Plan is a good starting point. If certain foods are unacceptable because of taste preferences or because they are not tolerated well, other alternatives can be explored. For example, if fluid milk is undesirable, cheese can be offered or dried milk solids can be added to soup, pudding, custards, and gravies. To increase sensory appeal, all foods should be well-prepared and attractively served. Tender, juicy foods cut into small pieces are often accepted more readily. Some people may require pureed meats and vegetables, but of a consistency that the food can be eaten with a spoon (16).

Because caloric requirements are lower but the need for other nutrients remains as high as earlier in adulthood, foods of high nutritional quality must be chosen whenever possible. Excess sodium consumption should be avoided to prevent fluid retention and elevation of blood pressure (21). Several surveys indicate that many of the elderly use dietary supplements (12,17). Some take supplements because they believe extra vitamins and minerals give them more energy or make them healthier. Others use them to prevent or treat colds, arthritis, and other problems. Many people simply want to ensure that their nutrient intake is adequate. Because food choices are often restricted in the elderly, a routine multivitamin supplement with iron might be beneficial (21). However, if they can be encouraged to consume a more varied diet, the money might be better spent on food.

FIGURE 13-4 Companionship at mealtime makes eating more enjoyable and encourages better eating habits. (Photograph by Ken Heyman).

The proper eating environment is as important to good dietary habits as providing good food. Eating is a social activity, and the elderly, like everyone else, enjoy the company of family, friends, or other peers at mealtime. If mealtime is something to look forward to, people will make a greater effort to plan and prepare good meals or eat the foods provided for them (Figure 13-4).

Several programs have been initiated by the federal government to improve the nutritional status of the elderly (21). The Meals-on-Wheels program delivers a hot meal to the homes of participating senior citizens 3 to 7 days a week, depending on the resources of the program. In some cases, food to be refrigerated for the evening meal or for breakfast is also delivered. In contrast, the Congregate Meals program attempts to meet the social as well as nutritional needs of the elderly. People are transported to a centrally located dining area and can participate in a variety of social, recreational, and educational experiences as well as a nutritious meal. The cost of the meals is based on the individual's ability to pay, but all senior citizens can participate regardless of income. Attempts by the

1. Certain special foods or nutrients retard aging.

2. Most older people are incapable of taking care of themselves and have lost interest in life.

Reagan administration to reduce federal spending will probably have profound effects on programs for the elderly during the early 1980s.

Supper clubs, churches and other social centers, and retirement communities also provide means for getting the elderly together for meals and social activities. Senior citizens in some cities have experimented with food-buying cooperatives, in which they pool their resources and younger volunteers help purchase and distribute food.

Nutritionally Related Problems

Obesity Obesity is a problem for many of the elderly. In several surveys, up to half the older people had body weights more than 10 percent above the desirable level. The HANES study, using skinfold thickness as a criterion, found that in the 45- to 74-year-old age group, 32.4 percent of the black women, 7.7 percent of the black men, 24.7 percent of the white women, and 13.4 percent of the white men were obese (10).

In the elderly, obesity frequently results from the maintenance of the higher caloric intake of earlier adulthood at a time when energy requirements have declined. Increasing physical activity will help solve this problem. It also will have beneficial effects on the heart and circulatory system, the respiratory system, and the strength of muscles and bones.

Atherosclerosis and Diabetes Mellitus Diabetes mellitus and the manifestations of atherosclerosis, such as heart disease and stroke, frequently occur in the elderly. However, both problems are the result of processes occurring throughout life, and steps must be taken much earlier to prevent them (see Chapters 2 and 3).

Osteoporosis Osteoporosis is a reduction in the mass of a bone without an alteration in its chemical composition. Thus the bone grows smaller or thinner, and as a result, it becomes more fragile and susceptible to fracture (2, pages 285–296). This disorder is becoming increasingly common among the elderly and is found more frequently in women than in men. Osteoporosis may have several causes, including prolonged calcium deficiency, hormonal imbalances, excess protein, and lack of physical activity (2, pages 285–296). Among the treatments are providing calcium, fluoride, and vitamin D supplements and hormonal therapy. However, permanent cure usually cannot be achieved.

Proper diet may contribute to the prevention of osteoporosis. Maintaining an intake of milk and dairy products or other good sources of calcium will prevent depletion of this mineral from bone. Vitamin D facilitates calcium absorption from the digestive tract. In addition, adequate fluoride intake, such as in fluoridated water, allows the incorporation of fluorine into the bone mineral, thereby increasing its resistance to decomposition.

Study Guide

SUMMARY

1. Because of the many physiological changes that occur, nutritional requirements may be altered by the aging process. Energy needs decrease as both the BMR and physical activity decline with age. Protein requirements, however, remain the same or may even increase slightly. Little is known about vitamin and mineral requirements in the elderly, and the RDAs for those people over the age of 50 are generally the same as for younger adults.
2. A variety of factors in aging may restrict food choices or interfere with the body's ability to utilize food. These include loss of teeth, decline in taste and smell, reduced digestive secretions, and loss of muscular strength and coordination. Living alone, reduced or fixed incomes, illness, apathy, medication, alcoholism, and poor food habits also contribute to poor nutrition in the elderly.
3. Providing an adequate diet for the elderly must take into account the particular problems and needs of each individual. The Basic Four Food Plan is a good starting point, and foods of high nutritional quality should be chosen from each group. To increase appeal, all foods should be well-prepared and attractively served in a proper eating environment. The Meals-on-Wheels and Congregate Meal programs are government programs that help provide these for the elderly.
4. Some problems of the elderly, such as obesity, atherosclerosis, osteoporosis, and perhaps diabetes mellitus, may result from poor dietary habits throughout adulthood, and a proper diet may delay or prevent their onset. However, no particular nutrient or type of food can retard the aging process.

STUDY QUESTIONS

1. Can any particular nutrient retard aging? In what ways can diet influence longevity?
2. Why does the energy requirement decline with age? How do the RDAs for the other nutrients for those over 50 years of age generally compare with those of younger adults? What implications do the answers to these two questions have for nutritional choices for the elderly?
3. List four physiological factors that can interfere with an elderly person's ability to utilize food and how they do so.
4. List four socioeconomic factors that can interfere with an elderly person's ability to utilize food and how they do so.
5. Why is it important not to stereotype elderly people when attempting to improve their dietary habits and nutritional status?
6. List some ways that food or the eating experience can be made more enjoyable to older people.
7. List four nutritionally related disorders common among the elderly. What changes in dietary habits during adulthood may help delay or prevent the onset of these problems?

SELF-TEST

Multiple choice: Select the one best answer.

1. Life span was extended by restricting food intake in
   a. Infant rats and mice
   b. Adult rats and mice
   c. Human infants
   d. Human adults
2. Impairment of stomach acid secretion may impair the ability to absorb
   a. Vitamin D
   b. Vitamin C
   c. Iron
   d. Riboflavin

3. Many older people need to avoid consuming too much
   a. Calcium
   b. Riboflavin
   c. Zinc
   d. Sodium
4. To reduce the occurrence of atherosclerosis and osteoporosis during old age
   a. Encourage major changes in the diets of all elderly people
   b. Choose a properly balanced diet throughout life
   c. Take vitamin and mineral supplements
   d. All of the above
5. Most people over the age of 65
   a. Continue to engage in their normal activities
   b. Are lonely and depressed
   c. Are confined to nursing homes
   d. Are senile

True-False

F 1. Vitamin E retards many of the basic processes of aging.
F 2. Dairy products should be avoided by most older people.
T 3. The need for most nutrients is about the same in the elderly as in younger adults.

SUGGESTED ACTIVITIES

1. Interview some elderly people you know and attempt to determine a typical day's diet and their particular likes and dislikes. Can you identify any nutrients that might be deficient in their diet? What foods might they enjoy that would provide these nutrients?
2. Explore local nutrition programs for the elderly. Some examples include:
   a. Invite a speaker from the Meals-on-Wheels or the Congregate Meals programs to talk to your class.
   b. Engage in volunteer work with Meals-on-Wheels, Congregate Meals, nursing homes, church groups, or a food-buying cooperative.

FURTHER READING

1. A readable discussion of the aging process:

   Shock, N. W.: "The Physiology of Aging," *Sci. Am.* **206**:100–110 (January 1962).

2. A detailed look at nutritional aspects of aging:

   Winick, M.: *Nutrition and Aging,* Wiley, New York, 1976.

3. This article explodes many myths about the elderly:

   Palmare, E.: "Facts on Aging—A Short Quiz," *Gerontologist* **17**:315–320 (1977).

NUTRITION CHALLENGES FOR THE 1980s

Throughout this book we have seen how important nutrition has become to everyone. A great deal of information has accumulated in the last few years. However, the field is still changing rapidly, and many major issues remain unresolved. As we look ahead into the 1980s, these issues assume even greater importance because many current problems could increase in magnitude during the next decade. However, the potential also exists to solve them: through well-planned research, appropriate economic programs and public health measures, and expanded nutrition education. Let us take a closer look at what may lie ahead.

The World Food Situation: Abundance or Scarcity?

From 1972 through 1975, the world experienced a major food crisis. It was sparked by poor harvests in the U.S.S.R. and southern Asia as well as severe drought across Africa south of the Sahara Desert and aggravated by the fact that in the early 1970s the United States had removed millions of acres of land from production in response to large surpluses and declining prices of grain. When the Soviet Union bought millions of tons of grain from the United States in 1972 and weather conditions resulted in poor harvests in the United States in 1974, world grain reserves plummeted to dangerously low levels. Prices soared. *World food crisis* became household words as millions of people in sub-Saharan African and

People are hungry more because they cannot get food than because there is not enough.

southern Asia faced starvation. Pessimists worried that the predictions of Thomas Malthus were finally coming true: that the world's population was nearing a size that could no longer be fed.

Improved weather conditions and record harvests in southern Asia, Canada, Australia, Argentina, and the United States eased the crisis in the second half of the 1970s, but some authorities warn that the respite is only temporary: sooner or later food production will not keep up with population growth. Furthermore, malnutrition has long been a problem among the poor, especially in the developing nations. An estimated 400 to 500 million people worldwide live on the edge of starvation, while more than a billion suffer from malnutrition to a degree that influences development or health (1,2) (Figure 14-1). Protein-energy malnutrition affects 100 to 200 million children under the age of 5 years (1,3) (Figure 14-2), and more than 100,000 children in the Far East alone go blind each year because of vitamin A deficiency. Are these problems beyond solution? Can we eliminate hunger and malnutrition among the world's poor? Is worldwide famine inevitable? In this section we will look at the current prognosis for the world food situation and the factors that will play a role in its outcome.

WILL DEMAND OUTSTRIP PRODUCTION?

The world's population is currently over 4 billion people (4), and it is increasing at a rate of about 2 percent annually (3). It is expected to reach about 5.4 billion by 1990 and between 6 and 7 billion by the year 2000 (3–5). At the present time, the rate of population growth is decreasing (5; 17, page 2) (Figure 14-3), and if this trend continues, the world's population could stabilize at 10 to 12 billion sometime in the next 100 years (30).

The world currently produces enough food to support its population (4,7,8). In 1977, grain production was high enough to provide 3000 kcal/day and 65 g/day of protein for every person on earth, and these figures do not include the additional amounts available from legumes, fruits and vegetables, fish, and forage-fed livestock (4). The Food and Agriculture Organization (FAO) of the United Nations estimates the world demand for food will increase at a rate of 2.4 percent annually through 1985, but food production will rise by 2.7 percent each year (3) (Table 14-1). Thus, barring a catastrophe, such as war or severe weather changes, caloric and protein production will still meet or exceed demand in the mid-1980s (5).

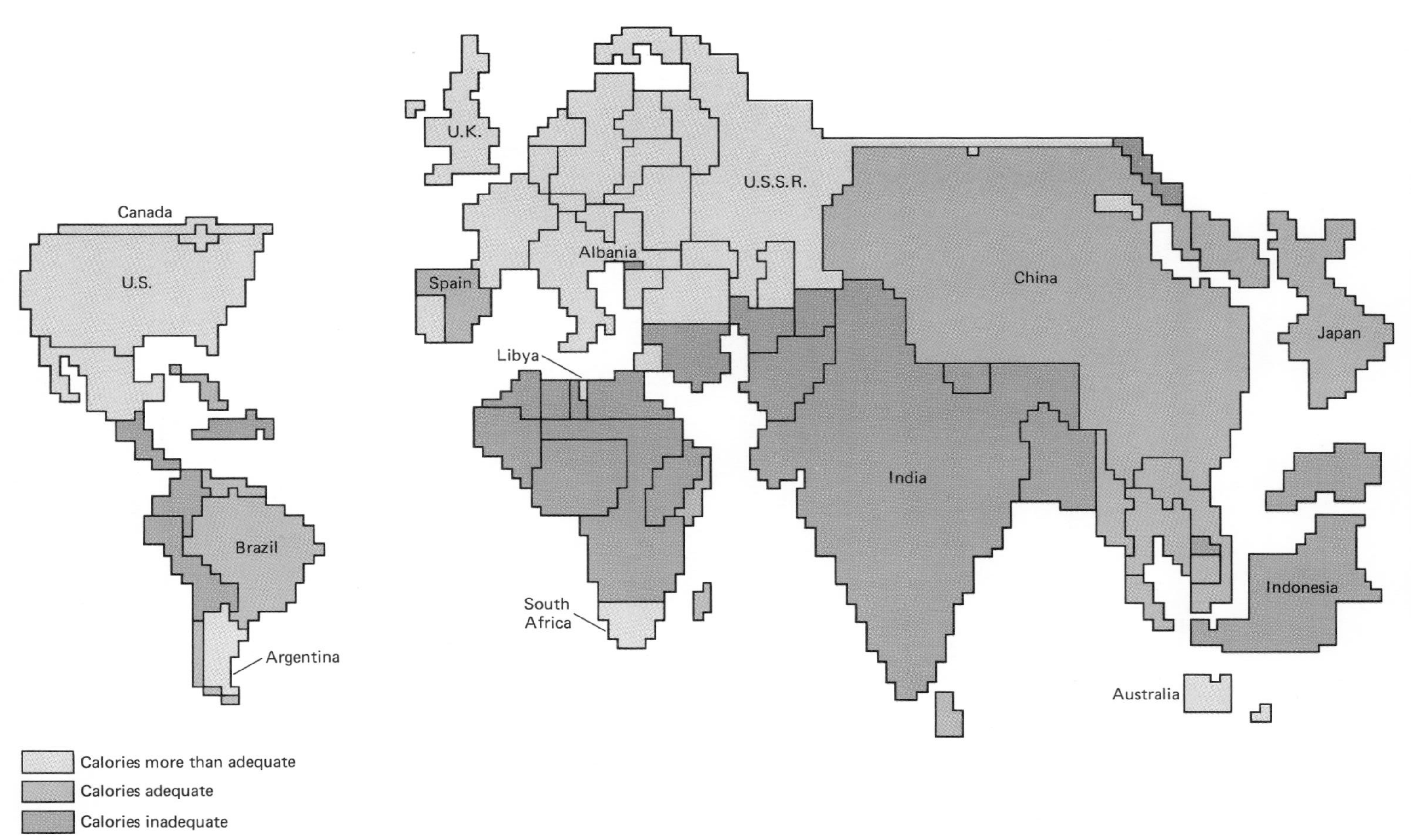

FIGURE 14-1
The Geographical Distribution of Malnutrition. In the countries with the darkest shading, average caloric intake is less than adequate. (Adequate is defined by the United Nations as 3000 kcal/day for males and 2200 kcal/day for females.) In the nations with intermediate shading, caloric intake is adequate or as much as 10 percent above adequate, and in the countries shaded slightly, average caloric intake exceeds the adequate level by more than 10 percent. [*Source:* J. Mayer, "The Dimensions of Human Hunger", *Scientific American* **235:**40–49 (September 1976). Copyright © 1976 Scientific American Inc. All rights reserved.]

FIGURE 14-2 Malnutrition is widespread in the developing nations. Here, hungry people wait in line for food in Bangladesh. (Photograph by David Austin, Stock, Boston, Inc.)

In most developing countries, however, the food situation is precarious, and it may deteriorate. During the mid-1970s, demand for grain in these nations exceeded production by 25 million tons annually (20, page 13). The FAO estimates that in the early 1980s, demand will increase faster than production by at least 1 percent each year (3) (Table 14-1). Estimates of the shortfall in the developing world by 1985 range from 60 million to 100 million metric tons of grain annually (6,9). Hundreds of millions of people, therefore, face hunger and malnutrition during the coming decade. The greatest challenge for the 1980s will be to raise the average level of food consumption among these people. What currently

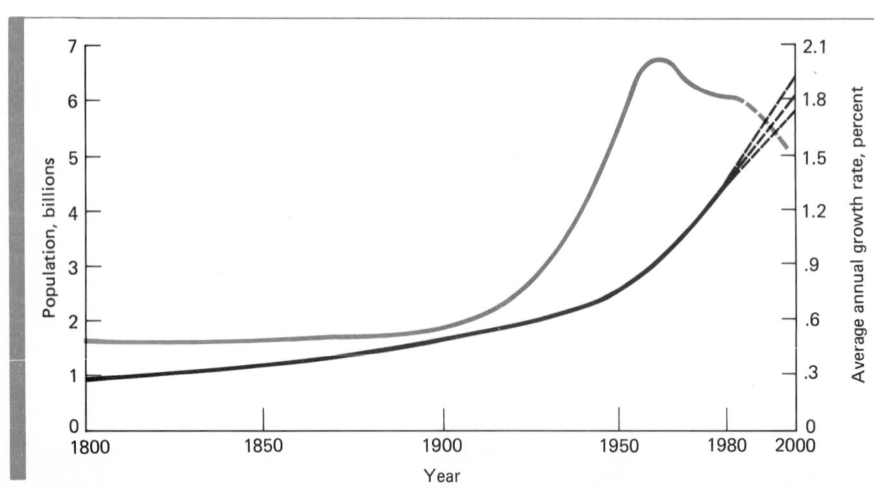

FIGURE 14-3 *Changes in World Population Growth.* World population is increasing (black line), but the rate of growth is declining (colored line). [*Source:* H. Mahler, "People", *Scientific American* **243**:67–77 (September 1980).]

limits their food supply? Can these factors be changed in the next decade? If so, how?

LIMITS TO PRODUCTION

On a worldwide basis, availability of land will not be an important restriction on food production. Of the 3.2 billion hectares of arable land in the world, only about half is currently in use (10,11,32). However, much of the best land is already being cultivated, and the costs of bringing new land into production are likely to be higher than for land now in use (20, pages 52–53). In addition, certain areas of the world, such as Bangladesh, Egypt, and parts of India, are nearing their limit of available land; these countries will have to rely on more intensive cultivation to produce more food. Opening new areas to agriculture will be restricted mainly to parts of Latin America and sub-Saharan Africa (11; 12, page 97; 16, pages 58–59).

Not only is land still available in the world, but much of the land currently in use does not produce to its full potential. Yields in the developing nations tend to be low (Figure 14-4). For example, corn yields in 112 of the developing nations average less than 3 metric tons per hectare (t/ha) and in 81 of these, yields average less than 1.5 t/ha. In contrast, corn yields in the United States average 5.8 t/ha; and in New Zealand, 7.2 t/ha (6). One authority estimates that if agricultural methods similar to those used in Iowa were applied worldwide, the present world population could be fed on only 170 million hectares rather than the 1.4 billion currently being utilized (10). Another factor restricting food production is that about 10 percent of the currently cultivated land is used to grow nonnutritive items, including rubber, cotton, coffee, tea, cocoa, and tobacco,

TABLE **14-1**

Projections of food demand and production to 1985

	Volume Growth Rates, Percent per Year	
AREA	FOOD DEMAND	FOOD PRODUCTION
All Developed Countries	1.5	2.8
Market economies	1.4	2.4
Eastern Europe and the U.S.S.R.	1.7	3.5
All Developing Countries	3.4	2.6
Market economies:	3.6	2.6
Africa	3.8	2.5
Far East	3.4	2.4
Latin America	3.6	2.9
Near East	4.0	3.1
Centrally planned economies	3.1	2.6
World	2.4	2.7

Source: Anonymous, "Assessment of the World Food Situation—Present and Future," *Food Nutr. (Roma)* **1**:7–40, 1975. Reprinted with permission of the Food and Agricultural Organization of the United Nations.

for export (12, page 96). Theoretically, the foreign exchange generated by selling these products can be used to buy food. However, depending on exports for revenue to buy food places a nation at the mercy of fluctuations in prices on the world market: if the price of an export commodity falls or if food costs rise, the ability to buy food is reduced. In addition, foreign exchange is often used to finance industrialization or to buy weapons for defense, while the poor continue to live in poverty.

One answer to the productivity problem has been the "Green Revolution," which began in Mexico in the 1940s and has since spread around the world. Its basis is the genetic improvement of grains, such as wheat, rice, and maize, to increase yields. For example, varieties have been developed that mature more rapidly, enabling a second and, in some cases, a third crop to be grown in one season. Another improvement was the development of strains of wheat and rice with shorter, stiffer stalks that can support the weight of more grain. However, use of these varieties requires large quantities of fertilizer, sophisticated irrigation systems, and knowledge of how to use them. Most small farmers do not have the capital to invest in these agricultural aids (12, pages 117–118; 15). One study found that production costs for the average Filipino rice farmer using traditional methods and seed varieties was about $20 per hectare. The costs rose to $220 per hectare when high-yield seed varieties and modern technology were adopted. Even though yields increased threefold and the return was four times that gained by traditional methods, the farmers still could not pay for the modern technology (12, pages 117–118). Large landholdings in the developing nations are generally no more productive (12, page 115). They are frequently divided into small plots worked by tenant farmers and sharecroppers. Rental rates often average 50 percent of the crop, and most tenants do not have leases. They constantly face the threat

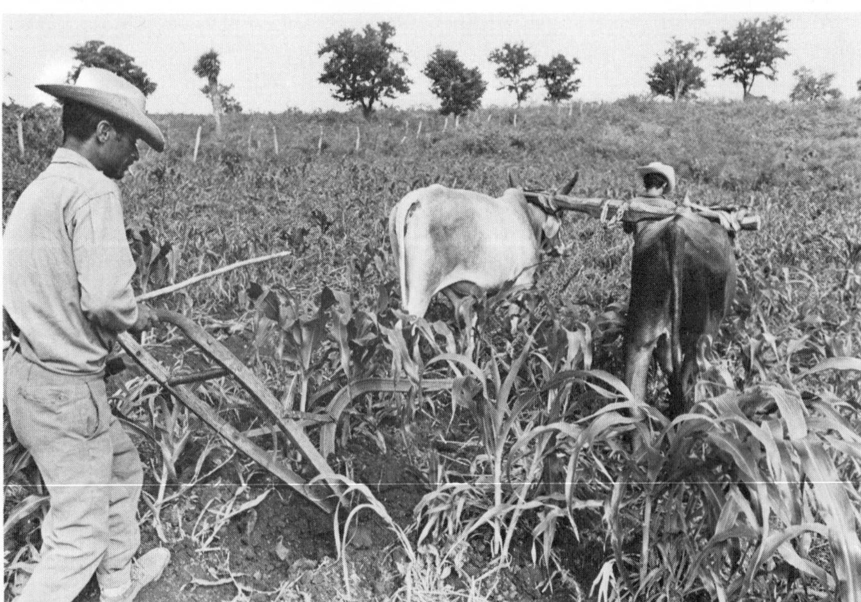

FIGURE 14-4 Antiquated farming methods are still widely used in the developing nations. (Photograph by John Running, Stock, Boston, Inc.)

of eviction, and rarely are they compensated for improvements they make on the land. Thus they have neither the capital nor the incentive to increase their productivity (15).

Not only are many modern agricultural methods currently too expensive for most of the world's farmers, but costs are expected to continue to rise in the future. Large amounts of energy are required in the manufacture of fertilizer and pesticides and to run machines and irrigation systems. The price of energy has spiraled upward throughout the 1970s and probably will continue to do so. In competing for available supplies, the developing nations generally come up short; the affluent countries can afford to bid prices up beyond their reach (5). Thus energy will be a limiting factor for agricultural expansion in these nations. Fertilizer is another agricultural input that will become increasingly expensive. Since petroleum is required for its production, fertilizer prices will generally rise along with those of oil. In addition, demand is increasing at a rate of about 5.5 percent annually, and the developing nations will again have difficulty competing with the affluent ones for limited supplies (5; 12, page 106; 16, pages 60–64).

Probably the most important limit to increased agricultural production is climate. Since the mid-1940s, a cooling trend has occurred and season-to-season weather has become more variable. Droughts and floods have become more frequent, and the monsoons in southern Asia have become less reliable in their timing and duration. One result was the famine of 1972 to 1975. Climatologists do not agree on the prospects for the future. Some believe the earth will warm up because of a "greenhouse effect," in which carbon dioxide released by human activities will hold heat to the earth. This will lead to greater precipitation and less variability in the weather. Other scientists believe a decline in sunspot activity will result in a cooling trend during the next 70 years, and weather will become drier and more variable. In either case, the effect on agricultural output will be profound, especially in areas with a short growing season or low water availability (21).

GETTING FOOD TO THE PEOPLE: THE DISTRIBUTION PROBLEM

That the world produces sufficient food to support its population but millions of people starve results largely from unequal distribution of food and income. A disproportionately large amount of food is used by the affluent countries. They consume an average of 45 percent more kilocal-

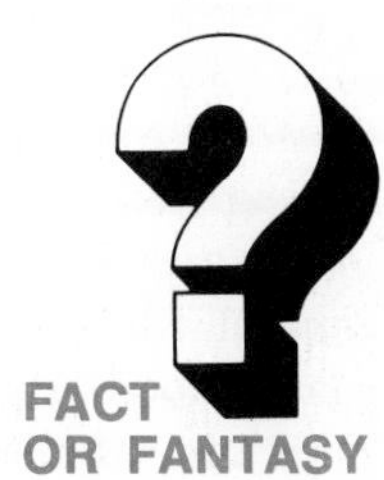

FACT OR FANTASY

1. The world is running out of food.

2. Shipping more food from the affluent nations to the developing countries will solve world food problems.

FIGURE 14-5 Although shipments of food to needy countries can save some people from malnutrition, they do not provide a long-term solution to the hunger problem. (Photograph by Jean-Claude Lejeune, Stock, Boston, Inc.)

ories per capita than the developing nations and almost three times as much meat, eggs, milk, fish, fruits, and vegetables (20, page 13). Per capita grain consumption in the United States and Canada is approaching 1000 kilograms annually, most of it fed to animals, while the developing world consumes only about 200 kg/year per person, most of it eaten directly (22). However, some experts argue that reducing grain consumption in the affluent countries (Figure 14-5) would not make any more grain available to the poorer areas of the world, because the surpluses would lower food prices and therefore profits for farmers in the developed nations. As a result, production would be cut back until market conditions were more favorable (16, page 51). There is also no guarantee that the food would ever reach the needy. Many developing nations export barley, soybeans, peanuts, fresh fruits and vegetables, sugar, bananas, coconut, meat, and fishmeal that could be used to feed humans or livestock in their own countries (13, page 15; 14). In 1975, for example, Brazil exported nearly all of its 10 million metric ton soybean harvest, while many of its own people were suffering from severe malnutrition (23). Many Central American countries have increased beef exports in recent years, despite a high incidence of malnutrition at home (12, page 127). As with nonfood agricultural exports, these are meant to generate foreign exchange. However, the money is seldom used to improve conditions for the poor (9).

Lack of adequate storage and distribution facilities limits the ability to market food in many developing nations. More than 10 to 20 percent of the total world grain harvest is lost to insects, rodents, mold, and spoilage during storage and transportation (10,32). In the developing countries, losses are much higher; in Africa, for example, as much as 25 to 30 percent of the food is spoiled annually (12, page 146). Moreover, lack of roads, railroads, and transportation vehicles hinders distribution of food. Food imported into Bangladesh, for instance, is likely to remain in warehouses in cities such as Dacca or Chittagong because it is difficult to transport it to where it is needed, especially during the monsoon season. Similar problems exist in much of Africa, where the populations are largely dispersed or nomadic (24).

Inadequate incomes among the poor contribute to the unequal distribution of food. Small landowners often grow barely enough food for themselves when the harvest is good, let alone having any to sell for additional income. When harvests are poor, their situation becomes precarious (3,9). Tenant farmers fare even worse, since they must give up a substantial part of their harvest to the landowner and seldom have money to buy additional food. Inability to find work, the difficulties of farm life, and the hope of employment in industry attract many rural people into the cities. The influx is too large to be accommodated, so most of these migrants cannot find jobs. They congregate in shanty towns with inadequate food, housing, and services. On the farm they could grow some food for their own use; in the city they must purchase all their food. With inadequate incomes and insufficient knowledge of sound buying practices, they cannot meet their nutritional needs.

LOOKING AHEAD

Some experts believe that unless a major catastrophe, such as war or adverse climatic changes, occurs, the world has the potential using conventional farming methods, to meet its food needs well into the next century

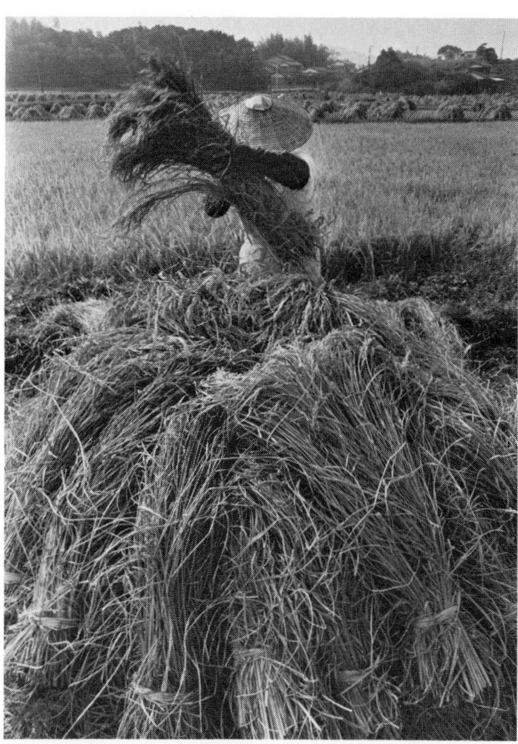

FIGURE 14-6
Intensive cultivation of very small farms in Japan, Taiwan, China, and South Korea has resulted in some of the highest yields of grain per acre in the world. (Photograph by George Bellerose, Stock, Boston, Inc.)

(13; 17, pages 293–313). The major problem will be managing agricultural resources for the maximum benefit of all. First, governments in the developing nations must make agricultural expansion a top priority and include it in their general development plans. A major failing in many of these countries has been the emphasis placed on industrialization and defense rather than on food production (17, page 207; 19). In addition, land reform must be undertaken in many areas and the land redistributed in a way that best meets the needs of the particular nation. For example, in Chile, farms of 40 to 80 hectares tend to be most productive (17, page 217). However, the highest yields of grain per unit of land in the world are found on small-scale holdings in Taiwan, Japan, China, and South Korea (15) (Figure 14-6). The farms in Japan and Taiwan average only 1 hectare in size (17, page 217).

We have already seen that the large-scale, energy-intensive farming methods used in the United States are not feasible in most of the developing nations. However, labor-intensive methods can be substituted for many of the inputs required for energy-intensive agriculture, especially on small farms. Since the cost of energy is high, using human labor for weeding, spraying, and harvesting may be a viable alternative. Multiple cropping (growing two or three successive crops on the same land) and intercropping (growing two crops simultaneously on the same land) also will increase productivity. Suitable technology, such as fertilizer, small machines, and more sophisticated irrigation systems, can be introduced where practical. Capital will have to be provided through government and international aid and by the farmers' banding together into cooperative organizations. Another important need is for extension systems to educate farmers. Finally, storage and distribution systems must be improved to provide markets for increased production. Not only will this increase profits for farmers and thereby provide the incentive to improve productivity, but it will facilitate the distribution of food to needy areas within each nation.

Although increased productivity and better distribution are important steps toward relieving hunger in the developing world, they will not help people who lack the money to buy food. Because 60 to 80 percent of the third-world population depends on agriculture for a living, much of the emphasis for increasing incomes should be directed toward the farming sector. For example, labor-intensive agricultural methods have the advantage of increasing employment, thereby keeping people on the farms and providing income with which they can buy food. Hopefully, as agricultural development progresses, demand for other consumer goods will rise, providing the impetus for industrial expansion and higher employment and incomes for the urban poor. As a temporary measure, subsidies may be needed to provide inexpensive food for the poor without reducing profits to farmers. One policy is a two-tiered pricing system in which the affluent pay more for a product, thereby allowing the poor to pay less. Such a system, involving wheat and rice, has been in operation in India for many years (12, pages 157–176).

The prognosis for the world food situation thus depends heavily on changing development priorities and reforming many institutions, such as food-distribution and land-tenure systems. Failure to do so will intensify current inequities and lead to increased malnutrition in the coming decades. However, if the necessary changes can be implemented and the population growth rate continues to decline, a balance between demand for food and its availability may be achieved in much of the world in the next century.

Nutrition in the United States: The Price of Progress

In contrast to people in the developing world, most Americans have become accustomed to an abundant and varied food supply. A number of nutritionists and government officials have boasted that the United States is the best-fed nation in the world. Nevertheless, many Americans suffer from malnutrition. Some cannot afford an adequate diet or lack the knowledge or motivation to make proper food choices. An even bigger problem, however, may be the abundance of food itself: as we have seen, considerable evidence has accumulated that suggests that current dietary patterns may contribute to the high incidence of obesity, heart disease, diabetes mellitus, high blood pressure, and certain types of cancer in the United States (see appropriate sections of Chapters 1, 2, 3, and 8). Many people also are concerned about the means by which we produce our food, claiming that they rob us of nutrients and add potentially hazardous chemicals to the food supply. During the 1970s we made substantial progress toward resolving some of these problems. But will current trends continue?

HUNGER IN THE UNITED STATES

In 1968, confidence that Americans are the best-fed people in the world was shaken by publication of *Hunger U.S.A.* by the Citizen's Board of Inquiry into Hunger and Malnutrition in the United States (25). The Board of Inquiry reported that between one-third and one-half of the poor people in this country were affected by hunger and malnutrition, and it identified 280 counties in which the situation was desperate enough to warrant a presidential declaration of national emergency. Cases of protein-energy malnutrition, rickets, and vitamin A and vitamin C deficiency, as well as widespread iron deficiency, were documented. In addition, federal, state, and local governments, medical institutions, charities, and our society as a whole were found to lack effective programs to improve the situation and little motivation to implement any. The Ten-State Nutrition Survey and preliminary results of the first Health and Nutrition Examination Survey (HANES), hearings by the Senate Select Committee on Nutrition and Human Needs, and the 1969 White House Conference on Food, Nutrition, and Health focused additional attention on the problem (Figure 14-7).

As a result of congressional action in the early 1970s, the federal gov-

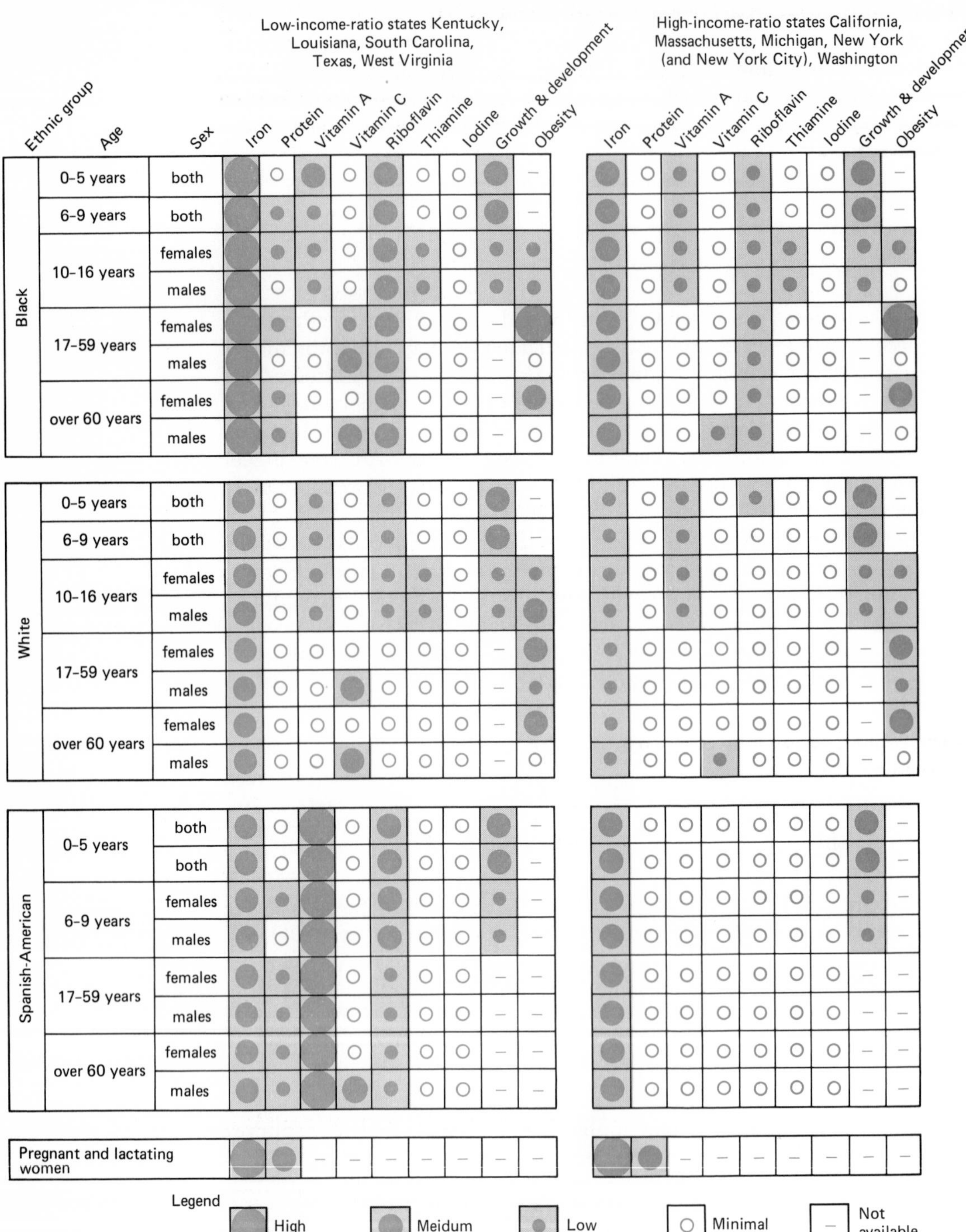

FIGURE 14-7

The Major Findings of the Ten-State Nutrition Survey. [*Source:* U.S. Dept. Health and Human Services, *Ten-State Nutrition Survey 1968–1970, Highlights,* Atlanta, GA, Center for Disease Control (1972), pp. 4–5.]

ernment increased its food aid to the underprivileged of this country. By 1972, some progress had been made (26), and this has continued into 1980 (27). By the first quarter of 1979, 18.4 million Americans were participating in the Food Stamp Program, as compared with 2.5 million in 1968. Child nutrition programs (School Breakfast, School Lunch, Summer Food Service, Child-Care Food, and Special Milk Programs) also had expanded considerably, with a budget exceeding $2.2 billion in fiscal 1977. The National School Lunch Program accounted for $2 billion of this amount. It reached 26 million children in 1977, 45 percent of whom received their meals free or at reduced prices. This compares with the 20 million children participating in the program in 1968, 15 percent of whom received their meals free or at reduced prices (27). The Special Supplemental Program for Women, Infants, and Children (WIC) was established in 1972, and its expenditures to improve the status of pregnant and lactating women, infants, and young children totaled about $259 million in 1977. The U.S. Department of Agriculture's Expanded Food and Nutrition Education Program (EFNEP), designed to improve food choices and preparation practices of low-income homemakers, also has been relatively successful, although it has been able to reach only 20 percent of its target population because of limited resources. Current data indicate that food assistance has been going where it is most needed: on the average, households in areas with the highest needs received substantially more food assistance than those in areas with higher incomes (27).

In the United States, malnutrition is far from being eliminated.

Despite the expansion of federal food aid to the poor, malnutrition in the United States is far from being eliminated. At the same time that aid has increased, rising food prices have reduced buying power. Although comprehensive data are lacking, it is likely that substantial numbers of low-income people, such as the poor in rural and urban areas, many of the elderly, migrant workers, and native Americans, still cannot buy sufficient food. Iron deficiency remains widespread, and deficiencies of zinc and folacin have been discovered among certain population groups.

Continued efforts to reach those still not served by aid programs would help reduce these problems in the future. However, budget cuts proposed by President Ronald Reagan in 1981 may greatly reduce food aid to the poor. Standards of eligibility for food stamps and free school lunches will probably be tightened, the cost of lunch for students who must pay will probably rise, and meal pattern requirements for school lunches may change. Funds for nutrition education, such as the WIC program, are also expected to decline.

As in the developing nations, the solution to hunger is not simply a matter of providing aid. A decisive victory will require attacking the problem at its roots: poverty and ignorance. Taming inflation, increasing employment and incomes, and expanding nutrition education will be the greatest contribution toward helping the poor share in the abundance of the American food supply.

THE DIET-DISEASE CONTROVERSY

The Dietary Goals issued by the Senate in 1977 have been considered by many to be a cornerstone of future American nutrition policy. Yet we have seen that the evidence linking diet with heart disease, diabetes mellitus, certain types of cancer, and high blood pressure is still controversial; many authorities do not advocate dietary modifications for most Americans as a means of fighting these problems. Many other nutritionists and influential members of Congress believe that the diet-disease link has been established firmly enough to warrant action at the present time. One step toward educating Americans about the recommended dietary changes was the publication of *Dietary Guidelines for Americans* by the Departments of Agriculture and Health and Human Services in 1980 (28). These recommendations were outlined in Chapter 1, and their controversial nature was discussed in Chapters 2, 3, and 8.

The surge of congressional and bureaucratic interest in nutrition, and nutrition-disease associations in particular, resulted in a dramatic increase in federal spending for research into these areas. The Office of Management and Budget estimated that in 1977, the United States government devoted $50 million toward nutrition research; by 1979, the USDA and National Institutes of Health alone planned to spend $120 million (29). In light of the fiscal policies of the Reagan administration, it is not certain that this flow of money will continue in the 1980s.

FOCUS 14-1 RESEARCH NEEDS FOR THE 1980s An important part of resolving current nutritional problems is the need for information. More money is being devoted to nutritional research than ever before. Here are some areas of greatest need (31):

1. Nutrient requirements:
   a. Especially for infants, children, adolescents, pregnant and lactating women, and the elderly
   b. Especially for fat and carbohydrate
   c. Especially for trace minerals
   d. Establishing what are optimal, as compared with adequate, levels of nutrient intake
   e. Effects of marginal intakes over a long period of time
2. Nutrient content of foods:
   a. Especially trace minerals
   b. Especially fiber
3. Availability to the body of nutrients in food
4. Nutrient toxicity
5. The diet-disease controversy: Conclusively establishing the role, if any, of diet in causing heart disease, diabetes mellitus, certain types of cancer, and high blood pressure
6. Toxicity of foreign compounds in food:
   a. Food additives
   b. Pesticides
   c. Antibiotics (from animal feed)
   d. Naturally occurring food toxins
7. Drug-nutrient interactions
8. Effects of early malnutrition on subsequent growth and mental development:
   a. Effect of early deprivation on physical and mental development
   b. Effect of overfeeding or obesity in early

life on body weight later on

9. Effects of new processing methods on the nutrient content of food (e.g., freeze-drying, microwave cooking)
10. Improved methods for monitoring the nutrient intake of the U.S. population
11. Methods of applying nutritional knowledge:
    a. Public health programs to improve nutritional status
    b. Nutrition education:
        (1) General public
        (2) Special population groups (e.g., pregnant and lactating women, children, the elderly)
        (3) Health professionals, including physicians, dentists, and nurses
        (4) Teachers at all grade levels

TRENDS IN FOOD PRODUCTION AND PROCESSING

Food technology has grown tremendously during the last two decades, resulting in an increasing number and variety of processed foods on our supermarket shelves (Figure 14-8). This trend will probably continue in the future. Although early efforts in food processing were devoted to improving the sanitary and microbiological quantity of food and extending shelf life, a major emphasis today is on convenience. Because of their active lifestyles, many Americans do not want to spend a lot of time preparing meals. In addition, increasing numbers of women are abandoning traditional roles and are entering the workforce. Thus demand for foods that

FIGURE 14-8
Processed foods are increasingly common in supermarkets in the United States, and the trend is expected to continue. (**A** Photograph by Russ Kinne, Photo Researchers, Inc; **B** Photograph by David Kramer, Photo Researchers, Inc.)

require a minimal amount of preparation can be expected to rise. Another advantage of many processed foods is their lower cost. For example, imitation orange juice products and processed cheese are less expensive than conventional juice and cheese. As food costs rise, more people will turn to these products. The potential exists to make many others, such as imitation meat products from textured soy protein. These will become more widely marketed as it becomes more profitable to do so. However, care must be exercised in using imitation foods, because they are not always nutritionally equivalent to the foods they replace.

As we saw in Chapter 9, many people are concerned about the effects of processing on the nutritional quality and safety of the food supply. As more information becomes available about human nutritional requirements and the composition of foods, particularly in terms of trace minerals, we will be better able to assess the practical impact of nutrient losses during processing. The Food and Drug Administration is currently taking a closer look at food additives and drugs in animal feed. Some additives, such as nitrites, and many antibiotics may be eliminated from food production in the next several years. Nevertheless, a substantial number of people have begun to move away from processed foods; they prefer to buy the so-called natural or organic products. However, continuation or growth of this "back-to-nature" movement will depend on whether consumers feel that the risks of processed foods outweigh their convenience and lower cost.

Study Guide

SUMMARY

Despite the fact that the world currently produces sufficient food to support its population, hundreds of millions of people still face malnutrition because of poor management of agricultural resources and inequitable distribution of income as well as food. World food production is expected to keep pace with growing demand, but unless changes are made, including shifting of priorities toward agricultural development, land-tenure reforms, increased incomes, and better distribution systems, the poor will continue to starve for a long time to come. Hunger exists in the United States as well, and its roots lie in poverty and ignorance. Although government food aid has reduced the problem in the past decade, only increased employment and incomes among the poor and expanded nutrition education programs will provide a permanent solution to the problem. Many current issues in nutrition, such as the diet-disease controversy and the effect of processing on the safety and nutritional quality of food, will continue to be important in the 1980s. Appropriate research will help point the way toward a resolution of these problems.

STUDY QUESTIONS

1. What factors currently lead to hunger in the developing nations, despite the fact that the world produces enough food to support its population?
2. What are some ways these factors could be altered?
3. What could make it difficult for these factors to be overcome in the next decade or so?
4. What has been done in the past to help alleviate hunger in the United States? What problems will be encountered in attempting to eradicate malnutrition in the United States during the 1980s?
5. What areas of nutrition do you think should be given more attention by researchers in the 1980s?

SUGGESTED ACTIVITIES

1. Keep abreast of the latest developments in nutrition by collecting articles from newspapers, news magazines, and government publications, as well as nutrition journals. Some suggested topics to look for:
   a. Climatic changes
   b. Agricultural reports about current harvests, both in the United States and abroad
   c. Political developments related to nutrition, such as grain sales to foreign countries and funding of public health and nutrition research programs
   d. Breakthroughs in the area of diet-disease relationships
   e. Introduction of new food products

FURTHER READING

1. The following publications look at different aspects of the world food situation and its prognosis:

Caliendo, M. A.: *Nutrition and the World Food Crisis,* Macmillan, New York, 1979.

Lappe, F. M., Collins, J., with Cary Fowler: *Food First: Beyond the Myth of Scarcity,* Houghton-Mifflin, Boston, 1977.

Center for Analysis of World Food Issues: *A Series of Papers on World Food Issues,* Cornell University, Ithaca, N.Y., 1979. This may be obtained by sending $2.00 to

Center for the Analysis of World Food Issues
Program in International Agriculture
Roberts Hall
Cornell University
Ithaca, New York 14853

Crossen, P. R., and Fredrick, K. D.: *The World Food Situation: Resource and Environmental Issues in the Developing Countries and the United States,* Resources for the Future, Inc., Washington, 1977.

Scrimshaw, N. S., and Taylor, L.: "Food," *Sci. Am.* **243:**78–88 (September 1980).

2. The original publications documenting hunger in the United States:

   Citizen's Board of Inquiry into Hunger and Malnutrition in the United States: *Hunger, U.S.A.,* Beacon Press, Boston, 1968.
   Citizen's Board of Inquiry into Hunger and Malnutrition in the United States: *Hunger, U.S.A., Revisited,* Southern Regional Council, Atlanta, Ga., 1972.

3. A description of the Dietary Guidelines for Americans:

   U.S. Department of Agriculture, U.S. Department of Health and Human Services: *Nutrition and Your Health—Dietary Guidelines for Americans,* 1980. This may be obtained from
   Superintendent of Documents
   U.S. Government Printing Office
   Washington, D.C. 20402

SELF-TEST ANSWER KEY

CHAPTER 2

Multiple choice

1.	b	6.	c
2.	d	7.	c
3.	c	8.	b
4.	d	9.	a
5.	a	10.	d

True-False

1.	T	6.	T
2.	F	7.	F
3.	T	8.	F
4.	F	9.	T
5.	F	10.	F

CHAPTER 3

Multiple choice

1.	c	6.	c
2.	d	7.	d
3.	d	8.	a
4.	b	9.	b
5.	a	10.	a

True-False

1.	T	6.	F
2.	F	7.	T
3.	F	8.	T
4.	T	9.	F
5.	T	10.	T

CHAPTER 4

Multiple choice

1.	d	6.	a
2.	a	7.	b
3.	c	8.	a
4.	b	9.	d
5.	c	10.	b

True-False

1. F
2. T
3. T
4. F
5. T

CHAPTER 5

Multiple choice

1.	c	6.	d
2.	a	7.	d
3.	a	8.	c
4.	d	9.	a
5.	c	10.	d

True-False

1. F
2. T
3. T
4. F
5. F

CHAPTER 6

Multiple choice

1. c	6. d
2. a	7. d
3. b	8. c
4. c	9. b
5. a	10. a

True-False

1. F
2. T
3. F
4. F
5. T

CHAPTER 7

Multiple choice

1. a	6. b
2. c	7. d
3. d	8. b
4. d	9. a
5. c	10. b

True-False

1. F
2. T
3. F
4. F
5. T

CHAPTER 8

Multiple choice

1. b	6. c
2. c	7. a
3. d	8. b
4. d	9. d
5. d	10. b

True-False

1. F
2. T
3. F
4. F
5. F

CHAPTER 9

Multiple choice

1. b	5. c
2. d	6. c
3. c	7. a
4. a	8. d

True-False

1. F	5. F
2. T	6. F
3. F	7. F
4. T	

CHAPTER 10

Multiple choice

1. a
2. c
3. c
4. a
5. a
6. d

True-False

1. T
2. F
3. F
4. T

CHAPTER 11

Multiple choice

1. b	5. a
2. c	6. d
3. a	7. d
4. d	8. b

True-False

1. T	5. T
2. F	6. F
3. F	7. T
4. T	

CHAPTER 12

Multiple choice

1. a
2. c
3. d
4. d
5. b
6. c
7. a
8. b
9. d
10. a

True-False

1. T
2. F
3. F
4. F
5. T
6. T
7. F
8. T

CHAPTER 13

Multiple choice

1. a
2. c
3. d
4. b
5. a

True-False

1. F
2. F
3. T

GLOSSARY

absorption The process by which the products of digestion pass from the digestive tract into the blood or lymph for distribution throughout the body.

aldosterone A hormone secreted by the adrenal cortex in response to decreased sodium or increased potassium concentrations in the extracellular fluid or decreased blood or extracellular fluid volume; it stimulates the kidney to reabsorb sodium from or secrete more potassium into the urine.

amino acids The subunits from which proteins are made; they are organic acids containing an amino ($-NH_2$) group.

anabolism Synthetic processes; those processes by which substances are built up from simpler ones.

anemia A reduction in the oxygen-carrying capacity of the blood.

aneurysm A localized swelling of a blood vessel resulting from a weakening of its wall.

anorexia nervosa A psychological disorder in which the person restricts food intake and loses body weight to the point of emaciation and even death.

antacids Drugs that neutralize stomach acid.

anthropometry The study of measurements made on the body, especially on a comparative basis.

antibodies Proteins synthesized in response to the presence of antigens in the body; the antibodies attack the antigen and render it harmless; they also persist in the body to protect it against further exposure to the antigen.

antidiuretic hormone (ADH) A hormone secreted by the posterior pituitary in response to a high concentration of solute in the extracellular fluid; it stimulates the kidney to reabsorb water from the urine.

antigen A foreign agent (bacterium, virus, foreign substance) that enters the body and stimulates the production of antibodies.

aplastic anemia A type of anemia in which the

bone marrow fails to produce enough red blood cells.

arachidonic acid A polyunsaturated fatty acid containing 18 carbon atoms and 4 double bonds.

arteriosclerosis A thickening and hardening of the walls of the arteries with a resultant loss of elasticity.

atherosclerosis A form of arteriosclerosis in which the thickening of the walls of the arteries is characterized by the accumulation of lipids, especially cholesterol, and connective tissue.

atherosclerotic plaque The patches of the arterial wall that are thickened and contain the lipid.

atom The smallest particle of matter that can exist by itself and still maintain its identity as an element.

autoimmune response A disorder in which the body produces antibodies that attack its own tissues.

balance studies A means of determining nutrient requirements in which the amount of a nutrient needed to balance that broken down by or excreted from the body is estimated.

basal metabolic rate (BMR) The energy needed to maintain life processes when at rest, but awake, and in the fasting state.

benefit-risk (cost-benefit) analysis A method of decision making in which the benefits of an action are weighed against its risks or hazards.

beriberi Thiamine deficiency characterized by impairment of nervous system function, edema, and/or wasting.

bile acids Substances synthesized from cholesterol by the liver and released into the small intestine in the bile; by emulsifying or dispersing fat, they increase the efficiency of triglyceride digestion by pancreatic lipase.

blanching Treatment of food with scalding hot water or steam to remove the skin, whiten, or inactivate enzymes; frequently used prior to canning or freezing food.

blastocyst A hollow ball of cells formed early in fetal development; it gives rise to the fetus and its supporting structures, such as the placenta.

blind experiment An experiment in which the subjects do not know whether they are receiving the treatment or not.

bolus A soft mass of chewed food.

bomb calorimeter An instrument used to measure the energy content of a food.

buffer A substance that can neutralize both acids and bases; in solution, it resists changes in pH.

calorie The energy needed to raise the temperature of one gram of water one degree Celsius.

carboxylation A chemical reaction in which carbon dioxide is added to a molecule.

carcinogen An agent which causes cancer.

carotenoid pigments Yellow-orange pigments, including alpha-, beta-, and gamma-carotene and cryptoxanthin found in plants; many are provitamins of vitamin A.

cassava A tuberous tropical plant with a starchy root that is used for food.

catabolism Degradative processes; those processes by which substances are broken down into simpler ones.

cell The smallest unit of life capable of functioning independently.

cellulose An indigestible polysaccharide composed of glucose subunits.

cephalin A phospholipid comprised of a diglyceride, phosphate, and ethanolamine.

cerebrovascular disease (stroke) Blockage of blood flow in an artery in the brain resulting from atherosclerosis or an aneurysm; owing to the death of brain tissue, one or more body functions may be partially or completely impaired.

chemical compounds Substances composed of two or more elements.

cholecystokinin-pancreozymin (CCK-PZ) A hormone produced by the small intestine in response to protein, fat, and their digestion products; it stimulates release of bile from the gall bladder and an enzyme-rich juice from the pancreas.

chyme The semifluid mass of partly digested food in the stomach and the small intestine.

chymotrypsin A pancreatic enzyme that digests proteins in the intestine; chymotrypsinogen is its inactive form.

coenzyme A nonprotein, organic substance usually derived from a vitamin that binds to an enzyme to activate it.

cofactor Any component, such as coenzymes and metal activators, required for the activity of enzymes; the term is most often used in connection with the metal activators of enzymes.

colostrum Immature milk secreted during the first few days of lactation; it is a thin, clear or yellowish fluid, and it contains antibodies that protect the infant against infections that enter the body through the digestive tract.

comedone A blackhead; the plug that clogs skin pores.

complete protein A protein containing sufficient amounts of all the essential amino acids.

conformation The structure into which a protein folds after it is synthesized.

conjugated protein A protein that has combined with a nonprotein compound.

constipation Infrequent passage of feces; the feces are usually dry and hard.

control enzymes Enzymes capable of being activated or inactivated by changing metabolic conditions in the body; they control the movement of material through biochemical pathways.

cornea The transparent covering of the front of the eye.

covalent bond A chemical bond formed by the sharing of two electrons between atoms.

cretinism The physical and mental retardation of a child owing to severe iodine or thyroid deficiency in its mother during pregnancy.

critical period The period of cell division in which a tissue or organ receives its full complement of cells; in some tissues, once this period has ended, no further cell division takes place and any defects present are permanent.

crude fiber A measure of the fiber content of a food; however, this analytical process underestimates the actual amount of fiber present.

cytoplasm The substance of a cell that lies outside the nucleus.

dental caries Tooth decay.

deoxyribonucleic acid (DNA) The substance that contains the instructions for protein synthesis and which can transmit them to succeeding generations of cells.

dextrins A polysaccharide composed of 10 to 20 glucose molecules; products of the partial digestion of starch, dextrins are used as thickening agents and to prevent sugar from crystallizing in candy.

diabetes mellitus A metabolic disorder in which the lack of insulin activity impairs the body's ability to use glucose for energy; catabolism of fat and protein are accelerated, and the concentration of glucose in the blood and urine increases.

diarrhea Frequent elimination of soft, watery feces resulting from the rapid movement of food through the digestive tract.

digestion The mechanical and chemical breakdown of food into its constituents, which can then be absorbed into the body.

diglyceride A lipid containing glycerol and two fatty acids.

disaccharide A sugar made up of two monosaccharides; for example, the disaccharide sucrose contains glucose and fructose.

diuretics Drugs that stimulate urination.

diverticular disease The formation of pouches, or "blowouts," in the wall of the large intestine; it is believed that these pouches result from an increase of pressure within the colon owing to slow movement of feces.

double-blind experiment An experiment in

which neither the subjects nor the researchers know which subjects are receiving the treatment and which are not.

edema Swelling caused by accumulation of fluid in the tissues.

electrolytes Elements capable of conducting an electric charge when in solution; the most abundant ones are sodium, potassium, and chloride, but the term includes calcium, phosphate, magnesium, and other elements.

element A substance that cannot be divided into simpler substances by chemical means.

emulsifying agents Substances that aid in the dispersion of lipids in water, for example, mono- and diglycerides, lecithin, and bile acids.

endogenous Originating within the body.

energy balance A state in which energy intake equals energy expenditure.

enrichment The practice of adding nutrients back to a food from which they have been removed by processing; generally applies to the addition of thiamine, riboflavin, niacin, and iron to refined-grain products.

enterokinase An enzyme produced by the small intestine which activates trypsinogen.

enzyme A biological catalyst, a protein that speeds up the rate of chemical reactions in the cell.

epidemiologic studies Studies that attempt to determine the factors which contribute to the occurrence of a disease in a population.

epiglottis A leaf-shaped piece of cartilage in the upper throat that deflects food away from the windpipe and into the esophagus.

epinephrine (adrenaline) A hormone produced by the adrenal gland in response to stress, danger, or hypoglycemia; it works to increase blood glucose concentration.

essential amino acids The nine amino acids the body cannot synthesize in sufficient quantities to meet its requirements and that must be obtained from the diet.

essential fatty acid A fatty acid that is required for growth and for maintenance of a healthy skin and which must be obtained in the diet because the body cannot synthesize it; generally refers to linoleic acid.

exchange list The grouping of foods in such a way that the content of a selected nutrient is roughly the same for all foods within a particular group; thus one food in the group can be substituted or exchanged for any other member without significantly altering the amount of that nutrient in the diet.

exogenous Originating outside the body.

extracellular fluid (ECF) The component of the total body water lying outside the cells.

fatty acid A hydrocarbon chain with a carboxylic acid (—COOH) group at one end.

feces The waste material expelled from the digestive tract; it consists of undigested and unabsorbed food, cells and secretions from the digestive tract, and bacteria.

ferric iron Iron in the oxidized (Fe^{3+}) state.

ferritin A substance in which iron is stored in the liver, spleen, and bone marrow; it consists of a protein, apoferritin, to which the iron binds.

ferrous iron Iron in the reduced (Fe^{2+}) state.

fetal alcohol syndrome (FAS) A condition found in many infants born to alcoholic mothers and characterized by growth retardation, birth defects, behavioral problems, and mental retardation.

fiber The component of food resistant to digestion by human enzymes.

flavoprotein The combination of a riboflavin coenzyme with an apoenzyme.

food additives Chemicals which, through their use in food processing or packaging, directly or indirectly become a component of or affect the characteristics of a food; intentional additives are those purposely added to a food; unintentional additives are those which migrate into the food as a result of growing, processing, or packaging.

food-composition table A table that lists the

components of a food, such as its content of kilocalories, protein, carbohydrate, fat, water, vitamins, and minerals.

fortification The addition of nutrients to a food that were not present or were present in small amounts before processing; the level of the nutrient in the final product is generally greater than in the original food.

fructose Also called levulose; a six-carbon monosaccharide found in sucrose, honey, and many fruits.

galactose A six-carbon monosaccharide that is a part of the milk sugar lactose.

gastric juice The digestive juice produced by the stomach; it contains hydrochloric acid, digestive enzymes (especially pepsin), and mucus.

gastrin A hormone produced by the stomach that stimulates the production of gastric juice.

gene The functional unit of heredity, a segment of DNA that contains the instructions for the synthesis of a particular protein.

genetic code The instructions in DNA that dictate the number, type, and sequence of amino acids used in the synthesis of a protein.

glucagon A hormone produced by alpha cells in the pancreas in response to hypoglycemia; it works to increase blood glucose concentration.

glucogenic amino acids The carbon skeletons of these amino acids can be used to synthesize glucose.

glucose Also called dextrose; a six-carbon monosaccharide found in sucrose, honey, and many fruits and vegetables; it is the major carbohydrate found in the body.

glucose tolerance factor (GTF) A chromium-containing substance needed for the normal catabolism of glucose by the body.

glycogen Form in which carbohydrate is stored in the body; composed of glucose molecules; it is found in the liver and muscles.

glycogen packing (carbohydrate loading) The practice of increasing glycogen reserves by depleting the body of glycogen about a week before an athletic event and then consuming a carbohydrate-rich diet for the 3 days prior to the competition.

glycoprotein The combination of a protein and a carbohydrate.

goitrogens Substances that produce goiter; many are found in foods and interfere with the utilization of iodine by the body.

generally recognized as safe (GRAS) Food additives which had been in use prior to the enactment of the 1958 Food Additive Amendment and which, in the opinion of qualified experts, are considered to be safe.

growth stage The last stage of fetal development in which organs and tissues increase in size owing to an increase in the number and size of their cells.

heat of combustion The amount of energy contained in a food; it is measured by a bomb calorimeter.

hematocrit The percent of the blood volume that is occupied by red blood cells.

heme A complex organic compound containing iron; it functions as part of hemoglobin, myoglobin, and several enzymes.

hemicellulose Undigestible polysaccharides composed of the sugars xylose, arabinose, glucose, mannose, and galactose.

hemochromatosis A genetic disorder in which the body absorbs an abnormally large amount of iron.

hemoglobin concentration The number of grams of hemoglobin contained in 100 milliliters (1 deciliter) of blood.

hemolytic anemia A type of anemia in which the red cells break in the bloodstream.

hemorrhage Bleeding.

hemorrhoids Swollen veins in the rectum, which may occur during pregnancy, chronic liver disease, from straining at stool, and from sudden increases in intraabdominal pressure.

hemosiderin A substance in which iron is stored in the liver, spleen, and bone marrow; it is protein in nature, but contains more iron than ferritin.

high-density lipoprotein (HDL) A lipoprotein involved in cholesterol transport in the blood; because relatively high levels of HDL appear to protect against atherosclerosis, cholesterol carried by these lipoproteins is said to be "good" cholesterol.

homeostasis The maintenance of stability or balance within a system.

hormone A chemical messenger, a substance secreted into the blood by an endocrine gland which influences the function of specific tissues.

hydrogenation (hardening) The process of adding hydrogen to unsaturated fatty acids, thereby saturating them and changing them from a liquid to a solid form.

hydroxyapatite The hard mineral part of bone composed of calcium and phosphate.

hyperactivity (hyperkinesis or hyperkinetic syndrome) A cluster of symptoms seen chronically in some children, including excessive activity, short attention span, limited ability to concentrate, impulsiveness, inability to delay gratification, and rejection of disciplinary measures.

hyperglycemia High blood glucose concentration.

hyperthyroidism High thyroid hormone output by the thyroid gland.

hypoglycemia Low blood glucose concentration.

hypothalamus A part of the brain located just above the pituitary gland; it controls body temperature, fluid and electrolyte balance, pituitary function, hunger, and other processes.

hypothyroidism Low thyroid hormone output.

immunologic Referring to the processes by which the body resists invasion by foreign agents, such as bacteria, viruses, and foreign substances.

implantation stage The earliest stage of fetal development beginning with fertilization of the ovum and ending with implantation of the blastocyst in the wall of the uterus.

incomplete protein A protein deficient or lacking in one or more essential amino acids.

inorganic Substances that do not contain carbon.

insensible water loss Fluid loss an individual is unaware of; it consists of water lost through the skin, except visible sweat, and water vapor lost from the lungs.

insulin A hormone produced by beta cells in the pancreas in response to hyperglycemia; it works to clear glucose from the blood.

intermediate compounds Substances that result from the partial breakdown of carbohydrate, fat, and amino acids (e.g., acetyl CoA and the TCA cycle compounds); intermediate compounds can be further catabolized for energy or used as substrates for the synthesis of other substances.

interstitial fluid The component of the extracellular fluid that bathes the tissues; it is found between cells.

intima The innermost layer of a blood vessel.

intracellular fluid (ICF) The component of the total body water lying within the cells.

intrinsic factor A protein produced by the stomach and required for vitamin B_{12} absorption in the small intestine.

in vitro "In glass"; experiments performed under artificial conditions on tissues removed from the living animal.

keratinization Formation of a protein called keratin; in vitamin A deficiency, mucus-secreting cells produce keratin instead of mucus, leading to a drying and hardening of epithelial tissue.

ketogenic amino acids The carbon skeletons of these amino acids can be used to synthesize fatty acids.

ketone bodies Substances resulting from the incomplete oxidation of fat when carbohydrates are deficient in the diet.

ketosis An accumulation of ketone bodies in the blood and their excretion in the urine.

kilocalorie (kcal) One thousand calories; the energy required to raise the temperature of a kilogram of water one degree Celsius.

kilojoule (kJ) The international metric unit of

energy; one kilojoule equals 4.2 kilocalories.

kwashiorkor A form of protein-energy malnutrition traditionally thought to result from deficiency of protein, but not kilocalories; it may be a failure to adapt physiologically to starvation.

lactase A digestive enzyme produced by the small intestine which breaks lactose down into its constituent sugars, glucose and galactose.

lacto-ovo-vegetarian A vegetarian who eliminates animal flesh from the diet, but consumes eggs, milk, and dairy products.

lactose A disaccharide made up of glucose and galactose; it is found in milk.

lactose intolerance An inability to digest lactose owing to a lack of the enzyme lactase in the intestine.

lacto-vegetarian A vegetarian who eliminates all animal products except milk and dairy products from the diet.

laxatives and cathartics Drugs that stimulate defecation.

lecithin A phospholipid composed of a diglyceride, phosphate, and choline.

letdown reflex The squeezing of milk from the lobules of the breasts forward into the sinuses from which it can be sucked by the infant.

lignin A noncarbohydrate component of fiber consisting mainly of phenylpropane subunits.

limiting amino acid The essential amino acid that is present in a dietary protein in the least amount relative to the body's need for it.

linoleic acid A polyunsaturated fatty acid containing 18 carbon atoms and 2 double bonds.

linolenic acid A polyunsaturated fatty acid containing 18 carbon atoms and 2 double bonds.

lipid Substances in the body and in food that are insoluble in water.

lipoprotein The combination of lipid and protein; lipoproteins function in the transport of lipids in the bloodstream.

lipositol A phospholipid made up of diglyceride, phosphate, and inositol.

low-density lipoprotein (LDL) A lipoprotein involved in cholesterol transport in the blood; because relatively high levels of LDL appear to enhance atherosclerosis, cholesterol carried by these lipoproteins is said to be "bad" cholesterol.

macronutrient elements Those present in the body in amounts greater than 0.005 percent of body weight and required in the diet in amounts greater than 100 mg/day.

maltase A digestive enzyme produced by the small intestine that breaks maltose down into its constituent glucose subunits.

maltose A disaccharide made up of two glucose molecules; it is produced by the digestion of starch.

marasmus A form of protein-energy malnutrition traditionally thought to result from deficiency of energy, including protein; it may be the body's normal means of adapting to starvation.

marbling The thin, often invisible wisps of fat in meat; because this fat increases the tenderness of the meat, heavily marbled meat is of a higher grade.

melanin The pigment that is largely responsible for the color of the skin, hair, and eyes.

messenger RNA (mRNA) The type of RNA that carries a copy of DNA's instructions for protein synthesis to the ribosome.

metabolic water Water formed in the body from the metabolism of other substances, such as the breakdown of carbohydrate, fat, and protein for energy.

metabolism The sum of all chemical reactions occurring within the body.

micronutrient (trace) elements Those present in the body in amounts less than 0.005 percent of the body weight and required in the diet in amounts less than 100 mg/day.

microvilli Tiny projections of the cells on the surface of the villi in the small intestine; they help increase the surface area of the intestine.

mitochondria The organelles in which respiration and energy production occur.

modified starch Starch that has been chemically and/or physically altered to meet the particular needs of a manufactured food product.

molecule A combination of two or more atoms.

monoglyceride A lipid made up of glycerol and one fatty acid.

monosaccharide A single sugar molecule, such as glucose, fructose, or galactose.

monounsaturated fatty acid A fatty acid containing one double bond; i.e., one pair of carbon atoms is not bound to the maximum possible number of hydrogen atoms.

mucopolysaccharide Polymer made up of nitrogen-containing sugars and other carbohydrate derivatives.

mutagen An agent that causes mutations.

mutual supplementation (complementation) Combining two or more incomplete proteins so that the essential amino acids lacking in each are provided by the others.

myelin sheath The lipid covering of most nerves in the body; it facilitates conduction of nerve impulses.

negative energy balance A state in which energy intake is less than energy expenditure.

negative feedback system A system that responds to a stimulus in a manner that counteracts or opposes the stimulus.

negative nitrogen balance Nitrogen intake is less than nitrogen output; it occurs in situations in which protein catabolism exceeds anabolism, such as starvation, certain disease states, and consumption of a low-quality protein.

net protein utilization (NPU) A means of measuring protein quality in which the amount of a given dose of protein nitrogen retained by the body is determined.

neurotransmitter substances Chemical substances secreted by nervous tissue which transmit impulses between nerve cells and carry out other functions.

nitrogen equilibrium (zero nitrogen balance) Nitrogen intake equals nitrogen output; the desirable state in healthy, nonpregnant, nonlactating adults.

nonessential amino acids The 13 amino acids that can be synthesized by the body in amounts adequate to meet body requirements.

nonheme iron Body iron not contained within the heme complex, including iron functioning as a cofactor for enzymes, plasma iron, and storage iron.

nucleus The membrane-enclosed cell structure that carries the genetic material and directs cell activities.

nutrients Substances required by an organism for growth, maintenance, and reproduction.

nutrition The study of the processes by which an organism obtains, assimilates, and utilizes food.

obesity Accumulation of excess body fat; a body weight greater than 15 to 20 percent above desirable weight.

oleic acid A monounsaturated fatty acid containing 18 carbon atoms and 1 double bond.

oral hypoglycemic agents Drugs that may be taken by mouth to lower blood glucose concentrations.

organ A structure that carries out one or more body functions.

organelle A specialized structure within a cell that carries out a particular function.

organic Chemical compounds that contain carbon (except carbon dioxide and carbon salts); in current usage, the term is often applied to those foods grown without the use of chemical fertilizers, pesticides, or, in the case of animal products, hormones and antibiotics.

organogenesis The stage of fetal development in which the tissues and organs differentiate.

organ system A collection of organs that act in a coordinated fashion to carry out body functions.

osmosis Movement of water across a membrane from an area of low solute concentration to one of high solute concentration.

osteomalacia A loss of bone mineral leading to a reduction in bone density, but not in bone size; one cause may be vitamin D deficiency.

osteoporosis A degeneration of the bones owing to loss of bone mineral in such a way that the bone decreases in size but does not lose density.

overweight A body weight greater than 10 percent above desirable weight.

oxidation-reduction reactions The transfer of electrons or hydrogen atoms from one molecule to another.

oxytocin A hormone produced by the posterior pituitary gland which stimulates the letdown reflex.

pack date The date on which a product was packaged.

palmitic acid A saturated fatty acid containing 16 carbon atoms and no double bonds.

pancreatic amylase A digestive enzyme synthesized by the pancreas which breaks down starch in the small intestine.

pancreatic lipase A digestive enzyme synthesized by the pancreas which breaks down triglycerides in the small intestine.

pectin A component of fiber made up of galacturonic acid, a derivative of galactose.

pellagra Niacin deficiency characterized by inflammation of skin exposed to sunlight, diarrhea, and mental disorders.

pepsin A digestive enzyme produced by the stomach which breaks down protein; pepsinogen is its inactive form.

peptic ulcer A localized erosion of the stomach lining caused by excess hydrochloric acid or a reduction in the mechanisms, such as mucus, that normally protect the lining.

peptide bond The chemical bond joining the amino acids in a protein.

peristalsis Propulsive movements of the digestive tract; the wall of the digestive tract contracts to form a ring, which pushes the food in front of it as it moves.

pernicious anemia An inability to absorb vitamin B_{12} owing to a lack of intrinsic factor; leads to a megaloblastic, macrocytic anemia and deterioration of the nervous system.

peroxide A compound in which an oxygen molecule (O_2) binds to another molecule, such as polyunsaturated fatty acid.

pH A measure of the acidity of a solution; a pH of 7.0 is neutral; greater than 7.0 is alkaline; less than 7.0 is acidic.

phospholipids Lipids composed of a diglyceride, phosphate, and any one of several other chemical substances.

photosynthesis The synthesis of carbohydrate from carbon dioxide and water, using sunlight as a source of energy.

physiological fuel value The energy available to the body from food; it is less than the heat of combustion because of incomplete digestion and absorption of carbohydrate, fat, and protein and the incomplete combustion of protein.

pica A craving for nonfoods, such as clay, dirt, laundry starch, ice, chalk, and ashes.

placebo A substance that is indistinguishable from another substance, but which does not have the activity of that substance; in experiments it is used so that the subjects do not know whether they are receiving the experimental treatment or not.

placenta The organ in which the maternal and fetal circulations come into close proximity to each other, allowing transfer of nutrients and oxygen to the fetus and removal of CO_2 and other wastes from the fetus.

plantain Bananas.

plasma membrane The membrane that encloses the cell.

polypeptide A chain of three or more amino acids.

polysaccharide Carbohydrates containing many monosaccharide subunits.

polyunsaturated fatty acid Fatty acid containing two or more double bonds; i.e., two or more pairs of carbon atoms are not bound to the maximum number of hydrogens possible.

positive energy balance A state in which energy intake exceeds expenditure.

positive nitrogen balance Nitrogen intake exceeds nitrogen output; it occurs in situations in which protein synthesis exceeds catabolism, such as growth, pregnancy, and lactation.

prolactin A hormone produced by the anterior pituitary gland which stimulates milk secretion by the mammary glands.

prostaglandins Hormonelike substances derived from the essential fatty acids that affect the contraction and relaxation of smooth muscles in blood vessel walls, blood pressure, and a variety of organ systems.

proteins Chains of amino acids.

provitamin A substance from which the body can synthesize a vitamin.

pull date The date after which a product should no longer be sold and should be removed from a store's shelves; the product can be used at home for several days after this date.

Recommended Dietary Allowances (RDAs) Standards of nutrient intake established by the Food and Nutrition Board of the National Academy of Sciences; they are the level of intake of essential nutrients thought to be adequate to meet the needs of nearly all healthy people.

replicate To produce a replica of something.

respiration The process by which oxygen is brought to the cell and used in the breakdown of carbohydrate, fat, and protein for energy and the resulting carbon dioxide is removed.

respiratory chain A biochemical pathway that accepts hydrogen atoms from other pathways and extracts their energy to produce ATP; at the end of the chain, the hydrogen combines with oxygen to form water.

retina The innermost layer of the eye containing the light-sensitive rods and cones responsible for receiving visual images.

rhodopsin The visual pigment in the rods responsible for the ability to see in dim light.

ribonuclease An enzyme that catalyzes the breakdown of RNA.

ribosome The cell structure in which protein synthesis occurs.

rickets A disease in children in which the bones fail to mineralize properly; one cause is vitamin D deficiency.

risk factors Any of a number of factors associated with the occurrence of heart disease.

salivary amylase (ptyalin) An enzyme produced by the salivary glands that digests starch.

saturated fatty acid Fatty acid containing no double bonds; i.e., all carbon atoms are bound to the maximum number of hydrogen atoms possible.

scurvy Vitamin C deficiency characterized by bleeding gums, joint pains, bruising easily, lethargy, and mental disorders.

sebum An oily substance produced by glands in the skin.

secretin A hormone produced by the small intestine in response to acidic chyme; it stimulates the release of a pancreatic juice rich in bicarbonate which neutralizes the acid.

sickle-cell anemia A genetic disorder found in black populations; the hemoglobin in the red blood cells is abnormal, and the cells twist into the characteristic "sickle" shape.

simple goiter Iodine deficiency in adults, resulting in enlargement of the thyroid gland.

simple proteins Proteins that combine with nothing or only with other proteins; simple proteins yield only amino acids when they are broken down.

single-carbon groups Molecules containing only one carbon atom, such as formyl (—CHO) and methyl (—CH_3) groups.

solute A dissolved substance.

specific dynamic action The increased energy output after a meal; it represents the energy needed to digest, absorb, and utilize food.

standard of identity A list of specifications for the manufacture of certain foods; since the required ingredients are published in the

Code of Federal Regulations, they need not be listed on the product label.

starch A polysaccharide composed of glucose molecules; in contrast to cellulose, it is digestible in the small intestine.

stearic acid A saturated fatty acid containing 18 carbon atoms and no double bonds.

steroids Any of a group of compounds the basic structure of which resembles cholesterol.

sucrase A digestive enzyme produced by the small intestine that breaks down sucrose into its constituent sugars, glucose and fructose.

sucrose A disaccharide made up of glucose and fructose; it is the common table sugar.

teratogen An agent that causes birth defects.

threshold dose A level of intake of a chemical above which hazardous effects occur and below which the individual is safe.

thrombosis Formation of a blood clot.

thyroxine Iodine-containing hormone secreted by the thyroid gland; it stimulates metabolism and growth and development.

tissues An aggregate of cells of the same type.

total body water (TBW) The sum of all the body fluids.

total dietary fiber All compounds resistant to the digestive enzymes of animals, including cellulose, hemicellulose, lignin, pectin, vegetable gums, and the indigestible products of food processing.

toxemia of pregnancy A complication of pregnancy characterized by vomiting, high blood pressure, edema, and high levels of the protein albumin in the urine.

transcription The process of copying the instructions on DNA onto mRNA.

transferrin The protein that transports iron in the blood plasma.

transfer RNA (tRNA) The type of RNA that carries amino acids to the ribosome.

translation The process by which the instructions on mRNA are used to synthesize a particular protein.

triglycerides Lipids made up of glycerol and three fatty acids.

true fiber The components of cell walls in plants: cellulose, hemicellulose, and lignin.

trypsin A digestive enzyme produced by the pancreas that breaks down protein in the small intestine; trypsinogen is its inactive form.

turnover A cycle of synthesis and breakdown.

underweight A body weight more than 10 percent less than ideal.

United States Recommended Daily Allowance (U.S.RDA) A derivation from the RDAs used for food-labeling purposes; for most nutrients it is the highest RDA listed for any population group (excluding pregnant and lactating women) in the 1968 Recommended Dietary Allowances.

urea The nitrogenous waste product resulting from the breakdown of amino acids.

vegan (strict vegetarian) A vegetarian who eliminates all foods of animal origin from the diet.

villi Protrusions of the inner wall of the small intestine; they help increase the surface area of the intestine.

vitamins Organic substances required in small amounts to facilitate growth, maintenance, and reproduction.

xerophthalmia A result of severe vitamin A deficiency, in which the cornea keratinizes and becomes opaque; eventually the structure of the entire eyeball may deteriorate.

Zen macrobiotic diet An extreme form of vegetarianism consisting of 10 stages, each of which is progressively more restrictive; at the highest level, the diet only permits consumption of cereal grains.

zygote The ovum (egg) after it has been fertilized by a sperm.

BIBLIOGRAPHY

CHAPTER 1

1. U.S. Department of Agriculture, U.S. Department of Health and Human Services: *Nutrition and Your Health, Dietary Guidelines for Americans,* Superintendent of Documents, Washington, 1980.
2. Food and Nutrition Board: *Recommended Dietary Allowances,* 9th ed., National Academy of Sciences, Washington, 1980.
3. Adams, C. F.: *Nutritive Value of American Foods in Common Units,* Agriculture Handbook No. 456, USDA, Washington, 1975.
4. Watt, B. K., and Merrill, A. L.: *Composition of Foods—Raw, Processed, Prepared,* Agriculture Handbook No. 8, USDA, Washington, 1963.
5. Pennington, J. A. T., and Church, H. N.: *Bowes and Church's Food Values of Portions Commonly Used,* Lippincott, Philadelphia, 1980.
6. Page, L., and Phipard, E. F.: *Essentials of an Adequate Diet,* Home Economics Research Report No. 3, USDA, Washington, 1957.
7. Davis, C. A., Fulton, L. H., Light, L., Oldland, D. D., Page, L., Raper, N. R., and Vettell, R. S.,: *Food: The Hassle-Free Guide to a Better Diet,* Home and Garden Bulletin No. 228, USDA, Washington, 1979.
8. King, J. C., Cohenour, S. H., Corruccini, C. G., and Schneeman, P.: "Evaluation and Modification of the Basic Four Food Guide," *J. Nutr. Ed.* **10:**27–29 (1978).
9. Commentary: "Dietary Goals for the United States (Second Edition)," *J. Am. Diet Assoc.* **74:**529–533 (1979).
10. Harper, A. E.: "Dietary Goals—A Skeptical View," *Am. J. Clin. Nutr.* **31:**310–321 (1978).

11. Olson, R. E.: "Are Professionals Jumping the Gun in the Fight Against Chronic Diseases?" *J. Am. Diet. Assoc.* **74:**543–550 (1979).
12. Hegsted, D. M.: "Dietary Goals—A Progressive View," *Am. J. Clin. Nutr.* **31:**1504–1509 (1978).
13. Goodhart, R. S., and Shils, M. E.: *Modern Nutrition in Health and Disease,* 6th ed., Lea & Febiger, Philadelphia, 1980, pp. 672–676, 685–696.
14. Health Services and Mental Health Administration: *Ten-State Nutrition Survey (1968–1972)*, Parts I–V, DHEW, Atlanta, GA., 1972.
15. Public Health Service: *Preliminary Findings of the First Health and Nutrition Examination Survey, United States, 1971–1972,* National Center for Health Statistics, Rockville, Md., 1974.

CHAPTER 2

1. Atkins, R. C.: *Dr. Atkins' Diet Revolution, The High Calorie Way to Stay Thin Forever,* Bantam Books, New York, 1972.
2. Yudkin, J.: *Sweet and Dangerous,* Peter H. Wyden, New York, 1972.
3. Reuben, D.: *The Save Your Life Diet,* Ballantine Books, New York, 1976.
4. Bloom, W. L., and Azar, G. J.: "Similarities of Carbohydrate Deficiency and Fasting," *Arch. Intern. Med.* **112:**333–343 (1963).
5. Goodhart, R. S., and Shils, M. E.: *Modern Nutrition in Health and Disease,* 6th ed., Lea & Febiger, Philadelphia, 1980.
6. Service, F. J.: "Hypoglycemia," *N.Y. State J. Med.* **78:**2122–2123 (1978).
7. Permutt, M. A.: "Is It Really Hypoglycemia? If So, What Should You Do?" *Med. Times* **108:**35–43 (1980).
8. Food and Nutrition Board: *Recommended Dietary Allowances,* 9th ed., National Academy of Sciences, Washington, 1980, pp. 32–33.
9. Committee on Nutrition, American Heart Association: "Diet and Coronary Heart Disease," *Nutrition Today* **9:**26–27 (1974).
10. U.S. Senate Select Committee on Nutrition and Human Needs: *Dietary Goals for the United States,* 2d ed., U.S. Government Printing Office, Washington, December 1977.
11. Anonymous: "Too Much Sugar?" *Consumer Reports* **43:**136–142 (1978).
12. Page, L., and Friend, B.: "Level of Use of Sugars in the United States," in H. L. Sipple and K. W. McNutt (eds.), *Sugars in Nutrition,* Academic, New York, 1974, pp. 93–107.
13. Marston, R., and Page, L.: "Nutrient Content of the National Food Supply," *National Food Review No. 5,* December 1978, pp. 28–33.
14. U.S. Department of Commerce, Bureau of the Census: *Statistical Abstracts of the United States,* 98th ed., Washington, 1977, p. 71.
15. Bray, G. A.: *Major Problems in Internal Medicine,* vol. 9: *The Obese Patient,* Saunders, Philadelphia, 1976.

16. Yudkin, J.: "Evolutionary and Historical Changes in Dietary Carbohydrate," *Am. J. Clin. Nutr.* **20:**108–115 (1967).
17. Tokuhata, G. K., Miller, W., Digon, E., and Hartman, T.: "Diabetes Mellitus: An Underestimated Public Health Problem," *J. Chronic Dis.* **28:**23–55 (1975).
18. Keys, A.: "Sucrose in the Diet and Coronary Heart Disease," *Atherosclerosis* **14:**193–202 (1971).
19. Walker, A. R. P.: "Sugar Intake and Diabetes Mellitus," *S. Afr. Med. J.* **51:**842–851 (1977).
20. West, K. M.: *Epidemiology of Diabetes and Its Vascular Lesions,* Elsevier, New York, 1978, pp. 248–262.
21. Cohen, A. M., Bavly, S., and Poznanski, R.: "Change of Diet of Yemenite Jews in Relation to Diabetes and Ischemic Heart Disease," *Lancet* **2:**1399–1401 (1961).
22. McGandy, R. B., Hegsted, D. M., and Stare, F. J.: "Dietary Carbohydrate and Serum Cholesterol Levels in Man," *Am. J. Clin. Nutr.* **18:**237–242 (1966).
23. Kuo, P. T., Feng, L., Cohen, N. M., Fitts, W. T., and Miller, L. D.: "Dietary Carbohydrates in Hyperlipemia (Hyperglyceridemia), Hepatic and Adipose Tissue Lipogenic Activities," *Am. J. Clin. Nutr.* **20:**116–125 (1967).
24. Grande, F.: "Sugar and Cardiovascular Disease," *World Rev. Nutr. Diet.* **22:**248–269 (1975).
25. Cohen, A. M.: "Effect of Dietary Carbohydrate on the Glucose Tolerance Curve in the Normal and Carbohydrate Induced Hyperlipemic Subject," *Am. J. Clin. Nutr.* **20:**126–130 (1967).
26. Danowski, T. S., Nolan, S., and Stephen, T.: "Hypoglycemia," *World Rev. Nutr. Diet.* **22:**288–303 (1975).
27. Richardson, J. P.: "The Sugar Intake of Businessmen and Its Inverse Relationship with Relative Weight," *Br. J. Nutr.* **27:**449–460 (1972).
28. Finn, S. B., and Glass, R. B.: "Sugar and Dental Decay," *World Rev. Nutr. Diet.* **22:**304–326 (1975).
29. Weiss, R. L., and Trithart, A. H.: "Between Meal Eating Habits and Dental Caries Experience in Preschool Children," *Am. J. Public Health* **50:**1097–1104 (1960).
30. Shannon, L. L.: "Sucrose—The Tooth's Mortal Enemy; Fluoride—The Tooth's Best Friend", *A.S.D.C. J. Dent. Child.* **44:**429–437 (1977).
31. Zita, A. C., McDonald, R. E., and Andrews, A. L.: "Dietary Habits and the Dental Caries Experience in 200 Children," *J. Dent. Res.* **38:**860–865 (1959).
32. Dalderup, L. M.: "Nutrition and Caries," *World Rev. Nutr. Diet.* **7:**72–137 (1967).
33. Van Soest, P. J.: "Component Analysis of Fiber in Food—Summary and Recommendations," *Am. J. Clin. Nutr.* **31:**S12–S20 (1978).
34. ———: "Dietary Fibers: Their Definition and Nutritional Properties, *Am. J. Clin. Nutr.* **31:**S75–S76 (1978).
35. Southgate, D. A. T.: "Dietary Fiber: Analysis and Food Sources," *Am. J. Clin. Nutr.* **31:**S107–S110 (1978).

36. Kelsay, J. D.: "A Review of Research on the Effects of Fiber Intake on Man," *Am. J. Clin. Nutr.* **31:**142–159 (1978).
37. National Dairy Council: "The Role of Fiber in the Diet," *Dairy Council Digest* **46**(1) (1975).
38. Kirwan, W. O., Smith, A. N., McConnell, A. A., Mitchell, W. D., and Eastwood, W. A.: "Action of Different Bran Preparations on Colonic Function," *Br. Med. J.* **4:**187–189 (1974).
39. Mendeloff, A. I.: "Dietary Fiber," in Nutrition Review (ed.), *Present Knowledge in Nutrition,* 4th ed., The Nutrition Foundation, Washington, 1976, pp. 392–401.
40. Trowell, H.: "The Development of the Concept of Dietary Fiber in Human Nutrition," *Am. J. Clin. Nutr.* **31:**S3–S11 (1978).
41. ———: "Definition of Dietary Fiber and Hypotheses that It Is a Protective Factor in Certain Diseases," *Am. J. Clin. Nutr.* **29:**417–427 (1976).
42. Burkitt, D. P., Walker, A. R. P., and Painter, N. S.: "Dietary Fiber and Disease," *J.A.M.A.* **229:**1068–1074 (1974).
43. Burkitt, D. P.: "Colonic-Rectal Cancer: Fiber and Other Dietary Factors," *Am. J. Clin. Nutr.* **31:**S48–S64 (1978).
44. Walker, A. R. P.: "Colon Cancer and Diet, with Special Reference to Intakes of Fat and Fiber," *Am. J. Clin. Nutr.* **29:**1417–1426 (1976).
45. Kelsay, J. L., Behall, K. M., and Prather, E. S.: "Effect of Fiber from Fruits and Vegetables on Metabolic Responses in Human Subjects, I: Bowel Transit Time, Number of Defecations, Fecal Weight, Urinary Excretions of Energy, and Nitrogen, and Apparent Digestibilities of Energy, Nitrogen, and Fat," *Am. J. Clin. Nutr.* **31:**1149–1153 (1978).
46. Connell, A. M.: "Natural Fiber and Bowel Dysfunction," *Am. J. Clin. Nutr.* **29:**1427–1431 (1976).
47. Devroede, G.: "Dietary Fiber, Bowel Habits and Colonic Function," *Am. J. Clin. Nutr.* **31:**S157–S160 (1978).
48. Spiller, G. A., Chernoff, M. C., Hill, R. A., Gates, J. E., Nassa, J. J., and Shipley, E. A.: "Effect of Purified Cellulose, Pectin, and a Low-Residue Diet on Fecal Volatile Fatty Acids, Transit Time, and Fecal Weight in Humans," *Am. J. Clin. Nutr.* **33:**754–759 (1980).
49. Phillips, R. L., Lemon, F. R., Beeson, W. L., and Kuzma, J. W.: "Coronary Heart Disease Mortality among Seventh Day Adventists with Differing Dietary Habits: A Preliminary Report," *Am. J. Clin. Nutr.* **31:** S191–S198 (1978).
50. Moore, W. E. C., Cato, E. P., and Holdeman, L. V.: "Some Current Concepts in Intestinal Bacteriology," *Am. J. Clin. Nutr.* **31:**S33–S42 (1978).
51. MacLennan, R., Jensen, O. H., Mosbeck, J., and Vuori, H.: "Diet, Transit Time, Stool Weight, and Colon Cancer in Two Scandinavian Populations," *Am. J. Clin. Nutr.* **31:**S239–S242 (1978).
52. Armstrong, B., and Doll, R.: "Environmental Factors and Cancer Incidence and Mortality in Different Countries, with Special Reference to Dietary Practices," *Int. J. Cancer* **15:**617–631 (1975).
53. Howell, M. A.: "Diet as an Etiological Factor in the Development of Cancer of the Colon and Rectum," *J. Chronic Dis.* **28:**67–80 (1975).
54. Visek, W. J.: "Diet and Cell Growth Modulation by Ammonia," *Am. J. Clin. Nutr.* **31:**S216–S220 (1978).

55. Wynder, E. L.: "Dietary Habits and Cancer Epidemiology," *Cancer* **43:**1955–1961 (1979).
56. Gori, G. B.: "Dietary and Nutritional Implications in the Multifactorial Etiology of Certain Prevalent Human Cancers," *Cancer* **43:**2151–2161 (1979).
57. Kritchevsky, D.: "Fiber, Lipids, and Atherosclerosis," *Am. J. Clin. Nutr.* **31:**S65–S74 (1978).
58. Van Itallie, T. B.: "Dietary Fiber and Obesity," *Am. J. Clin. Nutr.* **31:** S43–S52 (1978).
59. Trowell, H.: "Diabetes Mellitus and Dietary Fiber of Starchy Foods," *Am. J. Clin. Nutr.* **31:**S53–S57 (1978).
60. Anderson, J. W., and Ward, K.: "High Carbohydrate, High Fiber Diets for Insulin-Treated Men with Diabetes Mellitus," *Am. J. Clin. Nutr.* **32:**2312–2321 (1979).
61. Cummings, J. H.: "Nutritional Implications of Dietary Fiber," *Am. J. Clin. Nutr.* **31:**S21–S29 (1978).
62. Kelsay, J. L., Behall, K. M., and Prather, E. S.: "Effect of Fiber from Fruits and Vegetables on Metabolic Responses of Human Subjects, II: Calcium, Magnesium, Iron, and Silicon Balances," *Am. J. Clin. Nutr.* **31:**1876–1880 (1978).
63. Kelsay, J. L., Jacob, R. A., and Prather, E. S.: "Effect of Fiber from Fruits and Vegetables on Metabolic Responses of Human Subjects, III: Zinc, Copper, and Phosphorus Balances," *Am. J. Clin. Nutr.* **32:**2307–2311 (1979).
64. Sandstead, H. H.: "Influence of Dietary Fiber on Trace Element Balance," *Am. J. Clin. Nutr.* **31:**S180–S184 (1974).
65. McNutt, K. W.: "Perspective—Fiber," *J. Nutr. Ed.* **8:**150–152 (1976).
66. Anonymous: "High Fiber Diets and Colonic Disease," *Am. J. Nurs.* **77:**255 (1977).
67. Committee on Nutrition, American Academy of Pediatrics: "Should Milk Drinking by Children Be Discouraged?" *Pediatrics* **53:**576–582 (1974).
68. Kretchmer, N.: "Lactose and Lactase," *Sci. Am.* **227:**70–78, (1972).
69. Woodruff, C. W.: "Milk Intolerances," *Nutr. Rev.* **34:**33–37 (1976).
70. Simoons, F. J., Johnson, J. D., and Kretchmer, N.: "Perspective on Milk Drinking and Malabsorption of Lactose," *Pediatrics* **59:**98–109 (1977).
71. Pines, W. L., and Glick, N.: "The Saccharin Ban," *FDA Consumer* **11:** 10–13 (May 1977).
72. Morrison, A. S., and Buring, J. E.: "Artificial Sweeteners and Cancer of the Lower Urinary Tract," *N. Engl. J. Med.* **302:**537–541 (1980).
73. Hoover, R. N., and Strasser, P. H.: "Artificial Sweeteners and Human Bladder Cancer: Preliminary Results," *Lancet* **1:**837–840 (1980).
74. Smith, R. J.: "Latest Saccharin Tests Kill FDA Proposal," *Science* **208:**153–156 (1980).
75. Hoover, R. N.: "Saccharin—Bitter Aftertaste?" *N. Engl. J. Med.* **302:**573–574 (1980).
76. Talbot, J. M., and Fisher, K. D.: "The Need for Special Foods and Sugar Substitutes by Individuals with Diabetes Mellitus," *Diabetes Care* **1:**231–240 (1978).

77. Lee, C. K.: "Carbohydrate Sweeteners: Structural Requirements for Taste," *World Rev. Nutr. Diet.* **33:**142–197 (1979).
78. Lecos, C.: "Fructose: Questionable Diet Aid," *FDA Consumer* **14:**20–23 (March 1980).
79. Ylikahri, R.: "Metabolic and Nutritional Aspects of Xylitol," *Adv. Food Res.* **25:**159–180 (1979).
80. National Diabetes Data Group: "Classification and Diagnosis of Diabetes Mellitus and Other Categories of Glucose Intolerance," *Diabetes* **28:**1039–1057 (1979).
81. U.S. Department of Agriculture, U.S. Department of Health and Human Services: *Nutrition and Your Health, Dietary Guidelines for Americans,* Superintendent of Documents, Washington, 1980.

CHAPTER 3

1. Food and Nutrition Board: *Recommended Dietary Allowances,* 9th ed., National Academy of Sciences, Washington, 1980, pp. 31–38.
2. Committee on Nutrition, American Heart Association: "Diet and Coronary Heart Disease," *Nutrition Today* **9**(3):26–27 (1974).
3. Intersociety Commission for Heart Disease Resources: "Primary Prevention of Atherosclerotic Diseases," *Circulation* **42:**A55–95 (1970).
4. U.S. Senate Select Committee on Nutrition and Human Needs: *Dietary Goals for the United States,* 2d ed., U.S. Government Printing Office, Washington, 1977.
5. Bureau of the Census: *Statistical Abstracts of the United States,* 101st ed., U.S. Department of Commerce, Washington, 1980, pg. 78.
6. Isselbacher, K., Adams, R. D., Braunwald, E., and Petersdorf, R. G.: *Harrison's Principles of Internal Medicine,* 9th ed., McGraw-Hill, New York, 1980, pp. 1156–1166.
7. Stamler, J.: "Dietary and Serum Lipids in the Multifactorial Etiology of Atherosclerosis," *Arch. Surg.* **113:**21–25 (1978).
8. Kannel, W. B., and Dawber, T. R.: "Atherosclerosis as a Pediatric Problem," *J. Pediatr.* **80:**544–554 (1972).
9. Woolf, N.: "The Origins of Atherosclerosis," *Postgrad. Med. J.* **54:**156–161 (1978).
10. Davignon, J.: "The Lipid Hypothesis—Pathophysiological Basis," *Arch. Surg.* **113:**28–34 (1978).
11. Kolata, G. B.: "Atherosclerotic Plaques: Competing Theories Guide Research," *Science* **194:**592–594 (1976).
12. Enos, W. F., Holmes, R. H., and Beyer, J.: "Coronary Disease among United States Soldiers Killed in Action in Korea: Preliminary Report," *J.A.M.A.* **152:**1090–1093 (1953).
13. McNamara, J. J., Molot, M. A., Stremple, J. F., and Cutting, R. T.: "Coronary Artery Disease in Combat Casualties in Vietnam," *J.A.M.A.* **216:**1185–1187 (1971).
14. Gresham, G. A.: "Atherosclerosis in Man: Natural History and Effects," *Proc. Nutr. Soc.* **31:**303–305 (1972).

15. Carlson, L. A., and Bottiger, L. E.: "Ischeaemic Heart Disease in Relation to Fasting Values of Plasma Triglycerides and Cholesterol: Stockholm Prospective Study," *Lancet* **1:**865–868 (1972).
16. Kannel, W. B., Castelli, W. P., and Gordon, T.: "Cholesterol in the Prediction of Atherosclerotic Disease: New Perspectives Based on the Framingham Study," *Ann. Intern. Med.* **90:**85–91 (1979).
17. Albrink, M. J.: "Triglyceridemia," *J. Am. Diet. Assoc.* **62:**626–630 (1973).
18. Scanu, A. M.: "Plasma Lipoproteins and Coronary Heart Disease," *Ann. Clin. Lab. Sci.* **8:**79–83 (1978).
19. Wood, P. D., Haskell, W., Klein, H., Lewis, S., Stern, M. D., and Farquhar, J. W.: "The Distribution of Plasma Lipoproteins in Middle Aged Runners," *Metabolism* **25:**1249–1257 (1976).
20. Hjermann, I., Enger, S. U., Helgeland, A., Holme, I., Leren, P., and Trygg, K.: "The Effect of Dietary Changes on High Density Lipoprotein Cholesterol: The Oslo Study," *Am. J. Med.* **66:**105–109 (1979).
21. Hulley, S. B., Cohen, R., and Widdowson, G.: "Plasma High-Density Lipoprotein Cholesterol Level—Influence of Risk Factor Intervention," *J.A.M.A.* **238:**2269–2271 (1977).
22. Goodhart, R. S., and Shils, M. E.: *Modern Nutrition in Health and Disease,* 6th ed., Lea & Febiger, Philadelphia, 1980, pp. 1045–1070.
23. Astrup, D., and Kjeldsen, K.: "Carbon Monoxide, Smoking, and Atherosclerosis," *Med. Clin. North Am.* **58:**323–350 (1974).
24. Mann, G. V., Shaffer, R. D., and Rich, A.: "Physical Fitness and Immunity to Heart Disease in Masai," *Lancet* **2:**1308–1310 (1965).
25. Leon, A. S., and Blackburn, H.: "The Relationship of Physical Activity to Coronary Heart Disease and Life Expectancy," *Ann. N. Y. Acad. Sci.* **301:**561–578 (1977).
26. Joseph, J. J., and Bena, L. L.: "Cholesterol Reduction—A Long Term Intense Exercise Program," *J. Sports Med. Phys. Fitness* **17:**163–168 (1977).
27. Rosenman, R. H., Brand, R. J., Jenkins, C. D., Friedman, M., Straus, R., and Warm, M.: "Coronary Heart Disease in the Western Collaborative Group Study: Final Follow-Up Experience of 8½ Years," *J.A.M.A.* **233:**872–877 (1975).
28. Hatch, F. T.: "Interactions between Nutrition and Heredity in Coronary Heart Disease," *Am. J. Clin. Nutr.* **27:**80–90 (1974).
29. Glueck, C. J., and Connor, W. E.: "Diet-Coronary Heart Disease Relationships Reconnoitered," *Am. J. Clin. Nutr.* **31:**727–737 (1978).
30. Carroll, K. K.: "Dietary Protein in Relation to Plasma Cholesterol Levels and Atherosclerosis," *Nutr. Rev.* **36:**1 (1978).
31. Marston, R., and Page, L.: "Nutrient Content of the National Food Supply," *National Food Review No. 5,* December 1978, pp. 28–33.
32. Joosens, J. V., et al.: "The Pattern of Food and Mortality in Belgium," *Lancet* **1:**1069–1072 (1977).
33. McGill, H. C., and Mott, G. E.: "Diet and Coronary Heart Disease," in Nutrition Review (ed.), *Present Knowledge in Nutrition,* 4th ed., Nutrition Foundation, Washington, 1976, pp. 376–391.

34. Kannel, W. B., and Gordon, T.: *The Framingham Study,* Section 24: *Diet and the Regulation of Serum Cholesterol,* Department of Health, Education and Welfare, Washington, 1970.
35. Nichols, A. B., Ravenscroft, C., Lamphiear, D. E., and Ostrander, L. D.: "Daily Nutritional Intake and Serum Lipid Levels—The Tecumseh Study," *Am. J. Clin. Nutr.* **29:**1384–1392 (1962).
36. Stulb, S. C., McDonough, J. R., Greenberg, B. G., and Hames, C. G.: "The Relationship of Nutrient Intake and Exercise to Serum Cholesterol Levels in White Males in Evans County, Georgia," *Am. J. Clin. Nutr.* **16:**238–242 (1965).
37. Kahn, H., Medalie, J. H., Neufeld, H. N., Riss, E., Balogh, M., and Groen, J. J.: "Serum Cholesterol: Its Distribution and Association with Dietary and Other Variables in a Survey of 10,000 Men," *Isr. J. Med. Sci.* **5:**1117–1127 (1969).
38. Reiser, R.: "Oversimplification of Diet: Coronary Heart Disease Relationships and Exaggerated Diet Recommendations," *Am. J. Clin. Nutr.* **31:**865–875 (1978).
39. Kritchevsky, D.: "Diet and Atherosclerosis," *Am. J. Pathol.* **84:**615–632 (1976).
40. Watt, B. K., and Merrill, A. L.: *Composition of Foods—Raw, Processed and Prepared,* USDA, Washington, 1963.
41. Harper, H. A., Rodwell, V. W., and Mayes, P. A.: *Review of Physiological Chemistry,* 17th ed., Lange, Los Altos, Calif., 1979, pp. 335–336, 352.
42. U.S. Department of Agriculture, U.S. Department of Health and Human Services: *Nutrition and Your Health, Dietary Guidelines for Americans,* Superintendent of Documents, Washington, 1980.

CHAPTER 4

1. Marsten, R., and Page, L.: "Nutrient Content of the National Food Supply," *National Food Review No. 5,* December 1978, pp. 28–33.
2. Food and Nutrition Board: *Recommended Dietary Allowances,* 9th ed., National Academy of Sciences, Washington, 1980, pp. 39–54.
3. Sprinson, D. B., and Rittenberg, D.: "The Rate of Interaction of the Amino Acids of the Diet with Tissue Proteins," *J. Biol. Chem.* **180:**715–726 (1949).
4. Kopple, J. D., and Swenseid, M. E.: "Evidence that Histidine Is an Essential Amino Acid in Normal and Chronically Uremic Man," *J. Clin. Invest.* **55:**881–891 (1975).
5. Allison, J. B., Wannemacher, R. W., and Banks, W. L.: "Influence of Dietary Protein on Protein Biosynthesis in Various Tissues," *Fed. Proc.* **22:**1126–1130 (1963).
6. Allison, J. B., and Wannemacher, R. W.: "The Concept and Significance of Labile and Overall Protein Reserve in the Body," *Am. J. Clin. Nutr.* **16:**445–452 (1963).

7. Holt, L. E., Halac, E., and Kajdi, C. N.: "The Concept of Protein Stores and Its Implications in Diet," *J.A.M.A.* **181**:699–705 (1962).
8. Carroll, K. K.: "Dietary Protein in Relation to Plasma Cholesterol Levels and Atherosclerosis," *Nutr. Rev.* **36**:1–5 (1978).
9. Department of Health, Education and Welfare: *Preliminary Findings of the First Health and Nutrition Survey, United States, 1971–1972: Dietary Intake and Biochemical Findings,* DHEW, Rockville, Md., 1974, pp. 56–63.
10. Draper, H. H.: "The Aboriginal Eskimo Diet in Perspective," *Am. Anthropol.* **79**:309–316 (1977).
11. Margen, S., Chu, J. Y., Kaufmann, N. A., and Calloway, D. H.: "Studies in Calcium Metabolism, I: The Calciuretic Effect of Dietary Protein," *Am. J. Clin. Nutr.* **27**:584–589 (1974).
12. Robertson, W. G., Heyburn, P. J., Peacock, M., Hanes, F. A., and Swaminathan, R.: "The Effect of High Animal Protein Intake on Risk of Calcium-Stone Formation in the Urinary Tract," *Clin. Sci.* **57**:285–288 (1979).
13. Gray, G. E., Pike, M. C., and Henderson, B. E.: "Breast-Cancer Incidence and Mortality Rates in Different Countries in Relation to Known Risk Factors and Dietary Practices," *Br. J. Cancer* **39**:1–11 (1979).
14. Gori, G. B.: "Dietary and Nutritional Implications in the Multifactorial Etiology of Certain Prevalent Human Cancers," *Cancer* **43**:2151–2161 (1979).
15. Kannell, W. B.: "The Role of Cholesterol in Coronary Atherosclerosis," *Med. Clin. North Am.* **58**:363–379 (1974).
16. Beaton, G. H., and Bengoa, J. M. (eds.): *"Nutrition in Preventive Medicine: The Major Deficiency Syndromes, Epidemiology, and Approaches to Control," WHO Monogr. Series* **62** (1976).
17. Milner, R. D. G.: "Protein-Calorie Malnutrition," in Nutrition Review (ed.), *Present Knowledge in Nutrition,* 4th ed., The Nutrition Foundation, New York, 1976, pp. 428–436.
18. Behar, M., and Viteri, F.: "Protein-Calorie Malnutrition," *Prog. Food Nutr. Sci.* **1**:127–137 (1975).
19. Goodhart, R. S., and Shils, M. E.: *Modern Nutrition in Health and Disease,* 6th ed., Lea & Febiger, Philadelphia, 1980.
20. Alleyne, G. A. O., Hay, R. W., Picou, D. I., Stanfield, J. P., and Whitehead, R. G.: *Protein-Energy Malnutrition,* Arnold, London, 1977.
21. Church, M.: "Dietary Factors in Malnutrition: Quality and Quantity of Diet in Relation to Child Development," *Proc. Nutr. Soc.* **38**:41–49 (1979).
22. Rao, K. S. J.: "Evolution of Kwashiorkor and Marasmus," *Lancet* **1**:709–711 (1974).
23. Olson, R. E.: *Protein-Calorie Malnutrition,* Academic, New York, 1975.
24. McLaren, D. S.: "The Great Protein Fiasco," *Lancet* **2**:93–96 (1974).
25. Waterlow, J. D., and Payne, P. R.: "The Protein Gap," *Nature* **258**:113–117 (1975).
26. Olness, K.: "The Ecology of Malnutrition in Children, *J. Am. Med. Wom. Assoc.* **32**:279–284 (1977).

27. Food and Nutrition Board: *Improvement of Protein Nutriture,* National Academy of Sciences, Washington, 1974, pp. 184–200.
28. Bailey, K. V.: "Malnutrition in the African Region," *WHO Chron.* **29:** 354–364 (1975).
29. Hoorweg, J., and Stanfield, J. P.: "The Effects of Protein-Energy Malnutrition in Early Childhood on Intellectual and Motor Abilities in Later Childhood and Adolescence," *Dev. Med. Child. Neurol.* **18:**330–350 (1976).
30. Cravioto, J., and Delicardie, E. R.: "The Long Term Effects of Protein-Calorie Malnutrition," *Nutr. Rev.* **29:**107–111 (1971).
31. Cravioto, J., DeLicardie, E. R., and Birch, H. G.: "Nutrition, Growth, and Neurointegrative Development: An Experiment and Ecological Study," *Pediatrics* **38:**319–372 (1966).
32. Bressani, R.: "Upgrading Human Nutrition through the Improvement of Food Legumes," in M. Milner (ed.), *Nutritional Improvement of Food Legumes by Breeding,* Wiley, New York, 1975, pp. 349–380.
33. Orr, E.: "The Contribution of New Food Mixtures to the Relief of Malnutrition—A Second Look," *Food Nutr.* (*N.Y.*) **3**(2):2–10, (1977).
34. Kapsiotis, G. D.: "Single-Cell Protein," *Food Nutr.* (*N.Y.*), **4**(1–2):2–7 (1978).
35. Wallerstein, M. B., and Pariser, E. R.: "Fish Protein Concentrate—A Technological Approach that Failed," *Food Nutr.* (*N.Y.*) **4**(1–2): 8–14 (1978).
36. Nutrition Review (ed): *Present Knowledge in Nutrition,* 4th ed., The Nutrition Foundation, New York, 1976, pp. 453–458.
37. National Dairy Council: "Nutrition and Behavior," *Dairy Council Digest* **50**(5) (1979).

CHAPTER 5

1. Miller, A. T., and Blyth, C. S.: "Lean Body Mass as a Metabolic Standard," *J. Appl. Physiol.* **5:**311 (1953).
2. Mitchell, H. H.: *Comparative Nutrition of Man and Domestic Animals,* vol. 1, Academic, New York, 1962, p. 43.
3. Taylor, C. M., and McLeod, G.: *Rose's Handbook for Dietetics,* 5th ed., Macmillan, New York, 1949, p. 18.
4. Harper, H. A., Rodwell, V. W., and Mayes, P. A.: *Review of Physiological Chemistry,* 17th ed., Lange, Los Altos, Calif., 1979.
5. Bradfield, R. B., and Jourdan, M. H.: "Relative Importance of Specific Dynamic Action in Weight Reduction Diets," *Lancet* **2:**640–643 (1973).
6. Boothby, W. M., Berkson, J., and Dunn, H. L.: "Studies of the Energy of Normal Individuals: A Standard for Basal Metabolism, with a Nomogram for Clinical Application," *Am. J. Physiol.* **116:**468–484 (1936).
7. Boothby, W. M.: in W. S. Spector (ed.), *Handbook of Biological Data,* Saunders, Philadelphia, 1956.
8. Food and Nutrition Board: *Recommended Dietary Allowances,* 9th ed., National Academy of Sciences, Washington, 1980, pp. 16–30.

9. Anonymous: "Body Weight and Immunity—A Reciprocal Relationship," *Nutr. Rev.* **36:**41–43 (1978).
10. Keys, A., Brozek, J., Henschel, A., Mickelson, O., and Taylor, H. L.: *The Biology of Human Starvation,* University of Minnesota Press, Minneapolis, 1950.
11. Seifert, E.: "The High Calorie Diet," *Am. J. Clin. Nutr.* **12:**66–69 (1963).
12. Bruch, H.: *The Golden Cage—The Enigma of Anorexia Nervosa,* Harvard University Press, Cambridge, Mass., 1978.
13. Beeson, P. B., and McDermott, W.: *Cecil-Loeb Textbook of Medicine,* 13th ed., Saunders, Philadelphia, 1971, pp. 1742–1743.
14. Bruch, H.: *Eating Disorders; Obesity, Anorexia Nervosa and the Person Within,* Basic, New York, 1973.
15. Allon, N.: "The Stigma of Overweight in Everyday Life," in G. A. Bray (ed.), *Obesity in Perspective,* DHEW Pub. No. (NIH)75-708, Washington, 1973, pp. 83–102.
16. Bray, G. A.: *Major Problems in Internal Medicine,* vol. 9: *The Obese Patient,* Saunders, Philadelphia, 1976.
17. Van Itallie, T. B.: "Obesity: Adverse Effects on Health and Longevity," *Am. J. Clin. Nutr.* **32:**2723–2733 (1979).
18. Department of Health, Education and Welfare: *The Ten-State Nutrition Survey, 1968–1970,* DHEW Pub. No. (HSM)72-8131, Washington, 1972, pp. III–85.
19. ———: *Preliminary Findings of the First Health and Nutrition Examination Survey, United States, 1971–1972, Anthropometric and Clinical Findings,* DHEW Pub. No. (HRA)75-1229, Washington, 1974, pp. 15–17, 25–26, 58.
20. Goldblatt, P. E., Moore, M. E., and Stunkard, A. J.: "Social Factors in Obesity," *J.A.M.A.* **192:**1039–1044 (1965).
21. Garn, S. M., and Clark, D. C.: "Trends in Fatness and the Origins of Obesity," *Pediatrics* **57:**443–456 (1976).
22. Goodhart, R. S., and Shils, M. E.: *Modern Nutrition in Health and Disease,* 6th ed., Lea & Febiger, Philadelphia, 1980.
23. Lepkovsky, S.: "Regulation of Food Intake," *Adv. Food Res.* **21:**11–69 (1975).
24. Yaksh, T. L., and Myers, R. D.: "Neurohumoral Substances Released from Hypothalamus of the Monkey during Hunger and Satiety," *Am. J. Physiol.* **222:**503–515 (1972).
25. Gordon, E. S.: "Metabolic Aspects of Obesity," *Adv. Metab. Disord.* **4:**229–296 (1970).
26. Gurney, R.: "Hereditary Factor in Obesity," *Arch. Intern. Med.* **57:**557–561 (1936).
27. Winick, M.: *Childhood Obesity,* Wiley, New York, 1975, pp. 15–21.
28. Widdowson, E. M., and Dauncey, M. J.: "Obesity," in Nutrition Review (ed.), *Present Knowledge in Nutrition,* The Nutrition Foundation, Washington, 1976, pp. 17–23.
29. Garrow, J. S.: "Infant Feeding and Obesity of Adults," *Bibl. Nutr. Diet.* **26:**29–35, (1978).
30. Weil, W. B., Jr.: "Current Controversies in Childhood Obesity," *J. Pediatr.* **91:**175–187 (1977).

31. Poskitt, E. M. E., and Cole, T. J.: "Nature, Nurture, and Childhood Overweight," *Br. Med. J.* **1:**603–605 (1978).
32. Stunkard, A. J.: "Presidential Address, 1974: From Explanation to Action in Psychosomatic Medicine: The Case of Obesity," *Psychosom. Med.* **37:**195–236 (1975).
33. Schachter, S.: "Some Extraordinary Facts about Humans and Rats," *Am. Psychol.* **26:**129–144 (1971).
34. LeBow, M. D., Goldberg, P. S., and Collins, A.: "Eating Behavior of Overweight and Nonoverweight Persons in Natural Environment," *J. Consult. Clin. Psychol.* **45:**1204–1205 (1977).
35. Wagner, M., and Hewitt, M. I.: "Oral Satiety in Obese and Nonobese," *J. Am. Diet. Assoc.* **67:**344–346 (1975).
36. Rosenthal, B. S., and Marx, R. D.: "Differences in Eating Patterns of Successful and Unsuccessful Dieters, Untreated Overweight, and Normal Individuals," *Addict. Behav.* **3:**129–134 (1978).
37. Plutchik, R.: "Emotions and Attitudes Related to Being Overweight," *J. Clin. Psychol.* **32:**21–24 (1976).
38. Crisp, A. H., and McGuiness, B.: "Jolly Fat: Relation between Obesity and Psychoneurosis in General Population," *Br. Med. J.* **1:**7–9 (1975).
39. Mayer, J.: *Overweight: Causes, Cost, Control,* Prentice-Hall, Englewood Cliffs, N.J., 1968, pp. 76–77.
40. Armstrong, D. B., Dublin, L. I., Wheatley, G. M., and Marks, H. H.: "Obesity and Its Relation to Health and Disease," *J.A.M.A.* **147:**1007–1014 (1951).
41. Seltzer, C. C.: "Some Reevaluations of the Build and Blood Pressure Study, 1959, as Related to Ponderal Index, Somatotype, and Mortality," *N. Engl. J. Med.* **274:**254–259 (1966).
42. Goodman, N., Richardson, S. A., Dornbusch, S. M., and Hastorf, A. H.: "Variant Reactions to Physical Disabilities," *Am. Sociol. Rev.* **28:**429–435 (1963).
43. Walster, E., Aronson, V., Abrahams, D., and Rottman, L.: "Importance of Physical Attractiveness in Dating Behavior," *J. Pers. Soc. Psychol.* **4:**508–576 (1966).
44. Stunkard, A. J., and Mendelson, M.: "Obesity and the Body Image, I: Characteristics of Disturbances in the Body Image of Some Obese Persons," *Am. J. Psychiatry* **123:**1296–1300 (1967).
45. Anonymous: "Attitudes Toward and Perception of Obesity by Obese Subjects," *Nutr. Rev.* **27:**173–175 (1969).
46. Monello, L. F., and Mayer, J.: "Obese Adolescent Girls: An Unrecognized Minority Group," *Am. J. Clin. Nutr.* **13:**35–39 (1963).
47. Atkins, R. C.: *Dr. Atkins' Diet Revolution, The High Calorie Way to Stay Thin Forever,* Bantam, New York, 1972.
48. Council on Foods and Nutrition (AMA): "A Critique of Low Carbohydrate Ketogenic Weight Reduction Regimens—A Review of *Dr. Atkins Diet Revolution,*" *J.A.M.A.* **224:**1415–1419 (1973).
49. Lewis, S. B., Wallen, J. D., Kane, J. P., and Gerich, J. E.: "Effect of Diet Composition and Metabolic Adaptations to Hypocaloric Nutrition: Comparison of High Carbohydrate and High Fat Isocaloric Diets," *Am. J. Clin. Nutr.* **30:**160–170 (1977).

50. Hood, C. E. A., Goodhart, J. M., Fletcher, R. F., Gloster, J., Bertrand, P. V., and Crooke, A. C.: "Observations on Obese Patients Eating Isocaloric Reducing Diets with Varying Proportions of Carbohydrate," *Br. J. Nutr.* **24:**39–44 (1970).
51. Bloom, W. L., and Azar, G. J.: "Similarities of Carbohydrate Deficiency and Fasting," *Arch. Intern. Med.* **112:**333–337, 338–343 (1963).
52. Yudkin, J., and Carey, M.: "The Treatment of Obesity by the 'High Fat Diet': The Inevitability of Calories," *Lancet* **2:**939–941 (1960).
53. Kekwick, A., and Pawan, G. L. S.: "Fat Mobilizing Substance, F.M.S.," *Metabolism* **16:**787–796 (1967).
54. Consolazio, C. F., Matoush, L. O., Johnson, H. L., Nelson, R. A., and Krzwicki, H. J.: "Metabolic Aspects of Acute Starvation in Normal Humans (10 days)," *Am. J. Clin. Nutr.* **20:**672–683 (1967).
55. Drenick, E. J., and Smith, R.: "Weight Reduction by Prolonged Starvation," *Postgrad. Med.* **36:**A95–A100 (1964).
56. Johnson, D., and Drenick, E. J.: "Therapeutic Fasting in Morbid Obesity, Longterm Follow-Up," *Arch. Intern. Med.* **137:**1381–1382, (1977).
57. Harrison, M. T., and Harden, R. M.: "The Long Term Value of Fasting in the Treatment of Obesity," *Lancet* **2:**1340–1342 (1966).
58. Simeons, A. T. W.: "The Action of Chorionic Gonadotropin in the Obese," *Lancet* **2:**946–948 (1954).
59. Ballin, J. C., and White, P. L.: "Fallacy and Hazard: Human Chorionic Gonadotropin/500 Calorie Diet and Weight Reduction," *J. Am. Med. Assoc.* **230:**693–694 (1974).
60. Van Itallie, T. B.: "Dietary Fiber and Obesity," *Am. J. Clin. Nutr.* **31:** S43–S52 (1978).
61. Linn, R., and Stuart, S. L.: *The Last Chance Diet,* Bantam, New York, 1977.
62. Van Itallie, T. B.: "Liquid Protein Mayhem," *J. Am. Med. Assoc.* **240:**144–145 (1978).
63. Glick, N.: "Low-Calorie Protein Diets," *FDA Consumer,* March 1978, pp. 7–9.

CHAPTER 6

1. Food and Nutrition Board: *Recommended Dietary Allowances,* 9th ed., National Academy of Sciences, Washington, 1980, p. 69.
2. Isselbacher, K., Adams, R. D., Braunwald, E., and Petersdorf, R. G.: *Harrison's Principles of Internal Medicine,* 9th ed., McGraw-Hill, New York, 1980.
3. Goodhart, R. S., and Shils, M. E.: *Modern Nutrition in Health and Disease,* 6th ed., Lea & Febiger, Philadelphia, 1980.
4. Chernow, B.: "Diet and Heartburn," *J. Am. Med. Assoc.* **241:**2307–2308 (1979).
5. Levine, A. S.: "The Relationship of Diet to Intestinal Gas," *J. Med. Soc. N.J.* **76:**921–922 (1979).
6. Goodman, L. S., and Gilman, A.: *The Pharmacological Basis of Therapeutics,* 5th ed., Macmillan, New York, 1975.

7. American Pharmaceutical Association: *Handbook of Nonprescription Drugs,* 5th ed., American Pharmaceutical Association, Washington, 1977.
8. Spencer, H., and Lender, M.: "Adverse Effects of Aluminum-Containing Antacids on Mineral Metabolism," *Gastroenterology* **76:**603–606 (1979).
9. Corman, M. L., Veidenheimer, M. C., and Coller, J. A.: "Cathartics," *Am. J. Nurs.* **75:**273–279, 1975.
10. Morris, A. I., and Turnberg, L. A.: "Surreptitious Laxative Abuse," *Gastroenterology* **77:**780–786 (1979).
11. Hathcock, J. N., and Coon, J.: *Nutrition and Drug Interrelations,* Academic, New York, 1978.

CHAPTER 7

1. Zannoni, V. G., and Sato, P. H.: "Effects of Ascorbic Acid on Microsomal Drug Metabolism," *Ann. N.Y. Acad. Sci.* **258:**119–131 (1975).
2. Strut, J. C., and Chadwick, R. W.: "Ascorbic Acid Requirements and Metabolism in Relation to Organochlorine Pesticides," *Ann. N.Y. Acad. Sci.* **258:**132–143 (1975).
3. Food and Nutrition Board: *Recommended Dietary Allowances,* 9th ed., National Academy of Sciences, Washington, 1980, pp. 55–124.
4. Bieri, J. G., and Evarts, R. P.: "Gamma Tocopherol: Metabolism, Biological Activity, and Significance in Human Vitamin E Nutrition," *Am. J. Clin. Nutr.* **27:**980–986 (1974).
5. Sebrell, W. H., Jr., and Harris, R. S.: *The Vitamins,* vol. 5, 2d ed., Academic, New York, 1972, p. 256.
6. Sauberlich, H. E.: "Vitamin C Status: Methods and Findings," *Ann. N.Y. Acad. Sci.* **258:**438–450 (1975).
7. Pelletier, O.: "Vitamin C and Cigarette Smokers," *Ann. N.Y. Acad. Sci.* **258:**156–168, (1975).
8. Burgess, R. C.: "Beriberi: Epidemiology," *Fed. Proc.* **17**(Suppl. 2):3–56 (1958).
9. Center for Disease Control: *Ten-State Nutrition Survey, 1968–1970,* Part I: DHEW, Atlanta, Ga., 1972.
10. Armstrong, B. K., Davis, R. E., Nicol, D. J., VanMerwyk, A. J., and Larwood, C. J.: "Hematological, Vitamin B_{12} and Folate Studies on Seventh Day Adventist Vegetarians," *Am. J. Clin. Nutr.* **27:**712–718 (1974).
11. Sanders, T. A. B., Ellis, F. R., and Dickerson, J. W. T.: "Hematological Studies on Vegans," *Br. J. Nutr.* **40:**9–15 (1978).
12. Davidson, C. S.: "Scurvy," in P. B. Beeson and W. McDermott (eds.), *Cecil-Loeb Textbook of Medicine,* 11th ed., Saunders, Philadelphia, 1963, p. 1218.
13. "Vitamin A Deficiency and Xerophthalmia," *WHO Chron.* **30:**117–120 (1976).
14. Ramalingaswani, V.: "Knowledge and Action in the Control of Vitamin A Deficiency," *Ann. N.Y. Acad. Sci.* **300:**210–220 (1977).

15. Oomen, H. A. P. C.: Xerophthalmia," *WHO Monogr. Ser.* **62:**94–110 (1976).
16. Yaffe, S. J., and Filer, L. J.: "The Use and Abuse of Vitamin A," *Nutr. Rev.* **32**(Suppl.):41–43 (1974).
17. Pease, C. N.: "Focal Retardation and Arrestment of Growth in Bones due to Vitamin A Intoxication," *J. Am. Med. Assoc.* **182:**980–985 (1962).
18. Goodhart, R. S., and Shils, M. E.: *Modern Nutrition in Health andl Disease,* 6th ed., Lea & Febiger, Philadelphia, 1980.
19. Kuhnau, J.: "The Flavonoids, A Class of Semi-Essential Food Components: Their Role in Human Nutrition," *World Rev. Nutr. Diet.* **24:**117–191 (1976).
20. Lee, R. E.: "The Unique Role of Ascorbic Acid in Peripheral Vascular Physiology as Compared with Rutin and Hesperidin, a Micro-Manipulative Study," *J. Nutr.* **72:**203–209 (1960).
21. Anonymous: "Vitamin P," *Br. Med. J.* **1:**235–237 (1969).
22. Stacpoole, D. W.: "Pangamic Acid (Vitamin B_{15}), A Review," *World Rev. Nutr. Diet.* **27:**145–163 (1977).
23. Herbert, V.: "Pangamic Acid (Vitamin B_{15})," *Am. J. Clin. Nutr.* **32:**1534–1540 (1979).
24. Hawkins, D., and Pauling, L.: *Orthomolecular Psychiatry—Treatment of Schizophrenia,* Freeman, San Francisco, 1973, pp. 1–17.
25. Osmond, H., and Hoffer, A.: "Massive Niacin Treatment in Schizophrenia," *Lancet* **1:**316–319 (1962).
26. Denson, R.: "Nicotinamide in the Treatment of Schizophrenia," *Dis. Nerv. Sys.* **23:**167–172 (1962).
27. Ashby, W. R., Collins, G. H., and Bassett, M.: "The Effects of Nicotinic Acid, Nicotinamide, and Placebo on the Chronic Schizophrenic," *J. Ment. Sci.* **106:**1555–1559 (1960).
28. Ban, T. A.: "Nicotinic Acid in the Treatment of Schizophrenics," *Neuropsychobiology* **1:**133–145 (1975).
29. Wittenborn, J. R., Weber, E. S. P., and Brown, M.: "Niacin in the Long Term Treatment of Schizophrenia," *Arch. Gen. Psychiatry* **28:**308–315 (1973).
30. Task Force on Vitamin Therapy in Psychiatry, American Psychiatric Association: "Megavitamin and Orthomolecular Therapy in Psychiatry," excerpted in *Nutr. Rev.* **32**(Suppl.):44–47 (1974).
31. Pauling, L.: *Vitamin C and the Common Cold,* Freeman, San Francisco, 1970.
32. ———*Vitamin C, the Common Cold, and the Flu,* Freeman, San Francisco, 1976.
33. Stone, I.: *The Healing Factor—Vitamin C against Disease,* Grosset and Dunlop, New York, 1972.
34. Nutrition Review (ed.), *Present Knowledge in Nutrition,* 4th ed., The Nutrition Foundation, Washington, 1976, pp. 119–130.
35. Chalmers, T. C.: "Effects of Ascorbic Acid on the Common Cold—An Evaluation of the Evidence," *Am. J. Med.* **58:**532–536 (1975).
36. Dykes, M. H. M., and Meier, P.: "Ascorbic Acid and the Common

Cold—Evaluation of its Efficacy and Toxicity," *J. Am. Med. Assoc.* **231:**1073–1079 (1975).

37. Anderson, T. W.: "Large Scale Trials of Vitamin C," *Ann. N.Y. Acad. Sci.* **258:**498–504 (1975).
38. Coulihan, J. L., Kapner, L., and Eberhard, S.: "Vitamin C and Upper Respiratory Illness in Navaho Children," *Ann. N.Y. Acad. Sci.* **258:**498–504 (1975).
39. Lewis, T. L., Karlowski, T. R., Kapikian, A. Z., Lynch, J. M., Schaffer, G. W., and George, D. A.: "A Controlled Clinical Trial of Ascorbic Acid for the Common Cold," *Ann. N.Y. Acad. Sci.* **258:**505–512 (1975).
40. Miller, J. Z., Nance, W. E., Norton, J. A., Wolen, R. L., Griffith, R. S., and Ross, R. J.: "Therapeutic Effect of Vitamin C: A Co Twin Control Study," *J. Am. Med. Assoc.* **237:**248–251 (1977).
41. Barness, L. A.: "Safety Considerations with High Ascorbic Acid Dosage," *Ann. N.Y. Acad. Sci.* **258:**523–528 (1975).
42. Anonymous: "Vitamin C Toxicity," *Nutr. Rev.* **34:**236–237 (1976).
43. Ginter, E.: "Marginal Vitamin C Deficiency, Lipid Metabolism, and Atherogenesis," *Adv. Lip. Res.* **16:**167–220 (1978).
44. Creagan, E. T., Moertel, C. G., O'Fallon, J. C., Schutt, A. J., O'Connell, M. J., Rubin, J., and Frytak, S.: "Failure of High Dose Vitamin C to Benefit Patients with Advanced Cancer: A Controlled Trial," *N. Engl. J. Med.* **301:**687–690 (1979).
45. Shute, W., and Taub, H. J.: *Vitamin E for Ailing and Healthy Hearts,* Pyramid, New York, 1969.
46. Hodges, R. E.: "Vitamin E and Coronary Heart Disease," *J. Am. Diet. Assoc.* **62:**638–642 (1973).
47. Anderson, T. W., and Reid, D. B.: "A Double Blind Trial of Vitamin E in Angina Pectoris," *Am. J. Clin. Nutr.* **27:**1174–1178 (1974).
48. Gillian, R. E., Mondell, B., and Warbasse, J. R.: "Quantitative Evaluation of Vitamin E in the Treatment of Angina Pectoris," *Am. Heart J.* **93:**444–449 (1977).
49. Institute of Food Technologists' Expert Panel and Food Safety and Nutrition and the Committee on Public Information: "Vitamin E," *Nutr. Rev.* **35:**57–62 (1977).
50. Fried, J. J.: "The Glamorous Vitamin . . . E for Excess," *Family Health* **7:**26 (October 1975).
51. Tappel, A. L.: "Vitamin E," *Nutrition Today* **8:**4–12 (July/August 1973).
52. Farrell, P. M., and Bieri, J. G.: "Megavitamin E Supplementation in Man," *Am. J. Clin. Nutr.* **28:**1381–1386 (1975).
53. Anonymous: "Hypervitaminosis E and Coagulation," *Nutr. Rev.* **33:** 269–270 (1975).
54. Leonhardt, E. T. G.: "Effects of Vitamin E on Serum Cholesterol and Triglycerides in Hyperlipidemic Patients Treated with Diet and Clofibrate," *Am. J. Clin. Nutr.* **31:**100–105 (1978).
55. Leyden, J. J.: "Pathogenesis of Acne Vulgaris," *Int. J. Dermatol.* **15:**490–495 (1976).
56. Rasmussen, J. E.: "Diet and Acne," *Int. J. Dermatol.* **16:**488–492 (1977).

57. Heel, R. C., Brogden, R. N., Speight, T. M., and Avery, G. S.: "Vitamin A Acid: A Review of Its Pharmacological Properties and Therapeutic Use in the Topical Treatment of Acne Vulgaris," *Drugs* **14:**401–419 (1977).
58. Greenberg, D. M.: "The Vitamin Fraud in Cancer Quackery," *West. J. Med.* **122:**345–348 (1975).
59. Lewis, J. P.: "Laetrile," *West. J. Med.* **127:**55–62 (1977).
60. Herbert, V.: "The Nutritionally and Metabolically Destructive 'Nutritional and Metabolic Antineoplastic Diet' of Laetrile Proponents," *Am. J. Clin. Nutr.* **32:**96–98 (1979).
61. ———"Laetrile: The Cult of Cyanide-Promoting Poison for Profit," *Am. J. Clin. Nutr.* **32:**1121–1158 (1979).
62. *New York Times,* October 14, 1979, p. 44, col. 3.
63. Adams, C. F.: *Nutritive Value of American Foods in Common Units,* Agriculture Handbook No 456, USDA, Washington, 1975.
64. Orr, M. L.: *Pantothenic Acid, Vitamin* B_6 *and Vitamin* B_{12} *in Foods,* Home Economics Research Report No 36, USDA Washington, 1969.
65. Hardinge, M. G., and Crooks, H.: "Lesser Known Vitamins in Foods," *J. Am. Diet. Assoc.* **38:**240–245 (1961).
66. Perloff, B. P., and Butrum, R. R.: "Folacin in Selected Foods," *J. Am. Diet. Assoc.* **70:**161–172 (1977).
67. McLaughlin, P. J., and Weihrauch, J. L.: "Vitamin E Content of Foods," *J. Am. Diet. Assoc.* **75:**647–665 (1979).

CHAPTER 8

1. Goodhart, R. S., and Shils, M. E.: *Modern Nutrition in Health and Disease,* 6th ed., Lea & Febiger, Philadelphia, 1980.
2. Food and Nutrition Board: *Recommended Dietary Allowances,* 9th ed., National Academy of Sciences, Washington, 1980.
3. Harper, H. A., Rodwell, V. W., and Mayes, P. A.: *Review of Physiological Chemistry,* 17th ed., Lange, Los Altos, Calif., 1979.
4. FAO/WHO: "Calcium Requirements: Report of a FAO/WHO Expert Committee on Calcium Requirements," *WHO Tech. Rep. Ser.* **230** (1962).
5. Nordin, B. E. C. (ed.): *Calcium, Phosphorus, and Magnesium Metabolism,* Churchill-Livingstone, New York, 1976.
6. U.S. Senate Select Committee on Nutrition and Human Needs: *Dietary Goals for the United States,* 2d ed., Washington, 1977.
7. Lane, H. W., and Lerda, J. J.: "Potassium Requirements and Exercise," *J. Am. Diet. Assoc.* **73:**64–65 (1978).
8. Layrisse, M., and Martinez-Torres, C.: "Food Iron Absorption: Iron Supplementation of Food," *Prog. Hematol.* **7:**137–160 (1971).
9. Underwood, E. J.: *Trace Elements in Human and Animal Nutrition,* 4th ed., Academic, New York, 1977.
10. Nutrition Review (ed.), *Present Knowledge in Nutrition,* 4th ed., The Nutrition Foundation, Washington, 1976.

11. Prasad, A. S., and Oberleas, D.: *Trace Elements in Human Health and Disease,* vol. 1, Academic, New York, 1976.
12. Rheinhold, J. C.: "Phytate Destruction by Yeast Fermentation in Whole Wheat Meals," *J. Am. Diet. Assoc.* **66:**38–41 (1975).
13. Murphy, E. W.: "Provisional Tables on the Zinc Content of Foods," *J. Am. Diet. Assoc.* **66:**345–355 (1975).
14. Cummings, J. H.: "Nutritional Implications of Dietary Fiber," *Am. J. Clin. Nutr.* **31:**S21–S29 (1978).
15. Center for Disease Control: *Ten-State Nutrition Survey, 1968–1970,* Section 4: *Biochemical,* DHEW, Atlanta, Ga., 1972, p. IV-3–IV-8.
16. Garn, S. M., Smith, N. J., and Clark, D. C.: "The Magnitude and the Implications of Apparent Race Differences in Hemoglobin Values," *Am. J. Clin. Nutr.* **28:**563–568 (1975).
17. Public Health Service: *Preliminary Findings of the First Health and Nutrition Examination Survey, United States, 1971–1972,* National Center for Health Statistics, Rockville, Md., 1974.
18. Krupp, M. A., and Chatton, M. J.: *Current Medical Diagnosis and Treatment,* Lange, Los Altos, Calif., 1975, p. 1001.
19. Hambidge, K. M., Hambidge, C., Jacobs, M., and Baum, J. D.: "Low Levels of Zinc in Hair, Anorexia, Poor Growth, and Hypogeusia in Children," *Pediatr. Res.* **6:**868–874 (1972).
20. Elwood, P. C.: "The Enrichment Debate," *Nutrition Today* **12:**18–24 (July/August 1977).
21. Dahl, L. K.: "Salt and Hypertension," *Am. J. Clin. Nutr.* **25:**232–244 (1972).
22. Commentary: "National Nutrition Consortium Endorses Fluoridation," *J. Am. Diet. Assoc.* **70:**354 (1977).
23. Medical News: "Kelp Diets Can Produce Myxedema in Iodide-Sensitive Individuals," *J. Am. Med. Assoc.* **233:**9–10 (1975).
24. Prasad, A. S., and Oberleas, D.: *Trace Elements in Human Health and Disease,* vol. 2, Academic, New York, 1976.
25. Hadjimarkos, D. M.: "Effect of Selenium on Dental Caries," *Arch. Environ. Health* **10:**893–899 (1965).
26. Elwood, P. C., Waters, W. E., Green, W. J. W., and Sweetnam, P.: "Symptoms and Circulating Hemoglobin Level," *J. Chronic Dis.* **21:**615–628 (1969).
27. Leibel, R. L.: "Behavioral and Biochemical Correlates of Iron Deficiency," *J. Am. Diet. Assoc.* **71:**398–404 (1977).
28. Crosby, W. H.: "Who Needs Iron?" *N. Engl. J. Med.* **297:**543–545 (1977).
29. Gardner, B. W., Edgerton, V. R., Senewirtane, B., Barnard, R. J., and Ohira, Y.: "Physical Work Capacity and Metabolic Stress in Subjects with Iron Deficiency Anemia," *Am. J. Clin. Nutr.* **30:**910–917 (1977).
30. Pollit, E, and Leibel, R. L.: "Iron Deficiency and Behavior," *J. Pediatr.* **88:**372–381 (1976).
31. "Anatomy of a Decision," *Nutrition Today* **13:**6–8, 28–29 (January/February 1978).
32. Ast, D. B., Smith, D. J., Wachs, B., and Cantwell, K. T.: "Newburgh-

Kingston Caries-Fluorine Study, XIV: Combined Clinical and Roentgenographic Dental Findings," *J. Am. Dent. Assoc.* **52:**314–325 (1956).
33. Dunning, J. M.: "Current Status of Fluoridation," *N. Engl. J. Med.* **272:**30–34 (1965).
34. Newbrun, E.: "The Safety of Water Fluoridation," *J. Am. Diet. Assoc.* **94:**301–304 (1977).
35. Luke, B.: *Maternal Nutrition,* Little, Brown, Boston, 1979, pp. 75–83.
36. Vermeer, D. E., and Frate, D. A.: "Geophagia in Rural Mississippi: Environmental and Cultural Contexts and Nutritional Implications," *Am. J. Clin. Nutr.* **32:**2129–2135 (1979).
37. Prasad, A. S., Halsted, J. A., and Nadimi, M.: "Syndrome of Iron Deficiency Anemia, Hepatosplenomegaly, Hypogonadism, Dwarfism, and Geophagia," *Am. J. Med.* **31:**532–546 (1961).
38. Prasad, A. S., Miale, A., Farid, Z., Sandstead, H. H., Schulert, A. R., and Darby, W. J.: "Biochemical Studies on Dwarfism, Hypogonadism, and Anemia," *Arch. Intern. Med.* **111:**407–428 (1963).
39. Okcuoglu, A., Arcasoy, A., Minnich, V., Tarcon, Y., Cin, S., Yorukoglu, O., Demirag, B., and Renda, F.: "Pica in Turkey, I: Incidence and Association with Anemia," *Am. J. Clin. Nutr.* **19:**125–131 (1966).
40. "Mercury—A Water Pollutant of Concern but not Alarm," *N. Engl. J. Med.* **286:**840–841 (1972).
41. Adams, C. F.: *Nutritive Value of American Foods in Common Units,* Agriculture Handbook No. 456, USDA, Washington, 1975.
42. Sherman, H. C.: *Chemistry of Food and Nutrition,* 8th ed., Macmillan, New York, 1952, p. 227.
43. U.S. Department of Agriculture, U.S. Department of Health and Human Services: *Nutrition and Your Health: Dietary Guidelines for Americans,* Superintendent of Documents, Washington, 1980.

CHAPTER 9

1. Food and Nutrition Board: *Recommended Dietary Allowances,* 9th ed., National Academy of Sciences, Washington, 1980.
2. Page, L., and Phipard, E. F.: *Essentials of an Adequate Diet,* Home Economics Research Report No. 3, USDA, Washington, 1957.
3. Davis, C. A., Fulton, L. H., Light, L., Oldland, D. D., Page, L., Raper, N. R., and Vettel, R. S.: *Food—The Hassle-Free Guide to a Better Diet,* Home and Garden Bulletin No. 228, USDA, Washington, 1979.
4. King, J. C., Lohenour, S. H., Corruccini, C. G., and Schneeman, D.: "Evaluation and Modification of the Basic Four Food Groups," *J. Nutr. Ed.* **10:**27–29 (1978).
5. U.S. Senate Select Committee on Nutrition and Human Needs: *Dietary Goals for the United States,* 2d ed., U.S. Government Printing Office, Washington, 1977.
6. Tannenbaum, S. R. (ed.): *Nutritional and Safety Aspects of Food Processing,* Marcel Dekker, New York, 1979.

7. Harris, R. S., and Karmas, E.: *Nutritional Evaluation of Food Processing,* 2d ed., AVI Publishing, Westport, Conn., 1975.
8. Food, Drug and Cosmetic Act, Section 409(b)(2)(E).
9. Joint FAO/WHO Expert Committee on Food Additives: *Toxicological Evaluation of Certain Food Additives with a Review of General Principles and of Specifications,* FAO Nutrition Meetings Series No. 53, FAO, Rome, Italy, 1974.
10. Irving, G. W., Jr.: "Safety Evaluation of the Food Ingredients Called GRAS," *Nutr. Rev.* **36:**351–356 1978.
11. Kraybill, H. F.: "Proper Perspectives in Extrapolation of Carcinogenesis Data to Humans," *Food Tech.* **32:**62–64 (1978).
12. Schmidt, A. M.: "The Benefit-Risk Equation," *FDA Consumer* **8:**27–31 (May 1974).
13. Institute of Food Technologists' Expert Panel on Food Safety and Nutrition: "The Benefit-Risk Concept as Applied to Food," *Food Tech.* **32:** 51–56 (March 1978).
14. Food, Drug and Cosmetic Act, Section 409(c)(3)(A).
15. Mantel, N., Bohidar, N. R., Brown, C. C., Ciminera, J. L., and Tukey, J. W.: "An Improved Mantel-Bryan Procedure for 'Safety' Testing of Carcinogens," *Cancer Res.* **35:**875–882 (1975).
16. Reif-Lehrer, L.: "Possible Significance of Adverse Reactions to Glutamate in Humans," *Fed. Proc.* **35:**2205–2211 (1976).
17. Schaumberg, H. H., Byck, R., Gerstl, R., and Mashman, J.H.: "Monosodium L-Glutamate: Its Pharmacology and Role in the Chinese Restaurant Syndrome," *Science* **163:**826–828 (1969).
18. Olney, J. W.: "Brain Lesions, Obesity, and Other Disturbances in Mice Treated with Monosodium Glutamate," *Science* **164:**719–721 (1969).
19. ———: "Status of Monosodium Glutamate Revisited," *Am. J. Clin. Nutr.* **26:**683–689 (1973).
20. Stegnik, L. D., Reynolds, W. A., Filer, L. J., Jr., Pitkin, R. M., and Boaz, D. P.: "Monosodium Glutamate Metabolism in the Neonatal Monkey," *Am. J. Physiol.* **229:**246–250 (1975).
21. Fiddler, W.: "The Occurrence and Determination of *N*-Nitroso Compounds," *Toxicol. Appl. Pharmacol.* **31:**352–360 (1975).
22. Wogan, G. N., and Tannenbaum, S. R.: "Environmental *N*-Nitroso Compounds: Implications for Public Health," *Toxicol. Appl. Pharmacol.* **31:**375–383 (1975).
23. White, J. W., Jr.: "Relative Significance of Dietary Sources of Nitrate and Nitrite," *J. Agric. Food Chem.* **23:**886–891 (1975).
24. Glick, N.: "Bringing Home the (Nitrite-less) Bacon," *FDA Consumer* **13:**25–26 (May 1979).
25. *Code of Federal Regulations,* Title 21, Sections 74 and 81.
26. Lockey, S. D.: "Hypersensitivity to Tartrazine (F.D.&C. Yellow No. 5) and Other Dyes and Additives Present in Foods and Pharmaceutical Products," *Ann. Allergy* **38:**206–210 (1977).
27. Zlotlow, M. J., and Settipane, G. A.: "Allergic Potential of Food Additives: A Report of a Case of Tartrazine Sensitivity without Aspirin Intolerance," *Am. J. Clin. Nutr.* **30:**1023–1025 (1977).

28. Rose, T. L.: "The Functional Relationship between Artificial Food Colors and Hyperactivity," *J. Appl. Behav. Anal.* **11:**439–446 (1978).
29. Corwin, E., and Pines, W. L.: "Why FDA Banned Red No. 2," *FDA Consumer* **10:**18–23 (April 1976).
30. Ogilvie, M. L., Falten, E. C., Hauser, E. R., Bray, R. W., and Hoekstra, W. G.: "Effects of Stilbestrol in Altering Carcass Composition and Feed Lot Performance of Beef Steers," *J. Animal Sci.* **19:**991–1001 (1960).
31. Hecht, A.: "DES: The Drug with Unexpected Legacies," *FDA Consumer* **13:**14–17 (May 1979).
32. Jones, H. B., and Grenden, A.: "Environmental Factors in the Origin of Cancer and Estimates of the Possible Hazard to Man," *Food Cosmet. Toxicol.* **13:**251–268 (1975).
33. ———: "DES Banned in Cattle, Sheep." *FDA Consumer* **13:**2–3 (September 1979).
34. Rados, W., and Crawford, L.: "Watching the Food of Animals that Produce Food," *FDA Consumer* **13:**15–17 (October 1979).
35. McDean, L. D., and Speckman, E. W.: "Food Faddism: A Challenge to Nutritionists and Dietitians," *Am. J. Clin. Nutr.* **27:**1071–1708 (1974).
36. Commentary: "Soil Fertility and the Nutritive Value of Crops," *J. Am. Diet. Assoc.* **70:**469–470 (1977).
37. Underwood, E. J.: *Trace Elements in Human and Animal Nutrition,* 4th ed., Academic, New York, 1977, pp. 468–470.
38. Wasserman, M., Wasserman, D., Cucos, S., and Miller, J. H.: "World PCBs Map: Storage and Effects on Man and His Biologic Environment in the 1970's," *Ann. N.Y. Acad. Sci.* **320:**69–124 (1979).
39. Kimbrough, R. D.: "The Carcinogenic and Other Chronic Effects of Persistent Halogenated Organic Compounds," *Ann. N.Y. Acad. Sci.* **320:**415–418 (1979).
40. Bureau of the Census: *Statistical Abstracts of the United States,* 100th ed., Department of Commerce, Washington, 1979, p. 76.
41. Wynder, E. L.: "Dietary Habits and Cancer Epidemiology," *Cancer* **43:**1955–1961 (1979).
42. Hegsted, D. M.: "Optimal Nutrition," *Cancer* **43:**1996–2003 (1979).
43. Gori, G. B.: "Dietary and Nutritional Implications in the Multifactorial Etiology of Certain Prevalent Human Cancers," *Cancer* **43:**2151–2161 (1979).
44. Alcantara, E. N., and Speckmann, E. W.: "Diet, Nutrition and Cancer," *Am. J. Clin. Nutr.* **29:**1035–1047 (1976).
45. Visek, W. J.: "Diet and Cell Growth Modulation by Ammonia," *Am. J. Clin. Nutr.* **31:**S216–S220 (1978).
46. Thedogides, A.: "Cancer Cachexia," *Cancer* **43:**2004–2012 (1979).
47. Donaldson, S. S., and Lenon, R. A.: "Alterations of Nutritional Status: Impact of Chemotherapy and Radiation Therapy," *Cancer* **43:**2036–2052 (1979).
48. Goodhart, R. S., and Shils, M. E.: *Modern Nutrition in Health and Disease,* 6th ed., Lea & Febiger, Philadelphia, 1980, pp. 463–496.
49. Food and Nutrition Board: *Toxicants Occurring Naturally in Foods,* 2d ed., National Academy of Sciences, Washington, 1973.

50. U.S. Department of Agriculture, U.S. Department of Health and Human Service: *Nutrition and Your Health: Dietary Guidelines for Americans,* Superintendent of Documents, Washington, 1980.

CHAPTER 10

1. Food and Nutrition Board: *Recommended Dietary Allowances,* 9th ed., National Academy of Sciences, Washington, 1980.
2. Forbes, G. B., and Reina, J. C.: "Adult Lean Body Mass Declines with Age: Some Longitudinal Observations," *Metabolism* **19:**653–663 (1970).
3. *Code of Federal Regulations,* Title 21, Section 101 (1980).
4. Morrison, M.: "A Consumer's Guide to Food Labels," *FDA Consumer* **11:**4–7, 1977.
5. Shannon, B. M., and Parkes, S. C.: "Fast Foods: A Perspective on Their Nutritional Impact," *J. Am. Diet. Assoc.* **76:**242–247 (1980).
6. Anonymous: "Fast Foods OK with Nutrition Know-How," *Med. Times* **107:**21–22 (July 1980).
7. Lappe, F. M.: *Diet for a Small Planet,* revised ed., Ballantine, New York, 1975.
8. Committee on Nutrition, American Academy of Pediatrics: "Nutritional Aspects of Vegetarianism, Health Foods, and Fad Diets," *Nutr. Rev.* **35:**153–157 (1977).
9. Hardinge, M. G., and Stare, F. J.: "Nutritional Status of Vegetarians, 2: Dietary and Serum Levels of Cholesterol," *Am. J. Clin. Nutr.* **2:**83–88 (1954).
10. Sanders, T. A. B., Ellis, F. R., and Dickerson, J. W. T.: "Studies of Vegans: The Fatty Acid Composition of Plasma Choline Phosphoglycerides, Erythrocytes, Adipose Tissue, and Breast Milk and Some Indicators of Susceptibility to Ischemic Heart Disease in Vegans and Omnivore Controls," *Am. J. Clin. Nutr.* **31:**805–813 (1978).
11. Phillips, R. L., Lemon, F. R., Beeson, W. L., and Kuzma, J. W.: "Coronary Heart Disease Mortality Among Seventh Day Adventists with Differing Dietary Habits: A Preliminary Report," *Am. J. Clin. Nutr.* **31:**S191–S198 (1978).
12. Harding, M. G., and Stare, F. J.: "Nutritional Status of Vegetarians, I: Nutritional, Physical, and Laboratory Studies," *Am. J. Clin. Nutr.* **2:**73–82 (1954).
13. Hardinge, M. G., Chambers, A. C., Crooks, H., and Stare, F. J., "Nutritional Studies of Vegetarians, III: Dietary Levels of Fiber," *Am. J. Clin. Nutr.* **6:**523–525 (1958).
14. ADA Reports: "Position Paper on the Vegetarian Approach to Eating," *J. Am. Diet. Assoc.* **77:**61–68 (1980).
15. ———: "Vegetarian Diets," *Am. J. Clin. Nutr.* **27:**1095–1099 (1974).
16. Register, U. D., and Sonnenberg, L. M.: "The Vegetarian Diet," *J. Am. Diet. Assoc.* **62:**253–261 (1973).
17. Hines, J.: "Megaloblastic Anemia in an Adult Vegan," *Am. J. Clin. Nutr.* **19:**260–268 (1966).

18. Council on Foods and Nutrition, AMA: "Zen Macrobiotic Diets," *J. Am. Med. Assoc.* **218:**397 (1971).
19. Iber, E. L.: "In Alcoholism, the Liver Sets the Pace," *Nutrition Today* **6:**2–9 (January/February 1971).
20. Pawan, G. L. S.: "Metabolism of Alcohol (Ethanol) in Man," *Proc. Nutr. Soc.* **31:**83–89 (1972).
21. Goodhart, R. S., and Shils, M. E.: *Modern Nutrition in Health and Disease,* 6th ed., Lea & Febiger, Philadelphia, 1980, pp. 1220–1243.
22. Green, P. H. R., and Tall, A. R.: "Drugs, Alcohol, and Malabsorption," *Am. J. Med.* **67:**1066–1076 (1979).
23. McClain, C. J., Van Thiel, D. H., Parker, S., Badzin, L. K., and Gilbert, H.: "Alterations in Zinc, Vitamin A, and Retinol-Binding Protein in Chronic Alcoholics: A Possible Mechanism for Night Blindness and Hypogonadism," *Alcoholism: Clin. Exp. Res.* **3:**135–141 (1979).
24. Lieber, C. S.: "Alcohol, Nutrition, and the Liver," *Am. J. Clin. Nutr.* **26:**1163–1165 (1973).
25. Barboriak, J. J., and Meñahan, L. A.: "Alcohol, Lipoproteins, and Coronary Heart Disease," *Heart Lung* **8:**736–739 (1979).
26. Stephenson, P. E.: "Physiologic and Psychotropic Effects of Caffeine on Man," *J. Am. Diet. Assoc.* **71:**240–247 (1977).
27. March, D. C.: *Handbook: Interactions of Selected Drugs with Nutritional Status in Man,* American Dietetic Association, Chicago, 1977, p. 47.
28. Graham, D. M.: "Caffeine—Its Identity, Dietary Sources, Intake and Biological Effects," *Nutr. Rev.* **36:**97–102 (1978).

CHAPTER 11

1. Shanklin, D. R., and Hodin, J.: *Maternal Nutrition and Child Health,* Thomas, Springfield, Ill., 1979.
2. Burke, B. S., Hareling, V. V., and Stuart, H. C.: "Nutrition Studies during Pregnancy, IV: Relation of Protein Content of Mother's Diet during Pregnancy to Birth Length, Birth Weight, and Condition of Infant at Birth," *Pediatrics* **23:**506–515 (1943).
3. McFee, J. G.: "Anemia: A High Risk Complication of Pregnancy," *Clin. Obstet. Gynecol.* **16:**153–171 (1973).
4. Worthington, B. S., Vermeersch, J., and Williams, S. R.: *Nutrition in Pregnancy and Lactation,* Mosby, St. Louis, 1977.
5. Luke, B.: *Maternal Nutrition,* Little, Brown, Boston, 1979.
6. Hurley, L. S.: *Developmental Nutrition,* Prentice-Hall, Englewood Cliffs, N.J., 1980.
7. Food and Nutrition Board: *Recommended Dietary Allowances,* 9th ed., National Academy of Sciences, Washington, 1980.
8. Lechtig, A., Habicht, J. P., Delgado, H., Marcorell, R., Klein, R. E., and Behar, M.: "Effect of Food Supplementation during Pregnancy on Birth Weight," *Pediatrics* **56:**508–517 (1975).
9. Tafari, N., Nacye, R. L., and Gobezie, A.: "Effects of Maternal Undernu-

trition and Heavy Physical Work during Pregnancy," *Br. J. Obstet. Gynecol.* **87:**222–226 (1980).

10. Rosso, P.: "Placental Growth, Development, and Function in Relation to Maternal Nutrition," *Fed. Proc.* **39:**250–254 (1980).
11. Lindberg, B. S.: "Salt, Diuretics, and Pregnancy," *Gynecol. Invest.* **10:**145–156 (1979).
12. Goodhart, R. S., and Shils, M. E.: *Modern Nutrition in Health and Disease,* 6th ed., Lea & Febiger, Philadelphia, 1980, pp. 749–750.
13. Hurley, L. S., Dreosti, I. E., Swenterton, H., and Gowan, J.: "The Movement of Zinc in Maternal and Fetal Rat Tissues in Teratogenic Zinc Deficiency," *Teratology* **1:**216 (1968).
14. Dykes, M. H. M., and Meier, P.: "Ascorbic Acid and the Common Cold—Evaluation of Its Efficacy and Toxicity," *J. Am. Med. Assoc.* **231:**1073–1079 (1975).
15. *Code of Federal Regulations,* Title 7, Section 246.8 (1980).
16. Streissguth, A. P., Landesman-Dwyer, S., Martin, J. C., and Smith, D. W.: "Teratogenic Effects of Alcohol on Humans and Laboratory Animals," *Science* **209:**353–361 (1980).
17. Haworth, J. C., Ellestad-Sayed, J. J., King, J., and Dilling, L. A.: "Fetal Growth Retardation in Cigarette Smoking Mothers is Not Due to Decreased Maternal Food Intake," *Am. J. Obstet. Gynecol.* **137:**719–723 (1980).
18. Ericson, A., Kallen, B., and Westerholm, P.: "Cigarette Smoking as an Etiologic Factor in Cleft Lip and Palate," *Am. J. Obstet. Gynecol.* **135:**348–351 (1979).
19. Graham, D. M.: "Caffeine—Its Identity, Dietary Sources, Intake and Biological Effects," *Nutr. Rev.* **36:**97–102 (1978).
20. Corby, D. G.: "Aspirin in Pregnancy: Maternal and Fetal Effects," *Pediatrics* **62:**930–937 (1978).
21. Psiaki, D., and Olson, C.: *Current Knowledge on Breast Feeding,* Cornell University Cooperative Extension, Ithaca, N.Y., 1977.
22. Oseid, B.: "Breast-Feeding and Infant Health," *Semin. Perinatol.* **3:**249–254 (1979).
23. Fomon, S. J.: *Infant Nutrition,* 2d ed., Saunders, Philadelphia, 1974.
24. Filer, L. J.: "Early Nutrition: Its Long-Term Role," *Hosp. Pract.* **13:**87–95 (February 1978).
25. Woodruff, C. W.: "The Science of Infant Nutrition and the Art of Infant Feeding," *J. Am. Med. Assoc.* **240:**657–661 (1978).
26. Committee on Nutrition, American Academy of Pediatrics: "Iron Supplementation for Infants," *Pediatrics* **58:**765–767 (1976).
27. Fomon, S. J., Filer, L. J., Anderson, T. A., and Zeigler, E. E.: "Recommendations for Feeding Normal Infants," *Pediatrics* **63:**52–59 (1979).
28. Chandra, R. K.: "Immunological Aspects of Human Milk," *Nutr. Rev.* **36:**265–272 (1978).
29. Lamm, E., Delaney, J., and Dwyer, J. T.: "Economy in the Feeding of Infants," *Pediatr. Clin. North Am.* **24:**71–84 (1977).
30. Massey, L. K., and Davison, M. A.: "Effects of Oral Contraceptives on Nutritional Status," *Am. Fam. Physician* **19:**119–123 (January 1979).

31. Hathcock, J. N., and Coon, J.: *Nutrition and Drug Interrelations,* Academic, New York, 1978, pp. 151–187.
32. Hanson, J. W., Streithguth, A., and Smith, A.: "The Effects of Moderate Alcohol Consumption during Pregnancy on Fetal Growth and Morphogenesis," *J. Pediatr.* **92:**457–460 (1978).
33. Hanson, J. W., Jones, K. L., and Smith, D. W.: "Fetal Alcohol Syndrome: Experience with 41 Patients," *J. Am. Med. Assoc.* **235:**1458–1460 (1976).
34. Jones, K. L., Smith, D. W., Ulleland, C. N., and Streissguth, A. P.: "Pattern of Malformation in Offspring of Chronic Alcoholic Mothers," *Lancet* **1:**1267–1271 (1973).
35. Erb, L., and Andersen, B.: "FAS—Review of the Impact of Chronic Alcoholism on the Developing Fetus," *Clin. Pediatr.* **17:**644–649 (1978).

CHAPTER 12

1. Tanner, J. M., Whitehouse, R. H., and Takaishi, M.: "Standards from Birth to Maturity for Height, Weight, Height Velocity, and Weight Velocity: British Children, 1965," *Arch. Dis. Child.* **41:**454–471, (1966).
2. Fomon, S. J.: *Infant Nutrition,* 2d ed., Saunders, Philadelphia, 1974.
3. Nutrition Review (ed.): *Present Knowledge in Nutrition,* 4th ed., The Nutrition Foundation, Washington, 1976, pp. 453–458.
4. Timiras, P. S.: *Developmental Physiology and Aging,* Macmillan, New York, 1972.
5. Falkner, F., and Tanner, J. M. (eds.): *Human Growth,* vol. 3: *Neurobiology and Nutrition,* Plenum, New York, 1979, pp. 481–511.
6. Food and Nutrition Board: *Recommended Dietary Allowances,* 9th ed., National Academy of Sciences, Washington, 1980.
7. Goodhart, R. S., and Shils, M. E.: *Modern Nutrition in Health and Disease,* 6th ed., Lea & Febiger, Philadelphia, 1980.
8. Pipes, P. L.: *Nutrition in Infancy and Childhood,* Mosby, St. Louis, 1977.
9. Committee on Nutrition, American Academy of Pediatrics: "Commentary on Breast Feeding, Including Proposed Standards for Formulas," *Pediatrics* **57:**278–285 (1976).
10. Dykes, M. H. M., and Meier, P.: "Ascorbic Acid and the Common Cold—An Evaluation of Its Efficacy and Toxicity," *J. Am. Med. Assoc.* **231:**1073–1079 (1975).
11. Woodruff, C. W.: "Iron Deficiency in Infancy and Childhood," *Pediatr. Clin. North Am.* **24:**85–94 (1977).
12. Public Health Service: *Preliminary Findings of the First Health and Nutrition Examination Survey, United States, 1971–1972,* DHEW, Rockville, Md., 1974, p. 117.
13. Hambidge, K. M.: "The Role of Zinc and Other Trace Metals in Pediatric Nutrition and Health," *Pediatr. Clin. North Am.* **24:**95–106 (1977).
14. Committee on Nutrition, American Academy of Pediatrics: "Salt Intake

and Eating Patterns of Infants and Children in Relation to Blood Pressure," *Pediatrics* **53:**115–121 (1974).

15. Fomon, S. J., Filer, L. J., Anderson, T. A., and Zeigler, E. E.: "Recommendations for Feeding Normal Infants," *Pediatrics* **63:**52–59 (1979).
16. Worthington, B. S., Vermeersch, J., and Williams, S. R.: *Nutrition in Pregnancy and Lactation,* Mosby, St. Louis, 1977.
17. Anderson, T. A.: "Commercial Infant Foods: Content and Composition," *Pediatr. Clin. North Am.* **24:**37–47 (1977).
18. McLaren, D. S., and Burman, D.: *Textbook of Pediatric Nutrition,* Churchill/Livingstone, New York, 1976, pp. 358–359.
19. Pipes, P.: "When Should Solid Foods Be Fed to Infants?" *J. Nutr. Ed.* **9:**57–59 (1977).
20. Committee on Nutrition, American Academy of Pediatrics: "Iron Supplementation for Infants," *Pediatrics* **58:**765–767 (1976).
21. Cravioto, J., and Delacardie, E. R.: "Mental Performance in School Age Children," *Am. J. Dis. Child.* **120:**404–410 (1970).
22. Winick, M., Rosso, P., and Waterlow, J.: "Cellular Growth of Cerebrum, Cerebellum, and Brain Stem in Normal and Marasmic Children," *Exp. Neurol.* **26:**393–400 (1970).
23. ———: "Nutrition and Behavior," *Dairy Council Digest* **50**(5) (1979).
24. Martin, H. P.: "Nutrition: Its Relationship to Children's Physical, Mental, and Emotional Development," *Am. J. Clin. Nutr.* **26:**766–775 (1973).
25. Weil, W. B.: "Current Controversies in Childhood Obesity," *J. Pediatr.* **91:**175–187 (1977).
26. Himes, J. H.: "Infant Feeding Practices and Obesity," *J. Am. Diet. Assoc.* **75:**122–125 (1979).
27. Committee on Nutrition of the Mother and Preschool Child, FNB: "Fetal and Infant Nutrition and Susceptibility to Obesity," *Am. J. Clin. Nutr.* **31:**2026–2030 (1978).
28. Taitz, L. S.: "Obesity in Pediatric Practice: Infantile Obesity," *Pediatr. Clin. North Am.* **24:**107–115 (1977).
29. Anonymous: "Will a Fat Baby become a Fat Child?" *Nutr. Rev.* **35:**138–140 (1977).
30. Dubois, S., Hill, D. E., and Beaton, G. H.: "An Examination of Factors Believed to Be Associated with Infantile Obesity," *Am. J. Clin. Nutr.* **32:**1997–2004 (1979).
31. Morgan, J.: "The Preschool Child: Diet, Growth, and Obesity," *J. Hum. Nutr.* **34:**117–130 (1980).
32. Woolf, N.: "The Origins of Atherosclerosis," *Postgrad. Med. J.* **54:**156–161 (1978).
33. Committee on Nutrition, American Academy of Pediatrics: "Childhood Diet and Coronary Heart Disease," *Pediatrics* **49:**305–307 (1972).
34. Speer, F.: "Food Allergy: The 10 Common Offenders," *Am. Fam. Physician* **13:**106–112 (February 1976).
35. Eppright, E. S., Fox, H. M., Fryer, B. A., Lamkin, G. H., Vivian, V. M., and Fuller, E. S.: "Nutrition of Infants and Preschool Children in the North Central Region of the United States of America," *World Rev. Nutr. Diet.* **14:**269–332 (1972).

36. Beal, V. A.: "On the Acceptance of Solid Foods, and Other Food Patterns, of Infants and Children," *Pediatrics* **20:**448–456 (1957).
37. Bryan, M. S., and Lowenberg, M. E.: "The Father's Influence on Young Children's Food Preferences," *J. Am. Diet. Assoc.* **34:**30–35 (1958).
38. Committee on Nutrition, American Academy of Pediatrics: "Factors Affecting Food Intake," *Pediatrics* **33:**135–143 (1964).
39. Somers, A. P.: "Violence, Television, and the Health of American Youth," *New Engl. J. Med.* **294:**811–817 (1976).
40. Clancy-Hepburn, K., Hickey, A. A., and Nevill, G.: "Children's Behavior Responses to T.V. Food Advertisements," *J. Nutr. Ed.* **6:**93–96 (1974).
41. Gussow, J. D.: "Counternutritional Messages of TV Ads Aimed at Children," *J. Nutr. Ed.* **4:**48–52 (1972).
42. Program and Committee Staff, New York State Assembly: *Kids, Food, and Television: The Compelling Case for State Action,* Office of Research and Analysis, Program and Committee Staff, Albany, N.Y., 1977.
43. Senate Select Committee on Nutrition and Human Needs: *Edible T.V.: Child and Food Commercials,* U.S. Government Printing Office, Washington, 1977.
44. Lewis, C. E., and Lewis, M. A.: "The Impact of Television Commercials on Health Related Beliefs and Behaviors of Children," *Pediatrics* **53:**431–435 (1974).
45. Anonymous: "Cornell Counteracts Commercials," *Hum. Ecol. Forum* **10:**10, (Summer 1979).
46. Eppright, E. S., and Swanson, P. P.: "Distribution of Nutrients among Meals and Snacks of Iowa School Children," *J. Am. Diet. Assoc.* **31:**256–260 (1955).
47. *Code of Federal Regulations,* Title 7, Section 210.9 (1980).
48. *Code of Federal Regulations,* Title 7, Section 220.8 (1980).
49. *Code of Federal Regulations,* Title 7, Section 226.10 (1980).
50. Hill, M. M.: "School Lunch—A Tool for Nutrition Education," *World Rev. Nutr. Diet.* **14:**257–268 (1972).
51. Tuttle, W. W., Daum, K., Larsen, R., Salzano, J., and Roloff, L.: "Effect on School Boys of Omitting Breakfast," *J. Am. Diet. Assoc.* **30:**674–677 (1954).
52. Vyhmeister, I. B., Register, U. D., and Sonnenberg, L. M.: "Safe Vegetarian Diets for Children," *Pediatr. Clin. North Am.* **24:**203–210 (1977).
53. Fomon, S. J.: *Nutritional Disorders of Children—Prevention, Screening, and Follow-Up.* DHEW, Rockville, Md., 1976.
54. Neumann, C. G.: "Obesity in Pediatric Practice: Obesity in the Preschool and School-Age Child," *Pediatr. Clin. North Am.* **24:**117–122 (1977).
55. Nizel, A. E.: "Preventing Dental Caries: The Nutritional Factors," *Pediatr. Clin. North Am.* **24:**141–155 (1977).
56. Wender, E. H.: "Hyperactivity and the Food Additive Free Diet," *J. Fla. Med. Assoc.* **66:**466–470 (1979).
57. Feingold, B. F.: "Hyperkinesis and Learning Disabilities Linked to Artificial Food Flavors and Colors," *Am. J. Nurs.* **75:**797–803 (1975).
58. Institute of Food Technologists' Expert Panel on Food Safety and Nutri-

tion and the Committee on Public Information: "Diet and Hyperactivity: Any Connection?" *Food Tech.* **30:**29–34 (April 1976).

59. Connors, C. K., Goyette, C. H., Southwick, D. A., Lees, J. M., and Andrulonis, P. A.: "Food Additives and Hyperkinesis: A Controlled Double-Blind Experiment," *Pediatrics* **58:**154–166 (1976).
60. Harley, J. P., Matthews, C. G., and Eichman, P.: "Synthetic Food Colors and Hyperactivity in Children: A Double-Blind Challenge Experiment," *Pediatrics* **62:**975–983 (1978).
61. Marino, D. D., and King, J. C.: "Nutritional Concerns during Adolescence," *Pediatr. Clin. North Am.* **27:**125–139 (1980).
62. Greenwood, C. T., and Richardson, D. P.: "Nutrition during Adolescence," *World Rev. Nutr. Diet.* **33:**1–41 (1979).
63. Tanner, J. M.: "Earlier Maturation in Man," *Sci. Am.* **218:**21–27 (1968).
64. Richardson, B. D., and Pieters, L.: "Menarche and Growth," *Am. J. Clin. Nutr.* **30:**2088–2091 (1977).
65. Harnemann, R. L., Shapiro, L. R., Hampton, M. C., and Mitchell, B. W.: "Food and Eating Practices of Teenagers," *J. Am. Diet. Assoc.* **53:**17–24 (1968).
66. Thomas, J. A., and Call, D. L.: "Eating Between Meals—A Nutrition Problem among Teenagers?" *Nutr. Rev.* **31:**137–139 (1973).
67. Meyer, E. E., and Neumann, C. G.: "Management of the Obese Adolescent," *Pediatr. Clin. North Am.* **24:**123–132 (1977).
68. National Dairy Council: "Nutrition and Athletic Performance," *Dairy Council Digest* **46:**(2) (March/April 1975).
69. Astrand, P. O.: "Nutrition and Physical Performance," *World Rev. Nutr. Diet.* **16:**59–79 (1973).
70. Sufass, R. C.: "Nutrition for the Athlete," *N.Y. State J. Med.* **78:**1824–1825 (1978).
71. Rasch, P. J., and Pierson, W. R.: "Effect of a Protein Dietary Supplement on Muscular Strength and Hypertrophy," *Am. J. Clin. Nutr.* **11:**530–532 (1963).
72. Howald, H., Segesser, B., and Korner, W. F.: "Ascorbic Acid and Athletic Performance," *Ann. N.Y. Acad. Sci.* **268:**458–464 (1974).
73. Sharman, I. M., Down, M. G., and Norgan, N. G.: "The Effects of Vitamin E on Physiological Function and Athletic Performance of Trained Swimmers," *J. Sports Med.* **16:**215–223 (1976).
74. Than, T. M., May, M. W., Aung, K. S., and Tu, M. M.: "The Effect of Vitamin B_{12} on Physical Performance Capacity," *Br. J. Nutr.* **40:**269–273 (1978).
75. Costill, D. L., Bennett, A., Branan, G., and Eddy, D.: "Glucose Ingestion at Rest and During Prolonged Exercise," *J. Appl. Physiol.* **34:**764–769 (1973).
76. William, M. H.: *Nutritional Aspects of Human Physical and Athletic Performance,* Thomas, Springfield, Ill., 1976, p. 58.
77. Smith, N. J.: "Gaining and Losing Weight in Athletics," *J. Am. Med. Assoc.* **236:**149–151 (1976).
78. Mayer, J.: "A New Look at Old Formulas," *Fam. Health* **8:**38–40, 78 (October 1976).

79. Filer, L. J.: "Modified Food Starches for Use in Infant Foods," *Nutr. Rev.* **29:**25–59 (1971).
80. Phillips, W. E. J.: "Naturally Occurring Nitrate and Nitrite in Foods in Relation to Infant Methemoglobinemia," *Food Cosmet. Toxicol.* **9:**219–228 (1971).
81. National Center for Health Statistics: *Vital Statistics of the United States,* vol. 2, Public Health Service, Washington, 1950, p. 198.
82. Bureau of the Census: *Statistical Abstracts of the United States,* 101st ed., Dept. of Commerce, Washington, 1980.
83. Committee on Maternal Nutrition, Food and Nutrition Board: *Maternal Nutrition and the Course of Pregnancy,* National Academy of Sciences, Washington, 1970, pp. 139–162.
84. King, J. C., Cohenour, S. H., Calloway, D. H., and Jacobson, H. N.: "Assessment of Nutritional Status of Teenage Pregnant Girls, I: Nutrient Intake and Pregnancy," *Am. J. Clin. Nutr.* **25:**916–925 (1972).
85. Ferris, A. G., Lau, M. J., Hosmer, D. W., and Beal, V. A.: "The Effect of Diet on Weight Gain in Infancy," *Am. J. Clin. Nutr.* **33:**2635–2642 (1980).
86. McCallister, M., Rogers, C. S., and Taper, L. J.: "The Effect of Feeding Pattern on Weight Gain and Subscapular Skinfold Measurement in Infancy," *Fed. Proc.* **40:**906 (1981).

CHAPTER 13

1. Timiras, P. S.: *Developmental Physiology and Aging,* Macmillan, New York, 1972.
2. Rossman, I. (ed.): *Clinical Geriatrics,* Lippincott, Philadelphia, 1971.
3. Tappel, A. L.: "Vitamin E," *Nutrition Today* **8:**4–12 (July/August 1973).
4. Winick, M.: *Nutrition and Aging,* Wiley, New York, 1976, pp. 43–57.
5. Rowe, D.: "Aging, A Jewel in the Mosaic of Life," *J. Am. Diet. Assoc.* **72:**478–486 (1978).
6. Masore, E. J., Bertrand, H., Liepa, G., and Ya, B. P.: "Analysis and Exploration of Age-Related Changes in Mammalian Structure and Function," *Fed. Proc.* **38:**1956–1961 (1979).
7. Uauy, R., Scrimshaw, N. S., and Young, V. R.: "Human Protein Requirements: Nitrogen Balance Response to Graded Levels of Egg Protein in Elderly Men and Women," *Am. J. Clin. Nutr.* **31:**779–785 (1978).
8. Winick, M.: "Nutrition and Aging," *N.Y. State J. Med.* **78:**1970–1971 (1978).
9. Kohrs, M. B., O'Neal, R., Preston, A., Eklund, D., and Abrahams, O.: "Nutritional Status of Elderly Residents in Missouri," *Am. J. Clin. Nutr.* **31:**2186–2197 (1978).
10. Greene, J.: "Nutritional Care Considerations of Older Americans," *J. Natl. Med. Assoc.* **71:**791–793 (1979).
11. Krehl, W. A.: "The Influence of Nutritional Environment on Aging," *Geriatrics* **29:**65–76 (May 1974).
12. Guthrie, H. A., Black, K., and Madden, J. P.: "Nutritional Practices of

Elderly Citizens in Rural Pennsylvania," *Gerontologist* **12:**330–335 (Winter 1972).

13. Shock, N. W.: "Physiologic Aspects of Aging," *J. Am. Diet. Assoc.* **56:**491–495 (1970).
14. Clarke, M., and Wakefield, L. M.: "Food Choices of Institutionalized vs. Independent-Living Elderly," *J. Am. Diet. Assoc.* **66:**600–604 (1975).
15. Palmare, E.: "Facts on Aging—A Short Quiz," *Gerontologist* **17:**315–320 (1977).
16. Stiedemann, M., Jansen, C., and Harrett, I.: "Nutritional Status of Elderly Men and Women," *J. Am. Diet. Assoc.* **73:**132–139 (1978).
17. Grotkowski, M. L., and Sims, L. S.: "Nutritional Knowledge, Attitudes, and Dietary Practices of the Elderly," *J. Am. Diet. Assoc.* **22:**499–506 (1978).
18. O'Hanlon, P., and Kohrs, M. B.: "Dietary Studies of Older Americans," *Am. J. Clin. Nutr.* **31:**1257–1269 (1978).
19. National Institutes of Health, Public Health Service: *Our Future Selves,* DHEW Publication No. 77–1096, Washington, 1977, p. 9.
20. Young, V. R.: "Diet as a Modulator of Aging and Longevity," *Fed. Proc.* **38:**1994–2000 (1979).
21. Tempro, W. A.: "Nutritional Problems in the Aged: Dietary Aspects," *J. Natl. Med. Assoc.* **70:**281–283 (1978).
22. Myers, T. W.: "Nutritional Programming for the Elderly," *J. Natl. Med. Assoc.* **70:**335–338 (1978).
23. Sherwood, S.: "Sociology of Food and Eating: Implications for Action for the Elderly," *Am. J. Clin. Nutr.* **26:**1108–1110 (1973).

CHAPTER 14

1. Mayer, J.: "The Dimensions of Human Hunger," *Sci. Am.* **235:**40–49 (September 1976).
2. Scrimshaw, N. S.: "Global Use of the Instruments of Scholarship for the Conquest of Hunger—The World Hunger Program of the United Nations University," *Bibl. Nutr. Diet.* **28:**155–166 (1979).
3. Anonymous: "Assessment of the World Food Situation—Present and Future," *Food Nutr. (Roma)* **1:**7–40 (1975).
4. Timmer, C. P.: "Access to Food: The Ultimate Determinant of Hunger," *Ann. N.Y. Acad. Sci.* **300:**59–68 (1977).
5. Chancellor, W. J., and Goss, J. R.: "Balancing Energy and Food Production, 1975–2000," *Science* **192:**213–218 (1976).
6. Wortman, S.: "Food and Agriculture," *Sci. Am.* **235:**31–39 (September 1976).
7. Winikoff, B.: "Nutrition, Population, and Health: Some Implications for Policy," *Science* **200:**895–902 (1978).
8. Sanderson, F. H.: "The Great Food Fumble," *Science* **188:**503–507 (1975).
9. Sisler, D. G., and Blandford, D.: "'Rubber or Rice?'—The Dilemma of

Many Developing Nations," Paper No. 13, The Center for the Analysis of World Food Issues, Cornell University, Ithaca, N.Y., 1979.
10. Reville, R.: "The Resources Available for Agriculture," *Sci. Am.* **235:**165–178 (September 1976).
11. Van Wambeke, A. R.: "Land Resources and World Food Issues," Paper No. 2, *A Series of Papers on World Food Issues,* Cornell University, Ithaca, N.Y., 1979.
12. Caliendo, M. A.: *Nutrition and the World Food Crisis,* Macmillan, New York, 1979.
13. Lappe, F. M., and Collins, J., with Cary Fowler: *Food First: Beyond the Myth of Scarcity,* Houghton-Mifflin, Boston, 1977.
14. Olness, K.: "The Ecology of Malnutrition in Children," *J. Am. Med. Wom. Assoc.* **32:**279–284 (1977).
15. Cohen, J. M.: "Can Land Tenure Reform Lead to Increased Food Production?" Paper No. 12, *A Series of Papers on World Food Issues,* Cornell University, Ithaca, N.Y., 1979.
16. Economic Research Service: *The World Food Situation and Prospects to 1985,* Foreign Agricultural Economic Report No. 98, USDA, Washington, 1974.
17. Chou, M., Harmon, D. P., Kahn, H., and Wittwer, S. H.: *World Food Prospects and Agricultural Potential,* Praeger, New York, 1977.
18. Abbot, J. C.: "Adjustment of Food Distribution Systems to Meet Nutritional Needs," *Bibl. Nutr. Diet.* **28:**130–136 (1979).
19. Joint FAO/WHO Expert Committee on Nutrition: "Food and Nutrition Strategies in National Development," *WHO Tech. Rep. Ser.* **584** (1976).
20. Crossen, P. R., and Fredrick, K. D.: *The World Food Situation,* Resources for the Future, Inc., Washington, 1977.
21. Detheir, B. E.: "Problems of a Changing Climate," Paper No. 3, *A Series of Papers on World Food Issues,* Cornell University, Ithaca, N.Y., 1979.
22. Beaton, G. H., and Bengoa, J. M. (eds.): "Nutrition in Preventive Medicine—The Major Deficiency Syndromes, Epidemiology, and Approaches to Control," *WHO Monogr. Ser.* **62:**13–20 (1976).
23. Mayer, J., Chafkin, S. H., and Duke, R. C.: "Panel on Food, Nutrition, and Population Interactions," *Ann. N.Y. Acad. Sci.* **300:**5–16 (1977).
24. Robinson, K. L.: "International Food Aid," Paper No. 14, *A Series of Papers on World Food Issues,* Cornell University, Ithaca, N.Y., 1979.
25. Citizen's Board of Inquiry into Hunger and Malnutrition in the United States: *Hunger U.S.A.,* Beacon, Boston, 1968.
26. Citizen's Board of Inquiry into Hunger and Malnutrition in the United States: *Hunger U.S.A., Revisited,* Southern Regional Council, Atlanta, Ga., 1972.
27. Boehm, W. T., Nelson, P. E., and Longen, K. A.: *Progress Toward Eliminating Hunger in America,* Agricultural Economic Report No. 446, USDA, Washington, 1980.
28. U.S. Department of Agriculture, U.S. Department of Health and Human Services: *Nutrition and Your Health—Dietary Guidelines for Americans,* Superintendent of Documents, Washington, 1980.

29. Broad, W. J.: "Nutrition's Battle of the Potomac," *Nutrition Today* **14:**6–14 (July/August 1979).
30. Mauldin, W. P.: "Population Trends and Prospects," *Science* **209:**148–157 (1980).
31. ADA Reports: "ADA Outlines Research Needs at Congressional Hearing," *J. Am. Diet. Assoc.* **75:**692–695 (1979).
32. Scrimshaw, N. S., and Taylor, L.: "Food," *Sci. Am.* **243:**78–88 (September 1980).

READY REFERENCES

Ready Reference 1

NUTRITIVE VALUES OF THE EDIBLE PARTS OF FOODS

Dashes in the columns for nutrients show that no suitable value could be found although there is reason to believe that a measurable amount of the nutrient may be present.

	Food, Approximate Measure and Weight, g		Water, %	Food Energy, cal	Protein, g	Fat, g	Fatty acids: Saturated, Total, g	Fatty acids: Unsaturated, g: Oleic	Fatty acids: Unsaturated, g: Linoleic	Carbohydrate, g	Calcium, mg	Iron, mg	Vitamin A Value, IU	Thiamine, mg	Riboflavin, mg	Niacin, mg	Ascorbic Acid, mg
	Milk, Cheese, Cream, Imitation Cream; Related Products																
	Milk:																
	Fluid:																
1	Whole, 3.5% fat, 1 cup	244	87	160	9	9	5	3	Trace	12	288	0.1	350	0.07	0.41	0.2	2
2	Nonfat (skim), 1 cup	245	90	90	9	Trace	—	—	—	12	296	0.1	10	0.09	0.44	0.2	2
3	Partly skimmed, 2% nonfat milk solids added, 1 cup	246	87	145	10	5	3	2	Trace	15	352	0.1	200	0.10	0.52	0.2	2
	Canned, concentrated, undiluted:																
4	Evaporated, unsweetened, 1 cup	252	74	345	18	20	11	7	1	24	635	0.3	810	0.10	0.86	0.5	3
5	Condensed, sweetened, 1 cup	306	27	980	25	27	15	9	1	166	802	0.3	1,100	0.24	1.16	0.6	3
	Dry, nonfat instant:																
6	Low-density (1 1/3 cups needed for reconstitution to 1 qt), 1 cup	68	4	245	24	Trace	—	—	—	35	879	0.4	20[a]	0.24	1.21	0.6	5
7	High-density (7/8 cup needed for reconstitution to 1 qt), 1 cup	104	4	375	37	1	—	—	—	54	1,345	0.6	30[a]	0.36	1.85	0.9	7
	Buttermilk:																
8	Fluid, cultured, made from skim milk, 1 cup	245	90	90	9	Trace	—	—	—	12	296	0.1	10	0.10	0.44	0.2	2
9	Dried, packaged, 1 cup	120	3	465	41	6	3	2	Trace	60	1,498	0.7	260	0.31	2.06	1.1	—
	Cheese:																
	Natural:																
	Blue or Roquefort type:																
10	Ounce, 1 oz	28	40	105	6	9	5	3	Trace	1	89	0.1	350	0.01	0.17	0.3	0
11	Cubic inch, 1 in³	17	40	65	4	5	3	2	Trace	Trace	54	0.1	210	0.01	0.11	0.2	0
12	Camembert, packaged in 4-oz pkg. with 3 wedges per pkg., 1 wedge	38	52	115	7	9	5	3	Trace	1	40	0.2	380	0.02	0.29	0.3	0
	Cheddar:																
13	Ounce, 1 oz	28	37	115	7	9	5	3	Trace	1	213	0.3	370	0.01	0.13	Trace	0
14	Cubic inch, 1 in³	17	37	70	4	6	3	2	Trace	Trace	129	0.2	230	0.01	0.08	Trace	0
	Cottage, large or small curd:																
	Creamed:																
15	Package of 12-oz, net wt., 1 pkg.	340	78	360	46	14	8	5	Trace	10	320	1.0	580	0.10	0.85	0.3	0
16	Cup, curd pressed down, 1 cup	245	78	260	33	10	6	3	Trace	7	230	0.7	420	0.07	0.61	0.2	0

[a]Value applies to unfortified product; value for fortified low-density product would be 1500 IU, and the fortified high-density product would be 2290 IU.

NUTRITIVE VALUES OF THE EDIBLE PARTS OF FOODS

Dashes in the columns for nutrients show that no suitable value could be found although there is reason to believe that a measurable amount of the nutrient may be present.

	Food, Approximate Measure and Weight, g		Water, %	Food Energy, kcal	Protein, g	Fat, g	Fatty acids: Saturated, Total, g	Fatty acids: Unsaturated, g: Oleic	Fatty acids: Unsaturated, g: Linoleic	Carbohydrate, g	Calcium, mg	Iron, mg	Vitamin A Value, IU	Thiamine, mg	Riboflavin, mg	Niacin, mg	Ascorbic Acid, mg
	Uncreamed:																
17	Package of 12-oz, net wt., 1 pkg.	340	79	290	58	1	1	Trace	Trace	9	306	1.4	30	0.10	0.95	0.3	0
18	Cup, curd pressed down, 1 cup	200	79	170	34	1	Trace	Trace	Trace	5	180	0.8	20	0.06	0.56	0.2	0
	Cream:																
19	Package of 8-oz, net wt., 1 pkg.	227	51	850	18	86	48	28	3	5	141	0.5	3,500	0.05	0.54	0.2	0
20	Package of 3-oz, net wt., 1 pkg.	85	51	320	7	32	18	11	1	2	53	0.2	1,310	0.02	0.20	0.1	0
21	Cubic inch, 1 in^3	16	51	60	1	6	3	2	Trace	Trace	10	Trace	250	Trace	0.04	Trace	0
	Parmesan, grated:																
22	Cup, pressed down, 1 cup	140	17	655	60	43	24	14	1	5	1,893	0.7	1,760	0.03	1.22	0.3	0
23	Tablespoon, 1 tbsp	5	17	25	2	2	1	Trace	Trace	Trace	68	Trace	60	Trace	0.04	Trace	0
24	Ounce, 1 oz	28	17	130	12	9	5	3	Trace	1	383	0.1	360	0.01	0.25	0.1	0
	Swiss:																
25	Ounce, 1 oz	28	39	105	8	8	4	3	Trace	1	262	0.3	320	Trace	0.11	Trace	0
26	Cubic inch, 1 in^3	15	39	55	4	4	2	1	Trace	Trace	139	0.1	170	Trace	0.06	Trace	0
	Pasteurized processed cheese:																
	American:																
27	Ounce, 1 oz	28	40	105	7	9	5	3	Trace	1	198	0.3	350	0.01	0.12	Trace	0
28	Cubic inch, 1 in^3	18	40	65	4	5	3	2	Trace	Trace	122	0.2	210	Trace	0.07	Trace	0
	Swiss:																
29	Ounce, 1 oz	28	40	100	8	8	4	3	Trace	1	251	0.3	310	Trace	0.11	Trace	0
30	Cubic inch, 1 in^3	18	40	65	5	5	3	2	Trace	Trace	159	0.2	200	Trace	0.07	Trace	0
	Pasteurized process cheese food,																
	American:																
31	Tablespoon, 1 tbsp	14	43	45	3	3	2	1	Trace	1	80	0.1	140	Trace	0.08	Trace	0
32	Cubic inch, 1 in^3	18	43	60	4	4	2	1	Trace	1	100	0.1	170	Trace	0.10	Trace	0
33	Pasteurized process cheese spread, American, 1 oz	28	49	80	5	6	3	2	Trace	2	160	0.2	250	Trace	0.15	Trace	0
	Cream:																
34	Half-and-half (cream and milk), 1 cup	242	80	325	8	28	15	9	1	11	261	0.1	1,160	0.07	0.39	0.1	2
35	1 tbsp	15	80	20	1	2	1	1	Trace	1	16	Trace	70	Trace	0.02	Trace	Trace
36	Light, coffee or table, 1 cup	240	72	505	7	49	27	16	1	10	245	0.1	2,020	0.07	0.36	0.1	2
37	1 tbsp	15	72	30	1	3	2	1	Trace	1	15	Trace	130	Trace	0.02	Trace	Trace
38	Sour, 1 cup	230	72	485	7	47	26	16	1	10	235	0.1	1,930	0.07	0.35	0.1	2
39	1 tbsp	12	72	25	Trace	2	1	1	Trace	1	12	Trace	100	Trace	0.02	Trace	Trace
40	Whipped topping (pressurized), 1 cup	60	62	155	2	14	8	5	Trace	6	67	—	570	—	0.04	—	—
41	1 tbsp	3	62	10	Trace	1	Trace	Trace	Trace	Trace	3	—	30	—	Trace	—	—

	Whipping, unwhipped (volume about double when whipped):																
42	Light, 1 cup	239	62	715	6	75	41	25	2	9	203	0.1	3,060	0.05	0.29	0.1	2
43	1 tbsp	15	62	45	Trace	5	3	2	Trace	1	13	Trace	190	Trace	0.02	Trace	Trace
44	Heavy, 1 cup	238	57	840	5	90	50	30	3	7	179	0.1	3,670	0.05	0.26	0.1	2
45	1 tbsp	15	57	55	Trace	6	3	2	Trace	1	11	Trace	230	Trace	0.02	Trace	Trace
	Imitation cream products (made with vegetable fat):																
	Creamers:																
46	Powdered, 1 cup	94	2	505	4	33	31	1	0	52	21	0.6	200[b]	—	—	Trace	—
47	1 tsp	2	2	10	Trace	1	Trace	Trace	0	1	1	Trace	Trace[b]	—	—	—	—
48	Liquid (frozen), 1 cup	245	77	345	3	27	25	1	0	25	29	—	100[b]	0	0	—	—
49	1 tbsp	15	77	20	Trace	2	1	Trace	0	2	2	—	10[b]	0	0	—	—
50	Sour dressing (imitation sour cream) made with nonfat dry milk, 1 cup	235	72	440	9	38	35	1	Trace	17	277	0.1	10	0.07	0.38	0.2	1
51	1 tbsp	12	72	20	Trace	2	2	Trace	Trace	1	14	Trace	Trace	Trace	Trace	Trace	Trace
	Whipped topping:																
52	Pressurized, 1 cup	70	61	190	1	17	15	1	0	9	5	—	340[b]	—	0	—	—
53	1 tbsp	4	61	10	Trace	1	1	Trace	0	Trace	Trace	—	20[b]	—	0	—	—
54	Frozen, 1 cup	75	52	230	1	20	18	Trace	0	15	5	—	560[b]	—	0	—	—
55	1 tbsp	4	52	10	Trace	1	1	Trace	0	1	Trace	—	30[b]	—	0	—	—
56	Powdered, made with whole milk, 1 cup	75	58	175	3	12	10	1	Trace	15	62	Trace	330[b]	0.02	0.08	0.1	Trace
57	1 tbsp	4	58	10	Trace	1	1	Trace	Trace	1	3	Trace	20[b]	Trace	Trace	Trace	Trace
	Milk beverages:																
58	Cocoa, homemade, 1 cup	250	79	245	10	12	7	4	Trace	27	295	1.0	400	0.10	0.45	0.5	3
59	Chocolate-flavored drink made with skim milk and 2% added butterfat, 1 cup	250	83	190	8	6	3	2	Trace	27	270	0.5	210	0.10	0.40	0.3	3
	Malted milk:																
60	Dry powder, approx. 3 heaping tsp per oz, 1 oz	28	3	115	4	2	—	—	—	20	82	0.6	290	0.09	0.15	0.1	0
61	Beverage, 1 cup	235	78	245	11	10	—	—	—	28	317	0.7	590	0.14	0.49	0.2	2
	Milk desserts:																
62	Custard, baked, 1 cup	265	77	305	14	15	7	5	1	29	297	1.1	930	0.11	0.50	0.3	1
	Ice cream:																
63	Regular, approx. 10% fat, 1/2 gal	1,064	63	2,055	48	113	62	37	3	221	1,553	0.5	4,680	0.43	2.23	1.1	11
64	1 cup	133	63	255	6	14	8	5	Trace	28	194	0.1	590	0.05	0.28	0.1	1
65	3 fl oz cup	50	63	95	2	5	3	2	Trace	10	73	Trace	220	0.02	0.11	0.1	1
66	Rich, approx. 16% fat, 1/2 gal	1,188	63	2,635	31	191	105	63	6	214	927	0.2	7,840	0.24	1.31	1.2	12
67	1 cup	148	63	330	4	24	13	8	1	27	115	Trace	980	0.03	0.16	0.1	1
	Ice milk:																
68	Hardened, 1/2 gal	1,048	67	1,595	50	53	29	17	2	235	1,635	1.0	2,200	0.52	2.31	1.0	10
69	1 cup	131	67	200	6	7	4	2	Trace	29	204	0.1	280	0.07	0.29	0.1	1
70	Soft-serve, 1 cup	175	67	265	8	9	5	3	Trace	39	273	0.2	370	0.09	0.39	0.2	2

[b]Contributed largely from beta-carotene used for coloring.

NUTRITIVE VALUES OF THE EDIBLE PARTS OF FOODS

Dashes in the columns for nutrients show that no suitable value could be found although there is reason to believe that a measurable amount of the nutrient may be present.

	Food, Approximate Measure and Weight, g		Water, %	Food Energy, kcal	Protein, g	Fat, g	Fatty acids: Saturated, Total, g	Fatty acids: Unsaturated, g: Oleic	Fatty acids: Unsaturated, g: Linoleic	Carbohydrate, g	Calcium, mg	Iron, mg	Vitamin A Value, IU	Thiamine, mg	Riboflavin, mg	Niacin, mg	Ascorbic Acid, mg
	Yogurt:																
71	Made from partially skimmed milk, 1 cup	245	89	125	8	4	2	1	Trace	13	294	0.1	170	0.10	0.44	0.2	2
72	Made from whole milk, 1 cup	245	88	150	7	8	5	3	Trace	12	272	0.1	340	0.07	0.39	0.2	2
	Eggs																
	Eggs, large, 24 oz per dozen:																
	Raw or cooked in shell or with nothing added:																
73	Whole, without shell, 1 egg	50	74	80	6	6	2	3	Trace	Trace	27	1.1	590	0.05	0.15	Trace	0
74	White of egg, 1 white	33	88	15	4	Trace	—	—	—	Trace	3	Trace	0	Trace	0.09	Trace	0
75	Yolk of egg, 1 yolk	17	51	60	3	5	2	2	Trace	Trace	24	0.9	580	0.04	0.07	Trace	0
76	Scrambled with milk and fat, 1 egg	64	72	110	7	8	3	3	Trace	1	51	1.1	690	0.05	0.18	Trace	0
	Meat, Poultry, Fish, Shellfish, Related Products																
77	Bacon (20 slices per lb raw), broiled or fried, crisp, 2 slices	15	8	90	5	8	3	4	1	1	2	0.5	0	0.08	0.05	0.8	—
	Beef, cooked:[c]																
	Cuts braised, simmered, or pot-roasted:																
78	Lean and fat, 3 oz	85	53	245	23	16	8	7	Trace	0	10	2.9	30	0.04	0.18	3.5	—
79	Lean only, 2.5 oz	72	62	140	22	5	2	2	Trace	0	10	2.7	10	0.04	0.16	3.3	—
	Hamburger (ground beef), broiled:																
80	Lean, 3 oz	85	60	185	23	10	5	4	Trace	0	10	3.0	20	0.08	0.20	5.1	—
81	Regular, 3 oz	85	54	245	21	17	8	8	Trace	0	9	2.7	30	0.07	0.18	4.6	—
	Roast, oven-cooked, no liquid added:																
	Relatively fat, such as rib:																
82	Lean and fat, 3 oz	85	40	375	17	34	16	15	1	0	8	2.2	70	0.05	0.13	3.1	—
83	Lean only, 1.8 oz	51	57	125	14	7	3	3	Trace	0	6	1.8	10	0.04	0.11	2.6	—
	Relatively lean, such as heel of round:																
84	Lean and fat, 3 oz	85	62	165	25	7	3	3	Trace	0	11	3.2	10	0.06	0.19	4.5	—
85	Lean only, 2.7 oz	78	65	125	24	3	1	1	Trace	0	10	3.0	Trace	0.06	0.18	4.3	—
	Steak, broiled:																
	Relatively fat, such as sirloin:																
86	Lean and fat, 3 oz	85	44	330	20	27	13	12	1	0	9	2.5	50	0.05	0.16	4.0	—
87	Lean only, 2.0 oz	56	59	115	18	4	2	2	Trace	0	7	2.2	10	0.05	0.14	3.6	—

	Relatively lean, such as round:																
88	Lean and fat, 3 oz	85	55	220	24	13	6	6	Trace	0	10	3.0	20	0.07	0.19	4.8	—
89	Lean only, 2.4 oz	68	61	130	21	4	2	2	Trace	0	9	2.5	10	0.06	0.16	4.1	—
	Beef, canned:																
90	Corned beef, 3 oz	85	59	185	22	10	5	4	Trace	0	17	3.7	20	0.01	0.20	2.9	—
91	Corned beef hash, 3 oz	85	67	155	7	10	5	4	Trace	9	11	1.7	—	0.01	0.08	1.8	—
92	Beef, dried or chipped, 2 oz	57	48	115	19	4	2	2	Trace	0	11	2.9	—	0.04	0.18	2.2	—
93	Beef and vegetable stew, 1 cup	235	82	210	15	10	5	4	Trace	15	28	2.8	2,310	0.13	0.17	4.4	15
94	Beef potpie, baked, 4 1/4-in diam., weight before baking about 8 oz, 1 pie	227	55	560	23	33	9	20	2	43	32	4.1	1,860	0.25	0.27	4.5	7
	Chicken, cooked:																
95	Flesh only, broiled, 3 oz	85	71	115	20	3	1	1	1	0	8	1.4	80	0.05	0.16	7.4	—
	Breast, fried, 1/2 breast:																
96	With bone, 3.3 oz	94	58	155	25	5	1	2	1	1	9	1.3	70	0.04	0.17	11.2	—
97	Flesh and skin only, 2.7 oz	76	58	155	25	5	1	2	1	1	9	1.3	70	0.04	0.17	11.2	—
	Drumstick, fried:																
98	With bone, 2.1 oz	59	55	90	12	4	1	2	1	Trace	6	0.9	50	0.03	0.15	2.7	—
99	Flesh and skin only, 1.3 oz	38	55	90	12	4	1	2	1	Trace	6	0.9	50	0.03	0.15	2.7	—
100	Chicken, canned, boneless, 3 oz	85	65	170	18	10	3	4	2	0	18	1.3	200	0.03	0.11	3.7	3
101	Chicken potpie, baked 4 1/4-in diam., weight before baking about 8 oz, 1 pie	227	57	535	23	31	10	15	3	42	68	3.0	3,020	0.25	0.26	4.1	5
	Chili con carne, canned:																
102	With beans, 1 cup	250	72	335	19	15	7	7	Trace	30	80	4.2	150	0.08	0.18	3.2	—
103	Without beans, 1 cup	255	67	510	26	38	18	17	1	15	97	3.6	380	0.05	0.31	5.6	—
104	Heart, beef, lean, braised, 3 oz	85	61	160	27	5	—	—	—	1	5	5.0	20	0.21	1.04	6.5	1
	Lamb, cooked:[c]																
105	Chop, thick, with bone, broiled, 1 chop, 4.8 oz	137	47	400	25	33	18	12	1	0	10	1.5	—	0.14	0.25	5.6	—
106	Lean and fat, 4.0 oz	112	47	400	25	33	18	12	1	0	10	1.5	—	0.14	0.25	5.6	—
107	Lean only, 2.6 oz	74	62	140	21	6	3	2	Trace	0	9	1.5	—	0.11	0.20	4.5	—
	Leg, roasted:																
108	Lean and fat, 3 oz	85	54	235	22	16	9	6	Trace	0	9	1.4	—	0.13	0.23	4.7	—
109	Lean only, 2.5 oz	71	62	130	20	5	3	2	Trace	0	9	1.4	—	0.12	0.21	4.4	—
	Shoulder, roasted:																
110	Lean and fat, 3 oz	85	50	285	18	23	13	8	1	0	9	1.0	—	0.11	0.20	4.0	—
111	Lean only, 2.3 oz	64	61	130	17	6	3	2	Trace	0	8	1.0	—	0.10	0.18	3.7	—
112	Liver, beef, fried, 2 oz	57	57	130	15	6	—	—	—	3	6	5.0	30,280	0.15	2.37	9.4	15
	Pork, cured, cooked:																
113	Ham, light cure, lean and fat, roasted, 3 oz	85	54	245	18	19	7	8	2	0	8	2.2	0	0.40	0.16	3.1	—
	Luncheon meat:																
114	Boiled ham, sliced, 2 oz	57	59	135	11	10	4	4	1	0	6	1.6	0	0.25	0.09	1.5	—
115	Canned, spiced or unspiced, 2 oz	57	55	165	8	14	5	6	1	1	5	1.2	0	0.18	0.12	1.6	—

[c]Outer layer of fat on the cut was removed to within approximately 1/2 in of the lean; deposits of fat within the cut were not removed.

NUTRITIVE VALUES OF THE EDIBLE PARTS OF FOODS

Dashes in the columns for nutrients show that no suitable value could be found although there is reason to believe that a measurable amount of the nutrient may be present.

	Food, Approximate Measure and Weight, g		Water, %	Food Energy, kcal	Protein, g	Fat, g	Fatty acids: Saturated, Total, g	Fatty acids: Unsaturated, g: Oleic	Fatty acids: Unsaturated, g: Linoleic	Carbohydrate, g	Calcium, mg	Iron, mg	Vitamin A Value, IU	Thiamine, mg	Riboflavin, mg	Niacin, mg	Ascorbic Acid, mg
	Pork, fresh, cooked:[c]																
116	Chop, thick, with bone, 1 chop, 3.5 oz	98	42	260	16	21	8	9	2	0	8	2.2	0	0.63	0.18	3.8	—
117	Lean and fat, 2.3 oz	66	42	260	16	21	8	9	2	0	8	2.2	0	0.63	0.18	3.8	—
118	Lean only, 1.7 oz	48	53	130	15	7	2	3	1	0	7	1.9	0	0.54	0.16	3.3	—
	Roast, oven-cooked, no liquid added:																
119	Lean and fat, 3 oz	85	46	310	21	24	9	10	2	0	9	2.7	0	0.78	0.22	4.7	—
120	Lean only, 2.4 oz	68	55	175	20	10	3	4	1	0	9	2.6	0	0.73	0.21	4.4	—
	Cuts, simmered:																
121	Lean and fat, 3 oz	85	46	320	20	26	9	11	2	0	8	2.5	0	0.46	0.21	4.1	—
122	Lean only, 2.2 oz	63	60	135	18	6	2	3	1	0	8	2.3	0	0.42	0.19	3.7	—
	Sausage:																
123	Bologna, slice, 3-in diam. by 1/8 in; 2 slices	26	56	80	3	7	—	—	—	Trace	2	0.5	—	0.04	0.06	0.7	—
124	Braunschweiger, slice, 2-in diam. by 1/4 in, 2 slices	20	53	65	3	5	—	—	—	Trace	2	1.2	1,310	0.03	0.29	1.6	—
125	Deviled ham, canned, 1 tbsp	13	51	45	2	4	2	2	Trace	0	1	0.3	—	0.02	0.01	0.2	—
126	Frankfurter, heated (8 per lb purchased pkg.), 1 frank	56	57	170	7	15	—	—	—	1	3	0.8	—	0.08	0.11	1.4	—
127	Pork links, cooked (16 links per lb raw), 2 links	26	35	125	5	11	4	5	1	Trace	2	0.6	0	0.21	0.09	1.0	—
128	Salami, dry type, 1 oz	28	30	130	7	11	—	—	—	Trace	4	1.0	—	0.10	0.07	1.5	—
129	Salami, cooked, 1 oz	28	51	90	5	7	—	—	—	Trace	3	0.7	—	0.07	0.07	1.2	—
130	Vienna, canned (7 sausages per 5-oz can), 1 sausage	16	63	40	2	3	—	—	—	Trace	1	0.3	—	0.01	0.02	0.4	—
	Veal, medium fat, cooked, bone removed:																
131	Cutlet, 3 oz	85	60	185	23	9	5	4	Trace	—	9	2.7	—	0.06	0.21	4.6	—
132	Roast, 3 oz	85	55	230	23	14	7	6	Trace	0	10	2.9	—	0.11	0.26	6.6	—
	Fish and shellfish:																
133	Bluefish, baked with table fat, 3 oz	85	68	135	22	4	—	—	—	0	25	0.6	40	0.09	0.08	1.6	—
	Clams:																
134	Raw, meat only, 3 oz	85	82	65	11	1	—	—	—	2	59	5.2	90	0.08	0.15	1.1	8
135	Canned, solids and liquid, 3 oz	85	86	45	7	1	—	—	—	2	47	3.5	—	0.01	0.09	0.9	—
136	Crabmeat, canned, 3 oz	85	77	85	15	2	—	—	—	1	38	0.7	—	0.07	0.07	1.6	—
137	Fish sticks, breaded, cooked, frozen; stick 3 3/4 by 1 by 1/2 in, 10 sticks or 8-oz pkg.	227	66	400	38	20	5	4	10	15	25	0.9	—	0.09	0.16	3.6	—

138	Haddock, breaded, fried, 3 oz	85	66	140	17	5	1	3	Trace	5	34	1.0	—	0.03	0.06	2.7	2
139	Ocean perch, breaded, fried, 3 oz	85	59	195	16	11	—	—	—	6	28	1.1	—	0.08	0.09	1.5	—
140	Oysters, raw, meat only (13-19 med. selects), 1 cup	240	85	160	20	4	—	—	—	8	226	13.2	740	0.33	0.43	6.0	—
141	Salmon, pink, canned, 3 oz	85	71	120	17	5	1	1	Trace	0	167[d]	0.7	60	0.03	0.16	6.8	—
142	Sardines, Atlantic, canned in oil, drained solids, 3 oz	85	62	175	20	9	—	—	—	0	372	2.5	190	0.02	0.17	4.6	—
143	Shad, baked with table fat and bacon, 3 oz	85	64	170	20	10	—	—	—	0	20	0.5	20	0.11	0.22	7.3	—
144	Shrimp, canned, meat, 3 oz	85	70	100	21	1	—	—	—	1	98	2.6	50	0.01	0.03	1.5	—
145	Swordfish, broiled with butter or margarine, 3 oz	85	65	150	24	5	—	—	—	0	23	1.1	1,750	0.03	0.04	9.3	—
146	Tuna, canned in oil, drained solids, 3 oz	85	61	170	24	7	2	1	1	0	7	1.6	70	0.04	0.10	10.1	—
	Mature Dry Beans and Peas, Nuts, Peanuts, Related Products																
147	Almonds, shelled, whole kernels, 1 cup	142	5	850	26	77	6	52	15	28	332	6.7	0	0.34	1.31	5.0	Trace
	Beans, dry:																
	Common varieties as Great Northern navy, and others:																
	Cooked, drained:																
148	Great Northern, 1 cup	180	69	210	14	1	—	—	—	38	90	4.9	0	0.25	0.13	1.3	0
149	Navy (pea), 1 cup	190	69	225	15	1	—	—	—	40	95	5.1	0	0.27	0.13	1.3	0
	Canned, solids and liquid:																
	White with—																
150	Frankfurters (sliced), 1 cup	255	71	365	19	18	—	—	—	32	94	4.8	330	0.18	0.15	3.3	Trace
151	Pork and tomato sauce, 1 cup	255	71	310	16	7	2	3	1	49	138	4.6	330	0.20	0.08	1.5	5
152	Pork and sweet sauce, 1 cup	255	66	385	16	12	4	5	1	54	161	5.9	—	0.15	0.10	1.3	—
153	Red kidney, 1 cup	255	76	230	15	1	—	—	—	42	74	4.6	10	0.13	0.10	1.5	—
154	Lima, cooked, drained, 1 cup	190	64	260	16	1	—	—	—	49	55	5.9	—	0.25	0.11	1.3	—
155	Cashew nuts, roasted, 1 cup	140	5	785	24	64	11	45	4	41	53	5.3	140	0.60	0.35	2.5	—
	Coconut, fresh, meat only:																
156	Pieces, approx. 2 by 2 by 1/2 in, 1 piece	45	51	155	2	16	14	1	Trace	4	6	0.8	0	0.02	0.01	0.2	1
157	Shredded or grated, firmly packed, 1 cup	130	51	450	5	46	39	3	Trace	12	17	2.2	0	0.07	0.03	0.7	4
158	Cowpeas or blackeye peas, dry, cooked, 1 cup	248	80	190	13	1	—	—	—	34	42	3.2	20	0.41	0.11	1.1	Trace
159	Peanuts, roasted, salted, halves, 1 cup	144	2	840	37	72	16	31	21	27	107	3.0	—	0.46	0.19	24.7	0
160	Peanut butter, 1 tbsp	16	2	95	4	8	2	4	2	3	9	0.3	—	0.02	0.02	2.4	0
161	Peas, split, dry, cooked, 1 cup	250	70	290	20	1	—	—	—	52	28	4.2	100	0.37	0.22	2.2	—
162	Pecans, halves, 1 cup	108	3	740	10	77	5	48	15	16	79	2.6	140	0.93	0.14	1.0	2
163	Walnuts, black or native, chopped, 1 cup	126	3	790	26	75	4	26	36	19	Trace	7.6	380	0.28	0.14	0.9	—

[c]Outer layer of fat on the cut was removed to within approximately 1/2 in of the lean; deposits of fat within the cut were not removed.
[d]If bones are discarded, value will be greatly reduced.

NUTRITIVE VALUES OF THE EDIBLE PARTS OF FOODS

Dashes in the columns for nutrients show that no suitable value could be found although there is reason to believe that a measurable amount of the nutrient may be present.

	Food, Approximate Measure and Weight, g		Water, %	Food Energy, kcal	Protein, g	Fat, g	Fatty acids: Saturated, Total, g	Fatty acids: Unsaturated, g: Oleic	Fatty acids: Unsaturated, g: Linoleic	Carbohydrate, g	Calcium, mg	Iron, mg	Vitamin A Value, IU	Thiamine, mg	Riboflavin, mg	Niacin, mg	Ascorbic Acid, mg
	Vegetables and Vegetable Products																
	Asparagus, green:																
	Cooked, drained:																
164	Spears, 1/2-in diam. at base, 4 spears	60	94	10	1	Trace	—	—	—	2	13	0.4	540	0.10	0.11	0.8	16
165	Pieces, 1 1/2 to 2-in lengths, 1 cup	145	94	30	3	Trace	—	—	—	5	30	0.9	1,310	0.23	0.26	2.0	38
166	Canned, solids and liquid, 1 cup	244	94	45	5	1	—	—	—	7	44	4.1	1,240	0.15	0.22	2.0	37
	Beans:																
167	Lima, immature seeds, cooked, drained, 1 cup	170	71	190	13	1	—	—	—	34	80	4.3	480	0.31	0.17	2.2	29
	Snap:																
	Green:																
168	Cooked, drained, 1 cup	125	92	30	2	Trace	—	—	—	7	63	0.8	680	0.09	0.11	0.6	15
169	Canned, solids and liquid, 1 cup	239	94	45	2	Trace	—	—	—	10	81	2.9	690	0.07	0.10	0.7	10
	Yellow or wax:																
170	Cooked, drained, 1 cup	125	93	30	2	Trace	—	—	—	6	63	0.8	290	0.09	0.11	0.6	16
171	Canned, solids and liquid, 1 cup	239	94	45	2	1	—	—	—	10	81	2.9	140	0.07	0.10	0.7	12
172	Sprouted mung beans, cooked, drained, 1 cup	125	91	35	4	Trace	—	—	—	7	21	1.1	30	0.11	0.13	0.9	8
	Beets:																
	Cooked, drained, peeled:																
173	Whole beets, 2-in diam., 2 beets	100	91	30	1	Trace	—	—	—	7	14	0.5	20	0.03	0.04	0.3	6
174	Diced or sliced, 1 cup	170	91	55	2	Trace	—	—	—	12	24	0.9	30	0.05	0.07	0.5	10
175	Canned, solids and liquid, 1 cup	246	90	85	2	Trace	—	—	—	19	34	1.5	20	0.02	0.05	0.2	7
176	Beet greens, leaves and stems, cooked, drained, 1 cup	145	94	25	3	Trace	—	—	—	5	144	2.8	7,400	0.10	0.22	0.4	22
	Blackeye peas. See Cowpeas.																
	Broccoli, cooked, drained:																
177	Whole stalks, medium size, 1 stalk	180	91	45	6	1	—	—	—	8	158	1.4	4,500	0.16	0.36	1.4	162
178	Stalks cut into 1/2-in pieces, 1 cup	155	91	40	5	1	—	—	—	7	136	1.2	3,880	0.14	0.31	1.2	140
179	Chopped, yield from 10-oz frozen pkg., 1 3/8 cups	250	92	65	7	1	—	—	—	12	135	1.8	6,500	0.15	0.30	1.3	143
180	Brussels sprouts, 7–8 sprouts (1 1/4 to 1 1/2 in diam.) per cup, cooked, 1 cup	155	88	55	7	1	—	—	—	10	50	1.7	810	0.12	0.22	1.2	135
	Cabbage:																
	Common varieties:																

	Raw:																
181	Coarsely shredded or sliced, 1 cup	70	92	15	1	Trace	—	—	—	4	34	0.3	90	0.04	0.04	0.2	33
182	Finely shredded or chopped, 1 cup	90	92	20	1	Trace	—	—	—	5	44	0.4	120	0.05	0.05	0.3	42
183	Cooked, 1 cup	145	94	30	2	Trace	—	—	—	6	64	0.4	190	0.06	0.06	0.4	48
184	Red, raw, coarsely shredded, 1 cup	70	90	20	1	Trace	—	—	—	5	29	0.6	30	0.06	0.04	0.3	43
185	Savoy, raw, coarsely shredded, 1 cup	70	92	15	2	Trace	—	—	—	3	47	0.6	140	0.04	0.06	0.2	39
186	Cabbage, celery or Chinese, raw, cut in 1-in pieces, 1 cup	75	95	10	1	Trace	—	—	—	2	32	0.5	110	0.04	0.03	0.5	19
187	Cabbage, spoon (or pakchoy), cooked, 1 cup	170	95	25	2	Trace	—	—	—	4	252	1.0	5,270	0.07	0.14	1.2	26
	Carrots:																
	Raw:																
188	Whole, 5 1/2 by 1 in (25 thin strips), 1 carrot	50	88	20	1	Trace	—	—	—	5	18	0.4	5,500	0.03	0.03	0.3	4
189	Grated, 1 cup	110	88	45	1	Trace	—	—	—	11	41	0.8	12,100	0.06	0.06	0.7	9
190	Cooked, diced, 1 cup	145	91	45	1	Trace	—	—	—	10	48	0.9	15,220	0.08	0.07	0.7	9
191	Canned, strained or chopped (baby food), 1 oz	28	92	10	Trace	Trace	—	—	—	2	7	0.1	3,690	0.01	0.01	0.1	1
192	Cauliflower, cooked, flowerbuds, 1 cup	120	93	25	3	Trace	—	—	—	5	25	0.8	70	0.11	0.10	0.7	66
	Celery, raw:																
193	Stalk, large outer, 8 by about 1 1/2 in at root end, 1 stalk	40	94	5	Trace	Trace	—	—	—	2	16	0.1	100	0.01	0.01	0.1	4
194	Pieces, diced, 1 cup	100	94	15	1	Trace	—	—	—	4	39	0.3	240	0.03	0.03	0.3	9
195	Collards, cooked, 1 cup	190	91	55	5	1	—	—	—	9	289	1.1	10,260	0.27	0.37	2.4	87
	Corn, sweet:																
196	Cooked, ear, 5 by 1 3/4 in,[e] 1 ear	140	74	70	3	1	—	—	—	16	2	0.5	310[f]	0.09	0.08	1.0	7
197	Canned, solids and liquid, 1 cup	256	81	170	5	2	—	—	—	40	10	1.0	690[f]	0.07	0.12	2.3	13
198	Cowpeas, cooked, immature seeds, 1 cup	160	72	175	13	1	—	—	—	29	38	3.4	560	0.49	0.18	2.3	28
	Cucumbers, 10-oz, 7 1/2 by about 2 in:																
199	Raw, pared, 1 cucumber	207	96	30	1	Trace	—	—	—	7	35	0.6	Trace	0.07	0.09	0.4	23
200	Raw, pared, center slice 1/8-in thick, 6 slices	50	96	5	Trace	Trace	—	—	—	2	8	0.2	Trace	0.02	0.02	0.1	6
201	Dandelion greens, cooked, 1 cup	180	90	60	4	1	—	—	—	12	252	3.2	21,060	0.24	0.29	—	32
202	Endive, curly (including escarole), 2 oz	57	93	10	1	Trace	—	—	—	2	46	1.0	1,870	0.04	0.08	0.3	6
203	Kale, leaves including stems, cooked, 1 cup	110	91	30	4	1	—	—	—	4	147	1.3	8,140	—	—	—	68
	Lettuce, raw:																
204	Butterhead, as Boston types; head, 4-in diam., 1 head	220	95	30	3	Trace	—	—	—	6	77	4.4	2,130	0.14	0.13	0.6	18
205	Crisphead, as Iceberg; head, 4 3/4-in diam., 1 head	454	96	60	4	Trace	—	—	—	13	91	2.3	1,500	0.29	0.27	1.3	29
206	Looseleaf, or bunching varieties, leaves, 2 large	50	94	10	1	Trace	—	—	—	2	34	0.7	950	0.03	0.04	0.2	9

[e]Measure and weight apply to entire vegetable or fruit including parts not usually eaten.

[f]Based on yellow varieties; white varieties contain only a trace of cryptoxanthin and carotenes, the pigments in corn that have biological activity.

NUTRITIVE VALUES OF THE EDIBLE PARTS OF FOODS

Note: Dashes in the columns for nutrients show that no suitable value could be found although there is reason to believe that a measurable amount of the nutrient may be present.

	Food, Approximate Measure and Weight, g		Water, %	Food Energy, kcal	Protein, g	Fat, g	Fatty Acids: Saturated, Total, g	Fatty Acids: Unsaturated, g: Oleic	Fatty Acids: Unsaturated, g: Linoleic	Carbohydrate, g	Calcium, mg	Iron, mg	Vitamin A Value, IU	Thiamine, mg	Riboflavin, mg	Niacin, mg	Ascorbic Acid, mg
207	Mushrooms, canned, solids and liquid, 1 cup	244	93	40	5	Trace	—	—	—	6	15	1.2	Trace	0.04	0.60	4.8	4
208	Mustard greens, cooked, 1 cup	140	93	35	3	1	—	—	—	6	193	2.5	8,120	0.11	0.19	0.9	68
209	Okra, cooked, pod 3 by 5/8 in, 8 pods	85	91	25	2	Trace	—	—	—	5	78	0.4	420	0.11	0.15	0.8	17
	Onions:																
	Mature:																
210	Raw, onion 2 1/2-in diam., 1 onion	110	89	40	2	Trace	—	—	—	10	30	0.6	40	0.04	0.04	0.2	11
211	Cooked, 1 cup	210	92	60	3	Trace	—	—	—	14	50	0.8	80	0.06	0.06	0.4	14
212	Young green, small, without tops, 6 onions	50	88	20	1	Trace	—	—	—	5	20	0.3	Trace	0.02	0.02	0.2	12
213	Parsley, raw, chopped, 1 tbsp	4	85	Trace	Trace	Trace	—	—	—	Trace	8	0.2	340	Trace	0.01	Trace	7
214	Parsnips, cooked, 1 cup	155	82	100	2	1	—	—	—	23	70	0.9	50	0.11	0.12	0.2	16
	Peas, green:																
215	Cooked, 1 cup	160	82	115	9	1	—	—	—	19	37	2.9	860	0.44	0.17	3.7	33
216	Canned, solids and liquid, 1 cup	249	83	165	9	1	—	—	—	31	50	4.2	1,120	0.23	0.13	2.2	22
217	Canned, strained (baby food), 1 oz	28	86	15	1	Trace	—	—	—	3	3	0.4	140	0.02	0.02	0.4	3
218	Peppers, hot, red, without seeds, dried (ground chili powder, added seasonings), 1 tbsp	15	8	50	2	2	—	—	—	8	40	2.3	9,750	0.03	0.17	1.3	2
	Peppers, sweet:																
	Raw, about 5 per pound:																
219	Green pod without stem and seeds, 1 pod	74	93	15	1	Trace	—	—	—	4	7	0.5	310	0.06	0.06	0.4	94
220	Cooked, boiled, drained, 1 pod	73	95	15	1	Trace	—	—	—	3	7	0.4	310	0.05	0.05	0.4	70
	Potatoes, medium (about 3 per lb raw):																
221	Baked, peeled after baking, 1 potato	99	75	90	3	Trace	—	—	—	21	9	0.7	Trace	0.10	0.04	1.7	20
	Boiled:																
222	Peeled after boiling, 1 potato	136	80	105	3	Trace	—	—	—	23	10	0.8	Trace	0.13	0.05	2.0	22
223	Peeled before boiling, 1 potato	122	83	80	2	Trace	—	—	—	18	7	0.6	Trace	0.11	0.04	1.4	20
	French-fried, piece 2 by 1/2 by 1/2 in:																
224	Cooked in deep fat, 10 pieces	57	45	155	2	7	2	2	4	20	9	0.7	Trace	0.07	0.04	1.8	12
225	Frozen, heated, 10 pieces	57	53	125	2	5	1	1	2	19	5	1.0	Trace	0.08	0.01	1.5	12
	Mashed:																
226	Milk added, 1 cup	195	83	125	4	1	—	—	—	25	47	0.8	50	0.16	0.10	2.0	19
227	Milk and butter added, 1 cup	195	80	185	4	8	4	3	Trace	24	47	0.8	330	0.16	0.10	1.9	18

228	Potato chips, medium, 2-in diam., 10 chips	20	2	115	1	8	2	2	4	10	8	0.4	Trace	0.04	0.01	1.0	3
229	Pumpkin, canned, 1 cup	228	90	75	2	1	—	—	—	18	57	0.9	14,590	0.07	0.12	1.3	12
230	Radishes, raw, small, without tops, 4 radishes	40	94	5	Trace	Trace	—	—	—	1	12	0.4	Trace	0.01	0.01	0.1	10
231	Sauerkraut, canned, solids and liquid, 1 cup	235	93	45	2	Trace	—	—	—	9	85	1.2	120	0.07	0.09	0.4	33
	Spinach:																
232	Cooked, 1 cup	180	92	40	5	1	—	—	—	6	167	4.0	14,580	0.13	0.25	1.0	50
233	Canned, drained solids, 1 cup	180	91	45	5	1	—	—	—	6	212	4.7	14,400	0.03	0.21	0.6	24
	Squash:																
	Cooked:																
234	Summer, diced, 1 cup	210	96	30	2	Trace	—	—	—	7	52	0.8	820	0.10	0.16	1.6	21
235	Winter, baked, mashed, 1 cup	205	81	130	4	1	—	—	—	32	57	1.6	8,610	0.10	0.27	1.4	27
	Sweetpotatoes:																
	Cooked, medium, 5 by 2 in, weight raw about 6 oz:																
236	Baked, peeled after baking, 1 sweetpotato	110	64	155	2	1	—	—	—	36	44	1.0	8,910	0.10	0.07	0.7	24
237	Boiled, peeled after boiling, 1 sweetpotato	147	71	170	2	1	—	—	—	39	47	1.0	11,610	0.13	0.09	0.9	25
238	Candied, 3 1/2 by 2 1/4 in, 1 sweetpotato	175	60	295	2	6	2	3	1	60	65	1.6	11,030	0.10	0.08	0.8	17
239	Canned, vacuum or solid pack, 1 cup	218	72	235	4	Trace	—	—	—	54	54	1.7	17,000	0.10	0.10	1.4	30
	Tomatoes:																
240	Raw, approx. 3-in diam., 2 1/8 in high, wt. 7 oz, 1 tomato	200	94	40	2	Trace	—	—	—	9	24	0.9	1,640	0.11	0.07	1.3	42[g]
241	Canned, solids and liquid, 1 cup	241	94	50	2	1	—	—	—	10	14	1.2	2,170	0.12	0.07	1.7	41
	Tomato catsup:																
242	Cup, 1 cup	273	69	290	6	1	—	—	—	69	60	2.2	3,820	0.25	0.19	4.4	41
243	Tablespoon, 1 tbsp	15	69	15	Trace	Trace	—	—	—	4	3	0.1	210	0.01	0.01	0.2	2
	Tomato juice, canned:																
244	Cup, 1 cup	243	94	45	2	Trace	—	—	—	10	17	2.2	1,940	0.12	0.07	1.9	39
245	Glass (6 fl. oz), 1 glass	182	94	35	2	Trace	—	—	—	8	13	1.6	1,460	0.09	0.05	1.5	29
246	Turnips, cooked, diced, 1 cup	155	94	35	1	Trace	—	—	—	8	54	0.6	Trace	0.06	0.08	0.5	34
247	Turnip greens, cooked, 1 cup	145	94	30	3	Trace	—	—	—	5	252	1.5	8,270	0.15	0.33	0.7	68
	Fruits and Fruit Products																
248	Apples, raw (about 3 per lb),[e] 1 apple	150	85	70	Trace	Trace	—	—	—	18	8	0.4	50	0.04	0.02	0.1	3
249	Apple juice, bottled or canned, 1 cup	248	88	120	Trace	Trace	—	—	—	30	15	1.5	—	0.02	0.05	0.2	2
	Applesauce, canned:																
250	Sweetened, 1 cup	255	76	230	1	Trace	—	—	—	61	10	1.3	100	0.05	0.03	0.1	3[h]
251	Unsweetened or artificially sweetened, 1 cup	244	88	100	1	Trace	—	—	—	26	10	1.2	100	0.05	0.02	0.1	2[h]

[e]Measure and weight apply to entire vegetable or fruit including parts not usually eaten.

[g]Year-round average. Samples marketed from November through May, average 20 milligrams per 200-gram tomato; from June through October, around 52 milligrams.

[h]This is the amount from the fruit. Additional ascorbic acid may be added by the manufacturer. Refer to the label for this information.

NUTRITIVE VALUES OF THE EDIBLE PARTS OF FOODS

Note: Dashes in the columns for nutrients show that no suitable value could be found although there is reason to believe that a measurable amount of the nutrient may be present.

	Food, Approximate Measure and Weight, g		Water, %	Food Energy, kcal	Protein, g	Fat, g	Fatty Acids: Saturated, Total, g	Fatty Acids: Unsaturated, g: Oleic	Fatty Acids: Unsaturated, g: Linoleic	Carbohydrate, g	Calcium, mg	Iron, mg	Vitamin A Value, IU	Thiamine, mg	Riboflavin, mg	Niacin, mg	Ascorbic Acid, mg
	Apricots:																
252	Raw (about 12 per lb)[e] 3 apricots	114	85	55	1	Trace	—	—	—	14	18	0.5	2,890	0.03	0.04	0.7	10
253	Canned in heavy sirup, 1 cup	259	77	220	2	Trace	—	—	—	57	28	0.8	4,510	0.05	0.06	0.9	10
254	Dried, uncooked (40 halves per cup), 1 cup	150	25	390	8	1	—	—	—	100	100	8.2	16,350	0.02	0.23	4.9	19
255	Cooked, unsweetened, fruit and liquid, 1 cup	285	76	240	5	1	—	—	—	62	63	5.1	8,550	0.01	0.13	2.8	8
256	Apricot nectar, canned, 1 cup	251	85	140	1	Trace	—	—	—	37	23	0.5	2,380	0.03	0.03	0.5	8[h]
	Avocados, whole fruit, raw:[e]																
257	California (mid- and late-winter; diam. 3 1/8 in), 1 avocado	284	74	370	5	37	7	17	5	13	22	1.3	630	0.24	0.43	3.5	30
258	Florida (late summer, fall; diam. 3 5/8 in), 1 avocado	454	78	390	4	33	7	15	4	27	30	1.8	880	0.33	0.61	4.9	43
259	Bananas, raw, medium size,[e] 1 banana	175	76	100	1	Trace	—	—	—	26	10	0.8	230	0.06	0.07	0.8	12
260	Banana flakes, 1 cup	100	3	340	4	1	—	—	—	89	32	2.8	760	0.18	0.24	2.8	7
261	Blackberries, raw, 1 cup	144	84	85	2	1	—	—	—	19	46	1.3	290	0.05	0.06	0.5	30
262	Blueberries, raw, 1 cup	140	83	85	1	1	—	—	—	21	21	1.4	140	0.04	0.08	0.6	20
263	Cantaloupes, raw; medium, 5-in diam., about 1 2/3 lb, 1/2 melon	385	91	60	1	Trace	—	—	—	14	27	0.8	6,540[i]	0.08	0.06	1.2	63
264	Cherries, canned, red, sour, pitted, water pack, 1 cup	244	88	105	2	Trace	—	—	—	26	37	0.7	1,660	0.07	0.05	0.5	12
265	Cranberry juice cocktail, canned, 1 cup	250	83	165	Trace	Trace	—	—	—	42	13	0.8	Trace	0.03	0.03	0.1	40[j]
266	Cranberry sauce, sweetened, canned, strained, 1 cup	277	62	405	Trace	1	—	—	—	104	17	0.6	60	0.03	0.03	0.1	6
267	Dates, pitted, cut, 1 cup	178	22	490	4	1	—	—	—	130	105	5.3	90	0.16	0.17	3.9	0
268	Figs, dried, large, 2 by 1 in, 1 fig	21	23	60	1	Trace	—	—	—	15	26	0.6	20	0.02	0.02	0.1	0
269	Fruit cocktail, canned, in heavy sirup, 1 cup	256	80	195	1	Trace	—	—	—	50	23	1.0	360	0.05	0.03	1.3	5
	Grapefruit:																
	Raw, medium, 3 3/4 in diam.:[e]																
270	White, 1/2 grapefruit	241	89	45	1	Trace	—	—	—	12	19	0.5	10	0.05	0.02	0.2	44
271	Pink or red, 1/2 grapefruit	241	89	50	1	Trace	—	—	—	13	20	0.5	540	0.05	0.02	0.2	44
272	Canned, sirup pack, 1 cup	254	81	180	2	Trace	—	—	—	45	33	0.8	30	0.08	0.05	0.5	76
	Grapefruit juice:																
273	Fresh, 1 cup	246	90	95	1	Trace	—	—	—	23	22	0.5	[k]	0.09	0.04	0.4	92

No.	Food																
	Canned, white:																
274	Unsweetened, 1 cup	247	89	100	1	Trace	—	—	—	24	20	1.0	20	0.07	0.04	0.4	84
275	Sweetened, 1 cup	250	86	130	1	Trace	—	—	—	32	20	1.0	20	0.07	0.04	0.4	78
	Frozen, concentrate, unsweetened:																
276	Undiluted, can, 6 fl. oz, 1 can	207	62	300	4	1	—	—	—	72	70	0.8	60	0.29	0.12	1.4	286
277	Diluted with 3 parts water, by volume, 1 cup	247	89	100	1	Trace	—	—	—	24	25	0.2	20	0.10	0.04	0.5	96
278	Dehydrated crystals, 4 oz	113	1	410	6	1	—	—	—	102	100	1.2	80	0.40	0.20	2.0	396
279	Prepared with water (1 lb yields about 1 gal), 1 cup	247	90	100	1	Trace	—	—	—	24	22	0.2	20	0.10	0.05	0.5	91
	Grapes, raw:[e]																
280	American type (slip skin), 1 cup	153	82	65	1	1	—	—	—	15	15	0.4	100	0.05	0.03	0.2	3
281	European type (adherent skin), 1 cup	160	81	95	1	Trace	—	—	—	25	17	0.6	140	0.07	0.04	0.4	6
	Grapejuice:																
282	Canned or bottled, 1 cup	253	83	165	1	Trace	—	—	—	42	28	0.8	—	0.10	0.05	0.5	Trace
	Frozen concentrate, sweetened:																
283	Undiluted, can, 6 fl. oz, 1 can	216	53	395	1	Trace	—	—	—	100	22	0.9	40	0.13	0.22	1.5	[l]
284	Diluted with 3 parts water,		86														
	by volume, 1 cup	250	86	135	1	Trace	—	—	—	33	8	0.3	10	0.05	0.08	0.5	[l]
285	Grapejuice drink, canned, 1 cup	250	86	135	Trace	Trace	—	—	—	35	8	0.3	—	0.03	0.03	0.3	[l]
286	Lemons, raw, 2 1/8-in diam., size 165, used for juice[e]	110	90	20	1	Trace	—	—	—	6	19	0.4	10	0.03	0.01	0.1	39
287	Lemon juice, raw, 1 cup	244	91	60	1	Trace	—	—	—	20	17	0.5	50	0.07	0.02	0.2	112
	Lemonade concentrate:																
288	Frozen, 6 fl. oz per can, 1 can	219	48	430	Trace	Trace	—	—	—	112	9	0.4	40	0.04	0.07	0.7	66
289	Diluted with 4 1/3 parts water, by volume, 1 cup	248	88	110	Trace	Trace	—	—	—	28	2	Trace	Trace	Trace	0.02	0.2	17
	Lime juice:																
290	Fresh, 1 cup	246	90	65	1	Trace	—	—	—	22	22	0.5	20	0.05	0.02	0.2	79
291	Canned, unsweetened, 1 cup	246	90	65	1	Trace	—	—	—	22	22	0.5	20	0.05	0.02	0.2	52
	Limeade concentrate, frozen:																
292	Undiluted, can, 6 fl. oz, 1 can	218	50	410	Trace	Trace	—	—	—	108	11	0.2	Trace	0.02	0.02	0.2	26
293	Diluted with 4 1/3 parts water, by volume, 1 cup	247	90	100	Trace	Trace	—	—	—	27	2	Trace	Trace	Trace	Trace	Trace	5
294	Oranges, raw, 2 5/8-in diam., all commercial varieties,[e] 1 orange	180	86	65	1	Trace	—	—	—	16	54	0.5	260	0.13	0.05	0.5	66
295	Orange juice, fresh, all varieties, 1 cup	248	88	110	2	1	—	—	—	26	27	0.5	500	0.22	0.07	1.0	124
296	Canned, unsweetened, 1 cup	249	87	120	2	Trace	—	—	—	28	25	1.0	500	0.17	0.05	0.7	100
	Frozen concentrate:																
297	Undiluted, can, 6 fl. oz, 1 can	213	55	360	5	Trace	—	—	—	87	75	0.9	1,620	0.68	0.11	2.8	360
298	Diluted with 3 parts water, by volume, 1 cup	249	87	120	2	Trace	—	—	—	29	25	0.2	550	0.22	0.02	1.0	120
299	Dehydrated crystals, 4 oz	113	1	430	6	2	—	—	—	100	95	1.9	1,900	0.76	0.24	3.3	408

[e]Measure and weight apply to entire vegetable or fruit including parts not usually eaten.
[i]Value for varieties with orange-colored flesh; value for varieties with green-colored flesh would be about 540 IU.
[j]Value listed is based on product with label stating 30 milligrams per 6 fluid ounce serving.
[k]For white-fleshed varieties, value is about 20 IU/cup; for red-fleshed varieties, 1,080 IU/cup.
[l]Present only if added by the manufacturer; refer to the label for this information.

NUTRITIVE VALUES OF THE EDIBLE PARTS OF FOODS

Note: Dashes in the columns for nutrients show that no suitable value could be found although there is reason to believe that a measurable amount of the nutrient may be present.

	Food, Approximate Measure and Weight, g		Water, %	Food Energy, kcal	Protein, g	Fat, g	Fatty Acids: Saturated, Total, g	Fatty Acids: Unsaturated, g: Oleic	Fatty Acids: Unsaturated, g: Linoleic	Carbohydrate, g	Calcium, mg	Iron, mg	Vitamin A Value, IU	Thiamine, mg	Riboflavin, mg	Niacin, mg	Ascorbic Acid, mg
300	Prepared with water (1 lb yields about 1 gal), 1 cup	248	88	115	2	1	—	—	—	27	25	0.5	500	0.20	0.07	1.0	109
301	Orange-apricot juice drink, 1 cup	249	87	125	1	Trace	—	—	—	32	12	0.2	1,440	0.05	0.02	0.5	40[j]
	Orange and grapefruit juice:																
	Frozen concentrate:																
302	Undiluted, can, 6 fl oz, 1 can	210	59	330	4	1	—	—	—	78	61	0.8	800	0.48	0.06	2.3	302
303	Diluted with 3 parts water, by volume, 1 cup	248	88	110	1	Trace	—	—	—	26	20	0.2	270	0.16	0.02	0.8	102
304	Papayas, raw, 1/2-in cubes, 1 cup	182	89	70	1	Trace	—	—	—	18	36	0.5	3,190	0.07	0.08	0.5	102
	Peaches:																
	Raw:																
305	Whole, medium, 2-in diam., about 4 per lb,[e] 1 peach	114	89	35	1	Trace	—	—	—	10	9	0.5	1,320[m]	0.02	0.05	1.0	7
306	Sliced, 1 cup	168	89	65	1	Trace	—	—	—	16	15	0.8	2,230[m]	0.03	0.08	1.6	12
	Canned, yellow-fleshed, solids and liquid:																
	Sirup pack, heavy:																
307	Halves or slices, 1 cup	257	79	200	1	Trace	—	—	—	52	10	0.8	1,100	0.02	0.06	1.4	7
308	Water pack, 1 cup	245	91	75	1	Trace	—	—	—	20	10	0.7	1,100	0.02	0.06	1.4	7
309	Dried, uncooked, 1 cup	160	25	420	5	1	—	—	—	109	77	9.6	6,240	0.02	0.31	8.5	28
310	Cooked, unsweetened, 10–12 halves and juice, 1 cup	270	77	220	3	1	—	—	—	58	41	5.1	3,290	0.01	0.15	4.2	6
	Frozen:																
311	Carton, 12 oz, not thawed, 1 carton	340	76	300	1	Trace	—	—	—	77	14	1.7	2,210	0.03	0.14	2.4	135[n]
	Pears:																
312	Raw, 3 by 2 1/2-in diam.,[e] 1 pear	182	83	100	1	1	—	—	—	25	13	0.5	30	0.04	0.07	0.2	7
	Canned, solids and liquid:																
	Sirup pack, heavy:																
313	Halves or slices, 1 cup	255	80	195	1	1	—	—	—	50	13	0.5	Trace	0.03	0.05	0.3	4
	Pineapple:																
314	Raw, diced, 1 cup	140	85	75	1	Trace	—	—	—	19	24	0.7	100	0.12	0.04	0.3	24
	Canned, heavy sirup pack, solids and liquid:																
315	Crushed, 1 cup	260	80	195	1	Trace	—	—	—	50	29	0.8	120	0.20	0.06	0.5	17
316	Sliced, slices and juice, 2 small or 1 large, 1 large	122	80	90	Trace	Trace	—	—	—	24	13	0.4	50	0.09	0.03	0.2	8

317	Pineapple juice, canned, 1 cup	249	86	135	1	Trace	—	—	—	34	37	0.7	120	0.12	0.04	0.5	22[h]
	Plums, all except prunes:																
318	Raw, 2-in diam., about 2 oz,[e] 1 plum	60	87	25	Trace	Trace	—	—	—	7	7	0.3	140	0.02	0.02	0.3	3
	Canned, sirup pack (Italian prunes):																
319	Plums (with pits) and juice,[e] 1 cup	256	77	205	1	Trace	—	—	—	53	22	2.2	2,970	0.05	0.05	0.9	4
	Prunes, dried, "softenized," medium:																
320	Uncooked,[e] 4 prunes	32	28	70	1	Trace	—	—	—	18	14	1.1	440	0.02	0.04	0.4	1
321	Cooked, unsweetened, 17–18 prunes and 1/3 cup liquid,[e] 1 cup	270	66	295	2	1	—	—	—	78	60	4.5	1,860	0.08	0.18	1.7	2
322	Prune juice, canned or bottled, 1 cup	256	80	200	1	Trace	—	—	—	49	36	10.5	—	0.03	0.03	1.0	5[h]
	Raisins, seedless:																
323	Packaged, 1/2 oz or 1 1/2 tbsp per pkg., 1 pkg.	14	18	40	Trace	Trace	—	—	—	11	9	0.5	Trace	0.02	0.01	0.1	Trace
324	Cup, pressed down, 1 cup	165	18	480	4	Trace	—	—	—	128	102	5.8	30	0.18	0.13	0.8	2
	Raspberries, red:																
325	Raw, 1 cup	123	84	70	1	1	—	—	—	17	27	1.1	160	0.04	0.11	1.1	31
326	Frozen, 10-oz carton, not thawed, 1 carton	284	74	275	2	1	—	—	—	70	37	1.7	200	0.06	0.17	1.7	59
327	Rhubarb, cooked, sugar added, 1 cup	272	63	385	1	Trace	—	—	—	98	212	1.6	220	0.06	0.15	0.7	17
	Strawberries:																
328	Raw, capped, 1 cup	149	90	55	1	1	—	—	—	13	31	1.5	90	0.04	0.10	1.0	88
329	Frozen, 10-oz carton, not thawed, 1 carton	284	71	310	1	1	—	—	—	79	40	2.0	90	0.06	0.17	1.5	150
330	Tangerines, raw, medium, 2 3/8-in diam., size 176,[e] 1 tangerine	116	87	40	1	Trace	—	—	—	10	34	0.3	360	0.05	0.02	0.1	27
331	Tangerine juice, canned, sweetened, 1 cup	249	87	125	1	1	—	—	—	30	45	0.5	1,050	0.15	0.05	0.2	55
332	Watermelon, raw, wedge, 4 by 8 in (1/16 of 10- by 16-in melon, about 2 lb with rind),[e] 1 wedge	925	93	115	2	1	—	—	—	27	30	2.1	2,510	0.13	0.13	0.7	30
	Grain Products																
	Bagel, 3-in diam.:																
333	Egg, 1 bagel	55	32	165	6	2	—	—	—	28	9	1.2	30	0.14	0.10	1.2	0
334	Water, 1 bagel	55	29	165	6	2	—	—	—	30	8	1.2	0	0.15	0.11	1.4	0
335	Barley, pearled, light, uncooked, 1 cup	200	11	700	16	2	Trace	1	1	158	32	4.0	0	0.24	0.10	6.2	0
336	Biscuits, baking powder from home recipe with enriched flour, 2-in diam., 1 biscuit	28	27	105	2	5	1	2	1	13	34	0.4	Trace	0.06	0.06	0.1	Trace
337	Biscuits, baking powder from mix, 2-in diam., 1 biscuit	28	28	90	2	3	1	1	1	15	19	0.6	Trace	0.08	0.07	0.6	Trace
338	Bran flakes (40% bran), added thiamine and iron, 1 cup	35	3	105	4	1	—	—	—	28	25	12.3	0	0.14	0.06	2.2	0
339	Bran flakes with raisins, added thiamine and iron, 1 cup	50	7	145	4	1	—	—	—	40	28	13.5	Trace	0.16	0.07	2.7	0

[e]Measure and weight apply to entire vegetable or fruit including parts not usually eaten.
[h]This is the amount from the fruit. Additional ascorbic acid may be added by the manufacturer. Refer to the label for this information.
[j]Value listed is based on product with label stating 30 milligrams per 6 fluid ounce serving.
[m]Based on yellow-fleshed varieties; for white-fleshed varieties value is about 50 IU per 114-g peach and 80 IU per cup of sliced peaches.
[n]This value includes ascorbic acid added by manufacturer.

NUTRITIVE VALUES OF THE EDIBLE PARTS OF FOODS

Note: Dashes in the columns for nutrients show that no suitable value could be found although there is reason to believe that a measurable amount of the nutrient may be present.

	Food, Approximate Measure and Weight, g		Water, %	Food Energy, kcal	Protein, g	Fat, g	Fatty Acids: Saturated, Total, g	Unsaturated, g: Oleic	Unsaturated, g: Linoleic	Carbohydrate, g	Calcium, mg	Iron, mg	Vitamin A Value, IU	Thiamine, mg	Riboflavin, mg	Niacin, mg	Ascorbic Acid, mg
	Breads:																
340	Boston brown bread, slice 3 by 3/4 in, 1 slice	48	45	100	3	1	—	—	—	22	43	0.9	0	0.05	0.03	0.6	0
	Cracked-wheat bread:																
341	Loaf, 1 lb, 1 loaf	454	35	1,190	40	10	2	5	2	236	399	5.0	Trace	0.53	0.41	5.9	Trace
342	Slice, 18 slices per loaf, 1 slice	25	35	65	2	1	—	—	—	13	22	0.3	Trace	0.03	0.02	0.3	Trace
	French or vienna bread:																
343	Enriched, 1-lb loaf, 1 loaf	454	31	1,315	41	14	3	8	2	251	195	10.0	Trace	1.27	1.00	11.3	Trace
344	Unenriched, 1-lb loaf, 1 loaf	454	31	1,315	41	14	3	8	2	251	195	3.2	Trace	0.36	0.36	3.6	Trace
	Italian bread:																
345	Enriched, 1-lb loaf, 1 loaf	454	32	1,250	41	4	Trace	1	2	256	77	10.0	0	1.32	0.91	11.8	0
346	Unenriched, 1-lb loaf, 1 loaf	454	32	1,250	41	4	Trace	1	2	256	77	3.2	0	0.41	0.27	3.6	0
	Raisin bread:																
347	Loaf, 1 lb, 1 loaf	454	35	1,190	30	13	3	8	2	243	322	5.9	Trace	0.23	0.41	3.2	Trace
348	Slice, 18 slices per loaf, 1 slice	25	35	65	2	1	—	—	—	13	18	0.3	Trace	0.01	0.02	0.2	Trace
	Rye bread:																
	American, light (1/3 rye, 2/3 wheat):																
349	Loaf, 1 lb, 1 loaf	454	36	1,100	41	5	—	—	—	236	340	7.3	0	0.82	0.32	6.4	0
350	Slice, 18 slices per loaf, 1 slice	25	36	60	2	Trace	—	—	—	13	19	0.4	0	0.05	0.02	0.4	0
351	Pumpernickel, loaf, 1 lb, 1 loaf	454	34	1,115	41	5	—	—	—	241	381	10.9	0	1.04	0.64	5.4	0
	White bread, enriched:[o]																
	Soft-crumb type:																
352	Loaf, 1 lb, 1 loaf	454	36	1,225	39	15	3	8	2	229	381	11.3	Trace	1.13	0.95	10.9	Trace
353	Slice, 18 slices per loaf, 1 slice	25	36	70	2	1	—	—	—	13	21	0.6	Trace	0.06	0.05	0.6	Trace
354	Slice, toasted, 1 slice	22	25	70	2	1	—	—	—	13	21	0.6	Trace	0.06	0.05	0.6	Trace
355	Slice, 22 slices per loaf, 1 slice	20	36	55	2	1	—	—	—	10	17	0.5	Trace	0.05	0.04	0.5	Trace
356	Slice, toasted, 1 slice	17	25	55	2	1	—	—	—	10	17	0.5	Trace	0.05	0.04	0.5	Trace
357	Loaf, 1 1/2 lb, 1 loaf	680	36	1,835	59	22	5	12	3	343	571	17.0	Trace	1.70	1.43	16.3	Trace
358	Slice, 24 slices per loaf, 1 slice	28	36	75	2	1	—	—	—	14	24	0.7	Trace	0.07	0.06	0.7	Trace
359	Slice, toasted, 1 slice	24	25	75	2	1	—	—	—	14	24	0.7	Trace	0.07	0.06	0.7	Trace
360	Slice, 28 slices per loaf, 1 slice	24	36	65	2	1	—	—	—	12	20	0.6	Trace	0.06	0.05	0.6	Trace
361	Slice, toasted, 1 slice	21	25	65	2	1	—	—	—	12	20	0.6	Trace	0.06	0.05	0.6	Trace
	Firm-crumb type:																
362	Loaf, 1 lb, 1 loaf	454	35	1,245	41	17	4	10	2	228	435	11.3	Trace	1.22	0.91	10.9	Trace
363	Slice, 20 slices per loaf, 1 slice	23	35	65	2	1	—	—	—	12	22	0.6	Trace	0.06	0.05	0.6	Trace

364	Slice, toasted, 1 slice	20	24	65	2	1'	—	—	—	12	22	0.6	Trace	0.06	0.05	0.6	Trace
365	Loaf, 2 lb, 1 loaf	907	35	2,495	82	34	8	20	4	455	871	22.7	Trace	2.45	1.81	21.8	Trace
366	Slice, 34 slices per loaf, 1 slice	27	35	75	2	1	—	—	—	14	26	0.7	Trace	0.07	0.05	0.6	Trace
367	Slice, toasted, 1 slice	23	35	75	2	1	—	—	—	14	26	0.7	Trace	0.07	0.05	0.6	Trace
	Whole-wheat bread, soft-crumb type:																
368	Loaf, 1 lb, 1 loaf	454	36	1,095	41	12	2	6	2	224	381	13.6	Trace	1.36	0.45	12.7	Trace
369	Slice, 16 slices per loaf, 1 slice	28	36	65	3	1	—	—	—	14	24	0.8	Trace	0.09	0.03	0.8	Trace
370	Slice, toasted, 1 slice	24	24	65	3	1	—	—	—	14	24	0.8	Trace	0.09	0.03	0.8	Trace
	Whole-wheat bread, firm-crumb type:																
371	Loaf, 1 lb, 1 loaf	454	36	1,100	48	14	3	6	3	216	449	13.6	Trace	1.18	0.54	12.7	Trace
372	Slice, 18 slices per loaf, 1 slice	25	36	60	3	1	—	—	—	12	25	0.8	Trace	0.06	0.03	0.7	Trace
373	Slice, toasted, 1 slice	21	24	60	3	1	—	—	—	12	25	0.8	Trace	0.06	0.03	0.7	Trace
374	Breadcrumbs, dry, grated, 1 cup	100	6	390	13	5	1	2	1	73	122	3.6	Trace	0.22	0.30	3.5	Trace
375	Buckwheat flour, light, sifted, 1 cup	98	12	340	6	1	—	—	—	78	11	1.0	0	0.08	0.04	0.4	0
376	Bulgur, canned, seasoned, 1 cup	135	56	245	8	4	—	—	—	44	27	1.9	0	0.08	0.05	4.1	0
	Cakes made from cake mixes:																
	Angelfood:																
377	Whole cake, 1 cake	635	34	1,645	36	1	—	—	—	377	603	1.9	0	0.03	0.70	0.6	0
378	Piece, 1/12 of 10-in diam. cake, 1 piece	53	34	135	3	Trace	—	—	—	32	50	0.2	0	Trace	0.06	0.1	0
	Cupcakes, small, 2 1/2-in diam.:																
379	Without icing, 1 cupcake	25	26	90	1	3	1	1	1	14	40	0.1	40	0.01	0.03	0.1	Trace
380	With chocolate icing, 1 cupcake	36	22	130	2	5	2	2	1	21	47	0.3	60	0.01	0.04	0.1	Trace
	Devil's food, 2-layer, with chocolate icing:																
381	Whole cake, 1 cake	1,107	24	3,755	49	136	54	58	16	645	653	8.9	1,660	0.33	0.89	3.3	1
382	Piece, 1/16 of 9-in diam. cake, 1 piece	69	24	235	3	9	3	4	1	40	41	0.6	100	0.02	0.06	0.2	Trace
383	Cupcake, small, 2 1/2-in diam., 1 cupcake	35	24	120	2	4	1	2	Trace	20	21	0.3	50	0.01	0.03	0.1	Trace
	Gingerbread:																
384	Whole cake, 1 cake	570	37	1,575	18	39	10	19	9	291	513	9.1	Trace	0.17	0.51	4.6	2
385	Piece, 1/9 of 8-in square cake, 1 piece	63	37	175	2	4	1	2	1	32	57	1.0	Trace	0.02	0.06	0.5	Trace
	White, 2-layer, with chocolate icing:																
386	Whole cake, 1 cake	1,140	21	4,000	45	122	45	54	17	716	1,129	5.7	680	0.23	0.91	2.3	2
387	Piece, 1/16 of 9-in diam. cake, 1 piece	71	21	250	3	8	3	3	1	45	70	0.4	40	0.01	0.06	0.1	Trace
	Cakes made from home recipes:[p]																
388	Boston cream pie; piece 1/12 of 8-in diam., 1 piece	69	35	210	4	6	2	3	1	34	46	0.3	140	0.02	0.08	0.1	Trace
	Fruitcake, dark, made with enriched flour:																
389	Loaf, 1 lb, 1 loaf	454	18	1,720	22	69	15	37	13	271	327	11.8	540	0.59	0.64	3.6	2
390	Slice, 1/30 of 8-in loaf, 1 slice	15	18	55	1	2	Trace	1	Trace	9	11	0.4	20	0.02	0.02	0.1	Trace
	Plain sheet cake:																
	Without icing:																
391	Whole cake, 1 cake	777	25	2,830	35	108	30	52	21	434	497	3.1	1,320	0.16	0.70	1.6	2
392	Piece, 1/9 of 9-in square cake, 1 piece	86	25	315	4	12	3	6	2	48	55	0.3	150	0.02	0.08	0.2	Trace

[o] **Values for thiamine, riboflavin, and niacin per pound of unenriched white bread would be as follows:**

	IRON, mg	THIAMINE, mg	RIBOFLAVIN, mg	NIACIN, mg
Soft crumb	3.2	0.31	0.39	5.0
Firm crumb	3.2	0.32	0.59	4.1

[p] **Unenriched cake flour used unless otherwise specified.**

NUTRITIVE VALUES OF THE EDIBLE PARTS OF FOODS

Note: Dashes in the columns for nutrients show that no suitable value could be found although there is reason to believe that a measurable amount of the nutrient may be present.

	Food, Approximate Measure and Weight, g		Water, %	Food Energy, kcal	Protein, g	Fat, g	Fatty Acids: Saturated, Total, g	Fatty Acids: Unsaturated, g: Oleic	Fatty Acids: Unsaturated, g: Linoleic	Carbohydrate, g	Calcium, mg	Iron, mg	Vitamin A Value, IU	Thiamine, mg	Riboflavin, mg	Niacin, mg	Ascorbic Acid, mg
393	With boiled white icing, piece, 1/9 of 9-in square cake, 1 piece	114	23	400	4	12	3	6	2	71	56	0.3	150	0.02	0.08	0.2	Trace
	Pound:																
394	Loaf, 8 1/2 by 3 1/2 by 3 in, 1 loaf	514	17	2,430	29	152	34	68	17	242	108	4.1	1,440	0.15	0.46	1.0	0
395	Slice, 1/2-in thick, 1 slice	30	17	140	2	9	2	4	1	14	6	0.2	80	0.01	0.03	0.1	0
	Sponge:																
396	Whole cake, 1 cake	790	32	2,345	60	45	14	20	4	427	237	9.5	3,560	0.40	1.11	1.6	Trace
397	Piece, 1/12 of 10-in diam. cake, 1 piece	66	32	195	5	4	1	2	Trace	36	20	0.8	300	0.03	0.09	0.1	Trace
	Yellow, 2-layer, without icing:																
398	Whole cake, 1 cake	870	24	3,160	39	111	31	53	22	506	618	3.5	1,310	0.17	0.70	1.7	2
399	Piece, 1/16 of 9-in diam. cake, 1 piece	54	24	200	2	7	2	3	1	32	39	0.2	80	0.01	0.04	0.1	Trace
	Yellow, 2-layer, with chocolate icing:																
400	Whole cake, 1 cake	1,203	21	4,390	51	156	55	69	23	727	818	7.2	1,920	0.24	0.96	2.4	Trace
401	Piece, 1/16 of 9-in diam. cake, 1 piece	75	21	275	3	10	3	4	1	45	51	0.5	120	0.02	0.06	0.2	Trace
	Cake icings. See Sugars, Sweets.																
	Cookies:																
	Brownies with nuts:																
402	Made from home recipe with enriched flour, 1 brownie	20	10	95	1	6	1	3	1	10	8	0.4	40	0.04	0.02	0.1	Trace
403	Made from mix, 1 brownie	20	11	85	1	4	1	2	1	13	9	0.4	20	0.03	0.02	0.1	Trace
	Chocolate chip:																
404	Made from home recipe with enriched flour, 1 cookie	10	3	50	1	3	1	1	1	6	4	0.2	10	0.01	0.01	0.1	Trace
405	Commercial, 1 cookie	10	3	50	1	2	1	1	Trace	7	4	0.2	10	Trace	Trace	Trace	Trace
406	Fig bars, commercial, 1 cookie	14	14	50	1	1	—	—	—	11	11	0.2	20	Trace	0.01	0.1	Trace
407	Sandwich, chocolate or vanilla, commercial, 1 cookie	10	2	50	1	2	1	1	Trace	7	2	0.1	0	Trace	Trace	0.1	0
	Corn flakes, added nutrients:																
408	Plain, 1 cup	25	4	100	2	Trace	—	—	—	21	4	0.4	0	0.11	0.02	0.5	0
409	Sugar-covered, 1 cup	40	2	155	2	Trace	—	—	—	36	5	0.4	0	0.16	0.02	0.8	0
	Corn (hominy) grits, degermed, cooked:																
410	Enriched, 1 cup	245	87	125	3	Trace	—	—	—	27	2	0.7	150[q]	0.10	0.07	1.0	0
411	Unenriched, 1 cup	245	87	125	3	Trace	—	—	—	27	2	0.2	150[q]	0.05	0.02	0.5	0

	Cornmeal:																
412	Whole-ground, unbolted, dry, 1 cup	122	12	435	11	5	1	2	2	90	24	2.9	620[q]	0.46	0.13	2.4	0
413	Bolted (nearly whole-grain) dry, 1 cup	122	12	440	11	4	Trace	1	2	91	21	2.2	590[q]	0.37	0.10	2.3	0
	Degermed, enriched:																
414	Dry form, 1 cup	138	12	500	11	2	—	—	—	108	8	4.0	610[q]	0.61	0.36	4.8	0
415	Cooked, 1 cup	240	88	120	3	1	—	—	—	26	2	1.0	140[q]	0.14	0.10	1.2	0
	Degermed, unenriched:																
416	Dry form, 1 cup	138	12	500	11	2	—	—	—	108	8	1.5	610[q]	0.19	0.07	1.4	0
417	Cooked, 1 cup	240	88	120	3	1	—	—	—	26	2	0.5	140[q]	0.05	0.02	0.2	0
418	Corn muffins, made with enriched degermed cornmeal and enriched flour; muffin 2 3/8-in diam., 1 muffin	40	33	125	3	4	2	2	Trace	19	42	0.7	120[q]	0.08	0.09	0.6	Trace
419	Corn muffins, made with mix, egg, and milk; muffin 2 3/8-in diam., 1 muffin	40	30	130	3	4	1	2	1	20	96	0.6	100	0.07	0.08	0.6	Trace
420	Corn, puffed, presweetened, added nutrients, 1 cup	30	2	115	1	Trace	—	—	—	27	3	0.5	0	0.13	0.05	0.6	0
421	Corn, shredded, added nutrients, 1 cup	25	3	100	2	Trace	—	—	—	22	1	0.6	0	0.11	0.05	0.5	0
	Crackers:																
422	Graham, 2 1/2-in square, 4 crackers	28	6	110	2	3	—	—	—	21	11	0.4	0	0.01	0.06	0.4	0
423	Saltines, 4 crackers	11	4	50	1	1	—	1	—	8	2	0.1	0	Trace	Trace	0.1	0
	Danish pastry, plain (without fruit or nuts):																
424	Packaged ring, 12 oz, 1 ring	340	22	1,435	25	80	24	37	15	155	170	3.1	1,050	0.24	0.51	2.7	Trace
425	Round piece, approx. 4 1/4-in diam. by 1 in, 1 pastry	65	22	275	5	15	5	7	3	30	33	0.6	200	0.05	0.10	0.5	Trace
426	Ounce, 1 oz	28	22	120	2	7	2	3	1	13	14	0.3	90	0.02	0.04	0.2	Trace
427	Doughnuts, cake type, 1 doughnut	32	24	125	1	6	1	4	Trace	16	13	0.4[r]	30	0.05[r]	0.05[r]	0.4[r]	Trace
428	Farina, quick-cooking, enriched, cooked, 1 cup	245	89	105	3	Trace	—	—	—	22	147	0.7[s]	0	0.12[s]	0.07[s]	1.0[s]	0
	Macaroni, cooked:																
	Enriched:																
429	Cooked, firm stage (undergoes additional cooking in a food mixture), 1 cup	130	64	190	6	1	—	—	—	39	14	1.4[s]	0	0.23[s]	0.14[s]	1.8[s]	0
430	Cooked until tender, 1 cup	140	72	155	5	1	—	—	—	32	8	1.3[s]	0	0.20[s]	0.11[s]	1.5[s]	0
	Unenriched:																
431	Cooked, firm stage (undergoes additional cooking in a food mixture), 1 cup	130	64	190	6	1	—	—	—	39	14	0.7	0	0.03	0.03	0.5	0
432	Cooked until tender, 1 cup	140	72	155	5	1	—	—	—	32	11	0.6	0	0.01	0.01	0.4	0
433	Macaroni (enriched) and cheese, baked, 1 cup	200	58	430	17	22	10	9	2	40	362	1.8	860	0.20	0.40	1.8	Trace
434	Canned, 1 cup	240	80	230	9	10	4	3	1	26	199	1.0	260	0.12	0.24	1.0	Trace

[q]This value is based on product made from yellow varieties of corn; white varieties contain only a trace.

[r]Based on product made with enriched flour. With unenriched flour, approximate values per doughnut are: iron, 0.2 mg; thiamine, 0.01 mg; riboflavin, 0.03 mg; niacin, 0.2 mg.

[s]Iron, thiamine, riboflavin, and niacin are based on the minimum levels of enrichment specified in standards of identity promulgated under the federal Food, Drug, and Cosmetic Act.

NUTRITIVE VALUES OF THE EDIBLE PARTS OF FOODS

Note: Dashes in the columns for nutrients show that no suitable value could be found although there is reason to believe that a measurable amount of the nutrient may be present.

	Food, Approximate Measure and Weight, g		Water, %	Food Energy, kcal	Protein, g	Fat, g	Fatty Acids: Saturated, Total, g	Fatty Acids: Unsaturated, g: Oleic	Fatty Acids: Unsaturated, g: Linoleic	Carbohydrate, g	Calcium, mg	Iron, mg	Vitamin A Value, IU	Thiamine, mg	Riboflavin, mg	Niacin, mg	Ascorbic Acid, mg
435	Muffins, with enriched white flour; muffin, 3-in diam., 1 muffin	40	38	120	3	4	1	2	1	17	42	0.6	40	0.07	0.09	0.6	Trace
	Noodles (egg noodles), cooked:																
436	Enriched, 1 cup	160	70	200	7	2	1	1	Trace	37	16	1.4[s]	110	0.22[s]	0.13[s]	1.9[s]	0
437	Unenriched, 1 cup	160	70	200	7	2	1	1	Trace	37	16	1.0	110	0.05	0.03	0.6	0
438	Oats (with or without corn) puffed, added nutrients, 1 cup	25	3	100	3	1	—	—	—	19	44	1.2	0	0.24	0.04	0.5	0
439	Oatmeal or rolled oats, cooked, 1 cup	240	87	130	5	2	—	—	1	23	22	1.4	0	0.19	0.05	0.2	0
	Pancakes, 4-in diam.:																
440	Wheat, enriched flour (home recipe), 1 cake	27	50	60	2	2	Trace	1	Trace	9	27	0.4	30	0.05	0.06	0.4	Trace
441	Buckwheat (made from mix with egg and milk), 1 cake	27	58	55	2	2	1	1	Trace	6	59	0.4	60	0.03	0.04	0.2	Trace
442	Plain or buttermilk (made from mix with egg and milk), 1 cake	27	51	60	2	2	1	1	Trace	9	58	0.3	70	0.04	0.06	0.2	Trace
	Pie (piecrust made with unenriched flour): Sector, 4-in, 1/7 of 9-in diam. pie:																
443	Apple (2-crust), 1 sector	135	48	350	3	15	4	7	3	51	11	0.4	40	0.03	0.03	0.5	1
444	Butterscotch (1-crust), 1 sector	130	45	350	6	14	5	6	2	50	98	1.2	340	0.04	0.13	0.3	Trace
445	Cherry (2-crust), 1 sector	135	47	350	4	15	4	7	3	52	19	0.4	590	0.03	0.03	0.7	Trace
446	Custard (1-crust), 1 sector	130	58	285	8	14	5	6	2	30	125	0.8	300	0.07	0.21	0.4	0
447	Lemon meringue (1-crust), 1 sector	120	47	305	4	12	4	6	2	45	17	0.6	200	0.04	0.10	0.2	4
448	Mince (2-crust), 1 sector	135	43	365	3	16	4	8	3	56	38	1.4	Trace	0.09	0.05	0.5	1
449	Pecan (1-crust), 1 sector	118	20	490	6	27	4	16	5	60	55	3.3	190	0.19	0.08	0.4	Trace
450	Pineapple chiffon (1-crust), 1 sector	93	41	265	6	11	3	5	2	36	22	0.8	320	0.04	0.08	0.4	1
451	Pumpkin (1-crust), 1 sector	130	59	275	5	15	5	6	2	32	66	0.7	3,210	0.04	0.13	0.7	Trace
	Piecrust, baked shell for pie made with:																
452	Enriched flour, 1 shell	180	15	900	11	60	16	28	12	79	25	3.1	0	0.36	0.25	3.2	0
453	Unenriched flour, 1 shell	180	15	900	11	60	16	28	12	79	25	0.9	0	0.05	0.05	0.9	0
	Piecrust mix including stick form:																
454	Package, 10-oz, for double crust, 1 pkg.	284	9	1,480	20	93	23	46	21	141	131	1.4	0	0.11	0.11	2.0	0
455	Pizza (cheese) 5 1/2-in sector; 1/8 of 14-in diam. pie, 1 sector	75	45	185	7	6	2	3	Trace	27	107	0.7	290	0.04	0.12	0.7	4
	Popcorn, popped:																
456	Plain, large kernel, 1 cup	6	4	25	1	Trace	—	—	—	5	1	0.2	—	—	0.01	0.1	0

457	With oil and salt, 1 cup	9	3	40	1	2	1	Trace	Trace	5	1	0.2	—	—	0.01	0.2	0
458	Sugar coated, 1 cup	35	4	135	2	1	—	—	—	30	2	0.5	—	—	0.02	0.4	0
	Pretzels:																
459	Dutch, twisted, 1 pretzel	16	5	60	2	1	—	—	—	12	4	0.2	0	Trace	Trace	0.1	0
460	Thin, twisted, 1 pretzel	6	5	25	1	Trace	—	—	—	5	1	0.1	0	Trace	Trace	Trace	0
461	Stick, small, 2 1/4 in, 10 sticks	3	5	10	Trace	Trace	—	—	—	2	1	Trace	0	Trace	Trace	Trace	0
462	Stick, regular, 3 1/8 in, 5 sticks	3	5	10	Trace	Trace	—	—	—	2	1	Trace	0	Trace	Trace	Trace	0
	Rice, white:																
	Enriched:																
463	Raw, 1 cup	185	12	670	12	1	—	—	—	149	44	5.4[t]	0	0.81[t]	0.06[t]	6.5[t]	0
464	Cooked, 1 cup	205	73	225	4	Trace	—	—	—	50	21	1.8[t]	0	0.23[t]	0.02[t]	2.1[t]	0
465	Instant, ready-to-serve, 1 cup	165	73	180	4	Trace	—	—	—	40	5	1.3[t]	0	0.21[t]	[t]	1.7[t]	0
466	Unenriched, cooked, 1 cup	205	73	225	4	Trace	—	—	—	50	21	0.4	0	0.04	0.02	0.8	0
467	Parboiled, cooked, 1 cup	175	73	185	4	Trace	—	—	—	41	33	1.4[t]	0	0.19[t]	[t]	2.1[t]	0
468	Rice, puffed, added nutrients, 1 cup	15	4	60	1	Trace	—	—	—	13	3	0.3	0	0.07	0.01	0.7	0
	Rolls, enriched:																
	Cloverleaf or pan:																
469	Home recipe, 1 roll	35	26	120	3	3	1	1	1	20	16	0.7	30	0.09	0.09	0.8	Trace
470	Commercial, 1 roll	28	31	85	2	2	Trace	1	Trace	15	21	0.5	Trace	0.08	0.05	0.6	Trace
471	Frankfurter or hamburger, 1 roll	40	31	120	3	2	1	1	1	21	30	0.8	Trace	0.11	0.07	0.9	Trace
472	Hard, round or rectangular, 1 roll	50	25	155	5	2	Trace	1	Trace	30	24	1.2	Trace	0.13	0.12	1.4	Trace
473	Rye wafers, whole-grain, 1 7/8 by 3 1/2 in, 2 wafers	13	6	45	2	Trace	—	—	—	10	7	0.5	0	0.04	0.03	0.2	0
474	Spaghetti, cooked, tender stage, enriched, 1 cup	140	72	155	5	1	—	—	—	32	11	1.3[s]	0	0.20[s]	0.11[s]	1.5[s]	0
	Spaghetti with meat balls, and tomato sauce:																
475	Home recipe, 1 cup	248	70	330	19	12	4	6	1	39	124	3.7	1,590	0.25	0.30	4.0	22
476	Canned, 1 cup	250	78	260	12	10	2	3	4	28	53	3.3	1,000	0.15	0.18	2.3	5
	Spaghetti in tomato sauce with cheese:																
477	Home recipe, 1 cup	250	77	260	9	9	2	5	1	37	80	2.3	1,080	0.25	0.18	2.3	13
478	Canned, 1 cup	250	80	190	6	2	1	1	1	38	40	2.8	930	0.35	0.28	4.5	10
479	Waffles, with enriched flour, 7-in diam., 1 waffle	75	41	210	7	7	2	4	1	28	85	1.3	250	0.13	0.19	1.0	Trace
480	Waffles, made from mix, enriched, egg and milk added, 7-in diam., 1 waffle	75	42	205	7	8	3	3	1	27	179	1.0	170	0.11	0.17	0.7	Trace
481	Wheat, puffed, added nutrients, 1 cup	15	3	55	2	Trace	—	—	—	12	4	0.6	0	0.08	0.03	1.2	0
482	Wheat, shredded, plain, 1 biscuit	25	7	90	2	1	—	—	—	20	11	0.9	0	0.06	0.03	1.1	0
483	Wheat flakes, added nutrients, 1 cup	30	4	105	3	Trace	—	—	—	24	12	1.3	0	0.19	0.04	1.5	0
	Wheat flours:																
484	Whole-wheat, from hard wheats, stirred, 1 cup	120	12	400	16	2	Trace	1	1	85	49	4.0	0	0.66	0.14	5.2	0

[s]Iron, thiamine, riboflavin, and niacin are based on the minimum levels of enrichment specified in standards of identity promulgated under the federal Food, Drug, and Cosmetic Act.

[t]Iron, thiamine, and niacin are based on the minimum levels of enrichment specified in standards of identity promulgated under the federal Food, Drug, and Cosmetic Act. Riboflavin is based on unenriched rice. When the minimum level of enrichment for riboflavin specified in the standards of identity becomes effective, the value will be 0.12 mg/cup of parboiled rice and of white rice.

NUTRITIVE VALUES OF THE EDIBLE PARTS OF FOODS

Note: Dashes in the columns for nutrients show that no suitable value could be found although there is reason to believe that a measurable amount of the nutrient may be present.

	Food, Approximate Measure and Weight, g		Water, %	Food Energy, kcal	Protein, g	Fat, g	Fatty Acids: Saturated, Total, g	Fatty Acids: Unsaturated, g: Oleic	Fatty Acids: Unsaturated, g: Linoleic	Carbohydrate, g	Calcium, mg	Iron, mg	Vitamin A Value, IU	Thiamine, mg	Riboflavin, mg	Niacin, mg	Ascorbic Acid, mg
	All-purpose or family flour, enriched:																
485	Sifted, 1 cup	115	12	420	12	1	—	—	—	88	18	3.3[S]	0	0.51[S]	0.30[S]	4.0[S]	0
486	Unsifted, 1 cup	125	12	455	13	1	—	—	—	95	20	3.6[S]	0	0.55[S]	0.33[S]	4.4[S]	0
487	Self-rising, enriched, 1 cup	125	12	440	12	1	—	—	—	93	331	3.6[S]	0	0.55[S]	0.33[S]	4.4[S]	0
488	Cake or pastry flour, sifted, 1 cup	96	12	350	7	1	—	—	—	76	16	0.5	0	0.03	0.03	0.7	0
	Fats, Oils																
	Butter:																
	Regular, 4 sticks per pound:																
489	Stick, 1/2 cup	113	16	810	1	92	51	30	3	1	23	0	3,750[U]	—	—	—	0
490	Tablespoon (approx. 1/8 stick), 1 tbsp	14	16	100	Trace	12	6	4	Trace	Trace	3	0	470[U]	—	—	—	0
491	Pat (1-in³, 1/3-in high; 90 per lb), 1 pat	5	16	35	Trace	4	2	1	Trace	Trace	1	0	170[U]	—	—	—	0
	Whipped, 6 sticks or 2, 8-oz containers per pound:																
492	Stick, 1/2 cup	76	16	540	1	61	34	20	2	Trace	15	0	2,500[U]	—	—	—	0
493	Tablespoon (approx. 1/8 stick), 1 tbsp	9	16	65	Trace	8	4	3	Trace	Trace	2	0	310[U]	—	—	—	0
494	Pat (1 1/4-in³, 1/3-in high; 120 per lb), 1 pat	4	16	25	Trace	3	2	1	Trace	Trace	1	0	130[U]	—	—	—	0
	Fats, cooking:																
495	Lard, 1 cup	205	0	1,850	0	205	78	94	20	0	0	0	0	0	0	0	0
496	1 tbsp	13	0	115	0	13	5	6	1	0	0	0	0	0	0	0	0
497	Vegetable fats, 1 cup	200	0	1,770	0	200	50	100	44	0	0	0	—	0	0	0	0
498	1 tbsp	13	0	110	0	13	3	6	3	0	0	0	—	0	0	0	0
	Margarine:																
	Regular, 4 sticks per pound:																
499	Stick, 1/2 cup	113	16	815	1	92	17	46	25	1	23	0	3,750[V]	—	—	—	0
500	Tablespoon (approx. 1/8 stick), 1 tbsp	14	16	100	Trace	12	2	6	3	Trace	3	0	470[V]	—	—	—	0
501	Pat (1-in³, 1/3-in high; 90 per lb), 1 pat	5	16	35	Trace	4	1	2	1	Trace	1	0	170[V]	—	—	—	0
	Whipped, 6 sticks per pound:																
502	Stick, 1/2 cup	76	16	545	1	61	11	31	17	Trace	15	0	2,500[V]	—	—	—	0
	Soft, 2, 8-oz tubs per pound:																
503	Tub, 1 tub	227	16	1,635	1	184	34	68	68	1	45	0	7,500[V]	—	—	—	0
504	Tablespoon, 1 tbsp	14	16	100	Trace	11	2	4	4	Trace	3	0	470[V]	—	—	—	0

	Oils, salad or cooking:																
505	Corn, 1 cup	220	0	1,945	0	220	22	62	117	0	0	0	—	0	0	0	0
506	1 tbsp	14	0	125	0	14	1	4	7	0	0	0	—	0	0	0	0
507	Cottonseed, 1 cup	220	0	1,945	0	220	55	46	110	0	0	0	—	0	0	0	0
508	1 tbsp	14	0	125	0	14	4	3	7	0	0	0	—	0	0	0	0
509	Olive, 1 cup	220	0	1,945	0	220	24	167	15	0	0	0	—	0	0	0	0
510	1 tbsp	14	0	125	0	14	2	11	1	0	0	0	—	0	0	0	0
511	Peanut, 1 cup	220	0	1,945	0	220	40	103	64	0	0	0	—	0	0	0	0
512	1 tbsp	14	0	125	0	14	3	7	4	0	0	0	—	0	0	0	0
513	Safflower, 1 cup	220	0	1,945	0	220	18	37	165	0	0	0	—	0	0	0	0
514	1 tbsp	14	0	125	0	14	1	2	10	0	0	0	—	0	0	0	0
515	Soybean, 1 cup	220	0	1,945	0	220	33	44	114	0	0	0	—	0	0	0	0
516	1 tbsp	14	0	125	0	14	2	3	7	0	0	0	—	0	0	0	0
	Salad dressings:																
517	Blue cheese, 1 tbsp	15	32	75	1	8	2	2	4	1	12	Trace	30	Trace	0.02	Trace	Trace
	Commerical, mayonnaise type:																
518	Regular, 1 tbsp	15	41	65	Trace	6	1	1	3	2	2	Trace	30	Trace	Trace	Trace	—
519	Special dietary, low-calorie, 1 tbsp	16	81	20	Trace	2	Trace	Trace	1	1	3	Trace	40	Trace	Trace	Trace	—
	French:																
520	Regular, 1 tbsp	16	39	65	Trace	6	1	1	3	3	2	0.1	—	—	—	—	—
521	Special dietary, low-fat with artificial sweeteners, 1 tbsp	15	95	Trace	Trace	Trace	—	—	—	Trace	2	0.1	—	—	—	—	—
522	Home cooked, boiled, 1 tbsp	16	68	25	1	2	1	1	Trace	2	14	0.1	80	0.01	0.03	Trace	Trace
523	Mayonnaise, 1 tbsp	14	15	100	Trace	11	2	2	6	Trace	3	0.1	40	Trace	0.01	Trace	—
524	Thousand Island, 1 tbsp	16	32	80	Trace	8	1	2	4	3	2	0.1	50	Trace	Trace	Trace	Trace
	Sugars, Sweets																
	Cake icings:																
525	Chocolate made with milk and table fat, 1 cup	275	14	1,035	9	38	21	14	1	185	165	3.3	580	0.06	0.28	0.6	1
526	Coconut (with boiled icing), 1 cup	166	15	605	3	13	11	1	Trace	124	10	0.8	0	0.02	0.07	0.3	0
527	Creamy fudge from mix with water only, 1 cup	245	15	830	7	16	5	8	3	183	96	2.7	Trace	0.05	0.20	0.7	Trace
528	White, boiled, 1 cup	94	18	300	1	0	—	—	—	76	2	Trace	0	Trace	0.03	Trace	0
	Candy:																
529	Caramels, plain or chocolate, 1 oz	28	8	115	1	3	2	1	Trace	22	42	0.4	Trace	0.01	0.05	0.1	Trace
530	Chocolate, milk, plain, 1 oz	28	1	145	2	9	5	3	Trace	16	65	0.3	80	0.02	0.10	0.1	Trace
531	Chocolate-coated peanuts, 1 oz	28	1	160	5	12	3	6	2	11	33	0.4	Trace	0.10	0.05	2.1	Trace
532	Fondant; mints, uncoated; candy corn, 1 oz	28	8	105	Trace	1	—	—	—	25	4	0.3	0	Trace	Trace	Trace	0
533	Fudge, plain, 1 oz	28	8	115	1	4	2	1	Trace	21	22	0.3	Trace	0.01	0.03	0.1	Trace
534	Gumdrops, 1 oz	28	12	100	Trace	Trace	—	—	—	25	2	0.1	0	0	Trace	Trace	0

[s] Iron, thiamine, riboflavin, and niacin are based on the minimum levels of enrichment specified in standards of identity promulgated under the federal Food, Drug, and Cosmetic Act.
[u] Year-round average.
[v] Based on the average vitamin A content of fortified margarine. Federal specifications for fortified margarine require a minimum of 15,000 IU/lb of vitamin A.

NUTRITIVE VALUES OF THE EDIBLE PARTS OF FOODS

Note: Dashes in the columns for nutrients show that no suitable value could be found although there is reason to believe that a measurable amount of the nutrient may be present.

	Food, Approximate Measure and Weight, g		Water, %	Food Energy, kcal	Protein, g	Fat, g	Fatty Acids: Saturated, Total, g	Fatty Acids: Unsaturated, g: Oleic	Fatty Acids: Unsaturated, g: Linoleic	Carbohydrate, g	Calcium, mg	Iron, mg	Vitamin A Value, IU	Thiamine, mg	Riboflavin, mg	Niacin, mg	Ascorbic Acid, mg
535	Hard, 1 oz	28	1	110	0	Trace	—	—	—	28	6	0.5	0	0	0	0	0
536	Marshmallows, 1 oz	28	17	90	1	Trace	—	—	—	23	5	0.5	0	0	Trace	Trace	0
	Chocolate-flavored sirup or topping:																
537	Thin type, 1 fl. oz	38	32	90	1	1	Trace	Trace	Trace	24	6	0.6	Trace	0.01	0.03	0.2	0
538	Fudge type, 1 fl. oz	38	25	125	2	5	3	2	Trace	20	48	0.5	60	0.02	0.08	0.2	Trace
	Chocolate-flavored beverage powder (approx. 4 heaping teaspoons per oz.):																
539	With nonfat dry milk, 1 oz	28	2	100	5	1	Trace	Trace	Trace	20	167	0.5	10	0.04	C.21	0.2	1
540	Without nonfat dry milk, 1 oz	28	1	100	1	1	Trace	Trace	Trace	25	9	0.6	—	0.01	0.03	0.1	0
541	Honey, strained or extracted, 1 tbsp	21	17	65	Trace	0	—	—	—	17	1	0.1	0	Trace	0.01	0.1	Trace
542	Jams and preserves, 1 tbsp	20	29	55	Trace	Trace	—	—	—	14	4	0.2	Trace	Trace	0.01	Trace	Trace
543	Jellies, 1 tbsp	18	29	50	Trace	Trace	—	—	—	13	4	0.3	Trace	Trace	0.01	Trace	1
	Molasses, cane:																
544	Light (first extraction), 1 tbsp	20	24	50	—	—	—	—	—	13	33	0.9	—	0.01	0.01	Trace	—
545	Blackstrap (third extraction), 1 tbsp	20	24	45	—	—	—	—	—	11	137	3.2	—	0.02	0.04	0.4	—
	Sirups:																
546	Sorghum, 1 tbsp	21	23	55	—	—	—	—	—	14	35	2.6	—	—	0.02	Trace	—
547	Table blends, chiefly corn, light and dark, 1 tbsp	21	24	60	0	0	—	—	—	15	9	0.8	0	0	0	0	0
	Sugars:																
548	Brown, firm packed, 1 cup	220	2	820	0	0	—	—	—	212	187	7.5	0	0.02	0.07	0.4	0
	White:																
549	Granulated, 1 cup	200	Trace	770	0	0	—	—	—	199	0	0.2	0	0	0	0	0
550	1 tbsp	11	Trace	40	0	0	—	—	—	11	0	Trace	0	0	0	0	0
551	Powdered, stirred before measuring, 1 cup	120	Trace	460	0	0	—	—	—	119	0	0.1	0	0	0	0	0
	Miscellaneous Items																
552	Barbecue sauce, 1 cup	250	81	230	4	17	2	5	9	20	53	2.0	900	0.03	0.03	0.8	13
	Beverages, alcoholic:																
553	Beer, 12 fl oz	360	92	150	1	0	—	—	—	14	18	Trace	—	0.01	0.11	2.2	—
	Gin, rum, vodka, whiskey:																
554	80 Proof, 1 1/2 fl oz jigger	42	67	100	—	—	—	—	—	Trace	—	—	—	—	—	—	—
555	86 Proof, 1 1/2 fl oz jigger	42	64	105	—	—	—	—	—	Trace	—	—	—	—	—	—	—

556	90 Proof, 1 1/2 fl oz jigger	42	62	110	—	—	—	—	—	Trace	—	—	—	—	—	—	—
557	94 Proof, 1 1/2 fl oz jigger	42	60	115	—	—	—	—	—	Trace	—	—	—	—	—	—	—
558	100 Proof, 1 1/2 fl oz jigger	42	58	125	—	—	—	—	—	Trace	—	—	—	—	—	—	—
	Wines:																
559	Dessert, 3 1/2 fl oz glass	103	77	140	Trace	0	—	—	—	8	8	—	—	0.01	0.02	0.2	—
560	Table, 3 1/2 fl oz glass	102	86	85	Trace	0	—	—	—	4	9	0.4	—	Trace	0.01	0.1	—
	Beverages, carbonated, sweetened, non-alcoholic:																
561	Carbonated water, 12 fl oz	366	92	115	0	0	—	—	—	29	—	—	0	0	0	0	0
562	Cola type, 12 fl oz	369	90	145	0	0	—	—	—	37	—	—	0	0	0	0	0
563	Fruit-flavored sodas and Tom Collins mixes, 12 fl oz	372	88	170	0	0	—	—	—	45	—	—	0	0	0	0	0
564	Ginger ale, 12 fl oz	366	92	115	0	0	—	—	—	29	—	—	0	0	0	0	0
565	Root beer, 12 fl oz	370	90	150	0	0	—	—	—	39	—	—	0	0	0	0	0
566	Bouillon cubes, approx. 1/2 in, 1 cube	4	4	5	1	Trace	—	—	—	Trace	—	—	—	—	—	—	—
	Chocolate:																
567	Bitter or baking, 1 oz	28	2	145	3	15	8	6	Trace	8	22	1.9	20	0.01	0.07	0.4	0
568	Semisweet, small pieces, 1 cup	170	1	860	7	61	34	22	1	97	51	4.4	30	0.02	0.14	0.9	0
	Gelatin:																
569	Plain, dry powder in envelope, 1 envelope	7	13	25	6	Trace	—	—	—	0	—	—	—	—	—	—	—
570	Dessert powder, 3-oz package, 1 pkg.	85	2	315	8	0	—	—	—	75	—	—	—	—	—	—	—
571	Gelatin dessert, prepared with water, 1 cup	240	84	140	4	0	—	—	—	34	—	—	—	—	—	—	—
	Olives, pickled:																
572	Green, 4 medium or 3 extra large or 2 giant	16	78	15	Trace	2	Trace	2	Trace	Trace	8	0.2	40	—	—	—	—
573	Ripe, Mission, 3 small or 2 large	10	73	15	Trace	2	Trace	2	Trace	Trace	9	0.1	10	Trace	Trace	—	—
	Pickles, cucumber:																
574	Dill, medium, whole, 3 3/4 in long, 1 1/4 in diam., 1 pickle	65	93	10	1	Trace	—	—	—	1	17	0.7	70	Trace	0.01	Trace	4
575	Fresh, sliced, 1 1/2 in diam., 1/4 in thick, 2 slices	15	79	10	Trace	Trace	—	—	—	3	5	0.3	20	Trace	Trace	Trace	1
576	Sweet, gherkin, small, whole, approx. 2 1/2 in long, 3/4 in diam., 1 pickle	15	61	20	Trace	Trace	—	—	—	6	2	0.2	10	Trace	Trace	Trace	1
577	Relish, finely chopped, sweet, 1 tbsp	15	63	20	Trace	Trace	—	—	—	5	3	0.1	—	—	—	—	—
	Popcorn. See Grain Products.																
578	Popsicle, 3 fl oz size, 1 popsicle	95	80	70	0	0	0	0	0	18	0	Trace	0	0	0	0	0
	Pudding, home recipe with starch base:																
579	Chocolate, 1 cup	260	66	385	8	12	7	4	Trace	67	250	1.3	390	0.05	0.36	0.3	1
580	Vanilla (blanc mange), 1 cup	255	76	285	9	10	5	3	Trace	41	298	Trace	410	0.08	0.41	0.3	2
581	Pudding mix, dry form, 4-oz package, 1 pkg.	113	2	410	3	2	1	1	Trace	103	23	1.8	Trace	0.02	0.08	0.5	0
582	Sherbet, 1 cup	193	67	260	2	2	—	—	—	59	31	Trace	120	0.02	0.06	Trace	4

NUTRITIVE VALUES OF THE EDIBLE PARTS OF FOODS

Note: Dashes in the columns for nutrients show that no suitable value could be found although there is reason to believe that a measurable amount of the nutrient may be present.

	Food, Approximate Measure and Weight, g		Water, %	Food Energy, kcal	Protein, g	Fat, g	Fatty Acids: Saturated, Total, g	Fatty Acids: Unsaturated, g: Oleic	Fatty Acids: Unsaturated, g: Linoleic	Carbohydrate, g	Calcium, mg	Iron, mg	Vitamin A Value, IU	Thiamine, mg	Riboflavin, mg	Niacin, mg	Ascorbic Acid, mg
	Soups:																
	Canned, condensed, ready-to-serve:																
	Prepared with an equal volume of milk:																
583	Cream of chicken, 1 cup	245	85	180	7	10	3	3	3	15	172	0.5	610	0.05	0.27	0.7	2
584	Cream of mushroom, 1 cup	245	83	215	7	14	4	4	5	16	191	0.5	250	0.05	0.34	0.7	1
585	Tomato, 1 cup	250	84	175	7	7	3	2	1	23	168	0.8	1,200	0.10	0.25	1.3	15
	Prepared with an equal volume of water:																
586	Bean with pork, 1 cup	250	84	170	8	6	1	2	2	22	63	2.3	650	0.13	0.08	1.0	3
587	Beef broth, bouillon consomme, 1 cup	240	96	30	5	0	—	—	—	3	Trace	0.5	Trace	Trace	0.02	1.2	—
588	Beef noodle, 1 cup	240	93	70	4	3	1	1	1	7	7	1.0	50	0.05	0.07	1.0	Trace
589	Clam chowder, Manhattan type (with tomatoes, without milk), 1 cup	245	92	80	2	3	—	—	—	12	34	1.0	880	0.02	0.02	1.0	—
590	Cream of chicken, 1 cup	240	92	95	3	6	1	2	3	8	24	0.5	410	0.02	0.05	0.5	Trace
591	Cream of mushroom, 1 cup	240	90	135	2	10	1	3	5	10	41	0.5	70	0.02	0.12	0.7	Trace
592	Minestrone, 1 cup	245	90	105	5	3	—	—	—	14	37	1.0	2,350	0.07	0.05	1.0	—
593	Split pea, 1 cup	245	85	145	9	3	1	2	Trace	21	29	1.5	440	0.25	0.15	1.5	1
594	Tomato, 1 cup	245	90	90	2	3	Trace	1	1	16	15	0.7	1,000	0.05	0.05	1.2	12
595	Vegetable beef, 1 cup	245	92	80	5	2	—	—	—	10	12	0.7	2,700	0.05	0.05	1.0	—
596	Vegetarian, 1 cup	245	92	80	2	2	—	—	—	13	20	1.0	2,940	0.05	0.05	1.0	—
	Dehydrated, dry form:																
597	Chicken noodle (2-oz package), 1 pkg.	57	6	220	8	6	2	3	1	33	34	1.4	190	0.30	0.15	2.4	3
598	Onion mix (1 1/2-oz package), 1 pkg.	43	3	150	6	5	1	2	1	23	42	0.6	30	0.05	0.03	0.3	6
599	Tomato vegetable with noodles (2 1/2-oz pkg.), 1 pkg.	71	4	245	6	6	2	3	1	45	33	1.4	1,700	0.21	C.13	1.8	18
	Frozen, condensed:																
	Clam chowder, New England type (with milk, without tomatoes):																
600	Prepared with equal volume of milk, 1 cup	245	83	210	9	12	—	—	—	16	240	1.0	250	0.07	0.29	0.5	Trace
601	Prepared with equal volume of water, 1 cup	240	89	130	4	8	—	—	—	11	91	1.0	50	0.05	0.10	0.5	—
	Cream of potato:																
602	Prepared with equal volume of milk, 1 cup	245	83	185	8	10	5	3	Trace	18	208	1.0	590	0.10	0.27	0.5	Trace
603	Prepared with equal volume of water, 1 cup	240	90	105	3	5	3	2	Trace	12	58	1.0	410	0.05	0.05	0.5	—
	Cream of shrimp:																

No.	Food																
604	Prepared with equal volume of milk, 1 cup	245	82	245	9	16	—	—	—	15	189	0.5	290	0.07	0.27	0.5	Trace
605	Prepared with equal volume of water, 1 cup	240	88	160	5	12	—	—	—	8	38	0.5	120	0.05	0.05	0.5	—
	Oyster stew:																
606	Prepared with equal volume of milk, 1 cup	240	83	200	10	12	—	—	—	14	305	1.4	410	0.12	0.41	0.5	Trace
607	Prepared with equal volume of water, 1 cup	240	90	120	6	8	—	—	—	8	158	1.4	240	0.07	0.19	0.5	—
608	Tapioca, dry, quick-cooking, 1 cup	152	13	535	1	Trace	—	—	—	131	15	0.6	0	0	0	0	0
	Tapioca desserts:																
609	Apple, 1 cup	250	70	295	1	Trace	—	—	—	74	8	0.5	30	Trace	Trace	Trace	Trace
610	Cream pudding, 1 cup	165	72	220	8	8	4	3	Trace	28	173	0.7	480	0.07	0.30	0.2	2
611	Tartar sauce, 1 tbsp	14	34	75	Trace	8	1	1	4	1	3	0.1	30	Trace	Trace	Trace	Trace
612	Vinegar, 1 tbsp	15	94	Trace	Trace	0	—	—	—	1	1	0.1	—	—	—	—	—
613	White sauce, medium, 1 cup	250	73	405	10	31	16	10	1	22	288	0.5	1,150	0.10	0.43	0.5	2
	Yeast:																
614	Baker's, dry, active, 1 pkg.	7	5	20	3	Trace	—	—	—	3	3	1.1	Trace	0.16	0.38	2.6	Trace
615	Brewer's, dry, 1 tbsp	8	5	25	3	Trace	—	—	—	3	17	1.4	Trace	1.25	0.34	3.0	Trace
	Yogurt. See Milk, Cheese, Cream, Imitation Cream.																

[a]Value applies to unfortified product; value for fortified low-density product would be 1500 IU, and the fortified high-density product would be 2290 IU.
[b]Contributed largely from beta-carotene used for coloring.
[c]Outer layer of fat on the cut was removed to within approximately 1/2 in of the lean; deposits of fat within the cut were not removed.
[d]If bones are discarded, value will be greatly reduced.
[e]Measure and weight apply to entire vegetable or fruit including parts not usually eaten.
[f]Based on yellow varieties; white varieties contain only a trace of cryptoxanthin and carotenes, the pigments in corn that have biological activity.
[g]Year-round average. Samples marketed from November through May, average 20 milligrams per 200-gram tomato; from June through October, around 52 milligrams.
[h]This is the amount from the fruit. Additional ascorbic acid may be added by the manufacturer. Refer to the label for this information.
[i]Value for varieties with orange-colored flesh; value for varieties with green-colored flesh would be about 540 IU.
[j]Value listed is based on products with label stating 30 milligrams per 6 fluid ounce serving.
[k]For white-fleshed varieties, value is about 20 IU/cup; for red-fleshed varieties, 1,080 IU/cup.
[l]Present only if added by the manufacturer; refer to the label for this information.
[m]Based on yellow-fleshed varieties; for white-fleshed varieties value is about 50 IU per 114-g peach and 80 IU per cup of sliced peaches.
[n]This value includes ascorbic acid added by manufacturer.
[o]Values for iron, thiamine, riboflavin, and niacin per pound of unenriched white bread would be as follows:

	IRON, mg	THIAMINE, mg	RIBOFLAVIN, mg	NIACIN, mg
Soft crumb	3.2	0.31	0.39	5.0
Firm crumb	3.2	0.32	0.59	4.1

[p]Unenriched cake flour used unless otherwise specified.
[q]This value is based on product made from yellow varieties of corn; white varieties contain only a trace.
[r]Based on product made with enriched flour. With unenriched flour, approximate values per doughnut are: iron, 0.2 mg; thiamine, 0.01 mg; riboflavin, 0.03 mg; niacin, 0.2 mg.
[s]Iron, thiamine, riboflavin, and niacin are based on the minimum levels of enrichment specified in standards of identity promulgated under the federal Food, Drug, and Cosmetic Act.
[t]Iron, thiamine, and niacin are based on the minimum levels of enrichment specified in standards of identity promulgated under the federal Food, Drug, and Cosmetic Act. Riboflavin is based on unenriched rice. When the minimum level of enrichment for riboflavin specified in the standards of identity becomes effective, the value will be 0.12 mg/cup of parboiled rice and of white rice.
[u]Year-round average.
[v]Based on the average vitamin A content of fortified margarine. Federal specifications for fortified margarine require a minimum of 15,000 IU/lb of vitamin A.

Ready Reference 2

The American Dietetic Association Exchange Lists

Exchange lists provide a convenient means of planning diets, particularly if some component, such as carbohydrate, fat, or energy, must be restricted. Foods are grouped together according to their content of selected nutrients. For example, the ADA Food Exchange System, which was originally developed for diabetics, is based on the caloric, protein, carbohydrate, and fat contents of foods. There are six groups: milk, vegetables, fruits, bread, meat, and fat. Nearly every food normally consumed by Americans fits into one of these groups, except those containing large amounts of sugar, such as cookies, cakes, candies, soda, and alcoholic beverages, which are usually prohibited for diabetics. Because the caloric, protein, carbohydrate, and fat contents are roughly the same within each group, items can be substituted or exchanged for each other without significantly altering the composition of the diet with respect to these nutrients.

Suppose a dietitian wanted to plan a diet that provided 1500 kcal/day. He or she could specify the number of exchanges needed from each group to provide 1500 kcal/day and satisfy the requirements for other nutrients. The person could then choose the foods from each exchange group that satisfy his or her tastes. He or she could vary selections from day to day, and as long as the selections meet the required number of exchanges from each group, the person would obtain about 1500 kcal/day.

The exchange lists also can be used to estimate the caloric content of the diet. Take, for instance, the meal used as an example on page 135 in Chapter 5. According to the exchange list, 2 tablespoons of peanut butter equals one meat exchange plus 2½ fat exchanges, while the remainder of the meal represents 2 bread exchanges, 2 milk exchanges, and 1 fruit exchange. The caloric content of the meal can be calculated as follows:

1 meat exchange	X	55 kcal/exchange	=	55 kcal
2½ fat exchanges	X	45 kcal/exchange	=	113 kcal
2 bread exchanges	X	70 kcal/exchange	=	140 kcal
2 milk exchanges	X	80 kcal/exchange	=	160 kcal
1 fruit exchange	X	40 kcal/exchange	=	40 kcal
				508 kcal total

The exchange system shows that the person consumed about 508 kilocalories for the meal. A calculation done with Ready Reference 1 indicates consumption of about 570 kcal. Because of the difficulty in judging serving sizes (What exactly is one "small" apple?), the discrepancy between the exchange list and Ready Reference 1 values can be ignored.

LIST 1

Milk Exchanges (Includes Nonfat, Low-Fat, and Whole Milk). (One exchange of milk contains 12 grams of carbohydrate, 8 grams of protein, a trace of fat, and 80 calories.)

This list shows the kinds and amounts of milk products to use for one milk exchange. Those which appear in **bold type** are **nonfat.** Low-fat and whole milk contain saturated fat. The designation "omit _____ fat exchanges" indicates that those exchanges should be subtracted from the number of fat exchanges allowed under List 6.

Nonfat fortified milk	
Skim or nonfat milk	1 cup
Powdered (nonfat dry, before adding liquid)	1/3 cup
Canned, evaporated skim milk	1/2 cup
Buttermilk made from skim milk	1 cup
Yogurt made from skim milk (plain, unflavored)	1 cup
Low-fat fortified milk	
1% fat fortified milk (omit 1/2 fat exchange)	1 cup
2% fat fortified milk (omit 1 fat exchange)	1 cup
Yogurt made from 2% fortified milk (plain, unflavored) (omit 1 fat exchange)	1 cup
Whole milk (omit 2 fat exchanges)	
Whole milk	1 cup
Canned, evaporated whole milk	1/2 cup
Buttermilk made from whole milk	1 cup
Yogurt made from whole milk (plain, unflavored)	1 cup

LIST 2

Vegetable Exchanges. (One exchange of vegetables contains about 5 grams of carbohydrate, 2 grams of protein, and 25 calories.)

This list shows the kinds of **vegetables** to use for one vegetable exchange (one exchange is ½ cup).

Asparagus
Bean sprouts
Beets
Broccoli
Brussels sprouts
Cabbage
Carrots
Cauliflower
Celery
Cucumbers
Eggplant
Green pepper
Greens:
- **Beet**
- **Chards**
- **Collards**
- **Dandelion**
- **Kale**
- **Mustard**
- **Spinach**
- **Turnip**

Mushrooms
Okra
Onions
Rhubarb
Rutabaga
Sauerkraut
String beans, green or yellow
Summer squash
Tomatoes
Tomato juice
Turnips
Vegetable juice cocktail
Zucchini

LIST 2 (Continued)

The following **raw vegetables** may be used as desired:

Chicory	**Lettuce**
Chinese cabbage	**Parsley**
Endive	**Radishes**
Escarole	**Watercress**

Note: **Starchy vegetables** are found in List 4.

RR2

LIST 3

Fruit Exchanges. (One exchange of fruit contains 10 grams of carbohydrate and 40 calories.)

This list shows the kinds and amounts of **fruits** to use for one fruit exchange.

Apple	1 small	**Mango**	1/2 small
Apple juice	1/3 cup	**Melon**	
Applesauce (unsweetened)	1/2 cup	**Cantaloupe**	1/4 small
Apricots, fresh	2 medium	**Honeydew**	1/8 medium
Apricots, dried	4 halves	**Watermelon**	1 cup
Banana	1/2 small	**Nectarine**	1 small
Berries		**Orange**	1 small
Blackberries	1/2 cup	**Orange juice**	1/2 cup
Blueberries	1/2 cup	**Papaya**	3/4 cup
Raspberries	1/2 cup	**Peach**	1 medium
Strawberries	3/4 cup	**Pear**	1 small
Cherries	10 large	**Persimmon, native**	1 medium
Cider	1/3 cup	**Pineapple**	1/2 cup
Dates	2	**Pineapple juice**	1/3 cup
Figs, fresh	1	**Plums**	2 medium
Figs, dried	1	**Prunes**	2 medium
Grapefruit	1/2	**Prune juice**	1/4 cup
Grapefruit juice	1/2 cup	**Raisins**	2 tablespoons
Grapes	12	**Tangerine**	1 medium
Grape juice	1/4 cup		

Note: Cranberries may be used as desired if no sugar is added.

LIST 4

Bread Exchanges (Includes Bread, Cereal, and Starchy Vegetables) (One exchange of bread contains 15 grams of carbohydrate, 2 grams of protein, and 70 calories.)

This list shows the kinds and amounts of **breads, cereals, starchy vegetables**, and prepared foods to use for one bread exchange. Those which appear in **bold type** are **low-fat**. The designation "omit ____ fat exchanges" indicates that those exchanges should be subtracted from the number of fat exchanges allowed under List 6.

Bread			
White (including French and Italian)	1 slice	**English muffin, small**	1/2
Whole wheat	1 slice	**Plain roll, bread**	1
Rye or pumpernickel	1 slice	**Frankfurter roll**	1/2
Raisin	1 slice	**Hamburger bun**	1/2
Bagel, small	1/2	**Dried bread crumbs**	3 tbsp
		Tortilla, 6 inch	1

LIST 4 (Continued)

Cereal	
Bran flakes	1/2 cup
Other ready-to-eat unsweetened cereal	
Puffed cereal (unfrosted)	1 cup
Cereal (cooked)	1/2 cup
Grits (cooked)	1/2 cup
Rice or barley (cooked)	1/2 cup
Pasta (cooked)	3/4 cup
Spaghetti, noodles, macaroni	1/2 cup
Popcorn (popped, no fat added)	3 cups
Cornmeal (dry)	2 tbsp
Flour	21/2 tbsp
Wheat germ	1/4 cup

Crackers	
Arrowroot	3
Graham, 21/2 in^2	2
Matzoth, 4 x 6 inches	1/2
Oyster	20
Pretzels, 31/8 in long x 1/8 inch diameter	25
Rye Wafers, 2 x 31/2 inches	3
Saltines	6
Soda, 21/2 in^2	4

Dried beans, peas and lentils	
Beans, peas, lentils (dried and cooked)	1/2 cup
Baked beans, no pork (canned)	1/4 cup

Starchy vegetables	
Corn	1/3 cup
Corn on cob	1 small
Lima beans	1/2 cup
Parsnips	2/3 cup
Peas, green (canned or frozen)	1/2 cup
Potato, white	1 small
Potato (mashed)	1/2 cup
Pumpkin	3/4 cup
Winter squash, acorn or butternut	1/2 cup
Yam or sweet potato	1/4 cup

Prepared Foods	
Biscuit 2 inch diameter (omit 1 fat exchange)	1
Corn bread, 2 x 2 x 1 inch (omit 1 fat exchange)	1
Corn Muffin, 2 inch diameter (omit 1 fat exchange)	1
Crackers, round butter type (omit 1 fat exchange)	5
Muffin, plain small (omit 1 fat exchange)	1
Potatoes, french fried, length to 31/2 inches (omit 1 fat exchange)	8
Potato or corn chips (omit 2 fat exchanges)	15
Pancake, 5 x 1/2 inch (omit 1 fat exchange)	1
Waffle, 5 x 1/2 inch (omit 1 fat exchange)	1

LIST 5A

Meat Exchanges (Lean Meat). (One exchange of lean meat (1 ounce) contains 7 grams of protein, 3 grams of fat, and 55 calories.)

This list shows the kinds and amounts of **lean meat** and other protein-rich foods to use for one low-fat meat exchange. In the medium-fat and high-fat lists, the designation "omit ____ fat exchanges" means that those exchanges should be subtracted from the number of fat exchanges allowed under List 6.

Beef:	Baby beef (very lean), chipped beef, chuck, flank steak, tenderloin, plate ribs, plate skirt steak, round (bottom, top), all cuts rump, spare ribs, tripe	1 oz
Lamb:	Leg, rib, sirloin, loin (roast and chops), shank, shoulder	1 oz
Pork:	Leg (whole rump, center shank), ham, smoked (center slices)	1 oz
Veal:	Leg, loin, rib, shank, shoulder, cutlets	1 oz
Poultry:	Meat without skin of chicken, turkey, cornish hen, guinea hen, pheasant	1 oz
Fish:	Any fresh or frozen	1 oz
	Canned salmon, tuna, mackerel, crab and lobster	1/4 cup
	Clams, oysters, scallops, shrimp	5 or 1 oz
	Sardines, drained	3
Cheeses containing less than 5% butterfat		1 oz
Cottage cheese, dry and 2% butterfat		1/4 cup
Dried beans and peas (omit 1 bread exchange)		1/2 cup

LIST 5B

Meat Exchanges (Medium-Fat Meat). (For each exchange of medium-fat meat, omit 1/2 fat exchange.)

This list shows the kinds and amounts of medium-fat meat and other protein-rich foods used for one medium-fat meat exchange.

Beef:	Ground (15% fat), corned beef (canned), rib eye, round (ground commercial)	1 oz
Pork:	Loin (all cuts tenderloin), shoulder arm (picnic), shoulder blade, Boston butt, Canadian bacon, boiled ham	1 oz
Liver, heart, kidney, and sweetbreads (these are high in cholesterol)		1 oz
Cottage cheese, creamed		1/4 cup
Cheese:	Mozzarella, ricotta, farmer's cheese, neufchatel parmesan	1 oz 3 tbsp
Egg (high in cholesterol)		1
Peanut butter (omit 2 additional fat exchanges)		2 tbsp

LIST 5C

Meat Exchanges (High-Fat Meat). (For each exchange of high-fat meat, omit 1 fat exchange.)

This list shows the kinds and amounts of high-fat meat and other protein-rich foods to use for one high-fat meat exchange.

Beef:	Brisket, corned beef (brisket), ground beef (more than 20% fat), hamburger (commercial), chuck (ground commercial), roasts (rib), steaks (club and rib)	1 oz
Lamb:	Breast	1 oz
Pork:	Spare ribs, loin (back ribs), pork (ground), country style ham, deviled ham	1 oz
Veal:	Breast	1 oz
Poultry:	Capon, duck (domestic), goose	1 oz
Cheese:	Cheddar types	1 oz
Cold Cuts		41/2 x 1/8 inch slice
Frankfurter		1 small

LIST 6

Fat Exchanges. (One exchange of fat contains 5 grams of fat and 45 calories.)

This list shows the kinds and amounts of fat-containing foods to use for one fat exchange. To plan a diet low in saturated fat, select only those exchanges which appear in **bold type**; they are **polyunsaturated.**

Margarine, soft, tub or stick*	1 teaspoon
Avocado (4-in diameter)†	1/8
Oil, corn, cottonseed, safflower, soy, sunflower	1 teaspoon
Oil, olive†	1 teaspoon
Oil, peanut†	1 teaspoon
Olives†	5 small
Almonds†	10 whole
Pecans†	2 large whole

LIST 6 (Continued)

Peanuts†	
Spanish	20 whole
Virginia	10 whole
Walnuts	6 small
Nuts, other†	6 small
Margarine, regular stick	1 teaspoon
Butter	1 teaspoon
Bacon fat	1 teaspoon
Bacon, crisp	1 strip
Cream, light	2 tablespoons
Cream, sour	2 tablespoons
Cream, heavy	1 tablespoon
Cream cheese	1 tablespoon
French dressing‡	1 tablespoon
Italian dressing‡	1 tablespoon
Lard	1 teaspoon
Mayonnaise‡	1 teaspoon
Salad dressing, mayonnaise type‡	2 teaspoons
Salt pork	3/4 inch cube

*Made with corn, cottonseed, safflower, soy, or sunflower oil only.
†Fat content is primarily monounsaturated.
‡If made with corn, cottonseed, safflower, soy, or sunflower oil can be used on fat-modified diet.
Exchange lists from the *Exchange Lists for Meal Planning*, prepared by committees of the American Diabetes Association, Inc. and the American Dietetic Association in cooperation with the National Institute of Arthritis, Metabolism and Digestive Diseases and the National Heart and Lung Institute, National Institutes of Health, Public Health Service, U.S. Department of Health, Education and Welfare.

Ready Reference 3

Standards for Nutrient Intake

TABLE 1

Mean heights and weights and recommended energy intake (United States)

RR3

		Weight		Height		Energy Needs (with range)		
CATEGORY	AGE, YEARS	KILOGRAMS	POUNDS	CENTIMETERS	INCHES	KILOCALORIES		MEGAJOULES
Infants	0.0–0.5	6	13	60	24	kg X 115	(95–145)	kg X 0.48
	0.5–1.0	9	20	71	28	kg X 105	(80–135)	kg X 0.44
Children	1–3	13	29	90	35	1300	(900–1800)	5.5
	4–6	20	44	112	44	1700	(1300–2300)	7.1
	7–10	28	62	132	52	2400	(1650–3300)	10.1
Males	11–14	45	99	157	62	2700	(2000–3700)	11.3
	15–18	66	145	176	69	2800	(2100–3900)	11.8
	19–22	70	154	177	70	2900	(2500–3300)	12.2
	23–50	70	154	178	70	2700	(2300–3100)	11.3
	51–75	70	154	178	70	2400	(2000–2800)	10.1
	76+	70	154	178	70	2050	(1650–2450)	8.6
Females	11–14	46	101	157	62	2200	(1500–3000)	9.2
	15–18	55	120	163	64	2100	(1200–3000)	8.8
	19–22	55	120	163	64	2100	(1700–2500)	8.8
	23–50	55	120	163	64	2000	(1600–2400)	8.4
	51–75	55	120	163	64	1800	(1400–2200)	7.6
	76+	55	120	163	64	1600	(1200–2000)	6.7
Pregnancy						+300		
Lactation						+500		

Note: The data in this table have been assembled from the observed median heights and weights of children, together with desirable weights for adult men (70 in) and women (64 in) between the ages of 18 and 34 years as surveyed in the U.S. population (HEW/NCHS data).

The energy allowances for the young adults are for men and women doing light work. The allowances for the two older age groups represent mean energy needs over these age spans, allowing for a 2 percent decrease in basal (resting) metabolic rate per decade and a reduction in activity of 200 kcal/day for men and women between 51 and 75 years, 500 kcal for men over 75 years, and 400 kcal for women over 75 years. The customary range of daily energy output is shown in parentheses for adults and is based on a variation in energy needs of ±400 kcal at any one age, emphasizing the wide range of energy intakes appropriate for any group of people.

Energy allowances for children through age 18 are based on median energy intakes of children of these ages followed in longitudinal growth studies. The values in parentheses are tenth and ninetieth percentiles of energy intake, to indicate the range of energy consumption among children of these ages.

TABLE 2

Food and Nutrition Board, National Academy of Sciences, National Research Council recommended daily dietary allowances,[a] Revised 1980

(Designed for the maintenance of good nutrition of practically all healthy people in the United States.)

							Fat-Soluble Vitamins			Water-Soluble Vitamins							Minerals					
	AGE, YEARS	KILOGRAMS	POUNDS	CENTIMETERS	INCHES	PROTEIN, g	VITAMIN A, μg, RE[b]	VITAMIN D, μg, RE[c]	VITAMIN E, mg α-TE[d]	VITAMIN C, mg	THIAMINE, mg	RIBOFLAVIN, mg	NIACIN, mg NE[e]	VITAMIN B_6, mg	FOLACIN, μg[f]	VITAMIN B_{12}, μg	CALCIUM, mg	PHOSPHORUS, mg	MAGNESIUM, mg	IRON, mg	ZINC, mg	IODINE, μg
Infants	0.0–0.5	6	13	60	24	kg × 2.2	420	10	3	35	0.3	0.4	6	0.3	30	0.5[g]	360	240	50	10	3	40
	0.5–1.0	9	20	71	28	kg × 2.0	400	10	4	35	0.5	0.6	8	0.6	45	1.5	540	360	70	15	5	50
Children	1–3	13	29	90	35	23	400	10	5	45	0.7	0.8	9	0.9	100	2.0	800	800	150	15	10	70
	4–6	20	44	112	44	30	500	10	6	45	0.9	1.0	11	1.3	200	2.5	800	800	200	10	10	90
	7–10	28	62	132	52	34	700	10	7	45	1.2	1.4	16	1.6	300	3.0	800	800	250	10	10	120
Males	11–14	45	99	157	62	45	1000	10	8	50	1.4	1.6	18	1.8	400	3.0	1200	1200	350	18	15	150
	15–18	66	145	176	69	56	1000	10	10	60	1.4	1.7	18	2.0	400	3.0	1200	1200	400	18	15	150
	19–22	70	154	177	70	56	1000	7.5	10	60	1.5	1.7	19	2.2	400	3.0	800	800	350	10	15	150
	23–50	70	154	178	70	56	1000	5	10	60	1.4	1.6	18	2.2	400	3.0	800	800	350	10	15	150
	51+	70	154	178	70	56	1000	5	10	60	1.2	1.4	16	2.2	400	3.0	800	800	350	10	15	150
Females	11–14	46	101	157	62	46	800	10	8	50	1.1	1.3	15	1.8	400	3.0	1200	1200	300	18	15	150
	15–18	55	120	163	64	46	800	10	8	60	1.1	1.3	14	2.0	400	3.0	1200	1200	300	18	15	150
	19–22	55	120	163	64	44	800	7.5	8	60	1.1	1.3	14	2.0	400	3.0	800	800	300	18	15	150
	23–50	55	120	163	64	44	800	5	8	60	1.0	1.2	13	2.0	400	3.0	800	800	300	18	15	150
	51+	55	120	163	64	44	800	5	8	60	1.0	1.2	13	2.0	400	3.0	800	800	300	10	15	150
Pregnant						+30	+200	+5	+2	+20	+0.4	+0.3	+2	+0.6	+400	+1.0	+400	+400	+150	h	+5	+25
Lactating						+20	+400	+5	+3	+40	+0.5	+0.5	+5	+0.5	+100	+1.0	+400	+400	+150	h	+10	+50

[a]The allowances are intended to provide for individual variations among most normal persons as they live in the United States under usual environmental stresses. Diets should be based on a variety of common foods in order to provide other nutrients for which human requirements have been less well defined.

[b]Retinol equivalents; 1 retinol equivalent = 1 μg retinol or 6 μg β-carotene.

[c]As cholecalciferol; 10 μg cholecalciferol = 400 IU of vitamin D.

[d]α-tocopherol equivalents; 1 mg *d*-α-tocopherol = 1 α-TE.

[e]1 NE (niacin equivalent) is equal to 1 mg of niacin or 60 mg of dietary tryptophan.

[f]The folacin allowances refer to dietary sources as determined by *Lactobacillus casei* assay after treatment with enzymes (conjugases) to make polyglutamyl forms of the vitamin available to the test organism.

[g]The recommended dietary allowance for vitamin B_{12} in infants is based on average concentration of the vitamin in human milk. The allowances after weaning are based on energy intake (as recommended by the American Academy of Pediatrics) and consideration of other factors, such as intestinal absorption.

[h]The increased requirement during pregnancy cannot be met by the iron content of habitual American diets nor by the existing iron stores of many women; therefore the use of 30–60 mg of supplemental iron is recommended. Iron needs during lactation are not substantially different from those of nonpregnant women, but continued supplementation of the mother for 2 to 3 months after parturition is advisable in order to replenish stores depleted by pregnancy.

TABLE 3

Estimated safe and adequate daily dietary intakes of selected vitamins and minerals (United States)*

RR3

	AGE, YEARS	Vitamins		
		VITAMIN K, μg	BIOTIN, μg	PANTOTHENIC ACID, mg
Infants	0-0.5	12	35	2
	0.5-1	10-20	50	3
Children and adolescents	1-3	15-30	65	3
	4-6	20-40	85	3-4
	7-10	30-60	120	4-5
	11+	50-100	100-200	4-7
Adults		70-140	100-200	4-7

	AGE, YEARS	Trace Elements†					
		COPPER, mg	MANGANESE, mg	FLUORIDE, mg	CHROMIUM, mg	SELENIUM, mg	MOLYBDENUM, mg
Infants	0-0.5	0.5-0.7	0.5-0.7	0.1-0.5	0.01-0.04	0.01-0.04	0.03-0.06
	0.5-1	0.7-1.0	0.7-1.0	0.2-1.0	0.02-0.06	0.02-0.06	0.04-0.08
Children and adolescents	1-3	1.0-1.5	1.0-1.5	0.5-1.5	0.02-0.08	0.02-0.08	0.05-0.1
	4-6	1.5-2.0	1.5-2.0	1.0-2.5	0.03-0.12	0.03-0.12	0.06-0.15
	7-10	2.0-2.5	2.0-3.0	1.5-2.5	0.05-0.2	0.05-0.2	0.10-0.3
	11+	2.0-3.0	2.5-5.0	1.5-2.5	0.05-0.2	0.05-0.2	0.15-0.5
Adults		2.0-3.0	2.5-5.0	1.5-4.0	0.05-0.2	0.05-0.2	0.15-0.5

	AGE, YEARS	Electrolytes		
		SODIUM, mg	POTASSIUM, mg	CHLORIDE, mg
Infants	0-0.5	115-350	350-925	275-700
	0.5-1	250-750	425-1275	400-1200
Children and adolescents	1-3	325-975	550-1650	500-1500
	4-6	450-1350	775-2325	700-2100
	7-10	600-1800	1000-3000	925-2775
	11+	900-2700	1525-4575	1400-4200
Adults		1100-3300	1875-5625	1700-5100

*Because there is less information on which to base allowances, these figures are not given in the main table of RDA and are provided here in the form of ranges of recommended intakes.

†Since the toxic levels for many trace elements may be only several times usual intakes, the upper levels for the trace elements given in this table should not be habitually exceeded.

				Energy[a]			Water-Soluble Vitamins			
AGE	SEX	WEIGHT, kg	HEIGHT, cm	KILOCALORIES	MEGAJOULES[b]	PROTEIN, g	THIAMINE, mg	NIACIN, NE[f]	RIBOFLAVIN, mg	VITAMIN B_6[g], mg
0–6 mo	Both	6	—	kg X 117	kg X 0.49	kg X 2.2(2.0)[e]	0.3	5	0.4	0.3
7–11 mo	Both	9	—	kg X 108	kg X 0.45	kg X 1.4	0.5	6	0.6	0.4
1–3 yr	Both	13	90	1400	5.9	22	0.7	9	0.8	0.8
4–6 yr	Both	19	110	1800	7.5	27	0.9	12	1.1	1.3
7–9 yr	M	27	129	2200	9.2	33	1.1	14	1.3	1.6
	F	27	128	2000	8.4	33	1.0	13	1.2	1.4
10–12 yr	M	36	144	2500	10.5	41	1.2	17	1.5	1.8
	F	38	145	2300	9.6	40	1.1	15	1.4	1.5
13–15 yr	M	51	162	2800	11.7	52	1.4	19	1.7	2.0
	F	49	159	2200	9.2	43	1.1	15	1.4	1.5
16–18 yr	M	64	172	3200	13.4	54	1.6	21	2.0	2.0
	F	54	161	2100	8.8	43	1.1	14	1.3	1.5
19–35 yr	M	70	176	3000	12.6	56	1.5	20	1.8	2.0
	F	56	161	2100	8.8	41	1.1	14	1.3	1.5
36–50 yr	M	70	176	2700	11.3	56	1.4	18	1.7	2.0
	F	56	161	1900	7.9	41	1.0	13	1.2	1.5
51+ yr	M	70	176	2300[c]	9.6[c]	56	1.4	18	1.7	2.0
	F	56	161	1800[c]	7.5[c]	41	1.0	13	1.2	1.5
Pregnancy				+300[d]	1.3[d]	+20	+0.2	+2	+0.3	+0.5
Lactation				+500	2.1	+24	+0.4	+7	+0.6	+0.6

[a] Recommendations assume characteristic activity pattern for each age group.
[b] Megajoules (10^6 joules); calculated from the relation 1 kilocalorie = 4.184 kilojoules and rounded to 1 decimal place.
[c] Recommended energy intake for age 66+ years reduced to 2000 kcal (8.4 MJ) for men and 1500 kcal (6.3 MJ) for women.
[d] Increased energy intake recommended during second and third trimesters. An increase of 100 kcal (418.4 kJ) per day is recommended during the first trimester.
[e] Recommended protein intake of 2.2 g/kg of body weight for infants age 0 to 2 months and 2.0 g/kg of body weight for those age 3 to 5 months. Protein recommendation for infants 0 to 11 months assumes consumption of breast milk or protein of equivalent quality.
[f] 1 NE (niacin equivalent) is equal to 1 mg of niacin or 60 mg of tryptophan.
[g] Recommendations are based on estimated average daily protein intake of Canadians.
[h] Recommendation given in terms of free folate.
[i] Considerably higher levels may be prudent for infants during the first week of life to guard against neonatal tyrosinemia.

TABLE 4

Recommended daily nutrient intake (Canada), revised 1975

			Fat-Soluble Vitamins			Minerals					
FOLATE[h], μg	VITAMIN B_{12}, μg	VITAMIN C, mg	VITAMIN A, RE[j]	VITAMIN D, μg CHOLECAL-CIFEROL[k]	VITAMIN E, mg d-α-TOCOPHEROL	CALCIUM, mg	PHOSPHORUS, mg	MAGNESIUM, mg	IODINE, μg	IRON, mg	ZINC, mg
40	0.3	20[i]	400	10.0	3	500[m]	250[m]	50[m]	35[m]	7[m]	4[m]
60	0.3	20	400	10.0	3	500	400	50	50	7	5
100	0.9	20	400	10.0	4	500	500	75	70	8	5
100	1.5	20	500	5.0	5	500	500	100	90	9	6
100	1.5	30	700	2.5[l]	6	700	700	150	110	10	7
100	1.5	30	700	2.5[l]	6	700	700	150	100	10	7
100	3.0	30	800	2.5[l]	7	900	900	175	130	11	8
100	3.0	30	800	2.5[l]	7	1000	1000	200	120	11	9
200	3.0	30	1000	2.5[l]	9	1200	1200	250	140	13	10
200	3.0	30	800	2.5[l]	7	800	800	250	110	14	10
200	3.0	30	1000	2.5[l]	10	1000	1000	300	160	14	12
200	3.0	30	800	2.5[l]	6	700	700	250	110	14	11
200	3.0	30	1000	2.5[l]	9	800	800	300	150	10	10
200	3.0	30	800	2.5[l]	6	700	700	250	110	14	9
200	3.0	30	1000	2.5[l]	8	800	800	300	140	10	10
200	3.0	30	800	2.5[l]	6	700	700	250	100	14	9
200	3.0	30	1000	2.5[l]	8	800	800	300	140	10	10
200	3.0	30	800	2.5[l]	6	700	700	250	100	9	9
+50	+1.0	+20	+100	+2.5[l]	+1	+500	+500	+25	+15	+1[n]	+3
+50	+0.5	+30	+400	+2.5[l]	+2	+500	+500	+75	+25	+1[n]	+7

[j] 1 RE (retinol equivalent) corresponds to a biologic activity in humans equal to 1 μg retinol (3.33 IU) or 6 μg β-carotene (10 IU).

[k] One μg cholecalciferol is equivalent to 1 μg ergocalciferol (40 IU vitamin D activity).

[l] Most older children and adults receive vitamin D from irradiation, but 2.5 μg is recommended. This intake should be increased to 5.0 μg daily during pregnancy and lactation and for those confined indoors or otherwise deprived of sunlight for extended periods.

[m] The intake of breast-fed infants may be less than the recommendation but is considered to be adequate.

[n] A recommended total intake of 15 mg daily during pregnancy and lactation assumes the presence of adequate stores of iron. If stores are suspected of being inadequate, additional iron as a supplement is recommended.

Source: Reprinted by permission of the Director, Bureau of Nutritional Sciences, Canada, from Dietary Standards for Canada, Table 13, rev. 1975, by Committee for Revision of the Canadian Dietary Standard, Bureau of Nutritional Sciences, Health and Welfare, Information Canada, Ottawa, 1975.

TABLE 5

Recommended intakes of nutrients (WHO), 1974

AGE	BODY WEIGHT, kg	Energy[a] KILO-CALORIES	Energy[a] MEGA-JOULES	PRO-TEIN, g[a,b]	VITA-MIN A, μg[c,d]	VITA-MIN D, μg[c,f]	THIA-MINE, mg[c]	RIBO-FLAVIN, mg[c]	NIACIN, mg[e]	FOLIC ACID, μg[e]	VITA-MIN B_{12}, μg[e]	ASCOR-BIC ACID, mg[e]	CAL-CIUM, g[g]	IRON mg[e,h]
Children														
<1	7.3	820	3.4	14	300	10.0	0.3	0.5	5.4	60	0.3	20	0.5–0.6	5–10
1–3	13.4	1360	5.7	16	250	10.0	0.5	0.8	9.0	100	0.9	20	0.4–0.5	5–10
4–6	20.2	1830	7.6	20	300	10.0	0.7	1.1	12.1	100	1.5	20	0.4–0.5	5–10
7–9	28.1	2190	9.2	25	400	2.5	0.9	1.3	14.5	100	1.5	20	0.4–0.5	5–10
Male adolescents														
10–12	36.9	2600	10.9	30	575	2.5	1.0	1.6	17.2	100	2.0	20	0.6–0.7	5–10
13–15	51.3	2900	12.1	37	725	2.5	1.2	1.7	19.1	200	2.0	30	0.6–0.7	9–18
16–19	62.9	3070	12.8	38	750	2.5	1.2	1.8	20.3	200	2.0	30	0.5–0.6	5–9
Female adolescents														
10–12	38.0	2350	9.8	29	575	2.5	0.9	1.4	15.5	100	2.0	20	0.6–0.7	5–10
13–15	49.9	2490	10.4	31	725	2.5	1.0	1.5	16.4	200	2.0	30	0.6–0.7	12–24
16–19	54.4	2310	9.7	30	750	2.5	0.9	1.4	15.2	200	2.0	30	0.5–0.6	14–28
Adult man (moderately active)	65.0	3000	12.6	37	750	2.5	1.2	1.8	19.8	200	2.0	30	0.4–0.5	5–9
Adult woman (moderately active)	55.0	2200	9.2	29	750	2.5	0.9	1.3	14.5	200	2.0	30	0.4–0.5	14–28
Pregnancy (latter half)		+350	+1.5	38	750	10.0	+0.1	+0.2	+2.3	400	3.0	50	1.0–1.2	i
Lactation (first 6 months)		+550	+2.3	46	1200	10.0	+0.2	+0.4	+3.7	300	2.5	50	1.0–1.2	i

[a]Energy and Protein Requirements, Report of a Joint FAO/WHO Expert Group, FAO, Rome, 1972.
[b]As egg or milk protein.
[c]Requirements of vitamin A, thiamine, riboflavin, and niacin, Report of a Joint FAO/WHO Expert Group, FAO, Rome, 1965.
[d]As retinol.
[e]Requirements of ascorbic acid, vitamin D, vitamin B_{12}, folate, and iron, Report of a Joint FAO/WHO Expert Group, FAO, Rome, 1970.
[f]As cholecalciferol.
[g]Calcium requirements, Report of a FAO/WHO Expert Group, FAO, Rome, 1961.
[h]On each line the lower value applies when over 25 percent of calories in the diet come from animal foods, and the higher value when animal foods represent less than 10 percent of calories.
[i]For women whose iron intake throughout life has been at the level recommended in this table, the daily intake of iron during pregnancy and lactation should be the same as that recommended for nonpregnant, nonlactating women of childbearing age. For women whose iron status is not satisfactory at the beginning of pregnancy, the requirement is increased, and in the extreme situation of women with no iron stores, the requirement can probably not be met without supplementation.

Source: From Passmore, Nicol and Rao, "Handbook on Human Nutritional Requirements," WHO Monogr. Ser. 61, 1974, Table 1. Reprinted with permission.

Ready Reference 4

Nutritional Analyses of Fast Foods

	WEIGHT, g	KILOCALORIES	PROTEIN, g	CARBOHYDRATE, g	FAT, g	VITAMIN A, IU	VITAMIN B_1, mg	VITAMIN B_2, mg	NIACIN, mg	VITAMIN B_6, mg	VITAMIN B_{12}, μg	VITAMIN C, mg	VITAMIN D, IU	CALCIUM, mg	IRON, mg	POTASSIUM, mg	MAGNESIUM, mg	PHOSPHORUS, mg	SODIUM, mg
Burger Chef																			
Big Shef	186	542	23	35	34	282	0.34	0.35	5.4	—	—	2	—	189	3.4	384	—	278	622
Cheeseburger	104	304	14	24	17	266	0.22	0.23	3.2	—	—	1	—	156	2.0	220	—	198	535
Double cheeseburger	145	434	24	24	26	430	0.25	0.34	4.8	—	—	1	—	246	3.1	361	—	351	691
French fries	68	187	3	25	9	Trace	0.09	0.05	2.1	—	—	14	—	10	0.9	581	—	76	4
Hamburger, regular	91	258	11	24	13	114	0.22	0.18	3.2	—	—	1	—	69	1.9	210	—	102	393
Mariner Platter	373	680	32	85	24	448	0.37	0.40	7.3	—	—	24	—	137	4.7	1278	—	396	882
Rancher Platter	316	640	30	44	38	367	0.30	0.37	8.7	—	—	24	—	57	5.1	1370	—	326	444
Shake	305	326	11	47	11	10	0.11	0.57	0.3	—	—	2	—	411	0.2	548	—	319	167
Skipper's Treat	179	604	21	47	37	303	0.29	0.30	3.7	—	—	1	—	201	2.5	284	—	288	783
Super Shef	252	600	29	39	37	763	0.37	0.43	6.7	—	—	9	—	240	4.2	590	—	371	918

Source: Burger Chef Systems, Inc, Indianapolis, Ind, 1978 (analyses obtained from USDA Handbook No. 8).

	WEIGHT, g	KILOCALORIES	PROTEIN, g	CARBOHYDRATE, g	FAT, g	VITAMIN A, IU	VITAMIN B_1, mg	VITAMIN B_2, mg	NIACIN, mg	VITAMIN B_6, mg	VITAMIN B_{12}, μg	VITAMIN C, mg	VITAMIN D, IU	CALCIUM, mg	IRON, mg	POTASSIUM, mg	MAGNESIUM, mg	PHOSPHORUS, mg	SODIUM, mg
Burger King																			
Cheeseburger	—	305	17	29	13	195	0.08	0.16	2.20	—	—	0.5	—	141	2.0	219	—	229	562
Hamburger	—	252	14	29	9	21	0.08	0.10	2.20	—	—	0.5	—	45	2.0	208	—	119	401
Whopper	—	606	29	51	32	641	0.20	0.26	5.20	—	—	13.0	—	90	6.0	653	—	272	909
French fries	—	214	3	28	10	0	0.10	0.06	2.42	—	—	16.0	—	12	1.0	666	—	87	5
Vanilla shake	—	332	11	50	11	437	0.10	0.54	0.27	—	—	Trace	—	390	0.2	520	—	303	159
Whaler	—	745	18	69	46	141	0.09	0.09	1.04	—	—	1.3	—	70	1.0	130	—	91	735
Hot dog	—	291	11	23	17	0	0.39	0.15	2.00	—	—	0	—	40	1.4	170	—	117	841

Source: Chart House, Inc, Oak Brook, Ill, 1978.

	WEIGHT, g	KILOCALORIES	PROTEIN, g	CARBOHYDRATE, g	FAT, g	VITAMIN A, IU	VITAMIN B_1, mg	VITAMIN B_2, mg	NIACIN, mg	VITAMIN B_6, mg	VITAMIN B_{12}, μg	VITAMIN C, mg	VITAMIN D, IU	CALCIUM, mg	IRON, mg	POTASSIUM, mg	MAGNESIUM, mg	PHOSPHORUS, mg	SODIUM, mg
Dairy Queen																			
Big Brazier Deluxe	213	470	28	36	24	—	0.34	0.37	9.6	0.38	2.55	< 2.5	30	111	5.2	—	45	262	920
Big Brazier regular	184	457	27	37	23	—	0.37	0.39	9.6	0.34	2.29	< 2.0	31	113	5.2	—	42	223	910
Big Brazier w/cheese	213	553	32	38	30	495	0.34	0.53	9.5	0.35	2.89	< 2.3	36	268	5.2	—	47	359	1435
Brazier w/cheese	121	318	18	30	14	—	0.29	0.29	5.7	0.11	1.20	< 1.2	13	163	3.5	—	26	192	865

Nutritional Analyses of Fast Food (Continued)

	WEIGHT, g	KILOCALORIES*	PROTEIN, g	CARBOHYDRATE, g	FAT, g	VITAMIN A, IU	VITAMIN B_1, mg	VITAMIN B_2, mg	NIACIN, mg	VITAMIN B_6, mg	VITAMIN B_{12}, μg	VITAMIN C, mg	VITAMIN D, IU	CALCIUM, mg	IRON, mg	POTASSIUM, mg	MAGNESIUM, mg	PHOSPHORUS, mg	SODIUM, mg
Dairy Queen (continued)																			
Brazier cheese dog	113	330	15	24	19	—	—	0.18	3.3	0.07	1.22	—	23	168	1.6	—	24	182	—
Brazier chili dog	128	330	13	25	20	—	0.15	0.23	3.9	0.17	1.29	11.0	20	86	2.0	—	38	139	939
Brazier dog	99	273	11	23	15	—	0.12	0.15	2.6	0.08	1.05	11.0	23	75	1.5	—	21	104	868
Brazier french fries, 2.5 oz	71	200	2	25	10	Trace	0.06	Trace	0.8	0.16	—	3.6	16	Trace	0.4	—	16	100	—
Brazier french fries, 4.0 oz	113	320	3	40	16	Trace	0.09	0.03	1.2	0.30	—	4.8	24	Trace	0.4	—	24	150	—
Brazier onion rings	85	300	6	33	17	Trace	0.09	Trace	0.4	0.08	—	2.4	8	20	0.4	—	16	60	—
Brazier regular	106	260	13	28	9	—	0.28	0.26	5.0	0.13	1.03	< 1.0	13	70	3.5	—	23	114	576
Fish sandwich	170	400	20	41	17	Trace	0.15	0.26	3.0	0.16	1.20	Trace	40	60	1.1	—	24	200	—
Fish sandwich w/cheese	177	440	24	39	21	100	0.15	0.26	3.0	0.16	1.50	Trace	40	150	0.4	—	24	250	—
Super Brazier	298	783	53	35	48	—	0.39	0.69	15.6	0.69	4.97	< 3.2	65	282	7.3	—	61	518	1619
Super Brazier dog	182	518	20	41	30	Trace	0.42	0.44	7.0	0.17	2.09	14.0	44	158	4.3	—	37	195	1552
Super Brazier dog w/cheese	203	593	26	43	36	—	0.43	0.48	8.1	0.18	2.34	14.0	44	297	4.4	—	42	312	1986
Super Brazier chili dog	210	555	23	42	33	—	0.42	0.48	8.8	0.27	2.67	18.0	32	158	4.0	—	48	231	1640
Banana split	383	540	10	91	15	750	0.60	0.60	0.8	0.50	0.90	18.0	Trace	350	1.8	—	60	250	—
Buster bar	149	390	10	37	22	300	0.09	0.34	1.6	0.12	0.90	Trace	—	200	0.7	—	60	150	—
DQ chocolate dipped cone, sm.	78	150	3	20	7	100	0.03	0.17	Trace	0.04	0.36	Trace	Trace	100	Trace	—	16	80	—
DQ chocolate dipped cone, med.	156	300	7	40	13	300	0.09	0.34	Trace	0.08	0.60	Trace	Trace	200	0.4	—	24	150	—
DQ chocolate dipped cone, lg.	234	450	10	58	20	400	0.12	0.51	Trace	0.12	0.90	Trace	8	300	0.4	—	40	200	—
DQ chocolate malt, sm.	241	340	10	51	11	400	0.06	0.34	0.4	0.16	1.20	2.4	60	300	1.8	—	40	200	—
DQ chocolate malt, med.	418	600	15	89	20	750	0.12	0.60	0.8	0.20	1.80	3.6	100	500	3.5	—	80	400	—
DQ chocolate malt, lg.	588	840	22	125	28	750	0.15	0.85	1.2	0.30	2.40	6.0	140	600	5.4	—	80	600	—
DQ chocolate sundae, sm.	106	170	4	30	4	100	0.03	0.17	Trace	0.04	0.48	Trace	Trace	100	0.7	—	24	100	—
DQ chocolate sundae, med.	184	300	6	53	7	300	0.06	0.26	Trace	0.08	6.00	Trace	Trace	200	1.1	—	32	150	—
DQ chocolate sundae, lg.	248	400	9	71	9	400	0.09	0.43	0.4	0.12	1.20	Trace	8	300	1.8	—	40	250	—
DQ cone, sm.	71	110	3	18	3	100	0.03	0.14	Trace	0.04	0.36	Trace	Trace	100	Trace	—	8	60	—

DQ cone, sm.	71	110	3	18	3	100	0.03	0.14	Trace	0.04	0.36	Trace	Trace	100	Trace	—	8	60	—
DQ cone, med.	142	230	6	35	7	300	0.09	0.26	Trace	0.08	0.60	Trace	Trace	200	Trace	—	24	150	—
DQ cone, lg.	213	340	10	52	10	400	0.15	0.43	Trace	0.12	1.20	Trace	8	300	Trace	—	32	200	—
Dairy Queen parfait	284	460	10	81	11	400	0.12	0.43	0.4	0.16	1.20	Trace	8	300	1.8	—	40	250	—
Dilly bar	85	240	4	22	15	100	0.06	0.17	Trace	0.04	0.48	Trace	—	100	0.4	—	16	100	—
DQ float	397	330	6	59	8	100	0.12	0.17	Trace	—	0.60	Trace	—	200	Trace	—	—	200	—
DQ freeze	397	520	11	89	13	200	0.15	0.34	Trace	—	1.20	Trace	—	300	Trace	—	—	250	—
DQ sandwich	60	140	3	24	4	100	0.03	0.14	0.4	Trace	0.24	Trace	—	60	0.4	—	8	60	—
Fiesta sundae	269	570	9	84	22	200	0.23	0.26	Trace	—	0.90	Trace	—	200	Trace	—	—	200	—
Hot fudge brownie delight	266	570	11	83	22	500	0.45	0.43	0.8	0.16	0.90	Trace	Trace	300	1.1	—	40	250	—
Mr. Misty float	404	440	6	85	8	120	0.12	0.17	Trace	—	0.60	Trace	—	200	Trace	—	—	200	—
Mr. Misty freeze	411	500	10	87	12	200	0.15	0.34	Trace	—	1.20	Trace	—	300	Trace	—	—	200	—

Source: International Dairy Queen, Inc, Minneapolis, Minn, 1978. Dairy Queen stores in the state of Texas do not conform to Dairy Queen-approved products. Any nutritional information shown does not necessarily pertain to their products.

Kentucky Fried Chicken																			
Original Recipe dinner*	425	830	52	56	46	750‡	0.38‡	0.56‡	15.0‡	—	—	27.0‡	—	150‡	4.5‡	—	—	—	2285
Extra crispy dinner*	437	950	52	63	54	750‡	0.38‡	0.56‡	14.0‡	—	—	27.0‡	—	150‡	3.6‡	—	—	—	1915
Individual pieces† (Original Recipe)																			
Drumstick	54	136	14	2	8	30	0.04	0.12	2.7	—	—	0.6	—	20	0.9	—	—	—	—
Keel	96	283	25	6	13	50	0.07	0.13	—	—	—	1.2	—	—	0.9	—	—	—	—
Rib	82	241	19	8	15	58	0.06	0.14	5.8	—	—	< 1.0	—	55	1.0	—	—	—	—
Thigh	97	276	20	12	19	74	0.08	0.24	4.9	—	—	< 1.0	—	39	1.4	—	—	—	—
Wing	45	151	11	4	10	—	0.03	0.07	—	—	—	< 1.0	—	—	0.6	—	—	—	—
9 Pieces	652	1892	152	59	116	—	0.49	1.27	—	—	—	—	—	—	8.8	—	—	—	—

*Dinner comprises mashed potatoes and gravy, cole slaw, roll, and three pieces of chicken, either (1) wing, rib, and thigh; (2) wing, drumstick, and thigh; or (3) wing, drumstick, and keel.
†Edible portion of chicken.
‡Calculated from percentage of U.S. RDA.
Source: Nutritional Content of Average Serving, Heublein Food Service and Franchising Group, June 1976.

Long John Silver's																			
Breaded oysters, 6 pc.	—	460	14	58	19	—	—	—	—	—	—	—	—	—	—	—	—	—	—
Breaded clams, 5 oz	—	465	13	46	25	—	—	—	—	—	—	—	—	—	—	—	—	—	—
Chicken planks, 4 pc.	—	458	27	35	23	—		—	—	—	—	—	—	—	—	—	—	—	—
Cole slaw, 4 oz	—	138	1	16	8	—	—	—	—	—	—	—	—	—	—	—	—	—	—
Corn on cob, 1 pc.	—	174	5	29	4	—	—	—	—	—	—	—	—	—	—	—	—	—	—
Fish w/batter, 2 pc.	—	318	19	19	19	—	—	—	—	—	—	—	—	—	—	—	—	—	—
Fish w/batter, 3 pc.	—	477	28	28	28	—	—	—	—	—	—	—	—	—	—	—	—	—	—
Fryes, 3 oz	—	275	4	32	15	—	—	—	—	—	—	—	—	—	—	—	—	—	—
Hush Puppies, 3 pc.	—	153	1	20	7	—	—	—	—	—	—	—	—	—	—	—	—	—	—
Ocean scallops, 6 pc.	—	257	10	27	12	—	—	—	—	—	—	—	—	—	—	—	—	—	—
Peg Leg w/batter, 5 pc.	—	514	25	30	33	—	—	—	—	—	—	—	—	—	—	—	—	—	—
Shrimp w/batter, 6 pc.	—	269	9	31	13	—	—	—	—	—	—	—	—	—	—	—	—	—	—
Treasure Chest (2 pc. fish, 2 Peg Legs)	—	467	25	27	29	—	—	—	—	—	—	—	—	—	—	—	—	—	—

Source: Long John Silver's Seafood Shoppes, Jan. 8, 1978 (nutritional analysis information furnished in study conducted by the Department of Nutrition and Food Science, University of Kentucky).

Nutritional Analyese of Fast Food (Continued)

	WEIGHT, g	KILOCALORIES	PROTEIN, g	CARBOHYDRATE, g	FAT, g	VITAMIN A, IU	VITAMIN B_1, mg	VITAMIN B_2, mg	NIACIN, mg	VITAMIN B_6, mg	VITAMIN B_{12}, μg	VITAMIN C, mg	VITAMIN D, IU	CALCIUM, mg	IRON, mg	POTASSIUM, mg	MAGNESIUM, mg	PHOSPHORUS, mg	SODIUM, mg
McDonald's																			
Egg McMuffin	132	352	18	26	20	361	0.36	0.60	4.3	0.14	0.71	1.6	40	187	3.2	222	25	265	914
English muffin, buttered	62	186	6	28	6	106	0.22	0.14	6.4	0.03	0.02	< 0.7	8	87	1.6	66	13*	94	466
Hot cakes, w/butter & syrup	206	472	8	89	9	255	0.31	0.43	4.0	0.06	0.14	< 2.1	12	54	2.4	264	30	404	1071
Saugage (pork)	48	184	9	Trace	17	36	0.22	0.13	5.9	0.11	0.36	< 0.5	35	13	0.9	125	8	55	464
Scrambled eggs	77	162	12	2	12	514	0.07	0.60	0.4	0.16	0.76	< 0.8	60	49	2.2	144	11	167	207
Big Mac	187	541	26	39	31	327	0.35	0.37	8.2	0.22	1.89	2.4	37	175	4.3	386	38	215	962
Cheeseburger	114	306	16	31	13	372	0.24	0.30	5.5	0.10	0.97	1.6	14	158	2.9	244	24	134	725
Filet O' Fish	131	402	15	34	23	152	0.28	0.28	3.9	0.08	0.78	4.2	37	105	1.8	293	29	158	709
French fries	69	211	3	26	11	< 52	0.15	0.03	2.9	<0.01	0.01	11.0	< 3	10	0.5	570	23	49	113
Hamburger	99	257	13	30	9	231	0.23	0.23	5.1	0.11	1.03	1.8	11	63	3.0	234	21	88	526
Quarter Pounder	164	418	26	33	21	164	0.31	0.41	9.8	0.25	2.29	2.3	23	79	5.1	442	38	179	711
Quarter Pounder w/cheese	193	518	31	34	29	683	0.35	0.59	15.1	0.25	2.42	2.9	36	251	4.6	472	43	257	1209
Apple pie	91	300	2	31	19	< 69	0.02	0.03	1.3	0.08	0.01	2.7	5	12	0.6	39	7	23	414
Cherry pie	92	298	2	33	18	213	0.02	0.03	0.4	0.02	0.01	1.3	< 5	12	0.4	57	8	23	456
McDonaldland cookies	63	294	4	45	11	< 48	0.28	0.23	0.8	0.02	Trace	1.4	10	10	1.4	58	10	51	330
Chocolate shake	289	364	11	60	9	318	0.12	0.89	0.8	0.12	0.85	< 2.9	354	338	1.0	656	51	292	329
Strawberry shake	293	345	10	57	9	322	0.12	0.66	0.5	0.11	0.85	< 2.9	313	339	0.2	544	35	298	256
Vanilla shake	289	323	10	52	8	346	0.12	0.66	0.6	0.12	0.94	< 2.9	354	346	0.2	499	35	266	250

Source: "Nutritional analysis of food served at McDonald's restaurants," WARF Institute, Inc, Madison, Wisc, June 1977.

Taco Bell																			
Bean burrito	166	343	11	48	12	1657	0.37	0.22	2.2	—	—	15.2	—	98	2.8	235	—	173	272
Beef burrito	184	466	30	37	21	1675	0.30	0.39	7.0	—	—	15.2	—	83	4.0	320	—	288	327
Beefy tostada	184	291	19	21	15	3450	0.16	0.27	3.3	—	—	12.7	—	208	3.4	277	—	265	138
Bellbeefer	123	221	15	23	7	2961	0.15	0.20	3.7	—	—	10.0	—	40	2.6	183	—	140	231
Bellbeefer w/cheese	137	278	19	23	12	3146	0.16	0.27	3.7	—	—	10.0	—	147	2.7	195	—	208	330
Burrito supreme	225	457	21	43	22	3462	0.33	0.35	4.7	—	—	16.0	—	121	3.8	350	—	245	367
Combination burrito	175	404	21	43	16	1666	0.34	0.31	4.6	—	—	15.2	—	91	3.7	278	—	230	300
Enchirito	207	454	25	42	21	1178	0.31	0.37	4.7	—	—	9.5	—	259	3.8	491	—	338	1175
Pintos'N Cheese	158	168	11	21	5	3123	0.26	0.16	0.9	—	—	9.3	—	150	2.3	307	—	210	102
Taco	83	186	15	14	8	120	0.09	0.16	2.9	—	—	0.2	—	120	2.5	143	—	175	79
Tostada	138	179	9	25	6	3152	0.18	0.15	0.8	—	—	9.7	—	191	2.3	172	—	186	101

Sources: Menu Item Portions, July 1976, Taco Bell Co, San Antonio, Tex.
Adams, C.F., Nutritive Value of American Foods in Common Units, USDA Agricultural Research Service, Agricultural Handbook No. 456, November 1975.
Church, C.F., and Church, H.N., Food Values of Portions Commonly Used, 12th ed., Lippincott, Philadelphia, 1975.
Valley Baptist Medical Center, Food Service Department, Descriptions of Mexican-American Foods, NASCO, Fort Atkinson, Wisc.

Beverages																			
Coffee, 6 oz	180	2	Trace	Trace	Trace	0	0	Trace	0.5	—	—	0	—	4	0.2	65	—	7	2
Tea, 6 oz	180	2	Trace	—	Trace	0	0	0.04	0.1	—	—	1	—	5	0.2	—	—	4	—
Orange juice, 6 oz	183	82	1	20	Trace	366	0.17	0.02	0.6	—	—	82.4	—	17	0.2	340	18	29	2
Chocolate milk, 8 oz	250	213	9	28	9	330	0.08	0.40	0.3	—	—	3.0	—	278	0.5	365	—	235	118
Skim milk, 8 oz	245	88	9	13	Trace	10	0.09	0.44	0.2	—	—	2.0	—	296	0.1	355	—	233	127
Whole milk, 8 oz	244	159	9	12	9	342	0.07	0.41	0.2	—	—	2.4	100	188	Trace	351	32	227	122
Coca-Cola, 8 oz	246	96	0	24	0	—	—	—	—	—	—	—	—	—	—	—	—	40	20*
Fanta Ginger Ale, 8 oz	244	84	0	21	0	—	—	—	—	—	—	—	—	—	—	—	—	0	30*
Fanta Grape, 8 oz	247	114	0	29	0	—	—	—	—	—	—	—	—	—	—	—	—	0	21*
Fanta Orange, 8 oz	248	117	0	30	0	—	—	—	—	—	—	—	—	—	—	—	—	0	21*
Fanta Root Beer, 8 oz	246	103	0	27	0	—	—	—	—	—	—	—	—	—	—	—	—	0	23*
Mr. Pibb, 8 oz	245	93	0	25	0	—	—	—	—	—	—	—	—	—	—	—	—	28	23*
Mr. Pibb without sugar, 8 oz	237	1	0	Trace	0	—	—	—	—	—	—	—	—	—	—	—	—	28	37*
Sprite, 8 oz	245	95	0	24	0	—	—	—	—	—	—	—	—	—	—	—	—	0	42*
Sprite without sugar, 8 oz	237	3	0	0	0	—	—	—	—	—	—	—	—	—	—	—	—	0	42*
Tab, 8 oz	237	Trace	0	Trace	0	—	—	—	—	—	—	—	—	—	—	—	—	30	30*
Fresca, 8 oz	237	2	0	0	0	—	—	—	—	—	—	—	—	—	—	—	—	0	51*

*The values for sodium reflect value when bottling water with average sodium content is used, 12 mg/8 oz.
Table source: Anonymous, "Fast Foods OK with Nutrition Know-How," *Med. Times* 107:21–22 (July 1980).
Sources: Adams, C.F., Nutritive Value of American Foods in Common Units, USDA Agricultural Research Service, Agricultural Handbook No. 456, November 1975.
Coca-Cola Company, Atlanta, Ga, January 1977.
American Hospital Formulary Service, Washington, American Society of Hospital Pharmacists, Section 28:20, March 1978.

Source: Young, E.A., "Perspective on Fast Foods," *Public Health Currents*, 1981 (Ross Laboratories, Columbus, Ohio). Reprinted with permission.

Ready Reference 5

Costs of Activities in Kilocalories per Kilogram per Hour Exclusive of Basal Metabolism and the Influence of Food

ACTIVITY	ENERGY COST, kcal/kg/h
Bicycling (century run)	7.6
Bicycling (moderate speed)	2.5
Bookbinding	0.8
Boxing	11.4
Carpentry (heavy)	2.3
Cello playing	1.3
Crocheting	0.4
Dancing, foxtrot	3.8
Dancing, waltz	3.0
Dishwashing	1.0
Dressing and undressing	0.7
Driving automobile	0.9
Eating	0.4
Fencing	7.3
Horseback riding, walk	1.4
Horseback riding, trot	4.3
Horseback riding, gallop	6.7
Ironing (5-lb iron)	1.0
Knitting sweater	0.7
Laundry, light	1.3
Lying still, awake	0.1
Organ playing (30 to 40% of energy hand work)	1.5
Painting furniture	1.5
Paring potatoes	0.6
Playing Ping-Pong	4.4
Piano playing (Mendelssohn's songs)	0.8
Piano playing (Beethoven's "Appassionata")	1.4
Piano playing (Liszt's "Tarantella")	2.0
Reading aloud	0.4
Rowing in race	16.0
Running	7.0
Sawing wood	5.7
Sewing, hand	0.4
Sewing, foot-driven machine	0.6
Sewing, motor-driven machine	0.4
Shoemaking	1.0
Singing in loud voice	0.8
Sitting quietly	0.4
Skating	3.5
Standing at attention	0.6
Standing relaxed	0.5
Stone masonry	4.7
Sweeping with a broom, bare floor	1.4
Sweeping with a carpet sweeper	1.6
Sweeping with a vacuum sweeper	2.7
Swimming (2 mi/h)	7.9
Tailoring	0.9
Typewriting rapidly	1.0
Violin playing	0.6
Walking (3 mi/h)	2.0
Walking rapidly (4 mi/h)	3.4
Walking at high speed (5.3 mi/h)	9.3
Walking downstairs	*
Walking upstairs	†
Washing floors	1.2
Writing	0.4

*Allow 0.012 kcal/kg for an ordinary staircase with 15 steps without regard to time.
†Allow 0.036 kcal/kg for an ordinary staircase with 15 steps without regard to time.
Source: Taylor, C. M., and McLeod, G., *Rose's Laboratory Handbook for Dietetics*, 5th ed., Macmillan, New York, 1949, p. 18.

Ready Reference 6

Surface-Area Nomogram

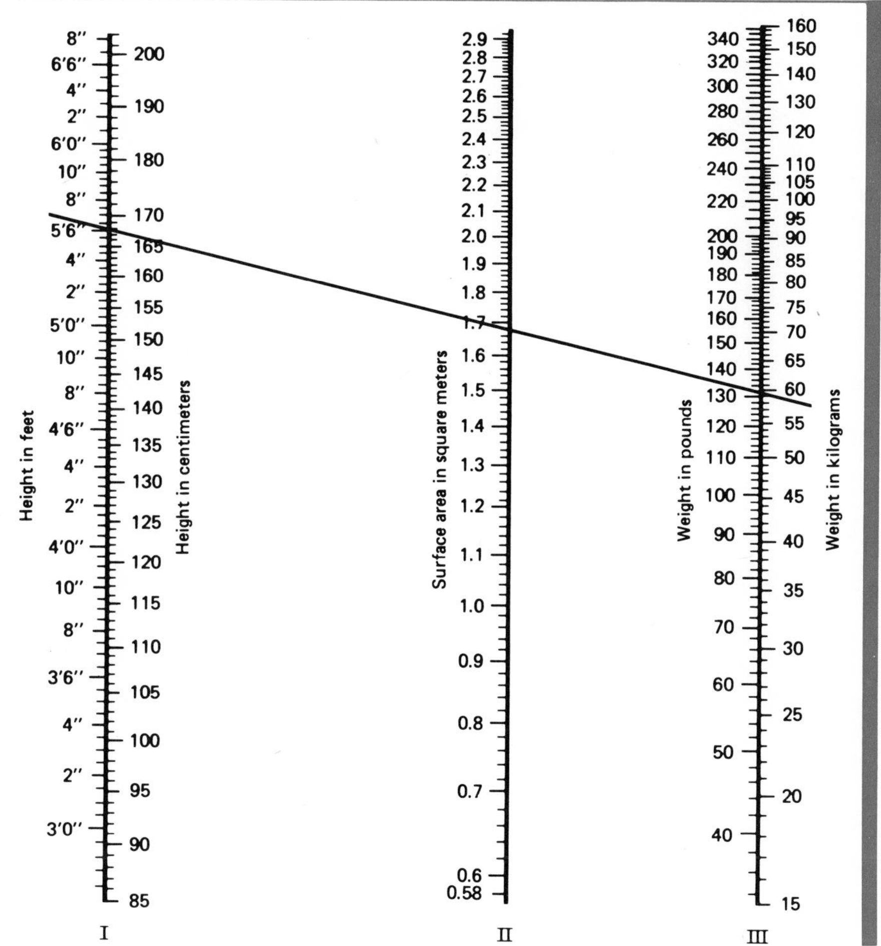

RR6

Ready Reference 7

Hourly BMR Based on Age and Sex

AGE	BMR (kcal/m²/h)	
	MALE	FEMALE
3	60.1	54.5
4	57.9	53.9
5	56.3	53.0
6	54.0	51.2
7	52.3	49.7
8	50.8	48.0
9	49.5	46.2
10	47.7	44.9
11	46.5	44.1
12	45.3	42.0
13	44.5	40.5
14	43.8	39.2
15	43.7	38.3
16	42.9	37.7
17	41.9	36.2
18	40.5	35.7
19	40.1	35.4
20	39.8	35.3
21	39.4	35.2
22	39.2	35.2
23	39.0	35.2
24	38.7	35.1
25	38.4	35.1
26	38.2	35.0
27	38.0	35.0
28	37.8	35.0
29	37.7	35.0
30	37.6	35.0
31	37.4	35.0
32	37.2	34.9
33	37.1	34.9
34	37.0	34.9
35	36.9	34.8
36	36.8	34.7
37	36.7	34.6
38	36.7	34.5
39	36.6	34.4
40	36.5	34.3
45	36.3	33.8
50	36.0	33.4
55	35.4	32.9
60	34.8	32.4
65	34.0	31.8
70	33.1	31.3
75 and above	31.8	31.1

Source: Spector, W.S., (ed.) *Handbook of Biological Data*, Philadelphia, W.B. Saunders, 1956, p. 259. Reprinted with permission of publisher.

Ready Reference 8

Examples of Daily Energy Expenditures of Mature Men and Women

TYPE OF ACTIVITY	Total Energy Expended, kcal/kg of body weight/h	
	MEN	WOMEN
Very light: Seated and standing activities, automobile and truck driving, laboratory work, typing, playing musical instruments, sewing, ironing	1.5	1.3
Light: Walking on level 2.5 to 3 mi/h, tailoring, pressing, garage work, electrical trades, carpentry, restaurant trades, cannery workers, washing clothes, shopping with light load, golf, sailing, table tennis, volleyball	2.9	2.6
Moderate: Walking 3.5 to 4 mi/h, plastering, weeding and hoeing, loading and stacking bales, scrubbing floors, shopping with heavy load, cycling, skiing, tennis, dancing	4.3	4.1
Heavy: Walking with load uphill, tree felling, work with pick and shovel, basketball, swimming, climbing, football	8.4	8.0

Source: Food and Nutrition Board, *Recommended Dietary Allowances*, 9th ed., National Academy of Sciences, Washington, 1980.

RR8

Ready Reference 9

Recommended Weights in Relation to Height*

Height		Men		Women	
FEET	INCHES	AVERAGE, lb	RANGE, lb	AVERAGE, lb	RANGE, lb
4	10	–	–	102	92-119
4	11	–	–	104	94-122
5	0	–	–	107	96-125
5	1	–	–	110	99-128
5	2	123	112-141	113	102-131
5	3	127	115-144	116	105-134
5	4	130	118-148	120	108-138
5	5	133	121-152	123	111-142
5	6	136	124-156	128	114-146
5	7	140	128-161	132	118-150
5	8	145	132-166	136	122-154
5	9	149	136-170	140	126-158
5	10	153	140-174	144	130-163
5	11	158	144-179	148	134-168
6	0	162	148-184	152	138-173
6	1	166	152-189	–	–
6	2	171	156-194	–	–
6	3	176	160-199	–	–
6	4	181	164-204	–	–

*Height without shoes, weight without clothes.

Source: Bray, G. A. (ed.), *Obesity in Perspective,* National Institute of Health, Bethesda, Md., 1973, p. 72.

Ready Reference 10

Vitamin Structures

Structures of Water-Soluble Vitamins

Ascorbic acid: vitamin C

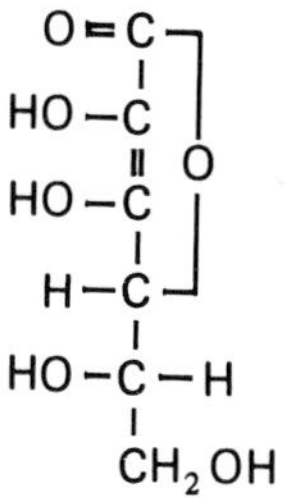

Riboflavin

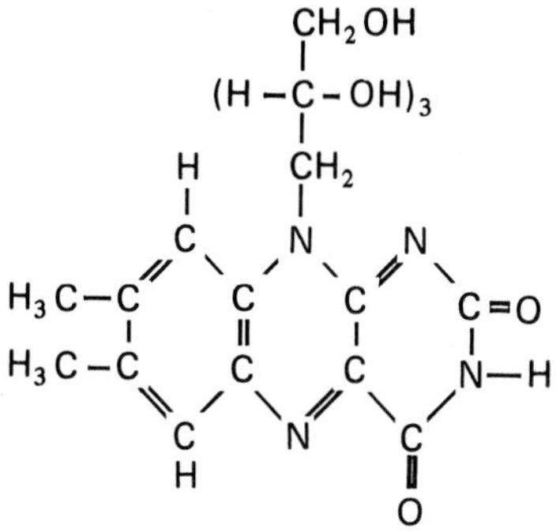

Thiamine: vitamin B_1

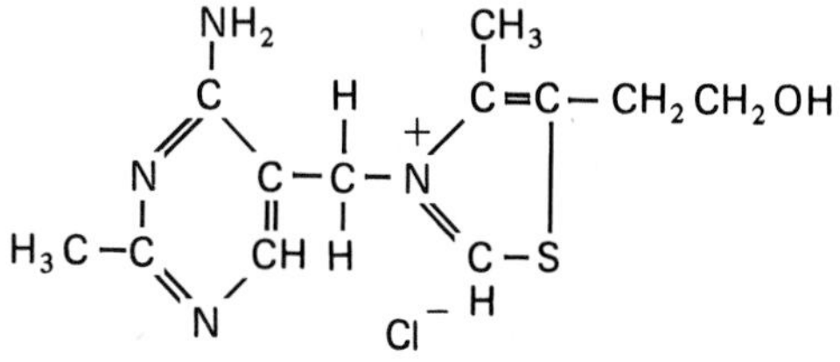

Niacin

Nicotinic acid

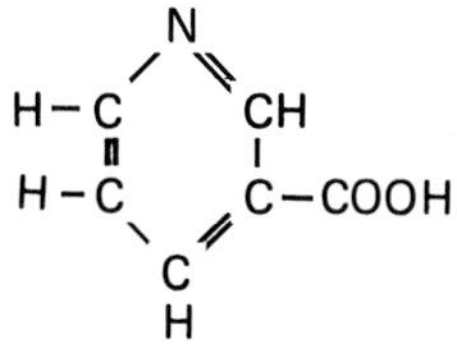

Nicotinamide

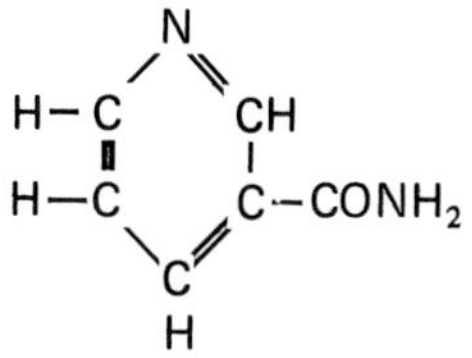

Vitamin B_6 group

Pyridoxine

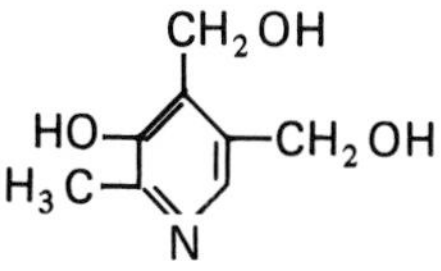

Pyridoxal

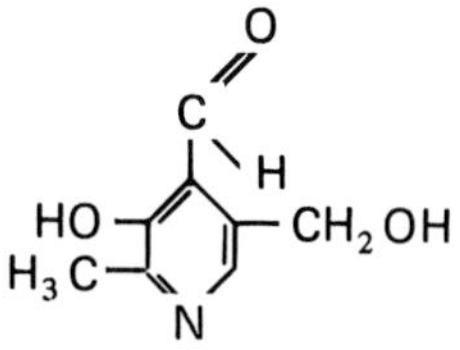

Pyridoxamine

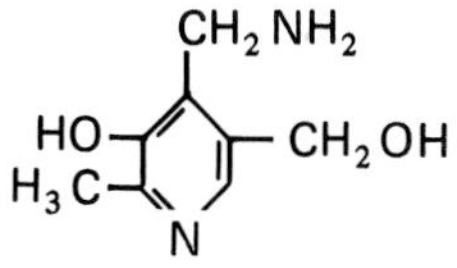

Pantothenic acid

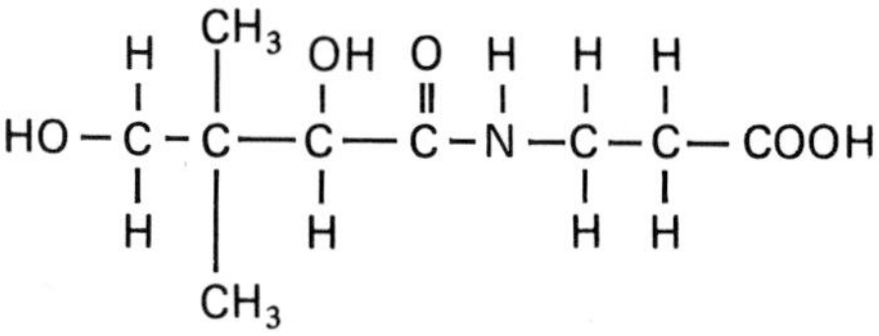

Structures of Water-Soluble Vitamins (Continued)

Folacin

(represented by monopteroylglutamic acid)

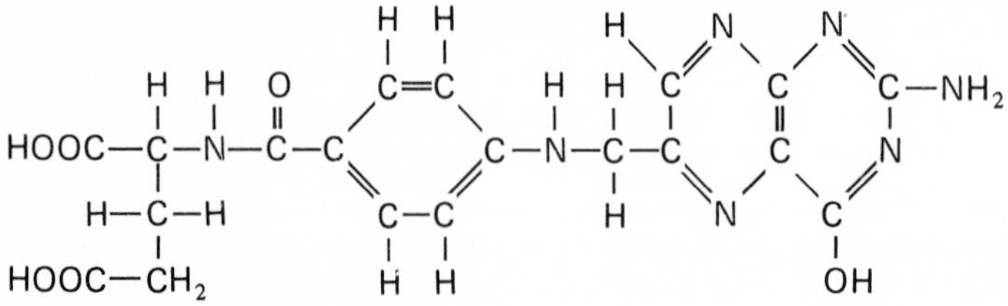

Biotin

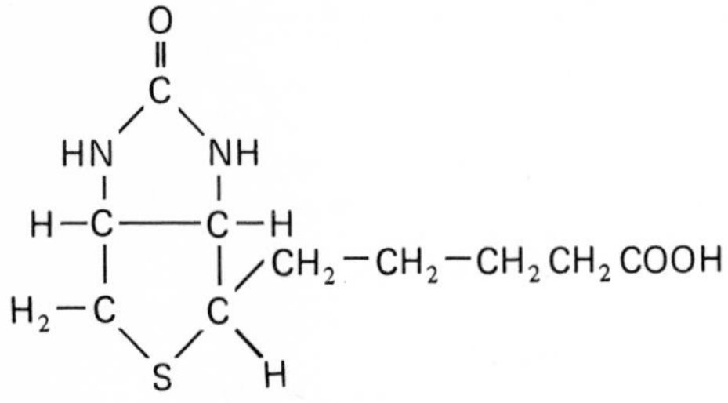

Vitamin B_{12}

(represented by cyanocobalamin)

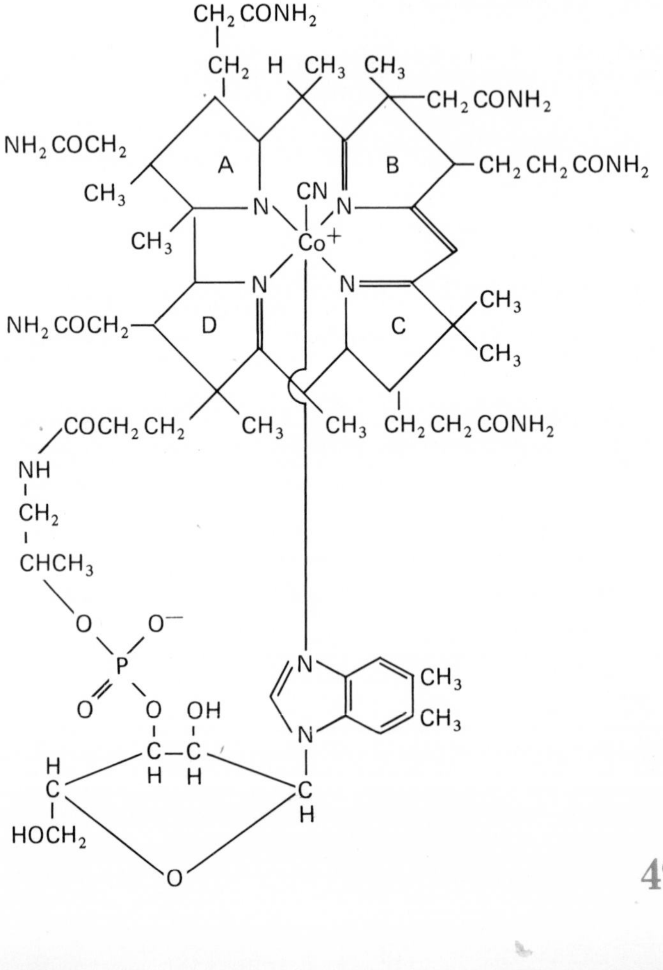

Choline

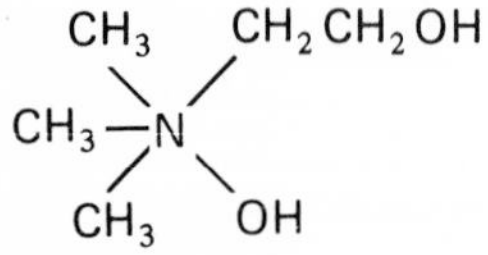

Vitamin A (represented by retinol)

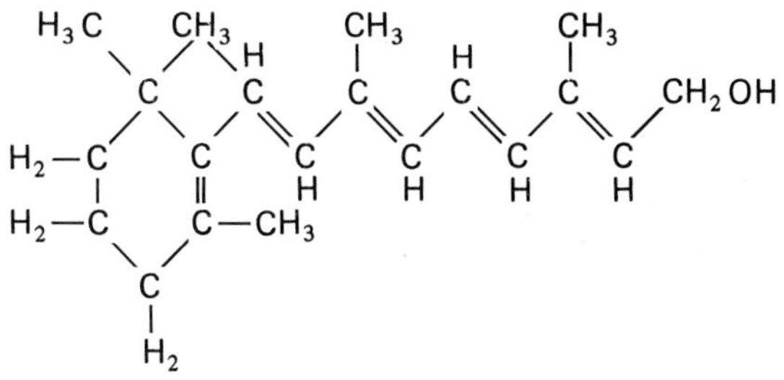

Beta-carotene (provitamin A)

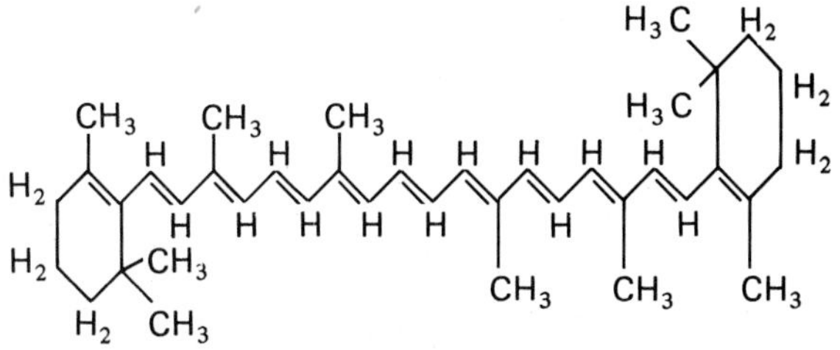

Vitamin D (represented by cholecalciferol, vitamin D_3)*

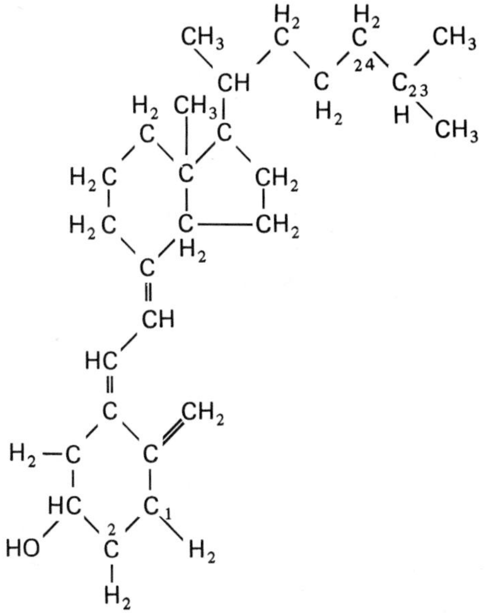

*The numbers of the carbon atoms involved in the biosynthesis of vitamin D hormone are shown.

Vitamin E (represented by alpha-tocopherol)

```
        CH3
        |
        C       O      CH3          H            H           CH3
      //  \   /   \   /             |            |            |
H3C—C      C       C——(CH2)3—C-(CH2)3—C—(CH2)3—C—H
    |      ||      |             |            |            |
HO—C       C      CH2           CH3          CH3          CH3
     \\   / \    /
        C      C             \___________________________________/
        |      H2                              R
       CH3
```

Vitamin K (represented by phytylmenaquinone, vitamin K_1)

```
              O
        H     ||
        C     C      CH3
      //  \  /  \   /
H—C       C      C            CH3 /                    CH3 \                         CH3
   |      ||     ||  H          |                        |                          /
H—C       C      C—C—C=C—( CH2—CH2—CH2—C— )CH2—CH2—CH2—C—H
     \\  /  \   /    H  |                        |                          \
        C     C           H                        H                           CH3
        |     ||
        H     O        \______________________________________________________/
                                                  R
```

Ready Reference 11

Amino Acid Structures

The part of each amino acid highlighted by the color box is the chemical group which is common to all amino acids.

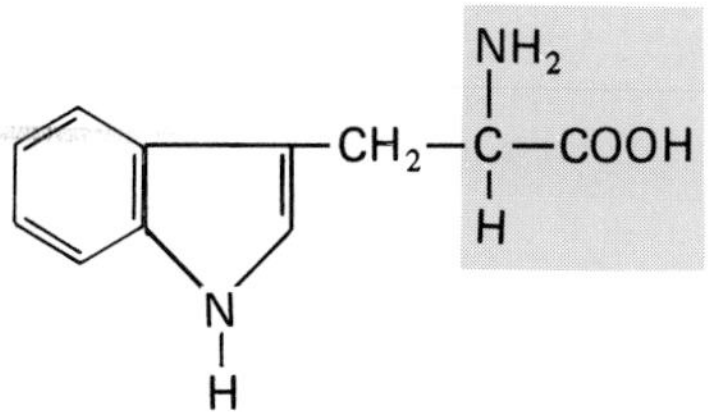

Tryptophan (TRP)

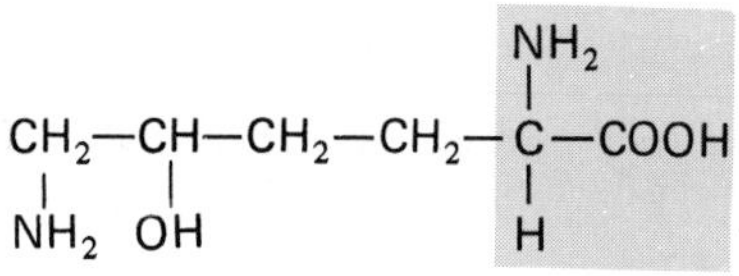

Hydroxylysine (HYL)

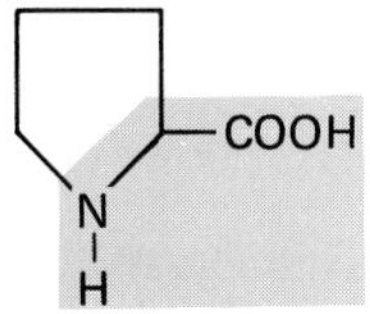

Proline (PRO)

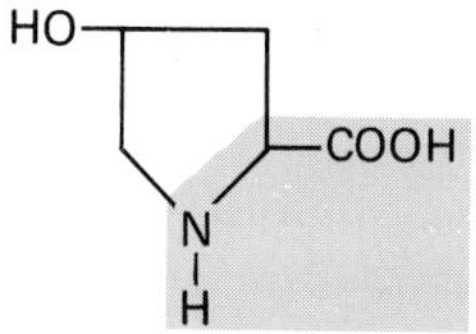

4-Hydroxyproline (HYP)

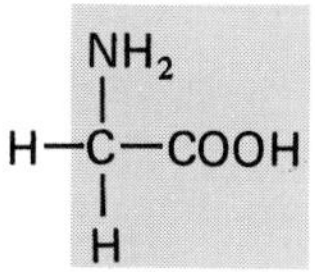

Glycine (GLY)

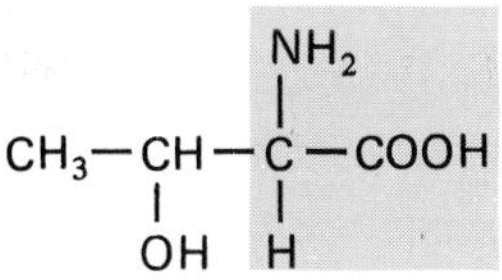

Threonine (THR)

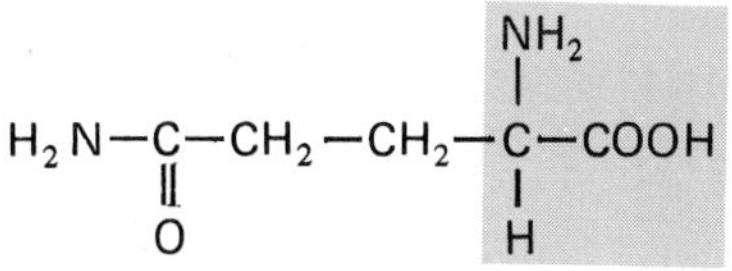

Glutamine (GLN)

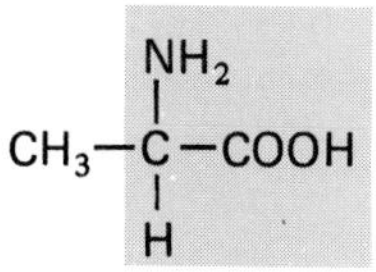

Alanine (ALA)

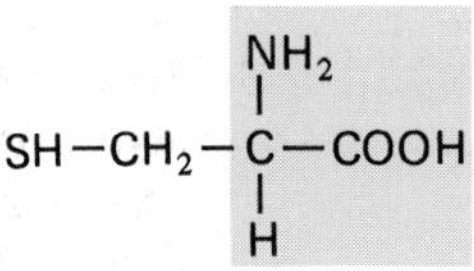

Cysteine (CYS)

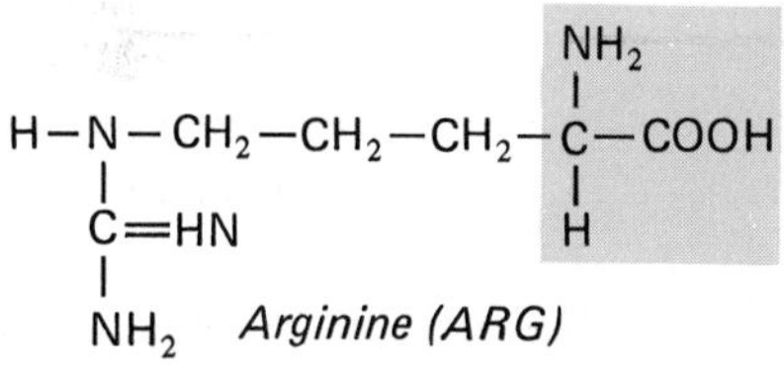

Arginine (ARG)

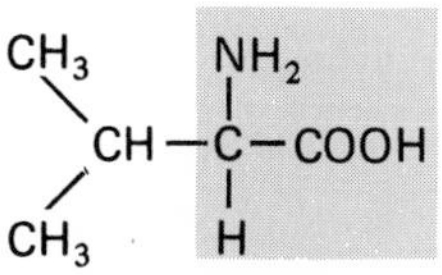

Valine (VAL)

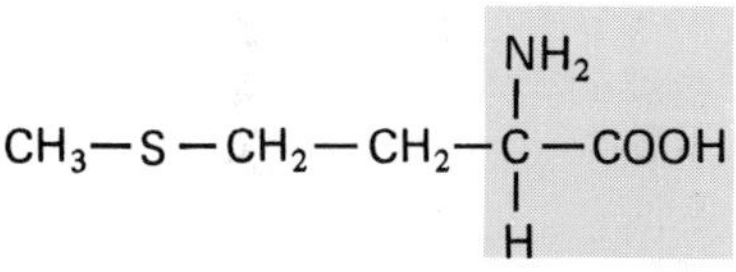

Methionine (MET)

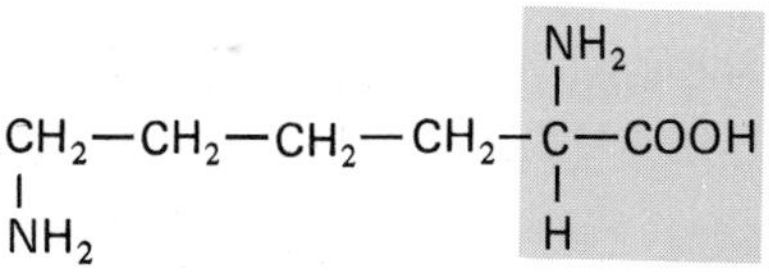

Lysine (LYS)

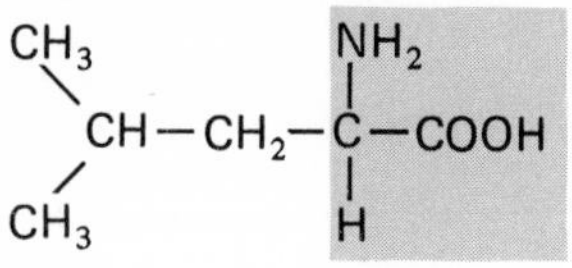

CH_3, CH_3 \ / $CH-CH_2-C(NH_2)(H)-COOH$

Leucine (LEU)

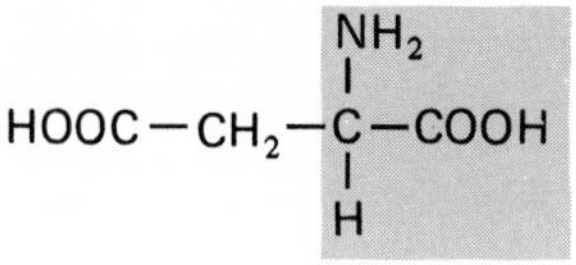

$HOOC-CH_2-C(NH_2)(H)-COOH$

Aspartic acid (ASP)

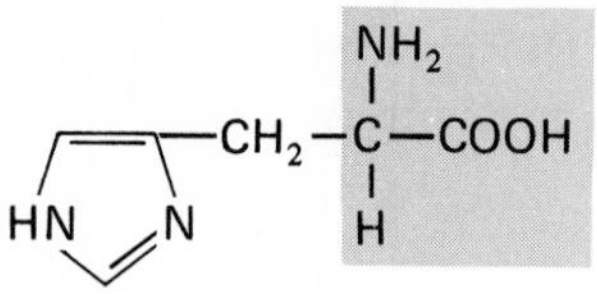

(HN, N ring)$-CH_2-C(NH_2)(H)-COOH$

Histidine (HIS)

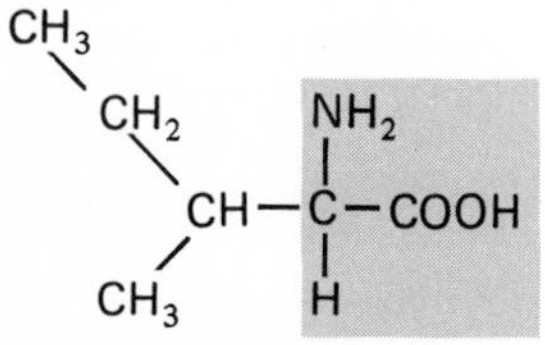

CH_3-CH_2, CH_3 \ / $CH-C(NH_2)(H)-COOH$

Isoleucine (ILE)

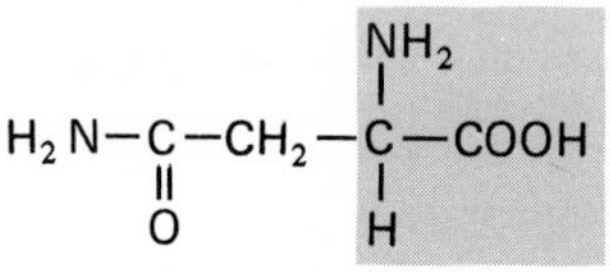

$H_2N-C(=O)-CH_2-C(NH_2)(H)-COOH$

Asparagine (ASN)

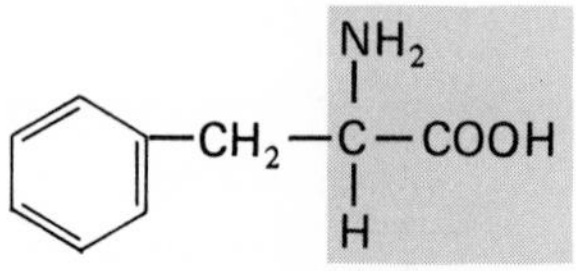

(benzene ring)$-CH_2-C(NH_2)(H)-COOH$

Phenylalanine (PHE)

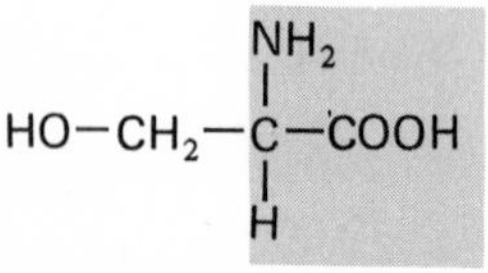

$HO-CH_2-C(NH_2)(H)-COOH$

Serine (SER)

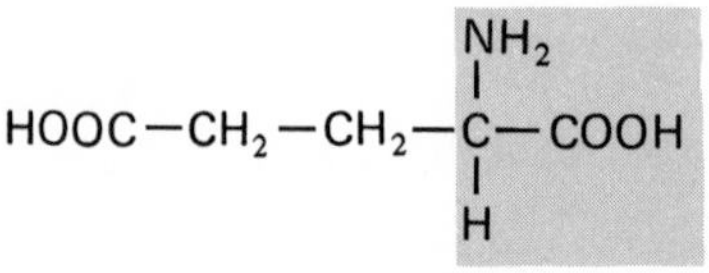

$HOOC-CH_2-CH_2-C(NH_2)(H)-COOH$

Glutamic acid (GLU)

$HO-$(benzene ring)$-CH_2-C(NH_2)(H)-COOH$

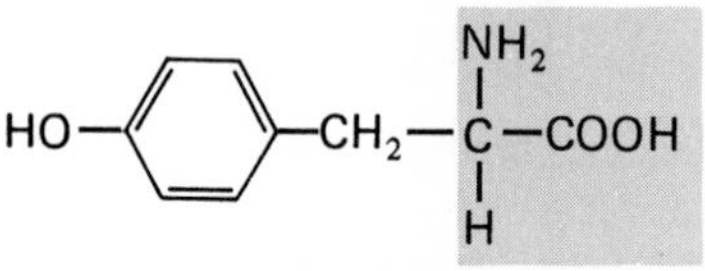

Tyrosine (TYR)

Ready Reference 12

Sucrose Content of Selected Foods

TABLE 1

Content of diet soft drinks

BRAND	SUCROSE, %	BRAND	SUCROSE, %
Miscellaneous		Shasta (continued)	
Diet 7-Up	0.00	Strawberry	0.00
Diet Royal Crown Cola	0.00	Red apple	0.00
Diet Pepsi Cola	0.00	Chocolate	0.06
Diet Dr. Pepper	0.00	Grapefruit	0.01
Tab	0.00	Golden Age Diet	
Fresca	0.00	Cola	0.00
Diet Rite Cola	0.00	Root beer	0.00
Shasta		Creme soda	0.00
Creme soda	0.00	Black cherry	0.00
Cherry cola	0.00	Strawberry	0.00
Grape	0.00	Weight Watchers	
Lemon lime	0.00	Chocolate	0.00
Orange	0.00	Orange	0.00
Ginger ale	0.00	Black cherry	0.00
Black cherry	0.00	Cola	0.00
Tiki	0.00	Root beer	0.00

Source: I.L. Shannon and W.B. Wescott, "Sucrose and Glucose Concentrations of Frequently Digested Foods," *J. Acad. Gen. Dent.* 23:37–43, 1975. Reprinted with permission.

TABLE 2

Sucrose of commercially available cheeses

BRAND AND TYPE	SUCROSE, %
Kraft Pasteurized Process Cheeses	
American	0.00
Brick	0.03
Swiss	0.00
Jalapeno	0.00
Onion Chive	0.18
Monterey Jack	0.00
Meunster	0.00
Cheez & Bacon	0.00
Sharp	0.00
Pimento	0.01
Hickory Farm	
Swiss on Rye	0.00
Hot Pepper	0.05
Cheddy Brew	0.00
Almond	0.00
Edam	0.00
Hickory Smoked	0.00
Samsoe	0.00
Butternip	0.00
Big Barn Cheddar	0.00
Butter Kaese	0.00
Gouda	0.00
Muenster	0.00
Belle Fleur	0.00

Source: I. L. Shannon and W. B. Wescott, "Sucrose and Glucose Concentrations of Frequently Ingested Foods," *J. Acad. Gen. Dent.* 23: 37–43, 1975. Reprinted with permission.

TABLE **3**

Sucrose content of fresh fruits and vegetables

ITEM	SUCROSE, %	ITEM	SUCROSE, %
Apple (Red Jonathan)	2.13	Onion (purple)	1.83
Apple (Red Winesap)	3.12	Orange	2.52
Apple (Red Delicious)	4.57	Peach	6.37
Apple (Yellow Delicious)	3.84	Pear (Bartlett)	1.13
Avocado	0.00	Pear (Peyote)	0.71
Banana	8.66	Pepper (Bell)	0.00
Cabbage (green)	0.00	Pineapple	4.49
Cabbage (red)	0.40	Plum	1.12
Carrot	5.38	Potato (Irish)	0.51
Cauliflower	0.00	Potato (sweet)	4.50
Celery	0.33	Prune	4.81
Cucumber	0.00	Radish	0.00
Grape (green)	0.79	Rutabaga	0.86
Grape (red)	1.46	Strawberry	0.86
Grapefruit	3.04	Tangelo	3.66
Lettuce	0.20	Tomato	0.00
Onion (white)	0.50	Turnip	0.82
Onion (yellow)	0.90		

*ND < 0.06% sucrose.
Source: I. L. Shannon and W. B. Wescott, "Sucrose and Glucose Concentrations of Frequently Ingested Foods," *J. Acad. Gen. Dent.* 23: 37-43, 1975. Reprinted with permission.

TABLE **4**

Content of commercially available luncheon meats

BRAND AND TYPE	SUCROSE, %	BRAND AND TYPE	SUCROSE, %
Oscar Mayer		Frey (continued)	
Fully Cooked Weiners	ND*	New England Sausage	ND
Beef Franks	ND	Excello Loaf	ND
Beef Variety Pak Bologna	ND	Luncheon Loaf	0.30
Variety-Pak Bologna	0.18	Olive Loaf	ND
Beef Variety Pak Cotto Salami	ND	Neuhoff	
Beef Variety Pak Salami for Beer	ND	Beef Bologna	0.24
Beef Variety Pak Beef Sausage	ND	Pork Shoulder Picnic	ND
Variety-Pak Honey Loaf	0.43	Spiced Luncheon Meat	0.35
Variety-Pak Old Fashioned Loaf	ND	Carl Buddig	
Variety-Pak Pickle and Pimiento Loaf	ND	Smoked Sliced Beef	0.51
Ham and Cheese Loaf	ND	Smoked Sliced Cooked Pastrami	0.71
Liver Cheese	ND	Smoked Sliced Ham	0.90
Rath		Sliced Cooked Corned Beef	0.61
Weiners	ND	Armour	
Bologna	ND	Hot Dogs	0.20
Cooked Salami	ND	Bologna	0.22
New England Sausage	ND	Spiced Luncheon Meat	0.24
Pickle Loaf	0.23	Olive Loaf	ND
Ham and Cheese Loaf	ND	Hormel	
Cooked Ham	ND	Weiners	ND
Liver Loaf	ND	Breast of Turkey	0.22
Frey		Miscellaneous	
Franks	ND	Swift's Premium Franks	ND
Bologna	ND	Cudahy Bar S Weiners	ND
Cotto Salami	ND	Corn Country Franks	0.19
Ham Sausage	0.31	Parade Beef Weiners	ND
		Kosher Zion Beef Franks	ND

*ND < 0.06% sucrose.
Source: I. L. Shannon and W. B. Wescott, "Sucrose and Glucose Concentrations of Frequently Ingested Foods," *J. Acad. Gen. Dent.* 23: 37-43, 1975. Reprinted with permission.

TABLE **5**

Sucrose content of commerically available crackers and wafers

BRAND AND TYPE	SUCROSE, %	BRAND AND TYPE	SUCROSE, %
Nabisco		Sunshine	
Triscuit	0.71	Hi Ho Crackers	3.74
Wheat Thins	4.41	Cheez-It	ND
American Harvest	1.00	Krispy Unsalted Tops Crackers	ND
Cheddar 'n Chips Cheese Thins	3.08	Krispy Saltines	ND
Buttery Flavored Sesame Snack	3.78	Sesame Bread Wafers	2.46
Sociables Savory	4.87	Honey Graham Crackers	16.09
Bacon Flavored Thins	4.33	Old London	
Chicken in a Biskit	0.79	White Melba Toast	ND
Ritz	3.23	Low Salt White Melba Toast	0.08
Cheese Nips	2.36	Wheat Melba Toast	ND
French Onion	6.14	Low Salt Wheat Melba Toast	0.10
French Accent	2.74	Rye Melba Toast	0.38
Meal Mates	3.23	Low Salt Rye Melba Toast	0.33
Uneeda Biscuit	0.14	Pumpernickel Melba Toast	ND
Graham Crackers	15.81	Sesame Rounds	0.12
Honey Maid Graham Crackers	16.69	Garlic Rounds	ND
Waverly Wafers	4.54	Onion Rounds	0.60
Escort Crackers	4.39	White Melba Rounds	ND
Cinnamon Treats	25.0	Manischewitz	
Ritz Cheeze	3.53	Matzo-Thins	1.06
Glazed Sesame Crisp	13.70	Egg n Onion Matzo Crackers	6.46
Nab Cheda Nut	3.32	Garlic Tams	4.14
Nab Cheese Sandwich	2.91	Tam Tams	5.79
Sea Rounds	0.23	Onion Tams	5.16
Premium Crackers	ND*	Unsalted Matzos	0.73
Premium Saltine Crackers	ND	Estee	
Cheese Tid Bits	0.42	Dietetic Cheese Thins	0.96
Keebler		Wasa Swedish Crispbread	
Club Crackers	5.74	Ry King Golden Rye	0.21
Town House Crackers	6.32	Ry King Lite Rye	1.52
Waldorf Low Sodium Crackers	ND	Ry King Seasoned Rye	0.26
Rye Toast	8.03	Ry King Brown Rye	0.28
Wheat Thins	8.23	Ralston Purina	
Onion Toasts	9.00	Original Ry Krisp Traditional	
Cheese Toasts	7.95	Scandinavian-Style	
Bacon Toasts	9.24	Whole-Rye Crackers	1.62
Cinnamon Crisp	32.03	Master	
Honey Graham Crackers	13.93	Dietetic Crackers	2.68
Zesta Saltine Crackers	ND	Topco	
		Gaylord Saltines	ND

*ND < 0.06% sucrose.

Source: I. L. Shannon and W. B. Wescott, "Sucrose and Glucose Concentrations of Frequently Ingested Foods," *J. Acad. Gen. Dent.* 23: 37–43, 1975. Reprinted with permission.

TABLE 6

Sucrose content of commercially available breads

BRAND AND TYPE	SUCROSE, %
Mrs. Bairds	
Rite Diet	ND*
Enriched White	ND
Early American Mixed Grain	ND
Wheat	0.07
New Orleans French	ND
Rainbo	
Roman Meal	0.13
Old Fashioned Enriched	ND
Country Crust Topped with Butter and Honey	ND
Sunbeam	
Enriched White Bread	ND
Old Fashioned Enriched French	ND
Old Fashioned Butter Split Enriched	ND
Cook Book	
Honey "V"	ND
Old Fashioned Enriched	ND
Wheat Bread	ND
German Rye	ND
French Enriched	ND
Oroweat	
Northridge Stone Ground 100% Whole Wheat	0.07
Northridge Honey and Egg	ND
Schwarzwolder Dark Rye	ND
Russian Style Rye	ND
Francisco Extra Sour Dough French Enriched	ND
Northridge Honey Wheat Berry	ND
Old Style Country Enriched	ND
Soya Bean	ND
Francisco French Enriched (Long Roll)	ND
Francisco French Thick Sliced Vienna	ND
Northridge Royal Raisin Nut	ND
Pepperidge Farm	
Sprouted Wheat	ND
Sprouted Rye	ND
Cracked Wheat	ND
Pumpernickel	0.06
White	ND
Wheat Germ	ND
Oatmeal	ND
Raisin Thin Sliced w/cinnamon	ND
El's	
Home Style Enriched	0.08
Rye	ND
El's (continued)	
Stone Ground 100% Whole Wheat	0.12
Pumpernickel	ND
Sidney Myers	
Dutch Maid Wheat	0.29
Dutch Maid Low Sodium	ND
Hearth Fresh 100% Whole Wheat	ND
Dutch Maid Honey Scotch	ND
Dutch Maid Vienna Rye	0.17
Chopped Onion	0.31
Hearth Fresh Pumpernickel	ND
American Prize Loaf "Nutty Brown"	ND
Hearth Fresh French	ND
Italian	ND
Circle French	ND
Hearth Fresh Jewish Sour Dough Rye	ND
Seedless Rye	ND
Buttermilk	ND
Potato	ND
Gluten	ND
Old Fashioned Cinnamon Loaf	3.44
Cottage	ND
Kroger	
Black Forest Rye	ND
Italian Style Enriched	ND
Buttercrust Enrich	ND
Thin Sliced Sandwich	ND
Rye Bread	ND
Sandwich Enriched with Buttermilk	ND
Mal-O-Soft White Enriched	ND
Bay's	
Old Style German Pumpernickel	ND
Sour Dough French	ND
Jewish Rye	ND
Cocktail Rye	ND
Scandinavian Dark Rye	ND
Hollywood	
Light Bread	ND
Dark Bread	ND
Aunt Martha's	
Old Fashioned Enriched	ND
Country Oven	
Village Bakery Thin Sliced Enriched	0.15
Sun Gold Sandwich Enriched	ND
Snyder's	
Peasant	ND
Cholmondley's	
English Muffin Loaf	0.15

*ND $<$ 0.06% sucrose.

Source: I. L. Shannon and W. B. Wescott, "Sucrose and Glucose Concentrations of Frequently Ingested Foods," *J. Acad. Gen. Dent.* 23: 37–43, 1975. Reprinted with permission.

TABLE 7

Sucrose content of commerically available snack foods

BRAND AND TYPE	SUCROSE, %	BRAND AND TYPE	SUCROSE, %
Frito Lay		Flavor Tree	
Fritos	0.77	Sesame Chips	0.39
Cheetos	0.36	Sesame Sticks	0.44
Doritos	1.74	Chedder Chips with Sesame	0.35
Potato Chips	1.06	Sta Krisp	
Ruffles Potato Chips	0.37	Potato Chips	0.13
Lay's Potato Chips	0.89	Corn Chips	0.48
Lay's Bar B. Q. Potato Chips	0.64	Jalepeno Corn Chips	0.56
Sour Cream and Onion Potato Chips	0.16	Tortilla Chips	ND
Taco Flavor Tortilla Chips	1.11	Bar B. Q. Tortilla Chips	2.15
Munchos Potato Crisps	ND*	Cheese Twists	0.14
Nacho Cheese Tortilla Chips	0.92	Morton's	
Funyun's Onion Flavor Snack	1.79	Barbeque Potato Chips	0.63
Rold Gold Pretzel Rods	0.53	Sour Cream and Onion Potato Chips	0.52
Bacon Nips	0.31	Tortilla Chips	0.71
Fried Pork Rinds	0.11	Taco Tortilla Chips	0.67
Nabisco		Cheese Baked Twistees	0.11
Diggers	2.24	Hot Diggity Dog	0.39
Chipsters	0.18	Kandi-roos	48.51
Korkers	0.34	Tacotoos	0.67
Doodads	0.99	Pizza 'potomus	0.91
Veri-Thin Pretzel Sticks	0.27	Pork Skins	ND
Dentler		Sidney Myers	
Facs Potato Chips	0.31	La Roseta Corn Chips	0.39
Facs Barbecue Potato Chips	0.12	La Roseta Tortilla Chips	0.72
Facs Corn Chips	0.42	San Tropez	
Facs B. B. Q. Corn Chips	0.59	Sesame Chips	0.49
Facs Pretzel Sticks	1.02	Onion and Garlic Sesame Chips	0.57
Facs Cheese Puffs	0.09	Sesame Sticks	0.41
General Mills		Miscellaneous	
Pizza Spins	1.26	Parkers Deluxe Assortment of Snacks	1.80
Bugles	1.95	Farmer Brown Wave Potato	0.33
Crisp-u-Taters	1.00	Laura Scudder's Scudderings	0.71
Chipos Potato Chips	0.75		
Chedder Taters	0.27		

*ND < 0.06% sucrose.

Source: I. L. Shannon and W. B. Wescott, "Sucrose and Glucose Concentrations of Frequently Ingested Foods," *J. Acad. Gen. Dent.* 23: 37–43, 1975. Reprinted with permission.

RR12

TABLE 8

Sucrose content of commerically available breakfast cereals

COMMERCIAL CEREAL PRODUCT	SUCROSE, %
Shredded Wheat (large biscuit)	1.0
Shredded Wheat (spoon-size biscuit)	1.3
Cheerios	2.2
Puffed Rice	2.4
Uncle Sam Cereal	2.4
Wheat Chex	2.6
Grape Nut Flakes	3.3
Puffed Wheat	3.5
Alpen	3.8
Post Toasties	4.1
Product 19	4.1
Corn Total	4.4
Special K	4.4
Wheaties	4.7
Corn Flakes (Kroger)	5.1
Peanut Butter	5.2
Grape Nuts	6.6
Corn Flakes (Food Club)	7.0
Crispy Rice	7.3
Corn Chex	7.5
Corn Flakes (Kellogg)	7.8
Total	8.1
Rice Chex	8.5
Crisp Rice	8.8
Raisin Bran (Skinner)	9.6
Concentrate	9.9
Rice Crispies (Kellogg)	10.0
Raisin Bran (Kellogg)	10.6
Heartland (with raisins)	13.5
Buck Wheat	13.6
Life	14.5
Granola (with dates)	14.5
Granola (with raisins)	14.5
Sugar Frosted Corn Flakes	15.6
40% Bran flakes (Post)	15.8
Team	15.9
Brown Sugar-Cinnamon Frosted Mini Wheats	16.0
40% Bran flakes (Kellogg)	16.2
Granola	16.6
100% Bran	18.4
All Bran	20.0
Granola (with almonds and filberts)	21.4
Fortified Oat Flakes	22.2
Heartland	23.1
Super Sugar Chex	24.5
Sugar Frosted Flakes	29.0
Bran Buds	30.2
Sugar Sparkled Corn Flakes	32.2
Frosted Mini Wheats	33.6
Sugar Pops	37.8
Alpha Bits	40.3
Sir Grapefellow	40.7
Super Sugar Crisp	40.7
Cocoa Puffs	43.0
Cap'n Crunch	43.3
Crunch Berries	43.4
Kaboom	43.8
Frankenberry	44.0
Frosted Flakes	44.0
Count Chocula	44.2
Orange Quangaroos	44.7
Quisp	44.9
Boo Berry	45.7
Vanilly Crunch	45.8
Baron Von Redberry	45.8
Cocoa Krispies	45.9
Trix	46.6
Froot Loops	47.4
Honeycomb	48.8
Pink Panther	49.2
Cinnamon Crunch	50.3
Lucky Charms	50.4
Cocoa Pebbles	53.5
Apple Jacks	55.0
Fruity Pebbles	55.1
King Vitaman	58.5
Sugar Smacks	61.3
Super Orange Crisp	68.0
MEAN	25.1
S. D.	19.16

Source: I. L. Shannon, "Sucrose and Glucose in Breakfast Cereals," *J. Dent. Child.* 41: 17–19, 1974. Reprinted with permission.

Ready Reference 13

Fiber Content of Selected Foods

FOOD	TOTAL DIETARY FIBER, G/100 G
Flours	
White, breadmaking	3.15
Brown	7.87
Wholemeal	9.51
Bran	44.0
Breads	
White	2.72
Brown	5.11
Hovis	4.54
Wholemeal	8.50
Breakfast cereals	
All-Bran	26.7
Cornflakes	11.0
Grapenuts	7.00
Readibrek	7.60
Rice Krispies	4.47
Puffed Wheat	15.41
Sugar Puffs	6.08
Shredded Wheat	12.26
Special K	5.45
Swiss breakfast (mixed brands)	7.41
Weetabix'	12.72
Biscuits	
Chocolate digestive (½ coated)	3.50
Chocolate (fully coated)	3.09
Crispbread, rye	11.73
Crispbread, wheat	4.83
Ginger biscuits	1.99
Matzo	3.85
Oatcakes	4.00
Semi-sweet	2.31
Short-sweet	1.66
Wafers (filled)	1.62
Leafy vegetables	
Broccoli tops (boiled)	4.10
Brussels sprouts (boiled)	2.86
Cabbage (boiled)	2.83
Cauliflower (boiled)	1.80
Lettuce (raw)	1.53
Onions (raw)	2.10
Legumes	
Beans, baked (canned)	7.27
Beans, runner (boiled)	3.35
Peas, frozen (raw)	7.75
Garden (canned)*	6.28
Processed (canned)*	7.85
Root vegetables	
Carrots, young (boiled)	3.70
Parsnips (raw)	4.90
Swedes (raw)	2.40
Turnips (raw)	2.20
Potato	
Main crop (raw)	3.51
Chips (fried)	3.20
Crisps	11.9
Potato (continued)	
Canned*	2.51
Peppers (cooked)	0.93
Tomato	
Fresh	1.40
Canned*	0.85
Sweetcorn	
Cooked	4.74
Canned*	5.69
Fruits	
Apples	
Flesh only	1.42
Peel only	3.71
Bananas	1.75
Cherries (flesh and skin)	1.24
Grapefruit (canned)†	0.44
Guavas (canned)†	3.64
Mandarin oranges (canned)†	0.29
Mangoes (canned)†	1.00
Peaches (flesh and skin)	2.28
Pears	
Flesh only	2.44
Peel only	8.59
Plums (flesh and skin)	1.52
Rhubarb (raw)	1.78
Strawberries	
Raw	2.12
Canned*	1.00
Sultanas	4.40
Nuts	
Brazils	7.73
Peanuts	9.30
Miscellaneous Foods	
Preserves	
Jam	
Plum	0.96
Strawberry	1.12
Lemon curd	0.20
Marmalade	0.71
Mincemeat	3.19
Peanut butter	7.55
Pickle	1.53
Dried soups (as purchased)	
Minestrone	6.61
Oxtail	3.84
Tomato	3.32
Beverages (concentrated)	
Cocoa	43.27
Drinking chocolate	8.20
Coffee and chicory essence	0.79
Instant coffee	16.41
Extracts	
Bovril	0.91
Marmite	2.69

Note: Value is sum of the noncellulosic polysaccharides, cellulose, and lignin.

*Drained.

†Fruit and syrup.

Source: Southgate, D. A. T., Bailey, B., Collinson, E., and Walker, A. F., "A Guide to Calculating Intakes of Dietary Fiber," *J. Hum. Nutr.* 30: 303–313, 1976. Reprinted with permission.

Ready Reference 14

A Form for Keeping a Diet Record

FOOD	SERVING SIZE	KILO-CALORIES	CARBO-HYDRATE	TOTAL FAT	SATURATED FAT	LINOLEIC ACID	CHOLES-TEROL
Total for Day							

CALCULATING KILOCALORIES OBTAINED FROM PROTEIN, CARBOHYDRATE, AND FAT

NUTRIENT	GRAMS PER DAY	TIMES KILOCALORIES PER GRAM	KILOCALORIES
Protein		4	
Carbohydrate		4	
Fat		9	
Total			

Calculating the Percent of Kilocalories Derived from Protein, Carbohydrate, and Fat

$$\text{Percent kcal from protein} = \frac{\text{kcal from protein}}{\text{total kcal}} \times 100$$

$$\text{Percent kcal from carbohydrate} = \frac{\text{kcal from carbohydrate}}{\text{total kcal}} \times 100$$

$$\text{Percent kcal from fat} = \frac{\text{kcal from fat}}{\text{total kcal}} \times 100$$

Calculating the P:S Ratio

$$\text{P:S ratio} = \frac{\text{grams linoleic acid}}{\text{grams saturated fat}}$$

Ready Reference 15

The Metric System and U.S. Equivalents

Metric abbreviations:
- micro- = 1/1,000,000th
- milli- = 1/1,000th
- centi- = 1/100th
- deci- = 1/10th
- deka- = 10
- hecto- = 100
- kilo- = 1000

Units of length:
- 1 millimeter = 0.03937 inch
- 1 centimeter = 0.3937 inch
- 1 meter = 39.37 inches
- 1 kilometer = 0.6214 mile
- 1 inch = 2.54 centimeters
- 1 mile = 1.609 kilometers

Units of mass or weight:
- 1 milligram = 0.0154 grain
- 1 gram = 15.43 grains or 0.03527 ounce avoirdupois
- 1 kilogram = 2.2 pounds avoirdupois
- 1 ounce = 28.35 grams
- 1 pound = 0.454 kilogram

Units of capacity:
- 1 milliliter = 0.034 fluid ounce
- 1 liter = 1.05 liquid quarts
- 1 fluid ounce = 29.6 milliliters
- 1 fluid quart = 0.946 liter

INDEX

Page numbers in *italic* indicate illustrations or tables.